THE ALPINE JOURNAL 1998

1. Annapurna North-West Ridge: the beginning of Cauliflower Ridge. (*Waldemar Soroka*) (p89)

THE ALPINE JOURNAL

1998

The Journal of the Alpine Club

A record of mountain adventure
and scientific observation

Edited by Johanna Merz

Assistant Editors:
José Luis Bermúdez and Geoffrey Templeman

Volume 103
No 347

Supported by the
MOUNT EVEREST FOUNDATION

Published jointly by
THE ALPINE CLUB & THE ERNEST PRESS

THE ALPINE JOURNAL 1998
Volume 103 No 347

Address all editorial communications to the Hon Editor :
Ed Douglas, 93c Junction Road, London, N19 5QX
e-mail ed_douglas@compuserve.com

Address all sales and distribution communications to:
Cordée, 3a De Montfort Street, Leicester, LE1 7HD

Back numbers:
Apply to the Alpine Club, 55 Charlotte Road, London, EC2A 3QT
or, for 1969 to date, apply to Cordée, as above.

First published in 1998 jointly by the Alpine Club and the Ernest Press
Typesetting by Johanna Merz
Illustration reproduction by Arneg, Glasgow
Printed and bound in Great Britain by St Edmundsbury Press Ltd,
Bury St Edmunds, Suffolk

A CIP catalogue record for this book is
available from the British Library

ISBN 0 948153 57 1

Foreword

The 103rd volume of the *Alpine Journal* will be my seventh as Editor and it will also be my last. As Doug Scott wrote to me recently, 'The seventh edition is a good one by which to leave – seven being a dominant number in our lives – seven days in the week, seven notes on the scale, seven colours of the rainbow, seven stars in the sky, seven continents, seven summits, the magnificent seven! etc. etc.'

There comes a time when it feels right to hand over to someone more closely in touch with today's mountaineering scene. Ed Douglas, who has agreed to take over the editorship from next year, is eminently well-qualified for the task, being not only an active climber but a talented journalist, as his widely-acclaimed *Mountain Review* bore witness.

I owe a tremendous debt of gratitude to Ernst Sondheimer, my predecessor, who, in 1988, gave me the opportunity to join his editorial team and taught me much about the art of editing. I am also sincerely grateful to my two Assistant Editors, José Luis Bermúdez and Geoffrey Templeman, who have compiled and expanded important sections of the Journal – without their help my task would have been impossible. I am grateful, too, to Roy Ruddle who transformed the Area Notes in my first five volumes; to Bill Ruthven who has meticulously carried out the laborious task of summarising the Mount Everest Foundation reports; to Ted Hatch for his beautiful maps; and to Christopher Russell who has kept us in touch, year after year, with our pioneering forebears.

Editing the *Alpine Journal* has been an immense privilege and one I have greatly enjoyed. During the last seven years the number of friends I have made worldwide has run into hundreds, as my swollen correspondence files testify. Indeed, I have received so much help from so many people that it might seem invidious to pay tribute to any of them individually without naming them all – which space would not allow. However, I would particularly like to thank George Band, Chris Bonington, Trevor Braham, Evelio Echevarría, Chuck Evans, Lindsay Griffin, David Hamilton, John Harding, John Hunt, Harish Kapadia, Paul Knott, Bill O'Connor, Roger Payne, Edward Peck, Kev Reynolds, Doug Scott and Michael Ward who have all not only made outstanding contributions to these volumes but have given me support and encouragement when most needed. Finally, the invaluable co-operation I have received from Peter Hodgkiss has extended far beyond the call of duty.

As I've said, limited space prevents me from mentioning by name the many other people who have so generously written for the *Alpine Journal* over the last seven years. Their names can be found in the 'Contributors' section at the back of every volume. As their mini-biographies show, these are all busy people who have freely given up their time to enrich these volumes. I offer my sincere thanks to them all.

Johanna Merz

Contents

THE BIG ISSUES

LOOKING BACK

SKETCH MAPS AND TOPOS

Illustrations

Appearing between pages 212 and 213

Appearing between pages 276 and 277

Indian Himalaya

ANDY CAVE

A World Apart

A tribute to Brendan Murphy
who died in an avalanche on Changabang, 3 June 1997

(*Plates 15–19*)

Momentarily I stepped outside myself, watching my exhausted legs trying to move quickly, my feet trying to hold steady on the snow-covered moraine. I stopped at a huge slab of granite to regain a grip on reality. Resting my sack against a tall cairn that Brendan had built the previous year, I took a sip of water. Minutes later, when I tried to lift the sack back onto my shoulders, a pain shot across my chest. Across the peaks and troughs of the glacier I could make out base camp, normally about an hour away. I jettisoned the rucksack and, in slow motion, using the ski poles to stabilise my jellied limbs, edged up to the first moraine ridge. By the time I reached the top the chest pain had returned and I was scared, but the rotting fish smell of festering frostbite forced me on. I had to get some medicine. I had to get there before they abandoned camp. I had to tell them what had happened.

After a full half-hour I had travelled only a pitiful 200m from the rucksack. I yelled into the approaching mist. There was no reply. The thought of only making it halfway, sleeping out without a sleeping-bag and refreezing my hands and feet frightened me enough to turn back. After almost twelve hours of wonderful sleep, I crawled out of my snow-covered sleeping-bag and stuffed it into the rucksack with my good hand. I felt refreshed inside, but still I walked like a delirious junky.

In my head I constructed the words I would say to the others. I was convinced they would see me a long way off in my conspicuous red suit and would become suspicious at the sight of just one red figure. As I wobbled down the final half-mile to base camp I felt intoxicated by the spring air.

A small red bird that had arrived with the warm temperatures sang and hopped to the side guiding me back into the camp. The overnight ice had not yet melted from the edge of the stream and I staggered straight across, crunching through it in my lead-heavy boots. I was grateful for the ski poles, which gave me dignity by allowing me to walk in a reasonably straight line. Once close enough I shouted a small 'hello', and immediately Narinda and Vikram, our liaison officer and cook, came out of the kitchen shelter. They held out their hands warmly but nervously. It had been eighteen long days. Narinda waited for my words, water welling in his eyes.

'Mick and Steve are coming,' I said. 'Brendan is dead.'

Brendan appeared to be annoyingly at ease with this acclimatising business. I appreciated that acclimatising was vital to our preparation for the route, but I found it tedious. All the slopes of the neighbouring cols and peaks were covered in loose snow topped by a hideous crust that made movement slow and dangerous. Consequently, we plodded up to 5700m on a boring but relatively safe slope on the unclimbed Dunagiri Parbat. Although uninspiring in itself, it gave exceptional views of our proposed route on Changabang's North Face.

The previous year Brendan had joined Roger Payne, Julie-Ann Clyma and Andy Perkins in an attempt on the same face. On that trip the four had climbed an impressive thin line of ice on the right-hand side of the face. Sadly, serious gastric illness floored Brendan's partner Andy Perkins, and eventually they were all forced down. This year, however, that line looked almost non-existent and there were more logical ice lines leading directly to the first icefield which would minimise the traversing. Of three possible lines Brendan and I chose the central one, as did Mick Fowler and Steve Sustad. Roger and Julie-Ann decided on the left-hand line.

Changabang provided a perfect objective for all of us. It wasn't exceptionally high but promised some excellent climbing. Julie-Ann and Roger are, of course, both seasoned Himalayan alpinists, with many trips to steep and remote peaks under their belts. Their impressive organisational skills were something of a novelty to the rest of us. Mick and Steve were blown away when they learned that we were to have a tablecloth for meals at base camp and delicious cakes to accompany our tea each afternoon. As is well known, Mick Fowler not only works as a taxman but is also one of the most prolific 'adventure' new route activists around. Steve Sustad, originally from Seattle but now living in Britain, is an exceptionally gifted mountaineer, although he hasn't such a high profile as Mick. Brendan Murphy had been on a number of trips to hard technical objectives. We first got to know each other well on a trip to climb the South Face of Gasherbrum IV in the summer of 1993. I liked his mixture of tenacity and good humour.

As well as offering potentially good climbing there were other reasons which made this mountain special. Changabang had symbolic status. The first ascent, by an Anglo-Indian team, was in 1974, followed a few years later by the monumental effort by Peter Boardman and Joe Tasker, a gripping account of which appeared in Boardman's book *The Shining Mountain*. Their amazing achievement was hailed as one of the most outrageous routes of its time. Subsequently, Alex McIntyre and John Porter teamed up with the Poles Voytek Kurtyka and Christoph Zurek to make the first ascent of the South Buttress. All these tales of committing, bold journeys inspired us. Many of those players were no longer alive, having lost their lives pushing the limits in various parts of the Himalaya. But their quest to climb in a lightweight style lives on and continues to influence the few people who still perform in this sphere.

I complained about the cold temperatures at such a modest height. After seeing photos and chatting to the team from the expedition of the previous spring, I had expected something quite different. They had relatively mild temperatures, good quality névé and some long spells of good weather. Brendan shook his head and said, as he did many times, 'This year it really is a different mountain.' And how true his words were. Out of 30 days there would be only one when it didn't snow. By 21 May we were ready for action. We had good clear weather every morning but storms every afternoon. Steve and Mick would follow two days behind and Julie-Ann and Roger a day or so behind them. We were all independent and didn't want to be too close to each other on the face, from the point of view of both falling rock and ice and the limited bivouac sites.

Climbing in Alpine style is an ambiguous term. In our case the definition seemed simple enough. We had two 60-metre ropes, an Alpine rack, eight to nine days' food, and ten days' gas. The only item we had that you probably wouldn't take to the Alps was our small tent. We hoped to pitch it on a series of tiny snow arêtes that dotted the bases of the various icefields on the face. We also had a hanging stove with a peculiar history. I had failed to locate my hanging stove at home and so brought along a standard one and then added bits of wire so that we could suspend it on bivouacs. To our surprise Metal Mickey, as we dubbed our construction, ended up being super-efficient.

One thing 'Alpine style' does *not* mean is lightweight. Despite close scrutiny of every item we carried, our sacks weighed 20 kilos. The climbing magazines and picture books can often lend an air of romanticism to Himalayan climbing, but for most of the time it is sheer damned hard work. We planned out our route so neatly – one hour across the glacier, two hours for the lower slopes up to the base of the first difficulties. How naïve we were, despite our joint experience of Himalayan climbing!

We left at 2am, spent three hours getting to the bergschrund and, being unroped, almost fell into it. The lower slopes proved to be anything but a walk. We arrived at what we considered to be the start of the climbing at 3pm, having broken two out of six ice screws and about to receive our baptism of what would become the daily storm.

Brendan led a meandering mixed pitch between two thundering powder chutes, eventually belaying by the left-hand chute. We searched in vain for a place to spend the night. Reluctantly I set off up the left-hand chute, which was not only extremely steep and rejected ice screws, but received regular surges of powder. Finally I made it onto easier ground, but by that time both my gloves were full of snow and my fingers numb. 'Great first night!', I thought, as we crawled onto a small ledge for the night. Down below, across the other side of the glacier, Fowler and Sustad watched our slow progress with surprise. Two days later they experienced a similar day and bivouacked in exactly the same place.

The next two days saw us edge upwards, tackling pitches that would have seemed demanding even at sea level. We had crossed the first icefield, a giant skating rink, tilted at 55°, with an almost impenetrable skin of steel that shattered and splintered until the sun softened it up. Getting in an ice screw took an eternity. We now had only three out of six functioning normally, with one that occasionally bit if persuaded by a violent beating. We had a mixture of 1987 Polish vintage titanium screws and slightly superior 1997 Ukraine ones. Often we were so wrecked after getting just one of these damn things halfway in, we would tie them off and, together with our ice tools, call it a belay. The constant avalanches had acted like giant polishing rags on the surface of the ice, making it much tougher than we had bargained for.

Dawn on day four saw us at the foot of the second icefield. This was important to Brendan, as we were at his team's high point of the previous year. The second icefield passed much more quickly than anticipated and led to a choice of two steep exits. The right-hand option looked like extremely steep ice with two thin sections. Yet, despite our serious lack of ice screws, it still looked preferable to the steep mixed line on the left. One pitch higher and the daily afternoon storm machine was warming up nicely. We had developed a theory that the spindrift came from the icefields but now, with no more big icefields above us and with spindrift sweeping the steep and giant walls out to our right, we realised the frailty of this theory. Snow must be picked from the slopes on the other sides and then swept down our route. Today the ferocity of the storm intensified to fever pitch. Brendan had just led an impressive pitch and now it was my turn.

The situation looked ugly and with ten good ice screws I would have been worried, but with just one tied off that Brendan hung on and two more on my harness, I climbed up full of fear. Absurd quantities of powder now thundered from above, pummelling us. The wind increased tenfold and violent thunder boomed from near the summit. I had climbed beyond the point of retreat.

Twenty metres above the belay I tried to place a screw. It would not bite. Tiring rapidly, I clipped into one of my tools. It held for a few seconds then ripped. Both crampons popped simultaneously and I fell onto my other tool. Then more spindrift swept upward, numbing my face. I struggled with the weight of the sack, the tip of my right tool staving off disaster. Regaining position, I managed to get the screw turning. At the halfway mark I tied it off and took a stance.

We were in the eye of an angry storm. Neck, nostrils, ears, gloves were packed with snow. When Brendan arrived he was retching with pain. I had never before seen him share his suffering so openly. Seeing this hard little bastard wince and groan made our predicament seem even worse, but he hacked on, up a brittle ice-filled corner.

I began talking to myself and flapping my arms to stay warm, but I was losing. I seconded the pitch screaming that I needed something to eat and was verging on hypothermia. Bren held out a food bar and I bit at it, with the wrapper still on. Night was approaching fast as I set off.

The angle eased, and the storm abated. I made it to the edge of the snow arête where we could bivvy. When I eventually reached the belay I had used all the functioning ice screws, and spent twenty minutes trying to beat in one of the damaged ones. Eventually I got it in partway and tied off my axes. I yelled a warning that the belay was shit. Normally Brendan is a super-meticulous, steady climber but, within minutes of his starting, I was yanked tight onto the belay and realised that all was not well. It was dark now and I made out a tiny light way below. After negotiating a 60ft pendulum, Brendan now climbed a more direct route up to the belay.

'That was lucky,' he said. 'I could have lost my head torch.'

At 11pm we crawled into our tent, psychologically and physically roasted. In the course of 15 years in the mountains, I had never experienced such a harrowing few hours. We were both frost-nipped on the fingers and I shivered, cold to the core.

The next day we rested. It was impossible to know what was running through Brendan's mind. He was a private person, and he kept chat to a minimum. After a day's rest I felt better. Brendan led three hard pitches that left us tantalisingly close to the groove system cutting through the final headwall. We fixed our two ropes and returned to our tent. Mick and Steve, who had set off two days behind, caught us up at this point. We were happy to see each other and exchange stories. Mick's typical enthusiasm uplifted us, but we were all worried about the danger of being too close. We considered joining forces, thinking it might be safer. Ultimately, however, we surmised that bivouacking in the steep upper grooves with a party of four might prove awkward and we were also reluctant to suddenly change systems. We all agreed that teaming up for the descent might prove beneficial. At that stage, though, we had no idea what surprises lay in store.

Reaching the groove system proper involved some of the most challenging climbing yet, and Mick and Steve, seeing our slow progress, opted for a relaxing day 'indoors'. But this was not to be. Brendan dislodged a large rock, which beamed in on their tent like a heat-seeking missile. Cringing on the belay, I feared the worst. Eventually Mick appeared and relayed that we had destroyed the back of the tent and that they were OK.

The afternoon snow began falling and filling the tent via this hole at such a rate that they considered descending. We felt dreadful. We moved into the grooves, which comprised especially hard brittle ice, and succeeded in making two more holes in their tent – events which elicited increasingly irate comments from below. I peered up at the next pitch. It looked long and hard. I tensioned off a knife blade and stabbed a tool into a blob of ice at the foot of a shallow groove and then followed an intermittent seam of ice over perfect granite. In terms of quality it was one of the best pitches either of us had ever done; I reached the belay knackered but buzzing.

The next morning I woke after a fitful night, and surveyed our surroundings. We were hemmed in by walls of El Cap stature. Huge arching corners, vast blank-looking sheets of icy granite and, here and there, a lonely crack that ran into some mad-looking roof. To be up in this world, to have overcome all that had been thrown at us, now elicited feelings of pride. Ice over perfect ice in a mind-blowing position – I led a long, hard mixed pitch.

Each pitch that day had a sting to it. The afternoon weather came in force, but we were so close to finishing the face that we bore it with extra patience. After negotiating a hideously loose aid section, we thought we could smell the top. But nothing came easily on this mountain. Brendan persevered up bold, powder-covered granite slabs that placed him within striking distance of the cornice. I joined him and then set to work on the final pitch to the ridge. What a pleasure to be hacking through the cornice after eight days' climbing.

The following morning it took me a while to register that it was in fact my birthday. To my surprise Brendan pulled out six Snicker bars. He had carried them up and never mentioned them. We celebrated with a whole chocolate bar each. We couldn't be too extravagant as we had virtually no food left. Fortunately, Mick and Steve had over-calculated their food and had agreed to help us out during the descent. Today the weather closed in at 8am and thwarted any possible attempts on the summit.

Instead, we passed the time by repitching the tent, as we had discovered that we were actually sleeping partly on a fragile snow mushroom, a section of which had disintegrated during the night leaving our feet unsupported. Throughout the day we chatted about all kinds of things. We had grown close during the climb and had become like an eccentric couple. We knew what soup or type of tea the other preferred, knew each other's aspirations and fears. Brendan, however, never talked without a purpose, and there was always a large part of him that seemed unknowable, that he had decided not to share.

I moaned that I was becoming too old for this sport. At 31 I had been at it ten years. But I also loved skiing and bouldering and, after all, you couldn't carry on doing this for too long, could you? Brendan didn't say much, but he too loved his rock climbing and spoke about how last summer, spent cragging in Britain, was one of his best. Philosophising high on that twisting corniced ridge seemed a luxury after the grinding face. That evening we ate our last meal. We had plenty of gas and enough drinks for another two or three days, but other than two chocolate bars each, eating was now officially over until we linked with the other two.

The first day of June dawned beautifully. I came out of the tent charged with energy. We carried light sacks and conditions underfoot were good. The summit looked close.

'I feel like I'm out for a trot in the park. Do you want me to take a bit of your gear?'

Brendan seemed to be moving more slowly, and he handed me the two water bottles to carry. After an hour or so we were forced onto the ridge proper. We put on the rope, primarily for psychological reasons. But less than a minute later an enormous section of ridge beside me snapped off and tumbled down the North Face. I teetered there, trying to control the surge of adrenalin racing through my veins. Brendan sat sixty metres away in a bucket seat, a leg on either side of the ridge.

Six pitches later the trusty afternoon cloud arrived. Our pace slowed and my earlier enthusiasm was virtually extinguished. A swirling mist enveloped us on the final ridge, robbing us of the magnificent views we had expected. The descent to the col between the horns of Changabang ate up one hour of our time. A layer of soft snow lay over brittle ice and, at the apex of the col itself, we sank almost to our waists. Giant rocks loomed out of the mist. We climbed out from between the horns and began the final, weary 200 metres in appalling visibility. At the summit we congratulated each other, then sat in the snow.

'I'm really chuffed,' Brendan said. The lack of food was taking its toll.

As we sat there the clouds dropped below us. Nanda Devi floated in front of us, Dunagiri behind, and in the distance the unmistakable Kamet. We wanted to linger but, with the descent down the twisting ridge still to come, we turned our backs on the summit. In the top of my rucksack I found the remnants of a broken biscuit, which we shared. I was amazed that Brendan still had some of his chocolate bar left.

Voices floated up through the clouds.

'Is that you Steve?' A lone figure stood on the ridge far below.

'Yes. How are you?'

'Good. And you?'

'Fine.' Suddenly the mist swept in and he disappeared.

Later there were two figures, this time 200ft lower and erecting a tent. It looked like a good place for a bivvy and I chided myself for not having spotted it for ourselves. Once close enough, Mick seemed eager to catch our attention. It seemed they had arrived at this wonderful camp spot by default. Steve had tripped on his balled-up crampons and dragged the two of them down. Mick had escaped unhurt, but Steve had been less fortunate. He lay in the tent with intense pain in his ribs and chest. Assured we could do nothing to help, we returned to our tent for the last of the instant soup.

Despite our fatigue, our minds were in a whirlwind. Exploring every avenue of escape, we concluded that everything hinged on the extent of Steve's injuries. Mick and Steve had a rough night: Steve was in pain, and Mick was perturbed by his partner's irregular breathing and groaning. They were glad that we were around to assist, and we were glad of them, as we had now begun to hallucinate about eating some of their mashed potato powder. The weather had been so consistently bad that the arrival of another poor day evoked no response. Fortunately Steve could move, albeit with great suffering. We spent a whole day getting ourselves to the Kalanka Col.

That evening Mick and Steve invited us for tea. Crammed into the back of their tent, we sat shaking with the excitement of eating. Steve prepared a wonderful dish of mashed potato, a meal that I will never forget. I even got to lick out the cooking pot. Now that *was* a birthday present!

If the climb had drawn Brendan and me together, the descent would draw the rest of us together more than we could ever have imagined. Ironically, back in the UK I hadn't climbed with Brendan that much. We moved in our own circles, meeting fairly regularly but rock-climbing together only occasionally. We had gelled socially on Gasherbrum IV and knew of each other's strengths. The number of people interested in such enterprises as Changabang's North Face is limited, and this often means that climbers have to search for climbing partners beyond their usual circle of friends. Good, successful partnerships are rare but, once established, the two can throw themselves, every two years or so, into adventurous enterprises requiring close co-operation and trust.

The next morning brought a biting wind. The simplest task took an eternity as I had to stop constantly to unfreeze my fingers. In near-zero visibility we started our descent, with enough food to last three or four days. For a while the sky cleared and the terrain proved straightforward. But as the weather closed in, it became difficult to find a safe route, and we did extremely well to locate a tiny flat area on the edge of the vast icefield we were aiming for. By this time we were all utterly exhausted, but from here just two or three abseils would see us into an easy gully and then down onto the Changabang Glacier. Mick abseiled first and I followed.

'It's too steep.' Mick shouted, just as I began. 'Too steep for Steve.'

Mick was right. Suddenly it became undercut, and a free-hanging abseil with broken ribs would have been dangerous. I climbed back out and Brendan volunteered to set up another anchor out to the right. He spent 20 minutes trying to get a screw in. There was a lot of névé but not much ice.

'I've got a bomber now,' he shouted across to us.

'He reminds me of Dick Renshaw,' said Steve. From what I had heard there were similarities: both were quiet, determined and tough but always with a gentleness and a disturbing modesty and selflessness.

'We used to call him the little angel,' Steve continued, 'because whenever there was a job to be done, a job that others didn't want to do, he would do it without any fuss.'

Seconds later a muffled noise came from above. Way up, an avalanche released and then another and another. These silent slides joined forces, heading straight for us. Time stood still. In a panic I began screaming and yelling.

'Brendan ... Brendan ... Brendan!'

I beat my axe into the slope up to the hilt and clipped in. The whiteness took an eternity to reach us. Brendan saw it coming but had no sling to clip into the ice screw. No rope. No second tool. Absolutely nothing. He tried to grab the screw. I turned away terrified.

Eventually it came. So quietly and so softly it took Brendan, sweeping him away to our right. Stunned I couldn't move at first and then started rocking my head, trying to control my anguish. The avalanche had stopped now, the debris sloughing to a halt just 20 metres away. Darkness was not far away and Mick and Steve led me down to a small safe spur where we would spend the night.

In reality Brendan had no chance of surviving, but still we shouted into the night. The next day we searched and shouted, and then saw the giant cliffs over which the avalanche had tracked. I shouted helplessly up into the deep empty basin ...

The next two days were the toughest any of us had ever dealt with. During the night, as I replayed the scene of Brendan disappearing, my thumb felt as if it was going to burst. The next morning an ugly black blister had appeared. Given reasonably stable weather, we aimed to cross first the Shipton Col and then the Bagini Pass. We estimated that they were both at around 5700m. If we stuck to one meal a day, our food supply might just see us through. Although attractive, the alternative descent down the Rishi Gorge had not been travelled for years and would take too long. We had no choice but to go for it and cross the two cols. We prayed for good snow conditions and a little luck. We had to get back to base camp soon. Steve and I needed a doctor and Roger and Julie-Ann would be desperately worried by now, assuming they had retreated and were waiting at base camp. In the event, foregoing a night's rest, visions of losing my infected thumb drove me to press on, leaving Mick and Steve below the face.

We began the long climb to the Shipton Col at 1am. I stared up at an unforgettable night sky. Between Nanda Devi and Changabang were great carpets of silver galaxies. Morning bathed the sacred mountain in a magical, golden light. I soothed myself by thinking how Brendan would rest in one of the most remote and beautiful mountain valleys on Earth. Soon the tiny spring flowers would be pushing their way through the thinning snow, carpeting the edges of the Changabang Glacier. Before reaching the col, I turned around one last time and said goodbye.

Summary: On 1st June 1997 Andy Cave and Brendan Murphy reached the summit of Changabang, 6864m, having made the first ascent of the North Face. Following a day behind, Mick Fowler and Steve Sustad reached the summit ridge on 1st June but Sustad slipped on 'balled up' crampons and the pair fell 200ft. Sustad sustained chest injuries and the four climbers teamed up to descend by the normal route on the south side of the mountain. At around 6000m an avalanche tragically hit Murphy while he was setting up an abseil and he was swept down the face. It was not possible either to locate or recover his body. Meanwhile Julie-Ann Clyma and Roger Payne spent 10 days on the face, reaching the Ice Tongue just above the second icefield. They sat out terrible storms there before abseiling off without incident.

JULIE-ANN CLYMA

Mountain of Dreams, Mountain of Sorrows

(Plates 15–19 and front cover)

Perhaps the most special mountain is the one that captures your imagination in your early climbing years – the one that is so big, so hard, so impossibly beyond your ability that it could only ever be a dream. For me, Changabang was such a mountain. And then the dream became a reality. Fifteen years after reading about the incredible ascent of the West Face by Peter Boardman and Joe Tasker, I found myself sitting above the Bagini Glacier and looking onto the North Face of that 'shining mountain'. Similar adjectives sprang to mind – steep, hard, technical – but now the 'impossible' was tempered to just 'improbable', and, as we looked closer, even the improbable began to seem possible.

May-June 1996

So it was that in 1996, by dint of good timing, good luck and persistent letter-writing, a team of four found itself with a permit to enter a controlled area and a chance to attempt this mountain of dreams. The team comprised Andy Perkins, Brendan Murphy, Roger Payne and me, and during May and June we made the first attempt on the North Face.

Because of environmental restrictions, the traditional approach to the mountain, following the Rishi Gorge into the Nanda Devi Sanctuary, has remained closed since 1982. So we approached from the north, to make our way up the Bagini Glacier and reach Changabang on the sanctuary rim from the outside. An impressive array of peaks surrounds this glacier, made all the more enticing by the ease of the approach – just two days' drive from Delhi to Joshimath, and then a two-day walk to Base Camp.

Once Base Camp had been established, our first task was to acclimatise and do a reconnaissance of the face. The main part of the North Face is a stupendous sweep of steep, clean granite, with improbable ice formations stuck randomly to it. The major lines of weakness lie on a buttress on the left side of the face, and while there appeared to be quite a selection of possible starts, there seemed only one likely finish. The key to any route would be to reach a central icefield, and then an upper snow spur which gives access to a groove system exiting onto the East Ridge – the junction with the original line of ascent of the mountain.

Our reconnaissance trips took us onto both the Bagini Col (5860m) and the unnamed col (*c*5690m) on which Peter Boardman and Joe Tasker had camped when they made their ascent of the West Face. This site was an excellent spot for viewing the starts of routes and we chose one that began on the right side of the obvious buttress. The route was a steep, thin ice runnel in a large corner system which appeared to lead in a continuous line to easier-angled mixed ground and then onto the edge of the central icefield. When planning the route, back in the UK, and looking at photographs of steep granite walls, it was decided that adopting a modified lightweight form of 'capsule style' would be the most appropriate. Hence, the four of us climbed co-operatively, with the two pairs sharing the leading and load-carrying.

On 3 June we set off from Advanced Base Camp at 5am, carrying all our rope and technical gear. We reached the bergschrund (*c*5450m) at around 7am and split into pairs. Roger and Brendan started on the route, with the intention of leading out all the rope, while Andy and I returned to camp to pick up food and tents and then carry as much gear as possible up to the high point established by the other two. By late afternoon about 350m of rope was out and most of our provisions sat at the end of it. We returned to ABC for the night and as we were all tired from our efforts we returned to Base Camp for a rest before making our main attempt on the route.

On 9 June we started back on the route. Unfortunately, the technical gear we had cached was now buried under several feet of fresh snow, as was the start of the rope, and an hour of digging was required to get it clear. Andy and Brendan then started up the ropes first in order to get to the high point, sort out the gear and go into the lead. Roger and I followed, carrying the heavier sacks and pulling up the ropes. Initial snow slopes led up to the thin ice runnel, which became progressively steeper. From the top of the fixed ropes Brendan and Andy led another two hard ice pitches. By then the heat of the sun had the couloir running with water and the whole team retreated off to the side onto small sloping rock ledges.

After a very uncomfortable night, Brendan and Andy led off again, pushing the route out to the top of the couloir and onto the mixed ground. The climbing was exceptionally steep with just adequate protection, and the couloir finished with a series of overhanging bulges. By the time Roger and I had reached this section, water was again cascading down and we finished the day soaked to the skin. We all met up together at the base of the mixed ground and spent an even more uncomfortable second night bivouacked on rock ledges.

On the third day Roger and I went into the lead and finished the section of mixed ground leading to a snow crest on the edge of the central icefield. This was really enjoyable climbing, with interesting moves and good protection. It was late afternoon before everyone was on the spur, and again no tent sites were immediately obvious. However, feeling in need of a proper rest, we spent four hours chopping inadequate ledges out of hard ice, and by 9pm we had the luxury of lying down flat.

Unfortunately, overnight Andy became ill with a severe case of diarrhoea (later diagnosed as arising from salmonella). It had already been decided that the next day should be a rest day, and this was now doubly important to enable him to recover. We spent the day in good weather, looking at the route ahead and catching up on food and fluid intakes. On the 13th we had hoped to move up, but Andy was still too weak and the weather had deteriorated, so we had another rest day.

It seemed from our analysis of the route that it would involve at least another three days' climbing from the spur to reach the summit, and then at least two further days for an abseil descent. With limited food and fuel, and with our porters due on 19 June, it was becoming imperative to start on the route again the following day. In a group discussion we went through all the possible options, and Andy indicated that he hoped he would be able to continue and that we would all move on as a team of four.

14 June dawned with high cloud and the promise of more bad weather, but with Andy a little improved we packed up camp and started the laborious process of traversing across the central icefield. This was the crux of the route in terms of commitment, as there would be no easy abseil off from this section if things went wrong, and in bad weather it was prone to constant spindrift avalanches from snow sloughing off the rock walls above. It was also a critical passage in leading to the upper snow spur, which we thought would lead to the technical crux of the route – to get off the tongue of ice and establish ourselves in the rock grooves leading to the East Ridge.

Roger led out from just above the campsite on a descending traverse. Two more pitches saw us into the middle of the icefield, with a good view of the difficult exit couloirs which would take us onto the upper snow spur. Unfortunately at this point it became clear that Andy was totally debilitated through his illness and that continuing up was out of the question. At the same time there was a sudden, rapid deterioration in the weather. There was little option but to return to the campsite on the spur, and we climbed back in heavy snowfall and spindrift avalanches. After an uncomfortable night with continued steady snowfall, the following morning dawned grey with more bad weather, and our summit attempt was over.

May-June 1997

While the 1996 attempt had ended in retreat, we were hardly back at Base Camp before our thoughts were turning to a rematch. The outstanding quality of the climbing in such a magnificent setting kept it foremost in our minds as an objective that could not be left unfinished. A year later we returned as a team of six. From the original expedition there were Roger and me; Brendan was this time joined by Andy Cave; and our numbers were completed by Mick Fowler and Steve Sustad. With the knowledge we now had of the type of climbing on the North Face, we were convinced that a route would go in Alpine style, and in 1997 we were committed to climbing as three independent pairs.

Returning to the same mountain was an unusual occurrence for us – but it had a definite advantage in that planning was much more straightforward.

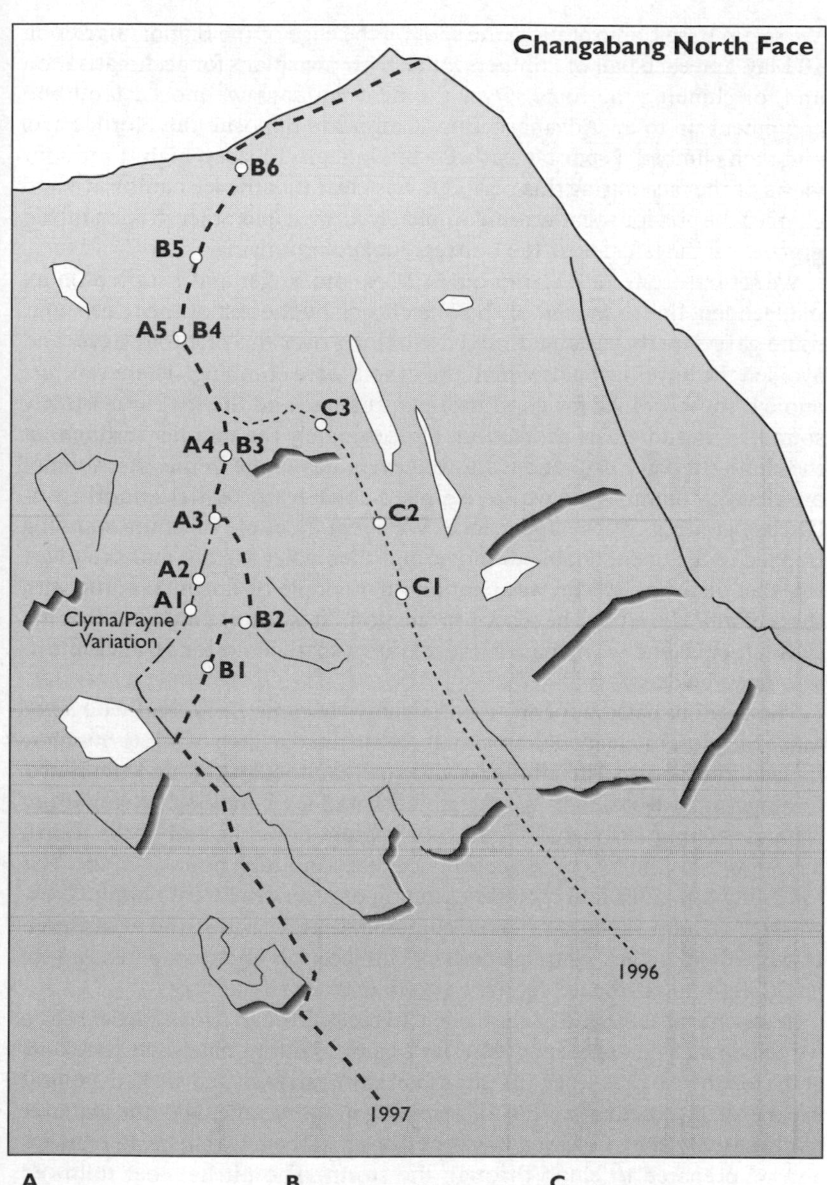

A
J-A Clyma, R Payne
26 May to upper icefield
on 30 May 1997

B
A Cave, B Murphy
23 May to summit on
1 June 1997

M Fowler, S Sustad
25 May to NE Ridge on
1 June 1997

C
J-A Clyma, B Murphy,
R Payne, A Perkins
9 June to central icefield
on 11 June 1996

We set up Base Camp at the same spot on the edge of the Bagini Glacier on 10 May, and each pair of climbers made their own plans for acclimatisation and for climbing the route. Over the next ten days we moved food and equipment up to an Advanced Base Camp site opposite the North Face, and then climbed a spur beneath Purbi Dunagiri to sleep high. From our views of the face during this period it was clear that the ice couloir we had climbed the previous year was incompletely formed, but other striking mixed grooves on the left side of the buttress looked promising.

We set out from Base Camp on 24 May, and Roger and I started on an independent line to the left of the one chosen by the rest of the team. Our route gave superb, sustained mixed climbing over the first four days, and avoided the lower icefields which the others were climbing. There was just enough snow and ice for good tool placements, and the rock was mainly sound, giving adequate protection. Unfortunately the weather throughout the climb was very bad, and it snowed every day. Late in the afternoon of our first day on the route we were pinned down by torrential spindrift avalanches pouring off the upper face. We spent a couple of hours standing trapped in the open, unable to move, and then when we did manage to get together on a small ledge we spent another couple of hours standing with the tent pulled over our heads for protection. It was not until 8pm that the snow stopped and we managed to excavate a small ledge for an uncomfortable open bivouac.

The weather pattern for the next few days became fixed, and we had to make the most of clear cold mornings, before increasingly wild storms blew in each afternoon. The climbing was steep and technical, and the route-finding totally absorbing. We moved back and forth, linking up runnels of ice and torquing through difficult rock passages. By the end of the fourth day we were at the foot of the central icefield – our high point of 1996. The following day (30 May) brought climbing of a very different nature. Now we were on hard, green ice and the climbing was precarious and exhausting. It was difficult to get secure placements for ice tools and crampons, and we had to fight to get the ice screws to go in more than halfway.

It was critical at the end of the icefield to break through a rock barrier before we could reach an upper snow spur for a camp. Unfortunately, we were only at the foot of the rock when the afternoon storm arrived, and we had a repeat experience of standing waiting for an easing in the weather with the tent over our heads. By 4pm, however, it was obvious that there was to be no reprieve, and we prepared to climb through the storm. The pitches that followed were the hardest so far – a strenuous mixed groove followed by a traverse on a blank slab. With gathering darkness, freezing temperatures, and a black eye from a bouncing ice axe, the climb was taking on the proportions of a major epic. Finally, at 11pm we crawled into our tents on the crest of the spur and the following day we took what felt to be a very well-deserved rest.

From this platform we could hear the occasional calls of the others as they continued up the final groove line to the East Ridge. From our own perspective, given the difficult conditions we had already encountered, we felt it was imperative that we should see some improvement in the weather before attempting this final part of the route, or else we could foresee serious cold injury or worse. Rather than improving, however, the weather worsened, with snow becoming constant throughout the following days. For three days we still entertained ideas of going up, despite problems clearing a blocked stove jet and me feeling increasingly ill with what seemed like bronchitis. But after the third night when three avalanches swept over the platform, collapsing the end of the tent, just getting back down safely became our prime objective.

On the fourth day we tried to descend, but this attempt was abandoned because of avalanches before the first abseil was completed, and we climbed back up to the tent platform. Eventually on 4 June we started down the North Face, and after one bivouac reached the glacier late on the 5th. After so many days on the vertical, it was hard to adjust to this suddenly horizontal world and I staggered unevenly across the glacier to reach Advanced Base Camp. There was a feeling of regret at having to retreat from the face again, but we also felt a strong satisfaction in the climbing we had achieved, in Alpine style and all free. Most of all, though, there was an overwhelming relief to have got back down safely.

Now, with our position secured, our thoughts turned to the predicament of the rest of the team. Assuming that the others must have reached the top and be descending the south side of the mountain in the same grim conditions we had endured, we could only imagine the exhausted state they would be in. With no sign of their return we could do little but descend to Base Camp and wait for news. This was swift in coming and tragic in content.

The next morning Andy arrived at Base Camp, soon followed by Steve and Mick. Brendan would not return, having been lost in an avalanche on the descent of the South Face. For us, the climbing of Changabang's North Face had encompassed the very best and the very worst of the climbing experience. We will not soon forget the struggle and the exhilaration of the climbing, but we have lost a friend, and everything else becomes meaningless in the face of that fact. We can only take some small comfort that Brendan climbed his sacred summit and rests in a beautiful place, looked over by the goddess, Devi.

Summary: In May/June 1996 Julie-Ann Clyma, Roger Payne, Brendan Murphy and Andy Perkins attempted the 1600m-high North Face of Changabang (6864m). On the traverse towards the upper icefield Andy Perkins became too ill to continue and they had to turn back from 6200m. In May/June 1997 they returned to the mountain with Andy Cave, Brendan Murphy, Mick Fowler and Steve Sustad. Clyma and Payne spent 10 days on the face, reaching the ice tongue just above the upper icefield. They sat out storms there before abseiling off and joining the rest of the team at Base Camp, where they learned of Brendan Murphy's tragic death.

JIM LOWTHER

The First Ascent of the Kullu Eiger

(Plates 2–4)

'Something technical but not too scary, something unclimbed, cheap and easy to get to, and in an interesting area.' That was my advice to Graham Little on the telephone in January 1996 when we pondered an alternative climbing objective in India at short notice, after our planned trip to Tibet had been called off. We had both been spoilt by years of climbing in pristine, little-known or unclimbed ranges in Greenland, Baffin Island and the Indian Himalaya and it was not easy to repeat, time after time, an expedition philosophy founded on 'exploration'.

However, Graham's knowledge of India, gained through seven previous trips, was bound to produce something interesting: he chose a jagged rock peak called Gupta in the Kishtwar region near the Kashmir Valley. In the rush to get things organised, the fact that a guerrilla war was quietly going on there had escaped our attention. So it came as a nasty surprise when, two days before our departure, we received a curt fax: 'Government of India has not accorded clearance to your expedition to Gupta Peak'.

What to do? Graham took on the job of dreaming up another objective, preferably in a place where there wasn't a war going on or Western hostages being kidnapped. Harish Kapadia put us in touch with Dr M S Gill, the President of the Indian Mountaineering Foundation, an unflappable man with impeccable connections. On our arrival in India we found that his invisible influence had cleared a path for us and bureaucrats hurried through the necessary paperwork in record time. As explained to us by a harassed clerk, 'It is as if a great weight has landed on us from above'.

So what was this new objective? Graham was able to produce a reassuring-looking photo-copy of a black and white photograph taken in 1970 of an Eiger-like mountain above the Parbati Valley, Himachal Pradesh. It had been named the Kullu Eiger by someone called Charles Ainger who was quick to spot the peak's resemblance to its Swiss namesake. Just the name of it was enough to get the adrenalin going. We tried to ignore Harish's throw-away comment, relayed to us on the day of our departure: 'Oh, Jim, you will know of course that this mountain of Graham's has just been climbed by some Italians.'

The fact that there are quite a number of 'Eigers' in the Indian Himalaya had escaped the attention of both of us. We accepted without question that the Italians had done it, but we doubted that they would have chosen the North Face route. This was the route favoured by our third climbing member, the youthful Scott Muir, who was on his first visit to the Himalaya.

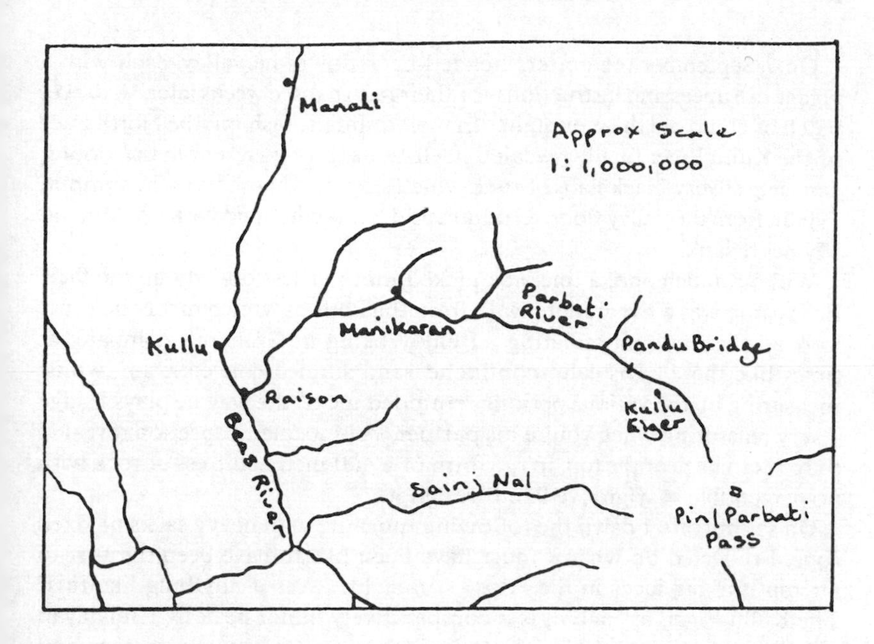

Aged 20, and with a Scottish winter climbing pedigree that already surpassed by far my own fitful career, his bold attitude to routes was complemented by his physical strength and raw climbing ability.

The three of us, plus 'base camp manager' John Findlay, departed from Delhi on 3 September 1996. Soon we were climbing up through the foothills in our chartered bus into the cleaner air of the Kullu Valley. At Manali, with its tacky chalet hotels, hundreds of trekking companies and goats with tinkling bells, we met our old friends Pasang and Prakash Bodh. In record time Pasang organised our supplies of base camp food and cooking utensils, and 25 porters appeared complete with their 'camping and wet weather gear'. Clouds enshrouded the hills and mountains and occasional rain warned us that the monsoon had life in it yet.

Our walk-in started from an offshoot of the main Kullu–Manali valley, at a pilgrimage town called Manikaran. Our porters swiftly settled into their daily routine. After breakfast, arguments would ensue over who would carry which load – surprising, as they were all the same weight. This initial burst of energy usually reached a pause after the first hour for a cigarette break or, for the more needy, a chillum of hashish. Not surprisingly, progress slowed to a snail's pace the more height we gained. The supplement that we had agreed to pay the porters for extra clothing and tentage had apparently been spent on something else, for at Pandu Bridge the incessant rain reduced our pathetic team to shivering groups crouching underneath rocks, with only their cigarettes for comfort. Scott's flapjack and a huge brew put spirit back into the team and mercifully the rain stopped for the last day into base camp.

On 7 September the porters headed back down the valley, each with a wadge of rupees and instructions for their return three weeks later. A darker patch of cloud hid the mountain. In melodramatic fashion, the North Face of the Kullu Eiger finally revealed itself to us through a rent in the clouds, exposing silvery-black slabs of rock which stretched above us to the summit, 1900m from the valley floor. Graham and Scott whooped with excitement. My heart sank.

Without much ado, a line was picked more or less directly up the face. Base camp was a five-minute walk from the bottom, which made the route look all the more intimidating. I enjoy being in Graham's company at times like these. His calm confidence and studied concentration whilst measuring up the various options reminded me of the way he plays bridge – very reassuring when you're his partner. A binocular inspection revealed the crux to be near the top, in the form of a 400-metre buttress of rock with no perceptible easy groove line through it.

On setting off at dawn the following morning with heavy sacks of fixed rope, I reflected on what it must have been like to have been the first to attempt the big faces in the Alps – on sight. Was it anything like this? The Kullu Eiger, at 5646m, is a comparatively minor peak by Himalayan standards, but therein lay its attraction: unvisited by the masses and unknown to all but a few.

A long scramble up talus took us to the start of the climb. Our plan was to use all our fixed rope – 300 metres of it – in securing a steep rock band at the bottom of the face and go Alpine from there. A promising twin-cracked groove fulfilled our hopes and gave classic, albeit vegetated, climbing up steep granite. Scott and Graham alternated the lead and I jumared behind them with a sack full of fixed rope. Whilst I grunted and cursed under the crippling load, the other two yipped and sang in delight as they padded up eight pitches. At the top we dumped the remaining gear and some gas cylinders and swiftly abseiled back down again in time for some chapatti and a bowl of *subjee* at base camp.

The following morning we scrambled up the talus again by the light of our head torches. I found it hard keeping up with Graham and Scott who seemed to be making it a race, or perhaps they were just keen to get going. Our sacks were cripplingly heavy and the ensuing jumar to the top of our fixed ropes left the tendons in my arms aching. We walked and scrambled up a series of vegetated ledges covered with strange Martian-looking plants, their purple flowers (*Saussurea simpsoniana*) festooned with what looked like thick cobwebs.

The sun had now swung round to shine on the North Face. This had the heartening effect of making our immediate surroundings seem less steep, but the way ahead, above a large icefield, would obviously be no pushover. Underneath a small buttress of rock in the lower icefield, we found a scoop large enough for the three of us to lie down in, with fantastic views of the Parbati Valley. Base camp lay beneath us as a green spot among a great

The North Face of Kullu Eiger, 5646m. (*Jim Lowther*) (p18)

3. Graham Little seconding Jim Lowther's pitch through the icicle overhang. (*Jim Lowther*) (p18)

4. Scott Muir and Jim Lowther on the summit of Kullu Eiger. (*Graham Little*) (p18)

number of white spots – the sheep and goats being herded back down the valley ahead of approaching winter. Great hammerhead clouds stretched like columns down either side of the valley. We brewed up in windless, perfect comfort, and admired the sunset from the warmth of our sleeping bags.

That night the unsettled conditions produced an eerily silent sheet-lightning display which dissipated by about 4am. Cloud had covered the face by morning, and it was only drizzling so we carried on. Soon we became stuck on some easy-angled slabs. Each of us harboured private doubts about how far we would get up the mountain which, with every passing hour, looked more and more serious. Our ungainly loads were becoming an annoyance so, forsaking his sack, Graham swore his way up the greasy slabs in rock boots. After three hours, he finally found a diagonal line that connected us to the main icefield. We had only run out one rope length and already half the day had passed.

We bombed up the icefield, front-pointing with two axes, and then ran out a rope length up to a much smaller icefield which, for some reason, became known as The Mask. It was foggy, damp and cold. The cloud build-up of the previous night obviously heralded a change in the weather pattern, so we dumped non-essential gear and abseiled back to our last bivvy for the night and a review of tactics.

On waking the following morning an inch of snow covered our bags and our minds were made up. Get down. I had barely wriggled out of my bag and Graham and Scott were already sauntering off downhill. For the second time we whizzed down the 350m-long abseil and clambered down the talus back to base camp for a supper of mutton and whisky followed by a game of bridge. We decided that we had not wimped out – for the next four days it rained at base camp and snow plastered the face.

All of us were consumed with that sense of anticipation brought about by the knowledge of a great task lying ahead. Now that we were established on the mountain, we just wanted to get on with it. Eventually, with time beginning to run out, we committed ourselves to a final push on the 16th. But first we decided upon a radical weight-saving strategy. We would leave our sleeping bags behind and rely upon our duvet jackets for warmth. We also took the little Gemini tent, and I slipped in a bivvy bag. As we probably wouldn't be able to sleep very well, Graham packed his *temazepam* sleeping tablets. We were driven by thoughts of making fast progress with super-light sacks on the technical ground that we knew lay above our high point.

We left the following morning, once again by the light of our head torches. I found myself going well – I could even keep up with Scott on the talus slope. Near the start of the fixed ropes we looked back down into the gloom. The solitary light from Graham's torch remained stationary. An hour later he had caught up with us and told us in slurred words that he wasn't fit to go on. The idea of continuing without him didn't appeal, so I voted that we go down. For an awkward moment Graham hesitated but, not wishing to be seen as a kill-joy, he elected to carry on in the hope of an improvement.

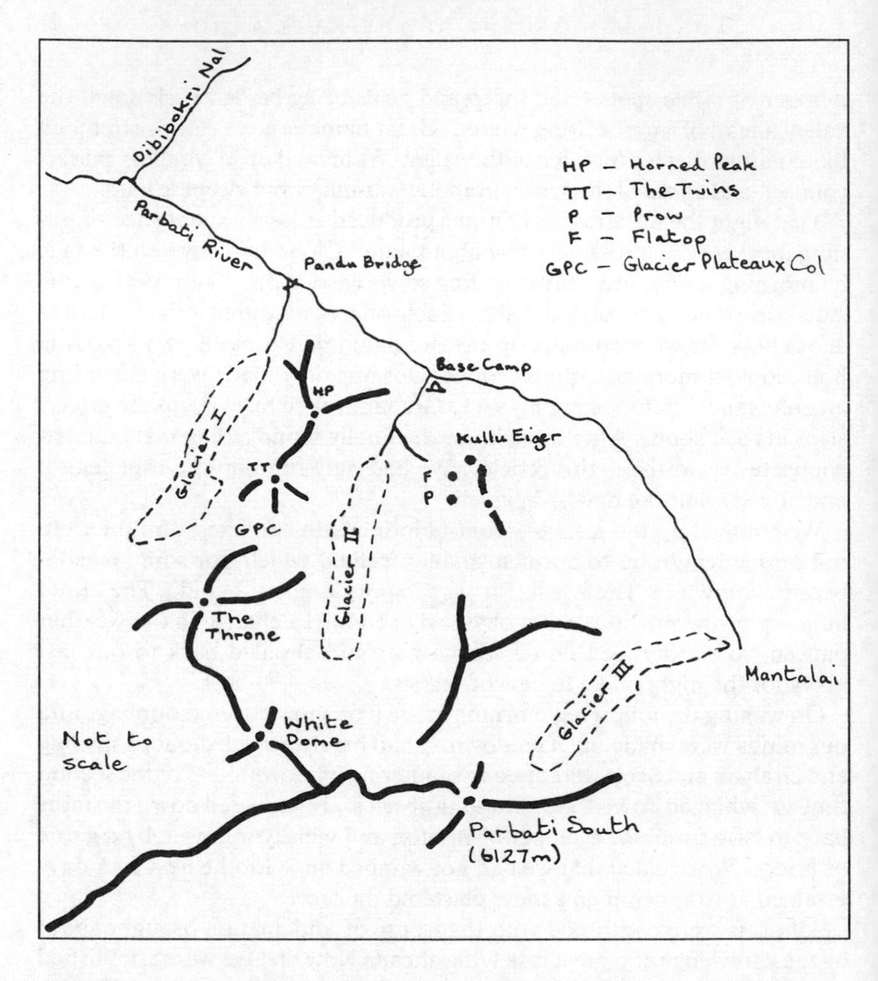

After our four days of rest and with lighter sacks, we were up the fixed ropes by noon and brewing-up at our first bivvy. Taking some of the food and gas cylinders we had left there from our previous attempt, we jumared up the fixed rope crossing the smooth slabs and from there stomped up the icefield, making The Mask by mid-afternoon. This brought us to the base of about 500 metres of intermittent steep grooves and ice-smeared rock. I belayed Scott whilst he started up a steep corner. Graham silently started clearing rocks and digging out the ice to form a tent platform.

The prospect of some good climbing had a therapeutic effect on Graham and he managed a very thin, scratchy grade V pitch up an ice-filled groove with a startling finish. Scott came through and struggled up the continuing groove which ran out, forcing him off left. In the declining light it was difficult to see what was going on, but we heard a grunt followed by expletives and he was off, slamming into the wall about two metres below. We decided to call it a day, so left the ropes in place and abseiled back down to the tent platform.

The Gemini tent is a squash for two and very intimate for three, but having no sleeping bags meant that we could actually fit in. Cooking outside the tent, I managed to throw the pan down the mountain. The other two were kind and made nothing of it (fortunately we had brought a spare). As Graham snored contentedly in his *temazepam*-induced sleep, Scott and I shivered our way through the night and longed for our sleeping bags. Unfortunately, the combined heat of our three bodies had little effect, so eventually, with Graham by then in a groggy half-awake state, we whiled away the rest of the night massaging our feet and praying for dawn.

Next morning the opposite side of the valley was bathed in light whilst our side was still frozen, but after jumaring up the ropes, warmth returned and our spirits rose as the blue sky of a clear day deepened. It was cold and crisp, sunny, and Alpine in feel. From the place of Scott's fall of the night before, I led through, after which Graham did another stunning pitch on rock and verglas. Scott led a groove of thickening ice – the colours of his clothing and flying splinters of ice catching the sun as shafts of light edged around the mountainside and shone obliquely across the North Face. Above him, curtains of icicles sparkled as they hung from two mild overhangs. I took the lead, brushing aside the first of these curtains, sending down debris below me to mute cries of warning from Graham who was still jumaring up the previous pitch. My axes sank in satisfactorily to their hilts as I swarmed up the plasticky ice through the first overhang and around the second. After a small chimney I stepped right and with heavy rope-drag was relieved to reach a small ledge for a belay. At close on grade V it wasn't the hardest pitch of the route, but it was the most satisfying.

Graham came up next. As he passed me, the plate of ice he was attached to shattered, falling away in spinning disks. Scott ducked down below and I looked up to see Graham still hanging on – from a solitary axe. He finished the pitch in double-quick time and disappeared for what seemed an age. Eventually his head poked over the top of an ice block, his face grinning. 'Do you want the good news, or the good news?' he asked. What he had found was an ice cave fit for kings, with room for a tent platform. The other bit of news was that he had spotted a corner system which would allow us to cut across to the left of the uppermost buttress on the face.

Scott and I quickly came up to join him and admired our prime piece of real estate and its view. I elected to hack out a platform while the other two started up the corner. Scott was the first up it. The crux was an overhanging block which he wriggled over by getting an axe placement into frozen gravel and heaving on it. They led out two more pitches and then abseiled down to the bivvy where I had a feast prepared of soup followed by oatcakes topped with Tartex pâté and cheese, then mackerel and shortbread, all washed down by mugs of fruit tea. Scott reckoned he didn't get better fare at his student flat in Edinburgh.

That night was the coldest I can remember. Confronted with another night of sleepless shivering, I popped a couple of Graham's pills and slept

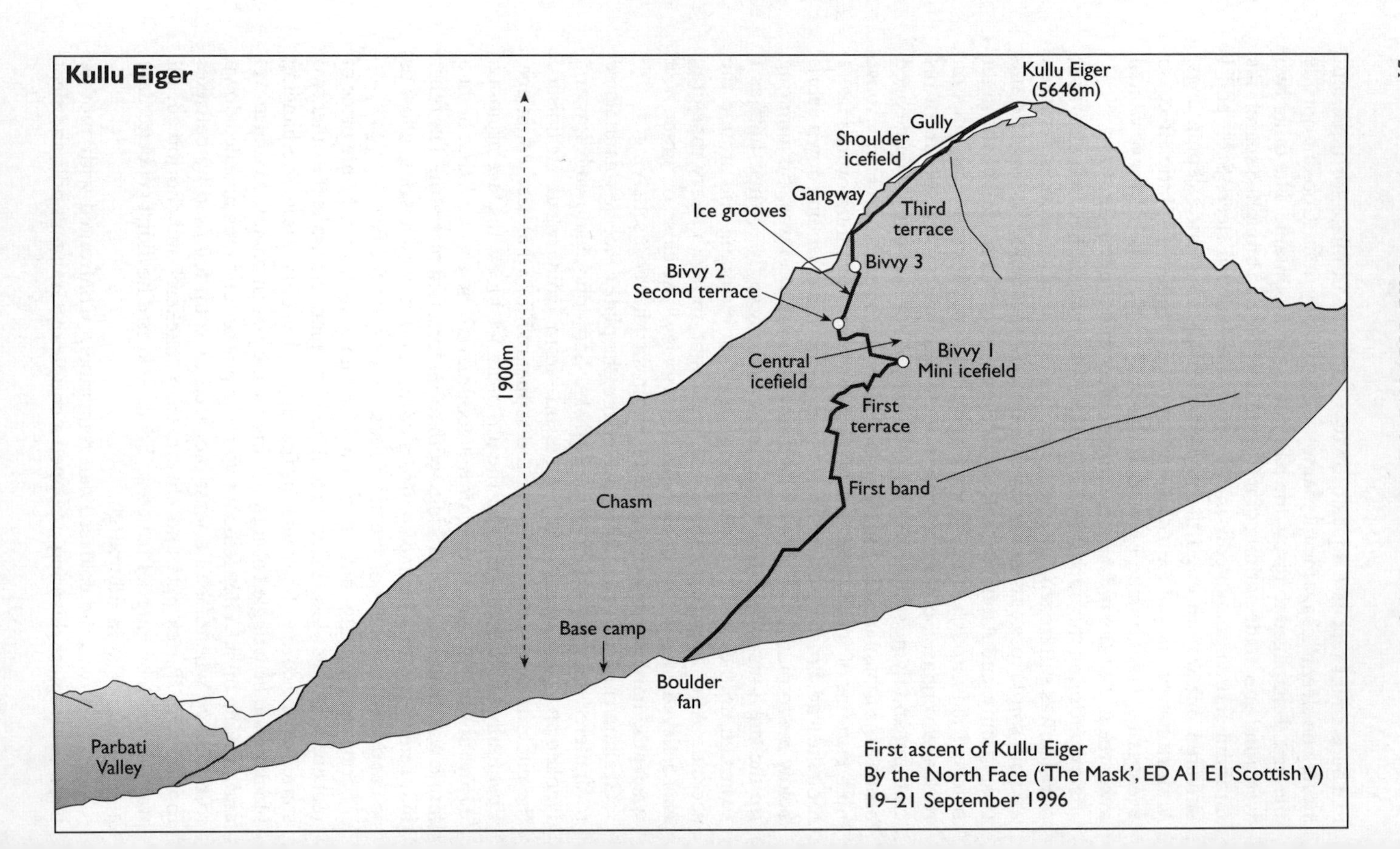

First ascent of Kullu Eiger
By the North Face ('The Mask', ED A1 E1 Scottish V)
19–21 September 1996

like a log until midnight. I woke up feeling like a stiff pair of jeans frozen into a board. I was sleeping ouside in my bivvy bag, but the others, in the Gemini, weren't faring much better. In the morning we waited for the sun before starting. Deciding it would be summit day, we left everything behind at the bivvy and succumbed to some more lightweight climbing advice from Graham. Last time it was sleeping pills, this time it was the suggestion that we take one water-bottle between us – and no stove.

We jumared the first three pitches and followed a ledge which progressively wound its way around the upper buttress. Above us a smooth wall offered us no hope of rapid progress. Graham carried on, inching his way round until he discovered the Gangway which got us onto a snowfield. We realised we had cracked it. Moving together we covered 300 metres on névé in rapid time. I took the lead through a shallow gully which offered an easy route through the mica schist which caps the summit. At a change of lead we finished the water and I began to get my dry cough which seems to dog me at high altitude. Graham continued up steep nine-inch-thick windslab and then brought us up onto the East Ridge.

The sun was strong as we walked up, across mica mud, to the summit. All of us knew at that moment that it hadn't been climbed before. I could hardly believe that we had done it. Around us was spread a vista of untouched mountains – a mountaineer's Nirvana, waiting to be tapped. To confirm our ascent we built a small cairn and posed for pictures in still and calm conditions, sleeves rolled up and the sun hot on our faces. I wasn't allowed to bring my Union Jack – we were supposed to be a Scottish expedition after all – so the St Andrew's flag was proudly produced by Scott, the most Scottish among us.

We took the rest of that day and all of the next to descend. As we reached the bottom of the 25th abseil we were greeted by the smiling faces of Pasang, Prakash and John who pumped our hands and slapped our backs – their sense of achievement as great as ours, and genuine. They thrust mugs of tea and chocolate into our hands and took our sacks for the final descent to base camp. A week later I walked out back to the roadhead, initially with John and then alone. I wanted to savour those last few days slowly. I spent a night in a shepherd's cave and three days in a village, doing nothing. It had been my best trip to date, on my hardest mountain. I had ended the trip with five very good friends and a wealth of experiences. I can think of nothing better.

Summary: The first ascent of the Kullu Eiger, 5646m, in the Parbati Valley, Himachal Pradesh, India. The 1900m North Face was climbed and the route named The Mask, at a grade of Alpine ED (E1, A1 and Scottish V). Graham Little, Jim Lowther and Scott Muir reached the summit at noon on 21 September 1996.

P M DAS

Qomolungma

The First Indian Ascent by the North Ridge/North-East Ridge

This article is a personal account of the Indo-Tibetan Border Police Expedition in April-May 1996. The author was Senior Deputy Leader of the 25-member expedition, though he did not belong to the organisation.

The going was hard. Every step was an effort and even changing the jumar clamp on the fixed rope required tremendous will-power. It was 19 April 1996 and this was my first attempt to reach the North Col at 7010m. We were a party of 19 people, including our star climbers, Smanla and Dorji, who were keeping me company on the fixed ropes. But while others moved ahead to dump their loads at the North Col, I soon realised that I was not yet fully acclimatised and turned back approximately 50ft below the last section of fixed rope. Back at ABC, I discovered that other members of the party were also feeling the altitude.

We had left New Delhi on 22 March and had travelled by road to Kathmandu. Crossing the border with Tibet at the Friendship Bridge, we reached Zhangmu where we were joined by our Chinese liaison officer Li Rui Hua, who had been deputy leader of the Chinese expedition to the NE Ridge in 1975; with him was interpreter Xu Chang. We and our 475 loads were transported in three trucks and two land cruisers. At Nyalam we spent a day acclimatising before continuing to Xigar at 4200m and the snow-covered Nyalam Thungla (5000m) – a flat, snow-covered field. The road ran east-west and here we enjoyed our first views of Qomolungma.

At the Shelkhar Hotel at Xigar we met teams from different countries planning to attempt Mount Everest by the same route as ourselves. Three nights later we drove for six hours over a reasonable dirt track, crossing a pass at 5500m with views of Shisha Pangma and Cho Oyu, to reach our Base Camp at Rongbuk on 5 April. Excellent views of the North Ridge and the NE Ridge dominated the landscape as we entered the Rongbuk Valley. We shared Base Camp with 14 other teams of various nationalities. Japanese and Russian teams were already camping there. Our own team was fit and eager to be on the move – the race to the summit was on.

The route from Base Camp at 5200m to Advanced Base Camp at 6400m runs up the East Rongbuk Glacier and is a long haul of 15km. Initially we found the going extremely tiring, so we set up two intermediate camps at 5700m and 5800m. But with the passage of time, and with the movement of yaks carrying loads up to ABC, the route became well-trodden and many of us were later able to go from Base Camp to ABC in one day.

During the period of acclimatisation at Base Camp I found plenty to do. The hospitable Li, our liaison officer, often entertained us to Chinese tea and biscuits at the permanent hut, equipped with television and a running mess, which the ChinaTibet Mountaineering Association (CTMA) has built for its liaison officers. I visited the historic Rongbuk Gompa which was destroyed by the Chinese during the Cultural Revolution and later rebuilt. I was able to stalk and photograph a herd of *nayan* which had taken up residence near Base Camp. The ceremonial *puja* was conducted by the Lamas of Rongbuk, culminating in the installation of prayer flags on a mound near our camp. I visited and photographed the memorial stone to George Mallory and Andrew Irvine who died while climbing the same route that we were about to attempt. We also visited the place where fourteen other memorial stones have been erected by various expeditions. They reminded us of the dangers we were about to face.

On 8 April I walked up to Camp 1 where I was able to photograph a family of *ram chakor* at very close quarters. The advance party, consisting of Smanla, Prem and Davinder, had already moved up to Camp 2 and would soon be establishing Camp 3. I got to know Jon Gangdal, the leader of the strong Norwegian team, and found that we had much in common. Not only were we the same age, but we discovered that we had the same mental approach to our task. We met frequently on the mountain to discuss a variety of subjects, ranging from Norwegian fjords to different climbing styles. Often we were joined by other members of his team, including Joseph Nezeriche – one of Czechoslovakia's most experienced 8000m climbers. This was a team that worked with enviable harmony and precision, so that eight of their ten members eventually reached the summit.

I occupied Camp 2 for the first time on 15 April after carrying a rucksack of 15kg. The next day, with a lighter sack, I took six hours to reach Camp 3, our Advanced Base Camp, at 6400m. This was overlooked by the North Col at the head of the East Rongbuk Glacier, up a steep ice/snow slope of 700m. Across the valley I could see the NE Ridge of Everest, ascending from the Raiphu La to the summit. On our right was Changtse, the beautiful North Peak of Everest, while extending southwards from the North Col to our left was the windy North Ridge up which we would soon be climbing.

On 18 April Mohinder Singh, our leader, complained of chest congestion and vomiting. Perhaps the altitude gain had been too fast for him. He went down for a rest. The route to the North Col having been opened by a combination of German, Norwegian and Indian teams, the plan was that five climbers, headed by Prem Singh, would establish a camp on the North Col, open the route to Camp 5 and return to ABC in three days. The rest of us would move up in support. So, on 21 April, I climbed the slopes above ABC, tackling the traverse up the final slopes to the North Col. Here I found, in addition to the Indian tents, some of the same Norwegian, German and Japanese teams who had earlier been working on lower portions of the route. They were now out in front, opening up the route from Camp 4 to Camp 5. On the higher slopes of the mountain the weather was clear. Camp 5 was eventually established on 27 April by Sangay Sherpa and a team of four. The rest of us returned to Base Camp in buoyant spirits.

Back at ABC on 29 April I found that the camp site had swelled with various expeditions of different nationalities camped in tiers, like a small rising village, along the glacier. There were the inevitable problems of toilets, hygiene and of melting water to drink, but it was clear that the Norwegian camp was the most efficiently organised. They had even installed a kerosene stove in their mess tent to warm themselves.

30 April was spent discussing tactics. Sangay Sherpa reported that, while opening the route to Camp 5 at 7800m, he had fixed 230m of rope, while the Japanese team had also fixed some parts. It was decided that from now on, groups of climbers would climb to the North Col, spend a night there, try to reach Camp 5 without oxygen and return to ABC. This exercise was to get fitter and more acclimatised before the summit attempts.*

On 2 May I reached the North Col, accompanied by Harbhajan Singh and five others. Looking up towards the summit I could see, etched clearly against the skyline, the First Step at 8498m, the Second Step at 8595m and the site for Camp 6 below the crest of the NE Ridge, at 8320m. The weather was clear and I was acclimatising well. I hoped soon to be on the summit with one of the assault teams. The party under Prem Singh was now returning from having carried loads to Camp 5 and they descended to ABC. Sangay Sherpa and Nadhre Sherpa, together with Kusang, the sirdar, again occupied Camp 5.

On 3 May I was ready early, but other members of our team had already left for Camp 5. However, the fixed rope was there and I clipped on and moved up at a slow but steady pace. In my rucksack was a load of oxygen cylinders which I intended to take as high as possible for the first summit team. We were lucky that on that particular day the sun was warm and there was no wind. The North Ridge is notorious for high winds and intense cold, but now it was pleasantly airy and I got a superb view of Norton's Couloir which looked a promising alternative in case the Chinese ladder (placed in 1975) was missing at the Second Step.

Soon I came across a group consisting of Wangchuk, Dorji and Norphel returning from Camp 5 after dumping their loads. They asked me to descend with them but I waved them on, hoping to carry my load as near to Camp 5 as possible. As I reached the end of the snow ridge at 7700m, with the camp now only a short distance away, suddenly all my usual energy seemed to evaporate. I asked myself: why continue if you are not enjoying the climb? Is it to prove that you are strong enough to reach your objective at any cost?

There was no suitable place to dump my load without the risk of theft (an unfortunate problem with so many expeditions on the same route), so I placed it behind a rock 100m lower down before returning to the North Col where a hot meal was waiting. I was soon joined by Harbhajan who

* *See note on acclimatisation on page 33.*

told me that the route to Camp 6 had been opened by Sangay, Nadhre, Kusang and Nima Sherpa. I descended to ABC the same day, withstanding a snowstorm on the lower slopes of the North Col and getting chilled to the bone by the time I reached camp, where Mohinder Singh was waiting with hot tea.

After establishing Camp 6, a reluctant Sangay was recalled to ABC. A great feeling of confidence now prevailed and most of the climbers were straining at the leash, though I warned them that we were ahead of schedule and that the weather was likely to break again shortly. Moreover, many members were suffering from dry coughs and needed to rest.

The summit teams were announced by Mohinder Singh in consultation with Harbhajan Singh and I heard that I would be leader of the third assault party. Harbhajan Singh was to lead the first party and Prem Singh the second. Beset with stomach trouble and a tiresome cough, I descended to Camp 2 where a satellite telephone had been installed. For the next few days we were able to communicate with the outside world, much to the relief of our families back in India.

On 7 May I was back in ABC and the first summit group, consisting of Smanla, Dorji Murup, Chewang Paljor, Wangchuk, Jodh Singh, Lobsang (who was suffering from mild frostbite on one finger) and Harbhajan Singh prepared for the assault. Harbhajan and Dorji moved up to spend the night on the North Col, while the rest of the first summit team climbed directly from ABC to Camp 5 in six hours on 8 May.

On 9 May we experienced some anxious moments as there was no radio contact with the assault group; we presumed that all was well and that they were occupying Camp 6. The route from Camp 5 to Camp 6 passed over the 'boiler-plate slabs' below the NE Ridge but was fairly straightforward. When Lobsang realised that frostbite was endangering all his fingers he decided to go down. Meanwhile, the second summit group, led by Prem Singh, moved up to occupy the North Col camp.

The First Assault: triumph and tragedy

On 10 May, we anxiously watched the movements of the summit team, camped at 8320m, through binoculars and a telescope. Cloudy weather meant that, despite their best efforts, they could only make a late start at 8.00am. This may have been crucial to the outcome. They then sorted out the jumble of old fixed ropes (the ITBP team was the first one in this season to work above Camp 6) and climbed towards the First Step at 8498m. When they ran out of fixed rope, Paljor volunteered to return to Camp 6 to collect some more rope and return.

Harbhajan, who was suffering from frostbitten toes, was moving slowly. With Jodh Singh and Wangchuk, he turned back near the First Step. Smanla, Dorji and Paljor (all Ladakhis) carried on fixing rope and ascended the Chinese ladder at the 30m Second Step, which they cleared by 3.40pm. The walkie-talkie at ABC crackled into life and Smanla informed Mohinder

Singh that the three Ladakhis were headed for the summit. There was an air of jubilation in all camps. But Harbhajan Singh, the assault leader, did not come on the air.

We were anxious as the weather was closing in, but at last, at 18.30hrs, Smanla announced over the walkie-talkie that the three of them had reached the top. Mohinder told them to look for the Chinese tripod and other items planted on the summit by earlier teams and to take photographs. Meanwhile, the second group, camping at the North Col, and the Norwegian team also camping there had seen our summit team a little short of the top and informed us accordingly over the radio.

By 7.00pm a storm was raging over the summit section and there was no radio contact. Mohinder was busy on the satellite telephone informing the organisers and others of the success, but we were anxious for the climbers to get back safely. Little did we realise that five climbers on the South Col route would perish in the storm at about the same time. At 7.30pm we noticed two head torches and the rapid movement of climbers descending. One of the beams spiralled downwards, towards the Second Step ... followed by darkness ... as they disappeared out of our lives ...

On 11 May ABC failed to get any response from the summit group at Camp 6. At 6.00am Prem Singh came on the air from the North Col to say that he was in touch with Camp 6 but had to inform us that the summit group had failed to reach the camp. At the top of the Second Step he had spotted a figure moving around and seemingly looking for a way down.

This was the day that the Japanese Fukuoka party of five were to make their summit bid. They had spent the night of 10 May at Camp 6. The ITBP began liaising with the Japanese leader at ABC for a possible rescue attempt. The Japanese leader was co-operative, and though there was no direct communication from ABC with the summit group, he was able to get in touch with them via Base Camp.

The Japanese team had made an early start, and between the First and Second Steps they had come across Dorji who, they said, was proceeding down slowly. He had refused to put on gloves over his frostbitten hands and was having difficulty in unclipping his safety karabiner at anchor points. The Japanese unclipped it for him before attaching him to the next stretch of fixed rope. Smanla was already dead and his body was seen lying above the Second Step as the Japanese team with their Sherpas moved up towards the summit slopes. It was not known whether Paljor had also been seen by the Japanese but in an account given later by one of the Sherpas in the Japanese party, he had been seen alive but delirious between the First and Second Steps. On their return from the summit, the Japanese team had passed Dorji again below the First Step, and assuming that he would be able to reach Camp 6, they carried on down. He must have died that afternoon and his body was found by later teams near Camp 6. The body of Paljor was not found and it is likely that he slipped and fell down the cliffs towards the Kangshung Face, on the eastern side of the mountain. During the course of the day, Wangchuk and Jodh Singh, who were in Camp 6, had made an attempt to move towards the First Step but were enfeebled by the altitude and returned after leaving four oxygen cylinders 100m short of the First Step. Prem Singh and his group had moved up to Camp 5 to assist the fatigued climbers in Camp 6.

The tragedy of the three doomed climbers brought home to us the truth that mountaineering at extreme altitudes is a very dangerous activity, demanding not only superior climbing skills but also good understanding of all the physiological and weather problems involved. Rescue at such altitudes can only be attempted at great risk to the lives of the rescuers themselves. The tactics of mountaineering at these heights is not the same as it is on peaks of 6000m and below; it involves a 'feel' for mountains beyond that of an average mountaineer. Leadership of a superior order is required and, above all, stronger team-work than is necessary on mountaineering expeditions at lower altitudes.

During the next few days there was much debate as to what should be done: should the expedition be called off or should a fresh assault be mounted? Advice was sought from the leaders of the British, Slovenian and Norwegian teams, who advised that the expedition should be called off, as had been done after similar tragedies on previous occasions. Most of our own team members agreed that, to honour the climb made by the three lost climbers, it would be a proper tribute to call off the expedition, even though the rest of the team were extremely fit and almost every remaining member was probably capable of climbing to the summit. However, after consulting with his headquarters over the satellite telephone, Mohinder announced that it had been decided to make one more assault.

Accordingly, Sangay Sherpa, Hira Ram, Tashi Ram, Nadhre and the sirdar Kusang, with the other Sherpas in support, moved up. Harbhajan's frostbitten toes were very painful and he was completely exhausted, despite having used oxygen on the descent. He and his two companions left for Base Camp where he spent an agonising period until the end of the expedition.

The Second Assault: success and a safe return

On 15 May the second group, led by Sangay Sherpa, moved up to Camp 5. On 16 May the group, consisting of four members and Kusang Sherpa, occupied Camp 6 where the summit teams of the Norwegian and Japanese groups were also camped. On 17 May the second group, along with the Norwegian and the Japanese teams, climbed in copybook style. We watched through a telescope at ABC as the climbers emerged from the Second Step, crossed over a snow field, ascended the fixed ropes on a rocky section at the top of the Great Couloir, before reaching the final summit slopes.

They were on the top by 9.55am and Sangay's voice came jubilantly over the walkie-talkie. They went through the summit rituals around the GPS prisms, the Chinese tripod and Smanla's prayer flags before turning back. The weather was stable and they descended to the safety of Camp 6 without difficulty. On the way down they spotted the body of Smanla lying prone above the Second Step, without jacket and crampons, about 20 metres away from their route. His rucksack was missing and so was his red Gore-Tex jacket. Lower down, they passed the body of Dorji lying under the shelter of a boulder near their line of descent, and close to Camp 6. His clothing was intact and his rucksack was by his side. Their bodies lay in their last resting places high up on Qomolungma – 'the finest cenotaph in the world'.

On 18 May the summit party moved down cautiously, bypassing Camp 4, and I received them with the others at ABC. They said that the only really difficult section on the route had been the upper part of the Second Step; other summit climbers' opinions of the route varied between 'difficult', 'dangerous' and 'not difficult but requires full concentration'.

Tashi Ram told me that he had placed on the summit a small plastic bottle given to him by me. The bottle contained a mixture of the holy waters of the Ganges, Hemkunt Sahib and Lake Gurudongmar of Sikkim.

I descended the same day, past three camps, reaching Base Camp by the late evening carrying a 10kg rucksack. The route was crowded with various teams going home. During the next few days the rest of the team wound up the high camps and most members were back in Base Camp by 20 May. There were signs that the weather was breaking. One after another the teams left Base Camp for their respective countries. After clearing the camp we paid a farewell visit to the memorial stones of Joe Tasker and Peter Boardman, Michael Rheinberger, Martin Joey and others whose bodies are still on the mountain, along with our three dead team mates. We laid a memorial stone for Smanla, Dorji and Paljor after I had arranged for it to be engraved in Kathmandu and delivered to Base Camp.

I asked myself: what has been gained in the last two months on this mountain? The physical and emotional strain had been enormous. I felt that the mountain had brought out the worst in us and that all our obsessions had been laid bare, overwhelming the time-tested qualities of the true mountaineer. I looked back on all the agony, pain and deaths, and the words of Jon Gangdal, the Norwegian team leader, who came to say goodbye to me, rang in my ears for a long time. He ought to have been very happy, he said, since eight of his ten-member team had reached the summit. Yet he told me that he had decided never to climb an 8000m peak again.

At the same time, I tried to take a more positive view. I looked back to all the friendships I had made with fellow climbers of different expeditions; to the interaction with so many fine climbers from different countries. We shared a common bond – that of the mountaineer away from his home, climbing in a remote corner of the earth on the highest mountain in the world, which taxes the human body and brain to the fullest. I realised that Qomolungma is a mountain which can change your life. A person makes history by setting foot upon it.

With Prem Singh, I left for Lhasa on 26 May in a land cruiser, with the task of procuring death certificates for our three comrades. The two of us spent four days in Lhasa being looked after by Gau Mauxing and Dou Chen, respectively Director and Deputy Director of the CTMA, and I was able to discuss with them matters of common interest to them, to the Indian Mountaineering Foundation and to our climbing fraternity. For Prem Singh, who is a Buddhist, it was a very special occasion, but for both of us it was a pilgrimage, as we visited the Potala and the monasteries of Dreypung, Sera, Norbulingka and Jorkhang.

Eventually, on 1st June, we flew from Lhasa to Kathmandu and on to Delhi where the rest of the team had arrived by road. Most of us were lean and thin. Stomachs had contracted, flesh was compact, muscles were hardened with usage; some wondered what had happened to our flab! I assured them, including those with first and second degree frostbite, that our normal shape would return in due course, for I had been through this process before.

The team now had to face the world of the press, receptions and controversies, but the climbers knew that 'the effect of Everest' would stay with them for ever.

Summary: A personal account, by the Senior Deputy Leader, of the first Indian ascent of the North Ridge/North-East Ridge of Everest. Three climbers – Smanla, Dorji and Paljor – died on the first summit assault but the second assault team reached the summit on 17 May 1996 and returned safely.

A NOTE ON ACCLIMATISATION

In the event, I found that there were three varied reactions of the climbers to our acclimatisation plan. The Ladakhis and those members who were of Sherpa origin seemed to settle down to any pattern of movement once they had spent two days at Camp 3. A second lot of fit plainsmen seemed to deteriorate with continued movement above Camp 4. The third lot – including two of the three women in the party – failed to acclimatise beyond Camp 3 and could not reach Camp 4. Those who chose to remain at Camp 3 to rest after working higher up, were not as refreshed as those who spent the same amount of time walking down to Camp 2 or Base Camp and then up again. A similar observation was made by some of my friends in other teams. Our wireless operator and doctor, who spent most of the expedition at ABC at 6400m, lost the maximum amount of weight.

APPENDIX

Some personal comments follow on assertions which have appeared in the press since this article was written, particularly those made by Joe Simpson in his book 'Dark Shadows Falling'. I make them simply as a climber who witnessed some of the events described and not on behalf of the ITBP.

National teams and team rivalry

None of the teams on the mountain were national expeditions in the strict sense of the word. Ours was an expedition composed of Indians and one Mongolian, organised by the Indo-Tibetan Border Police. Similarly, the 'Japanese' team was basically a team from Fukuoka and not a national team with members representing the country. To that extent avoidable controversies have arisen because of the loose usage of the names of the countries in the media.

No doubt there was eagerness amongst the different teams to be out front and to open the route on the mountain. It is only natural for climbers to prefer route-opening rather than following. For this reason, co-ordination meetings were held between the various team leaders at Base Camp and a tentative schedule had been evolved for route-opening.

More than any obvious rivalry between teams, what I did notice was an intra-team rivalry within our own large expedition. The three who perished were Ladakhi soldiers who competed with Sherpa soldiers of the ITBP to be first on the summit, and this compounded their problems.

The late start

For reasons mentioned in my article, a late start was made on 10 May. But many climbers have reached Everest's summit as late as 6pm, and have survived after a forced bivouac. In 1963 the American pair Unsoeld and Hornbein reached the top at 6.15pm after making the first ascent of the West Ridge. On the descent from the summit by the South Col route they joined Jerstad and Bishop who had themselves made a late start owing to a fire accident (*HJ25*, 64). The four were forced to bivouac at about 8600m, but all survived. There are innumerable other examples.

The first assault

It has been unjustly asserted that the three climbers of our first group failed to reach the summit, reaching only a point 500ft below it. In fact they were seen from ABC and from the North Col moving along the summit ridge well before the storm hit them. I myself overheard the radio communication between Smanla and Mohinder Singh, the leader, and the former declared that the three of them were on the top. Even if we assume that Smanla planted the prayer scarves short of the summit, he announced on the radio that he was going ahead in search of evidence of earlier expeditions. We accepted his claim in good faith. Their headlamps descending were visible to many of us at ABC on the East Rongbuk Glacier at about 7pm.

The allegation that they failed to reach the summit was made on the strength of a statement by the Fukuoka party that there was no evidence of footprints beyond that point. However, this unjustified assertion by a rival party is discounted by the evidence provided by the radio communication, which was heard by many climbers. Also, since the storm hit the NE ridge and the summit section thereafter, can we not assume that footprints would get obliterated?

No doubts on this issue were expressed by other teams before we left Base Camp. Our leader, Mohinder Singh, was given a certificate by the Chinese Chief Liaison Officer to the effect that the three dead climbers had indeed reached the summit. The Chinese LO was a seasoned Everest climber and was in charge of all the teams on the mountain.

Smanla and his two companions were not foolish and I think that Smanla was comparable, in temperament, to the legendary Hermann Buhl. He was in rank a Junior Commissioned Officer whose Himalayan experience was credited with more high summits than anyone else's on our expedition. It is therefore possible to assume that he took over the decision-making of the first assault group on the fateful day. Why did he make such a risky decision? The approach to risk in mountaineering has been well described by Dr Sol Ray Rosenthal who, after many years research, found 'that there is something in risk that enhances the life of the individual – something so real, something with such impact that people who have experienced it need to experience it again and again.'

Rescue attempts by the ITBP team

It has been alleged that the ITBP team mounted no rescue attempt of their own. The first assault group consisted of seven climbers: Smanla, Dorji, Paljor, Wangchuk, Jodh Singh, Lobsang, and Harbhajan Singh, their group leader. Lobsang turned back first with frostbitten fingers. On 10 May, at 3pm, Harbhajan Singh turned back, along with Wangchuk and Jodh Singh. Responding to directions from ABC, and despite their own fatigue, Wangchuk and Jodh Singh went back on 11 May in an attempt to help Dorji; they left some oxygen cylinders at a point beyond which their own tired bodies could take them no further. The second team, led by Prem Singh, moved up from the North Col and concentrated on rescuing the three survivors, having been told that the other three were already dead. I believe that all these team members did what they could to help their companions.

Finally, I should emphasise that had Indian mountaineers come across such a tragedy, I think they would most probably have abandoned their own summit attempt and concentrated on rescuing other climbers in distress, as in the 1984 Everest Expedition when they rescued the Bulgarians who had already completed their climb to the summit. It would not have been the first time that Indians had made such a sacrifice.

24 September 1997

ARUN SAMANT

In Pursuit of Gya

(*Plates 5–8*)

Early in 1983 Harish Kapadia noticed a high peak on a Survey of India map and was highly excited about his discovery. 'It is the highest peak in Himachal Pradesh,' he said, 'and nobody has even heard about it!' The peak was 6794m in height and was located at the tri-junction of Spiti, Ladakh and Tibet in the Lingti valley of the Lahul-Spiti district. Harish's excitement was infectious and we were all deeply involved in the pursuit of this unknown highest peak in Himachal Pradesh.

Books, journals, gazetteers, magazines, travel brochures – we left no pages unturned but came up with absolutely nothing. No photographs, no information, nothing. We could find no reports of any trekking parties, army patrols or local people even visiting the base of the mountain. Gradually our initial enthusiasm subsided. The point 6794m stared bleakly at us from the map like a big question-mark. We were even unsure of the correct spelling of the name of this elusive peak – Gya or Gyah? The only information we could find came from Tibetan scholars in Darjeeling, who interpreted the meaning of 'Gyah' as 'vast, great, widespread'. So we left Bombay on 20 June 1983 like a group of blind men in search of this highest, vast, great, widespread peak in Himachal Pradesh.

The road from Shimla to Lingti, our roadhead, runs initially along the great Sutlej river, across Kinnaur and later along the Spiti river. It is an engineering miracle. Most of the 394km road has been laboriously hewn out of the steep mountainside and is therefore susceptible to frequent landslides requiring constant maintenance. Tabo, Ki and Dankhar monasteries are encountered as the road passes through Spiti. The Tabo monastery is the one most revered by all Spitians. Established in AD 996, it is the most interesting monastery of that period and has been called 'The Jewel of the Himalaya'.

Owing to the monsoon rains, this road had been breached at a number of places and we were forced to make many transhipments of our luggage across the breaches. Luckily we managed to obtain priority over locals in obtaining seats in army vehicles at almost all these breakpoints. Often the vehicles were loaded to two or three times their normal capacity. Finally, at midnight on 25 June, we were unceremoniously deposited by a local bus at Lingti village, four days after we had hit the road at Shimla. By this time we were almost at the end of our tolerance level of patience after suffering the bad road ravaged by monsoon, the hard seats of army trucks, crowded buses in poor conditions and the ladies of Spiti who smelt of yak butter and chattered loudly and endlessly.

From Lingti we climbed up to Rama and Lalung (3660m), the last village in Lingti valley, with *khotas* carrying our loads. Lalung is regarded by geologists as a 'library' covering 250 million years of geological history, with its well preserved specimens of shales, ammonites and fossils. Here yaks were arranged for our onward journey towards Gya, about which none of the villagers, neither young nor old, seemed to have any knowledge. We pushed up along a high-level route south of the Lingti river. This route was familiar to the yak drivers since they used it in the summer to reach grazing grounds near Chaksachan La, north of the river. We camped below Zingu top (4390m), traversed the scree slopes of a tortuous gorge, crossed Shijbang Pass (4820m) and camped on grassy land beyond it. The route descended to the Shijbang nala, climbed up to Sasena, traversed high over Sibu, went down to cross the Sheru nala and climbed up to a camping ground at 4880m, where our luggage was deposited by the yak drivers.

This was our Base Camp and from here we scanned the horizon for elusive Gya in a northerly direction, as guided by the map. We saw a lovely huge peak, dome-shaped, serene and full of snow. Slightly to its right but far away we saw a majestic high rocky peak. There was a marginal difference between the compass bearings of the two peaks and this resulted in vigorous debate among ourselves about the true identity of Gya. Soon a consensus was reached and the closer large snow dome was proclaimed as the true Gya, as it fitted the interpretation of the word 'Gyah' which had been made by Tibetan scholars from Darjeeling. On the map Gya was about 35km from our Base Camp. Shekhar, being an airforce pilot, was better equipped than the rest of us to judge long distances with the naked eye. He said, 'That rocky peak appears to be 35km away, the snow dome is much closer. The rock tower must be Gya'. However, his sole dissenting voice went unheard, especially as the rocky peak was declared to be on the Tibetan side of the border.

The gorges leading to the base of our Gya looked formidable but, once at its base, it appeared to be easy to climb. One of the approach routes went from Base Camp to the Lingti river, crossed the river at Phiphuk, climbed up to Lashitanga and the Chaksachan La, and then descended to the Lingti once again. An alternative route would proceed to Detto-Numa in the east above us and then follow the Tangmor gorge to the Lingti river and proceed along it. We opted for the latter, which turned out to be a mistake. Though very beautiful, the Tangmor gorge was narrow with cliffs on both sides. Unfortunately sheer rock walls prevented us from progressing along the gorge and we were forced to retreat to Base Camp.

Though the expedition failed to reach its main goal of climbing Gya, many smaller peaks were climbed or attempted and it was an enjoyable experience for all of us.[1]

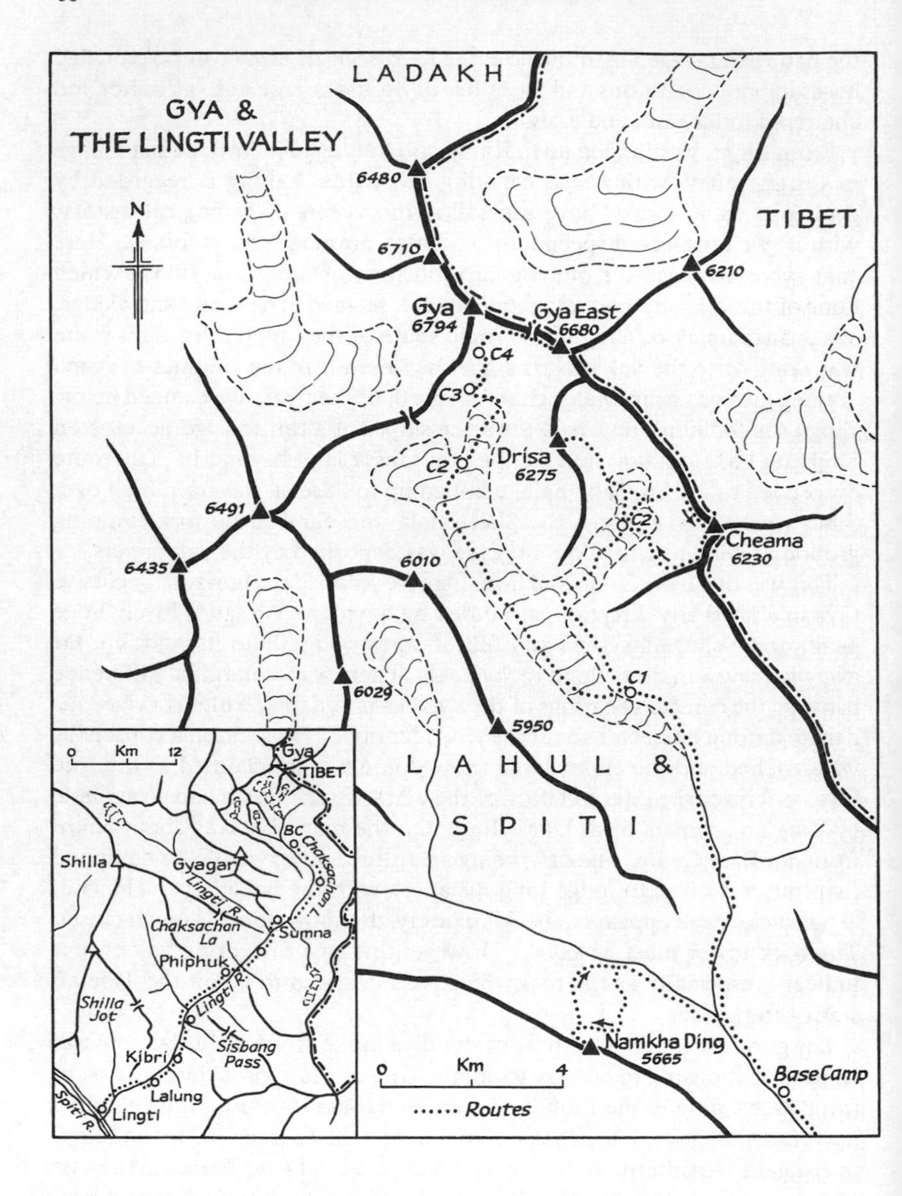
LADAKH
GYA &
THE LINGTI VALLEY
N
TIBET
6480
6710
6210
Gya
6794
Gya East
6680
C4
C3
Drisa
6275
C2
6491
C2
Cheama
6230
6435
6010
6029
C1
5950
LAHUL &
SPITI
0 Km 12
Gya
TIBET
BC
Chaksachan
Shilla
Gyagar
Lingti R.
Chaksachan
La
Sumna
Phiphuk
Lingti R.
Shilla
Jot
Sisbang
Pass
Kibri
Lalung
Spiti R.
Lingti
Namkha Ding
5665
0 Km 4
Base Camp
...... Routes

Led by Harish, we organised a second expedition to Gya during July and August 1987. Although I was deeply involved in the project from the beginning, unavoidable circumstances forced me to drop out at the last moment. The expedition followed the 1983 route up to Sheru. Going along the flooded Lingti river was impossible owing to its narrow passage through a gorge formed by steep walls. The team descended and crossed the Lingti river at Phiphuk, climbed up to Chaksachan La and again descended to the bed of the Lingti river. At some point during this approach march it dawned upon the team that the vast, dome-shaped, snow-capped peak which they were approaching was not Gya and that the true Gya was the more distant rocky peak. The dome-shaped peak was christened Gyagar (6400m).

The team now decided to try to go downstream along the Lingti river to its junction with the Chaksachan Lungpa and then to go upstream along the Chaksachan Lungpa to the base of the true Gya. Within a few kilometres the team was thwarted by deep gorges and flood water. They concluded that it was possible to go ahead only in winter or early summer. At those times the passes would be blocked lower down, hence the problem of the approach to Gya had to be left for a team with a year in hand!

The expedition turned around and concentrated on peaks at the head of the Lingti river. I received a telegram from Harish: 'Lingti fully explored. Gya identity solved. Climbed Parilungbi and five other peaks.' They had also attempted legendary Shilla and Gyagar. From the west ridge of Gyagar across the valley to the north, they clearly saw Gya at close quarters – a majestic rock monolith rising steeply about 1000 metres above the valley floor. It would defy the best rock climbers and to approach would require complicated logistic arrangements, they thought. It was an awe-inspiring view and a fitting finale to this successful expedition.[2]

In 1991 an Indian team from Delhi made the second ascent of Reo Pargial (Purgyil), 6816m, in Kinnaur. Gya, at 6794m, was relegated to the position of second highest peak of Himachal Pradesh.[3] In spite of this demotion my interest in Gya was undiminished. I believed that it might be possible to reach the base of the mountain by trekking all along the river bed at the end of winter when rivers were partially frozen, thus avoiding the high level route across the passes. It was also vital that the water level should remain fordable on the return journey.

At the end of another expedition, in 1994, we visited Lalung village on 1st September. We had a long chat with Lama Tashi and a villager named Pradhan about the best period to make the journey. We were told that April was the right month but we were advised to start the walk-out from the valley not later than the middle of May. During late winters villagers used a route along the river as far as Phiphuk and slightly beyond to fetch wood, but none of them had ever gone upstream beyond that point. However, two of them promised to persuade some of the villagers to carry loads for us all the way to the base of this mountain, Gya, which was unknown to them.

I returned to the Lingti valley in April 1996 with Dhiren Pania, Dhananjay Ingalkar from Bombay, and Pasang Bodh, Prakash Bodh andVinod Bodh from Manali. Our idea was to make an attempt on Gya (6794m), the highest peak on the axis joining Satopanth and Nun Kun.

We travelled by train from Bombay to Ambala and then by bus to snow-bound Lingti on 3 April. We walked with six yaks to Lalung (3600m) in the Lingti valley and remained four days there owing to heavy snowfall. This prompted the local porters to have second thoughts and desert us. Ultimately we were forced to agree to exorbitant rates and short daily marches. We walked along the partially-frozen Lingti river for four days with eight local porters instead of the required fourteen, covering only six or seven kilometres a day. The shortage of porters had forced us to cut down heavily on our food and equipment. At the end of the fourth day, having reached only about 5km beyond Phiphuk, the porters refused to go any further and we were stranded in the middle of nowhere, about 22km from the proposed site of our Base Camp. The ordeal of establishing Base Camp and identifying an alternative, high-level route for our return journey (in case the rivers became unfordable) had to be faced by three team members and just three permanent porters from Manali. Route-finding through the formidable Lingti gorge and the ferrying of loads consumed 11 unplanned additional days and much precious food. Base Camp (4800m) was not finally established until 24 April.

We approached the frighteningly steep and majestic 1000-metre rock and snow monolith, which formed the E face of the SSW spur of Gya (6794m), over the snout of the glacier by establishing two higher camps: Camp 1, at 5150m, was near the snout and Camp 2, at 5650m, was near the base of the wall of the peak. From Camp 2 a route was opened up on the wall proper through steep snow gullies to 6350m. Two 40-metre ropes were fixed at two separate, difficult locations; the rest of the climbing was free. Food, fuel and gear were also carried up and left at this high location for a proposed Camp 3 at about 6350m. The next day it snowed heavily for twelve hours, making any movement extremely hazardous.

On 2 May, after allowing the snow to settle for a day, Pasang, Dhananjay, Prakash and myself started climbing snow gullies to reach the site of Camp 3. By midday, however, when we had only reached the top of the first fixed rope, about halfway up, the weather turned foul. It had been snowing for the last half-hour as I climbed the fixed rope up a steep gully and had nearly reached its top. The cold wind was whipping through the gully and spraying my face with a spindrift of wet soft snow. As I pulled myself up on the rope to climb the last step to the stance above, I saw, to my horror, the ice screw anchoring the rope first move slowly and then come out with a sudden jerk. I fell. I slid down hitting Pasang Bodh, who was waiting for his turn to climb up the fixed rope, and slid further, faster and faster, somersaulted two or three times, getting choked with masses of snow in my mouth and nose.

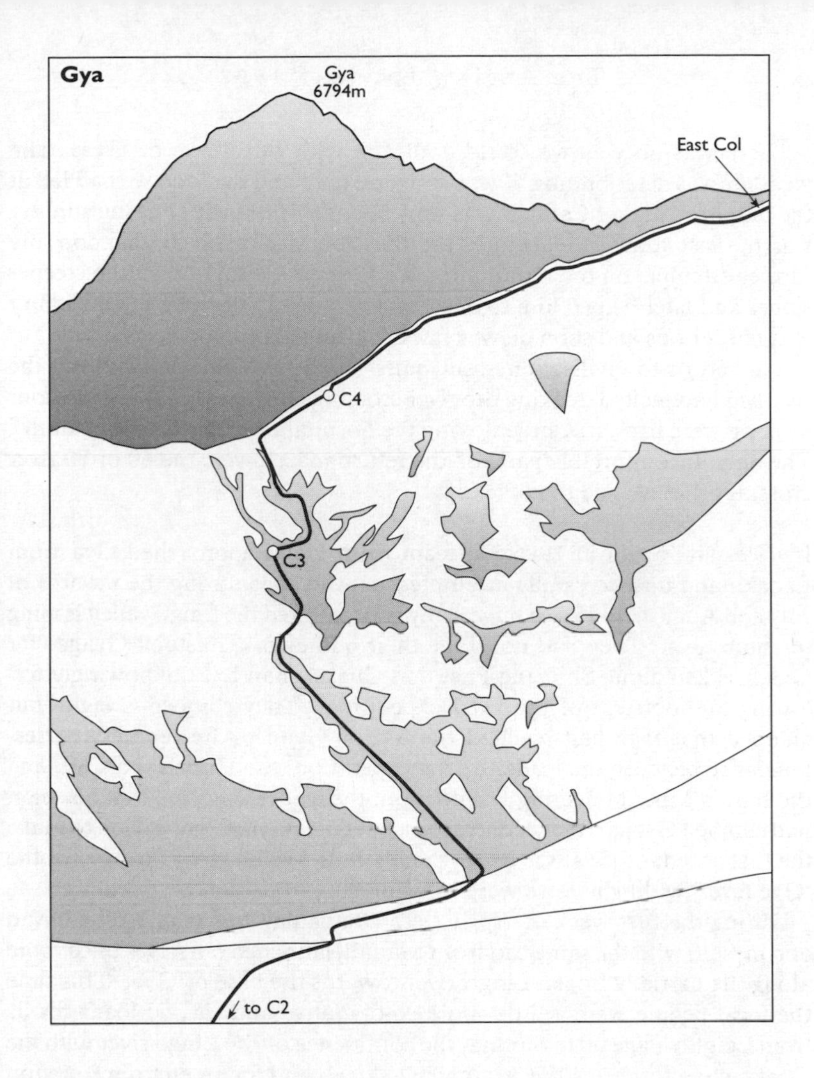

'This is it!' I thought, 'The end!'

Somehow I had managed to hold on to my ice axe, and in the correct 'self arrest' position I tried to push it into the snow slope. It failed the first time but it held during the next somersault. I kicked my boots into the soft snow to obtain some purchase on the slope. The entire sequence had gone by too fast for me to realise the consequences of what was happening. I looked up and saw that I had fallen perhaps 20 or 25 metres. I looked down to the black jagged rocks about 150m below me at the bottom of the slope. Adrenalin burst through my arteries with sudden mighty force and my body started shaking like the wings of a butterfly, my heart beating like wild drums and my lungs gasping for air. It must have been a full ten minutes before I was able to recover sufficiently to think and act normally. Slowly I climbed up to where Pasang was lying, crying in pain. Prakash and Dhananjay had climbed down from the top of the fixed rope.

There was no way we could continue with our climb of Gya. The weather was deteriorating, it was snowing hard and the food we had left at the proposed higher Camp 3 was now beyond our reach. Pasang's injury was the last straw. Reluctantly the decision was taken to abandon any further attempts on the mountain. We lowered Pasang down the steeper slopes and later helped him to descend to Camp 2. Fortunately his injury was not serious and soon he was back to being his usual cheerful self.

Our return to civilisation went quite smoothly. The snow along the riverbed had melted, making the river crossings relatively easy. In just four days we were back at Kibri enjoying the hospitality of the Choppel family. The only uncomfortable parts of the return march were the 60 or 70 river crossings that we had to make.[4]

In 1994 and again in 1996[5, 6] a team from Delhi approached Gya from Ladakh and unsuccessfully attempted its west face during the months of July and August. In 1995 a huge army team entered the Lingti valley hoping to climb Gya. They had not done their homework, mistook Gyagar for Gya, trekked along Shijbang Pass and Chaksachan La, unknowingly following the footsteps of the 1987 expedition. They climbed Gyagar[7] but claimed that they had reached the top of Gya.[8] After endless correspondence between the leader of the expedition, the Himalayan Club and the Indian Mountaineering Foundation, the leader accepted that his team had climbed Gyagar (the second ascent), and not Gya. Competition to make the first ascent of Gya was getting really hot. We knew of no cure for the 'Gya fever' with which we were now infected.

During the first week of April 1997 Dhananjay Ingalkar, Anil Chavan and myself, with the same trio from Manali, launched ourselves once more along the partially frozen Lingti river towards the base of Gya. This time the local people were a little more co-operative and carried loads for us from Lingti village up to Sumna, the confluence of the Lingti river with the Chaksachan Lungpa. We retained two locals and four men from Kumaón to help us. Within eight days from the roadhead we had established Base Camp at 4800m, together with all our loads, compared with the nineteen days we had needed the previous year to get only half the loads in place.

Camp 1 (5200m) and Camp 2 (5650m) were quickly set up, the rope in the gully was refixed and the attempt on Gya was immediately commenced. Pasang, Prakash, Vinod and myself left Camp 2 early on 22 April. We climbed the lower snow gully and the fixed rope, safely this time, and took just four hours to reach the camp below the bottom of the rock wall by midday. Camp 3 at 6050m offered great views towards Gyagar. The north face of Gyagar and its ridges looked steep, broken and extremely difficult to ascend or descend. The next day we wound up Camp 3, traversed to our right to the bottom of the gully and climbed it. The route alternated between snow gullies, rocks and scree ridges. Soft snow made the lower section easier to negotiate, but higher up a thin layer of snow on ice made progress difficult. Five hours of climbing brought us to a small patch of flat ground, at an altitude of 6300m, which could accommodate a tent. The site of Camp 4 was very exposed but safe from rock fall from the face above.

On 24 April Pasang, Prakash and myself climbed up the scree slope above Camp 4 to the base of the main rock wall and traversed upwards on a narrow ledge along its base. The ledge ended abruptly at the top of an ice wall. A rappel down the wall, a traverse along its base and a scramble up a vast scree slope brought us to a col on the SE ridge of Gya. A hard look at the summit ridge from the col was sufficient to convince us that it was not for us. It was broken up with rock gendarmes, snow cornices, ice flutings, all of which were too technical and dangerous for our team. The view northwards of Tso Moriri Lake and Tibet was fantastic. Rows of dark brown snow-capped peaks in Tibet looked like a mystically beautiful *tankha* hanging on the wall of a monastery.

We continued along the corniced ridge SE from the col and soon we were on the top of a 6680m peak. We decided to name this consolation peak 'Gya East'. The next day, starting from Camp 4, we descended directly to Camp 1 in ten hours, to be greeted by Anil and Dhananjay who had been busy, in the meantime, carrying out a recon-naissance of routes to 6275m and 6230m peaks SE of Gya.

We all descended to Base Camp for a much-needed rest, but we still had a week before the local porters were due up at Base Camp, and we made plans. Anil, Pasang, Dhananjay and Prakash decided to go back to Camp 1 to attempt 6275m and 6230m peaks, whereas Vinod and myself opted to try something on our own. Anil's group occupied Camp 1 on 29 April and the next day they established Camp 2 at 5750m on a subsidiary glacier between two peaks. On 1 May the four of them split into two teams. Anil and Pasang climbed the 45° E face of 6275m peak, which they named 'Drisa' (Yaksha), to gain a scree and snow ridge. They continued along the ridge to the bottom of a steep gully. They roped up to climb it and reached the summit ridge. The summit was gained at 11am, four hours after leaving Camp 2. The pair came down most of the way by the same route.

On the same morning Dhananjay and Prakash climbed a snow slope to a depression on the NW ridge of 6230m peak, climbed to a corniced high point on the ridge, descended to another col and climbed to the summit of the 6230m peak 'Cheama' (Twins) by 10.30am. Both the points reached appeared to have the same height. It was unsafe to return by the route of ascent, so the pair took a different line for the descent, first along the SW ridge and later over the W face to Camp 2.

Near Base Camp was a peak 5665m in height which involved a climb of about 850m and an interesting route to its top. On 30 April Vinod and I left the camp rather late for this peak. A 1½ hour walk brought us to the base of its north face. We scrambled up a scree slope and kicked our way up a 40° snow slope, until midday, to the base of the summit pyramid. The top was guarded by steep rock walls, except for a breach in its defences by the near-vertical snow gully. This steep gully was connected to the base of the summit pyramid by an exposed narrow ledge which was leaning outwards. Realising that we did not have sufficient time in hand to negotiate this crux section, go to the top and return, we decided to withdraw to Base Camp. Next day we made an early start. Helped by the footprints of the previous day we reached the base of the summit pyramid quite early. The ledge and the 60m gully had to be negotiated with utmost care in short belays. We were on the summit, 'Namkha Ding' (Garuda) by 2.30pm with great views of peaks, including Gyagar, all around. We descended the crux section, again on belays. Once at the base of the summit pyramid we glissaded down on our backs to the glacier below in just twenty minutes. It was the last day for me above Base Camp and I walked towards it at leisure, enjoying, absorbing and savouring everything around me.

This pursuit of Gya had been a long quest for me, both physically and mentally. Though the summit had eluded us, we had done our best and were content with the results. We had solved the riddle of the approach to Gya. We had completed a difficult route as far as Gya's SE Col, and we had made four interesting first ascents. On a personal level, I had been able to overcome the mental block caused by my fall in 1996. By climbing beyond the point where that happened, I finally rid myself of shackles of self-doubt about my own abilities. But now the time had come to close the chapter on Gya. During the last fourteen years it had occupied a special place in my mind. The vacuum left behind by its absence was frightening. It was difficult to look beyond Gya. What next? I had no immediate answer to this haunting question. My only recourse was to read and re-read the last paragraph of Maurice Herzog's book *Annapurna* to draw inspiration ...

> Annapurna, to which we had gone empty handed, was a treasure on which we should live the rest of our days. With this realisation we turn the page: a new life begins.

There are other Annapurnas in the lives of men.

REFERENCES

1 *The Himalayan Journal*, Vol 40, p 96
2 *ibid*, Vol 44, p 96
AJ93, 251, 1988/89
3 *The Himalayan Journal*, Vol 51, p 293
4 *The Himalayan Club Newsletter* No 50, p 66
5 *ibid*, No 48, p 20
6 *ibid*, No 50, p 66
7 *AJ 101*, 258, 1996
8 *The Himalayan Club Newsletter* No 50, p 63

JULIAN FREEMAN-ATTWOOD

The British Sikkim Expedition 1996

(Plates 29–32)

Prior to Indian partition in 1947 and the end of British rule, Sikkim, along with the Garhwal, was perhaps the best known and mapped of the Himalayan regions. Much of mountaineering significance was accomplished in those days but with the virtual closing of the Kingdom after partition, and even greater restrictions of travel after annexation by India in the early 1970s, this was an area waiting to be rediscovered. Indeed many worthwhile peaks of not inconsiderable technical difficulty are yet to be climbed.

Permission to travel in the Kingdom, even in the early days, was not a straightforward affair. The King had to be consulted indirectly through three British representatives, an arrangement which the monarch of the time was obliged to put up with in exchange for being largely left in peace. The climber most associated with these early explorations was the Aberdonian chemist Dr Alexander Kellas. He accomplished an incredible amount of climbing in six expeditions to the Kingdom between 1907 and 1920. Generally he operated alone with a loyal group of local porters whom he trained in basic Alpine skills. In 1910 he made ten first ascents above 20,000ft including Sentinel Peak (6490m), Pauhunri (7125m) and Chomo Yummo (6829m). His energy and tenacity must have been phenomenal; the previous year, for instance, he had twice attempted Pauhunri, getting within 200ft of the top.

During the inter-war years activity was centred more around Kangchenjunga than in the north of Sikkim. However, two climbs were made by returning Everesters: Shipton, Warren, Kempson and Wigram climbed Gurudongmar in 1936 (from the Tibetan plateau) and two years later Tilman, who was as he put it 'one of the rats deserting the sinking ship', broke away to climb and survey in North Sikkim. He crossed the Naku La to the west of Chomo Yummo and eventually climbed Chumangkang (6212m), one of the many fine peaks of North Sikkim lying to the south of the main Himalayan divide.

In 1945 Harry Tilly climbed Chomo Yummo and Wilfrid Noyce climbed Pauhunri which were both second ascents. As a result of interest in the area, two Himalayan Club huts were erected on either side of the Sebu La in the Lachen and Lachung valleys respectively. The Lachung hut was built at Yume Samdong where our base camp was eventually to be located but sadly both huts are now in ruins.

In 1949 Trevor Braham discovered a high pass linking the Kangkyong valley and glaciers with the Lachung valley to the west and recalls 'memories of old carefree days when one was happy enough to explore and never expected to climb a mountain at the first attempt'. No Western climber or walker has been to the north-east of Sikkim since Braham was there in the 1950s.

In 1962 the Chinese attacked the undefended northern border on many fronts and the Indian army drew an 'inner line' beyond which foreigners were not permitted. Several army expeditions were allowed in after the fighting but no Indian civilians. In 1972 Indira Ghandi sent in troops to annex Sikkim as an Indian State. Up to that point there had been a workable arrangement with the King with regard to Sikkim's defence, but the expansionist Ghandi took advantage of the fact that the King had rejected the representatives from Delhi (he was theoretically allowed to select his own Delhi politicians) and stormed the palace in Gangtok. The King's second wife was an American called Hope Cooke whose daughter Hope Leezum Namgyal (related also to the Kings of Bhutan) now runs a trekking group called Trek Sikkim. She remembers the day as a very young girl when the troops invaded, and as she is the only one of her family to live in the State, apart from her half brother the Crown Prince who lives in religious retreat, her contacts in Sikkim are widespread. This turned out to be invaluable to us. I had been in contact with Hope through Ed Webster the year before.

To bring this historical footnote up to date: in 1976 Harish Kapadia gained permission to enter North Sikkim and spent weeks tramping over the high passes including the Sebu La. By 1996 Indo-Chinese relations were less tense and it seemed that with a determined push the door might be opened. Doug Scott, our leader, was just the man for the job. He had several good contacts, not least Col. Balwant Sandhu who had been his liaison officer on several past trips. Doug had tried to get us into Arunachal Pradesh the previous year without success and began sending copious letters to Col. Badgel at the Indian Mountaineering Foundation (IMF) in Delhi.

Besides Balwant we had a great ally in Sunam Dubey, vice-president of the IMF, who kept our application moving through the endless bureaucratic corridors. It seemed we had to have permission from the IMF, the Home Office, the Foreign Office, the Sikkim State Government and not least the North-East Frontier Army Command. Lesser men than Doug would have retreated from the enormity of the job, especially with all of us constantly ringing him for updates. You could hardly blame us, since deadlines came and went with annoying regularity. Some members dropped out and the omens were not good. Other climbers had recently run foul of the military authorities' inner line permits, including Doug himself who had been turned away from Rimo II, Harish who had been turned away from the Terong Glacier in Siachen, Andrew Bett from Hanuman in Garhwal by the Forest Authority and finally Jim Lowther who had been told just before his expedition was due to leave for Kishtwar that his peak was now not available. Extraordinary that the authorities should use the phrase 'not available' as if the mountain had suddenly disappeared from the face of the Earth.

Just a week before our intended departure Doug contacted the IMF President Dr M S Gill. He was very busy at the time as India's chief election commissioner and therefore one of India's top civil servants. A series of forceful letters from all of us asked, not only about the permit itself, but also why it was that a simple 'yes' or 'no' decision had to be left until the very last moment when many irreversible arrangements, such as purchase of air fares, had already been made. Happily he took our letters to heart and took time off to sort things out despite the army complaining that they would be undertaking Sikkim manœuvres in the area and didn't particularly want us around. Our thanks are due to him and to General C S Nugyal, general secretary of the IMF, who, with Balwant, resolved the army problem. Our permit duly arrived and in the event we had a trouble-free expedition.

Besides Doug and myself the team consisted in the end of Lindsay Griffin, our *High* magazine mountain information editor, Phil Bartlett, a strong and very enthusiastic explorer/mountaineer, Mark Bowen from the USA who was a friend of Doug's, and Skip Novak, my sailing/mountaineering colleague from previous Antarctic trips. Two support trekkers, Paul Crowther (UK) and Michael Clarke (USA), completed the party.

We had decided on a post-monsoon expedition as the weather can be more settled at that time of year especially in the eastern Himalaya. As it turned out we were wrong in this particular year but as a rule it probably holds true. Having met Balwant and Sunam Dubey at the IMF in Delhi, and after a frantic few days shopping and packing, we left by train for New Jalpaiguri situated over 1000 miles east on the plains below Darjeeling. At Delhi station forty porters heaved our gear across endless tracks, inevitably to the furthest platform where everything was laboriously weighed. The train left exactly as they said it would at 5pm and arrived the next day promptly at 2.30pm. It had been a fascinating journey, to the accompaniment of Sunam describing the present-day political scene in India and Balwant recounting tales of the Raj. We rattled along across the endless Gangetic plain and on arrival at Jalpaiguri were met by Hope Leezum and her assistant from Trek Sikkim, Duguel. Some five hours later our jeeps rolled into Gangtok after crossing into Sikkim State territory. This was the first barrier, but the inner line was yet to come.

During the next few days Doug and Hope visited the various Ministries and Departments to pay over additional royalties to the Sikkim government and take on our liaison officer Lalit Basnet and four camp staff who would double as high-altitude porters if necessary. From Darjeeling came Pasang Namgyal Sherpa and Sungay Sherpa. Also from West Sikkim came Tenzing Norbu known as 'Lama' and from Gangtok, Narwang Zongda, one of the indigenous Lepcha people, who was known as 'Uncle'. Much of the gear we had brought from Delhi we now found was easily available in Gangtok. It is an amiable place, pleasanter than polluted Kathmandu, with houses crowded together on exceptionally steep slopes. Indeed with landslides and earthquakes (we felt a small tremor whilst there), the houses have a feeling of impermanence.

We set off up country on 27 September following the Tista River, the main drainage river of Sikkim. Just below its confluence with the Lachung Chu and Lachung Valley we passed across the inner line army border. Balwant sorted out everything in true 'Colonel' style and we were thankful to have him with us, as many a trip gets no further than this point. Some twelve miles upstream we stayed the night in an ex-colonial forestry Dak bungalow.

We soon discovered that there had been a considerable amount of environmentally destructive army road-building. Over the past 15 years a metalled road had been pushed up towards a high army camp at 4800m where the main pass, the famous Dongkya La, is guarded and where the original Chinese incursion occurred. The road workers in Sikkim are principally very poor Nepalese who have swamped the country in population terms and turned the Bhutias and Lepchas into a minority in their own country. Up in the fragile alpine zone, where even a small two-foot-diameter conifer (Deodar or Pine) will be some 200 years old, we watched in horror as many of these trees were cut down merely to melt tar to put on the road. We were basically watching the instant transformation of indigenous, virgin alpine forest into tarmacadam. There could never be a good enough reason for doing that in such a place, or indeed anywhere, and it didn't even make sense from a military point of view. The army people I talked to did not think that any permanent benefit could be derived from a metalled road, since landslides would sweep it away at frequent intervals.

After the trip, when we got to look behind the scenes, even more ugly facts came to light. The corruption in Sikkim State at government level seems to be so well known that I had no trouble finding people, mainly Lepchas and Bhutias, who were prepared to talk about it. It seems that the tarmacked road in the Lachung Valley, and the cutting of totally unsustainable amounts of timber, was instigated in large part by a corrupt forestry official who made a quasi-legal purchase of State (Reservation) Forestry land. Even in Sikkim, 'reservation' land is meant to belong to the state. The man in question, whose name is well known in the country, was a state minister at the time and also, to tie things up nicely for him, ran a trekking company to fill up the lodges he had established on the forest reserve.

Over in the west towards Kangchenjunga, another World Bank-aided dambuilding project resulted in a recent demonstration by monks and others, protesting at the violation of tribal land and environment, not to mention earthquake dangers. I was shown dreadful scars on a hillside where rock falls had taken away acres of trees – construction roads had been built across ground that anyone could see was unsustainable. It is doubtful whether they will even be able physically to keep the road open. Sikkim still has a lot more forest than Nepal, but that is misleading. Just at a time when we might have expected the dawn of a more enlightened era, the rot is setting in. To our mind it was a matter of save now or lose forever.

Base Camp was established by 1st October in a wide expansive valley of brown hillsides. We were practically in Tibet and saw fox, marmot and *bharal* (blue) sheep. We had much exploratory work and acclimatisation to do and over the next two weeks we split up at times into various parties. One of these forays took us into the Palo Chutang Valley which runs parallel to the south side of Gurudongmar and Sanglaphu.

Throughout this period the weather was very unsettled but we got a good view of Gurudongmar (6715m) and the col between it and Sanglaphu (6224m) from a 5575m peak we called 'the Coal Tip' (more accurately the north peak of the Lapchaten group). It was a monstrous heap of rubble but it became a good vantage point and a fine boulder-rolling location. The col between the two peaks was threatened by séracs on Sanglaphu – otherwise we would have found a feasible way up Gurudongmar. As it was we sighted another possible route up the south face but at a good deal harder technical standard. Nevertheless this was probably the best mountaineering line (along with the south ridge of Yulhekang 6429m) that we saw on the watershed peaks.

Leaving Gurudongmar alone for the present, we returned to base for a day and then set out with a few days' food to the Sebu Cho Lake below Chombu (6362m), our other permitted peak. Phil and Lindsay set off to look at Yulhekang and the Changme glacier leading up to it, including an ascent of Gurung, 5691m, followed by a recce over a glaciated col between Chombu and Chombu East (5745m). This latter recce proved very useful.

Meanwhile Doug, Skip and myself crossed the Sebu La (5352m) to do a thorough reconnaissance of Chombu and the Lachen Valley side of it. The La was apparently an old yak route linking the upper Lachung and Lachen valleys but glacial retreat meant we had to abseil down the western side of it. Not much hope here for a yak, we thought. Nevertheless, from the top we had stunning views of Chombu's north face, views of unclimbed Chungukang (5824m) and, not least, mighty views of Kangchenjunga's east face, together with the Nepal watershed peaks from 'The Twins', north to Jongsang, and beyond into NW Sikkim. We spent a night out at the NW end of Chombu but could see no feasible route on this difficult peak. The best way was probably on the Sebu Cho side where we had our camp.

On 14 October, now acclimatised, we set off to attempt Chombu East. As we crossed the glacier Col (5250m) onto the Rula Kang Glacier recced by Lindsay and Phil, we had good views of the Pauhunri massif to the east, along with two unclimbed 7000m peaks, a ruck of hard-looking unnamed 6500m peaks and the amazing looking Dongkya Ri (6190m). The other side of Pauhunri and the 7000m peaks would have been viewed by

Col. Younghusband on his way to Lhasa up the Chombi Valley in 1903 and by any other pre-war Everesters.

To the south of our col we looked into the very little-known country of central North Sikkim with a wealth of 5500m–6000m peaks. We descended what seemed a very long way before setting up camp under the SW side of our peak. We headed off at dawn, climbing some tricky moraine before donning crampons for the unnamed glacier fed by the south face of Chombu East. Apart from crevasses, this was straightforward until, after some hours, a 70° section landed us on a col at *c*5000m from which we could see our steepening ridge. We could now more or less look down onto our Base Camp and the hot springs at Yume Samdong. The inevitable morning clouds started rolling up the Tista River from the south and by the time we had climbed a further section of steep snow to the beginning of the long serrated rocky summit ridge, we were enveloped in what turned out to be a full-blown storm. To me the ridge was reminiscent of Mt Kenya's West Ridge, with towers to turn, abseils to be made and iced-up steep rocky gullies to be climbed. The wind blew into our faces and all the time, through swirling mist, the sharp-edged ridge could be seen dropping down either side for hundreds of feet. Anxious for a summit, we kept going. False top after false top came and went until we shuffled *à cheval* to a 30ft brèche. This was the crux (V) and especially difficult with crampons scraping through fresh snow onto the vertical rock. Beyond the brèche, the ridge levelled off and the summit was reached. We kept just off the true top in deference to the Gods and traditions of Sikkim.

Retreating the same way, which took nearly as long as the outward journey, we descended to about 400ft above the col in a complete whiteout, with huge dumps of snow falling. Tying two ropes together, three of us belayed Doug down whilst he tried to jump on, and avalanche, the slope below him. Unfortunately this didn't work, so we had no option but to plough on in trepidation and luckily emerged unscathed back onto the crevassed area, now with our outward tracks obliterated. We arrived back at our tents in late evening and next day waded back across the Rula Kang Col to Sebu Cho Lake feeling a little pleased with ourselves. It is worth mentioning that there was a Lower Sebu Lake which, as in many such Himalayan events, emptied after a natural moraine dam burst. The ensuing flood wave killed many people in the Lachung and Tista valleys.

Still with an eye on Chombu (main), we ascended from Sebu Cho managing to outflank a great lower icefall and put in a camp below the mountain's east face. After negotiating some tortuous moraine and scree slopes reminiscent of the Karakoram, we gained the upper glacier and made it, in good weather for a change, to the start of difficulties. We looked at a gully leading to the north ridge and at the east ridge itself, both of which looked hard. Nevertheless, the snow conditions were so obviously dangerous that there was no problem in making the decision to leave it alone for the time being.

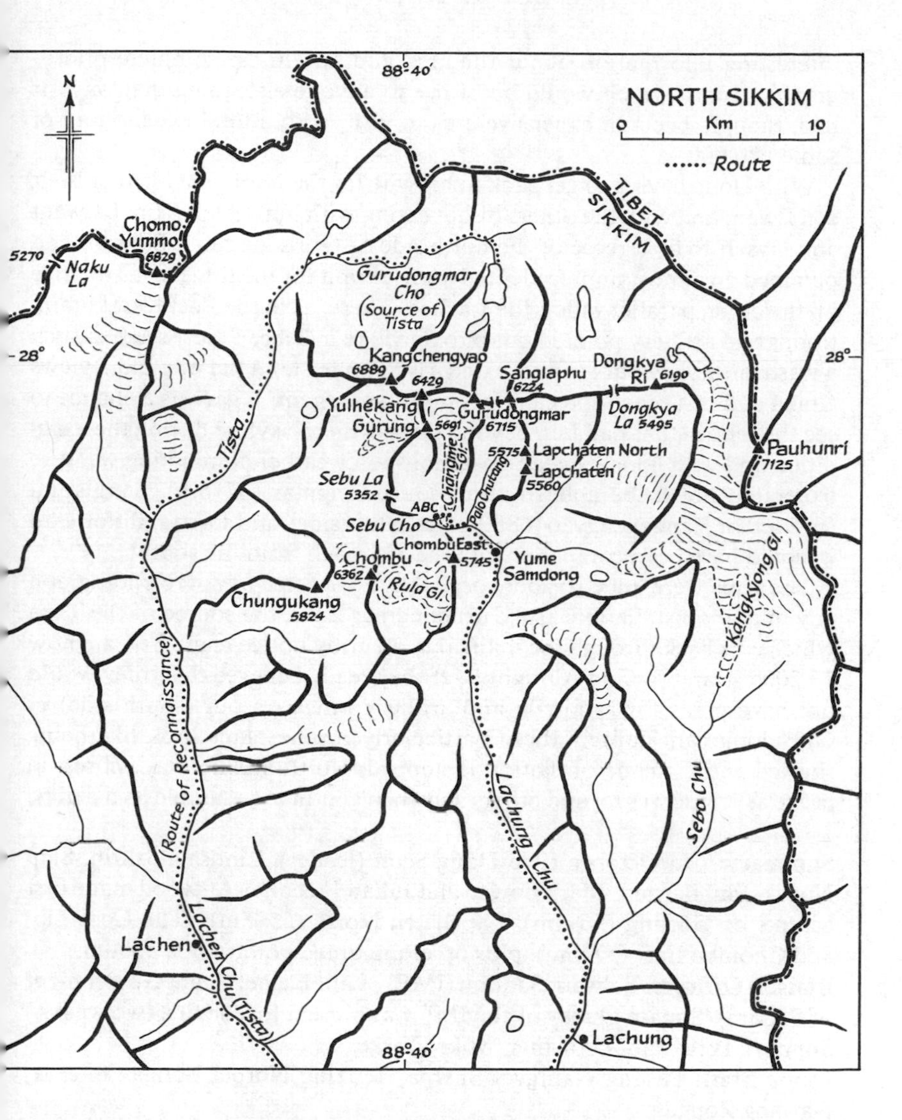

Our final plan was to have a go at Gurudongmar from the Palo Chutang Valley by the south ridge. After collecting food from Base Camp we established an Advanced Base Camp below the peak but three days of continuous bad weather and snow rendered the mountain unassailable and for that matter Chombu as well.

Time had now run out and whilst we would dearly love to have had another peak in the bag and felt a little disappointed, we had all worked long and hard on a fine exploratory expedition in country of rare beauty. It has to be said that the weather was not our friend and that snow conditions were particularly unconsolidated, but we had come back with a lot of interesting information about the area and an almost complete photographic record which would be of use to anyone else going that way. It had, though, been an expensive area to visit, with a total expenditure of some £20,000.

With Doug having to get back to his wife for the imminent birth of their son Ewan, and with the others disappearing with him, it left Skip, Balwant and myself to do a recce of the north side of Gurudongmar. Balwant had obtained an almost unprecedented army permit for the three of us to drive up the other, parallel valley, the Lachen. There, as in the East Karakoram, troops and artillery pointed out into nowhere in Tibet. It just seemed such a waste of money but I suppose one has to understand the way India views China and in a sense you can't entirely blame them. It gave us a chance to see the terrain that had lain beyond our northern skyline during the expedition and with good Tibetan post-monsoon weather dominating, we were frustrated not to be able to climb Gurudongmar (6715m), Sanglaphu (6224m) or Kangchengyao (6889m) from this side; and so straightforward it would have been compared with the approach from the south!

The army were unbelievably hospitable and trusted us not to photograph any military installations. At Gurudongmar Lake, the source of the Tista which cuts back through the main axis, an army notice read 'You are now 17,200ft nearer to God Almighty'. If they really believed that, they would not have plans for a missile and artillery range on our (south side) of Gurudongmar. Happily these particularly insane plans look like being shelved and if the deforestation is stopped, North Sikkim may yet rest in peace as it deserves to, and others may then continue to sample its delights.

Summary: In October 1996 Doug Scott (leader), Lindsay Griffin, Skip Novak, Phil Bartlett, Mark Bowen and Julian Freeman-Attwood made first ascents of Gurung (5691m), Lapchaten North (5575m), 'The Coal Tip' and Chombu East (5745m), plus other unnamed points circa 5500m.
Liaison Officers: Balwant Sandhu (IMF), Lalit Basnet (State Government of Sikkim) (Sunam Dubey of the IMF was present for the first two weeks.)
Support Trek: Paul Crowther, Mike Clarke.
Camp Staff: Pasang Namgyal Sherpa, Tenzing Norbu, Sungay Sherpa, Nawang Zongda.

The East Face of the SSE Spur of Gya, 6794m. (*Pasang Bodh*) (p36)

6. Negotiating a section of the Lingti Gorge in the Lahul-Spiti district of Himachal Pradesh, 1996. (*Dhiren Pania*) (p36)

Right
A view of the summit pyramid of Gya, 6794m, from below the col on its SE Ridge. (*Arun Samant*) (p36)

Below
From L: Gya, Gya East, Drisa and Cheama seen from the bottom of the summit pyramid of Namkha Ding. (*Arun Samant*)

9. Pundit Nain Singh, C.I.E., the first of the Pundits of Tibetan exploration. Survey of India, 1865-75. (*Alpine Club Library Collection*) (p61)

Note: C.I.E. stands for 'Commander of the Order of the Indian Empire'. This order of chivalry was inaugurated for those who worked in India. In the mid-19th century it was highly unusual for a village schoolmaster of lowly origin to be awarded such an honour.

10. Rai Bahadur Kishen Singh Milamwal, the 'A – K' of Tibetan exploration. Survey of India, 1869-83. (*Alpine Club Library Collection*) (p66)

11. Kunaling, 6471m. This unclimbed peak dominates the Bhagirath Kharak Glacier. It was referred to by Eric Shipton in *Nanda Devi*, chapters 12 and 13. (*Harish Kapadia*) (p53)

Right
Nilkanth, 6596m, seen from Deo Dekhni plateau. The NW ridge, by which it was first climbed by an Indo-Tibet Border Police team in 1974, is on the right. An earlier ascent, in 1961, was discounted. (*Harish Kapadia*) (p53)

Below
Shrak La (*centre right*), the pass between Bhagirath Kharak and Arwa valleys, first crossed by Shipton and Tilman in 1934. (*Harish Kapadia*) (p53)

14. 'Arwa Spires', 6193m, a group of steep granite spires in the Arwa Valley, have probably not been photographed before. (*Harish Kapadia*) (p53)

HARISH KAPADIA

In Famous Footsteps

A trek in the Garhwal

(*Plates 11–14*)

In 1934 two prolific explorers from England reached the Garhwal Himalaya. It was the beginning of an exploration which made them famous. They were Eric Shipton and H W Tilman, and they were trying to force an entry into the hitherto unknown Nanda Devi Sanctuary. In the summer of that year they discovered a route through the formidable Rishi Gorge and deposited some of their food and equipment there. When the monsoon arrived, they returned to Badrinath. Their intention was to spend some time elsewhere and then, when the monsoon had dispersed, return to the Sanctuary to complete their unfinished work.

In Badrinath they heard the Hindu legend about the journey of a temple priest from the Kedarnath Valley who, in a single day, crossed a high pass to worship at the Badrinath temple! Considering the terrain, this would have been a major mountaineering feat.

Supported by Sherpas, Shipton and Tilman decided to check the validity of the legend – with near-disastrous results. After crossing a difficult col at the head of the Satopanth Bank, they descended the Gundarpongi gad where they were trapped in dense, bear-infested forests. Being delayed for many days, they ran short of food and had to survive on bamboo shoots. They were lucky to survive this saga of hair-raising incidents, to eventually emerge at the village of Gaundar.

We thought that, by crossing the col at the head of the Satopanth Bank, they had perhaps misjudged the route referred to in the legend. But local information and modern maps revealed that there is a high col at the head of the Panpatia Bank further south. Perhaps this col could be crossed more easily. It leads down to Maindagalla tal on the ridge leading directly to Madhyamaheshwar temple and above the valley which trapped the Shipton-Tilman party. Perhaps this Panpatia Col, which can be reached directly from the temple, was the one referred to in the legend.

In 1984 a party of two trekkers from West Bengal, trying to repeat the 1934 Shipton–Tilman route, came up the valley from Madhyamaheshwar to Badrinath, perhaps via Panpatia Col, and were never seen again.

At Badrinath we met a priest whom we had already met on a previous journey. With a shaven head and a tilak on his forehead, the Panda (priest) sounded like the epitome of knowledge. I asked him about the old legend that the priest from the Kedarnath temple had worshipped at the Badrinath temple by crossing two high passes in a single day.

'In the days when the earth was flat,' he replied, 'it could have been true that the priest went from Kedarnath to Badrinath in a single day.'

This was before the days of the tectonic thrust, which is supposed to have created the range. Now Nilkanth has risen in between, blocking the route.

The priest added, 'This place is named Badri after a fruit that can grow only in a flat country. At present there are no badris growing here. So at one time this whole area must have been flat land.'

On the map it looked like an impossible terrain to traverse. 'It's hard to believe,' I protested, 'that it was possible to cross the range at all, let alone on the same day.'

'You must have faith in order to believe it. There was a route then and there will be a route now, if you look for it.' As an afterthought he added, 'But it is for the faithful only.' (1)

Bells were ringing and it was time to go to the Badrinath temple. I had bought a special ticket for Rs. 51 which entitled me to enter the temple individually rather than in a group. It was still a horrible experience – with dirt, pushing and crowds. I could not believe that the young Rawal performing the *puja* knew about the journey or could lead me to salvation. I came out less faithful than before. We were ready, though, to start our search for the legend, following Kipling's advice that there is something lost behind the ranges, go and find it.

In order to check out the legend, we decided to follow the Panpatia Valley. Talking to villagers, we found that almost everyone had heard the story. But they spoke of Kedarnath as an area and not specifically of the temple, which is situated some way off. On 31 May 1997, after three days of acclimatisation, the team was ready to enter the Panpatia Valley.

By 4 June we had reached the base of the icefall (4440m) in four easy stages: to Khirao village at 2840m, along the river at 3360m, to the snout at 3860m and thence to the foot of the icefall. Our intention was to reach the high col (5250m) to the south-west of the upper Panpatia Plateau. We hoped that crossing this would lead to the Madhyamaheshwar temple, via Maindagalla tal, and thence to Gupta Kashi (Kedarnath).

The icefall was attempted via three different routes, each ending in huge crevasse fields which would have required more equipment than we had

---

(1) There are several stories in the Himalaya which are for the faithful. The wall behind the ancient Yarma gompa in the Nubra Valley, Ladakh, is said to be shining with gold in the evenings, as per the local belief. When Professor Dainelli of the Italian expedition of 1929 tried to enquire scientifically he was told to look at it with faith. See 'My expedition in the Eastern Karakoram, 1930' by G. Dainelli in *Himalayan Journal, Vol. IV*, p. 46.

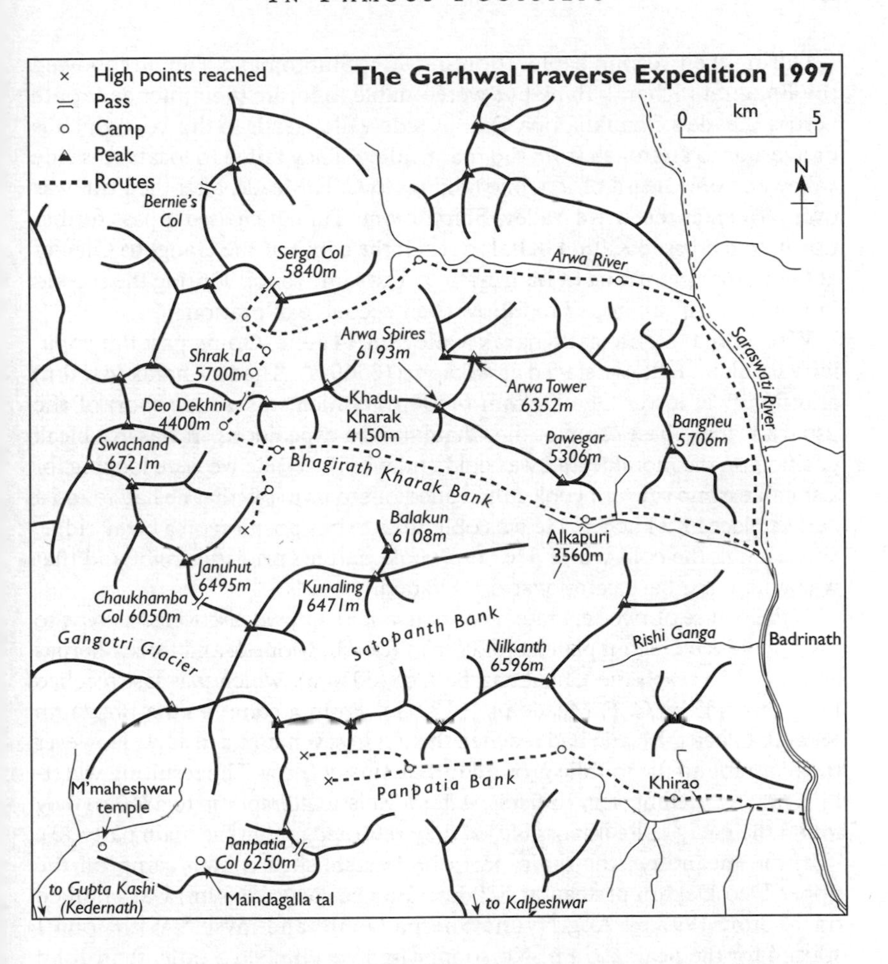

with us to be crossed safely. Finally a steep slope to the north gave us access, after fixing some ropes, to the higher plateau. However, it was observed that to reach the Panpatia Col it would be necessary to traverse almost 7km of highly crevassed ground. Reluctantly we gave up the idea. We returned by the same route to Badrinath on 13 June 1997.

There was another pass, however, from Khirao to Kalpeshwar, lower down the valley. This was the only other route which we thought could possibly enable us to cross over to the Kedarnath area.

We travelled to Joshimath for rest and to re-stock our rations. We visited Auli, a new ski resort developed above Joshimath. My enquiry as to why it is called Auli had a humorous explanation. Two lovers once visited Auli and in the mist the lady got lost, never to be found again. The gentleman kept shouting 'Auli! Auli!' which in the local language means 'Come! Come!' The tea-stall owner, who narrated the story to us, added with a grin, 'Now we are shouting Auli! Auli! to the tourists.'

During their second exploration in 1934, Shipton and Tilman followed the Bhagirath Kharak Bank but were unable to locate their intended route across Meade's Chaukhamba Col. A side valley leads to this col, which is dangerous to approach from the main valley. They failed to locate this side valley and only heard of it, while talking to C. F. Meade, after their trip was over. To enter the Arwa Valley, Shipton and Tilman crossed a pass further north, and crossed Kalindi Khal to reach the snout of the Gangotri Glacier at Gaumukh, returning to Badrinath by the same route. During the second half of our trip we hoped to follow their second exploration.

We entered the Bhagat Kharak Valley on 14 June. Going past the popular Vasudhara falls, we stayed at Alkapuri (3560m), Khadu Kharak (4150m) and finally at lower Deo Dekhni (4400m), which was a little short of the usual advanced base camp of the Chaukhamba expeditions. It was in a bleak position on the moraine and was cold and windy. While we were looking for a suitable camp site, our cook John called out to us to say that he had found a perfect place for a kitchen. He was oblivious to our position on a bleak ridge, shivering in the cold wind. He, as a cook, had his priorities right and that was where our base camp was established.

In the course of two separate reconnaissance trips, we discovered a route to the upper Deo Dekhni plateau (5200m). Rajesh, Monesh and three Sherpas attempted to reach the Chaukhamba Col (6050m), which was last reached from this side by C. F. Meade in 1912. (2) From a camp on the Bhagirath Kharak Glacier, Meade had reached the col in seven hours in July. However the team found the middle ground full of slushy snow. The resulting waterfalls made the climb very difficult. After a valiant attempt (up to 4850m) they found the going quite impossible, so they returned to join the main party. (3)

In the meantime, the main party had established a high camp on the upper Deo Dekhni plateau at 5200m. Bhagat Peak (5650m) was climbed on 19 June 1997 by Ang Nyima Sherpa (John) and myself. With John I started for the peak at 7am. No sooner had we climbed a little, than John unroped. He was looking for water, to be collected on our way back so that he could cook better meals! (Again he had his priorities right.) We climbed the ridge slowly, enjoying the view of Gods (Deo Dekhni) from the peak, and on our way back John collected more water for the kitchen.

Next day, after I had left for a rest at base camp, Kaivan and Mingma reached two peaks on the plateau with heights of 5360m and 5400m. Both were enjoyable climbs and they returned in about six hours.

Shipton and Tilman in 1934, like us, had failed to reach the Chaukhamba Col and had climbed to the Deo Dekhni plateau and crossed the Shrak La ('Pass of Rocks'), 5700m, to the north of this plateau. We reached this pass on 19 June (after 63 years). Next day, loads were ferried there and carried over to the other side.

---

(2) The col was reached by Simon Yearsley's team in 1995 from the Gantori Glacier. They camped on the col during their attempt on Chaukhamba I.

The entire team crossed the pass on 22 June. From here the eastern gully led steeply down to the valley floor with avalanches pouring down it. The broad western gully led down to the floor on the Arwa side without much difficulty. But by the time the entire party had reached the pass, it was too late to turn back; ropes had already been fixed down the eastern gully and loads lowered into the valley. We had overlooked Shipton's best advice: mountaineering is reconnaissance, reconnaissance and reconnaissance. Almost the entire gully had to be fixed with ropes and, as avalanches hissed by, narrowly missing us, we looked across at the easier broad valley which would have been the correct route. In the late evening, in heavy snowfall, we set up a camp on the glacier at 5400m. We descended to the end of this side valley and, in two days, were camping on one of the branches of the Arwa Valley (5280m). Again following the route of 1934, we entered a side valley and reached the next high col, which we named Serga Col ('Pass of Crevasses'), 5840m, on 25 June. Ahead we could see Birnies Col temptingly close, and far away was Kalindi Khal. The ground between us and the col was full of bergschrunds and crevasses which could have trapped our large party of 14 people. Very reluctantly we had to abandon the idea of crossing Birnies Col. This was not the year nor the time for crossing such passes.

Arwa had its charms. Explored by Frank Smythe, it has not received many visitors. Arwa Tower (6352m) and Arwa Spires (6193m) in the southern valleys, would test the best rock climbers.

I met the Panda again at the conclusion of our trip. 'I hope you found the route across the ranges,' he said. 'I was praying for your safety.' I was about to tell him that we found no route to confirm the truth of the legend. It might have been possible in earlier days, but not now. The legendary route led only to the Kedarnath area and not to the main temple. So he had been only half correct. Then I realised that you do not tell a learned priest that he knows only half-truths.

So I replied, 'Only with great difficulty will it be possible to find the route the priest went by.' As Aubrey Menen (in *Space Within the Heart*) had written, 'We generally find the truth, but never destroy the simple faith of simple people.' Perhaps some explorer some day will discover a route which will make it possible to cross the connecting ranges. Shipton and Tilman almost did it. After doing what we did and more, they returned to the Nanda Devi Sanctuary to complete their exploration there. But we were tired and looking forward to going home.

---

(3) Several times have I found this phenomena in my recent travels. The achievements and timings of earlier parties, like C. F. Meade's, do not seem to be possible nowadays. Today no one can reach the Chaukhamba Col from the Bhagat Kharak Glacier in 7 hours. I wonder whether early explorers were fitter and tougher, or whether the terrain has changed. Or possibly, because they had no return tickets booked and had more time, they were able to do things with less stress.

Members: Harish Kapadia (leader), Monesh Devjani, Rajesh Gadgil, Vijay Kothari and Kaivan Mistry.
Period: 25 May to 4 July 1997.
Areas: The Panpatia Valley, the Bhagirath Kharak Glacier and the Arwa Valleys, west of Badrinath temple, in the Central Garhwal.
Sponsored by: The Mountaineers, Bombay.

BIBLIOGRAPHY

1. Eric Shipton, *Nanda Devi* (for both the crossings).
2. C. F. Meade, *Approach to the Hills* (for Chaukhamba Col).
3. A. Heim and A. Gansser, *Throne of Gods* (climbs on the Bhagirath Kharak Glacier).
4. Frank Smythe, *Kamet Conquered* (exploration of the Arwa Valley).
5. Trevor Braham, *Himalayan Odyssey* (the Arwa Valley and Kalindi Khal).
6. Bill Aitken, *Mountain Delight* (for deaths of two Bengali trekkers).
7. *The Himalayan Club Newletter 38* (for deaths of two Bengali trekkers).
8. H. W. Tilman, 'Nanda Devi and the sources of the Ganges' in *The Himalayan Journal Vol. VII*, page 1.

MICHAEL WARD

The Survey of India and the Pundits

The Secret Exploration of the Himalaya and Central Asia

(Plates 9 and 10)

The Survey of India was one of the brightest jewels in the crown of the British in India. Its success was based on highly motivated, talented, well-trained and dedicated members of many races, a high proportion of whom died or were killed in its service. The number of British officers was always small but they more than made up for this by being highly effective. Their professionalism was in keeping with the ethos of the Indian Civil Service, which managed to administer a country of 250 million people with no more than about 2500 British members.

The contribution of the Survey of India to mountain exploration was formidable. In 1921, for example, during the first Everest Reconnaissance Expedition, E O Wheeler, later Surveyor-General of India from 1941 to 1946, discovered the key to the successful route on the north side of the mountain after Mallory had failed to investigate the East Rongbuk Glacier. Later that year Wheeler set up the world's highest survey station on the Lhakpa La (22,000ft), while H T Morshead, the other surveyor in the 1921 party, had already been on Kamet in 1920 with Kellas. Also in 1921 about 15,000 square miles of unknown southern Tibet were surveyed and a survey of northern Sikkim completed.

The roots of the Survey of India lay deep in the Vedic History of India: as early as the third century BC the art of survey had been described, and by the fifth century AD, Arya Bhat had calculated the earth's circumference at the equator to be 25,000 miles, less than 200 miles off the modern measurement. The Survey of India owed its birth to the appointment in 1797 by the East India Company of James Rennell as Surveyor General of Bengal. His first *Map of Hindostan*, printed in the UK, had reached India in 1783. A systematic survey had been set up in India even before the British Ordinance Survey had been established, while its scientific base, the Great Trigonometric Survey (GTS), had been undertaken before similar projects in France and the UK. The GTS owed much to the genius and resolution of William Lambton who started work in Madras in 1802. Early on he had found errors on existing maps of more than 40 miles in the breadth of the peninsula, together with many wrongly positioned towns.

After Lambton's death in 1823 he was succeeded by George Everest who completed the Great Meridional Arc from Cape Cormorin at the southern tip of India to Mussoorie, a distance of 2400km. This was the backbone of the gridiron system by which India was subsequently mapped.

The difficulties of working in a land of mountains, desert and jungle were awesome, with poor communications and the ever-present risk of attack by endemic disease, bandits and wild animals; moreover, instruments continually broke down. Sir George Everest, Surveyor General of India, particularly praised Momsin Hussain, 'the great repairer of instruments', without whose dedicated expertise so much of his survey work would have been impossible.

Eventually the Survey reached the unmapped ranges of the Himalaya and Karakoram which divided the subcontinent from Central Asia. The relatively favourable political climate of the time allowed teams to probe India's north-west boundaries, while access to the then independent kingdoms of Nepal, Sikkim, Bhutan, Assam, the North-East Frontier Agency and Tibet was largely unattainable. So the pundits were born.

Following the retirement of Sir George Everest in December 1843, Andrew Waugh was appointed both Surveyor General and Director of the Great Trigonometrical Survey. Between 1855 and 1865, some of the Survey's most important work was completed in Kashmir under the guidance of Captain T G Montgomerie, the originator of the pundits.

CAPTAIN T G MONTGOMERIE (1830-1878)

Montgomerie was gazetted in the Bengal Engineers and arrived in India in 1851. In the same year he joined the Great Trigonometrical Survey and in 1855 was put in charge of the Kashmir Survey, with W H Johnson as his second-in-command. The triangulation started in Kashmir's Pir Panjal. In 1856 a reconnaissance of Ladakh was made during which K2 was seen and its height, 28,265ft, calculated for the first time. The Kashmir survey continued throughout the Indian Mutiny of 1857, and in 1858 it was in Skardu. In 1861 it moved to Ladakh, where parties worked on the frontiers of Chinese Turkestan and Tibet, and in the Karakoram and the West Kun Lun Shan. By 1859 a map of 8000 square miles of Kashmir had been completed.

In 1865, during his first leave to the UK, Montgomerie was awarded the Founder's Gold Medal by the Royal Geographical Society. Though he was awarded this honour for his own personal achievements, it was to be for his initiative and enterprise in the use of the pundits that he would subsequently be remembered.

Although surveys covering 'several marches beyond the Karakoram Pass' had already been made, it was clear that different techniques would be needed to fill in the large blanks on the map of Tibet and Central Asia. As natives of India could cross the frontier freely, Montgomerie conceived the idea of training native surveyors disguised as traders or pilgrims, using concealed instruments; these men became famous as 'the pundits'.

Montgomerie first put forward his ideas in a Memorandum dated 20 August 1861. He suggested that to measure distance, surveyors should be required to walk 2000 paces to the mile. They were trained to do this by a British Sergeant-Major with a drum and a pace stick. To assist counting they carried a specially-designed Buddhist rosary with 100 beads rather than the usual 108. Every tenth bead was larger and represented 1000 paces, the smaller beads representing 100 paces. The results were inscribed and kept among the prayers in the cavity of the hand-held prayer wheel. Information about topography, culture and politics was also recorded. A compass could be placed in the semi-precious stone in the centre of the drum of the prayer wheel or in the head of a hollowed-out stick, which served also as a repository for gold and silver coins. A watch, boiling-point thermometer (for altitude), barometer and sextant were carried in various guises. After training at the Survey headquarters at Dehra Dun, each pundit was tested along a known route before being despatched on a mission. All Montgomerie's proposals were approved by the Government of India in 1863.

The first pundit, Abdul Hamid, was despatched to Yarkand the same year. Yarkand was chosen because not only was it an important centre, but its position had been incorrectly placed on contemporary maps and intelligence was needed about the region.

Hamid, a Moslem, already had some surveying knowledge, and after training for a month at Montgomerie's camp, he joined a caravan disguised as a trader. Leaving Leh on 23 August 1863 he crossed the Karakoram Pass and on 30 September reached Yarkand where he remained throughout the winter. Eventually the Chinese became suspicious so, with his friend Awaz Ali, he returned by the same route. Sadly, he died after eating poisonous rhubarb, but luckily his notes and instruments were rescued by W H Johnson, who happened to be camping close by.

This first secret journey was a great success from the point of view of the Survey, and Montgomerie capitalised on it by sending more pundits into Turkestan. The secret exploration of Central Asia now began in earnest. The two most outstanding pundits were Nain Singh and Kishen Singh.

NAIN SINGH (1830-1882)

For the initial exploration of Tibet and the independent Himalayan Kingdoms, Montgomerie selected Nain Singh and his cousin Mani Singh from Milam on the advice of Edmund Smyth, Education Officer of Kumaon. They were sons of the Singh family who had helped Moorcroft and Hearsey in their exploration of western Tibet in 1812.

Son of Lata Burha, Nain Singh was born in Milam in the Upper Johar Valley of Kumaon in 1830. Milam, situated at the foot of the glacier which is the source of the Gori Ganga river, is inhabited in summer only. Trade with western Tibet was in flour, rice and British manufactured goods, which were exchanged for wool, salt, gold-dust, ponies and borax. Each Johar

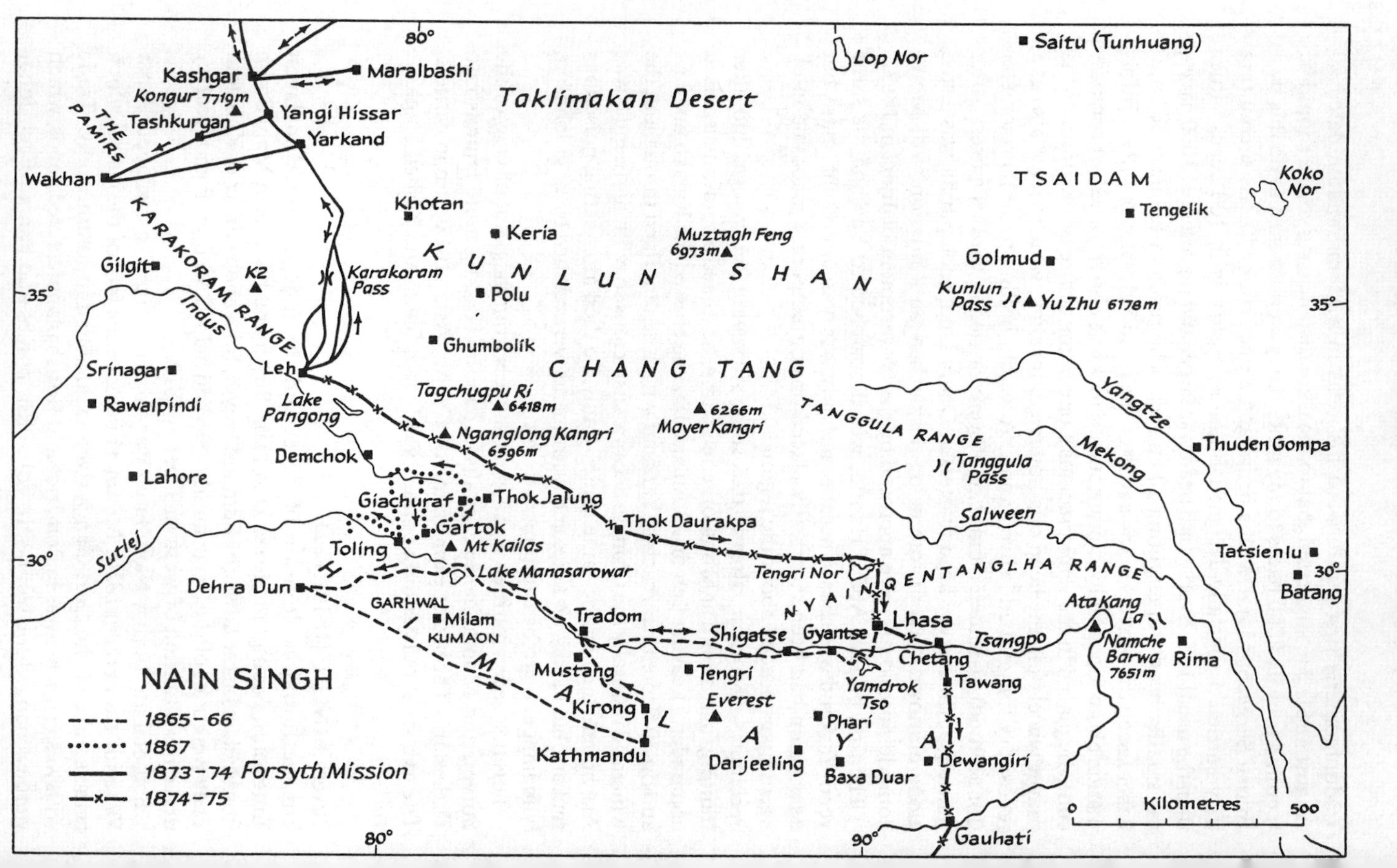
80°
Kashgar
Maralbashi
Kongur 7719m
Taklimakan Desert
THE PAMIRS
Tashkurgan
Yangi Hissar
Yarkand
Wakhan
Lop Nor
Saitu (Tunhuang)
TSAIDAM
Koko Nor
Tengelik
Khotan
Keria
Muztagh Feng 6973m
KUNLUN SHAN
Golmud
KARAKORAM RANGE
Gilgit
K2
Karakoram Pass
Polu
Kunlun Pass
Yu Zhu 6178m
35°
Indus
Ghumbolik
Srinagar
Leh
CHANG TANG
Yangtze
Rawalpindi
Lake Pangong
Tagchugpu Ri 6418m
6266m
Mayer Kangri
TANGGULA RANGE
Nganglong Kangri 6596m
Thuden Gompa
Mekong
Demchok
Tanggula Pass
Lahore
Giachuraf
Thok Jalung
Salween
Gartok
Thok Daurakpa
Toling
Mt Kailas
Tatsienlu
30°
Sutlej
Lake Manasarowar
Tengri Nor
NYAINQENTANGLHA RANGE
Batang
Dehra Dun
GARHWAL
Milam
KUMAON
Tradom
Shigatse
Gyantse
Lhasa
Ata Kang La
Tsangpo
Chetang
Namche Barwa 7651m
Rima
HIMALAYA
Mustang
Tengri
Yamdrok Tso
Tawang
NAIN SINGH
Kirong
Everest
Phari
1865-66
1867
Kathmandu
Darjeeling
Dewangiri
1873-74 Forsyth Mission
Baxa Duar
1874-75
0 Kilometres 500
90°
Gauhati

trader had a Tibetan colleague or *mitra* who was identified by the splitting of a stone, each keeping one half. Carrying this token, the Indian trader or a colleague would sell his goods in Tibet only to an individual who could marry up the other half of the stone.

Nain Singh, with his father, traded regularly in Tibet, became fluent in Tibetan and familiar with Tibetan customs and religious observances. With his cousin Mani Singh, he was with the Schlagintweit brothers between 1855 and 1857 and with Richard and Henry Strachey in western Tibet in 1858. Nain Singh then joined the education service and was headmaster of the Milam Government Vernacular School from 1858 to 1863. Both he and Mani Singh were then selected and trained as pundits at Dehra Dun.

1865–66 Kathmandu – Lhasa – Gartok

The first task assigned to Nain and Mani Singh was to make for Lhasa, and immediately they demonstrated qualities of initiative and enterprise. Providentially, some traders who had been robbed near Gartok in western Tibet asked them to act as their representatives in Lhasa in order to try to recover the goods. The direct route north from Kumaon to the Lake Manasarowar region, which followed the main route from Gartok to Lhasa, was impassable, so the cousins decided to go via Kathmandu which they reached on 7 March 1865. As the normal route by the Nyelam Valley to Tingri was also blocked by snow and landslides, they tried an alternative route via Kirong, but were stopped by suspicious border guards and returned to Kathmandu. Here they found a Bhotia merchant about to depart for Tibet again via Kirong, and the cousins split up. Mani decided it was too risky to travel to Kirong a second time; instead he carried out a route survey in north-west Nepal before returning to Dehra Dun.

Nain Singh persevered, and when the merchant for whom he was working reneged on his offer, Nain disguised himself as a Ladakhi merchant, complete with pigtail, and continued alone, joining a group of Bashari traders bound for Lake Manasarowar. On reaching the Tsangpo, he was told that this river flowed east and then turned south into India. At the time this information was of great geographical importance. Following the main trade route east he finally reached Lhasa in January 1866, having covered some 500 miles in 37 days. He rented a room and explored the city, making the first measured topographical observations since the visit in 1846 of Fathers Hue and Gabet.

Although 'forbidden' to Europeans, Lhasa was a thriving cosmopolitan centre visited by merchants from India, Sikkim, Bhutan, Nepal, Ladakh and further afield. Nain Singh had an audience with the Dalai Lama at Sera Monastery, and was able to observe closely the ceremonial details. When his funds were exhausted he supported himself by teaching. This was an unlikely occupation for a Bashari trader and his disguise was spotted by two Kashmiris, but luckily they remained silent and even lent him some money.

After three months in Lhasa Nain Singh returned to western Tibet with the same group of Kashmiris who had befriended him earlier. Instead of returning directly to Kathmandu, he continued towards the important trading centre of Gartok, crossed the Himalaya with difficulty and arrived in Dehra Dun on 27 October 1866. His report included the first survey of 1200 miles of the main trade route in southern Tibet. He also defined the course of the Tsangpo as far as the Kyi Chu tributary on which Lhasa lies. In addition he had collected innumerable climatic, topographical and political details which were of great value both to the Survey and to the Government of India. As a result, more money was made available for exploration in Tibet and Central Asia.

The pundits now started mining a rich seam of hitherto unavailable information with panache, bravery and intelligence. Once they had left Dehra Dun they received no support, and they had to rely for survival solely upon their own wit and cunning.

1867 Gartok – Thok Jalong goldfields – sources of the Indus and Sutlej rivers – Mt Kailas

The purpose of Nain and Mani Singh's next mission was to establish the position of the headwaters of the Indus and Sutlej rivers, explore the famed goldfields of Thok Jalong, and fill in a number of topographical gaps. An extra member was added to the party; this was Kalian Singh, one of Nain Singh's brothers.

The trio left Mussoorie on 2 May 1867 and travelled east through Badrinath, reaching Mana on 3 June. Crossing the Himalaya by the Mana Pass on 28 July, they passed close to Tsaparang where in 1624 Father Andrade had established the first Christian mission in Tibet. After crossing the Sutlej river at Toling, they headed north and east, to avoid Tibetan officials. On the desolate and bare 'antelope plains' they disguised themselves as Bashari traders, ostensibly selling coral in exchange for shawl wool (the soft underwool of the goat used in Kashmiri shawls). Unfortunately, at Giachuraf, some Tibetans pointed out that they could not possibly have come from Bashar, as all the routes across the Himalaya had been closed after an outbreak of smallpox. Moreover they were well past Gartok, the centre for exchanging shawl wool. Only by repeated protestations of innocence and the offer of large bribes were they allowed to continue. By this time Mani Singh's nerves were shredded and he was left behind as a hostage, whilst the other two continued their journeys separately – Kalian Singh towards Mt Kailas, and Nain Singh to the newly-worked goldfields of Thok Jalong.

The mine was a trench about a mile in length, 25ft deep, and with a width varying between 10 and 200 paces. A stream ran through the bottom of the trench, earth being sluiced into it and the soil being carried away leaving a residue of gold. At 16,000ft it was worked all the year round and tents were pitched below ground level to mitigate the almost continuous freezing wind. The gold was used for the many holy buildings of Tibet, particularly in

Lhasa, but to avoid suspicion Nain Singh only stayed for a short time and was not able to assess the annual output of the mine. Returning to Giachuraf he was reunited with Kalian who had confirmed that the eastern branch of the Indus, north of Mt Kailas, was the river's main source. Mani also rejoined them here and, with his cousin Nain, continued to Gartok before returning to Toling. Here they waited for Kalian who had surveyed the Indus as far as Demchok and crossed a high pass to the Sutlej valley before returning to Toling. Separating again, Nain Singh returned directly to Badrinath, whilst Mani and Kalian descended the Sutlej to Shipki, and then recrossed the Himalaya. All were reunited on British territory in November 1867.

Thus ended the first systematic survey of western Tibet. Montgomerie built on this by sending further pundits into southern, northern and eastern Tibet.

1873-74 Forsyth's Second Mission: Yarkand – Khotan – Polu – Pangong Lake – Leh

Nain Singh and Kalian Singh, with another member of the Singh family Kishen Singh, joined this mission which opened up some new ground. Politically, however, it was the most important ever to visit Central Asia, since it brought back a vast amount of information about a then little-known but strategically vital region where the empires and areas of influence of China, Russia and the British in India converged.

1874–75 Pangong Lake – North of the Gangdise Range – Tengri Nor – Lhasa – Tawang – Assam

This was Nain Singh's last mission. Captain Trotter, who had taken over from Montgomerie when the latter left India in 1873, despatched him to Lhasa by a route that crossed the Chang Tang from west to east, north of the Gangdise Range and the many lakes in that region. After nearly ten years of rigorous and dangerous work, Nain Singh was exhausted but he accepted this final mission before retiring to a well-earned government position and a pension.

The proposal of the Survey was that he should travel eastwards through the southern part of the Chang Tang, about 100-150 miles north of the Tsangpo and north of the Gangdise Range. Reaching Lhasa, he would join a caravan that went either south and east to Tatsienlu in China or north and east across the Tibetan Plateau to Xining, also in China, and from either place he would make for Beijing. If this proved impossible he was to return to India from Lhasa either by continuing down the Tsangpo or by going due south through Bhutan. In either case he would end up in British territory.

As Nain Singh was known in Leh from his previous government service, a subterfuge was used at the start of his journey. He was provided with a flock of sheep, ostensibly carrying merchandise to Yarkand over the Karakoram Pass, but at a certain point he would divert into western Tibet. His party consisted of Chhumbel (who later accompanied Kishen Singh on an epic four-year journey) and two Tibetans. At the last village before the Tibetan border the pundit and his companions changed into lamas' robes, and travelled along the north side of the Pangong Lake. They then continued parallel to but north of the Gangdise Range, befriended by khampa traders from eastern Tibet going in the same direction.

Nain was able to visit the gold mines at Thok Daurakpa. He identified the peak Aling Kangri for the first time and enjoyed extensive views of the north side of the Gangdise and later the Nyainqentanglha Range. After passing many lakes filled with brackish water, he arrived at the north-west corner of the largest of them, the Tengri Nor (Nam Co). Here he turned south and east, reaching Lhasa on 18 November 1874.

Unfortunately he was recognised by a merchant from Leh, so he sent two of his men back to Leh with all his notes and observations, whilst he himself stayed on for a few days before leaving with his other servants. To throw any potential pursuers off his track he left all his heavy gear in Lhasa, saying that he would return in a month or so. After a false start due north on the Xining Road, he doubled back as darkness fell and made for India. When he reached the Tsangpo he turned east for two days before crossing the river by boat. He estimated the current of the river by throwing logs into the stream and timing their descent over a fixed distance: by measuring the poles used for punting, he gained an idea of the depth of the river, which was 18-20 feet, and estimated its width at Tsetang where he crossed at about 500 yards. This was about 50 miles beyond the point to which the Tsangpo had been explored, and by taking bearings on distant peaks, he estimated its course for the next 50 miles or so. Following a tributary south, he crossed the Karkang La and entered Tawang just east of Bhutan. Here he was detained for two months by a local ruler but finally reached British territory on 1st March 1875.

Nain Singh's last survey had covered 1300 miles of virtually unexplored territory and the information gained about the goldfields and southern Chang Tang were verified by H Hayden in 1921, when further information about the Tsangpo River and Tawang was obtained. Exhausted now, after years of hazardous work, he retired to train further pundits. An excellent teacher, he was responsible for the instruction of the pundit Sarat Chandra Das, who provided a scholarly account of Lhasa and southern Tibet. The village of Rohilkhand, with a yearly revenue of 1000 rupees, was given to him as a pension. He died in 1882.

KISHEN SINGH (1851-1921)

Kishen Singh, the greatest of the pundits, died in 1921, the year of the first reconnaissance of Mount Everest, on which members of the Survey of India played such a notable part. A cousin of Nain Singh, Kishen too was born in Milam and in 1867 was summoned to Dehra Dun for training by T G Montgomerie and Nain Singh. In 1869, aged 18, he explored from Milam to Lake Rakas Tal, along the Karnali River to Kathan Ghat, a distance of 400 miles. In 1871 he was selected to explore the Nam Co Lake (Tengri Nor) just north of the Nyainqentanglha Range of southern Tibet.

1871–72 Shigatze – Namling – Nam Co – Lhasa

From Kumaon, Kishen Singh's party crossed the Himalaya, reached Lake Manasarowar and, evading robbers, took the main road, reaching Shigatze on 24 November 1871. Here they remained for twelve days, exploring the town and Tashilumpo Monastery, the seat of the Panchen Lama. They bought fifty sheep to carry their supplies to the region of the Nam Co and Kishen Singh exchanged his silver coins for gold ones which he placed in his hollowed-out walking-stick.

Leaving Shigatze on 6 December, they crossed the Tsangpo next day by raft to the north bank. At Namling ('garden of the sky'), which they reached on 14 December, there was a large monastery, about 200 houses, and a garrison of 100 soldiers. Here their tents were ripped apart by gale force winds, and they lost some time repairing them.

On 28 December they camped by a series of hot springs, part of a geothermal belt that crosses Tibet at about this latitude. The most spectacular of these were at Nai Sum Chuja, which they reached on 2 January 1872. Here the water of the Lahu River, a tributary of the Tsangpo, was so hot that it was unfrozen for three miles downstream. On one bank a jet of boiling water was thrown sixty feet into the air where it froze into a pillar of ice about thirty feet in circumference. The temperature of the water was 183° F, only a fraction below boiling point at that altitude.

After crossing the Khalamba Pass (17,200ft) they descended towards the Nam Co. To avoid being robbed, Kishen Singh deposited his goods at Dorkia Monastery, leaving three of his party to guard them. Over the next 15 days the rest of the party circumnavigated the Tengri Nor (Nam Co), returning to the monastery from which they had started. Though brackish and frozen in winter, the lake, at 15,200ft, contained fish. Many peaks of the Nyainqentanglha Range were visible to the south and east.

On 16 February they were attacked by armed robbers on horseback. Everything was taken except their instruments, which were not considered valuable. After listening to their pleas for mercy, the robbers gave them back a piece of cloth each, two sheep, two bags of food and one cooking vessel. This incident prevented them from continuing north to Xining, for in order to survive they had to find food and clothing. They all became so weak that Kishen Singh had to shorten his paces; begging all the way, they reached Lhasa on 9 March. Here Kishen Singh tried and failed to borrow money to go north to Xining, but after much difficulty he managed to obtain 150 rupees from a trader going west to Gartok, who insisted that he accompany him, taking his compass and anaeroid barometer (which he mistook for a watch) as surety. Finally, after a long and taxing journey, Kishen Singh reached Dehra Dun.

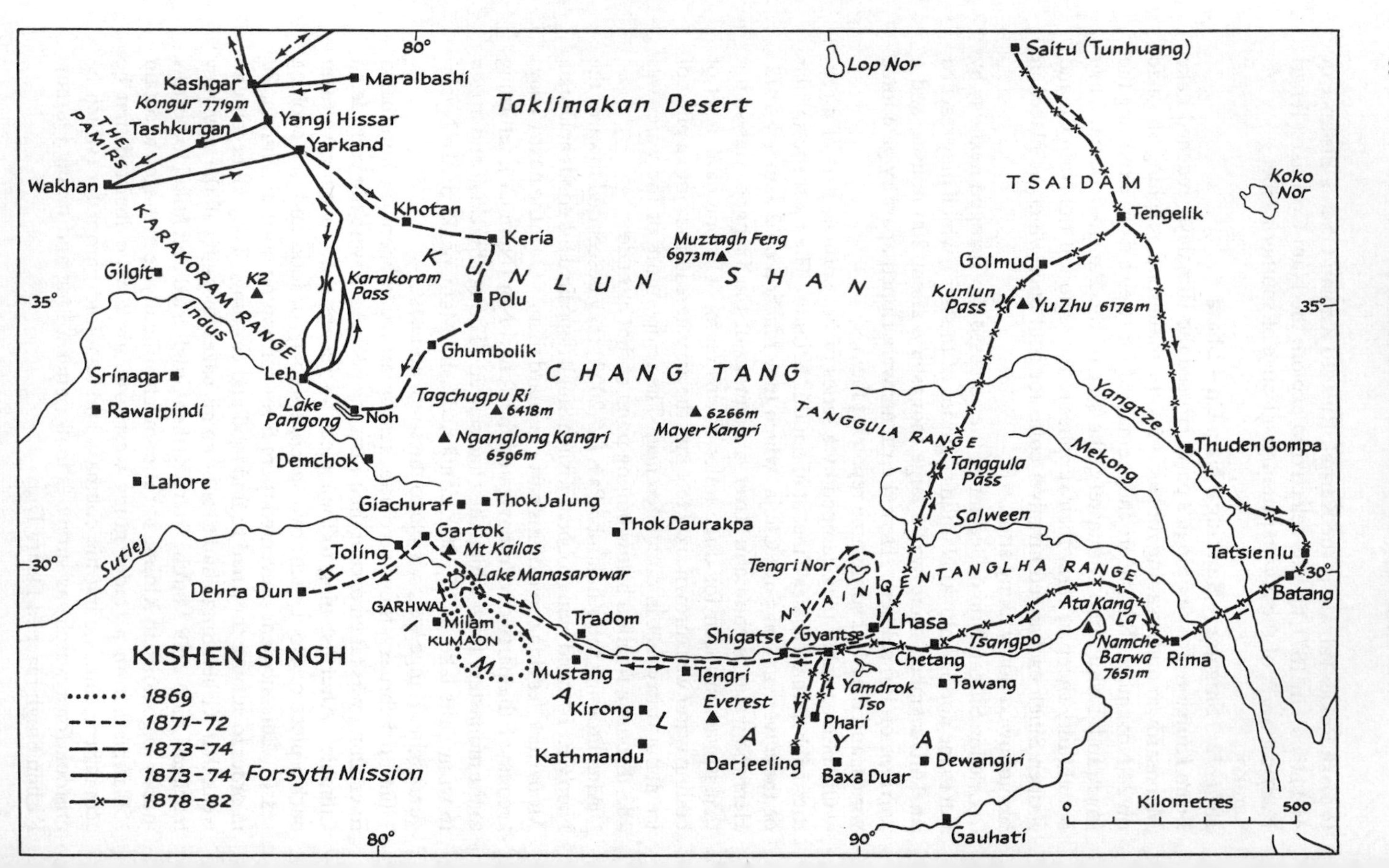
Saitu (Tunhuang)
Lop Nor
Kashgar
Maralbashi
Kongur 7719m
Taklimakan Desert
Yangi Hissar
Tashkurgan
THE PAMIRS
Yarkand
Wakhan
KARAKORAM RANGE
Khotan
Keria
TSAIDAM
Koko Nor
Tengelik
Muztagh Feng 6973m
Golmud
Gilgit
K2
Karakoram Pass
KUN LUN SHAN
Kunlun Pass
Yu Zhu 6178m
35°
Polu
Indus
Ghumbolik
Srinagar
Leh
CHANG TANG
Yangtze
Rawalpindi
Lake Pangong
Noh
Tagchugpu Ri 6418m
6266m
Mayer Kangri
TANGGULA RANGE
Nganglong Kangri 6596m
Thuden Gompa
Mekong
Demchok
Tanggula Pass
Lahore
Giachuraf
Thok Jalung
Salween
Thok Daurakpa
Gartok
Mt Kailas
Toling
Sutlej
Tengri Nor
Tatsienlu
30°
NYAINQENTANGLHA RANGE
Lake Manasarowar
Batang
Dehra Dun
Ata Kang La
GARHWAL
Milam
Tradom
Lhasa
KUMAON
Shigatse
Gyantse
Tsangpo
Namche Barwa 7651m
Rima
KISHEN SINGH
Mustang
Tengri
Chetang
HIMALAYA
Tawang
Yamdrok Tso
Everest
Kirong
Phari
Kathmandu
Darjeeling
Baxa Duar
Dewangiri
1869
1871–72
1873–74
1873–74 Forsyth Mission
1878–82
Kilometres
0
500
80°
90°
Gauhati

1873-74 Yarkand – Khotan – Polu – Noh – Pangong Lake – Leh

After taking part in Forsyth's Second Mission to Yarkand, Kishen Singh returned by a hitherto unknown route east of the already well-known Karakoram Pass (information about this route had been obtained some years earlier by R B Shaw from a native of the area). Before leaving Turkestan, Kishen Singh visited the Surghak goldfield, 160 miles east of Khotan. He then returned to Keriya and Polu. From here he followed the Polu (Keriya) River to the south for about 28 miles, making a 9000ft ascent to the Diwan Pass (17,500ft). After traversing the Ghumbolick Plain (17,000ft) he descended to Arash and crossed an unnamed pass over a range continuous with the Kun Lun. Continuing over a series of high plateaux containing numerous brackish lakes, he reached Noh. For the whole of this journey from Ghumbolik to Noh, a distance of 244 miles, he saw no one, though there were large herds of yak, antelope and *ovis ammon* (wild sheep). He was thus able to complete his route survey without interruption.

From Noh he tried to get to Rudok, an important village in western Tibet, but was prevented by the local inhabitants. Anticipating that his baggage would be searched, he buried all his instruments, returning for them some days later after he had persuaded the villagers to allow him to continue his journey to Leh. Following this lengthy exploration, he was too exhausted to join Nain Singh on his last expedition of 1874 through the southern Chang Tang, Lhasa, Tawang and the Tsang Po.

1878–82 Darjeeling – Lhasa – Chang Tang of Northern Tibet – Kun Lun Shan – Golmud – Tsaidam – Tunhuang – Eastern Tibet – Tatsienlu – Darjeeling

This was the most substantial and important journey in the history of Central Asian exploration. By 1878 the Survey of India had obtained a considerable amount of information about the Pamir, Kashgar and the approaches to Turkestan from the south via Leh and the Karakoram Pass. Southern and western Tibet were also fairly well known, but northern Tibet, the Chang Tang, Kun Lun mountains, the Tsaidam, eastern Tibet and the Chinese-Tibet borderlands were almost unknown. In 1846 Huc and Gabet had travelled to Lhasa from Xining through northern Tibet, and from Lhasa to Chamdo in Szechuan in China, but little geographical knowledge had been obtained.

J T Walker, who had taken over from Trotter, wrote in the *Proceedings of the Royal Geographical Society* in February 1888:

> Thus in the spring of 1878 I dispatched Pundit A–K [Kishen Singh] towards this region, directing him to strike directly across the great Plateau of Tibet into Mongolia, by any route from the south to north that he might find practical, and return by a parallel route over new ground. As he might very possibly strike one of the great routes to China and be tempted to find his way to the coast and return to India

> by the sea route to Calcutta, I particularly directed him to avoid China, of which the geography was well known, and make his way as far as practicable through Tibet, which was comparatively terra incognita.

Because of difficulties with the frontier guards in western Tibet, whose interrogations were extremely strict and thorough, Kishen Singh opted to cross into Tibet from Sikkim. He had with him his faithful companion Chhumbel and another servant, Ganga Ram. They left Darjeeling on 16 April 1878 and crossed through deep snow into Tibet by the Bod La. On 24 April they reached Chumbi, the summer residence of the Rajah (Gyalpo) of Sikkim and two days later were at Phari, where they enjoyed fine views of Chomolhari (Peak 1 of the Survey of India). On 21 August they reached Gyantse. After remaining here for a few days to exchange goods with traders from Nepal and China, they crossed the easy Karo La to reach the famous Yamdrok Tso ('Signet Ring Lake'). After crossing the Kampa La they descended a very steep path to the Tsangpo (100 paces wide) over which they went by the iron bridge at Chaksam and reached Khamba Barji where Kishen Singh started his survey. On 5 September he arrived in Lhasa where he replenished his merchandise.

Enquiring about a caravan to Mongolia, Kishen Singh was told that the next one would leave in February, but that no definite date had been fixed. A wait of over a year was imposed on him, but he put the time to good use, learning Mongolian and making a detailed survey of the city. He was also able to acquire valuable information on the customs, ceremonials and governance of the city which was subsequently used on Younghusband's mission of 1903-4. His knowledge of languages enabled him to speak freely without an interpreter; when robbed and destitute in the Tsaidam and Tunhuang, he was able to raise money by reciting from sacred books.

Eventually Kishen Singh and his party of six were able to join a caravan returning to Mongolia and they left Lhasa on 17 September 1879. Of the caravan's 105 members, 60 were Mongolians who, having ridden since birth, were able to stay on their horses even when dead drunk, whilst the Tibetans walked. All were armed, and they were preceded and followed by mounted scouts. Anyone who failed to keep up was left with food and water, but seldom survived. Each day, after a start at daybreak, a brief halt was made at 10am and camp was made at about 4pm. Overnight, horses were hobbled and a fire made from animal dung, a bellows being essential, as dung would not ignite without it.

Sixty miles north of Lhasa they crossed the Lani La (15,700ft) and started to cross the Chang Tang ('Northern Plain') which stretched to the Kun Lun Shan and covered 480,000 square miles. The world's largest plateau, and the highest at 15-16,000ft, the Chang Tang was almost wholly uninhabited except for nomads. No trees and very few shrubs grew on this plain, which was home to vast herds of wild yak, goats, antelope, sheep and, further north, 'Bactrian' camels. A week's march brought them, on 29 September, to the notable Shibden Gompa in the Province of Nakchuka. For the next 240 miles they passed no habitation.

On 8 October they crossed the Dang La (Tanggula Range) by a pass at 16,400ft. This east-west range is the main feature of the Chang Tang and separates the headwaters of the Yangtse Kiang to the north from the great rivers flowing to the south. Today the Lhasa–Golmud road crosses this range at 5120m. To the east and west there are extensive snowfields, with the highest peak at 6525m. The range is also the boundary between Tsinghai province, in which the north-east part of the plateau lies, and the Xizang autonomous region, which encompasses the rest. On 19 October they crossed a relatively minor range, the Koko Shili, and on 22 October met another caravan of 150 Mongolians on their way to Lhasa with 80 camels and 100 ponies. Here, whilst crossing an ice-covered and boggy river, Chhumbel lost a toe through frostbite, whilst a horse and a mule became fatally stuck in glutinous mud.

The next obstacle was the Kun Lun Range (Angirtakchia) which bounds the northern edge of the plateau. Kishen Singh correctly observed that this was the same range as the one that he had crossed over a thousand miles to the west on his return from the Forsyth Mission in 1873. On 27 October the Kun Lun Pass provided an easy passage and they dropped down into the Xidatan, a rift valley running straight from east to west on the north side of the Kun Lun Range. Continuing east and then north, they reached Naichi where they found a number of Mongolian yurts. They followed the Naichi River to Golmo (Golmud), which at that time was a nomad camp with 50 tents situated in a dense 'forest' of trees 6-7ft high. (Now it is a burgeoning industrial town in a key position on the road to Lhasa.) The Golmo nomads were most hospitable and Kishen Singh stayed with them for ten days after the caravan dispersed.

The clear air of the plateau had now changed to a murky haze; the landscape was one of sandy hills with many trees and shrubs covered with a salty-tasting dust, whilst the Bactrian camel of Central Asia had replaced the Tibetan yak as the main beast of burden.

Leaving Golmo, Kishen Singh went east to Tengelik, where his now diminished group was attacked by robbers. The Mongolians fled and he lost nearly all his possessions. Almost destitute, he continued north towards Saitu (Tunhuang). Fortunately at Yembi he met a Tibetan from Gyantse who, twenty years previously, had emigrated to Mongolia. He engaged Kishen Singh and his two companions, Chhumbel and Ganga Ram, to look after his camels in return for food. Here they remained for three months until, in July 1880, Ganga Ram deserted, taking with him almost all their remaining money and provisions. Still intent on reaching Tunhuang, both were hired to look after ponies and goats, but after five months they decided to move on, even with limited funds, and, if necessary, beg their way. On 3 January 1881 they joined a group going north and on their departure were very generously given a horse, warm clothing and provisions by their employer. Crossing the salty sand desert of the Tsaidam, they reached Sirthang and then on 8 January the outskirts of Tunhuang, the first town since Lhasa. Set in extensive green fields, it was an oasis with good water supplies and a largely Chinese population. The local people distrusted the two pundits, and they were detained in Tunhuang for seven months. By a lucky chance the head lama of Thuden Gompa, a large monastery near Darchendo (Tatsienlu) in the Derge Province of eastern Tibet, visited Tunhuang to see the Cave of the Thousand Buddhas (described so well by Aurel Stein). He obtained permission for them to leave as his servants, and they retraced their route, reaching Yemba on 15 August 1881.

Following J T Walker's instructions, they next went south through eastern Tibet and crossed the Kun Lun Range again by a pass 180 miles to the east of the Kun Lun Pass. Since he was now riding rather than walking, Kishen Singh had to adjust his pace-length figures. Gaining the Chang Tang once again, they crossed the headwaters of the Hwang-Ho River and five days later were at Thuden Gompa in the valley of the Yangtse Kiang, where they worked for the head lama. After two months their wages were paid and the lama gave them a letter to an influential friend at Kegudo, a town at the junction of the trade routes to Xining and Tatsienlu from Lhasa. Finally they reached their furthest point to the east – Tatsienlu (in China) – on 5 February 1882. Here Kishen Singh contacted Bishop Biet of the Franco-Catholic mission and on giving him a letter of introduction from General Walker, received some sorely-needed money. A letter was sent to Walker via the Abbé Desgordin of the Mission in India; this was the first news of the pundit for three years.

From Tatsienlu they went west to Batang and then Litang. Here smallpox was prevalent, so they took snuff prepared from the dried postules of patients as a prophylactic. Striking across the hitherto unexplored gorge country of south-east Tibet (so well described by the plant hunter F Kingdon Ward many years later) they reached the Zayul River which flowed into the Brahmaputra. At Sama they were only 30 miles from British territory, but would have been murdered if they had attempted to cross the country of the Mishmi tribes in between.

It was now the middle of May 1882 and Kishen Singh would have to go north and cross the main Himalaya by the Ata Kang La (15,300ft), a glacier pass, but as this was not immediately possible he went from village to village reciting the sacred books of Tibet to defray expenses. On 9 July he and his party crossed the Ata Kang La and regained the Plateau where, at Lhojong, they joined the Junglam, the official highway between Lhasa and China.

In the course of this excursion through south-east Tibet, Kishen Singh's observations left little doubt that the Tsangpo and Brahmaputra rivers were one and the same. Following the Kyi Chu River, on which Lhasa lies, they left the Junglam, struck south, and crossed the Tsangpo, reaching Khambarji on 17 October, 4½ years after they had left. Here Kishen Singh's survey ended. Both he and Chhumbel arrived in Darjeeling on 12 November 1882 'in a condition bordering on destitution, their funds exhausted, their clothes in rags and their bodies emaciated with the hardships and deprivations they had undergone'. The newly surveyed distance covered on this epic journey was 2800 miles which, added to the 1950 miles already surveyed by Kishen Singh on previous journeys, reached a total of 4750 miles, a feat never equalled or surpassed. Virtually all his survey notes and instruments were intact and when asked if he had any debts he said that he had none.

Kishen Singh faced a sad homecoming. On his return he found that his only son was dead and that his house had been broken up. He was kept on the books of the Survey at a salary of RS100 a month and retired in 1885 on the income from the village of Itarhi in the Sitapur district with the title of Raj Bahadur. Twenty years later Tom Longstaff met him in the village of Mansiari in Kumaon where the Milam Bhotias spent the winter.

Kishen Singh organised an expedition for J C Brown of the Geological Survey of India in 1905-6, but as the Tibetans had put a price of £500 on his head, he himself never went near the Tibetan frontier again.

Judge Usaris Ameer Ali, when Assistant Commissioner of Kumaon, visited Kishen Singh when he was in his seventies and found him very spry. An unassuming man, he kept chests full of books, diaries, maps and medals from the world's major geographical societies, but *not* the Royal Geographical Society which had only honoured Nain Singh.

It is difficult to overpraise Kishen Singh's epic final journey. His nationality and knowledge of Tibetan and Mongolian enabled him to explore regions which were inaccessible to Europeans. He provided the first route survey of eastern and northern Tibet, a description of the Chang Tang and of the Kun Lun range, an up-to-date survey of Lhasa, a description of Tunhuang, and information about the principal rivers of Tibet and of the gorge country of south-east Tibet. He also supplied details of the cultural and political facets of all the places through which he passed. All this was carried out secretly, and often when he was exhausted and in extreme danger. Truly Kishen Singh was the greatest of all the pundits.

THE PUNDITS

Abdul Hameed (Mahomed-I-Hameed)
Nain Singh (The Pundit, No 1)
Mani Singh (G.M., The Patwar)
Mirza Shuja (The Mirza)
Hyder Shah (The Havildar)
Ata Mahomed (The Mullah)
Kalian Singh (G.K.)
Hari Ram (M.H., No 9)
Ata Ram
Mukhtar Shah (M.S.)
Abdul Subhan (A–S)
Kishen Singh (A–K, Krishna)
Sukh Darshan Singh (G.S.S.)
Lama Serap Gyatso
Lala
Nem Singh (G.M.N.)
Kinthup (K.P.)
Rinzin Namgyal (R.N.)
Lama Ugyen Gyatso (U.G.)
Sarat Chandra Das (S.C.D.)
Alaga

CHRONOLOGY OF THE PRE-PUNDIT EXPLORERS

1774	A sepoy officer	Bengal
Later part of 18th century	Learned Muslims and Hindus	Central India, Hindu Kush, Chitral.
Early 19th century	Various Indians contributed to the compilation of the *Map of Hindostan.*	
1812	Mir Izzet Ullah	Leh, Karakoram Pass, Yarkand, Bokhara, Kabul.
1812-13	Harkh Dev Pundit used by Moorcroft. Measured paces used for the first time.	Western Tibet
1813	A Brahman used by J Hodgson	Ladakh, Western Tibet
1823-40	Agents used by C Wade, Political Officer in Ludhiana.	Punjab
1832	Mohammed Ali travelled with A Burnes.	Bokhara
1846	Ahmed Shah Nakshah Banda used summer route from Leh to Yarkand. Izzet Ullah used the winter route.	Ladakh, Karakoram Pass, Yarkand.
1855-57	Nain Singh, Mani Singh, Dolpa Singh with the Schlagintweit brothers.	Ladakh, Turkestan, Western Tibet.
1858	Nain Singh, Mani Singh with Moorcroft and Hearsey.	Western Tibet
1860	Abdul Mejid	Kokand. First recorded passage of the Pamirs.

CHRONOLOGY OF THE PUNDITS

1863	First pundit: Abdul Hameed (Mahomed–I–Hameed)	Leh, Yarkand
1864	Nain Singh and Mani Singh	Attempts to enter Tibet
1865	Pundit Munphool	Bokhara
1865-66	Nain Singh, Chhumbel, Mani Singh	Kathmandu, Tradom, Shigatse, Lhasa, Gartok, Milam
1867	Nain Singh, Mani Singh	Gartok, Thok Jalong. Headwaters of Indus and Sutlej rivers.
1856-68	Lama Serap Gyatso left China in 1856, and settled in Lower Tsang Po. Lived in Kongpo (south-east Tibet). Namcha Barwa mentioned.	
1868	Hari Ram	North of Everest
	Kalian Singh	Rudok, Thok Jalong, Shigatze
	Kalian Singh's Zaskari servant	visited Muktinath, Lo Mantang
1868-69	Mirza Shuja	Kabul, Kashgar, Yarkand, Leh
1869	Kishen Singh	Rakas Tal Lake, Karnali River
1870	Hyder Shah Ata Mahomed	Faizabad, Chitral
1871-72	Hari Ram	Tashirak, Tengri, Nyelam, Kathmandu.
	Kishen Singh	Kumaon, Shigatze, Tengri Nor, Lhasa, Gartok.
1872-73	Mirza Shusa murdered	? Bokhara

1873	Hari Ram	Kumaon, Kali Gandaki, Muktinath, Mustang, Tradom.
	Kishen Singh (2nd Yarkand Mission)	Khotan, Polu, Noh, Leh.
	Hyder Shah	First survey across Hindu Kush
	Nain Singh (2nd Yarkand Mission)	Leh, Yarkand, Khotan, Karakoram Pass.
1873-74	Ata Mahomed	Chitral, Wakhan, Yarkand.
1874	Abdul Subhan	Kabul, Wakhan, Oxus, Roshan.
1874-75	Nain Singh, Chhumbel	Leh, Thok Daurakpa, Tengri Nor, Lhasa, Tawang, Assam.
1875-76	Lala	Darjeeling, Shigatze, Tsona, Shigatze, Chumbi
	Ata Mahomed Sayid Amir	Gilgit
1876-77	Abdul Subhan	Udaipur
1877	Lala	Darjeeling, Lachen La, Darjeeling.
1878	Ata Mahomed	Swat River
1878-79	Nem Singh Kinthup	Darjeeling, Lhasa, Tsetang, Tsang Po to Gyala, Phari.
1878-81	Mukhtar Shah	Oxus River, Wakhan, Badakshan, Gilgit.
1878-82	Kishen Singh, Chhumbel	Darjeeling, Lhasa, across Chang Tang, Kun Lun Shan, Tsaidam, Tun Huang, East Tibet, Tatsienlu, Zayul (SE Tibet), Khambarji, Darjeeling.

1879	Rinzin Namgyal Nem Singh Alaga Sarat Chandra Das and Lama Ugyen Gyatso	Sikkim ? Upper Irrawady Jonsong La and Shigatze
1880	Nem Singh	Shigatze, Khamba Jong
1880-81	Sukh Darshan Singh	Popti La (Nepal-Tibet frontier), eastern Nepal
1880-82	Sarat Chandra Das Lama Ugyen Gyatso Phurchung	Shigatze, Lhasa
Before 1883	Bozdar	?
1883	Rinzin Namgyal	Sikkim, Talung Valley
1880-84	Kinthup A Chinese Lama	Tsangpo, Gyala, Olon, Darjeeling
1883-84	Lama Ugyen Gyatso (His third journey. The first two were with Sarat Chandra Das in 1879 and 1880-82.)	Shigatze, Lhobak, Kula Kangri (*alias* Kangri or Gangkar Puensum), Lhasa, Chumbi.
1884	Syud and Meah (with McNair) Rinzin Namgyal (with Tanner) The Hakim	NW Frontier West Nepal, Kumaon, Lipu Lek ?
1884-85	Rinzin Namgyal	Darjeeling, Jonsong Pass, Chorten Nyima La, Lachen, Darjeeling.
1885	Hari Ram	Sola Khumbu, Tengri, Kathmandu
1885-86	Rinzin Namgyal Phurba	Sikkim, East and West Bhutan, South Tibet.

1887-88	Rinzin Namgyal Tanner	West and Central Nepal, from tower stations outside its borders.
1888	Ata Mahomed	Afghanistan
1888-89	Rinzin Namgyal (with Needham)	To Sadiya on the Brahmaputra.He obtained information from Lama Ugyen Gyatso about Abors, Mishmi tribes and about the Tsangpo and Dihang rivers.
1891-92	Ata Ram (with Bower)	Across Tibet 50 miles N of Nain Singh's route of 1874. Traverse from Leh to Batang.
1892-93	Hari Ram and his son	Nepal and Tibet
1899	Rinzin Namgyal (with Freshfield)	Around Kangchenjunga

The external reconnaissance survey of Nepal from Tower stations outside its borders was completed by 1888. The Nepal detachment of the Survey of India worked inside Nepal from 1924-27, but with Indian surveyors only. Neither Europeans nor photographs were allowed.

The complete survey of Bhutan was completed by the Survey of India in 1971.

The survey of Sikkim was completed during the 1921 Everest Reconnaissance Expedition.

Everest was circumnavigated by Hari Ram in a series of journeys in 1871-72 and in 1885.

Kangchenjunga was circumnavigated by Rinzin Namgyal (with Douglas Freshfield) in 1899. The first circumnavigation of this peak had been completed by Rinzin Namgyal, leader of a survey team, in 1884-5.

The first 'modern' map of Tibet was published by the Royal Geographical Society in 1906.

BIBLIOGRAPHY

G F Heaney, 'Rennell and the Surveyors of India' in *Geographical Journal 134*, 318-327, Sept 1968.

R H Phillimore, *Historical Records of the Survey of India I-V*. Dehra Dun, 1945-58.

S M Chadha, *Survey of India Through the Ages*. 105 (DLI) Printing Group of Survey of India, 1990.

J B N Hennessey, *Report on the explorations in Great Tibet and Mongolia made by A–K in 1879-82 in connection with the Trigonometric Branch*. Survey of India, Dehra Dun, 1884.

S G Burrard, *Records of the Survey of India, Part I 1865-1879 and Part II 1879-1892*. Dehra Dun, 1915. Exploration in Tibet and neighbouring regions.

Indra Singh Rawat, *Indian Explorers of the Nineteenth Century*. Ministry of Information, Government of India. New Delhi, 1973.

D Waller, *The Pundits: British Exploration of Tibet and Central Asia*. The University Press of Kentucky, 1990.

Sarat Chandra Das, *Journey to Lhasa and Central Tibet*. Edited by W W Rockhill. John Murray, 1902.

Mir Izzet Ullah, 'Travels Beyond the Himalaya' in *Calcutta Oriental Quarterly Magazine*, 183-342, 1825.

Expeditions

ALAN HINKES

Challenge 8000

A progress report

(*Plates 20–22*)

It is not the critic who counts, not the man who points out how the strong man stumbled or where the doer of deeds could have done better. The credit belongs to the man who is actually in the arena; whose face is marred by dust and sweat and blood; who strives valiantly; who errs and comes short again and again; who knows the great enthusiasms, the great devotions, and spends himself in a worthy cause; who, at the best, knows in the end the triumph of high achievement; and who, at the worst, if he fails, at least fails while daring greatly, so that his place shall never be with those cold and timid souls who know neither victory nor defeat.

Theodore Roosevelt

Challenge 8000 is my endeavour to climb all fourteen 8000-metre peaks. Five people have succeeded, but no Briton. So far I have climbed nine, which has taken me ten years. In 1987 I climbed a new route on the north face of Shisha Pangma, 8046m, in a two-person lighweight, Alpine-style push. My partner was Steve Untch, an American. On the ascent we bivouacked at around 7800m with no tent – a tactic I have not been eager to repeat. Steve suffered frostbite to his feet and had several toes amputated. Sadly, he was killed on K2 in 1994.

My ascent of Shisha Pangma – my first ascent of an eight-thousander – coincided with Jerzy Kukuczka's fourteenth. Jurek, as he was known to his friends, was the leader of the Polish International Shisha Pangma Expedition. In addition to Steve and myself, several other nationalities were represented, such as Christine Colombel of France, Carlos Carsolio and Elsa Avila (now his wife) from Mexico, Ramiro Navarrete from Ecuador and Wanda Rutkiewicz from Poland. Jurek, along with Arthur Hazer, nicknamed Slon (elephant), also climbed a new route. Overall, it was a successful expedition and a good introduction for me to the tribulations, danger and suffering involved in climbing 8000-metre peaks. There were many problems, such as Tibetan yak herders stealing equipment and Chinese cooks who couldn't cook. Once on the mountain I began to understand why extreme altitude is called 'the death zone'. We survived avalanches, we were pinned down by fierce storms and heavy snowfalls, and I saw the savage toll that extreme cold and frostbite can exact on the human body. None of this deterred me and instead of returning to Britain, I went straight on to join Krzysztof Wielicki on the then unclimbed South Face of Lhotse. That expedition was hit by even worse weather, accidents and fatalities.

Since then I have been on twenty expeditions to 8000m peaks and have climbed nine of the fourteen eight-thousanders:

1987	Shisha Pangma, 8046m	1996	Everest, 8848m
1989	Manaslu, 8163m	1996	Gasherbrum I, 8068
1990	Cho Oyu, 8201m	1996	Gasherbrum II, 8035m
1991	Broad Peak, 8047m	1997	Lhotse, 8516m
1995	K2, 8611m		

At the time of writing, in November 1997, with only five 8000-metre mountains left to climb – Annapurna, Dhaulagiri, Nanga Parbat, Makalu and Kangchenjunga – the final goal looks more achievable, yet the nearer I get to it, the more daunting seems the challenge.

In the 1930s Ernest Hemingway wrote, 'There are only three true sports: bullfighting, mountain climbing and motor racing – the rest are merely games.' Traditional mountaineers have never thought of mountaineering as a sport – perhaps more as a way of life or a passion. Although there are similarities in the calculated risks taken in the three activities, there is no similarity in the income that they generate. Climbing eight-thousanders is expensive and, unlike motor racing, sponsorship is hard to come by. Despite this, I have managed to climb five eight-thousanders in the last two years: K2, Everest, Gasherbrum I (Hidden Peak), Gasherbrum II and Lhotse.

K2

I never really hatched a master plan to climb all fourteen eight-thousanders until I had summited eight and had only six to go. K2 took me three years to crack. I attempted the South-East (Abruzzi) Ridge in 1993, the North Face in 1994 and finally climbed the South-East Ridge in 1995. Although initially climbing with Alison Hargreaves, I made a rapid ascent, summiting on 17 July, three weeks after arriving at Base Camp. Leaving Alison at K2 Base Camp with the American expedition, I returned home with an uneasy feeling, almost a premonition, that a disaster was going to happen. However, I was shocked and unprepared for the magnitude of the tragedy which followed a few days later, when a ferocious storm left seven dead, including Alison.

Back in Britain after climbing K2, I was invited by Benoît Chamoux to join him on Kangchenjunga. I had been on several expeditions with Benoît but I felt in need of a rest, so I declined his offer. Sadly, Benoît and his climbing partner Pierre Royer were killed on Kangchenjunga.

15. Changabang 1996. Brendan Murphy (*back*) and Andy Perkins (*front*) at the Bagini Col. (*Julie-Ann Clyma*) (p12)

16. Brendan Murphy approaching the ice couloir, the start of the 1996 route. (*Julie-Ann Clyma*) (p12)

17. Roger Payne climbing through difficult mixed ground on the lower part of the route in 1997. (*Julie-Ann Clyma*) (p3)

18. Brendan Murphy climbing the ice tongue. (*Andy Cave*) (p3)

19. Andy Cave's frostbitten thumb is treated by Julie-Ann Clyma at base camp. (*Roger Payne*) (p3)

20. The South-East Ridge of Everest seen from Lhotse. The last 900m: South Col (note tent village), South Summit, Hillary Step and Summit. (*Alan Hinkes*) (p83)

Alan Hinkes on the summit of Gasherbrum II in 1996. Mustagh Tower on the left, K2 to the right. (*Alan Hinkes*) (p83)

Lhotse – South Col – Everest seen from Makalu at 6400m. (*Alan Hinkes*) (p83)

23. Kyrghyz horsemen in the Ak-Su Valley, Pamir Alai Range. *Right* Our cook Artyk. (*Paul Pritchard*) (p109)

24. Dave Green and Paul Pritchard on the summit of the Wall of Dykes. (*Paul Pritchard*) (p109)

Dave Green leading on the final day of *The Great Game*, the Russian Tower behind.
(*Paul Pritchard*) (p109)

26. Gasherbrum I seen from Base Camp. (*David Hamilton/High Adventure collection*) (p197)

27. Gasherbrum II, III and IV seen from *c*7500m on GI. Muztagh Tower and the Ogre visible on extreme left edge. (*David Hamilton/High Adventure collection*) (p197)

Everest, Gasherbrum I (Hidden Peak) and Gasherbrum II

The deaths of Alison and Benoît affected me greatly and I had seriously to consider my feelings for dangerous, high-altitude mountaineering. However, the passion I felt won through, and in the pre-monsoon of 1996 I went to the north side of Everest to make a documentary about Brian Blessed's attempt on the mountain. I reached the summit on 19 May, a week after nine people were killed on the mountain, six on the south side and three on the north side, by a vicious storm. I only had time for a few days' rest in Britain before heading out to the Karakoram again.

In July I climbed Gasherbrum I and Gasherbrum II, alone and unsupported, although of course there were other expeditions on both mountains.

Lhotse

The first of my 'last six' eight-thousanders was Lhotse which, at 8511m, is only 100 metres lower than K2. Lhotse, which means 'South Peak', is the fourth highest eight-thousander. It is on the opposite side of the South Col from Everest and shares the same route through the Khumbu Icefall and Western Cwm. I planned to ascend Lhotse alone. Of course, the Icefall would be fixed for the Everest expeditions and there would be plenty of other people around for company. Tyne Tees TV were sending a two-man crew to Base Camp for a week; then it was up to me to film myself. Most people at Everest/Lhotse Base Camp were attempting Everest. The area was a vast mêlée of nationalities, literally hundreds of people. There were a few others attempting Lhotse, notably a Russian expedition which hoped to traverse to Lhotse Middle, still the highest unclimbed summit in the world.

I had bought a place on the Mal Duff permit and shared Mal's Base Camp facilities. I had known Mal for twenty years and it was an unexpected and grievous blow when he died in Base Camp of a heart attack on 23 April 1997.

My master plan was to climb Lhotse in late April or early May, transfer from Lhotse Base Camp to Makalu Base Camp by helicopter, climb Makalu in mid-May and transfer to Kangchenjunga by helicopter to climb it in late May. I would then move to Pakistan and Nanga Parbat before returning to Nepal for Dhaulagiri and Annapurna in September/October.

I arrived in Lhotse Base Camp in mid-April; all the other expeditions were already well under way. There was a route through the Icefall, a track up the Western Cwm and fixed ropes on the Lhotse Face. All that I had to do was acclimatise and bear off right from the fixed ropes up the final 600m summit gully on Lhotse. My master plan went well until early May and I was on line for a quick summit attempt. Unfortunately, the weather window did not materialise, and the wind was too strong for a summit bid. I ended up hanging about in Base Camp at 5300m. Some people went off trekking for a few days, others went home – they had had enough and were worn out. I was acutely aware that my time for climbing three eight-thousanders in one season was running out. I was also losing my fitness and becoming debilitated. Although 'high-altitude rot' was creeping in, trekking down to a lower altitude might have meant missing a weather window. I thus chose to linger in Base Camp, playing the Himalayan waiting game.

Towards the end of May the weather started to improve and I felt that the time was right to make an ascent. I moved up to the Western Cwm on 20 May, rested and got a 'feel' for the mountain and conditions. On 22 May I set off for my tent at 7400m, the usual Camp 3 for Everest. I intended to leave before midnight and push straight to the top, ignoring the usual Camp 4 at 7800m. In the bitter cold Himalayan night my tent, sleeping-bag and warm brews of tea and coffee were hard to leave and I didn't set off until around 2am or later. It was a clear, calm, bright, moonlit night. Once I had got going it felt warm, despite being –20°C, and I stripped off my hat as I plodded up the Lhotse Face and pulled over the Yellow Band.

It was well after dawn when I reached the gully. Five climbers – three Russians, a Dane and a Canadian – were ahead of me. The Russian team had already fixed rope up the lower part of the gully. It was now bitterly cold, as the west face of Lhotse doesn't get the sun until late afternoon. I could see the wind picking up on the ridge crest above but the sky was clear and my instinct was to push on. At around midday I caught up with the five climbers ahead of me. They had stopped fixing with 200m still to go.

I took over and forged ahead. The rock on either side was black shale, shattered and sloping downwards. Finding a solid anchor on which to fix the rope was difficult and time-consuming and it was past 2pm when I reached the col at the top of the gully. Below me the three Russians and the Dane continued, but the Canadian chose to descend. At the col I went left up the ridge to the summit, discovering on the descent that it would have been easier to zigzag up the broken wall and avoid a difficult and exposed move on the ridge. I relished the unique and spectacular view to the South Col and the last 900m of Everest. In the opposite direction the fluted narrow Lhotse Ridge disappeared towards Nuptse. Two of the three Russians and the Dane followed me to the top.

From the summit I chatted on my radio to a friend who had just climbed Everest and was safely back at the South Col. It was now 3pm, the weather was fine and the wind not too strong. I filmed for Tyne Tees TV and took some stills before bailing out back down the fixed ropes to the relative safety of Camp 3 at 7400m on the Lhotse Face. A lot of people summited on Everest on 23 May 1997; it was a good mountain day.

An attempt on Makalu

Back down in Base Camp on 24 May I had the problem of trying to get a helicopter in to take me to Makalu, climb the mountain and get to Kangchenjunga before 31 May. I now realised that Kangchenjunga was off and that even Makalu was an unlikely prospect. On 27 May a small, four-seater helicopter eventually made Base Camp and took me as far as Lukla. The next day, 28 May, a big Russian helicopter took me to Makalu. It was getting late in the season now and the monsoon was beginning to encroach into the Himalaya, engulfing the mountains in cloud, rain and snow.

Whereas on Lhotse I had climbed alone, on Makalu I had intended to climb with an American friend, Fabrizio Zangrilli. He was already at Base Camp when I arrived and had acclimatised up to 6500m or so. Whereas on Lhotse I had over 200 people for company, most of them climbing Everest, here on Makalu there were no other expeditions. A large Russian team, led by an old friend of mine, Sergei Efimov, had just left in the helicopter that had brought me in. This team had climbed a superb new route on the right side of the West Face, joining the West Pillar near the top. When the Russians left there was no one else on the mountain. We were alone. It was a stark contrast with the hundreds of people at Lhotse/ Everest Base Camp.

There is no serious icefall on Makalu comparable with the Khumbu Icefall on Everest. It is possible to climb completely alone, without a support team to fix ladders up séracs and across crevasses. However, there is a long and extremely arduous approach to the mountain. Fabrizio had already made several lengthy trips up the glacier and lower slopes before I arrived. Food levels had become precariously low but I had brought with me, just in time, fresh supplies of potatoes, oil for chips, eggs, coke, beer, bananas and lots more. Fabrizio was raring to go, but he is no gung-ho, do-or-die merchant. He could also see that conditions were far from perfect, that it was late in the season, temperatures were rising and rockfall was an increasing risk, as were monsoon storms. We were pushing our luck, but we still made a concerted effort up to around 7300m.

Then Fabrizio was struck on the side of his face by a lump of ice which knocked him out for a while. At this point we decided that the risk was becoming too great. It was time that we left Makalu. We stripped the slopes of all that we could and descended to Base Camp to wait for the helicopter to take us out to Kathmandu. We waited on tenterhooks for a few days before it finally arrived in a break in the monsoon clouds. It had cost a few thousand dollars, but it would have taken over a week to walk out with porters through leech-infested monsoon-soaked foothills.

This was my second attempt at Makalu – my third, if you count the trek to Makalu Base Camp in 1996 when I met with an accident in the foothills – but I could accept this temporary retreat. No mountain is worth a life, returning is part of the achievement, and the summit is only a bonus.

A bizarre accident on Nanga Parbat

I met up with Fabrizio again in Islamabad for the usual round of Ministry meetings and briefings. We intended to climb the Kinshofer Route on the Diamir Face. The trek to Base Camp up the Daimir valley is very short – only 2½ days. The lower valley was extremely hot – the whole of Pakistan had been experiencing high humidity, with temperatures over 40°C, and scores of locals had died. Dehydration and heat-stroke were a serious threat and by the time we reached Base Camp on 17 July we were drained. The campsite is on a pleasant grassy area at 4000m, which is low for an eight-thousander. It was a splendid spot, providing a welcome respite from the usual discomfort of camping on ice and moraine. The route ahead was in full view, just as the Eigerwand is from Alpiglen. A few ascents had already been made and there were three expeditions at Base Camp still attempting it. A couple of days' rest were necessary before an acclimatisation foray to 7500m. A dump of essential equipment, such as ropes, food, stove, tent, and down suits, was left on the lower snow slopes. All this was stolen, which meant that an ascent was not possible until we had either tracked it down or replaced it. Some of the gear was eventually returned damaged and unusable.

The event which finally brought our attempt to an end was more bizarre even than the theft. On 22 July I sneezed on some flour or dust from a burnt crust on a chapati – and prolapsed a disc in my back. I rolled on the ground in extreme agony and could not even crawl. Earlier, I had strained my back a little, but I had no previous history of back problems. It was an extraordinary and salutary accident. With few anti-inflammatory drugs or painkillers with me, I was stranded for ten days at 4000m. After struggling down 700m, a helicopter eventually managed to reach me and I was flown to Islamabad for treatment. I had lost 10kg.

Challenge 8000 is still on and I will be returning to the Himalaya to climb my remaining five 8000m peaks: Annapurna, Dhaulagiri, Nanga Parbat, Makalu and Kangchenjunga.

Summary: Yorkshireman Alan Hinkes aims to become the first Briton to climb the fourteen eight-thousanders. This is his 'Challenge 8000'. He climbed his first 8000-metre peak – Shisha Pangma – in 1987. Between 1987 and 1997 he climbed a further eight. In November 1997 five eight-thousanders remain to be climbed before he achieves his goal.

WALDEMAR SOROKA

Annapurna North-West Ridge

Translated from the Polish by Ingeborga Doubrawa-Cochlin

(Plate 1)

In the 1996 post-monsoon season (15 August to 31 October) an expedition from the Polish Trojmiasto Mountaineering Club arrived in the Central Himalaya. The objective of the expedition was the main summit of Annapurna (8091m). During the three years spent in preparation, the heaviest burden fell on the shoulders of Krzysztof Tarasewicz and Waldemar Soroka, the two members who first thought of the idea of climbing this 8000-metre peak.

The thirteen members of the expedition left Poland on 15 August 1996. After completing the formalities and buying in extra food and equipment, we left Pokhara on 22 August, with 10 porters, for the North Sanctuary. The effects of the monsoon persisted and during the whole trek we were plagued by incessant rain and leeches. We spent the final four days trekking along isolated paths and building improvised rope bridges across treacherous rivers, before reaching Base Camp on 3 September.

On 5 and 6 September Jan Szulc and Andrzej Zieleniewski flew in by helicopter with three tons of food and equipment. Helicopter transport is very popular in Nepal and often cheaper than hiring traditional porters. In our case, the use of a helicopter was absolutely essential, given the harshness of the terrain and the fact that our porters were terrified at the prospect of returning over difficult river crossings without our help. So they decided to give up part of their wages in order to return by helicopter.

We had planned to attempt Annapurna from the north by the Dutch route of 1977, but after consulting Józef Nyka we decided to try to establish a new route on the North-West Ridge. Previously only two routes to the main summit from the north had been established – the Dutch route and the French route. The North Face of Annapurna is not visible from Base Camp, so we postponed our decision about which route to choose until we had established Camp 2 under the 2½km-long Wall of Annapurna at 2500m.

The choice of route to Camp 1 was decided by Marciniak/Terzeul and Soroka/Tarasewicz on 7 September. These two pairs maintained their respective partnerships throughout the expedition. One day later Kochanczyk, Marciniak, Soroka, Tarasewicz, Terzeul and Tonsing established Camp 1 at 5100m. Kochanczyk descended to Base Camp and the remaining five climbers set up Camp 2 at 5700m on the following day.

After spending the night there, they returned to Base Camp. 300 metres of rope were fixed between Camps 1 and 2 on the same route as that followed by the first conquerors of the mountain in 1950.

The most active participant in setting up the camps was Slawa Terzeul. In July 1996 he had climbed Gasherbrum II and was therefore better acclimatised than the rest of us. On the day that Camp 2 was set up, Kochanczyk and Turowiecki came up to Camp 1 and, the next day, deposited a load on the route to Camp 2. Between 9 and 12 September loads were brought up to the camps, but unfortunately very heavy snow made it impossible to go higher.

From the moment that we set up Base Camp we had been plagued by various illnesses. As a result, both Urbanowicz and Litwin were prevented from climbing until nearly the end of September. Later, Szulc, Sicinski and Kochanczyk were unable to climb for the same reason.

After watching avalanches thundering down the Wall several times a day, we came to the conclusion that, in those conditions, attempting either the Dutch or French routes was out of the question. We were fully aware now that our team of climbers was not as strong as we had thought. Nevertheless, we decided to attack the North Ridge.

On 16 September Marciniak,Tarasewicz and Terzeul tried to reach Cauliflower Ridge (the name chosen by the French in 1950). At about 10am, at Camp 2, I spotted an avalanche on the upper part of the North Wall which, after a short time, expanded to an immense size. The whole four-kilometre width of the Wall seemed to disintegrate and disappear downwards. After snatching a few photos I rushed to take shelter in my tent, fearing that I had little chance of surviving the onslaught. Luckily the tent was protected by a very high snowy ridge protruding from the Wall. Another empty tent next to mine was completely destroyed. During the next few minutes the hurricane-force winds continued to rage. Then suddenly they stopped and everything went quiet.

I started to dig myself out from under the snow and spoke to Marciniak on the radio. He was relieved to hear from me. Having seen the avalanche from above, they had all feared I would be dead. Marciniak, Tarasewicz and Terzeul planned to set up Camp 3, using over 250m of fixed ropes. But it snowed heavily all night and we were afraid of another avalanche. So Soroka and Tarasewicz went down to Base Camp, while Marciniak and Terzeul, in spite of the dangers, continued towards Camp 3. On the way, just above Camp 2, another avalanche broke loose above them, but they managed to jump for cover into a crevasse. The same avalanche hit Soroka and Tarasewicz as they descended to Base Camp, but they too managed to escape from it.

Eventually Camp 3 was established on 18 September. One day later Marciniak and Terzeul set up fixed ropes on the ice peak (called by us 'Alpamayo') 120m high and 70° steep. On 20 September Tarasewicz and Soroka climbed from Base Camp to Camp 2 without stopping. During the following days Szulc, Kochanczyk, Tarasewicz and Soroka tried to place fixed ropes on the Cauliflower Ridge, but overhanging snow of the consistency of sugar made the work impossible. We tried to dig down to the ice, but after probing to a depth of about two metres without success, we decided to give up.

Between 1 and 4 October the weather deteriorated still further and it started snowing heavily. While trying to find a way under 'Alpamayo', Sicinski, Soroka, Tarasewicz and Tonsing were caught in another avalanche and fell about 100m. Fortunately, apart from suffering minor injuries and losing some equipment, no serious damage was done.

Meanwhile, an expedition from Belgium had arrived at Base Camp on 21 September. They attempted, without success, first the Dutch and then the French routes and finally the North-West Ridge route that we ourselves were following. All their attempts were unsuccessful. One of the Belgians, Pascal Debrouwer, joined our team and, together with Marciniak, Soroka, Tarasewicz and Terzeul, remained at Camp 3 in a struggle against the weather. At Camp 2, Turowiecki had become dangerously ill and had decided to go down to Base Camp to avoid the avalanches. After that, Camp 2 was completely buried under snow and only faint traces of it were visible. Altogether over two metres of fresh snow fell at that time.

We found out later from Elizabeth Hawley, Reuter's correspondent in Kathmandu, that the huge amounts of snow had forced over 70% of all expeditions that year to withdraw from the Nepal Himalaya. At one point Terzeul, realising how small were our chances of reaching the summit, brought all his gear down to Base Camp and decided to leave the expedition. But after a heated discussion he changed his mind and finally agreed to join those who were in favour of continuing the assault on the mountain.

The long Cauliflower Ridge, stretching over 600m, was at last conquered on 11 October by Marciniak and Terzeul. The next day Camp 4 was established at 6500m. Just above that point the ridge became a very steep ice-rock pillar, so after three days of rope-fixing, Marciniak, Terzeul and Soroka (for part of the time) finally established Camp 5 at 7100m. While this was going on, Tarasewicz had climbed up from Base Camp to Camp 3 in one day. Then, along with Sicinski, Soroka and Turowiecki, he climbed to Camp 5 on 15 October. Turowiecki then went back to Camp 4 while Marciniak and Terzeul fixed ropes on the route to the rocky bastion. On 17 October Marciniak and Terzeul were trying to find a passage through the barrier, while Sicinski, Soroka and Tarasewicz fixed 150m of rope above Camp 5. Then Sicinski returned to Camp 4.

During those last few days, the wind was gusting strongly, sometimes at hurricane force, and the temperature dropped to below –25°C. We were very worried about our tents which were already torn. Tarasewicz and Soroka had mild frostbite on their toes. Szulc climbed to Camp 5. On 19 October Marciniak conquered the 100m-high rock barrier which was about grade 6 in difficulty. Tarasewicz climbed to 7400m but Soroka had to return owing to frostbite.

On 20 October, in spite of hurricane-force winds, Marciniak and Terzeul started to attack the summit. They left at 7am and by 10 o'clock had reached the rock barrier. The rocky slabs, in a tile-like formation, were covered in snow and with slopes of between 30° and 40°, were difficult to negotiate. Finally, at 3pm they were standing on the summit of Annapurna.

They spoke with Base Camp, took several pictures and posed with the flag celebrating the 1000th anniversary of Gdansk. Slawa Terzeul filmed the event. After leaving the summit, they descended to Camp 5 and at about 9pm the weather started to deteriorate. So Soroka and Tarasewicz called off their planned second attempt on the summit via the North-West Ridge. During the night one of our tents had been torn apart. The following morning at about 6am we started our descent in hurricane-force winds. Marciniak, Soroka and Tarasewicz reached Base Camp at 10pm that evening. Terzeul stayed at Camp 2. Below Camp 1 Marciniak sustained an injury to his right knee which was to make it impossible for him to leave Base Camp with the caravan.

On 22 October, Tonsing left Base Camp in order to organise a helicopter air lift for Marciniak. The same day the rest of the team descended to Base Camp. But the weather continued to deteriorate. After a 16-metre snowfall, the route back to Lete was practically cut off and our provisions of food and fuel were nearly finished. The weather made it impossible for any helicopter to fly in.

Eventually, on 18 October at 4pm, all the members of the expedition arrived safely back in Pokhara. At the subsequent press conference, Elizabeth Hawley described our achievement – a new route on the North-West Ridge of Annapurna – as the best climb in the Nepal Himalaya in 1996.

Summary: Between 15 August and 31 October 1996 a Polish team attempted the French and Dutch routes on Annapurna. 13 climbers took part: Michal Kochanczyk, Wojciech Litwin, Andrzej Marciniak, Waldemar Sicinski, Waldemar Soroka (the leader), Jan Szulc, Krzysztof Tarasewicz (deputy leader and principal organiser), Wladyslaw Terzeul (from Ukraine), Antony Tonsing (USA), Jan Turowiecki, Miroslaw Urbanowicz, Andrzej Zieleniewski (doctor) and Andrzej Grotha (radio-telegrapher, who had to return to Poland owing to illness). In addition, between 30 September and 13 October, there was also a film crew from Polish TV on the mountain. Subsequently, in seriously bad weather, Andrzej Marciniak and Wladyslaw Terzeul reached the summit via the North-West Ridge at 3.30pm on 20 October. They celebrated the 1000th anniversary of Gdansk by taking pictures with the Polish flag. The following pair, Soroka and Tarasewicz, abandoned their attempt owing to deteriorating weather.

JONATHAN PRATT

Lhotse 96: Controversy in the Shadow of Everest

(*Plate 28*)

As Lhotse and Everest share the same route up to 7500m, our expedition to Lhotse in 1996 became inextricably involved with the thirteen expeditions operating on Everest. In many respects we were shielded from the tragedy that took place there, yet our mere proximity enmeshed us within it. On that fateful day, David Sharman and I climbed the Lhotse Face to where our route parted from the Everest trail. Just below Camp 4 we met Tim Horvath and Steve Koch on their way down. The day before, their companion, Chantal Mauduit, had persuaded them to leave their sleeping bags behind and share a tent between three; consequently they had spent a grim night huddled together struggling to keep warm. At 8.30am they had set out for the top but Tim and Steve, cold and exhausted, had turned back, leaving Chantal to carry on alone.

As David and I established ourselves in the tent, clouds enveloped the mountain and it started to snow. We had just got the tea made when Chantal appeared; she was dusted with fresh snow, but looked exhilarated. Breathlessly, she described her climb, the first female ascent of Lhotse: she had reached the top at 2pm in clear weather, but had to descend immediately in the face of a threatening storm. She wished us good luck, and headed down to spend the night at Camp 3.

We made a radio call and talked with the rest of the expedition, who were over on Pumori. We told them of Chantal's success and they encouraged us: 'You guys should do well tomorrow: lots of people topped out on Everest today. We could see them queuing up at the Hillary Step through the telescope.' Little did we realise that, as we spoke, several people were losing their lives on the mountain.

During the night David was quite sick and the next morning he was seriously under par when we set off for our summit attempt. The first part of our climb was across the exposed Lhotse Face, and although the sky was clear a vicious wind scythed across the icy slope. I followed Chantal's footprints to the start of the couloir that cuts through the cliffs directly to the summit, but David was struggling to keep up. As I waited, I looked over towards Everest. I could make out the dots of several climbers moving up from the South Col.

'That's a bit odd,' I thought, 'they must have left Camp 4 at about 10am – far too late for a summit attempt.' I watched them for a while, then David came up and I thought no more about it. David was feeling pretty ill so, almost with relief, we turned back. As we descended to Base Camp we found ourselves amongst a stream of climbers coming from Everest. They were moving agonisingly slowly and, without a word, we abseiled past them; it was only when we reached Camp 3 that we learned of the tragic events on Everest and the deaths of five climbers. With modern communications the rest of the world had already heard all about it, while we were completely unaware that anything unusual had happened.

Unfortunately, we did not avoid controversy. Chantal had reached the summit alone, and even before she had got back to Base Camp people were expressing doubts about her ascent. On her way down she had met one of the Sherpas who had helped rescue her on Everest in 1995. When she told him that she had reached the top of Lhotse, he had just snapped, 'You lie,' and walked away. Many others clearly felt the same. The cause of the ill-feeling was that, the year before, Chantal had attempted to climb Everest without oxygen but had collapsed near the summit and had to be helped down. Most of the people involved were on Everest again; they resented her return this year and were looking for an excuse to discredit her. For instance, some people at Camp 2 had seen her, wearing a yellow suit, disappear into the clouds around Camp 4 at 1pm and reappear only two or three hours later – obviously not enough time for her to have been to the summit. This accusation made no sense at all, because Chantal had left Camp 4 at 8.30am and had met David and me at 5.30pm on her way down. Tim, Steve and David were all wearing yellow suits just like Chantal's; her detractors must have seen David climb into the clouds below our tent, and Tim or Steve coming down a few hours later. Sadly, months later, this bogus 'evidence' was still being used to discount Chantal's ascent.

Despite all the deaths, it didn't take long for things on Everest to revert to normality, and the teams that had not yet made their attempts at the summit returned to the mountain to carry on where they had left off. We, too, returned to have another go at Lhotse.

Dan Mazur and Chris Shaw pushed ahead, but instead of going up to the uncomfortable tent in the rocks that we had used before, they dug a better platform into the Lhotse Face some 200m lower at 7800m. Unfortunately, they expended more energy on the task than they realised and the next morning felt unable to make a bid for the top. Instead, they descended.

On 21 May, Scott Darsney and I moved up for our turn at the summit. During the night, a disaster with a water bottle got us out of bed early and with perfect conditions we made excellent progress up the couloir. Near the top I stopped to take a photo, and as I fumbled with the pack, I dropped my bag of extra clothing. Amazingly, Scott, who was 50m below, caught it just as it flew over his head.

At 3pm, I reached the top. The summit was a knife-edge of snow, impossible to stand on, so I stood on some rocks just below it and reached up and touched the top with my hand. Crouched there, waiting for Scott, I studied Lhotse's West Ridge. As I looked at it, I started to wonder if I really was on the summit. That other point along the ridge appeared to be quite a bit higher than the one I was standing on. If it *was* higher, then Lhotse would still be unclimbed. Except that Tomo Cesen, who had climbed the South Face, would surely have come over that peak, wouldn't he? He said he had reached the ridge about 1000ft away and gained the summit after what he called 'a straightforward traverse'. But he said he had climbed just *below* the crest on the south side – in which case he would not have climbed that other peak.

Looking over to the ridge which Cesen was supposed to have traversed, his description didn't appear to make a lot of sense: crossing that ridge would be extreme, and the obvious way to go would be on the north side. It was when the Russians, who climbed the South Face in 1990, saw this part of the ridge that the first doubts about Cesen's climb were raised. I reflected on the differences between Cesen's and Chantal's ascent. He had used someone else's summit photos; he had acclimatised in an unprecedentedly short time; his description of the summit ridge was questionable, and there were several other inconsistencies. In fact, there was significant evidence against him, and nothing to back up his claim. However, things were very different in Chantal's case. It had taken me the same time to climb the couloir as she had taken; I found her description of the route, especially the top, fitted exactly with what I had encountered, which was quite different from descriptions that people who had done the route in previous years had given us; the weather was good, and she had been climbing very strongly up to then. Essentially, everything pointed to her having reached the top, and there were no facts to suggest that she hadn't.

Scott came up to the top, and realising that time was running short we quickly started down. Our progress was laborious and it wasn't until midnight that we reached our tent. We had just got the tea brewing when we were disturbed by someone outside; it was Dan Mazur coming up for another attempt at the top. After descending to Camp 3, he had decided to return for one last try. We gave him a cup of tea, and wished him good luck, little realising that it would be the only drink he would have for the next 20 hours. He assured us that he would call us on the radio when he got safely back to Camp 3.

The next day, as Dan made his summit bid, Scott and I descended to Camp 2 to wait for him. We expected him to call in at about 5pm, but the radio remained stubbornly silent. All through the night we kept looking up hoping to see a tell-tale light, but there was only darkness, and our calls on the radio failed to elicit any response. Finally, we decided there was nothing we could do but try to get some sleep. At midnight, a soft voice on the radio slowly nudged me awake; Dan had finally got back to Camp 3.

But our worries were not yet over. Talking to Dan on the radio the next morning, we realised that he was far from well. He sounded confused and exhausted, and although he said he was going to come down immediately, by mid-afternoon he still hadn't left the tent. The IMAX team were camped only twenty yards away, and we asked them to check on him, but they refused. For Scott, the worry of waiting was becoming too much, and he was starting to get quite agitated. Suddenly, I heard him calling the IMAX team on the radio, telling them that we would pay for some Sherpas to help bring Dan down. I had to quickly intercede, 'Hold on, let's not get carried away. It's only Dan up there, we don't want to spend any money on him!' Of course I knew that, however bad Dan might be feeling, he always had the reserves to get down without assistance.

Eventually, after much persuasion, the IMAX group agreed to send a Sherpa over-to his tent and ask Dan to call us on the radio. As night fell, he finally came down and, after a short rest, was restored to his usual bubbly self. His toes were a little frostbitten, and one of them stubbornly refused to thaw out. In the end, Dan lost just the very tip of that toe.

It was not until we were back in Base Camp that I thought to ask Dan if he had reached the top.

'Well, I don't know,' he replied, 'do you think you stood on the true summit?'

'I'm not entirely sure. Why?'

'Well, that summit along the ridge looked a lot higher to me. It just seems rather convenient that the summit everyone goes to is pretty easy, and that other one looks pretty difficult.'

The map showed Lhotse as 8501m and the other point as 8499m. Rather too close for comfort.

'Just think,' taunted Scott, 'If that other peak really is higher, we'll have to come back and climb it all over again!'

Did I stand on the top of Lhotse, or was that more western peak the real summit? When I got home, I contacted Bradford Washburn who was involved with the most recent survey of Everest. They had used fixing from the space Shuttle, and overflown the area by Learjet. Brad was adamant that we had reached the true summit. Since I don't really want to go back and climb Lhotse again, I suppose I had better believe him – but I don't! It's much more fun to think that the world's fourth highest peak is still unclimbed.

Summary: Chantal Mauduit made the first female ascent of Lhotse on 10 May 1996. Jonathan Pratt and Scott Darsney reached the summit of Lhotse on 22 May 1996, and Dan Mazur on 23 May 1996.

PAUL MOORES

Cerro Torre

(*Plates 36–38*)

My first visit to Patagonia was in 1993 with Doug Scott, Tut Braithwaite and Sandy Allen, when we failed to climb Fitzroy. It taught me that a slightly different approach might be necessary to climb routes in this part of the world. Traditionally, 'big mountain' siege tactics were employed here, using fixed ropes and camps, but it seemed that there ought to be a better way of maximising time and effort. I remember thinking that, if I ever returned, I must arrive ready to go climbing right away. This would mean being fit in all aspects: for climbing rock or ice, walking fast, carrying big rucksacks in wind and rain, and being prepared for uncomfortable bivouacking ... When was the last time I did all those things? Two years later, Adrian Burgess and I met up to put theory into practice on Cerro Torre.

Several times we had climbed up to the Col of Patience from Bridwell Camp, only to be turned back by ferocious winds. This preliminary section, which took about eight hours to climb, was similar in length and grade to the Frendo Spur. This time, we were five people crammed into a tight snow burrow high on the Col, looking straight out over the 1500m South Face of the mountain and only 50 metres from the first rock pitch. Setting out at 2.30am came hard. It meant getting up just after midnight to start cooking breakfast and getting ready. Any attempt to organise ourselves the night before was difficult in the cold confined space of the ice cave; it made for an abrupt start. It's never easy to rock-climb by head torch in big boots and carrying a heavy pack.

I was partnering Max Berger, a young Austrian guide we had only just met. He had arrived in Patagonia with his friend Luis almost three weeks before us and they had tried Cerro Torre several times already. With only frost-nipped toes to show for their effort, Luis had decided it was not his idea of fun any more, so Max asked if he could climb with us. Aid Burgess and I had originally planned to climb together while Mark Wilford soloed something else – it didn't really matter what so long as we were all climbing. After much discussion around the fire in Bridwell Camp, it was agreed that Aid would partner Mark, and I would partner Max.

Max had been up this part of the climb three times already, and the first four rope lengths went by reasonably quickly, though climbing with a new partner in the dark, and on 'the most difficult mountain in the world' (as many have described it) was daunting. There was no time to stop and enjoy the dawn. We moved as fast as we dared, all the while scanning the horizon for approaching clouds. Patagonia's notorious weather disciplines you to monitor constantly what is happening.

Max asked me to take over the lead on the next pitch as he felt I would be quicker. It was an icy, narrow chimney, awkward and strenuous, leading to some scary iced-up slabs which continued for four rope lengths. This sort of climbing eats up time. The next section comprised thin overhanging cracks leading to a hanging undercut like a diving board with a 1000m void below it. We started to traverse the Maestri bolt ladder which veers horizontally above the void for three and a half pitches. It was intimidating at first but I found I got used to it; and it was certainly no easier for the second. As I belayed Max across the last of these pitches, great blocks of ice the size of piano stools came ricocheting down a shallow couloir over my right shoulder. I had to duck and dive to avoid being hit, all the time thinking that there couldn't possibly be a way to cross under this constant barrage. It was just too dangerous.

Suddenly it occurred to me that we might have to retreat, that we weren't going to get up this climb after all. My first reaction was one of sheer relief – we could go down! Then came feelings of disappointment. After that, for some unknown reason, I 'got brave', just as Max arrived at the stance. Realising that the sun had strengthened sufficiently to loosen the snow and ice from the headwall hundreds of feet above, and that this all seemed to be funnelling directly towards us, we started counting. By studying the rate at which the blocks came flying down, we could choose the best moment to cross the couloir.

It worked. We escaped being pounded to death, and set up our next stance on a pedestal beneath another overhanging wall. Water was pouring down this section, and I could see us getting soaked to the skin, our clothes freezing like boards. This took the edge off any enthusiasm we might have felt. Tied onto the smallest of ledges, and only able to move one at a time, we struggled into waterproof jackets and trousers. As we climbed, water found its way into every seam and aperture and streamed down our necks and sleeves. But once we had reached the end of the pitch, the sun dropped behind Cerro Torre and within a few minutes the water subsided. It was nearly 4pm and we had been on the go for almost 14 hours. Surely the top of the headwall could not be far now?

Ahead, the climbing was mixed – icy corners, hands on rock, feet on ice – but still steep, and all the anchors were hidden under ice. We started to move together, trusting one another not to fall. Soon the climb opened up on to a steep, icy slope. We needed to traverse right for three rope lengths. Armed with only one ice tool each, this operation felt very precarious. After that we were back on straight vertical ice, which is far less hazardous than any traversing. The final headwall was at last getting closer but we still had a long way to go. Three more difficult ice pitches followed, each with vertical sections, and we came upon a leaning tower with Maestri's bolts spaced every two metres or so.

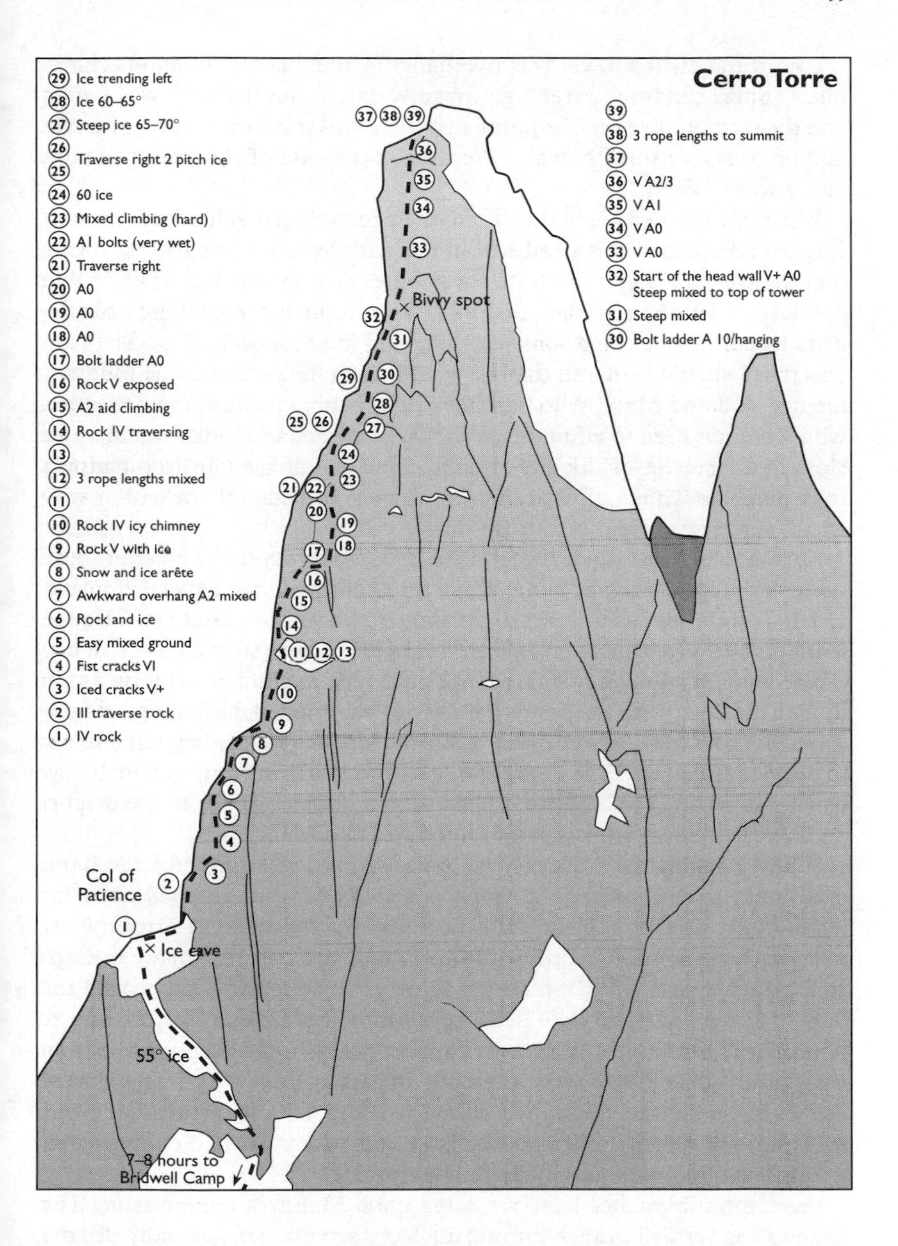

The East Face of Cerro Torre showing Cesare Maestri's 1971 bolted route up the SE Ridge variation to the top of the headwall. UIAA numerical gradings.

Unfortunately the tower was overhanging, making for strenuous climbing. Things certainly weren't getting any easier, but the light was fading and the temperature was dropping fast. This tower led to steep icy grooves and on to a very small brèche. We were at the base of the headwall now, and it was 9.30pm.

When Max joined me in the dim light he remarked that his friend Robert Jasper had climbed this headwall in the dark by head torch so, knowing that the weather might not hold for another day, we set out: HVS/5.9 in the dark! I left my rucksack tied to a piton in the brèche, taking only the head torch. Max carried some clothing and food for both of us. The plan was that I should lead and that he would clean the pitches as he followed me up. Aid and Mark, who had been right behind us from the outset but who were not keen to climb on in darkness, decided to look for a bivouac close to the brèche. Mark ended up hacking into an ice mushroom atop a rock pinnacle which, after about 45 minutes, provided them with a very small, slippery, icy platform to sit on.

Meanwhile, I was still trying to lead up loose rotten rock and after some difficulty I found a stance in the dark. Max followed; then I was off again. Cerro Torre's headwall is approximately 300m high – about six full rope lengths. We were starting up the second pitch when, after 25m, I reached a very blank section and couldn't work out how to climb it. Out on a thin limb in the dark, with an icy wind blowing, fear gripped me and my imagination ran riot. Max, who had no desire to lead the pitch either, left it to me to decide what to do. The thought of Aid and Mark brewing up 60m below us left me wanting to descend, which we did, abseiling back to the brèche.

'There's no room over here,' shouted Aid and Mark.

Whilst hanging onto the end of our abseil ropes, Max and I set about excavating a small ledge. The slope was about 65° and dropped away for 2000m into dark emptiness, with no room for the slightest error. After what seemed hours of cutting into iron-hard ice, we had made enough space for two backsides. Side by side we sat, tied to the rope. I held the lighted stove and pan while Max kept filling it with small pieces of ice. After two or three hot drinks and snacks we shivered through the long early hours. At 4.30am we started the process again and by 5.30 we were away. By some miracle the weather was still good and, returning to our high point in the daylight, the climbing didn't look too bad either. Even with a head torch, darkness can hide so much.

Five fantastic pitches later we came upon Maestri's compressor. The headwall is vertical orange granite and so steep that ice generally doesn't form on it. A compressor the size of a small table stuck out at an ugly, incongruous angle. Atmospheric ice had formed on it, forcing us to make bizarre ice moves in the middle of the blank rock wall. Above the compressor, Maestri had smashed the heads off all his bolts during his descent, leaving minute stubs of mild steel punctuating the pitch. This made for some very spooky climbing, as we tried to re-use the holes and stubs with sky hooks, tying off the metal remnants. This was the most difficult pitch by far, but mercifully the last one as it brought us to the top of the headwall. The top of the mountain was much larger than I had imagined it, and we had to climb three rope lengths back from the edge, traversing behind mushrooms of ice, to reach the summit.

We'd climbed it! We could see most of the ice cap, but lenticular clouds were streaking the horizon and racing towards us. How lucky we had been! We spent 15 minutes on top waiting for Aid and Mark; then we could hang about no longer. Clouds were beginning to engulf the summit, coating us with hoar frost. We met the other two a pitch below the top of the headwall and we all congratulated each other on our success. They would be on the summit soon. They caught up with us again on the long abseil back to our ice cave on the Col of Patience. By now the storm had really set in and the descent was treacherous, requiring eight hours of total concentration, with icy, shredded ropes.

Summary: In November 1995 an ascent of Cerro Torre (3128m) in Patagonia was made via the SE Ridge variation (Maestri's 1971 bolted route) by Paul Moores with Max Berger (Austria). They completed the route by climbing the ice mushroom – a variable build-up of atmospheric ice that rises above the rock plinth at the top of the headwall. They circled clockwise round the back of the mushroom, where they reported a relatively easy 3-pitch climb to the summit. The 39-pitch route was graded 5.10/A2. The following pair, Adrian Burgess (UK/US) and Mark Wilford (US), reached the top of the headwall (ie the end of the rock pitches) in the first stages of deteriorating weather and, in mist, continued for a full pitch up the 30° to 40° snow/ice slope. They reversed the route when conditions became unacceptably dangerous. This was the first time that British mountaineers had reached the summit and summit plinth of Cerro Torre after several notable attempts.

NOEL CRAINE

On the Central Tower of Paine

(*Plates 39–41*)

The wind, the background and director of every Patagonian foray, whips through the trees. The sounds, subtly different in each area from Tower to valley, are a constant accompaniment. The aim is to get high when it drops, to use the opportunities, rare yet golden, that arrive between front after front of bad weather. Yesterday the wind picked up with fresh vengeance, a small yet powerful blast of a few hours laced snow and sound sufficient to force one to dig deep. The forest answers back with creaks and groans and the roar of surf. A beautiful place, tentative yet full of life, evolution at the extreme edge. The huge tree-trunks found in the sheltered spots drop in size with increased altitude, sheltering the occasional orchid cluster, becoming ever smaller before giving way to moss, lichen and finally rock, snow and ice. Ever changing yet in our human life span so barren. Who knows the past or future colonisation of this place? We live in just one frame of the film. The bird life one respects for the audacity of living in such an environment, the unexpected patrolling fox, bold in its visits to base camp.

And so here I lie, tired and aching, eating and resting. Slowly the route takes shape. Initially it seems distant, gradually a picture develops, lessons are learned, plans change, weather dictates the pace.

Diary entry, 24th January 1997

The phone never stopped ringing in the last week before our departure. Attempting to co-ordinate myself (hard enough), Simon (an island of sanity) and Strappo (professionally disorganised) was a fair old challenge. Inevitably we made it, successfully negotiating New Year in Buenos Aires and arriving in the Torres National Park having lost nothing but sleep. Simon assumed the role of expedition treasurer, while Strappo and I concentrated on buying provisions, including essentials like red wine, lemon, sugar and Pisco. Horses were procured, rucksacks packed and an attempt on base camp launched.

Stage one was reasonably successful: loaded with vast amounts of food and climbing gear, we reached our first objective – the 'Campimento Japanese'– early in January 1997. Our base camp, situated amongst tall trees on the bank of the river Ascensio, was a fine venue. Graced by a hut made of rough-hewn timber and tarpaulin, it provided clean water and shelter from the wind, and was to become both a relaxing home and the scene of a few of its own little adventures.

Our initial objective, the South Ridge on the South Tower of Paine, was 'occupado' by a team of Swiss climbers. Three years previously they had arrived on Baffin Island to find their objective, the route that Paul Pritchard, Steve Quinlan, Jordi Tosa and myself were privileged to climb, similarly occupied. Our pleasure at meeting our Swiss friends again made up for our slight disappointment about the route, and we turned our attention instead to the Ascencio Valley on the west side of the Torres.

An initial load-carrying foray up the moraine and into the wind revealed a beautiful objective – a new line on the huge orange wall, left of *Wild Wild West*. We huddled behind boulders in an attempt to hold binoculars steady enough to trace a potential line. Previously climbed as the start to the Basque route *Kanterarik ez*, a series of grooves and cracks led, with a little imagination and the odd pendulum, to a snaking overhanging groove line gracefully winding its way towards the broken ground that led to the summit towers. We agreed that the line looked feasible and safe from objective danger. All we needed were a couple of weeks' good weather.

Base camp was shared with a small number of other teams. Chilean, British, Swiss, American, Canadian and Brazilian climbers appeared over the ensuing weeks, each group having its own objectives, ideas and brand of entertainment. Thankfully the atmosphere was good, there were no character clashes and an enjoyable blend of international humour developed. With the exception of 'les Swiss', all the other teams were sensibly attempting the Alpine-style routes which abound in the area. With a total of half-a-dozen climbable days over two months, this was probably not a bad idea. We lacked such insight and convinced ourselves that this year would be different. Needless to say we were spectacularly wrong.

To climb a 'big wall' one must first reach its base. Photographs tend to shrink approach gullies – or maybe one just ignores them in the general enthusiasm to tackle the route. In this case we had not really thought much about the logistics of getting ourselves and our gear to the base of the wall. Fortuitously a 3000ft snow gully appeared, as if by magic, a day before we set off. This gully was to become a well-trodden route, and changed its character to suit our mood. On certain days it would yield only to the crampon and axe, giving tiring but fast névé for two hours; on other days it would remain unfrozen and offer three hours of wallowing. On special occasions it would dramatically avalanche, leaving boiler-plate slabs and an arduous and circuitous approach up the north gully as the only option. For the return journey, conditions permitting, our efforts were rewarded with a very fast bum slide and stupendous views.

Early attempts were encouraging: on our first time up the gully we had reasonable weather, though high winds. We managed just two pitches, carrying huge loads, followed by a rapid bum slide back to our bivvy. After supper and rehydration and oh so short a sleep, we reloaded and toiled up again, this time in better weather, as the wind dropped and the sun came out. Simon led a beautiful technical bridging pitch of about E4 on good rock, and after two more easier pitches we were at the ledges: at last we had reached a feature! Full 60-metre pitches were the way to go, speeding things up and dramatically reducing the number of belays. A large rack, however, was required for this approach. An hour of hauling saw us reunited with the haul sack, and as the sun was rapidly being replaced by snow and wind and conditions became more and more like the Cairngorm plateau, we abseiled back down the fixed ropes, wrestling with knots and cold fingers, and wondering whether the sun and chalk bags of a few hours previously had all been a dream. Later, down on the moraine, drenched and cold, we reminded ourselves that, as Patagonian weather goes, the previous 24-hour spell of good weather was something to be grateful for.

During the next few weeks the weather remained unremittingly bad. The rain that swept base camp turned to snow, branches collapsed off trees (one landed on Strappo's tent, thankfully missing him). When the last of the Pisco was gone the true desperation of our situation became apparent – surely the weather *had* to improve. Time and time again we went through the routine of the 2am, 4am and 6am weather checks. We tried bivvying on the moraine, below the North Tower. We attempted to dig a tent into the moraine ... each time the wind laughed at our efforts, and after two tents had been wrecked, and we had been sent scurrying back to base from the moraine, the gully and the wall, we began to examine our sanity.

Each bivvy received a name. The boldest effort, a little two-man tent made cosy by the presence of three, became known as 'the prayer flag'. It didn't last long – in fact we used it for one night only before it was claimed as its own by the ice and wind. And then the real *pièce de résistance*: a night out in an A5 double portaledge fly, with no sleeping-bags or mats or supper. Balanced on a dubious snow ledge directly below the tower, it was memorable, companionable ... and wonderfully ineffective.

During a window sandwiched between a huge snowstorm that buried everything – necessitating hours of digging to recover essential gear from the base of the fixed ropes – and an equally vicious mix of ice and wind, we managed to reach the base of the wonderful snaking groove line after a fine lead in a high wind from Strappo and some cold pendulums and frantic scrabbling from myself. Hanging on a rather dubious nut braced at the end of a successfully latched pendulum, I looked back at Simon and Strappo, shivering, uncomplaining, distant, while waves of spindrift swept down between us. I realised it was time to bail.

Our retreat down the fixed ropes came not a moment too soon, as spindrift or *viento blanco* piled down, almost suffocating us in its intensity. We needed to concentrate and relax, and keep moving when we hit the gully, since the avalanche risk was increasing by the minute. Base camp beckoned and we descended to the pleasures of the valley. We were down to lentils and rice but, although gratefully eaten, this was not quite what one had hoped for. However, base camp was a welcome contrast to the constant wind battering on the moraine.

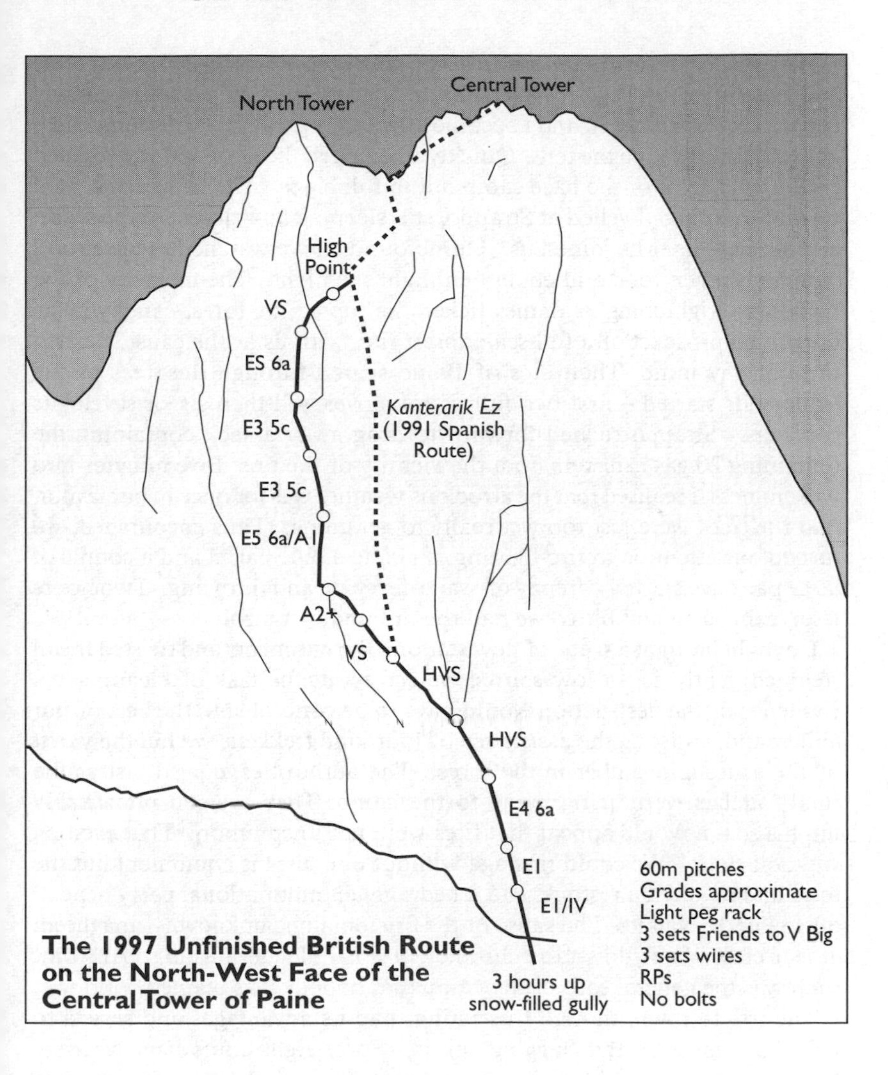

The 1997 Unfinished British Route on the North-West Face of the Central Tower of Paine

We finished our late supper and sat talking before drifting off to our tents and much-needed sleep. At 1.30am I was awoken by a shout. Slowly consciousness kicked in and I became aware of a great roaring sound and a golden glow through the tent. Quickly I unzipped the door and was greeted by the wild sight of the base camp hut in full blaze. The Canadians were up and shouting. I yelled at Strappo, still sleeping and closest to the blaze, and seconds later he joined us. Dumbfounded, we watched the beautiful wooden shelter, food and equipment light the night. The intensity of the blaze was frightening as flames licked the top of the forest canopy. The horrifying prospect of a full-scale forest fire, with us as the cause, flashed through my mind. Then arcs of flame seared through the trees as the explosions started – first two full petrol stoves and then six or seven gas canisters. Strappo rushed forward to drag away a sack containing the remaining 20 gas canisters from the vicinity of the fire. Five minutes into wakefulness, I realised that the atrocious weather was for once in our favour, that the trees were just too wet really to get going. Thus encouraged, we turned our attention to fire-fighting. Seizing a blue barrel and a couple of large pans, we started a frenzy of water-ferrying and throwing. Two hours later, exhausted and filthy, we had the fire under control.

Daylight brought a scene of devastation. Burnt timbers and twisted metal steamed gently as, in low spirits, we set about the task of cleaning up. Evidence of the destruction would have to be concealed to the best of our ability and, enlisting the assistance of four kind trekkers, we hid the worst of the ashes and timber in the forest. The authorities arrived just as the final touches were being made to the camp. They seemed remarkably unphased – it would appear that fires were not uncommon. That evening we took stock. We could manage without our surplus equipment but the food loss required a restock, and a bedraggled multinational party headed off to Puerto Natales. The cause of the fire remained unknown – maybe an ember blown back down the chimney or a candle left burning. Anyway, such was the general ease of the camp that nobody was blamed.

The trip to town, though frustrating, had its advantages and served to refuel our muscles and flagging spirits. Forty-eight hours later we were back, having managed to get from Puerto Natales to the moraine in a day. With only a few more days available to us we decided to forsake the comfort of the forest, move wholesale up onto the moraine and sit out any storms within sight of the tower. Despite being only an hour or so closer, the advanced base camp had the advantage of being an instant weather station – the 2am weather check could be performed without leaving our pit. For four or five days we lay in ever-increasing squalor and listened to the wind, the food became more like grit, stubble grew, the books were read, the adventures of Don Quixote finished. Finally the wind relented, the spindrift ceased to encase the mountain in its swirling shroud and we were off.

In the early hours one tends not to feel one's best and as we slogged up the gully for the thirteenth time our emotions were low. When the dawn came our enthusiasm increased, and three hours later I was swinging on a windy belay after leading a beautiful pitch – a perfect, clean, crack in a gently overhanging corner, long and sustained and with not too many footholds. My hands were numb, and in places snow mixed with chalk and scraped my knuckles. There was more of the same for Strappo, this time with a little more ice in the corner and a short blank section that succumbed to the charm of RPs. And then it was Simon's turn again.

We really felt we were motoring, swinging leads working well together. This is why we do it, why we try again and again. Simon's pitch, we hoped, would lead us to easier ground – a deep chimney gently overhanging and closing to a difficult exit. He paused, tried the move free and with a muffled cry of frustration rising up through three pile jackets and a Gore-Tex, resorted to an aid point; we didn't hold it against him and minutes later we were jugging up to join him.

All day the wind had been blowing hard. These were borderline conditions, just bearable, the constant march of high cirrus and tell-tale mackerel skies promised us that bad weather was very close. We convened on a small ledge and discussed our options. Darkness was only 30 minutes away and the weather should, by rights, be about to turn ugly. I suggested caution, since getting benighted in a big storm high up and a long way from the fixed ropes was to be avoided. We descended into the night, knowing that, by accepting a huge jumaring effort, we should be able to top out next time.

Sliding down the pitch-black ropes I saw stars ... this wasn't right, the pattern was not being followed. Later, on the moraine, exhausted and speechless, we realised that the clouds, reliable signs for six weeks, had deceived us. Searching for a reason, we realised that the signals were the end of a front rather than an imminent storm. We had climbed through a weak depression and now we sat, completely wasted, dehydrated and gutted, in a period of fine weather. The torture did not last long. By midday next day the wicked winds had returned, but the damage had been done ... we could have summited.

Picking ourselves up mentally, we realised we had one more go left in us. Sadly, at the eleventh hour, Strappo had to leave us and return home; we missed him greatly. We needed his random bouts of wild enthusiasm and his non-stop entertainment during the long bivouacs. It was with mixed feelings that Simon and I prepared for one more go. The knowledge that we could have topped out, the lack of a third member of the team, and our mental weariness made the inevitable routine of early start, slog and jumar seem even more daunting than usual.

The weather kept us pinned down for a couple of days and then at 2am all seemed quiet and the nausea returned as I stumbled over boulders and up into the gully. Simon always seems so irritatingly fit and efficient. I struggled to keep up with him and, in the darkness, watched his head torch slowly creep away up the steep slope.

... Crash and cordite ... rockfall ... my early morning reverie is disturbed and I run in full adrenalin-inspired action across the gully to avoid a fusillade of large rocks, the first such incident on the whole trip. The sudden exertion sends my heart racing; I feel sick and nearly pass out. Simon is OK above the rockfall and is shouting enquiries as to my health. After a few minutes rest I continue, with heavy limbs, the slow, unrelenting, uphill plod.

In the first rays of dawn, when a beautiful triangle of sunlight illuminates the Escudo, our spirits lift. We are high enough now to see over the ridges, and the explosions of orange cloud inspire us to press on. We choose to ignore the lazy wind and the high cirrus. We reach the ropes, stop, drink, check and double check: spare film, food, head torch. Then the slow rhythm of jumaring takes over from the long haul of the gully; right shoulder scrapes against the groove eating through Gore-Tex. Pitch after pitch, and then Simon, ahead as ever, stops and looks concerned as I near the belay. He points at the next rope – it looks strange around its upper anchor. We fear a fraying has occurred over an edge, but it still holds body weight. We take stock and find that we have, purely by chance, five rocks, one RP and a few spare krabs.

I free the fixed rope on the pitch below and tie into it as if leading. Simon belays and I commence a worrying jumar. Like a card player, I don't want to play my trump cards too soon. I place the first of the wires and jumar on. Fifty feet out from the belay I'm beginning to think the rope may last, though the runners have dwindled. A large fall onto a non-stretch rope may be fine for some, but I wish to avoid it. Leaning back I scrutinise the belay, and the realisation hits me with the change of perspective. Not only is the rope I am on looking bad but the next rope is completely absent from the crux pitch. A short length of a few feet flaps around the upper belay – in a moment I realise it's all over. We will not reach the summit. Our rack and lead ropes are up at the top, and our spirits way down below. I abseil back to Simon and together we begin the long road back to the rest of our lives.

Summary: Noel Craine, Roger 'Strappo' Hughes and Simon Nadin made 13 attempts on the Central Tower of Paine between 8 January and 10 March 1997. Their aim was to climb a new line between the 1963 Bonington/ Whillans Route and the huge corner system to the right. They also aimed to make an entirely free ascent of the Central Tower, something that has yet to be achieved. They followed a line up an S-shaped crack and corner system as far as the junction with the 1991 Spanish route *Kanterarik ez.* Leaving their climbing ropes and equipment at this high point, the three descended in appalling weather to await the next fine day. When this day occurred (Hughes having been obliged to return home), Craine and Nadin found that the rope at the eighth and crux pitch had been shredded and blown off the face by the wind. Unable to ascend past this point, and with all their gear above, the two had no option but to give up the climb. The line, on which no bolts were placed, remains to be completed to the summit.

PAUL PRITCHARD

Ak-Su: The Wall of Dykes

(Plates 23–25 and back cover)

With cheap air travel and easy access to all parts of the world, we are now in the golden age of exploration. Pre-war climbers couldn't go to Patagonia, the Himalaya and the Arctic all in one year! Yet as far as free climbing walls go, the mountains of the world are virtually untouched. It's an arena that offers a vast amount of exploration, which was why my friends and I chose to visit the Ak-Su valley in Kyrghyzstan. In 1996 Lynn Hill, Alex Lowe and Conrad Anker brought back tales of huge cliffs more featured than the polished walls of Yosemite and eminently free-climbable. The low altitude was also a bonus, as strenuous free climbing can be hard enough at sea level. The highest peak in the area, Pik Pyramidalniy, is only 5510m and the granite spires are all under 5000m.

In recent years free climbing of big walls has become increasingly popular. One of the first ground-breaking achievements was Kurt Albert's and Wolfgang Gullich's free ascent of the *Slovene Route* on Trango Tower in the eighties. In Yosemite, Skinner and Piana pioneered what is possible on El Capitan's Salathé Wall and Lynn Hill's one-day free ascent of The Nose is already legendary. The Americans and the Germans dominated the scene until mid-September 1997, when Yuji Hirayama made the first single push and fourth free ascent of the Salathé Wall (V 5.1 3b) in 37½ hours. The British have made forays onto shorter walls but we hadn't touched the really big stuff. It was with this in mind that Noel Craine, Johnny Dawes, Dave Green and I packed our sacks for Ak-Su.

We arrived at Heathrow with thirty minutes to go before the plane took off. Noel went to the long-stay car park and then to buy the crucial American dollars whilst we found the weighing scales and started repacking in a futile attempt to beat the pitiful 20 kilo allowance. Although we each had 50 kilos we were determined not to pay any excess. All the hardware went into our pockets, the usual scam, and we each put on our Gore-Tex suit and mountain boots. As there was no one else at the check-in I assumed that we had arrived early and that the queue would start building up soon, so when Noel arrived we waddled to the desk to be there first. The woman behind the counter looked us up and down in bewilderment.

'Surely you're not here for the Tashkent flight?'

'Yes. Is something wrong?'

'You're too late. It's about to take off.' Panic set in amongst our team as we saw our dream of climbing in Ak-Su melt away.

'But we're an important expedition to the Pamir Alai mountains,' we lied.

'I'll see what I can do,' sighed the woman, reaching for her mobile phone. 'If you rush to the gate they might just let you on.'

And so they never found out the weight of our grotesquely heavy bags and we struggled off, very smug with our uncontrollable trolleys. Unfortunately, at the X-ray machine they pulled the Dawes apart. The metal detector went crazy because of all the camming devices in his pockets and his bags seemed to be full of offensive weapons – pegs and such.

We stumbled onto the plane, sheepish, realising we had held up 300 people for half an hour, and settled into our seats for aperitifs.

'Has everybody still got their passports?' I enquired by the by.

'I have,' said Noel.

'I have,' said Dave.

Johnny rummaged around and began frantically slapping at his pockets. 'Mine's gone. Oh God!'

Ropes and hardware were scattered around the cabin, to stares from fellow passengers, but to no avail. As the crew prepared for take-off it became obvious that we couldn't leave. They would never let him into Uzbekistan without a passport. Noel and Johnny ran down the aisle to stop the plane as Dave and I discussed the possibility of deserting our teammate. Next minute the doors had been opened again and the Dawes was in the hold rooting through everybody's bags. No luck though, and the other travellers were now looking irate. In a last attempt to save his trip the Dawes ran back to the gate – and there it was, in a trolley, sandwiched between the *Tibetan Book of the Dead* and *The Secret Life of Plants*. With sighs of relief and a surprisingly relaxed response from the cabin crew we took off for Central Asia.

Almost at the end of our flight, we were somewhere over Kazakhstan and I had been staring down at the patterns in the desert below for hours. I asked the steward what was the name of the desert and he sighed, 'That is no desert; that is the Aral Sea.' We were astounded. We had always read and seen film of 'the greatest environmental disaster in the world', but at home you can feel a bit of sadness and then forget about it and carry on with your dinner. Seeing it for real, albeit from a safe distance, left a lasting impression on us. Later we were to discover from locals that the drying up of the Aral Sea had had a dramatic effect on the climate of the Pamir mountains, with less precipitation than in previous times. To us climbers this seemed a good thing but to the Kyrghyz, trying to grow chick peas and tobacco, not so.

On landing in Tashkent we were met by our interpreter and cook Artyk, a mild-mannered lad with Tartar looks, who was to give us much entertainment and grief over the coming month. Shopping for our supplies in the 30° heat was a blur of noise and colour. We sped from one giant market to another past vast empty squares where Soviet troops used to march, no doubt. Statues of Lenin and hammer and sickle murals were conspicuous in a city which had so obviously embraced capitalism.

It soon transpired that Artyk had never been shopping. At home his mother did all that, he told us, so the catering was left to the team. He was also shocked when we bought no meat. The reason for his being upset became more evident at our base camp when he admitted that the only food he knew how to cook was, in fact, meat. One refreshing aspect of walking around Tashkent was the anonymity we could retain, as a white people, compared with people from other Asian countries. In ex-Soviet Asia there are many White Russians. Stalin sent them here in the thirties in his great plan to mix up all the races and break down ethnic pride. Today, as a tourist in this Central Asian city, nobody even casts you a second glance.

The following morning we hit the road for the mountains. What we were told would be a six-hour drive turned out to take twenty hours from Uzbekistan, through Tadjikistan and into Kyrghyzstan. At the Tadjik-Kyrghyz border a slimy looking official swaggered over and shook our hands. Slung over his shoulder was a rifle with a Rambo sticker on the butt. Quickly he whipped the offensive weapon into his hand and thrust it towards Noel, who jumped back in fright. The archetypal border official laughed out loud and spat his gum into the dust. He only wanted Noel to play with his gun. When the bored guards learnt we were alpinists they invited us to climb the vertical mud crag above their remote dwellings. It looked quite appealing but the thought of them taking pot shots at us led us to decline.

We arrived in the village of Katran in the middle of the night and stayed at the horseman's house, which was hastily reorganised to cater for us. Our lack of Kyrghyz or Russian caused many misunderstandings – for instance, when Johnny, who was worried that we had taken the horseman's young daughter's room, enquired, with all the right sign language, if they were going to sleep with us. We could always count on Johnny, or the Loose Canon as he had become known, to get us into trouble, but we could also count on him to test all the scary-looking food. He would tuck into the salads and unpasteurised dairy products with relish. The problem was that when he became violently ill we had no way of telling exactly which meal was responsible.

We awoke in a sunny, peaceful mountain village and staggered out into the street, rubbing our eyes. At the roadhead we chilled out in an apple orchard, wrestling and bouldering with our horsemen. Then a game was played not too dissimilar to British Bulldogs but on horseback. One rider holds onto a dead goat whilst all the other riders try to relieve the said rider of his goat in a high-speed chase. In the absence of a dead goat a rolled up blanket was used, and in the absence of a proficient horseman, I was used. My horse galloped through the dense orchard, egged on by the whoops and whips of the horsemen as they gave chase, but before they could catch me I was dragged through an apple tree and I found myself hanging from a branch for a second and then lying in the dirt.

Without too many injuries we began our trek into the mountains. Our agent had told us that it was a one-day approach to our base camp, and then this was mysteriously extended to three days. We were told a road had been washed away but this didn't ring true as we knew that another team of Brits had gone in the other way. Things became even more mysterious as we passed very friendly sheep herders in some valleys but met with outright hostility in other valleys. Much later we were to discover that we were passing through pockets of Tadjik teritory within Kyrghyzstan and that thousands of people had been killed in the Ferghana Valley region since the collapse of communism. The fighting had been over border disputes, and bad feeling lingers between these people.

On our second day of walking we passed over a high col and ate bread and lard with a herdsman. There then followed a long uphill day through gorges and past nomads who sold us yoghurt and cream. As we entered the Ak-Su valley we were overawed at the sight of the mountains of rock. It was like walking into Yosemite but with bigger walls and only about fifteen other folk.

As we rolled into camp in a dwarf juniper forest we met the only other climbers there – a hotshot American team of two women and two guys. They were shocked to see us arriving with our horsemen friends.

'What are you doing with those guys?' asked Steph, who glared at the men as they kept their distance.

'They're the ones who robbed us at knifepoint!' Another mystery. These men who had been our good friends turned out to be bandits in their spare time! We swapped addresses, promised to send photos, bade our farewells and they galloped away, rifles slung over their shoulders.

We were to climb as two independent teams, so Dave and I wandered off to search for a likely objective. We hadn't walked long when we stopped and gawped at the giant block of granite to the right of the Russian Tower. It was over a thousand metres high and seamed with quartz dykes of all colours. As far as we could later ascertain nobody had ever climbed to its sharp little summit but, most importantly, the face looked like it might go all free. We acclimatised on Small Tower with a seven-pitch 5.10 and were delighted to find the rock featured with chicken heads and ripples.

After a rest at camp, where Artyk cooked the worst food any of us had ever eaten, Dave and I escaped across the river to the wall. It began easily enough on the lower apron in cracks but as they ran out the climbing became scary friction. At a giant detached flake we fixed the ropes and rappelled off. We hadn't brought a portaledge to the Ak-Su because we wanted to go light and fast but we now regretted our decision, as we found no natural ledges bigger than a house brick on the whole wall. At night we shivered in camp and sang Barry Manilow songs, which led to complaints from our American friends. They had already been here five weeks and wondered why we had come so late in the season. In perfect weather the Americans had done numerous climbs but now, in September, the season was coming to an end. We had only decided to come on this trip shortly before we left and a friend, an old hand on Kyrghyzstan, told us September would be fine. The horsemen assured us that we would have to cut our trip short if we were to have any hope of getting all our kit out on horseback, because the snows were coming. The pressure was on for us to get up our wall fast.

We scrounged a fixing rope off the Americans and went back up to fix a couple more pitches. In a flying chimney Dave became allergic to the lichen and lowered off with swollen eyes. I took over and back and footed out into space. Then came more scary face and friction, drilling the odd bolt miles out on gritty smears. But now we had run out of rope again on an overhanging wall, with nowhere to sleep. It seemed there was no way out.

Meanwhile Noel and Johnny had enjoyed making the second ascent of the Americans' route *Black Magic* on Center Pyramid but had decided to leave early for home. The cold was too much. Dave and I had to stay and luckily for us they gave us three more ropes to fix. While Noel and Johnny made numerous boulder problems in the valley, waiting for the horsemen to take them out, we tackled the crux pitches of the route.

Dave was leading up to the central arch feature of the wall when he hit a blank wall. He moved up and down for an age and then pronounced, 'It's no good, Paul. I'll have to drill some bat hooks.' As he was on the second bat move his hammer deflected off the top of the drill and fractured his thumb. In pain he lowered to the hanging belay.

'You'll have to go up, I can't grip the drill anymore.' I moved onto the face and, with the hooks for protection, I found a circuitous and tenuous free way with a downward traverse on tiny razor edges to reach a ladder of good little holds. I pulled an overhang and found a perfect pancake flake running the rest of the 60 metres.

'It looks easy now Dave,' I shouted down. But as Dave led through, horizontally round a corner he shouted back, 'No it isn't, Paul.'

Back down we had to go to see to Dave's hand. The daily jumaring was becoming a dangerous chore. We had come to get away from this kind of thing and here we were, yet again, fixing. Jugging over one huge, sharp-lipped roof in particular was quite terrifying, spinning in the air and seeing the river below our feet.

The hardest pitch was now to come. I aided up a thin seam on copperheads to fix protection for a desperate, thin face sequence. I lowered down, composed myself and pulled off the moves to reach a fingertip layback flake in an incredibly exposed position. Another 60m higher and I belayed on easier ground. Dave seconded stoically with a hurting hand. The next pitch looked easier and Dave could cope as long as there was no jamming. A beautiful 70m simo pitch ran us out of all our rope. The top was 700m of confusing slabs away and next time up we would go for the top.

At camp we ate sheep and rice, drank vodka which said 'Fit for human consumption' on the label and said goodbye to Noel, Johnny and the Americans. Now it was just Artyk, Dave and I.

We crawled out early, but not too early as it was too freezing to climb, and made the long jumar back to our high point. We had only packed six chocolate bars, two litres of juice and spare jackets. We didn't have much time left and it had to be today. Dave led off in the morning chill and made a 200m runout leftwards traverse on a friction slab. Our route seemed never to go upwards, the dykes always leading us left or right. We had hit many blind alleys and were now going all over the place.

I led an easier straight-up pitch at last and then Dave had to take us 60m back right. It was noon, but around the next bulge we knew we would be into the upper corner system. I made one more pitch, flying now, and as Dave led out another we began to simo-climb for 400m until we hit a sharp arête. In a spacey position we simoed in the sunshine to the summit, where we were met by two weasels who were very curious to see the new arrivals.

We had a stunning view of the Pamir Alai range, Bird Peak looking particularly fine as a future hit. To the west was Peak 4810m and the wonderfully-named One Thousand Years of Russian Christianity and, to the north, the Russian Tower. Surrounded by all this rock we were sad that we would have to leave for home, but I knew I would be coming back.

The descent gully was dangerous but quick and at dusk we were back at camp. I made the mistake of celebrating with Alumbec the horseman by chewing some of his tobacco, which turned out to be laced with opium and ground glass. Dave took to it well but I had to hide in my tent trying to control that violent spinning feeling. But I was content to have done what we had set out to do.

We still had a couple of days before we could leave so Dave and I went and explored the Kara-Su valley next door. We found miles of rock in a more rugged terrain than the Ak-Su. I walked alone up the glacier to watch the avalanches coming off Pyramidalniy and there, close to 4000m, I found a steam-driven tractor on the lateral moraine. Further up I found mine workings and machinery. What were they mining in such a desolate place?

Back at our bivouac I found that my new rope had disappeared out of my rucksack. There were a handful of dzo herders in the valley but I couldn't really go casting accusations. All the herders were descending from the mountains now and we were following them. I discovered that the workings up above the glacier were a mica mine which, I was informed, was used for making car windscreens!

Almost at the roadhead Dave and I were way ahead of the team when we came across a caravan of herders bringing their homes down to the valleys on the backs of their horses. On closer inspection Dave noticed that the loads were strapped on with my new Beal 8.6mm rope neatly chopped up and divided between all the horses! I started shouting at the herder and pointing at the rope. 'My rope. This my rope!' The herdsman stood and smiled with his rifle over his shoulder. Dave and I looked at each other in bewilderment, looked back at the man and then we too broke into broad smiles. What else could we do?

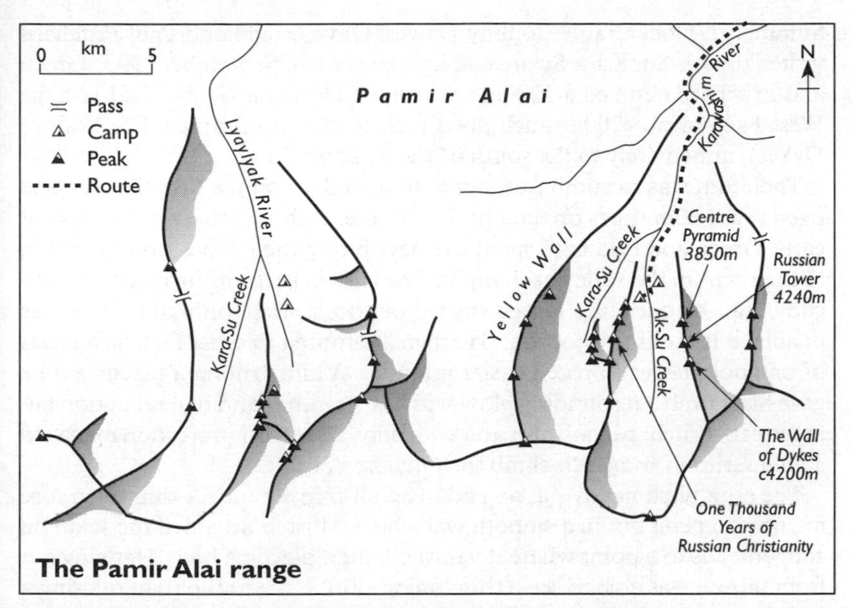
0 km 5
Pass
Camp
Peak
Route
Pamir Alai
N
Lyaylyak River
Karavshin River
Kara-Su Creek
Yellow Wall
Kara-Su Creek
Ak-Su Creek
Centre Pyramid 3850m
Russian Tower 4240m
The Wall of Dykes c4200m
One Thousand Years of Russian Christianity
The Pamir Alai range

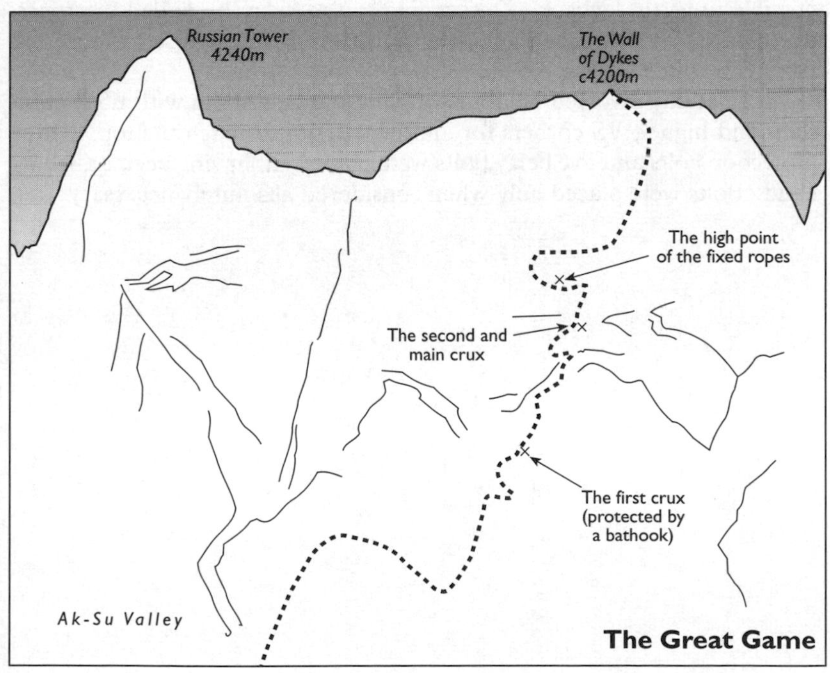
Russian Tower 4240m
The Wall of Dykes c4200m
The high point of the fixed ropes
The second and main crux
The first crux (protected by a bathook)
Ak-Su Valley
The Great Game

Summary: Noel Craine, Johnny Dawes, Dave Green and Paul Pritchard visited the Ak-Su/Kara-Su area of Kyrghyzstan in September 1997. Green and Pritchard climbed a 1200m new route (*The Great Game*, 5.12b) on the West Face of a *c*4200m unclimbed rock formation (named The Wall of Dykes) immediately to the south of the Russian Tower.

Their aim was to climb free, but with no ledges on the face the climbers fixed seven 60m ropes on their proposed line. After Craine and Dawes left early, Green and Pritchard spent five days fixing their ropes, coming down to their tent in the valley each night. The easiest sections involved HVS 5a climbing. At one stage Green started out on a pitch, only to find he was unable to free climb a section. He then attempted to cross this via a series of bathook moves to reach easier ground. While drilling a placement he gave his thumb a resounding blow with the hammer and had no option but to retreat. Pritchard took over and with only a hook for protection managed a bold series of moves to climb the pitch free at E4.

The crux pitch nearly put an end to an all-free ascent. A thin seam rose up, only to peter out in a smooth wall above. Pritchard aided the seam on copperheads to a point where it vanished, then placed a bolt. Hanging out from this he was able to see a thin 'onion skin' flake to the right offering a possible fingertip layback. Descending to the belay he pulled the ropes, free climbed the seam to the bolt and made a hard traverse to reach the flake. The pitch went at E5 6b.

The final day involved 18 hours of climbing beginning with E3 friction slabs and higher, VS corners for another *c*650m to reach the top. Three protection bolts and five belay bolts were placed, all having been drilled by hand. Bolts were placed only when considered absolutely necessary.

3. Looking along the West Ridge of Lhotse. Is the other (west) peak higher? Tomo Cesen supposedly came along below the crest of the ridge on the south side (*L side in the photo*). Nuptse behind. (*Jonathan Pratt*) (p95)

Left

29. The British Sikkim Expedition: Chombu, 6362m, seen from the Sebu La, with Skip Novak (*L*) and Doug Scott.
(*Julian Freeman-Attwood*) (p45)

Below

30. Sanglaphu, 6224m, Gurudongma 6715m, and Kangchengao, 6889r seen from the Tibetan (north) sid of Gurudongmar Lake.
(*Julian Freeman-Attwood*) (p45)

Above
1. Skip Novak on the pinnacle ridge of Chombu East. (*Doug Scott*) (p45)

Right
2. Julian Freeman-Attwood just short of the summit of Chombu East, 5745m, in deference to the traditions of Sikkim. (*Doug Scott*) (p45

36. Cerro Torre, 3128m, (Patagonia) seen from Bridwell Camp. (*Paul Moores*) (p97)

37. The ice cave at the Col of Patience. *L to R* Mark Wilford, Aid Burgess, Paul Moores. (*Paul Moores collection*) (p97)

8. Max Berger leading the overhanging pillar, with the headwall of Cerro Torre (*upper left*). (*Paul Moores collection*) (p97)

39. The W Face of the Central Tower of Paine, Patagonia. The route climbs the wall below the heavy ice encrustings. (*Noel Craine*)

40. Simon Nadin climbing on lower slabs. (*Noel Craine*) (p102)

41. Simon climbing the penultimate pitch before the high point. (*Noel Craine*) (p102)

LOUISE THOMAS

Beatrice

The First Ascent of the South-East Face

We were a team of three women: Kath Pyke, Glenda Huxter and myself. The choice of people was simple – women inspired by the mountain, women prepared to attempt a new route at altitude and women with some concept of big wall climbing. Believe me, there are not many of them. So I was delighted when both Glenda and Kath agreed to join me. Despite all our plans and promises, the first opportunity we had to climb together was actually on Beatrice itself. The first time that we even coincided in the same room was only 24 hours before we left. These facts did not affect our ability to work together. We each contributed something different, making, I believe, a strong and supportive team

As women in a Muslim country, we were anxious about how we should behave and also about how we would be treated. Our anxiety increased with the stories recounted by friends and fellow climbers who had already visited Pakistan. Fortunately our anxiety was unfounded. We were very well treated and well looked after and experienced no bureaucratic nightmares. We all felt that it was important to respect the Pakistani culture, so we wore the traditional 'shalwar-chemise' while in the towns and cities and kept arms, legs and head covered when in company. As a result, we were rarely harassed, although we were occasionally the subject of curiosity.

In less than a week we had arrived in Islamabad, collected freight, permits and food, travelled the Karakoram Highway to Skardu and continued by jeep up the Hushe Valley, from where we began our walk-in.

During the three days' walk from Kunde at just under 3000m through Hushe and then on up to Base Camp at 4100m we were carrying the heaviest loads possible, partly to save on porters but also to demonstrate that we were able to put some effort in ourselves. We tended to walk very fast and Glenda began to suffer from the effects of altitude. As a team we felt that it was important to support any member who was not well and not expect them to carry such big loads as the rest of us, nor force them on regardless. I believe that the women's team felt more at ease with this policy than the men's team (who were going to pursue a different line on the mountain) and more able to appreciate the frustration of the person who is ill.

Arriving at Base Camp was a stunning experience. The glacier through which we had been weaving gave way to a flat almost grassy meadow with streams running through it. At the far end the porters waited to greet us with singing and dancing. Ibrim, our cook and guide, had already laid out tea and goodies for our arrival. Rocky peaks surrounded us and we were thrilled that our chosen mountain, Beatrice, looked dominating and beautiful.

After establishing Base Camp it was decided to keep two porters to help transport equipment up to Advanced Base, without a rest day. We decided on an early start to avoid the heat of the day. Fortunately no matter how early we left, Ibrim was always ready with porridge and chapattis. We all carried loads up by different routes to try and identify the best way through the horrible scree and big rolling boulders.

Two or three hours later we were all lying in various states of exhaustion on a moraine rib at the side of the glacier – our site for Advanced Base. Glenda was now feeling distinctly poorly and so descended back to base with Twid and Grant who were also suffering from the heat and altitude. Kath, Steve and I continued up onto the glacier to try to find a route through and to get a better look at the face. We were eager to identify some possible lines. Three hours later we had not reached the base of the wall. We were between huge crevasses, relatively secure but not willing to go further with our minimal kit. We sat on a hump-backed lump of glacier, necks straining, eyes upwards. The face looked hard, very hard. There were lines to the left that looked promising but what mainly caught our attention was a stunning overhanging crack that cut the main face. There was a potential stopper, as overlapping roofs guarded the bottom of the whole of the main face walls. We turned tail and in about a third of the time descended to base to report back.

What to report? I imagine, in our hearts, we had all hoped that, after a little jaunt across the glacier, we would be able to identify a line of weakness running from bottom to top. But there is always a good reason why something so stunning as this wall remains untouched. What if we had to join the lads to break through the bottom roofs? Glenda may have been feeling unwell but she was utterly depressed by the thought. 'It's very important that we should do it on our own,' she said. We looked at the cracks on the left, discussing tactics and climbing rotas. All were irrelevant in the end. If you were fit enough, you climbed. Our plan was that Kath and I would have a leisurely day walking to Advanced Base. This would allow us to make a start on a line. Glenda was now dealing with a resting heart rate of 110 and feeling exhausted by any exertion. She would remain at base, carrying loads if she improved. On the lads' side, both Twid and Grant appeared to be suffering from altitude. So Steve joined Kath and me at Advanced Base.

We rose early hoping to make a start climbing. Through the boulders Twid appeared, not wanting to let Steve down. Four on the rope was a definite improvement through the crevasses. Soon we reached our hump-backed lump of ice and studied the wall again. Suddenly there was no need for further uncertainties as the mountain released a torrent of icy rock and water down our once hopeful corner. The roofs were the only answer. There was only one way through.

The glacier seemed to extend and grow, the wall never seeming to arrive. Finally we kicked our way up a steep tongue of snow to reach the base. We teetered below the wall, hacking ledges to stand on. The plan was to break through the roofs and weave a way up onto an apparent ledge from which two possible lines continued. Our action plan was simple: lead for 1½ hours, then lower off for the next person.

Twid began free climbing, then aiding, breaking through the first roof. It was my turn next to tackle the second and biggest roof. I tried to sound totally at ease, eager to get on with it. In fact I was terrified. What if I was incapable of 'doing my bit'? Quickly I reached the roof; it was seamed with blind cracks. I placed a downward-pointing knifeblade to move up on; it groaned. The hopeful-looking crack up left yielded nothing but a small RP. Trying to convince myself that my heart's pounding was due to the altitude, I gently moved up. It all held and I was up over the roof, my time up, my turn over. Next, Steve made his way up into a hopeful crack system on the left. Unfortunately the rock was loose and he had to keep climbing just to find a good belay. Our first day's climbing was over and four weary souls made a quick descent to boil-in-the-bag meals and cosy sleeping-bags.

The next day Grant appeared and replaced a now suffering Twid. We made another early start back to the wall. This time it was Kath and Grant's turn to push the way. Grant's lead took him back in line with our start, making it possible to fix 100m of rope to the snow. Altitude was making us all slow, so I jumared to help them just in time to follow Kath on an excellent pitch that took us to our ledge and future bivvy site. Despite our early starts, by the end of the day we were always fighting the fading light. Kath and I organised the stance as best we could with ropes and gear. We surveyed the ledge, which was generally more of a slab with some very precarious boulders perched around apparently defying gravity. Memorising what we could, we slid down the ropes and back to the tents.

Twid was waiting with tea and supper, keen to hear how we had progressed. We were happy to have reached the ledge. The line the lads were contemplating looked inspiring. It appeared to be a continuous overhanging crack. From the ledge, Kath and I had been able to identify a corner system which looked feasible as far as we could see. It was difficult to surmise what would happen higher up. However, we decided it was our best option.

A rest day was now definitely needed. We felt a little more relaxed, as a start had been made and our next move would be to get established on the wall. As we sat supping tea and making plans in the dark, a head torch glimmered through the scree; it was Glenda. We were really pleased to see her as we had been concerned that she might have got worse or be miserable on her own at Base Camp. She had not been miserable, as Ibrim and Zakir had been delighted to have someone to look after. Unfortunately she did not seem a lot better, though, and had developed a horrendous cough.

In the morning Grant, Kath and Steve descended to base for a rest. Twid and I slept late before heading up the glacier carrying loads. Glenda accompanied me to see how she would feel. She did not feel well and everything was a tremendous effort. Being ill on a trip must be the most soul-destroying experience. You have to cope not only with feeling lousy but also with the even worse feeling that you can't contribute, that you are left behind on your own, wondering what you can do and contemplating how much it has cost you to feel ill in a far-off land.

Back at Advanced Base we lazed in the sun, which soon disappeared behind steadily thickening clouds. We knew the signs – a front was approaching. Quickly we bundled kit into tents, grabbed everyone's sleeping-bags and stumbled our way down to Base Camp. Ibrim was delighted – lots of people to look after and cook for. He celebrated with chips. The rain began as we huddled into the kitchen-dining area that had been built for us out of tarpaulins, boulders and climbing tape. Over tea I nursed a minor cut shin that I had sustained when a boulder had rolled while I had been standing on it. Kath then revealed a badly-swollen and bruised ankle where her foot had become pinned between two boulders on the descent. She was probably lucky not to have broken it.

Next day the mountains began to crash and boom, as avalanches tumbled down. We felt very safe in our camp but still it snowed and snowed. We read, played cards, watched endless chess challenges and felt the weariness of inactivity. When two of us returned to Advanced Base a day or two later, the Ferrino tent had completely vanished under several feet of snow. Beside it the Super Nova remained standing, if slightly squashed. If it too had collapsed, we might have had great difficulty finding our kit.

Finally, after eight days of rain and snow, the clouds dispersed, mountains began to appear plastered in white, and we made our plans to return to the wall. Although the poor weather had been frustrating it had made us take our time. Glenda had taken antibiotics in case she had an infection, and for the first time she began to feel well. The enforced rest had given her time to recover and Kath's ankle time to heal. Now all six of us headed up to Advanced Base Camp ready to go onto the wall. Ibrim and Zakir sent us off after a fantastic pizza. We were on our way.

After digging out the tents we went to sleep full of hope and woke to yet more snow. Emotions were mixed and tempers fraught – ought we to wait or push? Was it worth breaking trail? Fortunately we packed sacks and for six hours waded through the snow, burrowing out a trail. The once innocuous glacier appeared an unfriendly and intimidating beast, with its dangers so well hidden. We were grateful for the security of numbers on the rope. Exhausted by our efforts we reached the dump zone and retreated. It took us a full day to recover.

Finally we woke to a different morning, cold and clear. We made quick progress up our trail to the base of the wall, but despite this the final trail-breaking in the heat of the day, through untouched snow, while ferrying loads, took till late afternoon. With little daylight left, we began to jumar and haul bags up to our ledge. Darkness crept onto us as we reached our high point. It was no longer a ledge but a snow slope and all our equipment and ropes were buried. Eventually, late in the night, we drank hot brews in sleeping-bags on our temporary ledges. It had been worth the effort.

Sun and falling ice woke us. The day was spent establishing a really good camp. We hacked out ledges, constructed mighty anchors, hung the portaledge, and made a funnel to collect water as the snow melted. Finally there was nothing left to do but to begin climbing. Glenda led off, making tentative moves over loose rock into a corner. Once established, she settled down to a long pitch of good climbing at about 5b. Kath followed and then continued on above. While they pushed out nearly 100m I came close to a heart attack trying to fit our Karrimor storm fly over the portaledge. Relieved when eventually the ledge was squeezed in, I was dismayed to discover that the zips were on the outside only! The girls returned happy and excited to have made progress, with promises that my pitch looked great.

We would wake early in order to jumar in the cool before the early sun hit our route. The bad weather seemed to mark a change of season – although it was still warm in the sun, at all other times it was freezing. The lower section of the route ran beneath a huge chimney couloir. In the cool it was safe but as the sun hit its ice-filled cracks, we would be showered with ice and small rocks. Glenda and I reached the top of the ropes with the sun. The warmth was lovely, the climbing steady, but as time progressed, the urgency of falling ice changed the mood of the climbing. Nearing the end of the rope a solid, huge spike appeared perfectly situated out to the side under a sheltering wall. Glenda joined me, then launched back into the firing-line before escaping out left. She called down that it looked not too bad, but then went quiet. Desperate moves faced her, with minimal protection. Glenda had recovered! The pitch took her onto what we hoped would be more ledges and possible bivvy sites. The ledges were non-existent and we found nothing but piles of teetering, huge loose blocks. Carefully we climbed up towards the steep corner above. By midday we had lost the sun and although this made the lower corner much safer, it was freezing. We fixed our ropes as carefully as possible and abseiled to bed and waiting tea. The steep corner looked possible if aided, and this was what I had to psyche myself up for next day. I was excited, nervous and totally committed. For several days we worked on the corner. I was slow but we made progress. The crack became awkward, not yielding easily to gear. Pegs would rip, nuts gave way to pee nuts and RPs. These would then not fit into the crack but needed mashing. While I whittled away, reminding myself to breath gently and stand lightly on my étriers, Kath or Glenda would patiently encourage, even after hours hanging in a harness in horrendous cold.

Each day we would return to the ledge and the third person would be ready with hot tea and meals. There was a marked difference between the two teams living on the wall. Other than brief greetings the lads rarely talked to us. We could have been from another planet speaking a strange language! They were never unfriendly but they would climb, eat and sleep. Because we girls were smaller, we could all snuggle into the double portaledge for meals and gossip, making life on the wall a very sociable experience. The other factor was that we felt weary but healthy, whereas Twid was still being sick and Grant, too, was feeling unwell.

Every day we were hopeful that we would see a breakthrough, an easing and a way to the top. After a slow start, with some hard aiding, the lads had suddenly made progress. Breaking through the difficulties, their crack had finally kicked back into steady free climbing. They were ready to go for the summit. Grant and Twid were still suffering, so they decided to return to base for a rest before the final push. As snow began to fall we decided to go down as well. By descending, we hoped to get a look at the face, but cloud moved in quickly. It was Friday night and in a week we would have to have moved all our kit back to Advanced Base. I felt pleased with what we had achieved but very unsure of the outcome. Would we have enough time to finish the route?

We three rested on Saturday but made an early start on Sunday. Again, as we crossed the glacier, the clouds obliterated our view of the face. The snow began as I jumared the first rope. I waited for Kath as we tried to haul up some extra equipment. It was snowing above me and water began to pour down the ropes and freeze. Kath struggled as her jumars began to slip on the ice-covered ropes. Through the mist I could see the lads arriving. 'GO HOME! GO DOWN!' I screamed. Of course they took one look and had no intention of coming up. Fortunately Glenda, who was at the base of the wall, was able to retreat with the lads. Kath and I decided to get up to the shelter of the ledges as quickly as we could.

The next hour was like a dream. It was freezing, raining and snowing, and we were aware of the dangers of getting really cold and wet. I rushed to ascend the final rope, pushing the jumar aggressively to cut through any ice, but ice was not the problem and my action turned slush into ice as the jumar clattered down the rope into my chest. I took a big breath and calmly placed prussiks around the ropes.

On Monday we woke to a calm silence after a fitful night. The sun warmed the ouside of the ledge and the orange of the canopy gave the impression of a fine day. We disturbed the peace, beating the snow off the shelter and fighting with the outside zips. On the other side, the lads' camp was a torrent of water on their back wall, with icicles decorating the base of their ledges. We spent a sunny few hours drying our kit. Below us we could spy the same process happening at Advanced Base. Just as we began to contemplate the others' return, the clouds tumbled in again, the sun vanished and it began to snow.

On Tuesday, early sunshine dragged us from our beds. Being on the wall gave us a day in hand. Up the ropes we went, tentatively, checking for damage. The corner still continued, not relenting, not easing. I settled down and began aiding. Above me placements appeared to dwindle, but I kept on trying until eventually something would hold and I would move up. Occasionally a good Friend placement would remind me how useless the other pieces had been. Up on the wall we were able to watch a little trail tracing its way through the glacier. The minute figures gave some scale to the huge holes among which they were weaving their way. Glenda was waiting at the ledge. The good news was that we had reached the top of the corner, the bad news was that the wall did not ease and the crack lines that we had been heading for still looked hard. There was, however, a flake line out left.

On Wednesday we were woken by the lads heading off before dawn. I did not want to move. Earlier than I wanted, I was back on the ropes heading upwards. Glenda moved left to the flakes, easy climbing drawing her away from the cracks and the solace of protection, while scary moves drove her back to find a belay. We made progress. For the first time the whole face appeared and we were able to watch the lads on a huge expanse of wall, and then disappearing over the top. We were thrilled for them but worried by the sounds of retching. The sun had gone, I was freezing, but Glenda was prepared to do one more pitch. Her hands were numb as the rock drew the heat away and not even adrenalin could put heat back into them. She moved left again into another crack. From this belay, flakes continued above and although we still could not see if they would take us to the top, we had to hope.

That night Twid, Steve and Grant returned safely to the ledges. They had been to the top of the wall. Their route sounded brilliant. They were subdued by fatigue.

Thursday was our last opportunity. We planned to rise at 4am but at 3am I was woken by cold wet flakes of snow landing on my face. We closed the flaps and went back to an unhappy sleep. Discussions restarted at 6am. Could we afford to wait? What if the weather continued to snow? Would we be able to ascend our ropes to retrieve the climbing gear? Eventually we decided to go up and retrieve it. We would all jumar up in case the weather improved.

Going up the ropes, it became apparent that this would have to be our last effort, as we were all too tired to do it again. As Kath and I reached our previous high point, the snow stopped. Kath led off, aiming for a triangular niche that promised to become a belay, but it was useless and she sounded worried. But with the aid of pegs, an anchor was constructed and we were on our way again. A black fault line was reached which continued up. The fault was loose but continuous and by 3pm we were below a final corner and steep cracks that led to the summit. As Glenda headed up, suddenly she became aware of how exhausted she felt and how tired her muscles were. Kath and I willed her on. At 5.45pm we were on the top of the wall, perched on a tiny pinnacle. Chuffed to bits, we watched the clouds dispersing to reveal mountains layered with mountains.

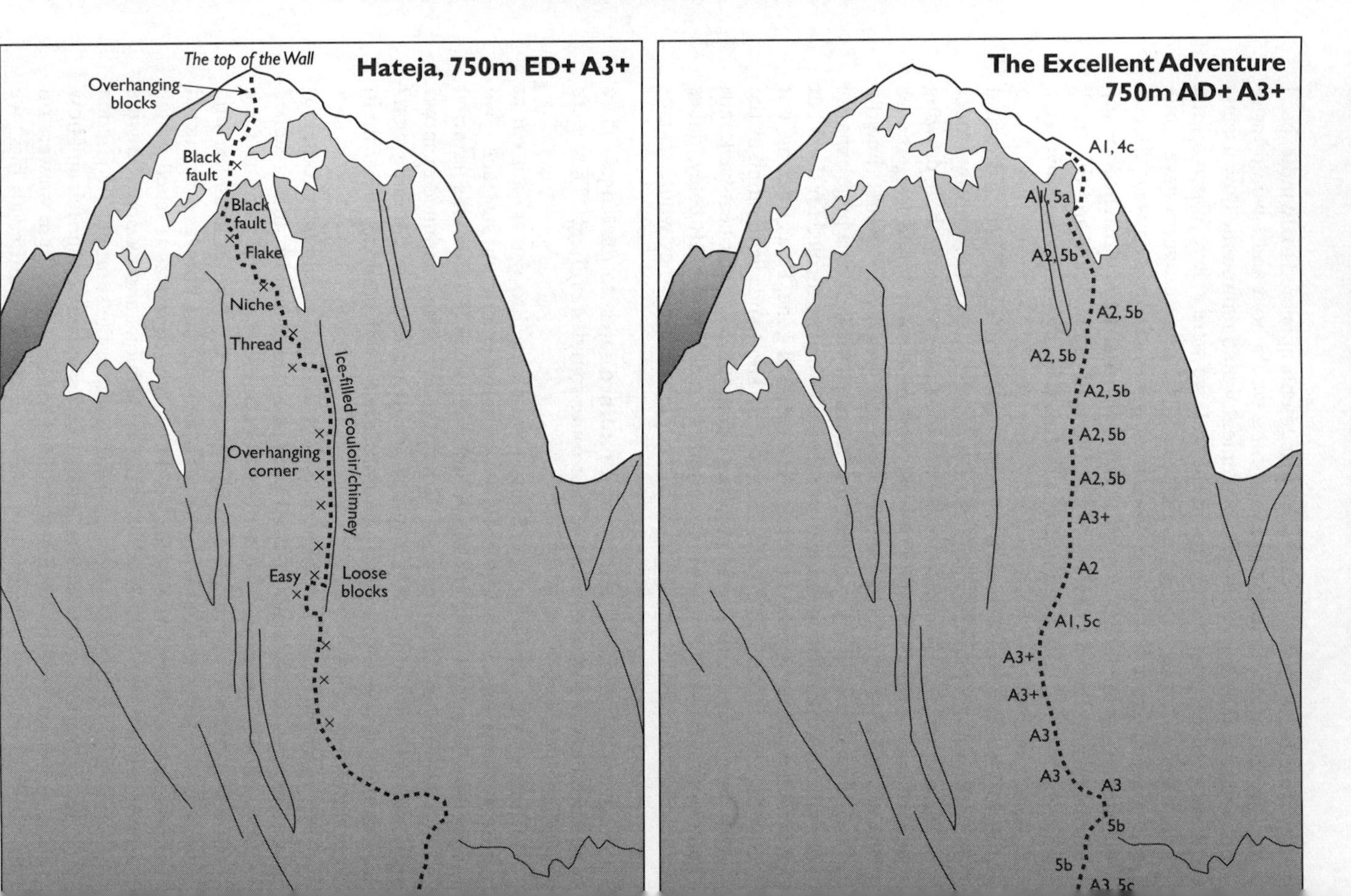
Hateja, 750m ED+ A3+
The top of the Wall
Overhanging blocks
Black fault
Black fault
Flake
Niche
Thread
Ice-filled couloir/chimney
Overhanging corner
Easy
Loose blocks
The Excellent Adventure
750m AD+ A3+
A1, 4c
A1, 5a
A2, 5b
A2, 5b
A2, 5b
A2, 5b
A2, 5b
A2, 5b
A3+
A2
A1, 5c
A3+
A3+
A3
A3
A3
5b
5b
A3 5c

We wanted to stay. We wanted this moment to last for as long as possible – but, as ever, darkness made its call.

The top is never the end. We cleaned as much as we could and finally looked in dismay at the amount of kit that we were going to have to abseil with and carry in a day to Advanced Base. Kath and I touched down on the snow and hauled our kit over some cathedral-sized holes to wait for Glenda. Approaching the roofs, Glenda glanced below to discover that the rope had shredded. The weight of her and her kit would strip it. But having seen it in time, she was able to deal with it.

Finally we stood on the snow, too hot and too tired. We each had a huge sack and haul bag with ledges and ropes spewing out. Our next attempt at death was to tie ourselves together to cross the wet glacier, each dragging a beast of a sack. One slip and we would be catapulted into any waiting hole. Eventually we took a grip of ourselves and resorted to shuttling kit to the dry glacier where we were able to drag the beasts.

We abandoned all but the essentials above Advanced Base and headed in the dusk to Base Camp. I had felt little emotion until, looking down the final scree, I saw Ibrim and Zakir, followed by the lads, heading up to meet us. I felt silly, as tears welled up at the sight of them. I sniffed them back and was saved as Ibrim produced the teapot and three mugs. Hugs and tea all round. We were definitely down.

Summary: The Joint North Wales Expedition achieved two new routes on Beatrice, 5800m, in the Charakusa Basin, Pakistan. During 12 days in August/September 1997 Louise Thomas, Glenda Huxter and Kath Pyke climbed *Hateja* ('Strong-willed, determined lady') (750m, ED+ A3+). Starting from a portaledge camp 150m up the wall, they moved left into a corner, giving some excellent free climbing between 5b and 6a. After 200m the corner led to an area of loose blocks above which another corner began. This overhung and provided several days of aid climbing. When the corner started to blank out they launched left, moving from corner to cracks as each turned blank. On their last possible day to complete the route, the trio awoke to heavy snow. Despite this the rock remained dry. As yet another corner blanked out, they moved into a black fault-line and by 5.45pm all three were sitting on the top of the wall.

Meanwhile Steve Meyers, Mike 'Twid' Turner and Grant Farquhar climbed a stunning crack that began from the same ledge 150m up the wall and continued to the top. *The Excellent Adventure* (750m, ED+ A3+) involved 300m of aid climbing before kicking back to give gradually easing free climbing. Seven days were spent fixing ropes from a portaledge camp on the wall before the final push to the summit.

PAT PARSONS

The Gimmigela Adventure

(*Plates 33–35*)

The outcome of any adventure is, by definition, uncertain. If that were not the case, there would be little point in doing it. In the spring of 1997 Gimmigela provided the adventure of a lifetime for fourteen British Servicemen. The mountain kept us guessing right to the end and even the day before the summit, after five gut-busting weeks, I felt sure we were staring defeat in the face. The weather was deteriorating and time running out. However, by the skin of our teeth we achieved our goal.

I had been looking for such a mountain for some time. Remote and isolated, Gimmigela was still a virgin 7000m peak in 1993. I couldn't believe my luck, therefore, when the Nepalese authorities made it available for mountaineering. Kit Spencer, an old friend of mine in Kathmandu, told me this news in December 1994, and so it was that Gimmigela became our expedition objective. My dreams of a first ascent were soon dashed, however, when I heard that the Japanese had climbed it, just a few months earlier, from the Sikkim side. Imagine my dismay when I heard of their second ascent in 1995, this time from the Nepalese side. Nevertheless, it was still a remote and relatively unknown peak and therefore a worthy objective.

Despite being in the shadow of Kangchenjunga's north face, Gimmigela stands alone and has its own character. It is a beautiful mountain to look at but proved deceptively difficult to climb. Perhaps the greatest surprise was the quality of the climbing. Although loose in places, this followed the most compelling line and was continually steep and exciting.

The idea of leading an expedition had been in the back of my mind for some time. Over the years, I have gained much from the Royal Navy and Royal Marines Mountaineering Club (RN&RMMC) and the time seemed right to put something back in. I half-seriously asked my appointer for the time off to do the trip and, to my astonishment, he agreed. My bluff was called and the game was on! For such a venture, the team is all-important and we were blessed with a good one. Most of its members came from the Club (RN&RMMC) with two Army members and one from the RAF. For the most part we were a happy and harmonious group and worked well together. As one might expect from such a gathering, humour was in abundance and there were few dull moments.

The aim of the expedition was to make the first British ascent of Gimmigela, ideally by a new route. My unstated objectives, in order of priority, were to get everybody back in one piece, to summit and still to be talking to each other afterwards. Thankfully, all these aims were achieved.

The approach march to Gimmigela (and to Kangchenjunga) was described by Peter Boardman as one of the most beautiful treks in the Himalaya. It is now a recognised trekking route, but owing to its length and altitude it is, thankfully, infrequently done. After a high-level start at Basantapur, the middle section drops down to the Tamur and Ghunsa Kholas through steep, spectacular valleys.

The character of the route changes markedly above Ghunsa, as do the porterage charges. Ghunsa, at 3430m, is the last permanent habitation before base camp, and the route above is steep and difficult – a fact not lost on the inhabitants, who charge exorbitant porterage prices to negotiate it. Sadly, many expeditions simply throw money at the problem to avoid confrontation and delay, further inflating prices (up to Rs 400 per day). We calculated that it would have cost us no more to fly all our kit into base camp in a single helicopter lift, which is readily available from Kathmandu. Unless they are careful, the inhabitants of Ghunsa will price themselves out of the market. Pointing out this fact to them had a miraculous effect on their porter prices.

From Ghunsa to Pangpema, the going is often difficult and a yak fell to its death crossing a dangerous scree slope between Ghunsa and Kambachen. Pangpema, a summer yak pasture at 5139m, is an ideal base camp location. At the confluence of the Kangchenjunga Glacier, it is set in magnificent surroundings with stunning mountain views. Particularly impressive were Wedge Peak and, of course, Kangchenjunga itself. Normally a remote and isolated spot, this season we shared Pangpema with four other expeditions: Spanish, Slovakian, American/British and Korean, all attempting the big prize: Kangchenjunga's North Face.

Our plan, which had evolved from photos back in the UK, was to climb Gimmigela's South-West Ridge. It appeared to offer the most natural and the safest line to the summit, a fact confirmed when we saw it. The route followed the true line of the ridge from foot to summit and had never been attempted before. (The Japanese climbed the NW Face from the col between Cross Peak and Gimmigela).

As a Services team, I wanted to get as many people as high as possible, so that all might benefit equally. We therefore elected to climb in traditional style using tented camps and fixed ropes. In any case, the nature of the route mitigated against an Alpine-style ascent, the ridge being over three kilometres long from glacier to summit. In the event, about 1500m of rope were fixed (and stripped after the climb). No high-altitude porters were used and oxygen was taken (but not used) for medicinal purposes only. We divided the team into two climbing groups, led by Tug Wilson and Ted Atkins respectively. Initially, the two groups alternated between lead climbing and supporting and this even-handed approach was partly responsible for the slow rate of progress early on. Later, less democratic measures were adopted.

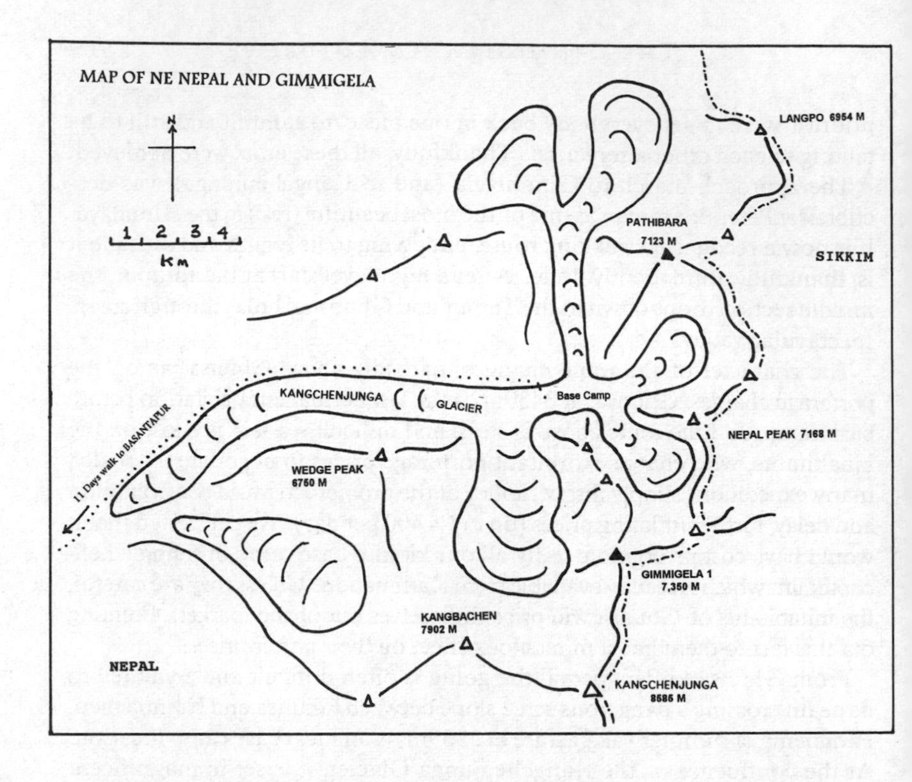

The route from Base Camp to Advanced Base Camp is some six kilometres long and, for the most part, follows the Kangchenjunga Glacier. It was the most frequently travelled part of the entire route, with most members traversing it at least a dozen times. It was also mind-numbingly tedious, the only relief being the staggering mountain views in every direction. From Base Camp a 400ft descent was made down onto the main glacier – this was a real gut-buster on the return trip. Once on the glacier, the first section resembled a trek through a 'Dr Who' set with enormous, scree-covered ice penitents frequently covered with fresh snow.

The next section was on snow and ice and followed the main glacier towards Kangchenjunga. Flatter than the first section, the going was easier, especially after a hard freeze. However, during the heat of the day, the glare and heat were intolerable, so early starts were the order of the day. Latterly, as winter receded, some small crevasses opened up and rivers appeared from nowhere across the main track. To cross them we were frequently wading up to our knees.

Initially, ferrying a load from Base Camp to ABC in a single push was too much. We therefore established a temporary campsite where loads could be dumped before the final long steep push up glacial moraine the following day. ABC itself was in a magnificent position overlooking the main glacier, with stunning views of Pangpema, Drohmo, Wedge Peak, Ramtang and of course, Kangchenjunga's North Face just a stone's throw away – or so it appeared.

Advanced Base Camp (Camp 1) was sited as high and as close as possible to the foot of the route. This followed a steep snow gully, a loose and exposed rock ridge and a short snow field. The ridge comprised towers of shattered blocks perched amongst razor-sharp slates. The climbing was precarious, Scottish II/III with moves of Hard Severe. The fixed rope was in constant danger of being cut and the entire line was eventually moved into the adjacent gully (where it was avalanched instead!). A variety of protection devices were used to secure the rope to the shattered rock.

A characteristic problem with this part of the route was one of perspective. From BC it looked like an easy 45° plod. In reality, it was steep and sustained mixed climbing all the way to Camp 2, some 800m above. This was the hardest part of the climb and took 17 days to complete. From below, the route looked grossly foreshortened and the cry 'Camp 2 tomorrow' every day for 10 days became slightly wearing. Halfway up, the lead climbers frequently became 'lost' in the vastness of the mountain and found it difficult to judge their relative positions and, indeed, the way ahead. Only by standing back (on the other side of the Kangchenjunga Glacier) could the full picture be seen and the key gully leading to Camp 2 identified.

As the route progressed it took more and more time to reach the previous day's high point. Progress, already hindered by daily afternoon snowstorms, slowed right down. A halfway camp known as 'Intermediate' was therefore established precariously on the ridge above the first snowfield. The line up to this point was climbed and descended many times and much time was spent improving, replacing and doubling the fixed ropes where necessary. From ABC to Intermediate took, on average, about four hours to climb.

Above Intermediate, the climbing changed in character. Far from easing off, as we had fervently hoped it would, it became steeper. The exposed and very steep mixed ridge above Intermediate was climbed for about 500ft before we realised it was a dead end. It was therefore stripped and the focus shifted to a very steep ice gully, spotted from the other side of the glacier. For over 300m the gully steepened until it reached the near-vertical 'Ice Monster', so named after its gleaming eyes and gaping crevasse for a mouth. The run-out from the gully was even longer – some 1000m straight down onto the Kangchenjunga Glacier. From Intermediate, it took a further six days to reach the Ice Monster, which proved to be the key to the route as it led up to Camp 2 and the main Gimmigela ridge. Towards the end, the load carriers were able to complete a carry from ABC to Camp 2 in a single day. Indeed, they had to, to keep the supply route open.

Camp 2 was not established until 26 April, over three weeks after our arrival at Pangpema. It was increasingly clear that at this rate we would not summit in the next two weeks, which we needed to do if we were to strip the mountain before our departure. We were barely halfway up! A rethink was needed and the existing teams reorganised. From now on, three pairs of the strongest lead climbers were selected to push hard until they reached the summit. Each pair would rotate the lead for three days and then be replaced without losing momentum. The rest of the team were dedicated to supporting the leaders and a plan was drawn up detailing individual duties over the next two weeks. Of course, its success depended upon the weather.

Camp 2, at 6350m, was perched on an excellent site with views of Makalu and into Tibet. The climbing above was open snow and ice on the main SW ridge of Gimmigela. Up to this point the whole route had been fixed; above, it would only be fixed on the steepest sections. The conditions improved with height as the winds blew away any fresh snow before it could settle. We now used only our lightest equipment, fixing 6mm ropes to reduce weight, swapping the comfort of Quasar tents for tiny Gemini assault tents and eating only freeze-dried rations. As the route progressed along the ridge and the lines of communication extended, so it became harder to support the lead climbers.

The wind and cold intensified. We had to keep moving on this magnificent knife-edged ridge with few breaks for chocolate or drinks. Twice, teams failed to reach Camp 3 because of the severity of the winds and were forced to turn back. It was here that Paul Hart was blown off; he fell a full rope length but was held by his partner, Marty Hallett. Camp 3 was established at 6700m on 4 May by Tug Wilson and Larry Foden. It was the same site as the Japanese had used some 18 months earlier and marked the end of the new ground. The route above followed their general line to the summit.

Clinging to a steep slope with an alarming degree of exposure, Camp 3 had atmosphere. But it was not as comfortable as Camp 2 and the Gemini tents were coffin-like compared with the Quasars below. Time now presented a new pressure, the amount left being measured in days. We had completed the difficult climbing but, as we climbed higher, each day brought worsening conditions. Defeat was staring us in the face.

The first summit bid, starting from Camp 3, was, perhaps, a little ambitious. And there were other problems: for instance, a huge tower on the ridge above, christened 'The Cioch', blocked the way to the summit. The team set off full of characteristic, if unfounded, optimism – into the wind. After eight hours The Cioch had still not been reached and visibility became limited by driven snow. Ted Atkins and Rob Magowan pressed on and climbed The Cioch; however, the day was nearly done and with no summit in sight, they turned back to face the long retreat to Camp 3.

A higher camp was required for the next team to have any chance of summiting. Despite deteriorating conditions and against all expectations, Pea Peacock and Bert Lane established Camp 4 at 7050m the following day. They were now above any fixed ropes and on their own. After a delayed start on 10 May, they set off into a gale. They elected to drop down from the main ridge onto the south side of the mountain, effectively bypassing The Cioch.

The climbing was initially across a highly unstable, avalanche-prone slope some 3000ft above the upper Kanch glacier. The wind was gusting up to 90 mph, adding to the sense of commitment. Time was running out and exhaustion setting in as they reached the first false summit. Pressing on, the wind forced them to drop down from the ridge until they reached a final steep ice gully leading to the summit ridge. The pair eventually summited at 1600hrs after a supreme effort and an epic climb.

My diary entry for 10 May captures the changing mood at Base Camp: from despondency to jubilation.

> On my way down from ABC I kept looking back up at the mountain. There was a jet-stream plume coming off the summit and my heart sank. No chance of the summit today and time is running out like sand through my fingers. I knew that Pea and Bert had made a late start this morning because of the wind and, no doubt, they would soon be turning back. I hope they make it down to their tent OK in this wind. When I got to BC Huan Davies told me they were 250m from the summit on their last radio call. Better news than I had ever dared hope for. At 1240, Pea calls up to say he is just 5m from the summit and is bringing Bert up to join him. He'll call again when they're both up. UNBELIEVABLE! Jubilation and congratulations all round. I grab the satcom and call up CinC Fleet (the Royal Navy Headquarters in Northwood). Create a bit of a stir by asking to speak to the First Sea Lord, (the expedition Patron), I had forgotten it's Saturday! Eventually persuade the Duty Fleet Controller that I'm serious and I am given Admiral Slater's home number. He is expecting my call in a couple of minutes.
>
> A tense and silent hour later, Pea calls to say he is still an hour from the summit and the wind is horrendous. DEJECTION! It must have been a false summit – I thought it was too good to be true! The tension in Ted's Shed is palpable for the next hour. Pea's next call does nothing to reassure us. He is now just two pitches from the summit but on a pitch of 'grade V'. I leave the shed for some relief. Looking through the telescope the summit is clagged in. Then, all of a sudden it clears, and yes, there they are! Two tiny figures crawling up to the summit! We really have done it this time! In two minutes Admiral Sir Jock Slater is personally congratulating Pea and Bert who, naturally enough, think it is a wind-up!

The commitment shown by Nigel Lane and Neil Peacock on their successful summit bid was inspirational. Despite all odds, they eventually made it to the summit and staggered back down to their tent just as darkness fell. The second bid was made two days later by the remaining four lead climbers: Ted Atkins, Rob Magowan, Larry Foden and Tug Wilson. The conditions were still cold but less windy and it did not snow. They took a slightly different line but the climbing was excellent and they enjoyed the stunning summit views denied to the first team.

We climbed Gimmigela with just one day to spare and were extremely lucky to get the necessary weather windows during a prolonged period of poor weather. The same weather caused three out of the four international expeditions on Kangchenjunga to fail. Our concern now was to get everyone down safely – always the most dangerous part. It was also our intention to bring everything from the hill down to Base Camp. In the event we left only a short section of fixed line on the Ice Monster. Everything else was recovered and carried out.

We left Pangpema on 18 May and were some four hours out of Base Camp when a shocked and breathless Tom Herries from Jonathan Pratt's Kangchenjunga Expedition caught us up. He explained that Roddy McArthur had fallen over an ice cliff and actually landed in their Camp 3. Roddy had been ill for a couple of days and was making his way down by himself when he fell. Tom actually witnessed the fall through a telescope and was not optimistic about Roddy's chances. Nevertheless, we used our satcom to call for a helicopter in the hope that Roddy was still alive. Luckily, he was. We saw him the following day in Ghunsa when his helicopter briefly touched down on its way to Kathmandu. Luckily, he made a full recovery.

Already, with the immediate demands and deadlines of work, a unique adventure is fading into a memory. But what a memory: one to be treasured for the rest of our days. My one regret is that Gimmigela kept us so busy that we were unable to explore the hidden delights that the area so obviously holds. I would love to return to Pangpema to fully explore the area and possibly to climb Pathibara (Pyramid Peak) which we actually had a permit for, but time ran out. At 7123m this fine peak still awaits an ascent from the Nepalese side. I believe the British Services may go to Kangchenjunga for a Millennium expedition but, for me at least, exploring the lesser peaks provides the greater sport and adventure, and from what I saw, there is sport and adventure in abundance in the Pangpema area of north-east Nepal.

Summary: The British Services Gimmigela Expedition, led by Royal Marine Pat Parsons, made the third ascent and first British ascent of this 7350m peak lying on the Nepal/Sikkim border just north of Kangchenjunga. They climbed the SW Ridge, over 3km in length, with a vertical height gain of 2150m. Nigel Lane and Neil Peacock (Royal Marines) summited on 10 May. Two days later Ted Atkins (RAF), and Royal Marines Larry Foden, Rob Magowan and Tug Wilson reached the summit. Before leaving Pangpema Base Camp on 18 May, the mountain was stripped of fixed ropes and garbage.

Ski Mountaineering

VADIM VASILJEV

Skiing the Clouds in the Karakoram

(*Plates 59–62*)

Three years ago, just after the Transpamirs Ski Expedition (an account of which appeared in the 1995 *Alpine Journal*), all the members of that expedition were extremely enthusiastic about making another trip, and this time we were determined to ski among the highest mountains in the world. However, none of us expected that it would take so long to make our dreams come true: obstacles to our plans seemed to appear faster than we were able to overcome them.

Perhaps our hardest task was to decide on the team itself. So many factors needed to be considered, including families, businesses, fitness, technical skills and previous experience. In the end, it became obvious that there would be significant advantages in settling for a team of only two members. At the same time, we knew that this was probably a rash decision bearing in mind that, in an emergency, we would have to rely solely on an alert satellite beacon and a rescue helicopter.

As our starting date approached we became less concerned about possible emergencies, as other more pressing matters had to be tackled. In addition to the usual problems over money, transport and equipment, we faced some obstacles which were unique to Pakistan. The rules about the restricted zones dictated that we would have to take along an approved guide, but it appeared that none existed with the necessary skiing skills. Moreover all satellite devices, even for rescue purposes, were strictly prohibited, and no insurance policy would be accepted as a deposit for a possible rescue helicopter. We had no alternative, therefore, but to stay within the open zone, without a guide, and to rely for success solely on our own skills, experience and stamina and, with luck, good weather.

We decided that the best time to go would definitely not be during the warmer months of April or May. These months usually produce a lot of foggy and snowy days, which are no fun and can be very dangerous. Both of us were familiar with the skills involved in fighting intense cold, so low temperatures were not a deterrent for us. February, we decided, was the optimum month to go, and we would ignore any adverse social factors such as Ramadan and Government elections which both occurred in that month.

The object of the expedition was to cross the Biafo–Hispar Glacier – the largest glacier system in Eurasia – via Snow Lake and the Hispar La.

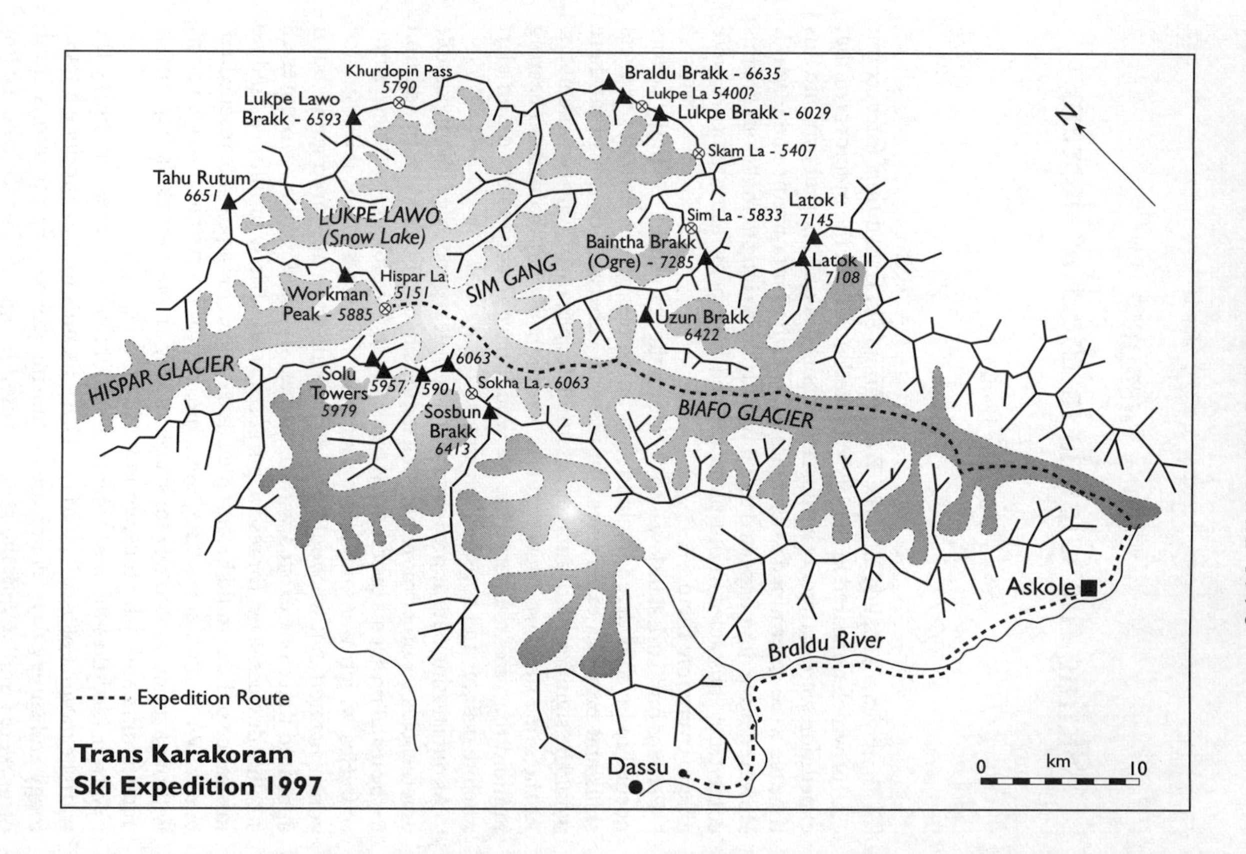
Khurdopin Pass
5790
Braldu Brakk - 6635
Lukpe La 5400?
Lukpe Brakk - 6029
Lukpe Lawo
Brakk - 6593
Skam La - 5407
Tahu Rutum
6651
Latok I
7145
Sim La - 5833
LUKPE LAWO
(Snow Lake)
Baintha Brakk
(Ogre) - 7285
Latok II
7108
SIM GANG
Hispar La
5151
Workman
Peak - 5885
Uzun Brakk
6422
6063
HISPAR GLACIER
Solu
Towers
5979
5957
5901
Sokha La - 6063
Sosbun
Brakk
6413
BIAFO GLACIER
Askole
Braldu River
Expedition Route
Trans Karakoram
Ski Expedition 1997
Dassu
0
km
10
N

Obviously, as a two-man expedition, we had to be completely self-contained and self-dependent; there would be no possibility of outside assistance or rescue. Although we knew that February would be the coldest season in the mountains, we took with us lightweight rations and the minimum of gear. Probably we were the first to ski in that area during February. We certainly met no other skiers or climbers during our trip.

It still sounds strange, but the best flight connection from St Petersburg to Islamabad was via London and Manchester by British Airways. Early in the morning of 29 January 1997 we landed in Islamabad, and thanks to the assistance of Ashraf Aman (the first Pakistani to climb K2) we quickly made all the necessary arrangements: Skardu flight booking, Ministry of Tourism briefing, and even an interview for *The Nation*.

If you are flying to Skardu, remember to look out of the right-hand window. The view of Nanga Parbat is spectacular. I still can't understand how the pilot managed to fly so low in the narrow Indus river valley, but at 8000m we were able to examine the Rakhiot face of the mountain as if it were a photograph in a book.

In Scardu we obtained everything we needed at low rates. Our hired jeep was a converted Russian GAZ (a good sign perhaps!) but it was able to take us only as far as somewhere above Dassu where a carpet of fresh snow prevented the vehicle from venturing further. This meant that our expedition route would be 40km longer than we had expected. We had hoped to be able to drive as far as the road head at Askole, but now we had to carry our 50kg loads for three extra days to reach our planned starting point. At Askole we were lucky to hire porters for the first three stages to the campsite at Mango. It was a wonderful feeling to be carrying only a third of our full load! The porters were hardworking and polite, and we enjoyed our three-day trek across the moraines.

Above Mango there was enough snow for us to start skiing with pulks in perfect weather at –25°C ; the lack of wind enabled us to reach Sim Gang Glacier on the ninth day of the trip. Our overnight camp was at about 5000m and then the weather started deteriorating. Our tent was soon weighed down with hoar frost and rocked by a strong wind. The cold was so intense that it was almost impossible to sleep. At 3.45am, after a rotten night, we started moving, but when the sun rose we felt ready to attempt the Hispar La Pass.

Snow conditions were reasonably good at first, though we had problems with the altitude combined with a strong head wind and an extremely low temperature (–35°C). But at least we were moving. Soon visibility deteriorated and we had to use a compass to maintain our direction. By noon there was a complete whiteout, so we decided to pitch the tent and take a lunch break.

Early on the eleventh day we made our first attempt on the pass. We zigzagged up the steep, undulating terrain near the foot of the pass until suddenly we found ourselves engulfed in powder snow. We tried moving over to the right where the snow was more solid but where the icefall had formed itself into menacing séracs. The nearer we came to the icefall the more dangerous the snow conditions became, so we had to retreat to the central area again. Some guys like powder skiing, provided they are going downhill. We were going uphill and needed something more stable to ski on.

We managed to pick out a route between the crevasses but several times the slope creaked alarmingly as if it were about to avalanche. For several hours we pressed on, trying to stifle our fears, and by 3.40pm we had almost reached the saddle. The highest point of the Hispar La (5151m) was only 150m away. The only remaining problem was how to cross a heavily crevassed area by precarious snow bridges covered with deep powder snow. I made three attempts to cross a snow bridge, but on each occasion my skis simply dug more deeply into the powder until the rope stopped them from falling any further. Eugene made two attempts on the right, with the same result. The snow was so unstable that it felt like skiing the clouds. The vast Hispar Glacier lay in front of us, while behind us lay eleven days of activity on the route and three years of preparations. Now we were faced with the impossible decision of whether to risk forcing a crossing of a dangerously crevassed area or of retreating. Who can accurately assess the right balance between a calculated and an unjustifiable risk?

Trying to reach a decision in these highly dangerous conditions, I recalled some similar situations I had been in before. The last one took place in February 1992 during an expedition in the Eastern Sayan range near Lake Baikal in Siberia. We were caught by an avalanche and one member of the party broke both a rib and a ski. Over the next three days the rest of us managed to convey the injured member to safety, and he was lucky to survive. Our situation was different now: we had no team mates to help us and no possibility of rescue. The choice was between putting our lives at serious risk and retreating. We decided to turn back and live a little longer.

Our ski descent to the foot of the pass was soon accomplished and we pitched camp, intending to make another attempt, further left, the next day. But morning brought with it a total whiteout through which we struggled for two more hours. These were the first and last hours of our second attempt on the Hispar Pass. We devoted most of the rest of the day to a review of our schedule and resources. The distance ahead, across the pass, was now shorter than the way we had come but was, of course, totally unpredictable. We knew that we had just enough food and fuel left to get back to Dassu in seven days. The next morning we started our descent.

On the thirteenth day we enjoyed magnificent views around Snow Lake and the Sim Gang Glacier, towards Sosbun Brakk and the Ogre. We skied in cloud for the next two days, assuring us that our decision to return had been the right one. Despite the weather we were moving fast and on the late evening of the fifteenth day we enjoyed the cry of a coyote near the Biafo snout. The great chaos of the Biafo moraines was now over and the trail down by the riverside began.

Two days later, we telephoned our former driver who picked us up late that evening in Haiderbad village below Dassu. After three hours' drive we found ourselves back in the Karakoram Inn in the centre of Skardu. Unfortunately, we had not achieved our main objective, which was to cross the Hispar La. Instead, we had climbed it and accomplished our main purpose, which was to come back alive.

Summary: The Trans Karakoram Ski Expedition 1997: two Russian skiers, Vadim Vasiljev and Eugene Orlov, tried to cross the Biafo–Hispar glacier system, the largest in Eurasia, via the Hispar La at 5151m. On 10 February this lightweight expedition reached the saddle, 150m from the top of the pass, but was forced to turn back owing to extremely dangerous snow conditions and avalanche risk. The route of 220km (140km on skis) was covered in 17 days. This expedition was probably the first February attempt to cross the Hispar La.

We are grateful to the Russian Geographic Society, British Airways, W L Gore & Associates, GmbH, Salewa-Russia, On-Top, Valvik, Krupskaya Confectionery Factory and Adventure Tours Pakistan who supported the expedition.

J G R HARDING

'Ski Mountaineering *is* Mountaineering ...'

What exactly is 'ski mountaineering'? You can't improve on Arnold Lunn's definition: 'The marriage of two great sports, mountaineering and skiing'. Lunn chose this order of words advisedly. To him mountains were sacrosant but ski mountaineering was the synthesis of mountain adventure. The sport has a broad parish and includes both Alpine and Nordic disciplines. But it is not simply a matter of climbing up mountains or cols on ski and then schussing or wedelning down them. In its purest form it is a winter voyage in which you explore new country, climbing peaks en route. To steer a safe passage ski mountaineers must possess the full range of skiing skills and techniques (arguably more difficult to master than those of climbing *per se*); they must have a thorough knowledge of snowcraft, avalanche evaluation, navigation and weather and be blessed with a climber's temperament and basic skills. Objective dangers are an unavoidable hazard.

Ski mountaineering is not a soft option. Stomping uphill for hours on end with a heavy pack in zero visibility to reach some blizzard-swept col or peak, and then getting down the other side safely through crust and crud, is as demanding as most mountain experiences.

Although improvements in equipment and avalanche safety devices have been spectacular, the ski mountaineer's basic kit – skis, sticks, skins and boots – has changed little over the years. Ski mountaineering is the most environmentally friendly of all mountain sports. It requires no infrastructure and leaves no tracks. In all, it combines the exhilaration of skiing with the drama of mountaineering. Yet, in Britain at least, it remains a Cinderella.

Why should this be? Statistics tell their own story. There are literally tens of thousands of active British skiers and mountaineers. The Ski Club of Great Britain (SCGB), representing but a fraction of British participants, has 24,500 members. The British Mountaineering Council has over 31,500. By comparison, it would be difficult to muster a thousand active British ski mountaineers. This state of affairs is somewhat mystifying given the British contribution to mountaineering generally and as the initiators of Alpine competition skiing. On the Continent, in America and in New Zealand, ski mountaineering competence is now regarded as an essential part of the all-round mountaineer's portfolio of skills, and is a prerequisite for UIAGM qualification. But in Britain the sport is still regarded as only an optional extra to mainstream mountaineering. History may provide some clues to this peculiarly British paradox.

Although the Norwegians have been using ski for millennia, Alpine skiing is little more than 100 years old. The spread of Nordic skiing was largely brought about by Norwegian emigrés (who popularised the sport in America and Australia long before it caught on in the Alps) and to Nansen's 1888 ski crossing of Greenland. But to cope with Alpine conditions, Norwegian skis and bindings had to be refashioned. In those days, the serious skier needed to know his snowcraft, and was reliant on skins, rather than lifts, to get himself uphill. To put chronology into perspective, the High Level Route between Chamonix and Zermatt was first accomplished on ski in 1911 by Professor F Roget and Marcel Kurz – 19 years before the first World Downhill Championships were run.

At this dawn of Alpine skiing, the British were up with the rest. Sir Arthur Conan Doyle's 1894 ski crossing of the Mayenfedler Furka, linking Davos with Arosa, was one of the earliest Alpine ski traverses. In 1908, a 20-year-old Oxford undergraduate, Arnold Lunn, launched himself on his personal mountain crusade. In that year he founded both the Oxford University Mountaineering Club and the Alpine Ski Club – the first of all mountain clubs to require a ski mountaineering qualification. In that year, too, he and Cecil Wybergh traversed from Montana to Villars in four days, to make the first guideless British Alpine ski tour.

In later years, Lunn was to become the 'father' of downhill racing, the inventor of slalom, the prime promoter of skiing as an Olympic sport, the founder and editor of the *British Ski Yearbook* (from 1920 to 1974) before being knighted for his services to skiing. But he remained at heart a mountaineer and, above all, a ski mountaineer. In 1909, aged 21, he had suffered a 100ft fall on Cader Idris which left one leg two inches shorter than the other. This injury was to give him pain for the rest of his life yet, within two years of the accident, he had climbed the Dent Blanche in ten hours from the hut and, three years later, had made the first *integrale* crossing of the Oberland. In 1917 he crowned a remarkable decade with his historic ski ascent of the Dom with Joseph Knubel.

During the 'Golden Age' of ski mountaineering, which Lunn dated from Wilhelm Paulke's first ski traverse of the Oberland glaciers in 1897 to his own ascents of the Wellenkuppe and Dom in 1917, several British ski mountaineers were prominent and Lunn's Alpine Ski Club (which he intended as a bridge between the Alpine Club and the SCGB) was the catalyst for much pioneering activity. Lunn persuaded Sir Martin Conway, mountaineering's first knight and a former AC President, to be the ASC's first President. Conway was an all-rounder famous not only for his exploration of the Karakoram (1892) and Andes (1898) but also for his complete traverse of the Alps (1894) and pioneer ski crossing of Spitsbergen (1896 and1897). Lunn also recruited, as early members, a clutch of leading mountaineers including Paulke, W R Rickmers, Tom Longstaff, Geoffrey Winthrop Young and Claude Schuster, along with the High Level Route pioneers Roget and Kurz.

Rickmers, in particular, was one of Lunn's exemplars. A future RGS Gold Medallist for his contributions to Central Asian mountain exploration, Rickmers had himself become an early convert to ski mountaineering and in 1903 had made the first ski ascent of the Cima di Rosso with his Scottish wife. As a German, he achieved the unparalleled distinction of twice being elected to the Alpine Club and twice deselected as a result of two world wars, before ending up as an Honorary Member. In 1903 Rickmers read a Messianic paper to the AC entitled 'The Alpine Skee and Mountaineering'. In this, he prophesied that 'skee' would 'rejuvenate the Alps' and that AC members should try this wonderful new sport for themselves because 'skiing *is* mountaineering...the best method of mountaineering in the snow'. (*AJ21, 442-455, 1903*). Few AC members took heed of Rickmer's message. In 1911, the year of Roget's first HLR Alpine ski traverse, Amundsen reached the South Pole on ski. Scott's exhausted team came in over a month later. They had never mastered the technique of skiing. Scott had always reckoned that it was better to slog it out to the Pole on foot.

With some notable exceptions, the inter-war years were not generally a period of marked distinction for British alpinism. Much the same could be said for British ski mountaineering. The Eagle Ski Club (ESC) was founded at Maloja in 1925, but overall the 1920s were lean years save for the achievements of Lunn's parties and those of certain resolute ladies such as Maud Cairney, who made the first winter ascent of the Gabelhorn in 1928, and Marjorie Pugh with her Valaisian and Central Alpine traverses of 1928 and 1929. The 1930s saw a gradual increase in guided Alpine touring by ASC members (faithfully recorded in the *British Ski Year Book*) and also the publication of a classic avalanche study – Gerald Seligman's *Snow Structure and Ski Fields*. Further afield, the British were more ambitious. Frank Smythe, always a keen ski mountaineer, almost reached the summit of Ramthang Peak (6700m) on ski in 1930; R L Holdsworth established a height record for a ski ascent by reaching Meade's Col (7138m), below Kamet, in 1931; and Sir Norman Watson, E B Beauman, Clifford White with Camille Couttet made the first ski crossing of British Columbia's Coast Range from Lake Tatla to Knight Inlet, via the Fury Gap, in 1934.

At the same time, this traditionalist era was marked by a mood of growing animosity and bizarre conflict between Britain's skiers and climbers. The Old Guard of the Alpine Club regarded Lunn as an *arriviste* for promoting the new-fangled sport of skiing and, by extension, ski mountaineering. The anti-ski faction found a formidable champion in Colonel E L Strutt, President of the AC from 1935 to 1938 and Editor of the *Alpine Journal* from 1927 to 1937, who was notorious for resisting any sort of mountaineering innovation, whether crampons, pitons or ski. Lunn's mountaineering credentials were impeccable, yet he was to suffer the ignominy of being blackballed from Alpine Club membership, before becoming an Honorary Member in 1961. Paradoxically, Lunn's magisterial *Century of Mountaineering* (Allen & Unwin, 1957), commissioned by the Swiss

Foundation for Alpine Research as a centenary tribute to the Alpine Club, remains the only historical monograph written about the Club to date. Yet, until Edward Smyth's sympathetic centenary portrait of Lunn, written 15 years after his death (*AJ94, 214-216, 1989-90*), the Club's only memorial to this most distinguished Honorary Member was the sparse obituary contributed by his close skiing friend James Riddell (*AJ80, 298, 1975*).

The outstanding British ski mountaineer of the immediate pre- and post-war years was the artist, writer and botanist Colin Wyatt who also happened to be an international skiing and ski jumping champion and all-round mountaineer with a taste for exploration. Early in his life, Wyatt had concluded that the Alps had become 'blatantly commercial', so he undertook a series of pioneer ski mountaineering journeys to wilder parts such as the Atlas, Scandinavia (Sareks to North Cape), Albania, the Rockies, the Australian Alps, Baffin Island and Kashmir.

But his *tour de force* was a 1936 visit to New Zealand at the invitation of the NZ Ski Council. With the legendary Hermitage guide Mick Bowie, Wyatt made first ascents of Mts Annan and Wilsyck, climbed a clutch of other peaks in the Mount Cook area and then made ski mountaineering history with the first double winter traverse of the Main Divide, crossing westwards via Graham's Saddle and the Franz Joseph Glacier and then returning up the Fox Glacier across Pioneer Pass. Wyatt's New Zealand visit induced the birth of ski mountaineering there (*see AJ49, 87, 1937*), yet old prejudices die hard and the man himself remains a little-known and enigmatic character whose achievements went largely unrecognised. His lyrical book *The Call of the Mountains* (Thames & Hudson, 1952) is a ski mountaineering classic, but was carpingly reviewed in *AJ59*, 361, 1953-54. His death in 1977 passed without an AJ obituary.

After the Second World War, British ski mountaineering reached its nadir. Austerity, travel restrictions imposed by currency controls and a dearth of young people with the requisite skills and experience prompted Gerald Seligman to postulate at the Eagle Ski Club's 1951 AGM that the club might either have to close or be put into cold storage. The sport appeared to have sunk without a trace in the annals of British mountaineering. R L G Irving's *A History of British Mountaineering* (Batsford, 1955) makes only one reference to ski mountaineering (and then in a Scottish context) while in the *Alpine Journal*'s 1957 *Alpine Centenary*, there are no references to ski mountaineering save in Lunn's magnanimously good humoured article 'Alpine Controversies'.

The ski mountaineering fraternity had become complacent and out of touch. But there were some stirrings. In 1956 that most eloquent of mountain writers Robin Fedden, an expert skier who had only recently been converted to mountaineering as result of his Pyrenean journeys, wrote *Alpine Ski Tour* (Putnam, 1956). Fedden's taut description of the High Level Route was an inspiration to many aspirant ski mountaineers at a time when no unguided British party had completed the High Level Route's full course. Fedden has a special place in British ski mountaineering history as the first Briton to attempt a continuous ski traverse of the Central Pyrenees. He did this in 1977 at the age of 65 with only three more years to live.

If one event can be fixed to mark the revival of British ski mountaineering, it was the Eagle Ski Club's appointment in 1960 of a long-standing Alpine Club member, Neil Hogg, to become its Honorary Swiss Secretary. In 1962, on the joint initiative of the ESC and SCGB, Hogg organised a ski mountaineering training meet at Koncordia with the assistance of such Swiss guides as the peerless Hermann Steuri. These meets were to become ESC annual events and the training ground for a new generation of ski mountaineers. They precipitated a series of ambitious 1960s Alpine tours, usually led by Terry Hartley, culminating in ski ascents of Monte Rosa, Mont Blanc, Piz Bernina, Finsteraarhorn, Dom and Aletschhorn. They also created a vigorous new climate which induced several active mountaineers, including Alan Blackshaw, Dick Sykes, John Peacock and Jeremy Whitehead, to have a go at ski mountaineering. Hartley's 1969 expedition to Iran's Elburz Mountains broke new ground, and in 1972 Alan Blackshaw and six other amateurs completed the first British ski traverse of the Alps. Blackshaw's parties followed this up with an historic North–South Scandinavian traverse on Nordic skis between 1973 and 1977.

By now, several other British ski mountaineers were entering the field to pioneer new routes. Between 1975 and 1984 Guy Sheridan's parties made the first ever Nordic ski traverses of Iran's Zagros Range, a 600km stretch of Zanskar and a section of Yukon's Mackenzie Range. Hamish Brown began his methodical exploration of the Atlas on ski and in 1982 John Cleare made the first ski ascent of Muztagh Ata (7545m). From 1981 onwards, the Eagle Ski Club became the focus of British ski mountaineering in sponsoring bi-annual pioneer ski mountaineering expeditions to Kashmir, Greenland, Alaska, Kulu, New Zealand, Mount Waddington, the Caucasus, Nepal, Svalbad and Baffin Island. On many of these Rob Collister played a leading role, with David Williams, Rodney Franklin and Rupert Hoare often in the van. Derek Fordham has been pre-eminent in the Arctic while, nearer home, others* have unearthed unusual prizes in the remoter reaches of the Pyrenees, Spain, Greece and Turkey. In 1996 John Kentish, Steve Jennings and Phil Wickens completed the ambitious Central Caucasus ski traverse previously attempted by David Hamilton. In 1997 Polly Murray and Andy Salter made the first telemark ski descent of Mt McKinley.

Many other British ski mountaineers have pioneered new routes in remote places. The Eagle Ski Club, which has had a 100% increase in membership (currently some 660) over the past 30 years, flourishes. In 1998 it sponsored 18 Alpine or Nordic tours and five Scottish meets. Indeed, Sassenachs have discovered what the Scots have always known – that in a good season Scotland has something unique to offer the ski mountaineer. A new, and in some cases not so new, generation of British professionals – Peter Cliff, Rob Collister, Fred Harper, David Hamilton, Eric Langmuir, Bill O'Connor and Nigel Shepherd, to name but a few – has emerged to instruct and guide.

* *Notably the author himself. Ed.*

What of the future? To fix the place of British ski mountaineering in today's world frame is beyond the scope of this article, but it has to be accepted that in terms of participant numbers and technique we hardly compete. Frenchmen took most of Europe's blue ribands years ago with Leon Zwingelstein's 1933 Alpine traverse and Charles Laporte's 1968 Pyrenean traverse.

In the daring arena of extreme skiing, where ski descents are made of hard ice routes and the smallest mistake can prove fatal, Frenchmen such as Sylvain Saudan (the Spencer, Whymper and Gervasutti couloirs); Cachat-Rosset (South Face Grandes Jorasses, North Face Tour Ronde, Couturier Couloir Aiguille Verte); Anselme Baud and Patrick Vallenant (North Faces of the Aiguille Blanche and Aiguille du Midi) in the 1960s and 1970s opened new frontiers. In 1978 a Japanese, Yuichiro Miura, skied off Everest's South Col into the Western Cwm, and in 1992 Pierre Tardivel made a record-breaking descent from Everest's South Summit (8760m). In 1997 an Italian, Hans Kammerlander, having climbed Everest from the Tibetan side, descended his ascent route on ski to make the round trip from his 6400m base camp and back in 23½ hours.

British successes, though more modest, have been substantial, especially in the field of exploratory ski mountaineering where initiative and imagination are key factors and where the amateur still has some advantages over the professional in being able to choose his own place and time. In spite of these achievements the conversion rate of climbers to ski mountaineering remains disappointing. In 1990 the Alpine Ski Club, the only British ski club for which it is necessary to qualify, proposed a merger with the Alpine Club to enhance the status and scope of British ski mountaineering. Sadly, in the event, negotiations between the two clubs foundered over detail. Yet although the attitude of some Britons to ski mountaineering remains equivocal, this form of mountaineering will continue to attract climbers in search of new horizons and skiers who want to lift their game beyond the piste.

As it has always been for mountaineering generally, the quintessence of ski mountaineering achievement is exploration and the pursuit of new routes. And there is still considerable scope for ski mountaineering exploration, both near and further afield. With a sense of *déjà vu*, one can only paraphrase a basic truth enunciated by our illustrious pioneer members Rickmers and Lunn, almost one hundred years ago: 'Ski mountaineering *is* mountaineering – the marriage of two great sports.'

Above and Below the Snow-line

42. Western Nepal: the Karnali River which forms the western limit of Mugu district.
(*Kev Reynolds*) (p157)

43. Taktsang monastery, Bhutan, with *Rhododendron arboreum* and prayer flags. (*Ernst Sondheimer*) (p149)

44. *Rhododendron falconeri ssp eximium*. (*Ernst Sondheimer*) (p149)

45. The pyramid of Namche Barwa, 7756m, glimpsed from the Temo La. (*Ernst Sondheimer*) (p149)

46. *Primula whitei*. (*Ernst Sondheimer*) (p149)

47. Peaks of the Central Cordillera Real seen from above the Jankho Kkota lake and mining road (*Lindsay Griffin*) (p163)

48. On the SE Face of Pacokeuta, Central Cordillera Real. (*Lindsay Griffin*) (p163)

Right
Excellent conditions on the SE Face of Pacokeuta, Central Cordillera Real, Bolivia. (*Lindsay Griffin*) (p163)

The Central Cordillera Real seen from the Island of the Sun on Lake Titicaca: *left* Chearoco, *centre* Chachacomani, *far right* the long flat-topped peak of Jallawaya. (*Lindsay Griffin*) (p163)

51. Stratified mountain and Rangdom Monastery, Zanskar, 1983. (*Sidney Nowill*) (p228)

. Tikse Gompa, Ladakh. (*Sidney Nowill*) (p228)

. Elaine Brook and friend near Rangdom, Zanskar, 1983. (*Sidney Nowill*) (p230)

54. Mulbek Gompa, Ladakh, in 1987. Built on a massive block of limestone, it is approached by a steep path, lined with prayer-flags, which winds behind the back of the aiguille. (*John Jackson*) (p225)

55. Buddhist Lamas and an apprentice monk at Mulbek. Robes the colour of old red wine. (*John Jackson*) (p225)

ERNST SONDHEIMER

A Plant Addict in the Eastern Himalaya

(*Plates 43–46*)

I can't remember when I first began to notice the flowers of the mountains; it was certainly a long time ago, and it must have been in the Alps. Some places stand out in the memory: bright yellow sulphur anemones in profusion by the snowfields on the way to the Muretto Pass; looking down on Lake Geneva far below and finding vast sheets of little crocuses where the snow had just melted; the Piz Terri in July, the ridge aglow with purple saxifrage; sheets of the Mont Cenis bellflower (*Campanula cenisia*), of the palest blue imaginable, covering high screes in the Graian Alps where nothing else would grow.

With advancing age and receding climbing power I started trying to grow alpine beauties in the garden, learning the hard way that many of them simply refuse to come down from the heights, and exulting on the occasions when I managed to make one of them feel at home. But the Himalaya! My friends were always going off on exciting expeditions there, but it seemed that these fabled regions were not for me – they were too far away, too expensive, too time-consuming; and I knew that my wife Janet would not want to come along. I had indeed read about the Himalayan exploits of the great plant collectors, Joseph Hooker, George Forrest, Frank Kingdon-Ward and the rest, and I knew well that many rhododendrons, primulas and other treasures are at home in the Himalaya. But the mountains themselves felt as inaccessible as ever.

Bhutan

All that changed towards the end of 1992 when Livia Gollancz, my neighbour and friend, mentioned that she was planning to join a botanical trek in Bhutan the following spring. Would I be interested in coming along? She showed me the prospectus: it was headed 'The Rhododendron Trek to Bhutan', and the plan was to drive across the country stopping several times to go on treks over passes. The leader was to be Ian Sinclair from the Younger Botanic Garden in Argyll, and his description started: 'Bhutan is undoubtedly the botanical paradise of the Himalaya'. How could this fail to grip my imagination? It's now or never, I said to myself. When I mentioned the matter to Janet, she was unexpectedly encouraging, murmuring something about gathering rosebuds ... That was all I needed, and I hastily booked myself in, before she could change her mind.

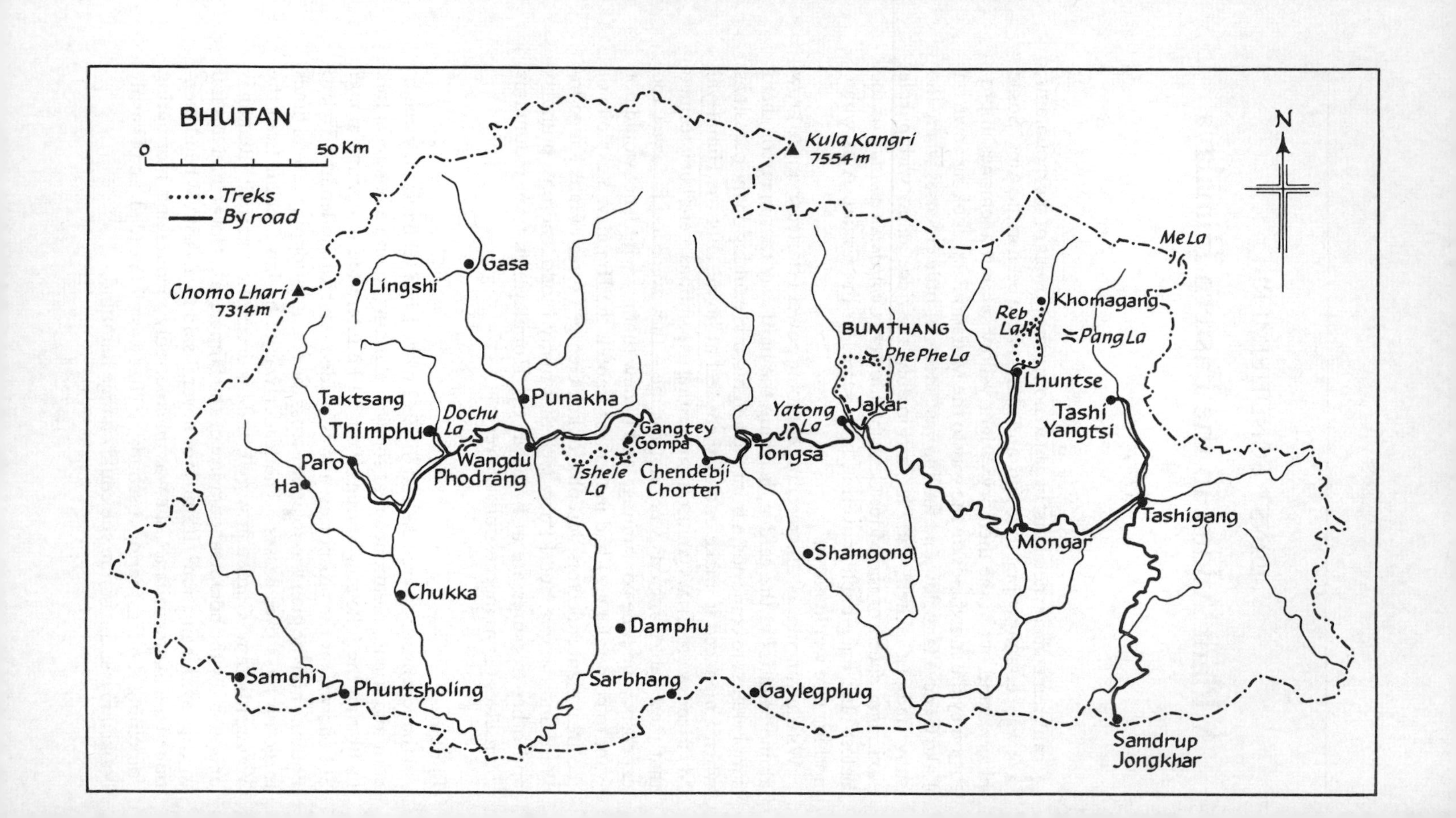
BHUTAN
0
50 Km
Treks
By road
N
Kula Kangri
7554 m
Chomo Lhari
7314 m
Gasa
Lingshi
Me La
Khomagang
Reb Lake
Pang La
BUMTHANG
Phe Phe La
Lhuntse
Tashi Yangtsi
Taktsang
Punakha
Thimphu
Dochu La
Gangtey Gompa
Yatong La
Jakar
Paro
Wangdu Phodrang
Tshele La
Chendebji Chorten
Tongsa
Ha
Tashigang
Mongar
Shamgong
Chukka
Damphu
Samchi
Phuntsholing
Sarbhang
Gaylegphug
Samdrup Jongkhar

From the accounts I had read in the *Alpine Journal,*[1] I knew that the mysterious Kingdom of Bhutan was still remote from the world, unspoilt, with very few tourists. Furthermore, this trip was to be neither a climbing expedition, suitable for hard men only, nor a brief 'cultural visit' such as was normally on offer, but was evidently a very special opportunity, under the auspices of Himalayan Kingdoms, to see and study those wonderful plants. I also realised uneasily that I would undoubtedly be among experts, and my deplorable ignorance in matters botanical would be all too obvious; but I hoped to learn a lot. I did find out, before we left, that not many plant-collectors had been to Bhutan. The earliest was W Griffith, way back in 1838; later ones included Frank Kingdon-Ward in the 1920s; but the most important were Frank Ludlow and George Sherriff, who visited Bhutan seven times in the 1930s and 1940s.[2] They introduced many of the popular plants growing in our gardens.[3] More recently, A J C Grierson and D G Long of the Edinburgh Botanic Garden have been there and are producing a *Flora of Bhutan*, part of which has been published.[4]

Our trip turned out to be in every way delightful. We were a harmonious party of ten, efficiently looked after by the staff of the Bhutan Tourism Corporation. We drove by mini-bus along the single rough mountain road, only completed in the 1980s, which traverses the country from west to east. It crosses numerous passes linking the valleys which run from north to south. This is the 'Middle Kingdom' where most of the population live, between the main Himalayan chain to the north and the subtropical jungle merging into the Indian plain to the south. Here the altitude ranged from 1500m to 3600m, and most of the time we were in forest, almost entirely untouched. Amongst the trees the chir pine (*Pinus roxburghii*), the blue pine (*Pinus wallichiana*), spruce, hemlock (*Tsuga dumosa*) and the Himalayan birch (*Betula utilis*) with its beautiful bark were much in evidence. Our skilful, patient driver was willing to stop every few hundred yards so that we could pile out to admire some rarity or other. On the treks our luggage was carried by ponies, and there were riding ponies for those who were ill, tired, or just too slow or lazy.

On 22 April 1993 we flew into Paro and were taken to the idyllic Olathang Hotel. The next day, before driving to the diminutive capital Thimphu, we went on the obligatory uphill walk towards Taktsang monastery, the famous 'Tiger's Nest', high on its sheer cliff. Here we first saw the tree-rhododendron *Rh. arboreum*, with blood-red flowers (*Plate 43*). Later on we would see it again, growing up to thirty metres high. We also admired *Rh. virgatum*, with delicate pale pink flowers; in contrast to most of the other plants seen, this likes dry conditions. (Bhutan has a moist climate, much wetter than Nepal, for example.) A pretty blue gentian might have been *G. pedicellata* – the Himalayan spring gentians are hard to identify.

From Thimphu we drove to Gangtey Gompa, a monastery set on a hilltop, where our first trek was to start. This drive took us over the Dochu La, in gentle rain, where masses of *Daphne bholua* filled the air with scent.

The forest floor was covered with myriads of wild strawberries. Beautiful yellow *Rh. falconeri* (*Plate 44*) could be seen everywhere, and the occasional *Magnolia campbellii* gleamed white in the gloomy mist. *Rh. griffithianum* had large white, fragrant, bell-shaped flowers. There was much excitement when *Primula whitei* (*Plate 46*), the lovely blue primula which wins many prizes at our flower shows, was seen, growing happily like our own primroses, on the banks flanking the road; and again when we spotted *Bryocarpum himalaicum*, a charming plant looking like a yellow soldanella.

The two-day Gangtey Gompa trek took us over the Tshele La (3300m) and finished with an exciting ride in an open box-car down 1200 metres into the valley. At the start of the trek we crossed meadows studded with a little purple primula, *P. erythrocarpa*, a Bhutanese relation of *P. denticulata*, and hedges of the yellow-flowered laburnum-like shrub *Piptanthus nepalensis*. Later we saw *Rh. kesangiae*, a very beautiful newly described species, named after Bhutan's Queen Mother, which has deep rose trusses; and, growing in a bog, there was yellow *Primula smithiana*.

Over the next two days we drove via the ancient capital Tongsa to Jakar in the centre of the country. On the first day we stopped for lunch at Chendebji Chorten, a big white religious monument, where *Rh. lindleyi* was growing epiphytically on the hemlock trees. It has huge white blossoms, and a sweet scent. Next day *Arisaema nepenthoides* with its mottled greenish-brown spathe, with white stripes on the back, was an exciting find. Later on we stopped, in rain and mist, on the Yatong La. Some of our members disappeared into the undergrowth and came back clutching purple trusses; this was *Rh. hodgsonii aff.*, never before described. Climbing Everest could hardly have felt more of a triumph, and the plant was thoroughly studied and measured (though not by me!) for most of the following night.

Our second trek was the popular Bumthang trek which crosses the Phe Phe La (3450m). Here we saw the Himalayan giant lily *Cardiocrinum giganteum*, not yet in flower; anemones in the forest (*A. obtusiloba*, white and blue); and, by the Sacred Lake of Mabartsho, yellow tree paeonies, a variety of *Paeonia lutea*. Then came a long day's drive from Jakar to Mongar, over several passes, with frequent stops for photography. The day provided a feast of rhododendrons, among them yellow *Rh. cinnabarinum ssp. xanthocodon* (one of Joseph Hooker's introductions), cream and pink *Rh. flinkii* and scarlet *Rh. argipeplum*. The rare *Rh. pendulum* was photographed by one dare-devil leaning over the edge of a cliff, with another belaying him by sitting on his legs. We also saw *Arisaema griffithii*, a fearsome-looking plant resembling a cobra about to strike.

The original intention had been to finish with a week's trek over the Pang La, a remote high pass in the east of the country, in the footsteps of Ludlow and Sherriff, but at the last moment permission was withdrawn, either because conditions were too difficult or because the Bhutanese just didn't want us to go there – probably both. So our third trek was a more modest one over the Reb La, on the way to the Pang La, which as far as we knew had also not been visited by Westerners since the days of Ludlow and Sherriff. We started along a level valley, with cannabis much in evidence, and camped high, in a field above the last village. Next day the weather was uninviting, but more lovely rhododendrons consoled us on the way to the pass: *Rh. keysii*, red with yellow tips, was the most interesting. *Coelogyne corymbosa* (white orchids) were seen in the trees on the long descent from the pass; and on the walk-out next day there were fine tree ferns and bright blue *Iris decora*.

We then drove eastwards to Tashigang, the main town in East Bhutan, and finally south to the dreary border town Samdrup Jongkhar. A brilliant yellow clump of orchids by the roadside was *Dendrobium densiflorum*, and there were more rhododendrons: *Rh. maddenii*, sweetly scented, and the unusual *Rh. dalhousiae ssp rhabdotum* which has red stripes down each flower. As we departed into India and the real world, this intoxicated visitor felt that it had been a 'Rhododendron Trek' indeed and, quite apart from the wondrous plants, he will remember Bhutan as an unspoilt Shangri La with ravishing landscape, beautiful buildings, no beggars and simple, gentle and cheerful people. Long may it remain so.

Tibet

After such a feast, the Himalaya had surely nothing comparable to offer to the plant enthusiast. Or had it? Anne Chambers, our expert on alpines in Bhutan, had mentioned Kingdon-Ward's book *The Riddle of the Tsangpo Gorges.*[5] This tells about the great Tsangpo river which, coming from the high plateau of Tibet, forces its way through the Eastern Himalaya in a big loop around the mysterious high mountain Namche Barwa (7756m), unclimbed until 1992, to become the Brahmaputra in the plains of India: the 'riddle' being the legend that there must be a huge waterfall somewhere in the deep impenetrable gorge. But it was chapter headings such as 'The Paradise of Primulas' and 'In the Rhododendron Fairyland' which stimulated more dreams ... and the Doshong La, where the weather was always evil, was the place where these marvels were to be found. Kingdon-Ward was there in 1924, and Ludlow and Sherriff had also explored the region. In recent years botanists had been hoping to make a return, but it was not until 1995, after at least one false start, that a party from the UK was at last able to go. This was under the auspices of Exodus Travels, and Anne was a member of the party. I tried hard not to feel jealous! When I heard that a similar trip was planned for 1996 I succumbed, with (admittedly) some trepidation. I would be three years older than in Bhutan, and the trek would be tougher: the 1995 party had found the Doshong La under many metres of snow and only half of them had managed the crossing. For 1996 ice axes and crampons were recommended.

On 28 May 1996 our party of fourteen, accompanied by a group of Sherpas from Nepal, arrived at Gonggar airport, 120km south of Lhasa, and were met by our Tibetan staff, with four land-cruisers and a lorry for

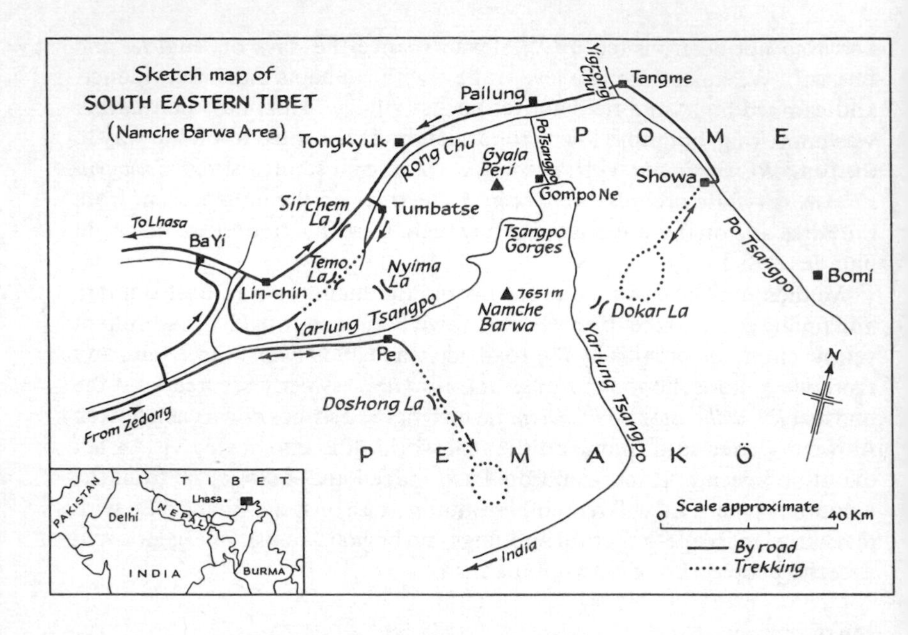

the tents and luggage. Our botanical leader was Kenneth Cox, a leading expert on rhododendrons, who had brought his equally expert father Peter; and David Burlinson of Exodus, whose enthusiasm for Tibet had made the trip possible, also came along. This time we started at a height of 3500m (and felt it!) and reached nearly 5000m on the trip; thus the plants to be seen were mostly different from those encountered in Bhutan. The next three weeks amply fulfilled our expectations: Kenneth Cox's list of plants seen comprises over 250 species, including 64 different rhododendrons, and I can only mention a few of the most exciting discoveries.

For two days we drove east along rough roads, following the Tsangpo river; gradually the arid landscape turned green, and trees and cultivated fields appeared. Eventually we camped in an idyllic forest clearing to the north of the Doshong La: masses of orange-yellow *Primula chungensis* grew in boggy ground nearby, and aptly-named bright yellow *Rhododendron wardii* filled the forest. A reconnaissance towards the pass confirmed that the snow was deep and soft, but we were declared fit for the crossing which was successfully accomplished the following day. A young Tibetan guide was assigned to me as minder, and his physical and moral support proved crucial as I plodded along, hours behind everyone else. The season was late, and flowering plants were sparse in the clearings, but creeping scarlet *Rhododendron forrestii* remains in the memory. The campsite down on the other side, where we stayed for three nights, was dank and the rain was incessant; nevertheless, when we explored the valley below we found many treasures, among them Kingdon-Ward's pale yellow 'daffodil primula' *P. falcifolia*, so-called after its scythe-shaped leaves, which is endemic to the

Doshong La. All that rain meant lots of new snow on the pass, and our return threatened to become an epic. As we had no permission from the Chinese authorities to travel into Pemakö, south from the pass, I still wonder what would have happened if any of us had failed to get back across. Fortunately I will never know.

Now the weather cleared, and remained good for the rest of the trip. Another two days of driving took us across the Tsangpo, through the green and beautiful Rong Chu Valley and eastwards into the district of Pome. On the way we admired *Clematis montana*, with huge white blooms some with pink-striped edges, drifts of yellow *Rhododendron wardii* and lovely purple *Primula tanneri ssp tsariensis*. We camped at Showa, by the Po Tsangpo river which is a tributary of the main Yarlung Tsangpo. Local porters were recruited with difficulty – there is no trekking tradition in this remote part of Tibet – but a gang consisting mainly of women and young boys was eventually assembled; fortunately their load-carrying capacity was astounding. Two days' uphill trek through superb untouched forest – elsewhere in Tibet excessive logging was all too sadly evident – took us to a camp, still in forest, below the Dokar La: this pass, which leads to the Tsangpo Gorge, was crowned with huge cornices and was evidently quite out of bounds. At the camp, as we watched the clouds disperse, a glittering icy peak, Jhulong, slowly began to dominate the view. Plants seen on this trek included blood-red *Rhododendron sanguineum*, the yellow poppy *Meconopsis pseudo-integrifolia*, the remarkable striped *Daiswa violacea* and the woodland orchid *Calanthe tricarinata*. Special thrills were *Omphalogramma tibeticum*, a primula-related rarity with deep violet trumpets, and the brilliant red *Lilium paradoxum*, discovered by an intrepid member on a daring solo scramble up steep scree. We may have been the first Westerners ever to have approached so close to the Dokar La.

We returned to the Rong Chu Valley where we stayed for three nights, botanising and recuperating. Whilst there we visited Tumbatse, the village which had been Kingdon-Ward's base; it had largely preserved its Tibetan character. Here a gracious old lady invited us into her house and offered us the inevitable butter tea, which is not nearly so disagreeable as popular opinion would have it. Then we were ready for another long day's walk, which turned out to be a most enjoyable finale. It took us over the Temo La on a good track; there was no snow, the sun was shining and I could stroll along at my own pace. From the pass Namche Barwa revealed itself as a fearsome-looking pyramid (*Plate 45*). On the long descent there were more lovely plants, including the dark red, striped ladies' slipper orchid *Cypripedium tibeticum*, a clump of blue poppies by a stream (*Meconopsis betonicifolia*, the emblem of the Himalaya), and beautiful *Primula cawdoriana*, with downward-pointing mauve tubular flowers, named after the Earl of Cawdor who accompanied Kingdon-Ward on his 1924 expedition.

Finally, on the long drive back to Lhasa, further excitements awaited us when we stopped on the last high pass, the Manshung La (4800m):

among them a curious member of the crucifer family called *Solms-Laubachia*, with pale blue flowers, and, much more striking, soft hairy cushions carrying forget-me-not-like sessile flowers of intensest blue, *Chionocharis hookeri*.

Kingdon-Ward spoke the truth. This remote corner of the Himalaya, with its wealth of rare and beautiful plants, its imposing mountains and its gentle people who are trying to preserve their customs and religion under difficult circumstances, left deep and enduring impressions. I hope to return one day, even if it means waiting for my next incarnation.

REFERENCES

1. *AJ91*, 94-100, 1986; *AJ94*, 38-51, 1989/90.
2. Michael Ward, 'Exploration of the Bhutan Himalaya' in *AJ 102*, 222-223, 1997.
3. H R Fletcher, *A Quest of Flowers. The plant explorations of Frank Ludlow and George Sherriff*. Edinburgh University Press, 1975.
4. Review of *Flora of Bhutan, Vol I* by A J C Grierson & D G Long. (Royal Botanic Garden, Edinburgh) in *AJ94*, 288-289, 1989/90.
5. F Kingdon-Ward, *The Riddle of the Tsangpo Gorges*. Arnold, 1926.

KEV REYNOLDS

Nepal's Farthest West

(*Plate 42*)

> In Nepal one can live off the country in a sombre fashion, but it is no place in which to make a gastronomic tour.
>
> *H W Tilman*

On the final pass of our epic traverse of the hidden land of Dolpo late in 1995, I sat hunched against the wind gazing west across a maze of folding blue ridges and hinted valleys to a block of snow and ice that seemed suspended in the sky. It appeared to have no connection whatever with the earth, but hung there in the distance, a misty veil between skybound glacier and blue foothill, a mountain divorced from its roots.

'What's that?' I gasped.

Kirken tapped the side of his nose and let his voice drop to a whisper, as though afraid someone would overhear. 'Saipal,' he said. Then, breathless with anticipation, 'I need to go there.'

It was the way he spoke of his need to go there that caught my imagination. It was not simply a desire, a vague wish or a dream, but an urgent, desperate craving, as though he had a duty to fulfil. No, not a duty, it was more personal than that; more a necessity to see yet another part of this globe-trotting Sherpa's own country, before it was altered for all time by the incipient tide of change led by the outside world's sometimes questionable aid programmes.

On that November pass, with frost-nip in the air, a dream was born. From my dream and Kirken's need, plans took shape so that 16 months and a clutch of faxes later, he and I, plus five of his lads who had opted to join us as porters, spilled from an overcrowded Third World bus at the roadhead of Gukuleswar, 10km from the Indian border, and wondered what madness had taken hold of the land.

Wherever we looked smoke rose from cooking fires; there were tents and awnings and a bustling, jostling, good-natured gaggle of brilliant saris and dazzling teeth, a cacophonous swell of laughter and chatter, of bells and trumpets and belching buffalo, of shrill cries and raucous greetings hurled against a background of rushing water, as the Chamliya River surged over a makeshift causeway destined not to last the day. We had arrived in the high fever of a major Hindu festival and it seemed every son and daughter of the Far West had converged on Gukuleswar to celebrate. Clearly this was no place in which to unwind from three days and nights of travel on broken roads before heading for the high country and our vague eastward traverse. When I gazed over five thousand bobbing heads to the north-east, wild-looking hills rose to unseen mountains that had thrilled me at daybreak that morning when we had lurched over yet another foothill ridge.

A week later we cowered at the foot of unseen Api with clouds at shoulder-height and snow drifting round us. Five splendid days of trekking had brought us to this rarely visited corner of the Himalaya where Nepal, India and Tibet converge at unmarked borders. It had been unbearably hot down at Gukuleswar, but up here things were different. Avalanches boomed through the swirl of twilit midday and a blast of arctic wind bent our resolve. Over a communal pot of garlic soup and a chunk of fruit cake from home, we altered out plan. Instead of trying to link the glaciers that swirled from Api, Nampa and the 'big' 6000m peaks that spread east to Saipal, we would concede to the prevailing conditions and cross a little south of the main block. Personally that suited me fine, for we would now be touching base every few days with remote settlements in isolated valleys. I had long ago realised that mixing with the people of Nepal gives as much lasting pleasure as the mountains themselves.

So we backtracked for two days, crossed and recrossed the extraordinary gorge of the Chamliya River to its eastern side and found ourselves in a village at about 3000m stuffing between us 8 kilos of potatoes and 18 boiled eggs in the midst of a group of snotty-nosed toddlers who hacked and coughed and sneezed with generous distribution. To the north, Api's unmistakable signature blazed white above the valley clouds. Local men turned the soil with wooden ploughs. Behind them children threw down handfuls of manure, while women pressed potatoes into the dung for a summer crop. The last harvest had been a good one, hence the feast of rapidly dwindling food spread before us, and it presented vain hope that such would be the case throughout our traverse.

As a sirdar and trekking agent Kirken has organised some outstanding treks off the beaten track. He is a man whose judgement I trust completely, and after listening to him grilling the village elders with regard to a possible onward route, I took it for granted that he understood all the directions offered in this curious dialect. Perhaps it was the directions that were misleading, the unwise wisdom of people who didn't really know but who were reluctant to admit it. Whatever the reason, my confidence began to wane as a couple of hours later we were plunging down a near-vertical jungle into a ravine barely twenty paces wide in its bed, then attempting to scramble up the other side, using rhododendron roots as handholds and hauling each other through tangles of vegetation. Thinking all would be well when at last we emerged from the jungle, we were dismayed as snow began to fall from a leaden sky, but at least the gradient eased as I suddenly ploughed ahead in excitement on discovering what appeared to be a vague trail, or trough, through a snowfield.

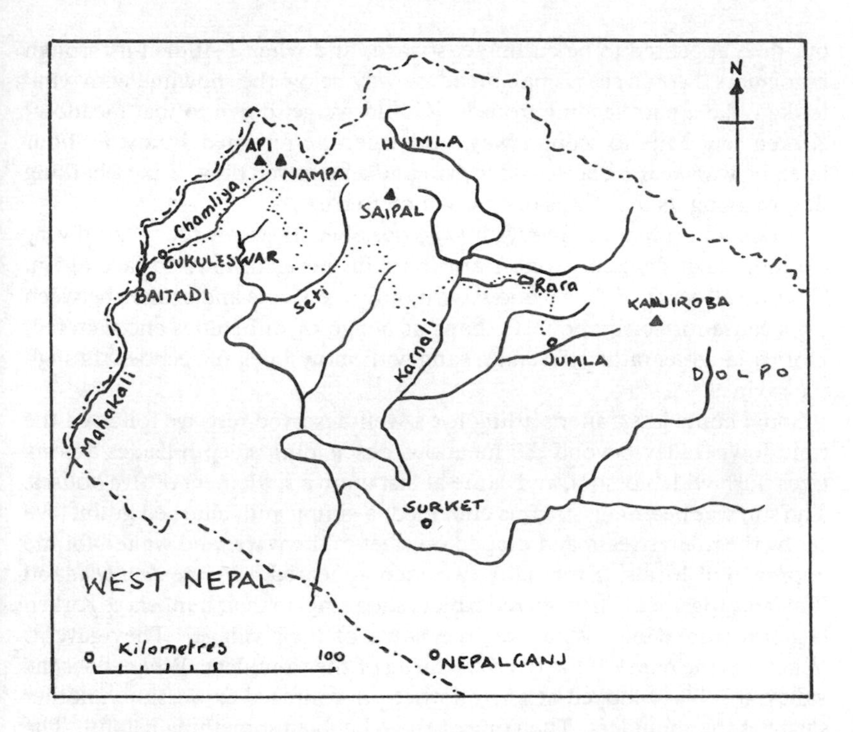

The trail led on a meandering course, topped a crest and bore left. Light was fading fast now and the snow falling heavier than before. There was no indication of what lay ahead, behind or below. Our world shrank to a few paces, but I pushed on anyway, afraid that if we stopped now the meandering course of the trail would disappear in the snow and we would be stuck. Then Kirken's voice called me back. Of course, he was right. It was too dangerous to continue, it would be completely dark in half-an-hour and our best bet was to return to the crest and dig our tents into the snowfield on the other side.

It continued to snow throughout the night, and although it had eased when day broke, we were snug within a blanket of cloud and visibility was down to a few metres. The boys were unconcerned and waves of laughter rose and fell from their crowded shelter. In recollection it was the sound of their laughter that accompanied every tricky moment, every dangerous situation, and every joyous hour upon the trail.

When the cloud lifted we scanned the far side of the ridge which plummeted into a savage glen. There was no sign of the trail we had followed yesterday, and I offered a silent prayer of thanks that we had stopped when we did. To have continued looked now to have been a suicidal option. Yet where were we to go? The map, which had unaccountably mislaid a couple of 6000m peaks, did not bother to include the valley spread before us. I checked with the compass. That valley was flowing roughly south, but then appeared to be curling eastward, and when I studied it through binoculars, I could see a small meadow way below the snowline with what looked like a path leading from it. Could we get down to that meadow? Kirken sent Mila to scout a way, and when he returned almost an hour later, he was wearing both a wide grin and a furrowed brow. Like a barking dog wagging its tail, I was unsure which to trust.

Kirken interpreted. 'He says it *looks* possible. If we are lucky. And very careful.' That descent is one I am thankful never to have to face again. That we all reached the meadow with only a few cuts and bruises between us is cause for celebration. Perhaps as a sign of difficulties encountered, Dorje's laughter rattled the crags, sang with snowslides and echoed through the ravines.

Some hours later, after settling for a well-deserved rest, we followed the trail down valley beyond the meadow, descending steep hillsides among trees flush with blossom, and came at last upon a settlement of five houses. The sun was beaming, streams chuckled, a simple mill churned grain. We sat by the main stream and dipped our feet in the water and waited for the approach of locals. Eventually two men appeared. We ate *daal bhat* and drank tea together. They offered a pipe, squatting on their hunkers as Kirken began the quizzing. What was the name of their village? They gave it. What was the name of the river? A shrug of the shoulders. Where does the valley go? They looked at one another. A confused expression, another shrug of the shoulders. Then one of them babbled something helpful. The gist of it was: 'If you go downstream for one day you will come to another village.' That was the extent of their world. A day's walk downstream.

So we followed the stream down valley and, sure enough, after a camp on a scrub terrace, came to another village. The same questions, the same uncertainties. But as our valley was now digging itself in a south-westerly trend away from where we wanted to go, Kirken encouraged one of the villagers, a hunter, to lead us over the eastern wall of mountains where, hopefully, we would be able to resume the traverse. It was an interesting morning's climb to a wooded saddle from which we gained a fine panorama of Himalayan snow peaks stretching in a line that included Indian massifs as well as Api, Nampa, the nearer Kapchuli and a jostling array of summits missing from the map. A woodpecker rattled a nearby branch, primulas poked through snow pockets, and all the world was as it should be; untroubled and untroubling.

Instead of descending the far side of the saddle, the hunter led us off to the right, twisting among trees to gain height over a bluff on a vague trail we would never have found by ourselves. Up and up it went, frustratingly, but then at last we were chasing downhill in a mad dash onto an open meadow that ought to have had a stream running through it, but didn't. We had not seen water since breakfast, and the boys were growing thirsty. The hunter led us on for another hour, then stopped on a high hillside overlooking a vast southern view where one *lekh* after another folded down to blue-hinted valley systems shimmering in the afternoon sunlight. He pointed to a gully cutting south-east and suggested that was where we should aim for. Then he was gone and we were left to our own devices in a trailless landscape that seethed with insect life.

That night on a shelf by a stream I poured sweat and hacked through the dark hours with the onset of a fever that later turned into a racking chest infection, courtesy, no doubt, of the snotty kids at the potato feast. At last we came to the Seti River, followed it upstream for a day and a bit towards Saipal, then cut off to the east on a trail that wound onto a fine *lekh* dotted with villages. A glen cut into the *lekh*, and through it ran several streams. Terraces fanned across the hills, and I remember the rich greenery of young millet, the brilliant scarlet of a woman bent double at work in the fields, buffalo complaining at the day, the far-off laughter of children. Ah, to be wandering again through such a land with little idea where you are!

One morning early, before light had properly stolen through the hills, I heard what I took to be rainfall – though no rain was touching the tent. I looked out to see in the gloom a vast flock of sheep and goats pushing along the dusty trail, their cloved hooves softly tap-tapping as imitation rain. Each animal wore a double pannier of rice, and in their wake stepped wild-eyed Humla herders, their worldly belongings carried in bundles across their shoulders.

For countless generations the people of Humla have been making long trading journeys over the Himalayan divide, using their goats and sheep as juggernauts. Now we had stumbled upon their trail, and for the next few days we shared with them the valleys, passes, river crossings and sometimes the night camps too. What privilege there was in that! What joy to cough the same dust, to drink the same ginger soup-like tea, to be bruised by the same rock-hard panniers as the animals bullied each other to pass on trails too narrow for comfort. What delight to witness an ancient procession that owed its ancestry to other millennia, unchanged and unchanging. Of a night I would sit and watch the campfires spark and crackle. Only the stars, it seemed, were older than this.

I lost all sense of time as the traverse continued, the map no longer trusted. Directions were taken by word of mouth from one village to the next, one valley to the next. It was the journey that mattered, the daily act of trekking through a land untouched by the West, among peoples for whom technology had virtually ended with the millstone. And there were other considerations too, beyond that of trying to commit mountain vistas to memory. Our food supplies had dwindled, and although we had confidently expected to be able to live off the land, those villages we came upon had little to spare. Their's was a millet and barley land. There were no more potatoes, rice was hard to come by, chickens and goats impossible to obtain. At one remote teahouse Kirken haggled for five bantam eggs. In another valley we managed to get two fish – each no more than eight inches long – but they did not go far between the seven of us, no matter how much I prayed for a miracle of Biblical proportions. Our rations were halved and as a consequence each successive pass doubled our efforts.

Then we were among the people of Mugu, whose language Kirken spoke well, and they directed us to the valley of the Khanyer Khola, the river which, despite what several authorities claim, flows from Rara Lake. Two days of wandering through the valley brought us to the shores of this beautiful stretch of water, and suddenly we knew the end of our traverse of the Farthest West was nearly over. Hungry and weak I lay by my tent and gazed across the lake to snow peaks filling the far horizon, and imagined I had been transported to Switzerland. Serene is the most apt adjective to describe this glorious place with its unspoilt forests, open grasslands, crystal water and far views, and when we departed it was with reluctance, delaying to absorb the magic of sunrise before breaking off to the south for the crossing of our last two passes.

A couple of days later we stumbled down the never-ending trail to Jumla, passing a group of perspiring trekkers heading uphill bound for a week-long circuit of Rara. As light was fading I came upon a lady doctor from New Zealand who, with her husband, was working at Jumla's leprosy clinic. She was eager to talk and we chatted for some time in the litter-strewn street. As I was about to leave in order to catch Kirken and the boys who were being swallowed by the darkness, I remembered it was Good Friday.

'Happy Easter for Sunday,' I said

'Easter? On Sunday? Oh yes, so it is! Say – you wouldn't have any Easter eggs, would you?'

Easter eggs? I wished ...

Author's note: Should any AC members be interested in undertaking 'off the beaten track' (or more conventional) journeys through the Nepal Himalaya, I can highly recommend Kirken Sherpa at Himalayan Paradise & Mountaineering Pvt Ltd, GPO Box 5343, Chabahil, Kathmandu, Nepal. Fax: 00977 1 471103

LINDSAY GRIFFIN

The Mystery of Vinowara

Exploratory Climbing in the Cordillera Real

(*Plates 47–50*)

The first expedition in the history of mountaineering to use the uncooperative llama for transport took place in Bolivia's then largely unexplored Cordillera Real. During that very successful Austro-German expedition of 1928, which knocked off three of the 6000m 'giants' in this Royal Range, Ahlfeld and Hein made the first ascent of a prominent snow and ice peak that they believed to be the highest in the range of mountains south of Chachacomani (6074m). They christened their peak Vinowara, after the marshy plain where they set up their base camp south-east of the mountain. However, their published survey of the area still left it unclear as to where exactly they had climbed.

No mountaineers were subsequently to set foot in this Vinowara Group until 1964, when Ichiyou Mukou's Tokyo University of Foreign Studies Expedition approached from the altiplano to the west and, somewhat confusingly, claimed the first ascents of both Vinowara and Jallawaya. The latter was a neighbouring mountain to which the Japanese gave a height of 5940m. Existing reference sources, such as the less than accurate *Southern Cordillera Real* by Pecher and Schiemand and *Cordillera Real de los Andes* by the legendary French alpinist Alain Mesili, have added to this confusion by talking about the 'Vinohuara Group'. This name has also been adopted by Jill Neate in her scholarly work *Mountaineering in the Andes.* Both the IGM and a more recent but less accurate Cordova map to the region introduced a new spin to the puzzle by referring to the range as Warawarani or Keakeani and designating the East Summit of Jachcha Pata as the highest at 5670m.

With such a confusing situation in existence, this little-known range of mountains, having almost 50 tops above 5000m between the Chachacomani Pass and the Jankho Kkota Valley, seemed an ideal spot for an exploratory expedition tackling new routes and unclimbed summits. OTT Expeditions and their resident agent in La Paz, Juan Villerroel, head of the loosely formed Bolivian Association of Guides, thought so as well and so a small commercially-organised expedition was born. In contrast to many of the high-profile commercial operations that command attention these days, it was hoped that the Bolivian adventure would be more in the spirit of traditional mountaineering, as well as having a minimal impact on the area.

Fortunately for exploratory mountaineers, though perhaps not for commercial operators, it is only a small minority that wants to climb peaks of which no one has ever heard. It was therefore a delight that our eventual three 'clients', Brian Gebruers, Dave Liddall and Robert Hester, were all competent climbers with Alpine experience who wanted something different.

Formerly known as a country of political instability (187 coups in its 157 years of independence), and for romantic revolutionaries (Che Guevara) and staggering economic inflation (around 24,000 percent in 1985), Bolivia has now established itself as a stable democracy, though with a per capita income of around $900 it still remains one of the poorest countries in the World. I had first visited Bolivia shortly after the Falklands conflict, climbed peaks at both ends of the Real and been enchanted by both the country and its people. Although my experiences in 1982 had involved a total transport strike, a blockade of the city and finally a military coup, I would later still consider La Paz to be perhaps my favourite city.

By 1996 things had changed. The city had undoubtedly got to grips with the 20th Century and a number of the small wood-built shops had been transformed into glass-fronted boutiques. The bowler-hatted women in traditional dress still sat knitting on the pavement, though their wares tended to be more in the line of Walkmans rather than the characteristic chicken wings, birds' eggs or sheep's heads. Even the old witches' market seemed to be a trifle short on the infamous dried llama foetus. However, the atmosphere was still full of life, colour and friendly hospitality, leaving me once again favourably impressed. And I still enjoyed the lazy luxury of 'convenience acclimatisation' – the ability to acclimatise to an altitude of *c*3700m by rigorously following a wonderfully decadent programme of simply lying in bed or spending hours relaxing in the various cafés and bars.

Inevitably, the place also has its downside. In 1982 El Alto was the world's highest international airport, its super-long runway set in splendid isolation on the windswept altiplano directly above the bowl of La Paz. However, around the start of this decade a bad summer drought, followed by a year of heavy floods, resulted in a massive crop failure which forced *campesinos* from the altiplano to take up residence on the fringes of the capital. By 1996 the conurbation of El Alto was the fourth largest and the fastest growing city in Bolivia.

The large *campesino* community also has the highest infant mortality rate in South America. Those who survive could benefit from the now compulsory primary education system but in fact only 2% either make it or are allowed to make it through school. University courses are scheduled for a regulatory five years but generally last much longer; student unrest is rife and colleges can often shut down for six months at a time. Rich kids, not surprisingly, get sent to the USA. La Paz now has a resident English mountaineering expert in the form of ex-Walsall newspaper journalist Yossi Brain.

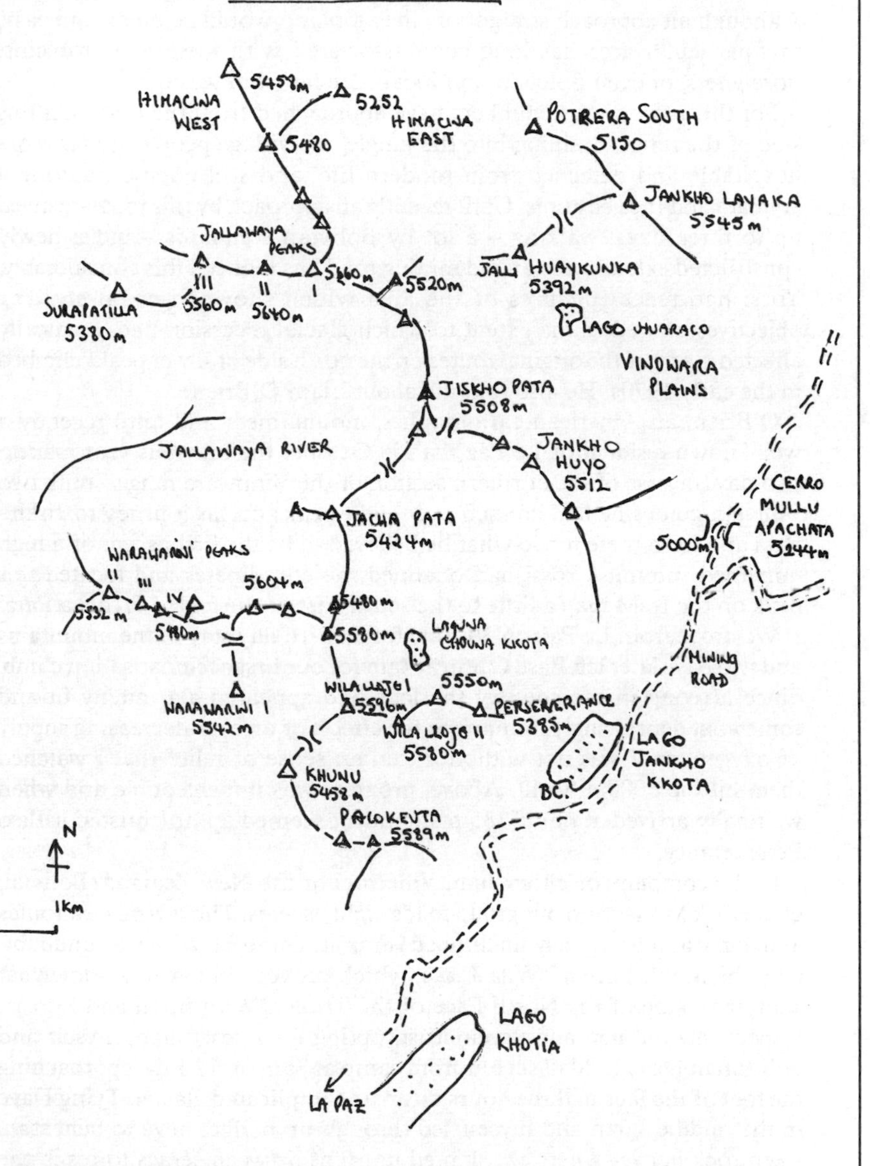

CENTRAL CORDILLERA REAL
5458m
5252
HIMACINA WEST
HIMACINA EAST
5480
POTRERA SOUTH
5150
JANKHO LAYAKA
5545m
JALLAWAYA PEAKS
III
II
I
5660m
5520m
JALLI HUAYKUNKA
5392m
SURAPATILLA
5380m
5560m
5640m
LAGO JHUARACO
VINOWARA PLAINS
JISKHO PATA
5508m
JALLAWAYA RIVER
JANKHO HUYO
5512
CERRO MULLU APACHATA
5244m
JACHA PATA
5424m
5000m
WARAWARNI PEAKS
II
III
IV
5604m
5480m
5532m
5480m
5580m
LAGUNA CHOUNA KKOTA
MINING ROAD
WARAWARNI I
5542m
WILA LLOJEI
5596m
5550m
PERSEVERANCE
5385m
WILA LLOJE II
5580m
LAGO JANKHO KKOTA
BC.
KHUNU
5458m
PALOKEUTA
5589m
N
0
1KM
LAGO KHOTIA
LA PAZ

Yossi had recently visited our proposed area and was able to talk knowledgeably about a new access road. In the past, one of the main deterrents to visiting the Vinowara region had been the relatively lengthy access time. Although an approach straight off the altiplano would be quick and easy, this particular area has long been associated with *campesino* problems. Foreigners, or even Bolivian non-locals, are far from welcome.

For this reason most climbers have approached from the east. On this side of the range, draining into the jungle, the village people are far more hospitable and detached from modern life, and still pursue traditional Aymara and Inca customs. Until recently an approach by this route involved up to three days' walking – a lot by Bolivian standards – but a newly constructed extension to an old mining road has reduced this considerably. Yossi had recent pictures of the area which showed several enticing objectives as well as the extent to which glacial recession had drastically affected many of the original routes on the north side of lower peaks climbed in the early 1970s. He also told me about Liam O'Brien.

O'Brien, an American cartographer, mountaineer and until recently a well-known resident of La Paz, had in October the previous year made a two-day traverse of the northern section of the Vinowara range. With two Bolivian guides he had crossed over eight peaks on his journey to Jiskho Pata and from there made what he believed to be the first ascent of a high unnamed summit. Yossi had obtained the coordinates and located this peak on the IGM map a little to the south-east of the fabled Jachcha Pata.

We drove from La Paz on 30 June for a 15-16 day stay in the mountains and two days later left Base Camp at 4am for our first acclimatisation climb. Since arriving in the country the lads had appeared alarmingly fit and somewhat depressingly immune to the effects of an ever-decreasing supply of oxygen, so it was not without a certain sense of relief that I watched them hit the 5000m 'wall'. Above, progress was imperceptible and when we finally arrived at our *c*5385m summit it seemed apt to christen it Pico Perseverance.

In the company of either Juan Villerroel or the New Zealand/Bolivian guide Erik Monasterio our group made eight ascents. Three were new routes and one was a previously unclimbed summit. Our best route was undoubtedly the South Face of Wila Lloje, which proved similar to a somewhat shorter version of the North Face of the Triolet. With Brian and Robert, respectively oil man and psychiatrist, opting for a rest, Juan, myself and policeman Dave Liddall set out from camp at 7am on 12 July, approaching the foot of the face in three hours up an uncomplicated glacier. Tying Dave in the middle, Juan and myself led through up perfect névé to beneath a steep rock barrier where we slanted up right between séracs to reach the centre of the face. Conditions changed as we met classic Andean snow. Almost bottomless unconsolidated powder can lie at angles up to 70° and is decidedly unnerving to climb at first, until you realise that after a month or so of generally fine weather it is just not going to avalanche

– a phenomenon seemingly peculiar to the Andes. Odd strips of ice proved technically harder but offered some security in the form of ice screw belays. Higher, the sun had crusted a thin veneer over the powder, making climbing relatively straightforward but belays largely illusory. Only deadmen the size of dustbin lids would have offered any security, so it was very definitely a case of the leader shall not fall. At one point I suggested to our rugged policeman that our best form of security would be to clove-hitch him round the waist and bury him horizontally as a belay. Being a bit of a spoil-sport he made some pathetic excuse and we were forced to continue as before, tip-toeing on egg shells to the summit.

The long equatorial night began as we set off on our descent, attempting to reverse the original 1970 Japanese route northwards into an unknown valley. Once off the glacier it was nice to be able to relax slightly and leave route finding to our hawk-eyed local. Eighteen hours after leaving we stumbled back to our camp and collapsed into bed.

With only three days remaining and a promise to keep to the other members, a much needed rest was not on the programme. After six hours' sleep we all breakfasted, repacked and set off on a journey through the northern part of the range. Initially we reversed the previous night's struggle, this time threading a better route through rough ground and moraine, admiring the spectacular mountain scenery in glorious weather. 1½ days and several glaciers later we had clipped the summit of Jiskho Pata and were setting up camp below the south-east face of a prominent fin-like peak which Yossi had marked as O'Brien's coordinates.

Never knowing what the morrow might bring, Brian and I set off that afternoon in an attempt to reach Jachcha Pata. A col, some moderate but icy slopes, steeper mixed ground and a plod up a glacier bowl led to beneath the summit ridge. A 60° slope with a steeper mushy exit gave access to easier ground and we walked up to where the ridge became steep and rocky. After one false start we took it direct – a great scramble in crampons up an exposed crest of rough blocky granite to a summit with no cairn. We felt very much in the heart of the range. The great bulk of Sir Martin Conway's 'Chisel Peak' (Chachacomani) lay close at hand. Clouds swept up from the jungle, yet to the west the view extended uninterrupted over the altiplano to Lake Titicaca and beyond. Strangely, a superb high peak rose to the north-east. Not on any map, its location has baffled me ever since. We arrived back at camp after dark. Next morning's plans to bag O'Brien's peak before walking out to the Vinowara plains were unfortunately thwarted by illness.

On our return to the UK I managed to track down O'Brien's report. Lo and behold his coordinates did not match the fin at all but the East Summit of Jachcha Pata which we had climbed. He had also done some detective work. Replotting, enlarging and superimposing existing expedition maps, he quickly realised that the Vinowara and Jallawaya of the Japanese were in fact the 5458m Himacina West and the 5670m Jachcha Pata, the heights of all the peaks climbed by this 1964 expedition having been overestimated by *c*250m. The Austrian Vinowara corresponded exactly to Jiskho Pata (5508m) – perhaps they had limited visibility on reaching the summit. As Jachcha Pata actually lies above the source of the Jallawaya River, it would seem that the original Japanese name for this 5670m peak is perfectly appropriate. With such a strong tradition of naming a mountain range after its highest peak, it seems logical that we should henceforth refer to this region as the Jallawaya Range and so put an end once and for all to the confusion that has reigned here for the last 70 years.

Summary: Brian Gebruers, Lindsay Griffin, Dave Liddall and Robert Hester accompanied throughout by either Juan Villerroel or Erik Monasterio explored the Jallawaya Range of the Cordillera Real in July 1996. Eight ascents were made: Pico 5385m (Pico Perseverance: F+), Cerro Wila Lloje II (5580m: PD), Pico 5550m (new route via South-East Couloir), Cerro Pacokeuta East and Main (5565m and 5589m: PD+/AD–), Warawarini IV (*c*5480m: first ascent of mountain), Pico 5580m (new route via West Couloir: AD+ Scottish III), Cerro Wila Lloje (5596m: new route up South Face: TD– 65-70°) and Jallawaya I (5,670m: PD+).

JIM CURRAN

Once In A Blue Moon

(Plates 56–58)

If you were brought up, like me, on a diet of early *Mountain* magazines, you may understand my misgivings when, for the first time in June 1996, I lurched out of a car hire parking lot at San Francisco airport, aiming for the correct strand of the spaghetti complex of freeways that leads to Yosemite Valley. I remembered stunning black and white photos of soaring walls, flared cracks and holdless slabs on which gaunt, hollow-cheeked hard men like Warren Harding and Royal Robbins stared, wild eyed, over bottomless voids. Why then was I, in the last throes of middle age, heading for this Mecca of world climbing? The answer lay with my companion. It was all Mac's fault.

Ian McNaught-Davis is a devout – what is the right word? – 'Americaphile' who has climbed and skied extensively from the Gunks in the east to the Valley in the west. He had assured me that we were heading for a feast of easy classics, tailor-made for our declining powers. I wasn't totally convinced. Two days later, in Tuolumne Meadows, my worst fears were realised. An Achilles tendon injury, originally acquired playing geriatric pub cricket in Sheffield, had flared up on an innocuous little route on Lambert Dome. The weather was awful (it was actually snowing gently), and I was tempted to cut my losses and go home. Then Mac, inspired, suggested a drive down through Death Valley to Las Vegas and a couple of days climbing on the sandstone of the nearby Red Rock Canyon.

Even to an old cynic like me, Las Vegas was a bit of a shock. I could cope with most of its garish excesses, but the sight of all those blue-rinsed, semi-transparent old ladies endlessly feeding the slot machines was beyond my comprehension. Couldn't someone explain to them that they weren't *ever* going to win?

After a gruesome night in a cheap motel, which obviously it wasn't, we took the local climbing guidebook's advice and got a fantastically cheap midweek deal in the Las Vegas Hilton (no kidding). We wanted one really excellent climb and after the drive and a day off, my ankle had miraculously improved. We chose a route called *Tunnel Vision*. It was 800ft long and graded 5.7 – well within our capabilities (or so we thought). In retrospect, it was an eccentric choice on grounds of shape alone, as it consisted mainly of flared chimneys and various unspecified subterranean ramblings.

Many years ago, when I was merely fat, Mo Anthoine had inveigled me into climbing the detestable *Monolith Crack*, a party piece he had perfected in his days as an instructor at Ogwen Cottage. Like Winnie the Pooh on his ill-fated visit to his friend Rabbit, I had become inextricably stuck. It was only Mo's ability to make me laugh that enabled me, through some strange convulsion of stomach muscles, to wobble up and break surface with a sigh of relief and a vow never, ever, to go near such a route again. Now, in a kind of ecstasy of self-delusion, we stood at the foot of what appeared to be about ten *Monolith Cracks* stacked on top of each other. Anyone in the State of Nevada could have told us that we were about to make a big mistake.

After two or three relatively easy pitches Mac set off on what was to be the lead of the trip: up an imposing flared chimney that looked horrifyingly unprotected. Eighty feet of squirming brought him to a point where the chimney narrowed and both walls overhung. Mac was seriously worried: 'If I can get some decent protection in you can lower me off – this is absolutely desperate.' After fiddling around for ages, the unwelcome news fluttered down that it was useless. Not trusting it, Mac climbed a few feet higher and at last slotted in a perfect nut.

'Might as well carry on now,' he muttered, before shooting up the last twenty feet to a belay and a whoop of delight. (From him, I scarcely need add, not from me.) Strangely, though, I climbed through the lower constrictions quite easily. Knowing that I was even bigger than Mac, I had watched him carefully and managed to unlock the combinations without too much trouble. Relieved, I started the steep moves at the top. I was appalled. What Mac had made look so easy I found to be the living end. Apoplectic with fury, wasted energy and the desertion of every bit of technique I ever possessed, I was hauled onto the ledge by Mac, only for him to have to endure a tirade of abuse instead of the congratulations he richly deserved. He heard me out.

'Oh Jim, I do enjoy your company' was his disarming remark, accompanied by a beatific smile, as I subsided into grumpy silence.

Above this the climb was easier, although increasingly peculiar as we climbed through a weird landscape of sandstone features vaguely reminiscent of the Old Man of Hoy. We arrived at the pitch that gave the climb its wholly appropriate name. Mac's lead again, and he disappeared into the bowels of the earth behind a monstrous flake. Eventually a faint shout, followed by a piercing whistle, jerked me back to reality. I disentangled the belay and set off to see what was coming next. Or rather not see, for I was immediately plunged into inky darkness. As the ropes led upwards I followed, wondering where I was going, until I could hear Mac somewhere up to my left.

'Walk along the ledge.'

'Oh really?'

'Well, I think it's a ledge.'

Blindly I groped, shuffled and slithered towards his voice. Suddenly there was a flash as Mac took a picture, which later provided us with the only visual evidence of the whole pitch. I emerged into daylight on the other side of the flake. After that, two long pitches led to the top and partial satisfaction, for the route description of the descent was incredibly complicated. Amazingly, though, we got it right for once and a couple of hours later the blue-rinsed old ladies in the foyer of the Hilton were treated to the sight of two grinning dust-encrusted climbers in torn and dirty T-shirts, carrying their ropes, boots and racks of gear to the lift. In the London Hilton we wouldn't have made it through the door. Here we could have carried ice axes, worn crampons and full down suits and nobody would have batted an eyelid.

Two days later we were back in Yosemite and Mac's master plan was revealed. *Snake Dike* is on Half Dome and is a route Mac had failed on with his son Simon several years previously. Ominously it was again graded 5.7, which seemed to cover a multitude of sins .

Half Dome, seen from the viewpoint of Glacier Point, is a wonderful but wholly misleading sight. The huge, apparently vertical, blank face in front of you is in fact a slab set at a gentle angle and easing all the way to the top. We decided to bivvy near the foot of the route and plodded up the Half Dome trail past the impressive Vernal and Nevada Falls in the heat of the afternoon, carrying, as usual, ridiculously heavy sacks. Our prospective bivouac site was not exactly cramped – about three acres of flat ground – but Mac and I stayed sufficiently close together to assuage our terror of bears, but far enough apart for him not to resort to extreme violence at my snoring. (At one campsite, during a sleepless night, Mac had seriously considered tying all the guy ropes of my tent to the hire car and towing me out of earshot.)

Just before we settled down we were surprised by the arrival of three young superfit Californian climbers; two youths and a girl. They explained that they were off to do a nocturnal ascent of *Snake Dike*, to celebrate a 'blue moon'. I, for one, was unaware that such a thing existed outside popular songs, but was informed that the phenomenon occurs when there is a full moon twice in the same calendar month. Tonight would be such an occasion and, what's more, would happen in a cloudless sky. They invited us to join them, which we declined without too much trouble, and wished them well before settling down to sleep in what, as the moon rose, seemed like broad daylight.

At dawn (which was noticeably darker than the rest of the night) we set off, and I could easily understand how Mac and Simon had got lost, particularly as they had strayed into an area of fallen trees blown down in a recent storm. This time we found the devious trail, which was still in shadow, leading to the foot of the route.

What can I say about such a superb climb? Like all classics it takes the easiest line through a huge area of much harder rock. It is never much more than good British VS but, and it is a significant 'but', the protection is minimal. Those who shudder at the mention of the world 'bolt', should get themselves on the upper pitches which are probably no more than Severe but have only one bolt runner between each bolted stance. There is no natural protection at all. The climbing is exactly the same standard throughout, move for move, but feels much harder as the fall potential grows, particularly if, like Mac, you fail to notice a protection bolt and climb past it, giving a possible 100-metre fall, plus rope stretch, if you come off just below its stance!

In fact Mac was climbing really well, as he had done the entire trip, whereas I had long succumbed to the 'Oh God, what am I doing here?' syndrome, a question that was not difficult to answer as far as the view was concerned. What a stupendous place! Once you are above the valley, Yosemite is as wild and beautiful as anywhere in the world. Here, the views across to Glacier Point and down towards the unmistakable profile of El Cap, now below us, were sublime.

As we gained height the angle eased. Suddenly, in the middle of a long run-out, I made an amazing discovery: I could stand up and walk! After another pitch we unroped but kept our rock boots on all the way to the top, for a slip here would be both embarrassing and, shortly afterwards, terminal. The last few hundred feet seemed to take forever. It was scorchingly hot and windless. I was puffing, but of course Half Dome is nearly 9000ft high. Could I be about to succumb to the lowest ever case of pulmonary oedema?

Eventually we arrived at the flat summit, along with dozens of hikers who had flogged up the Half Dome Trail and braved its extraordinary and rather frightening line of ladders up the final few hundred feet. Descending them, against the panic-stricken hordes coming up, was interesting, with one severe case of hysterics to contend with. Luckily Mac quickly calmed me down and the descent passed off without further incident. We were happy and fulfilled.

Later I read the account of the first ascent of *Snake Dike* in Steve Roper's excellent *Camp IV – Recollections of a Yosemite Rockclimber*. As you may imagine it was a bit of an anti-climax to find it described as 'a perfect beginner's climb'. I will never be a hollow-cheeked, wild-eyed hard man. Ah well ... so what?

The Big Issues

Note: The views expressed in this section are those of the individual authors and do not necessarily reflect the views of the Alpine Club, the *Alpine Journal* or the Editor.

Leader-placed protection techniques
This term covers the placement and subsequent removal of nuts and Friends for protection while free-climbing a route. Even hand-placed pitons can be treated as nuts. It does not encompass preplacement of nuts from an abseil, though this is preferable to placing bolts. Although the old American/ Alpine style of piton placement and removal could be described as leader-placed protection, this process is largely moribund on free climbs and the term is thus not generally intended to embrace those past protection methods, though they did rely on weaknesses in the rock and thus demanded a full range of skills from the user (unlike bolting, or clipping in-situ bolts). In free climbing, piton use for making solid belays might still be considered a valid (though unfashionable) technique on certain types of cliffs (eg loose sea cliffs).

KEN WILSON

A Future for Traditional Values?

Will rock climbing degenerate into 'theme park exercise'?

(*Plate 71*)

The rigging of rock climbs and mountain routes with bolts, stanchions, abseil anchor rings and fixed ropes makes them safer, easier to follow, and simple in retreat, thereby eliminating the need to carry heavy gear – nuts and pitons, plus the mountaineering equipment for devious descents. Pat Littlejohn's article in last year's *Alpine Journal* (*AJ102, 184-187, 1997*) described the 'theme park' attitude to climbing which is now spreading all over the world, despite the existence of excellent portable protection equipment. In the same volume Paolo Vitali offered a defence of bolt placement and even of retrobolting (*AJ102, 181-183, 1997*). The climbing world is thus facing a choice. Should mountains and cliffs be allowed to remain, wherever possible, free from fixed gear, thus retaining their basic character and challenge, or should the trend towards 'theme park' rigging be accepted as inevitable – a process which will, if uncontested, eventually result in all climbs involving awkward rock climbing being bolted?

These two articles made a stimulating contribution to a somewhat overdue debate to which I have been asked to contribute. As a modest climber, my views on harder climbing may lack the authority of a major participant. However, a modest climber, well versed in British, European and American rock-climbing mores, is perhaps better placed to comment on the pros and cons of leaving cliffs free from fixed gear. The easier climbs derive much of their challenge from the absence of fixed protection, and their character would be dramatically changed by any equipping policy.

The origins of leader-placed protection techniques*

The development of nut and other leader-placed protection devices during the last 40 years is one of the great success stories of climbing, in that these devices have allowed countless cliffs to be explored without the mass use of ironmongery. They originated from techniques applied during the first ascent of the East Buttress (*Piggot's Climb*) of Clogwyn Du'r Arddu in North Wales in 1927. Chockstones with slings wrapped round them and linked to the climbing rope, first by threading and later with karabiners, provided some protection for climbs in Britain until the early 1960s. (Slings draped over spikes were also used.) At that point it was discovered that reamed engineering nuts fitted to slings would do the same job with greater economy.

* See note on opposite page.

There followed three decades of steady nut development, culminating in the invention of the Friend and a variety of similar camming devices.

There had already been 40 years of rock-climbing development in Britain when *Piggot's Climb* was pioneered. Most of the easier lines had been done and climbers were eyeing the steeper buttresses; some were even considering placing pitons in order to protect their climbs. Thereafter a strong movement took place to avoid the use of pitons. Climbers worked hard to find subtle routes up the cliffs, with places to rest and spikes that they could use (together with chockstones) to provide some form of protection. A strict code developed that 'the leader must not fall' and that he/she should always be able to climb down whatever had been ascended. This policy may have prevented British climbers from reaching the high technical standards that were being achieved in the Alps, but it did lay the foundations for a purer form of rock climbing. The rejection of pitons during the inter-war years resulted in hundreds of interesting and challenging rock climbs being pioneered in Britain, with standards averaging S/VS (5.5–5.7 or Alpine 5) and a few as high as HVS/5b (5.9 or Alpine 6). What the climbs lacked in technical difficulty they amply repaid in intricacy and excitement.

In the Eastern Alps the great piton debate was conducted during the years before and after the First World War. Throughout the inter-war years piton protection assisted the development of rock climbing in the Alps and probably also on the the smaller training cliffs (*Klettergarten*) of mainland Europe. It is important to realise that many of the Alpine pioneers used pitons sparingly, as their soft metal meant that they deformed easily and, once placed, they were best left where they were. This had a rationing effect on their use and many of the Eastern Alpine rock climbs of the period, by climbers such as Solleder, Wiessner, Steger, Carlesso, Andrich, Tissi, Comici and Cassin, were still very bold and exceptional ascents. In the Western Alps some climbers like Armand Charlet resisted the use of the piton, while others (Allein, Greloz, Roch, Lambert and Gervasutti) had no such qualms.

Thus, while Britain shunned the piton, Europe adopted it. This was understandable in view of the sheer scale of the cliffs involved. Anyone setting out on a big Alpine rock climb in the thirties would have been very unwise to do so without carrying pitons, if only for retreat. Those tackling the much smaller British cliffs, however, chose to adopt a more sporting approach which, in hindsight, still looks surprisingly bold on routes like *Great Slab* on Cloggy or *Great Eastern* on Scafell. Two distinct sporting traditions developed, as was demonstrated so forcefully by the *Munich Climb* incident on Tryfan in 1936 when visiting German climbers used pitons on a British first ascent. Outraged local experts immediately removed them.

The postwar position

After the Second World War there was a slight increase in piton use in Britain. For about 25 years they were used sparingly on the hardest climbs but once nuts had been fully developed they were systematically removed, though they did continue to have a role, particularly for belaying, in sea-cliff exploration. There was also a brief period when post-war climbers practised aid climbing to prepare themselves for the big routes on the Dru, the Tre Cime and, later, Yosemite. This took place on a few clearly defined cliffs and, in general, did not disrupt the mainstream cragging tradition.

In the Alps British free-climbing prowess (developed on gritstone and on Clogwyn Du'r Arddu) was demonstrated on the West Face of the Aiguille de Blaitière by Joe Brown and Don Whillans by a new climb which subsequent parties were soon forced to rig with fixed aid points (wooden wedges). There were many good continental climbers around at that time. Their best performances were in the Dolomites where climbers like Aste, Sussati, Phillip, Brandler, Hasse and later Messner, Gogna and Cozzolino established fine routes in good style. Other climbers, of lesser ability, were forcing climbs with hundreds of pitons and bolts, however, and were even placing bolts to overcome the difficult sections of existing climbs. This incurred the wrath of Reinhold Messner whose essay 'Murder of the Impossible' (*Mountain 15, 1971*) was a stinging rebuke of such practices and stiffened Eastern Alpine ethics at a time when they threatened to get totally out of hand.

The international growth of leader-placed protection techniques

British nut protection techniques received a massive boost in the late 1960s when they were adopted by leading American climbers. American protection techniques (which involved constant placing and removing of pitons on both free and aid climbs) were causing such damage to cliffs that it was clear that something had to change. Ironically, the piton removal ethic had been prompted by the conservation ideas of John Muir and the Sierra Club. Yosemite climbers were seeking to avoid leaving their cliffs littered with old pitons, as in the Alps. This led to the development of hard metal pitons that could be used and removed again and again. The popular routes thus got more and more scarred, so enlightened climbers like Royal Robbins and Yvon Chouinard started to use nuts brought over from Britain. Once Chouinard and his partner Tom Frost began to manufacture and market them (with more sophisticated designs and skilful, conservation-linked, publicity) their adoption throughout the United States, for both aided big-wall climbing and conventional crag climbing, was rapid.

By that time the main European rock climbs were littered with pitons that had proliferated after the first ascents. But when European climbers, plus those from other climbing nations, began visiting the United States in large numbers to sample its large-scale rock climbs, they soon accepted the superior ethics they found there and took them back to their own countries. The 1970s therefore saw fledgling leader-placed protection movements beginning in France, Germany, Italy and Switzerland.

There followed a period when a few major Alpine rock climbs were pioneered using leader-placed protection techniques, notable examples being the Pumprisse in the Kaisergebirge and rock routes on the Charmoz by

Cordier and the south side of Mont Blanc by Italian teams. The whole process was strengthened worldwide, particularly on smaller cliffs, by travelling climbers such as Henry Barber, John Allen, John Ewbank, Kim Carrigan, Pete Livesey and Ron Fawcett who demonstrated fierce free climbing using these techniques. Unfortunately this 'ultra-pure' phase in the 1970s and early 1980s was too short to take deep root in most countries. It should have led to novices being introduced to the techniques at an early stage. Unfortunately this did not happen. *Klettergarten* remained piton-rigged and young climbers seem not to have been encouraged to learn the new techniques.

Parties carried nuts but often these were seen as gear for experts, rather than fundamental gear for all climbers. Despite the enlightenment of a few, the mass of European climbers never changed their ways. From the early days, they expected rock climbs to be fully pitoned (just as hill walks were waymarked). The piton at least had to use cracks and was thus guided to some extent by what the mountain had to offer. But during the 1970s climbers seem to have got out of the habit of carrying hammers and pitons, and thus be able to take responsibility for their own protection or abseil anchors.

Meanwhile, with good protection, standards had rocketed, a process also aided by the advent of climbing walls. The big international proving grounds like Yosemite and Verdon encouraged the best climbers to demonstrate their skills. Soon conventional local cliffs seemed too easy. It was clear that, provided good protection could be found, far steeper cliffs could be tackled. Leader-placed protection was difficult and strenuous to place securely in such situations. Moreover, these steeper cliffs (they were often limestone) were frequently crackless. Bolts were the answer.

The bolt gun arrives

This was the position in the early 1980s. At that moment an important new invention became easily available – the cordless power drill. This was a device that allowed the rapid and efficient placing of bolts, particularly when dangling down an overhanging cliff or, when lightweight versions appeared, leading Alpine rock climbs. A number of cliffs in southern France were developed in this way with some very hard and spectacular climbs. Soon climbers everywhere were rigging up their own local overhanging cliffs and 'working' their own set of desperate routes.

It is doubtful whether this type of climbing could ever have proliferated without the power drill: previously walls of this type had been unclimbable unless they had already been ascended by aid climbers, eg Ravenstor and Kilnsey. Even top-roping was not feasible, as the pendulums involved would have been too great. The problem was that the power drill was soon applied to cliffs that might have been climbed without it. As such its appearance may come to be seen as a black day for climbing.

Hitherto, the bolt, piton and leader-placed nut had reached a satisfactory balance. The bolt was tiresome to place, thereby limiting its use, and nut techniques had developed to such a point of sophistication that they rendered pitons, apart from the thinnest blades, virtually unneccessary. Various short-cuts for aid climbing, such as bat hooks, bashies and rivetting, had developed but all were precarious. The nut and the Friend were poised to conquer the world. Had they done so, it would have been a tremendous boon to both adventurous climbing and conservation.

In Britain most of our cliffs enjoy this sublime state. Walk to the bottom of Cloggy or Stanage and the situation is the same today as it has always been: a cliff without any sign of iron – either bolts or pitons. The guidebook must be read, however. The route must be located and assessed and judged constantly as one progresses, with an eye to its exact line and its protection possibilities. Thus the outcome and the attendant quality of adventure remains in doubt until the route is finally climbed and its secrets divulged. Moreover, in conservation terms, our cliffs remain free from paraphernalia. Even on hard limestone cliffs like Rubicon Wall, some very bold routes had been done without it. The same boast could be made (in general) of places like the Shawangunks and large tracts of Yosemite.

Sport climbing and the cordless drill

The cordless drill has changed all that. A new generation of hard over-hanging climbs was developed, resulting in very demanding, highly spectacular but generally safe 'sport climbing'. Some climbers liked this, as they could still appear to be performing at top levels without taking any great risks or undergoing any arduous inconvenience.

If these developments had remained on the very overhanging cliffs they would have presented no great problem. But they spread to other cliffs. Big semi-Alpine cliffs were tackled and, worst of all, the smaller crags, often with quite easy climbs, were also fitted up. Each of these 'sport' cliffs was also rigged to allow quick abseil descents or lower-offs, thus enabling climbers to escape in the face of bad weather or to avoid awkward, circuitous, and frequently dirty and dangerous descents – the previous prosaic inconveniences of the sport. Thus, freed from rock climbing's tiresome and time-consuming aspects, a new sort of sybaritic climber began to develop who expected to be confronted solely with the route. At a stroke there developed a breed of sun-worshipping activists secure in their own technically focused world.

A number of groups popularised this type of climbing. Firstly there were leading technical climbers (in Britain these included many who had a fine adventure climbing record) who wished to concentrate on pushing the frontiers of technical difficulty, free from the 'distraction' of risk. In France this group acquired high publicity and glamour which soon led to demands for easier climbing to be protected in the same manner so that everyone could take part. The cliff protection organis-ation, COSIROC, took these demands to heart and instituted a bolt-equip-ping programme on many cliffs, all in the name of *egalité*.

In Britain those actually toting power-drills (with one or two exceptions) tended to come from the group that some people have referred to as 'B team climbers' – those who are not in the top rank but who would like to be seen as such. This is an important group, as they were the ones who, in the past, made an informed and appreciative audience that identified and lionised the greatest climbs and sought to repeat them. In effect, they cemented the culture. With the appearance of very hard and serious adventure climbs, like *Indian Face*, *Beau Geste*, *The Bells, the Bells* and *End of the Affair*, it may be that this group psychologically surrendered, admitting that the game had become too tough to emulate. Sport climbing provided the way out: the opportunity to excel but without the now awesome risks.

Instructional groups and outdoor centres also yearned to place bolts. In Britain bolts appeared (but were quickly removed) on some training crags – amidst genuine outrage. It is clear that those involved in using cliffs for novice training would like to fix anchor points at the top, but in Britain the established ethical conventions do not allow it. Elsewhere the conventions are less rigorous.

The removal of the allegedly tiresome inconveniences and discomforts of the sport also encouraged more women to take up climbing. Bolt-protected sport climbing (particularly in the controlled climbing-wall setting) has clearly proved a female attraction where previously there had been (for whatever reason) far more circumspection. Sport climbing removes the need to hang around to securely place 'tiresome' nuts. Clipping quick draws to bolts on sunny cliffs or in warm gymnasiums rigged up for easy descents is an altogether more user-friendly activity. Female nimbleness, dexterity and better power-to-weight ratios could thus be fully exploited on the actual climbing. At the same time there are male climbers who now avidly climb with their wives and girlfriends in a sport-climbing setting but steer clear of major adventure climbs, with the possibility of long falls onto dodgy gear. There are, of course, many notable exceptions to these generalisations. I know a number of women climbers who are just as obsessive about their next big adventure leads (in all grades) as any male enthusiast. There are, in addition, groups of extremely bold and innovative female climbers who are actually taking the lead in hard traditional new-route exploration (where previously women had been notable by their absence). It may be that this has been facilitated by the more comprehensible entries to the sport provided by climbing walls, sport climbing and competitions. Alternatively, it may just be a manifestation of the fact that women are now beginning to challenge men in many of the hitherto male-dominated sporting activities.

Another group seems particularly enthusiastic about bolted climbs – ageing experts. These types got hooked on the buzz of the adventurous 'big scene' in their youth and wish to continue to climb on hard rock but without the adventure risks. This group often includes some of the boldest participants of the past, who for some reason seem unconcerned to see the old values steadily being dismantled.

How the bolting changed climbing

In Britain the new bolt-protected rock climbs were (until recently) put up mainly on very hard and steep cliffs, most other cliffs having already been developed with a matrix of traditional rock climbs, recorded in guidebooks and protected by tradition. This was not the case on many continental cliffs where much of the small crag climbing, piton-abused from the start, seems to have failed to generate a respectful tradition and history. This situation was made worse by the absence, for the smaller cliffs, of official guidebook systems. In Britain these are published by the main clubs and edited by climbers of long experience and bent on ethical rectitude, but in Europe this type of official guidebook tradition is focused only on the main Alpine areas – the guides of the CAF, CAS and CAI being exceptional in terms of quality and historical accuracy. Many of the smaller cliffs have been left to private *ad hoc* publishing ventures with little on-going tradition and continuity. Good guidebooks are essential if there is no obvious signs of passage, such as a line of fixed pitons or bolts. Such climbs and guidebooks also encourage more careful study and assessment of the cliff. On the continent descriptions in one language are more difficult to popularise for crags where multi-lingual solutions are sought – here the ubiquitous topo guide, giving the grade and general position of each anonymous line of bolts, is a further convenience provided in the rise of sport climbing. With the absence of this culture-of-care ethic, many European cliffs rapidly succumbed to the bolting made possible by the cordless drill. Now, in Britain, private guidebooks, imbued with the sport-climbing culture, are beginning to appear, offering a supposedly 'modern' ethic that is starting to bypass the traditional approach.

Another factor should be mentioned – the advent of the package-tour, low-stress holiday. Climbers of an adventurous bent, who might normally seek to test themselves against one of the great rock or Alpine routes (with all the heart-searching commitment that involves), are happy to patronise safe sport climbing in places like Costa Blanca, Majorca or Tenerife.

In more central areas of Europe, despite the presence of a regular local clientele, the cliffs are being steadily bolted. Saulges, for example, is a typical limestone cliff near Le Mans with climbs of all grades. It was originally developed by aid climbers; the routes are now mainly free but all are bolt protected. On a quick visit I sampled two routes, both based on easily nut-able cracks, both 'well' bolted, to use the usual weasel word. While I was there I witnessed an instructor toting a large box of drilling equipment for bolting a face of manifestly easy climbing.

On the Martinswand in the Vosges, a sort of hillside Bosigran with plenty of nut-able cracks, Jean Pierre Bouvier noted in his guidebook *Rock Climbing in France* that the pitons had been removed to encourage nut use, but when I visited the cliff in the late 1980s new bolts sprouted everywhere.

Near Landeck, a band of crags called *Affenhimmel*, above the main road to the east of the town, offers Tremadog-style climbing of some interest, with many cracks and obvious lines with an average VS/HVS standard.

The recently-developed cliff was 'well' bolted and each route was paint-marked, numbered and titled. I asked the opinion of an obviously old and experienced climber who was there with his son: 'Surely this is terrible?' I suggested. 'It's only a training crag,' he shrugged. 'It won't happen in the mountains.' Herein lies the cultural difference between (mainland) European and British climbing. Many European climbers never seem to have regarded their smaller valley cliffs as a valuable resource on which to develop a climbing system of real rigour. The lower Dauphiné cliffs around Briançon, for example, were recently all retrobolted and this was announced as a triumph by local guides who value the convenience and safety as they ply their trade.

In northern Europe, at least, it seems that rigour increases the further one travels away from the Alps. Britain, Fontainebleu, Brittany, Saxony and areas of Scandinavia, for example, maintain tough ethics. There are exceptions to this, however. Freyr in Belgium is pretty raddled when it should, in the 1970s, have developed an ethic akin to the Avon Gorge or Tremadog. The cliffs of northern France are a curious mishmash of mixed ethics (Mortain, Clecy, Ile-aux-Pies etc), and Le Saussois which should have an ethic as tough as High Tor or Stoney Middleton is steadily succumbing to the bolt. Val de Mello in Italy, an area that developed demanding slab climbing in the 1970s (like Tuolumne or Etive), is now, if Paolo Vitali is correct, to be subjected to retrobolt protection. St Victoire in Provence, for years an area of challenging ethics, now sprouts new bolts all across its lower tier. Sooner or later these will spread to the cliffs of the upper tier.

At this point, I must mention the minimalist bolted routes of the Remy brothers, Kaspar Ochsner and Michel Piola. These can be found on the big limestone escarpment cliffs and the granite walls and slabs of Central Switzerland (Salbit, Graue Wand, Bühlenhorn, Grimsel, Fiesch, etc) and on convenient facets in the Chamonix Aiguilles (Grépon, Charmoz, Blaitière, Petites Jorasses, Grand Capucin, etc). These climbs, with bolts usually placed on the lead (initially by hand, but later utilising lightweight power drills) also involve the use of nuts and Friends. They allow spectacular climbing in big mountain settings where the lightly-rigged climber can cavort on cliffs where, hitherto, he/she might have been climbing, with some aid points, wearing boots and carrying a sack.

Such convenience climbing, epitomised in the guide *Schweiz Extrème*, has gained rapid popularity. The climbs are long and demanding, with challenging run-outs between the bolts where nuts and Friends can be used for some extra protection, as allowed by the rock. Colleagues who regularly patronise the routes on the Grimsel, Fiesch and the big Swiss limestone cliffs speak highly about their quality. It is clear, however, that notwithstanding their initial frugal bolting ethic, this type of climbing is leading to far more heavily bolted imitations and even retrobolting. Illustrations of some of the routes show bolts appearing in positions that can clearly be protected by nuts and it seems likely that the bolting will steadily proliferate so that eventually only quick-draws will be required.

Thus European rock climbing has changed. We now have a mixture of heavily bolted lower cliffs and partially bolted semi-Alpine cliffs. How long will it be before the great Alpine rock climbs on the Drus, the Jorasses, the Eckpfeiler, Frêney and Brouillard faces of Mont Blanc, the Tre Cime, the Badile and the Civetta are bolted up for convenience climbing?

Does climbing reflect a changing cultural preoccupation?

This new simplification of the rock-climbing experience may be a reflection of a broader cultural change. Climbing in the past, be it challenging rock climbing or alpinism, was lauded for the demands it made on good judgement and courage and steadiness in the face of adversity. This might involve poor protection, awkward route-finding in ascent and descent, loose rock, bad visibility, difficult weather and, in the Alps, uncomfortable bivouacs, stonefall, avalanches and blizzards – a veritable obstacle course of problems. Tackling and overcoming such problems, in addition to the actual technical difficulties of the climb, were considered the measure of one's ability and competence as a climber – all-round skills that we all sought to perfect. Nowadays many of these matters are regarded as tiresome distractions that impede 'enjoyment' (a constantly used word by apologists) of the technical aspect of the sport. Bolting has provided an easy solution to the problems posed by 'the awkward bits'. Climbs can be completed, free from excessive risk, and quite quickly. This, in turn, allows light logistics and even faster movement. The whole logistical equation is being changed by adapting the mountain or crag to allow fast movement.

Malte Reopper has just produced an elegant book *Sport Climbing in the Alps* which records some of the more challenging Central Swiss bolt-protected climbs. In discussing the possibility of a co-edition with him, I pointed out that the illustrations of the Hammerbruch in the Salbitschijen showed climbers protected by bolts placed alongside obviously nut-able cracks. He admitted, with regret but no fiery outrage, that this and other Salbit climbs had been unnecessarily retrobolted and that these included the classic West Ridge. Thus we have the whole Alpine rock saga beginning again: climbs done initially with a small number of bolts but later sprouting more as repeat parties seek greater security. Had the power drill not existed, this whole sad process would have been avoided.

Is bolt-protected climbing really Climbing?

Can people who ascend pre-equipped routes claim to be really climbing? Being a 'Climber' is a proud term that implies the ability to conduct oneself safely over mountain and cliff terrain by one's own skill. I do not believe that those who carry no nuts and pitons and who expect mountain routes to be bolted and rigged for their convenience are taking part in 'climbing' in the true meaning of the word: 'extreme mountain exercise' might be a more accurate term. Climbing walls, equipped in this manner, have now developed at such a pace that they too are introducing a whole new dynamic to the sport. They have, of course, the advantage of allowing climbers to train up to peak exercise fitness in a warm and very sociable atmosphere. The downside is that the invention of the fully-bolted climbing wall (taking over from the more judgement-demanding bolt-free bouldering walls) may now prove to be as fundamental a change in climbing as the invention of the heated indoor swimming pool must have been in that sport. Prior to that there was, perhaps, a breed of doughty lake and river swimmers as attuned to the vagaries and dangers of water as mountaineers and rock climbers are to avalanche conditions and loose crags. Once the swimming pool was invented, speeds and techniques no doubt improved, but the price was a totally controlled, safe, predictable and regulated environment.

Competitions have also exerted a thoroughly unhelpful dynamic on the sport. Having easily identifiable 'champions' is ideal for commerce, the media and those who have entered the sport seeking experiences and rewards akin to athletics. Such events are also valued by such diverse bodies as the various Alpine Resort Tourist Boards and the UK National Indoor Arena. Even the central bureaucratic organisations of climbing – the BMC, the UIAA, the FFM, etc – have adopted them, allegedly only with reluctance, 'to control and guide them and prevent them falling under the influence of other bodies who have less interest in climbing mores'. After ten years of such events it is now clear that the BMC and the UIAA actually like having competitions to administer.

The competitions themselves have some useful spin-offs; participants have noted their sociability, their opportunities for exotic overseas travel and their discipline in making controlled sustained leads in strenuous situations. I believe the negative aspects of such events greatly outweigh the alleged benefits. Most damagingly they provide a regular illustration of climbing as an extreme and very safe sport whereas the reality (in Britain at least) is that it is invariably much easier and much more dangerous. They portray climbers as fierce competitors whereas the reality is that the danger demands a high degree of realistic judgement that discourages rash competition. They convey a totally inaccurate image of the sport as a safe activity, most perniciously to youngsters and their parents, but also to the authorities and, perhaps ominously, to insurance companies.

Soon, after conventional crag accidents, coroners, police and politicians will begin to ask 'Why weren't the cliffs bolted as we have seen on televised competitions?' Soon there will be pressures to propel the sport into a safer mould and these will be eagerly supported by those who wish sport climbing to grow. The traditional challenge (danger) will come to be seen as a bad thing. Bolt protection will gain more and more approval in that it will allow more people of all ages and sexes to take part and allow complete concentration on performance, and thus transform the sport into something more like conventional athletics.

Climbing walls and competitions, with their attendant advertising and media hype, are already generating a new breed of people who actually believe they are going 'climbing'. In the United States, I understand, this group is now very large and they are moving outside to bolted crags on which they can continue (often at a very high standard) with the make-believe that they are 'climbers'. The crunch comes when they decide to visit normal cliffs, that are not rigged and that demand the full panoply of climbing skills. There, for a time, they find themselves undertaking a steep learning or revulsion experience which can sometimes end in disaster.

Exactly the same thing has happened in the Eastern Alps where classic climbs in ranges like the Dachstein and the Gesäuse are now considered not well enough protected for the new breed of climbing-wall-trained climbers. If this was merely a temporary phase while they learned their craft, it might be shrugged off (we all arrive by diverse routes) but this new group, and particularly their parents and attendent instructors, will soon expect training cliffs to be rigged like climbing walls. This has already happened in Switzerland and France. Swiss climbing hut wardens and their regular guides now seek their adjacent rock climbs to be rigged up to attract wall-trained climbers. This was certainly the dynamic that led to cliffs like the Graue Wand and the Salbit West Ridge being retrobolted. For the same reason we can soon expect this treatment for all the major Dolomite classics and the North Ridge of the Badile (probably the face as well), the 'Flat Iron' of Pizzi Gemelli, the Cengalo and eventually (I fully expect) many of the rock routes of Chamonix, such as the North Ridge of the Aiguille de l'M and the Papillons Arête. In 1997 there were plans to completely rig up the Zmutt Ridge. If that occurs and is accepted, all other sections of difficult rock on classic Alpine climbs are likely to be rigged.

In Britain how long will places like the Idwal Slabs and Milestone Buttress be able to retain their challenging aspects (particularly their awkward descents) once the rigged wall generation really begins to exert a serious influence? This new breed will expect the mountains to be safe from all technical hazards – they will not understand, and decry as 'élitist', an attitude that wishes to retain a mountain's or a crag's classic difficulties.

Is the old sport worth saving?

Why should we seek to keep the Zmutt Ridge tough? Why shouldn't the Idwal Slabs, the Badile North Ridge and the other great classics be retro-bolted? Why should we resist the establishment of bolt-protection of cliffs that might easily be climbed without it?

Stephen Venables, in a recent article in *High*, described the deeply satisfying challenge of a climb like the Zmutt (in its unequipped state) and its ability to leave those that rise to its challenge with a profound sense of achievement (and this from one who has climbed a new route on Everest). How can we convince the villagers of Zermatt that they risk destroying the equivalent of a priceless 'old master' if they despoil the Zmutt?

There is nothing élitist in taking a stand that maintains the intrinsic challenges in sports. In seeking to protect our sport's proven characteristics we are merely informed aesthetes jealously protecting an exquisite art form. The beauty of the sport thus protected is that quite easy climbs can continue to offer high challenge to the person of matching experience or fitness. In this manner, far from being élitist, a sport that takes care to preserve the full character of its environmental challenges, remains demanding at all levels and thus quintessentially egalitarian. A sport rigged up for safety and performance will probably soon become highly élitist, and at the same time be performance-obsessed and conformist.

Have the climbing magazines properly defended the sport?

The battle for the soul of climbing is thus joined. The rest of the world looks to Europe to resolve it, though America, as always, has a key role to play. In the eighties, competitions and power-drilling swept the States, unrestrained by those best placed to strike a cautionary note. Royal Robbins and others, including myself, pleaded with Michael Kennedy to take a harder line, in his otherwise fine magazine *Climbing*, on the spread of rap-bolting across cliff after cliff. Instead he pursued a policy of appeasement and gave heavy coverage to both sport 'exercise' and competitions.

In Britain all the magazines have adopted a similar role, with adverts, news items and features about the spread of sport 'exercise' and competitions, whilst at the same time under-stressing the really major rock-climbing developments. There should have been a far more spirited degree of editorial enquiry and censure of factors that were clearly damaging climbing. At least the official British guidebooks have maintained a sturdy defence of our traditions.

In Europe the magazines have all uniformly swooned over competitions and have been equally eager to carry body-beautiful features about the largely unimportant activities of the sport climbers (exercisers). This state of affairs recently reached a nadir with the Italian magazine *Alp*'s proposal to head a consortium of trade sponsors to rebolt Piola's routes on the Grand Capucin.

Readers may feel that this article is unduly strident, but at least it cannot be deemed hypocritical or inconsistent. When I edited *Mountain* we were proud to follow the lead of *Alpinismus* and *Ascent* and, earlier, the *Alpine Journal* tradition set and maintained by Percy Farrar, Edward Strutt and T Graham Brown. These publications were fearless in spotlighting humbug and falsehood, and at giving poor climbing, particularly where ethical lapses were involved, the savage press it deserved. The disgraceful Maestri bolt route on Cerro Torre got such coverage in *Mountain*, though care was taken to give ample space and enquiry to the counter view.

Recently, *High* (*No 154, page 18*) carried the story of a fine rock climb discovered and climbed by a group of guides in traditional style on a crag above the Piansecco Hut in Switzerland. It seems it was about HVS, solid and well protected with nuts and Friends. Shortly afterwards, the same guides came along and retrobolted it to create a guiding allurement for themselves and the hut. Why were those responsible not prominently identified and pilloried by the climbing press? Why did normal climbers not immediately go out and strip the bolts? Why did the authorities responsible for the environment not protest as they surely would have done in the United States? Indeed in the United States there have already been National Parks that have banned the power drill, and the Mohonk Trust (who administer the Shawangunks) have to their credit always resisted bolting. The power drill is now banned in Yosemite National Park. It is quite clear that power-drilling activity represents a grave threat to the mountain environment, not least in all the remote big-wall areas, such as Baffin, Greenland, Baltoro, Patagonia.

Is there a future for traditional climbing values?

In preparing this piece, I have been warned not to be too negative. Some of my friends take the view that my alarmist comments are too gloomy, and that there are signs of a renewal of proven and basic values. They point out many examples of fine adventurous and innovative climbing. It was a relief to publish Paul Pritchard's *Deep Play* – a book which celebrates this new spirit – and I know that there are groups with the same inspirational approach to climbing in each of the main climbing nations. Neverthess I believe that the overall trend is very much towards 'equipping' and, as the appetite for adventurous climbing dies out among the masses, the élite will soon be starved of the peer-group support that sustains and encourages them.

In the belief that the traditional approach to climbing is infinitely more rewarding, I would like to propose three immediate actions that might help to put a brake on this drift towards the 'theme park' type emasculation of mountaineering and rock climbing.

(1) The UIAA should forge a world mountaineering policy outlawing the power drill. This could then be presented to the National Parks as an environmentally desirable policy, ensuring that no further expeditions to the great walls of Greenland, Baffin, Patagonia and the Baltoro are able to use it. Following this move, the European and American National Parks should also be encouraged to adopt the policy. This would not eliminate sport climbing, but it would surely redress the balance and make it far more difficult for it to proliferate. It would also serve notice to equipment advertisers that mass bolting is not environmentally respectable.

(2) The Maestri bolt route on Cerro Torre should be removed by a posse of the world's top big-wall climbers (ideally including several Italians). The same team could then join forces to make the first ascent of the true SE Ridge climb to which Maestri should have applied his famed rock-climbing talents in the first place, instead of indulging in all those tawdry compressor-bolting activities.

(3) The 'convenience' routes above various Alpine huts, eg the South Face of Cassino Baggio above the Piansecco Hut (*see High 154, page 18*), those by the Salbit Hut including the West Ridge, the Niedermann Route on the Graue Wand and the ancient rope-rigged route on the Dent du Géant should all have their bolts, ropes and the like removed, ideally under the aegis of the main national clubs. Ideally the Mitteleggi Ridge, the Hörnli, the Italian Ridges of the Matterhorn and all the newly-invested *via ferrate* should also be de-rigged but their future might be the subject of a special conference.

The debolting of the Cerro Torre climb would be seen by all as a dramatic international rejection of power drilling in the mountains. If the Géant's ropes were removed it would reinvest one of Italy's greatest peaks with the status it truly deserves.* The result of these three policies would be to strike a massive international blow for real climbing values and to put a brake on the advance of bolting and rigging.

In conclusion, I would like to quote from a letter written by Royal Robbins to the Editor of *Les Alpes* on 3 January 1995 after Robbins had heard that routes on the cliffs above Leysin, of which he had made the first ascents in 1964 with George Lowe, had been turned into sport climbs:

> It makes me sad to realize that every route that is retrobolted is another nail in the heart of a great and noble craft to which we respond because it brings out the best in us, and causes us to grow until we are big enough to face the challenges of the mountains, rather than bring those challenges down to our level. Retrobolting removes risk. It removes uncertainty. Both are key elements in true climbing adventure. I can only hope that future generations will recognize what the great climbers of the past have taught us: It's not getting to the top that counts. It's the way you do it, and that they will undo the damage that this misguided generation has wrought.

I should add that Claude Remy had told me, at the 1994 BMC Conference, that if Royal Robbins complained about the retrobolting at Leysin, he would personally debolt the routes and return them to their original state. Royal duly provided this letter. As far as I am aware the bolts are still there.

---

* Note: The de-rigging of the Dent du Géant would have an educative effect on the whole Alpine-climbing community. The Italians believe that it was always rigged, whereas it was originally climbed free from ropes (though not to the highest point) by J J Maquignaz and his family and only rigged up afterwards for political and commercial reasons. Other parties had previously tried to climb it properly, and W W Graham made a true first ascent to the highest point soon after it had been rigged, avoiding most of the fixed ropes. If the Géant ropes were removed, it would return one of the greatest Alpine 4000m peaks to its natural difficulty, making the achievement of that goal an ascent of real prestige.

DOUG SCOTT

Fame and Fortune

Risk, responsibility, and the guided climber

Near the entrance to most Buddhist Monasteries there is a painting of the wheel of life. At the hub of the wheel is a symbolic explanation for all our suffering. There is a pig representing our ignorance, a cockerel representing greedy desires and a snake representing the anger within us. In our ignorance, we become attached to our desires for such things as fame, fortune and power over others. But no sooner have we gratified one set of desires than we set off in pursuit of others, and anyone or anything that seems to thwart the attainment of those desires evokes in us responses of anger and malice.

It is so easy to get on this treadmill of life, but much harder to get off it, as evidenced by myself at 56 still reaching out to an audience for attention, still wanting a slice of the action and acclaim, and still planning new routes on unclimbed Himalayan peaks. There are those, however, whose ambitious desires outstrip their own ability, so that they have to pay others to help them achieve their goals – a hollow victory if they succeed and a course of action that has caused a great deal of suffering to others. When things go wrong or when there is an accident, there are those, too, whose first thought is 'Who shall I blame?' and the second 'How can I make some money out of it?'

The whole of life is an adventure. If it had not been there would be no evolution, no progress. A number of situations have arisen recently where risk-taking and its consequences have not been fully understood and accepted. As a result, the financial cost of adventurous pursuits has increased and the spontaneous initiative to adventure has been diminished.

Climbing Walls

A young woman, Kim Touch, had been to the Philadelphia Rock Gym on many occasions. She knew it was potentially dangerous, she had signed all the disclaimers. She fell only three feet whilst bouldering, breaking her wrist, even though there was adequate floor padding. The wrist didn't mend well and so she instructed her lawyers to sue the owners of the climbing wall for compensation. The owners were tempted to pay up in order to avoid the loss of their 'no claims' bonus, escalating insurance costs for the future and to save time and trouble contesting the claim. However, the plaintiff's case was so outrageous that they and their insurers decided to take her on. The case has yet to go to court, but whichever way it goes the climbing wall owners know that they have already lost $2500 and that it will be more difficult to get reasonable insurance cover next time. This woman suspected that all this would happen but she did not reckon on her opponents having the courage to fight the case.

Crag Climbing with Guides

A novice climber fell to his death whilst being lowered down Lovers Leap Rocks in Northern California. Four anchors had been placed around a block by his climbing instructor. They all pulled when the block moved and the student fell to his death. His wife subsequently sued. The case eventually found its way to the Appeal Courts where the judge displayed amazing insight with the statement: 'Falling, whether because of one's own slip, a co-climber's stumble, or an anchor system giving way, is the very risk inherent in the sport of mountain climbing and cannot be completely eliminated without destroying the sport itself.' The court decided in favour of the defendants and in effect in favour of climbing. In making a judgement, the courts have to balance the fact that the plaintiff is assumed to know of the risks, against possible negligence on the part of the guides. The student here had signed his disclaimers and the instructors were found to have set the anchors 'within the sport's norms'. Had the instructors not done so, the outcome could have been very different.

Two years ago, in Britain, Martin Pope, after thirty days of climbing experience, and after three outings with British Mountain Guide David 'Cubby' Cuthbertson, followed Cuthbertson up a climb of HVS standard and himself led successfully a V-Diff and a Severe climb. Cuthbertson allowed him to select his own gear and lead another V-Diff. He was rightly trying to instil into his client a degree of self-reliance, albeit in a very controlled environment. Pope fell, all his runners failed and he ended up in hospital with spinal injuries. Later he sued his guide for negligence. The case went against the plaintiff. The judge held that 'if you are going to engage in rock climbing you must acknowledge and accept the risks you take and not expect to off-load your responsibility onto others. I believe that Mr Pope thought that having paid for a guide he was entitled to have his safety guaranteed. To engage in what even he regarded as a high risk sport in that frame of mind was foolish.'

It should be noted that the judge was helped enormously to come to this decision by the extremely articulate evidence given by the expert witness, guide and former head of the Mountain Leader Training Board, Iain Peter.

Alpine Climbing with Guides

Not so fortunate was David 'Smiler' Cuthbertson. He was found negligent in a widely reported High Court case that took place seven years after an accident on the north face of the Tour Ronde in July 1990 when his client and friend Gerry Hedley died.

It would be interesting to trace in full the humble beginnings of guiding in the Alps through to modern times, but here is a very brief potted history. At first the foreigner hired the more adventurous of the local villagers living below his peak – woodsmen, chamois hunters, crystal hunters – more or less as a servant to help him find the easiest way and to hump his load up to the mountain. The local people gradually took on more responsibilities for the actual climb, arriving at the point where climbers such as Geoffrey Winthrop Young treated the local people as equals and friends.

Nowadays there is a presumption that when you hire an Alpine guide you are hiring someone to take care of you and all aspects of the climb, roped together all the way. However, in the case of Cuthbertson and his client Hedley, a situation had developed over the years, leaning towards the style of Winthrop Young, where the client had gained enough experience to suggest that he should lead some of the route. Hedley had led some of the earlier pitches, but had been slow, so much so that Cuthbertson took over the lead and, two pitches later, with the sun striking the rocks above and with a potential for stonefall, he hurriedly left his client belayed to one ice screw and moved quickly out of the fall line of the face, to the safety of a rocky section. On the way ice broke off beneath his crampons and he fell, pulling his client with him. Cuthbertson suffered only a broken knee while, sadly, Gerry Hedley was killed.

Last year the case came to court and the judge found in favour of the plaintiff, Gerry Hedley's son, who, at the time of the accident, had not yet been born. The British Mountain Guides suspended Cuthbertson while they conducted their own enquiry. In September last year they found that Smiler was 'not at fault' and he was reinstated as a full BMG guide. Thus ended a 'seven-year nightmare' for Cuthbertson and his family.

However, a black cloud still hangs over the future of British guiding in the Alps. This case should never have gone against the guide in the first instance. The court could find absolutely no evidence of negligence up until that last fatal belay. Until then every care and consideration had been responsibly taken by Cuthbertson. Suddenly, at that point, danger was threatening, decisions had to be made fast by the man on the spot and Cuthbertson took them in what he considered to be the best interests of his client and himself.

Back in Britain, seven years later, the judge made his decision based on comments made by the plaintiff's expert witness, experienced climber and fellow BMG guide Alan Fyffe, that Cuthbertson was negligent in that he only placed one ice screw instead of two. Alpine climbers everywhere have debated that judgement. But even if Cuthbertson had made the wrong decision in the fast-moving and dangerous situation he was in, that could happen to anyone, as everyone who climbs must know. None of us is infallible nor can Alpine climbing be reduced to an exact science, as the judge had assumed. Without gross negligence or criminal intent, there was absolutely no case to answer.

With the benefit of hindsight, Cuthbertson was badly served by his own BMG body. In failing to conduct an enquiry immediately after the accident, they left a vacuum that was filled by all manner of ill-informed opinion.

If they had found, as they found later, that Cuthbertson was not negligent, then it would have been a tremendous boost to his case and given a lot of credence to his own expert witness. But, in fairness to the British Mountain Guides, they are a relatively young organisation maturing in response to crises that confront them from time to time, including the other David Cuthbertson accident. Now no doubt they will learn through the experience of the accident on the Tour Ronde.

It seems to me, from having enquired into this case at some length, that the BMG are as yet uncertain what their role is: are they a company of friends, a professional association or a trade union of guides? At times they attempt to be all three but they did not fulfil any of these three roles to Cuthbertson's satisfaction. He had not until the end received the wholehearted backing of any individual guide and in fact some had already suggested that he should not be fully reinstated. After the accident they were quite content for Cuthbertson to continue guiding for another 1500 days until his suspension last September. They also completely failed to anticipate the importance of the court case and prepare for a possible negative outcome.

Someone had to be an expert witness for the plaintiff, as well as for the defence, and the fact that Allen Fyffe gave answers to leading questions that were not countered by Cuthbertson's defence was hardly Fyffe's fault. With the case going against Cuthbertson, Fyffe has come in for a degree of criticism from his peers. Fyffe gave his opinion that two ice screws should have been placed in the belay. It was up to the defence team to state the obvious: that one of the great challenges and attractions of Alpine climbing is that every climb is different from the one the day before and that on big ice faces there is no right or wrong way, but only what is appropriate at the time. The conditions may be such that no belay at all is necessary and that the team should move rapidly together.

The main point is that danger and the risk of accident are an inherent part of Alpine climbing. The client knew this and accepted the dangers when he signed up to climb with Cuthbertson. The case should have been thrown out of court regardless of the fact that a bereaved mother and son would receive no award from an insurance company. Despite the fact that the husband and wife were negligent themselves in not taking out personal accident cover, the wife's situation evokes considerable sympathy. Which of us can say, if we had been in her position, that we would not have done exactly as she did? The fact remains that, as a result of this case, every British Mountain Guide going off to the Alps with his clients will do so with a lot more circumspection, be that little bit less adventurous and will have had to increase his charges to meet increased insurance premiums.

Guiding in the Himalaya

Last year my own Specialist Trekking Co-operative was involved in litigation after a trek to Rara Lake in West Nepal. It was a *Trail Walker* 'special offer' trek and so the seven clients were accompanied by Chris Fenn, appointed by the magazine. The sirdar running the trek was Tej Badhur, a very experienced Tamang who had trekked all over the Himalaya with myself, other friends and many clients, to everyone's satisfaction. On this occasion, on reaching Rara Lake, the sirdar decided, in consultation with Chris Fenn, that they should return to Jumla by the same route, with interesting variations, instead of returning by a different route to Jumla, thus making a complete circular trek as advertised. The reasons for the change of plan were that two of the trekkers had been ill and a further one was very slow. Moreover, they were already two days behind schedule owing to international airline delays. The return trek was completed to everyone's satisfaction at the time. In fact, one of the trekkers who was later to become one of two plaintiffs against STC, wrote a glowing article in *Trail* immediately after his return, saying how much he had enjoyed the trek.

The sirdar had not done the trek before but he was quite certain that he would have had no problem in completing the itinerary as advertised, and in fact showed his metal by carrying out the variations, as requested, despite the fact that he had not done them previously. Two of the clients seized on this point, that the sirdar had no previous knowledge of the route, and made it the basis of a claim for £500 each through the Small Claims Court. The plaintiffs lost in view of the overriding consideration that the planned route needed to be curtailed to ensure that the trekkers should not miss their international flight home. The judge also seemed to be impressed that the plaintiffs had been thoroughly briefed well in advance that trekking in the Himalaya was no ordinary holiday and was for the enthusiast, implying that only the unexpected was to be expected on such holidays.

Our relief at the favourable outcome can be imagined. We had spent so much time and money preparing the case; it had filled our minds with worry, off and on, for eight months. It had given me a first-hand inkling as to how Smiler Cuthbertson and others must have suffered during the period of waiting for their cases to come to court. Those who accept money to take people into the mountains take on enormous responsibilities and are very exposed. Even if the case is won, there is no compensation for travel and other actual costs, nor for time lost. The insurance company loses a great deal more if they take on the case and provide a solicitor. It would certainly have been in the short-term interests of Sun Alliance to have settled out of court. They too were very courageous in taking on the litigants.

Trekking Peaks

A few months ago I was contacted by a client, who had been on a trek with another trekking company, to provide photographic evidence and statements so that he could take them to the Small Claims Court. In this case the client had paid the trekking company to be taken on a trek to climb unclimbed trekking peaks. In the event there was an accident and the team as a whole was not sufficiently fit, and so the Western leaders curtailed their activities and failed to complete all that was advertised. The trekker who contacted me told me that he and a companion were fit and could see that it would be easy for them to climb one of the peaks concerned. I asked him why he didn't just go and do it. He said that the Western leader was not keen and so he backed off. I asked him why he didn't just tell the leader that he and his friend would climb the peak on their own responsibility. He had no answer.

It is my opinion that as soon as people pay money to go off to the mountains, they often absolve themselves from all further responsibility for taking risks and facing up to uncertainties. There are many instances in the mountains these days where this syndrome is becoming more and more apparent, and never more so than on Everest.

Everest with Guided Parties

Suddenly it strikes certain people who have been successful in other spheres of life that they would like to climb Everest, even though in some cases they have had no previous climbing experience. With their 'can do' mentality they have fat enough wallets to make them think they can buy anything, even reaching the top of Everest and getting down safely. After paying a guide or a guiding organisation huge amounts of money, currently around $65,000 a time, off they go onto the mountain, as little more than a dog on a leash.

In good weather a lot of them 'succeed'; in bad weather many of them do not and remain up there or come back terribly mutilated. The accruing publicity from such disasters only seems to encourage more non-climbers to sign up for the mountain, egged on no doubt by such claims as that of a Frenchman who climbed Everest and declared afterwards that it was the first mountain he had climbed. He was lucky with the weather and with his own ability to acclimatise but, as we saw in the summer of 1996, when the weather comes in, terrible things can happen high on Everest, even to climbers who have earned every right to be there by a long apprenticeship climbing elsewhere, but especially to clients on commercial expeditions.

The first of the genre was the high-profile and somewhat flamboyant Texan tycoon, Dick Bass, aged 55, who bought his way onto a Norwegian expedition and paid for his guides David Breashers and Ang Phurba to take him to the summit. He reached the summit and thus completed his quest to be both the oldest man to climb Everest and the first to climb the Seven Summits. The other six of the Seven Summits seem to have been the only climbing that he had done previously. Bass made it because he was canny enough to make certain that he was roped to two good men all the way to the summit. After his ascent in 1985, and his obvious enjoyment of the achievement, Dick Bass became quite evangelical about the benefits of climbing high and his success had the effect of encouraging a lot more non-climbers to follow the same trail. Guiding organisations were subsequently set up to meet this demand for climbing high in the Himalaya.

There are many non-climbers who go where they should not go and consequently put their guides and Sherpas at risk. In 1994, Australian business man Michael Rheinberger, aged 53, who had attempted Everest seven times before, now found himself with the summit in his sights. He was accompanied by the experienced New Zealand guide, Mark Whetu. Despite good weather Rheinberger was going desperately slowly. One guide had already turned back because of the slow pace, but Whetu became caught up in Rheinberger's obsession to be on the summit of Everest. They reached the summit after sunset and bivouacked 20 metres below the top. The next morning was cold and windy. After descending only 900ft to just below the Second Step, Rheinberger, by now blind, delirious and unable to walk, could go no further. Whetu had to leave him to save himself. Two days later he made it into advanced base camp with badly frostbitten feet. The client had not seemed to mind at all that he might lose his life to achieve his goal. Now Whetu was left behind, maimed physically and consumed with guilt for having abandoned his client whilst there was life left in him.

Thanks to the writing skills of Jon Krakauer, as evidenced in his book *Into Thin Air*, we are given a personal account of the worst day ever on Everest, 10 May 1996, when altogether eight climbers died. Krakauer was one of 240 climbers and Sherpas from 14 expeditions occupying a sprawling city of tents on the Khumbu Glacier. Among their number were men and women with little or no climbing experience – relative newcomers to the sport who had paid experienced Himalayan guides up to £42,000 to get them to the top of Everest. Although Krakauer had paid to go on Rob Hall's commercial Everest expedition, he was himself a very experienced climber. Yet he too succumbed to the dangerous client/guide dependency syndrome. Rob Hall and his guides were strong characters with proven track records and the clients 'had been specifically indoctrinated not to question our guides' judgement'. In his book he tells us how, for safety's sake, a responsible guide will always insist on calling the shots, for he cannot afford to allow clients to make important decisions independently. Thus the clients have to abandon their usual self-reliance and personal responsibility. This state of affairs is one which he says will haunt him for the rest of his life, when he recalls 'the ease with which I abdicated responsibility – my utter failure to consider that Andy might be in serious trouble'. Here he is referring to Andy Harris, a guide who was suffering from *hypoxia.* If that can happen to a serious mountaineer who signs on to a commercial expedition, then it is obvious that the effect on the inexperienced client is going to be at least as dramatic, if not more so.

The other commercial outfit on the mountain, Scott Fischer and his Mountain Madness team, were also well disciplined, at least up to the South Col. From reading the various accounts it would seem there was some competition, albeit friendly, between Rob Hall and Scott Fischer to get as many clients to the summit as possible. If this is true, it may explain why Fischer carried on when he was sick from some long-standing liver complaint and Rob Hall went on to the summit long after his prearranged return time of 2pm. In fact he didn't get to the summit until after 4pm. With one head guide incapacitated with sickness and the other isolated because of the late hour of his ascent, the rest of the team floundered around. The probability is that, had the weather stayed fine, all the clients and guides would have got down safely. But when the storm blew in, it dangerously compounded the cocktail of errors that had been developing all day.

The fittest and most experienced man on the mountain was probably Scott Fischer guide, Anatoli Boukreev. He believed that clients should be as fit and able as the organisers and leaders themselves. 'If client cannot climb Everest without big help from guide,' he maintained, 'this client should not be on Everest otherwise there can be big problems up high.' He reached the summit without oxygen and, rather than stand around getting hypothermic and losing strength, he descended to the South Col so that he could be of more use to those coming down late in the day. In his book Krakauer is very critical of Boukreev and yet it was Boukreev who had gone out solo into the blizzard sweeping across the South Col when no other guide, client or Sherpa had the strength or courage to do so. He probably saved three lives and he also went back up the following day, from the South Col to 27,600ft, to try to rescue his friend Scott Fischer. He found him dead.

Whilst Krakauer and some of the other clients may have found Boukreev's rapid descent to the South Col ahead of his clients irresponsible, his peers in the American Alpine Club conferred on him the David A Sowles Memorial Award which is given to climbers who distinguish themselves, with unselfish devotion and personal risk, to assist a fellow climber imperilled on the mountain. This award – justly given for the care and consideration Boukreev had shown to others – must have healed some of the wounds inflicted on him by the criticism he had received. Sadly, he died on Christmas Day 1997 whilst attempting Annapurna's South Face.

Boukreev was a strong, self-realised man who had relatively little respect for the formal rules and regulations of guiding, but who knew from experience what the right approach and attitude should be. Every committed Himalayan climber will concur with that approach. What has to be made certain is that the client signing up for a commercial venture on Everest knows what is expected of him. It should be pointed out to clients that in the Himalaya, particularly high on Everest, conditions are different from the Alps where the guide is roped to the client most of the time and makes most of the decisions. In the Himalaya this is not always possible. The commercial organisations will be peddling a dangerous and unreal myth if they advertise or imply that they can get anyone fit enough to the summit and down again safely. Of course, there can be no guarantees. How can there be when there are so many very accomplished climbers who have come to grief high on Everest?

DAVID HAMILTON

The Great Himalayan Circus

(Plates 26 and 27)

On 9 July 1997 at 12.05pm I stood on the summit of 8068-metre Gasherbrum I (Hidden Peak). This was my first 8000-metre peak and most likely my last. I felt little of the elation which has accompanied summit success on lesser mountains during my climbing career. Instead, the scenes that I had witnessed filled me with despair for the future of mountaineering in the Himalaya.

On returning from leading a successful expedition to Tirich Mir in the autumn of 1995, I began the search for my next big objective. An 8000-metre peak in Pakistan seemed to be the obvious choice. K2 and Nanga Parbat were quickly ruled out for being too dangerous. I then dismissed Broad Peak and Gasherbrum II for being too popular. This left only Gasherbrum I. With only one previous British ascent (at that date) and a moderately technical route, it seemed to be an ideal choice. I could hardly hope to have the route or the peak completely free of other climbers, but recent history indicated that GI was unlikely to be crowded. On each of my three previous expeditions to high peaks in the Karakoram there had been only one party on the mountain. I valued the atmosphere of self-reliance and solitude that this had added to the climbing experience.

The sight of Gasherbrum Base Camp was an unwelcome shock. More than 150 climbers and 50 local staff were spread over 1000m of moraine. Mess tents bristled with aerials, microwave dishes and satellite telephones. Solar-powered laptop computers processed images from digital still and video cameras before they were beamed out via the internet to various expedition web sites. Doctors came equipped with hundreds of kilos of supplies, ready to run MASH-style field hospitals. Helicopters of the Pakistan Army roared overhead daily.

There was a lively Base Camp social scene complete with endless gossip, intrigue and tea parties. Some people enjoyed BC life so much that they never felt inclined to go onto the mountain at all. Some groups were so over-sponsored that they seemed to have a different coloured down jacket for each day of the week. I cannot pretend to have felt at home in the village atmosphere of BC, but this seems to be the future of Himalayan climbing. The only choice open to those wanting to climb the highest peaks is to accept it or stay at home.

My disquiet at sharing a crowded Base Camp became insignificant compared with my rising concern about activities on the mountain. There were several very competent climbers and a few well organised, responsible teams. They were the exceptions. The general standard of safety being observed was dismally low. Many climbers were happy to plan an ascent in a style which I regard as ethically unacceptable, deliberately profiting from the efforts of others with no intention of making any contribution themselves.

Between Base Camp and Camp 2 there are two crevasse fields to be negotiated. In recent years there have been several fatal falls in this area. This is well documented in expedition reports and should have been known to all the climbers attempting the Gasherbrum peaks. Yet of the 15 expeditions on GI and GII, only three regularly roped together on this section. Two members of other groups suffered large falls into crevasses, resulting in broken limbs and helicopter evacuations. Some groups fixed several hundred metres of unnecessary rope on flat easy ground in the icefall. This gave a false sense of security to unroped climbers, as the weak anchors were incapable of holding a serious crevasse fall.

On GI the steep gully between Camps 2 and 3 was a natural funnel for debris falling from the upper face. Climbers ascending this section were threatened by stonefall for 6 to 8 hours, yet my party were the only group on the mountain wearing helmets. The large number of climbers moving about on the mountain led to a lackadaisical attitude towards co-ordination within the various expeditions. Often members of one team had little idea where their colleagues were nor who they were climbing or camping with. Good weather meant that most of these lapses went unpunished.

It could be argued that the climbers taking these risks had made rational choices and had accepted responsibility for their actions. My belief is that the 'casual' attitude adopted on the mountain was a direct consequence of there being so many people about. People were cutting corners and taking unnecessary risks in the belief that someone else would help them out if they had a problem. The poorly prepared groups on the mountain were, in effect, assuming that the better resourced and organised groups would provide a free rescue service for them. This mentality is bound to lead to avoidable accidents as well as causing acrimonious disputes between members of different expeditions.

Throughout my climbing career I have always believed that the style in which you climb is more important than the simple fact of reaching the summit. For many groups in the Himalaya this is clearly not the case. In the scramble to claim an 8000-metre summit a variety of shameful tactics are being employed. There are 'climbers' who, through lack of physical strength or technical expertise, are clearly incapable of climbing the mountain using their own resources. Rather than admit this and go home, they employ high-altitude porters to do all the work for them. These porters break trail, establish camps, melt snow, cook food, fix ropes, and drag their employers, like so much baggage, up the mountain. Anyone who ascends a peak in this style does not deserve to be called a 'climber'.

Another variety of ethically suspect mountaineering was practised by the 'jumar brigade'. These were often experienced climbers with several 8000-metre peaks to their credit. Typically involved in the race to be the first from their country to bag all the 8000-metre peaks, these climbers arrived at Base Camp several weeks after the other expeditions. Thus they found the route through the lower icefall had been established, the route adequately marked, trail broken, camps established and ropes fixed on the more technical sections. With a bit of fitness and acclimatisation, these climbers were able to pull themselves up other people's fixed ropes, bag the summit and be back in Base Camp within a few days: much to the delight of their sponsors and their domestic media. But is this the way that we want mountaineering to develop? Is this a healthy or an ethically desirable style of climbing?

The scenes I witnessed on summit day served to reinforce the views which I had formed on the earlier stages of the climb. The 'leading female climber' of a SE Asian nation was manhandled to the summit by two strong porters. One pulled on a short rope from the front while the other pushed from behind. Smiling summit photographs were procured for the sponsors back home, before she was led back to the top camp in a semi-conscious state by her loyal porters. Descending from the summit, I was surprised to find a group of 'late starters' still heading upwards several hours behind the main group, and risking possible benightment on their descent. Fortunately the climbers concerned were lucky – this time!

This is just a brief summary of some of the incidents that occurred on GI in 1997. I have already blotted much of the expedition from my mind, preferring to remember happier and more satisfying summits from my eleven seasons in the Karakoram. I am tempted to turn my back on the 8000-metre circus and search for more rewarding ascents on other peaks. But is simply turning away from this issue any sort of solution? Is it not the case that the death of traditional mountaineering values on the world's largest peaks is an issue which concerns all climbers, and demands our consideration?

The practice of 8000-metre peak-bagging is leading to a distorted and debased form of mountaineering in the Himalaya. This can have no other effect than to damage the sport of mountaineering in all the world's mountain ranges. The high media profile of attempts on 8000-metre peaks means that this aspect of the sport is the one that the public sees. The sport is thus defined in the public perception by what happens on the big-name peaks. They are attractive to advertisers and sponsors for the simple fact that they are the biggest. For climbers they have the added bonus of offering a high chance of success, on a known route, with many other expeditions present. Therefore repeat ascents on these mountains attract a disproportionate amount of the sponsorship money available to climbers, and disadvantage those wishing to pursue more innovative objectives. Moreover, high-profile accidents on these peaks, involving multiple deaths, are instantly world-wide news and reflect badly on climbing as a whole.

Everest has already been lost. What happens on that mountain can no longer claim to have any connection with the sport of mountaineering as practised by hundreds of thousands of grass-roots adherents around the world. The rush to collect 8000-metre peaks is a dead-end activity which is distorting the sport of mountaineering. The true custodians of mountaineering's spirit are surely the unsung army of climbers, pursuing unheralded projects, who savour the quality of their experiences. If we focus too easily on quantifiable goals we risk allowing a diminished form of the sport to be the yardstick by which all other ascents are measured.

Can this process be stopped? Or should we stand back and accept these developments as the inevitable face of progress? What is at stake is the extent to which the future of mountaineering can be influenced by climbers themselves. Nothing less than an ethical reappraisal of high-altitude mountaineering will do. Drastic measures are needed to focus attention on the problems and create a climate in which a structure for a sustainable future can be developed. If we do not fight for control, the sport will mutate into something unrecognisable.

The world of rock climbing in Britain provides an example of a sport whose participants have rejected what is technologically possible in favour of what is deemed to be ethically desirable. It would be technically possible to make all classic British rock climbs into *via ferrate*, creating safer, easier and more family-friendly routes. But in order to preserve the essential nature and ethic of rock climbing in this country, our climbing community has chosen *not* to do this. It is doubtful if such a self-regulating ethic could be introduced in the Himalaya. There is no unanimity of approach even amongst Western climbers, and the differing cultural outlook and economic imperatives of Asian climbers and the mountain communities are unlikely to be reconciled.

During eighteen years of climbing I have learned to appreciate the mountain environment as a source of many rich and diverse experiences. Each of us approaches the sport from our own unique perspective, and we are all changed in different ways by our experiences. Mountaineering has taught me an appreciation of wilderness areas, how to work with others in difficult situations, how to develop the skills of self-reliance, and how to temper ambition with prudence and the knowledge of one's own limitations. Joining the crowds on 8000-metre peaks contributes to few of these qualities. For many it is a purely physical activity which, like exercising on a treadmill, may build strong leg muscles but does little for the mind.

As I sit pondering these issues in the garden of Skardu's K2 hotel, an army helicopter thunders overhead bearing the bodies of six Japanese climbers killed in an avalanche that struck their base camp. In a season when friends of mine have been killed on the mountains, how important is it to get worked up about 'abstract' issues of style? Should I not simply be thankful for a successful and incident-free season, and leave the agonising for someone else? I am prepared to ask the questions. I have no answers.

JOE SIMPSON

Dead Man Waving

The climber lying on the Col never realised how close he had come to being saved. It was a mercy of sorts. At one point in the long night hands had pulled at him, voices harried him, frozen fingers had groped vainly for his fluttering pulse, felt for the slightest zephyr of damp breath at his lips. Then he was alone again, unaware that his colleagues from their tents on the Col had found him and then left him for dead.

No one came out to hold the dying man, to still his piteous waving arm with a gentle hand. No one took his pulse or checked his vital signs. No one acknowledged his last despairing movement, knelt by him and had the humanity to hug him. They let him die alone for reasons best known to themselves.

These events happened in May 1992 when four Indian climbers had left Camp 3 on the Lhotse Face and made an abortive attempt to reach Camp 4 on the South Col in a day of strong winds and intense cold. By nightfall two climbers had retreated to the safety of Camp 3 whilst their two colleagues were seemingly lost. Camped on the South Col that day were members of an Indian Border Police Expedition as well as five members of a Dutch expedition, led by Ronald Naar, and their Sherpas. In his book, *Alleen De Top Telt* (Only the Summit Counts), Ronald Naar states that in the night he heard 'a fearful scream above the sound of the roaring wind'. One of their Sherpas went out to search for the source. He found nothing, and nor did the Indian Border Police team who had also heard the cries. Everyone then retired to sleep.

At first light, about six o'clock, a female member of the Indian Border Police expedition visited the Dutch tents to inform them that they had found a 'casualty' and needed help. When asked what sort of help was required, the climber hesitated before other members of the Indian Border Police team appeared and reported that the victim had died. He was one of the missing climbers who had set out from Camp 3 the previous day. Clearly the anguished screams in the night had not been imagined.

Naar writes that the woman, named as Santosh, was in some confusion about what had happened.

She tells him: 'My colleagues gave him oxygen to revive him but now he is beyond help they say. He is already dead it seems.'

'But what has happened?' Naar asks her.

'I have no idea. But the others have decided to go down.'

The Indian team and their Sherpas then left the South Col and descended towards the Western Cwm. The Dutch had no reason to believe that the man was anything other than dead and didn't bother to check the corpse lying close to their tents. For them, it would be unimaginable to think that anyone might abandon a living team member.

The retreating Indians then came across the body of the second missing climber hanging on the fixed ropes leading down to Camp 2 from the South Col. Hypothermia and exhaustion had killed him some time during the night. Perhaps it was his screams everyone had heard – anguished cries for help from a man lost and exhausted in the darkness. In their swift descent from the Col the Indians left the climber hanging on the rope. One of the Dutch team was to say later how they were consequently forced to climb over the man's body on later ascents to the Col until someone eventually cut him free in the hope that he would fall into the Western Cwm. Unfortunately the body became jammed in rocks a short distance below the ropes. It appears that no further effort was made by his team mates or other expeditions to bury or retrieve the body. Neither was any attempt made to cover or bury the body lying on the col.

Meanwhile, back on the Col, the Dutch had a brief discussion about what they wanted to do. The weather was too cold and windy for a summit attempt that day. They knew that to stay on the Col would be a heavy drain on their strength and resilience. A quick retreat to Camp 2 in the Western Cwm to recuperate and wait for an improvement in the conditions was obviously the better idea but for the moment they prevaricated. Settling back into their sleeping bags, they rested for the next four hours until one of their Sherpas crawled outside to relieve himself. He was soon back, pale-faced and visibly shaken.

'There is a dead body waving over there,' he says to a startled Ronald Naar. The Dutch leader peers out of the tent and sees the body lying amidst the snow-drifted rocks. Every now and then one of the man's arms comes up very slowly in an eerie sort of salute before it is lowered slowly back to his side. Perhaps the familiar sound of voices drifting over from the tents had triggered the almost superhuman effort to wave one hand. A feeble, slow wave. A plea. Help me. Hold me, please. Whatever signal pulsed through his enfeebled body, slowly his arm began to move.

There were five Dutch climbers and two Sherpas in residence on the Col, sufficient to drag the man into a tent. One might have expected their instinctive reaction to be to rush to the poor man's aid; to try and drag him into the tents, maybe revive him with oxygen and fluids. After all, he was only between twenty and thirty metres from the their tents. Instead there followed a bizarre radio conversation between Ronald Naar and the expedition doctor at base camp. Having established that dead men cannot make involuntary movements, Naar asked about the man's physical condition. The experts at base camp advised him that since the man had lain exposed to the fury of the elements for so long, it would be quite impossible to revive him or do anything to save him. This may very well be true, but it could only really be verified by a physical examination of the victim.

No one made any attempt to do this. On discovering that the Indian was alive and waving, the two Sherpas were distressed by what had happened, convinced in a fatalistic way that a man returning from the dead was a very serious omen.

'He is a dead man and he calls us,' Nima tells Naar. 'Our religion says a calling dead man means we should follow. We too must die.'

The Sherpas wanted to descend as soon as possible. One of the Dutch climbers, Hans Anterbosch, was also adamant that he wanted to leave. Naar left his tent to go to the adjacent tent and discuss the situation, glancing across as he went at the silent figure lying on his back, waving feebly. No one went across to examine the victim. In the shelter and relative comfort of their tent the Dutch climbers came to the conclusion that the core temperature of the man lying outside must be so low that to do anything – move him, feed him fluids or try to administer oxygen – would almost certainly kill him. The man had lain there since possibly as early as 1.30am after climbing all day in stormy conditions – nearly nine hours exposed to the killing wind. It was now four hours since his Indian colleagues had pronounced him dead. After Hans and another Dutch climber had left with the Sherpas, the remaining three filmed each other discussing what should be done.

Later, I watched their video in hushed despair, thinking all the time of the poor man dying alone barely a rope-length from the nylon walls in the background. I find it astounding that they made no attempt to examine the dying Indian.

'That man walked into his own death,' Ronald Naar writes in *Alleen de Top Telt* (Only the Summit Counts). 'I don't want any of us to get hurt. It makes no sense to try and rescue him.'

'But he is still human. He still lives, and we have to do something, don't we?' Hans van Meulen, a Dutch team mate, cries out in despair. Naar is adamant that nothing should be done; and his view prevails. It is too dangerous, he says, and although he understands their distress, he insists that nothing be done.

They did not go outside again until the following morning when the three Dutch climbers made their attempt on the summit, stepping past the man's frozen body on their way. They were forced to retreat some hundred metres below the South Summit.

In the spring of 1996 a vicious storm swept across the summit region of Everest, with tragic results. Eight climbers died during that night and early the following day, but many more survived the horrendous conditions. The laudable behaviour of both victims and rescuers stands in stark contrast to the expediency of the decision taken by Ronald Naar. In that storm, an American climber, Seaborn Beck Weathers, was abandoned on the South Col by rescuers who were overwhelmed by the conditions and the number of victims needing help. They simply couldn't find him in the dark and assumed that he must be dead.

Having slumped in a comatose state, the American revived over twelve hours later in daylight and staggered to the safety of the tents on the Col. He suffered severe frost injuries, with the loss of his right hand and part of his nose, but he survived. He had spent more than thirty hours at or above the Col, without oxygen for most of that time, and had survived through a long night of ferocious winds and plummeting temperatures. He was alive despite suffering considerably more trauma than the Indian climber in 1992.

The weather that night was appalling, with blizzard whiteout and freezing temperatures that were far more extreme than the relatively benign conditions in 1992. Rescue attempts were conducted in the stormy darkness of the night at distances from the tents far in excess of the thirty yards that separated the Indian climber from safety and warmth. The same day a Taiwanese climber, Makalu Gau, was revived and rescued from a forced open bivouac over a thousand feet above Camp 4 on the Col. Like Beck Weathers he also suffered dreadful frostbite injuries but nevertheless survived.

It shows clearly what utter nonsense it is to act upon a medical prognosis made in base camp as to the life expectancy of anyone on the South Col without making a physical examination. When the victim is a stone's throw away and you have warmth, shelter, oxygen, food and seven people capable of helping, then failure to go and take a close look at him seems highly questionable. In truth, all that the Dutch base camp doctors could do over the radio was to speculate on the dying Indian's condition and, however well meant this may have been, it was never going to be more than guesswork. It was however enough to justify Ronald Naar's insistence that his duty was not to risk the safety of his team in any attempt to save the man. The decision, it might be noted, also meant that they could pursue an unsuccessful summit attempt the following day.

When I learned of this awful death on the South Col I thought that it was a one off. A single example of climbers behaving badly that would never happen again. I was wrong.

On the evening of 10 May 1996, on the Tibetan side of Everest, three Indian climbers were trapped by that same vicious storm. The following morning two Japanese climbers and their three Sherpas made their summit bid via the North Face and NE Ridge of Everest from a high camp at 8300m. The Japanese party left early in the morning, determined to reach the summit in time to get back to their high camp before dark. They estimated that the ascent would take no longer than ten hours. By 8am they had reached their first big obstacle, the First Step, where they found, to their dismay, one of the Indian climbers slumped in the snow. It should have been no surprise since they must have known of the Indian's summit attempt and their failure to return the night before. The man was conscious, although clearly in a bad way, severely frostbitten and mumbling incoherently. The two Japanese climbers insisted on continuing with their summit bid. The Sherpas, who are all too often and easily bullied into acting against their wishes, went with them. No liquid, oxygen or food was offered. Five fit, well-equipped oxygen-breathing climbers just moved on past the stricken man.

One and a half hours later the Japanese came to the Second Step, and it took them more than an hour to scale the 80ft-high rock buttress as the metal caving ladder, draped down it by a Chinese expedition years before, had partly come away. This sort of climbing is an extreme and exhausting undertaking at 8650m. When at last they hauled themselves over the top of the rock wall they came upon the remaining two Indians, also slumped in the snow, some thirty feet from the edge of the step. One man was unconscious and close to death, while the other was conscious and crouched in the snow as if attempting to get up and climb. The Japanese did not speak to the Indians or examine them in any way. They carried on for another fifty metres before stopping for a brief rest and to change their oxygen bottles. They even took in a little food and liquid nourishment within sight of the dying Indians. By 2.30pm, after a further 3½ hours climbing, Hiroshima Hanada and Eisuke Shigekawa had fulfilled their dream – one they were prepared to stop at nothing to achieve. Helping others had no part in the dream into which they had bought.

They happily radioed news of their triumph to their team in base camp unaware of the storm of horrified protests that their behaviour induced. It was at first reported that the five climbers descended safely to their high camp, passing the now dead bodies of the two climbers at the Second Step and the comatose but living man at the First Step. Later the Japanese changed their story, claiming that at least one of the climbers above the Second Step was still alive, and that one of their staff, Pasang Kami Sherpa, who on that day had achieved his fourth ascent of the mountain, had helped the ailing Indian down the Second Step. Presumably the Sherpa then had to leave the Indian because he was unable to help him any further on his own. In all of this, one wonders why nothing had been done by the Indian team to mount some sort of rescue of their own.

Richard Cowper, a member of the British 1996 North Ridge Everest Expedition, organised by the commercial trekking and climbing company Himalayan Kingdoms, interviewed both the Japanese climbers immediately they reached base camp. Writing in the *Financial Times*, Cowper reported Eisuke Shigekawa as saying in response to being asked why they had done nothing: '...above eight thousand metres is not a place where people can afford morality'. This is a shocking reflection on some of today's big mountain-climbing ethics. His partner, Hiroshi Hanada, apparently distressed, added in faltering English: 'They were Indian climbing members – we didn't know them.'

The leader of a Norwegian expedition was quoted as saying: 'Friendship, closeness to nature, building up a relationship with the mountain has gone. Now it is attack, in old fashioned siege style, and climbers have to reach the top at any price. People are even willing to walk over dead bodies to get to the top ... I shall never come back.'

Brian Blessed, the former star of the BBC Television serial 'Z-cars', was making his third unsuccessful attempt to climb the mountain with Himalayan Kingdoms. He was reported in *The Times* to have been outraged by the behaviour of the Japanese and had been quoted as saying in his usual theatrical manner: 'Everest stank of death ... with climbers running around like headless chickens, desperate to reach the summit first. I was horrified that such a high mountain experienced the lowest common denominator in human behaviour.' It was an emotional response from a man unashamed to wear his heart on his sleeve. Yet there is some truth in what he said. He claimed that when the Japanese team held a victory party, he went into their tent, ripped down their national flag, threw it to the ground and pissed on it. If this is true, then good for him.

The other expeditions at the base camp were outraged by the Japanese, who seemed unconcerned at all the fuss and immediately dispatched two more climbers and three Sherpas to the summit two days later. They climbed past the frozen body at the First Step and confirmed that it lay only one hundred metres above the high camp. The majority of climbers in the base camp were appalled by the behaviour although a few – more pragmatic and hard-nosed than others – felt that it would have been impossible anyway to get the victims down without grave risk. For purely practical considerations, there was nothing to be done. I wonder how they would feel if they found themselves needing help in such circumstances?

It was probably hopeless to attempt rescuing the climbers at the Second Step, but even so, it appears that a single Sherpa managed to get one man down what in reality is the hardest section of the route. If the man at the First Step was in fact alive when the Japanese returned from the summit some eight to nine hours later, then it is unforgivable that they did absolutely nothing. That climber had survived a savage storm and a long night in an exposed position, yet he had still been strong enough when first found at eight in the morning to survive the entire day without liquid or oxygen.

Surely if the Japanese climbers had had the decency to abandon their ambitions and, with their three Sherpas, had worked together, they could have saved at least one life. Four people could have worked at reviving the man sufficiently to get him moving with their assistance just as three Sherpas did with Makalu Gau from a similar height on the south side on that same day. The fifth climber could have descended to the high camp to get some essential supplies: spare oxygen, a stove, some hot drinks. They could have radioed base camp to explain the situation and request that help be sent up from the lower camps. They could have tried. It would have been desperately hard work, and would not have been without risk, but it would have had a chance of success. They seemed to have forgotten a certain moral duty.

Frankly, I find it unimaginable that they possessed such a narrow-minded, almost insane obsession with the summit, that they could find it in themselves to ignore a dying man. Even if the victim will inevitably die, does that mean you should offer him absolutely nothing, not a drop of fluid, a comforting presence? How can anyone climb past a dying man and still think reaching the summit is worth anything?

To date a quite ghastly number of corpses have accumulated on or above the South Col. In 1993 at least five corpses were visible on the Col – three Nepalese, one Indian, and one Yugoslav. There were also two more Sherpas to be seen lying on the slopes above at 8400m. It was suggested that there may have been more, as four Indian climbers had died and been left there in October 1985. By 1994 it was estimated that there were as many as nine bodies on or near the Col. There is nothing noble about the way they have been abandoned. They are not mute, poignant testimony to an enduring spirit of adventure; they are simply the losers, abandoned by the winners.

Bodies have been left on mountains all over the world. Because these bodies lie in inaccessible or impossibly dangerous positions, they cannot be buried. But the South Col of Everest is not inaccessible. Corpses beside which people camp are not exactly hard to reach. It has been shown that, with care, it is not too dangerous to retrieve them from this spot nor too exhausting to attempt some form of burial.

The truth is that it is expedient not to do anything. Who wants to waste time, energy, and the vast amounts of money they have spent trying to climb the mountain on retrieving corpses? As we all know, expediency is the essence of convenience, and that's what helps you get up Everest.

On 22 April 1993, Pasang Lhamu became the first Nepalese and 17th woman to summit on Everest. She descended very slowly, taking five hours to reach the South Summit where she was benighted and forced to bivouac with her companions Pemba Norbu and Sonam Tshering Sherpa. The following morning Pemba left her with her companion and descended alone to the South Col to get oxygen supplies for Pasang. The weather worsened, and despite repeated attempts, no one could reach the stricken climbers. Pasang Lhamu died, and in so doing became a national heroine. Eighteen days later her body was found near the South Summit and lowered down to the South Col by a team of Russian climbers. It was then brought down to base camp by a SW Face Korean team. Whether a reward had been offered for the recovery of this national heroine, or Everest climbers had suddenly got an attack of the moralities, is not clear. She was eventually taken back to Kathmandu for national mourning.

Never before had a body been recovered from such a height on the mountain. The Russians and Koreans had proved the lie of expediency. Not only did they retrieve her body safely but they got it all the way back down to Kathmandu for cremation and last respects. What does that say about those who continue to climb in the full knowledge that they will be camping beside corpses? Not a great deal. When they do so they cannot claim to be surprised.

If you have spent mortgage-sized amounts of money to climb a mountain, then perhaps respect for the dead does become a secondary concern. Some clients have paid commercial companies as much as $65,000 to be guided to its summit. Would it be so bad to say, 'Well, damn it, he isn't going anywhere for a while so I may as well climb to the top and then do something about him when I get down again.' And then, when you get back to the Col, you can always say, 'Hell, I'm so knackered; it would kill me if I tried to do anything for that poor guy now, but at least I thought about it.' Yes, at least you did.

It is not enough to say that these incidents are rare and exceptional occurrences. It does not matter if the mess may have since been cleaned up. The fact that we ever let it get into such a deplorable state remains a shameful legacy. Too many Everest climbers have in the past been prepared to accept the mess on the South Col as an acceptable price to pay. Commercial companies, and those guides who have first-hand knowledge of the state of the mountain, have been prepared to sell and lead trips through a field of tattered tents, oxygen cylinders and abandoned corpses.

Karl Huyberecht's shocking picture taken on the South Col in spring 1989 is a damning indictment of high-altitude mountaineering and its motives. In the foreground, almost unnoticed, as if casually tossed aside, lies the body of a man wearing a red down suit, face down amidst the rubble. For as far as one can see the bleak barren rocks of the Col are dotted with bright yellow oxygen bottles. Shredded tents, half-buried under drifts of ice-hard snow, with skeletal poles pointing bleakly at the sky, added splashes of colour to a dirty scene. It looks like a scene from a battlefield.

A record eleven climbers died on Everest in the spring season of 1996. Eighty-four climbers reached the summit, which makes a fatality rate of one in seven. Nevertheless, the average historical fatality rate still makes the Spring season of 1996 a safer-than-average year. At this rate how many climbers will have died on the mountain after another twenty years of hundreds of climbers attempting Everest each season? One hundred? Two hundred? Will the area of the South Col and above begin to resemble some grisly charnel house?

Some climbers have risked their lives, others have died, selflessly attempting to rescue fellow mountaineers, regardless of fault or criticism. Others have sat by and zipped the door shut on a man's final lonely end. Some have tried to climb the mountain in the purest style by new routes while the majority seem to care not at all for such fine ethical notions and reduce the mountain's height and seriousness by breathing bottled oxygen and hauling up on fixed ropes. Some say they are cheating, others think it is perfectly acceptable.

I understand why people might want to climb Everest. An ascent of the highest peak will always have a great deal of social cachet. For the professional climber, an Everest ascent is a significant addition to his or her mountaineering *curriculum vitae*, and so be bound to increase the chances of sponsorship or employment as a guide. Although diminished in reputation, Everest is still regarded by an ill-informed general public as the ultimate mountaineering achievement. In most countries an ascent of Everest is still held to be an heroic endeavour. Such national acclaim can be a source of considerable wealth and prestige for the opportune climbers lucky enough to make a first ascent for their country. Few, if any, of these Everest climbers ever make any comment about the state of the mountain or the style of ascents.

There have been calls for a complete ban on climbing Everest, citing the quite plausible argument that there is nothing left to be proved by an ascent other than to massage the egos of rich clients whose motives leave a lot to be desired. Sagamartha, 'Mother of the Universe', as the Sherpas call Mount Everest, or Chomolungma, 'Goddess Mother of the Wind', as she is known to the Tibetans, is now no more than '...an old whore made sordid and debauched by her clientele', according to Jim Crumley, author of *Among Mountains*. I can sympathise with Crumley's view that it is time for Everest to be made inviolate, closed to all suitors for all time, to become a sanctuary to be honoured, admired and respected rather than abused for profit and ego. 'It will take the marshalling of world opinion,' Crumley writes, 'but to restore Everest's sanctity should be as high a priority of nature conservation as saving the tiger.' If he is correct, then it is a frightening analogy, given that the tiger, despite all international efforts at conservation, is today on the verge of extinction.

While Jim Crumley reasoned that it was time to apply the wise philosophy of conservation to a mountain crying out for respect and sanctity, he rightly overruled any temptation to argue that expeditions provide vital economic resources for an impoverished nation. Such economic arguments are deceptively facile. Trekkers would still come in their droves to view an 'Everest made sacred again'.

Does paying mortgage-sized amounts of cash to be led up a mountain, regardless of the style or the inherent moral principles behind climbing, become something laudable? When you can zip shut a tent door in sight of a dying man or believe that 8000 metres is really 'no place for morality', then perhaps it is time for all climbing on the mountain to cease, or at the very least be confined to the handful of mountaineers capable of climbing it without oxygen.

I can only guess at how close I came to dying in Peru in 1985 when my climbing partner Simon Yates was forced to cut our rope and I plunged into the crevasse on Siula Grande. Although there was a lot of pain and anguish and hardship during the four days in which I struggled to survive, it is the dreadful loneliness that still deeply unsettles me. Much of what I did at that time was instinctive; but what kept me going for so long when all seemed lost was the desperate desire for company. I went beyond caring whether I lived or died so long as I did not have to die alone. I wanted a hand to hold, a voice to hear. I craved for some human contact that might alleviate the terrifying emptiness of those days spent slowly dying.

Looking back rationally now as a mountaineer, I can see no reason why Simon Yates should have attempted to rescue me. Indeed, at the time I really thought it to be an impossible task, and if that were so then any such attempt would be suicidal. I was 6000m up on a remote mountain with a badly shattered knee. We had run out of food and gas that morning and there were no mountain rescue teams or helicopters to call upon. As a two-man team, climbing Alpine-style with no other climbers in the vicinity, we always knew that even a minor accident could be a death sentence. Suddenly we were forced to confront a situation of our own making, one that we had hoped would never happen. We found ourselves in a game that no one was likely to win – so much so that it became *how* we strove to play the game that counted in the end.

When the testing moment came, I looked into the eyes of a friend and wondered what he was thinking, what he was going to do, whether he would leave me to die or help me. It seemed to take a very long time while my life hung in the balance of another man's thoughts.

Simon had a way out. I did not. It would have been reasonable for him to climb down alone, leaving me to my fate. No one would have had any right to criticise him for such a course of action. He would probably have been able to descend the mountain safely on his own, although it would have been an extreme undertaking. He chose instead to try to rescue me single-handed in an audacious and exceptional piece of mountaineering requiring skill, experience beyond his years and, above all, courage.

... Lights came on in the blackness, and a head torch spurted a sodium yellow light beam into the night, and I fell off my boulder and wept as heavy footfalls crunched in the gravel and voices shouted in the dark. Strong arms grabbed me and pulled me towards the lighted tents. Simon grinned and swore at me in shock – to see a dead man moving. He looked old and haggard and care-worn. After he settled me gently against the soft down sleeping bags he zipped the tent door closed against the dark shadows of a frightening night.

(The author's latest book *Dark Shadows Falling* was published by Jonathan Cape in 1997. The book is reviewed by Trevor Braham on pages 314-316.)

Looking Back

5. Jim Curran seconding *Tunnel Vision* at Red Rock Canyon, Las Vegas. (*Ian McNaught-Davis*) (p169)

57. *Snake Dike* on Half Dome, Yosemite. (*Jim Curran*) (p171)

8. Half Dome, Yosemite. (*Jim Curran*) (p171)

66. The Cambridge University Mountaineering Club meet in the Hurrungane, 1932. *Back row from L* B K Harris, P D Baird, A M Greenwood. *Middle row* A R Wilson, B C Harvey, A J S Stewart, A L Cram. *Front row* J A Ramsay, E H L Wigram, E A M Wedderburn. (p213)

Below
7. The bergschrund on the Jervvasstind. First stage. *Climber*: E H L Wigram. (*Ashley Greenwood*) (p213)

Above
68. The bergschrund on the Jervvasstind. Second stage. *Climbers*: P D Baird (*top*), A L Cram (*bottom*). (*Ashley Greenwood*) (p218)

69. The West Hurrungane from Mohn's Skar, with Austanbotntind (*centre L*) and Store Ringstind (*centre R*). X ... X shows new route on Nordre Dyrhaugstind, 2147m. (*Ashley Greenwood*) (p218)

70. Store Skagastølstind (Storen) from Mohn's Skar, Slingsby's route on the first ascent. (*Ashley Greenwood*) (p218)

ASHLEY GREENWOOD

Norway 1932

The Cambridge University Mountaineering Club meet in the Hurrungane

(*Plates 66–70*)

When my wife and I arrived at Turtagrø in July 1970, I was delighted to see that the original wooden fretwork building, where our CUMC party had stayed nearly 40 years earlier, was still standing, albeit as an annexe to a new hotel. It had been 98°F on an August day in 1932 when some of our party met at Kings Cross to catch the train to Newcastle – the hottest day on record in London at that time. At Newcastle we boarded the *SS Venus* for Bergen and the sea was calm enough for us to enjoy the ship's considerable culinary delights. After a night in Bergen we took the Bergen–Oslo express to Myrdal, and walked the 20km down to Flåm. From there we travelled by fjord steamer to Skjolden, at the head of the Sognefjord, and walked up to the mountain hotel of Turtagrø at the north end of the Hurrungane range in the Jotunheimen. On both these walks our baggage was transported by Stolkjaerre (anglicised by us into 'Stockjerry') – a sort of glorified wheelbarrow pulled by a horse.

The Turtagrø Hotel is at about 900m, and the mountains run from about 1800m to 2400m. At that time the hotel was fairly basic as regards washing and sanitary facilities, but it was clean and the food was excellent. Norway was much cheaper than anywhere in the Alps. Unfortunately Turtagrø is at the northern end of the range and a 2½ hour walk was required to reach the climbing area.

On the first day we all climbed the Store Skagastølstind (Storen), 2403m, by the ordinary route from the Bandet, a col between it and the Dyrhaugstinden. This consisted of an easy ridge followed by a straightforward but sensational traverse leading to Heftye's chimney, situated above a short overhang and difficult to reach without a shoulder hoist. The chimney itself was easy, as were the slabs above it, which led in a short time to the summit on which we emerged from a sea of cloud above which only the highest peaks were visible. Alastair Wilson's party had started at 4am. The rest of us set out much later, after a seven o'clock breakfast; but fortified by bacon and eggs, porridge and all kinds of fish dishes, we had almost caught them up by the time we reached the foot of Heftye's chimney. They never made the same mistake again. We found that in the 12 hours between an 8am start and 8pm dinner, most of the local climbs could be accomplished.

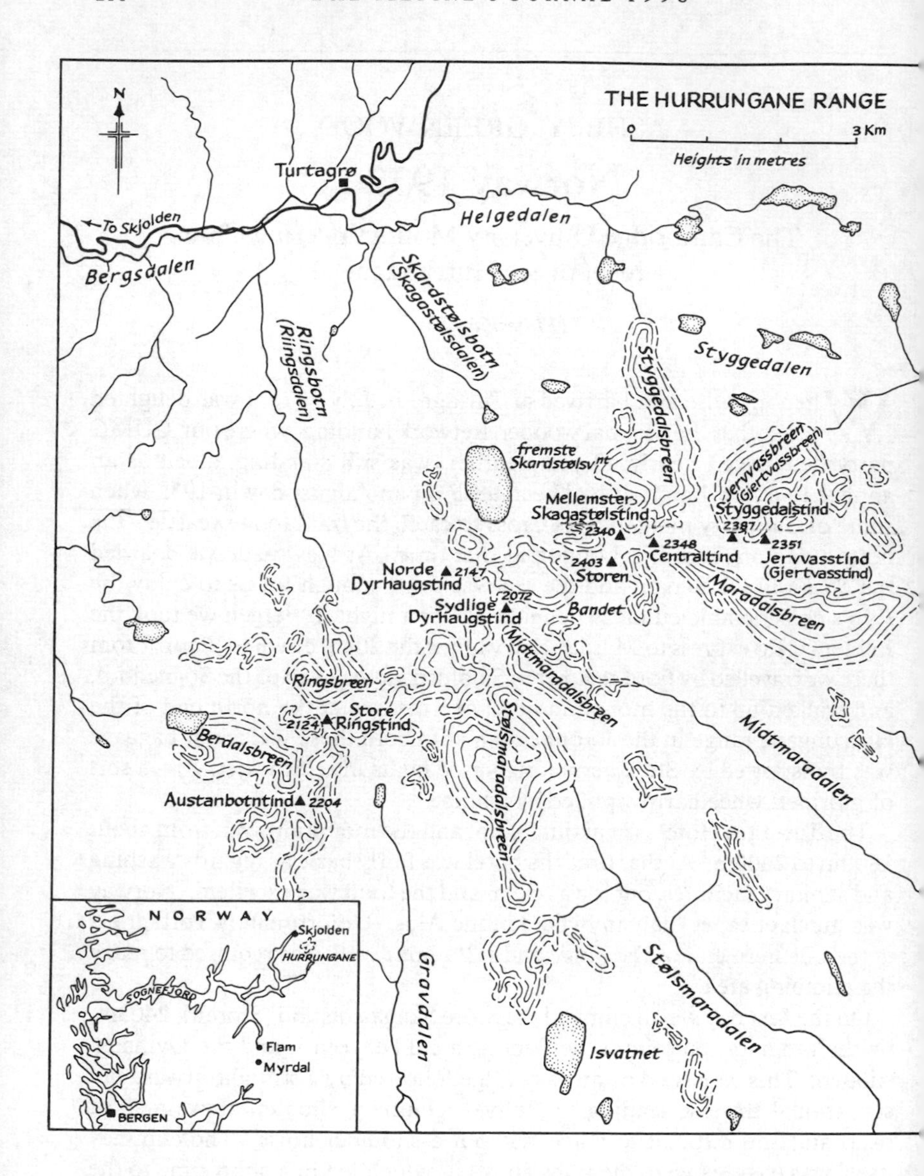

The next day Sandy Wedderburn led me and another member of the party up the NE ridge of Sydlige Dyrhaugstind, 2072m, from the Bandet. This was a delightful climb, now labelled Difficult, consisting of chimneys connected by traverses to and fro until you come to a point where, when my wife and I repeated the climb 38 years later, the guidebook (non-existent in 1932) directed us to go 'slap op ryggen', an expression which even with our ignorance of Norwegian we could not fail to understand. Soon after that we emerged from another chimney onto the summit ridge, easy but sensational, along which we walked and scrambled until we could descend easily into the Skardstølsbotn and so back to Turtagrø, where we learned that Pat Baird and Alastair Cram were missing. As they had not returned by 10.30pm a search party set out, with deep curses, to look for them. Contact was made in the dark by voice, but physical contact had to await dawn. Having climbed the Mellemster Skagastølstind, they had been overtaken by darkness, with a difficult place called the Skaret (a V cleft) between them and the top of the route down to the valley. It was a fine night and they were unharmed.

Everyone took a rest day after this, and on the following day I accompanied Sandy Wedderburn on an attempt on Storen by its NW arête. Moving together most of the way, we climbed for about 2000ft up the arête, fairly steep and exposed, on rather rotten rock. By then we were in mist and confronted by steep and rather holdless slabs. While I watched apprehensively from a small stance with an inadequate belay, Sandy progressed for about 30ft on small holds before coming to an impasse. Unable to get any higher or to see any other feasible route, he faced a daunting descent, but luckily he was able to traverse to a small spike of rock from which a short abseil took him down the trickiest part. However, when he had reached a point directly above me, he put his foot on a loose ledge. Warning me to move aside, he held it in position long enough for me to do so. Then down it came with a crash, loosening a lot of adjacent rock; in a cloud of dust, it bounced once and then descended 2000ft to the glacier below, leaving behind a sulphurous smell. We continued our descent without incident and arrived back for dinner at 8pm, to find that the tenth member of the meet had just arrived from England, having missed the ship at Newcastle. This was B K (Brian) Harris, the schoolmaster who had introduced me to rock climbing in North Wales just over a year before. He was an ex-member of the CUMC, of the vintage era of Jack Longland and Ivan Waller.

The weather had been fine till now and remained so for a further two or three days. Six of us now embarked on a very long ridge traverse starting with Storen and proceeding over the Vesle Skagastølstind (2325m), the Centraltind, and two peaks of the Styggedalstinder to the Jervvasstind, 2351m (first climbed by W C Slingsby in 1876), from the top of which we would return to Turtagrø by a pass and a different valley. We understood that this expedition had been done only once before. Harris opted out of this and took a party to the Austanbotntind which they climbed in perfect weather, having spent the night in a *saeter* (herdsman's hut). We six walked up to the Bandet on which there was a primitive hut. It was draughty and there were only three bunks and five blankets. I shared a bunk with Pat Baird and had the better of it, as our one blanket, though long enough for me, was too short for his 6 foot 4 inches, so that his feet stuck out all night. At 2am we got up and cooked a large breakfast of porridge and bacon and eggs, and at 4.15am we set off minus Sandy Wedderburn who had developed a bad foot. I was paired with Alastair Cram, while Edmund Wigram,

Wilson and Baird formed the other party. This time we traversed Storen, descending to Mohn's Skar, thus reversing Slingsby's route of first ascent in 1876. The descent to the Skar, though appearing formidable, was only moderately difficult. From the Skar stretched several kilometres of delightful ridge climbing over the intervening peaks, never difficult but always narrow and sensational, with steep drops on both sides.

Just after midday we found ourselves at the Jervvasskaret, 500ft below the top of the Jervvasstind. 'The top in half to three-quarters of an hour', we thought; but we had miscalculated by five hours. First there was a bergschrund with a vertical lip, which Wilson attacked from a snow bridge until ominous cracks and subsidence put an end to that. The only other possibility seemed to be a spot where a rock outcrop cut into the bergschrund, leaving a narrow chimney between the rock and ice. Reaching this by a delicate traverse, Wigram climbed the chimney using holds on the rock on one side and cutting steps on the other, and debouched onto a slope of mixed rock and snow, emerging onto a good platform at the end of his 120ft of rope. We all followed separately and our sacks were hauled up. These manœuvres had taken two hours. The final slope, 360ft long, was of hard ice at 45° to 50°. The old climbing books, which most of us had read with some scepticism, referred to 'pitiless' ice slopes, but this was the reality. We had no crampons and it took Wigram 40 or 50 blows to cut each step. At the end of 3¼ hours he reached the top, by which time all our 360ft of rope was out, the last of the party was just leaving the platform, and the other three were strung out at intervals on the ice slope. It was 5.30pm.

After five minutes on top we began the easy descent, stopped to eat, and by 8pm were off the mountain. Of the return to Turtagrø the less said the better. First we had to cross a col, then followed 9km of the valley. There may have been a path, but by the light of candle lanterns in the dark it was hard to find. Wigram led, and every time he stopped he fell asleep, and so did we. Sometimes he fell asleep while actually walking. For me it was torture, as I had sprained my ankle on the descent when jumping from a short ice glissade (there was no snow on the Jervvasstind, only ice) onto an up-sloping rock. We reached Turtagrø at 12.45am, too tired even to appreciate the *aurora borealis* which accompanied us all the way.

Two days later Sandy Wedderburn had designs on a new route on the Nordre Dyrhaugstind (2147m), by a ridge which descends onto the Skagastøls Glacier and is easily recognisable by the tongue of rock which projects onto the glacier at the bottom. This we were able to reach by a finger of ice. The climbing was easy until we reached an overhanging nose, which we surmounted by means of elbows, chests, stomachs and knees. Then it was easy again until we reached a bouldery platform above which the ridge rose at a high angle, the crux of the climb. Wedderburn led and progressed easily for about 15ft. Then the difficulties began and he disappeared from our view. Almost imperceptibly the rope inched out, and showers of moss, earth and stones descended on us. With about 50ft of rope out, there was a long pause; then another 30ft of rope moved slowly up; another long pause followed before the rope began to run out again, inch by inch. At last, after a further 15 minutes, Sandy announced that he had reached a belay. With no intermediate protection, on unknown and difficult ground, he had run out 105ft of rope. I followed and found it delicate and difficult all the way. There were very few handholds and every move had to be thought out. It took me 25 minutes to climb the pitch, and the most difficult part was at the end. Ramsay's comment when he arrived after another 25 minutes was 'Sandy, you're mad, utterly and completely mad'. Above this pitch the angle eased off, but the rock was extremely loose and rotten. Another 500ft brought us to the summit ridge of the Nordre Dyrhaugstind, and so back to Turtagrø.

The weather now broke, and a party of us climbed the Store Ringstind (2124m) in thick cloud, by an easy glacier route. The retaining wall of the glacier at the summit was strictly vertical. We threw stones over and heard nothing. My wife and I tried to repeat this climb in 1970, but the glacier had retreated so much that to get to it we were faced with smooth glacier-worn rocks which we could not climb.

We left Turtagrø the following day and walked down to Skjolden where we caught a fjord-steamer which took us the whole way to Bergen. We crossed the North Sea again on the *Venus*, and from Newcastle I made my way by train to Hunstanton, where my parents were staying at a hotel noted for its excellent cuisine – just the place to satisfy a post-climbing-holiday appetite.

Edmund Wigram, who was a doctor, took part in the 1935 and 1936 Everest expeditions. During the former, which was a reconnaisance, he climbed six peaks of 22,000ft or thereabouts. He was killed climbing with his wife shortly after the end of the Second World War, when he fell off *Faith* on the Idwal Slabs.

Sandy Wedderburn pioneered, among other notable climbs, the first ascent of the Mitre Ridge on Beinn a'Bhuird, Cairngorms, at the same time as, but not by the same route as, the one described in Ken Wilson's *Classic Rock*. He was killed while serving with the Lovat Scouts in Italy at Christmas 1944, when he fell while sliding down marble banisters in a hotel in Aquila degli Abruzzi, and broke his neck.

Pat Baird took Canadian nationality; as a Colonel in the Canadian Army, he became a well-known expert on the Arctic regions of Canada. He died in 1984.

Alastair Cram was a Scottish lawyer. After war service he became a judge in Kenya. His death was recorded in the 1995 *Alpine Journal*.

Brian Harris had a long career as a schoolmaster at Haileybury and Oundle. I was his first climbing pupil, but many others followed. He lives in Shropshire at the foot of the Long Mynd.

ROBIN HODGKIN

Masherbrum in 1938

(*Plates 63–65, 80*)

In January 1938 I was in Grenoble, learning French and geography during the week and skiing at the weekends. My parents thought I ought to be doing an education diploma if I was going to teach. The Grenoble agenda seemed to be a better idea; especially as there was a possibility of going to the Himalaya or Karakoram before 'settling down'. I had been polite to Colonel Strutt in Edinburgh and friendly with Dr Longstaff at the Alpine Club. There had been some talk of joining Tilman on an unconventional approach to Everest. Then James Waller's letter arrived:

R.A.Mess, Jhansi,
U.P., India

1/1/38

Dear Hodgkin

I have just had a letter from Dr Longstaff, enclosing your letter to him, by which I see that it is on the cards that you might like to join up for our show this year. Of course it is impossible to decide right away, and as a matter of fact, I can only be tentative from this end too, as we have asked a number of men, and many of them are uncertain. As however you are interested, and if you did decide you would like to come, I am almost certain there would be a vacancy. I will give you an outline of the plan and party.

At present Jock Harrison and Roberts (J.O.M., Alpine Club) and I are certainties, if we can get leave. Roberts will only get 2 months leave so cannot be in for the whole climb. Brotherhood (R.A.F.) who was with me on our Peak 36 climb in 1935 is trying to get out from England, but his leave is very uncertain. He has asked a friend called [Reggie] *Cooke, whom I do not know, and who is apparently keen to come but does not know whether he can manage getting out from home. Harrison has asked a man called, I think, Lloyd-Brown* [T Graham Brown], *but I do not know whether he can come, or anything about him.*

From that you see that at present we only have two certainties for the whole climb. I am aiming at a party of 5; 3 is the minimum possible; 6 the maximum.

The mountain is MASHERBRUM, 25660 ft, in the Karakoram, approached from the south and not from the Baltoro glacier. We know practically nothing about the mountain, beyond the fact that I have seen it, and have gathered some photographs of it. From the photos it appears that a rock route might be practicable for most of the way; this is to be desired as Karakoram snow conditions are heavy, to say the least of it! It will however be necessary to make a thorough reconnaissance of the south and east faces, and we are allowing a fortnight to do this, with long leave climbers only.

Travelling hard it will take a fortnight to reach the mountain from Srinagar in Kashmir. The advance party (recce party) proposes leaving Srinagar about the end of April and starting the recce about mid-May. The short leave members start about mid-May and arrive at the beginning of June. The climb takes place in June and is based on a 23 climbing day plan; it should be finished by the end of June, and must be finished by Mid-July, as the monsoon comes then ...

The plan is to do everything as light and simply as possible. It is proposed to have a party of ten carriers for higher camps, if they can get there. They will be Darjeeling men, Gurkhas and possibly locals. The plan does not really allow of prolonged seige tactics, as I think that deterioration is a big factor on this sort of expedition, where comfort has to be greatly sacrificed to lightness and economy. Consequently, although no detailed plan can be made till after the recce, I visualise the climb being in two stages. 1. The stocking of an advanced Base at between 20000 and 22000 feet, probably in two or three carries and descents for recuperation. 2. The assault from the stocked advanced base. As there are two summits and the higher has to be reached over the lower [not so], *it is probable that the highest camp will have to be not far short of 25000 feet, and we are prepared for 8 camps above Base, at about 13000 feet.*

We are trying to keep the climb hush-hush beforehand, and are very definitely against any Press stunting at any time. Nobody except those actually asked knows the objective. The party is going out for the purpose of "sightseeing, shooting and climbing".

The whole thing is run as a soviet. I am merely organiser and general sorting house. I am seeing to buying expedition equipment. We already have a great deal of what is necessary and expenses will be mostly food and transport. Copies of all party letters are sent to all members and for God's sake don't think I look upon myself as that mystic being "the Leader". If we have a large party I think a technical leader is definitely required, but suggest that he is best chosen by the party after we have shaken down, and got each other's measure on the mountain. I shall have to go on as general organiser, but that is merely the quartermaster branch. I propose spending a good deal of time photographing and cinema-ing. The technical leader should be the best climber and fellow with most guts; the latter the most important!

I am sending this Air Mail to France and a copy to the Alpine Club. I should be very glad to hear if you are interested. I hope by the time I hear from you that I shall be in a position to know exactly who has signed on and who hasn't. Frankly, with your qualifications, your Caucasus show, and Dr Longstaff's and Col Strutt's recommendation, I am much more anxious to get you to join than I am the rather unknown quantities in Brotherhood's and Harrison's friends, but unfortunately they were asked first. I think it very unlikely that Brotherhood and the two friends will all be able to come, in which case I do hope you will give us a try. [In the event, Brotherhood did not come.] *Harrison, Roberts and I are all as keen as mustard, but I would hesitate to call us an experienced trio, and your joining would add great strength to the party. We are out to do something really worth while.*

Incidentally I do not think you would find us very Empire Builder! We don't unfortunately run to brain in the army, but I think you would like all the chaps in the party, and I am sure that Harrison and Brotherhood would not ask any one who was not of the best. The team business is rather important, I think, don't you? There shall be no names, but on Peak 36 we had a fellow who is the very nicest I know. He started with the queer idea that all men are brothers, even our black brethren, who really aren't, though they are good blokes in their way, and was shocked at our language. By the end he wasn't, and I don't know what his friends must have thought about mountaineering when he got back!

Would you be so good as to let me know how all this strikes you by Air Mail, as time is none too long? The best for the New Year.

Yours,

James Waller (J. Waller, Lieut. R.A.)

The eccentric 'anti-racist' was, of course, Lieut. Hunt. The rest of this note will be a few comments on the accuracy of James Waller's forecasts, on the interesting mixture of attitudes which the expedition embodied and on some of the surprising friendships which awaited me; and then, finally and briefly, what happened.

Graham Brown – 'Call me Tim'

At sea level Tim Graham Brown could be very pleasant. He gave me lunch at the Atheneum and told me about the scientific work he was doing on hush-hush accoustic devices for detecting German bombers. This not-quite-true tale was probably part of the disinformation screen that was then being put up to confuse the public about the true purpose of the radar installations that were appearing on southern and eastern coasts.

On the P&O liner *Strathnaver*, outward bound for Bombay and the Far East, Graham Brown was good company. He talked a bit about that villain F S Smythe but more about Nanda Devi in 1936; how he *should* have been on the assault party, and I can't quite recall the reason why he wasn't. And advice about girls:

'Watch out for that lass at the swimming pool, Robin, not too much "spooning"'. That was a new word to me and I don't think that G.B. quite realised how inexperienced this young mountaineer was.

'Yes, and watch out for that friendly Indian girl. Mixed marriages with natives can be pretty disastrous ... etc.'

The trouble was that Parvati Kumaramangalam was the most charming person on the boat and beautiful, with South Indian, wiry hair and a wonderful smile. She was a year younger than me and knew many of my Quaker cousins in Oxford; all of them, like her, communistically inclined. Most of us, young idealists of the 1930s, were tinged that way, though some followed alternative allurements and adventurous scents – mountains, scientific research or the Spanish Civil War.*

It was the last evening before we reached Bombay. Parvati and I were leaning over the rail. The sun was down and the Southern Cross was swinging up over the phosphorescent wake. We talked of our hopes, friends, plans. Then she came up with a suggestion.

'Pop into my cabin, Robin, after supper. I'd like to show you something.' This certainly seemed to be an interesting proposition and I didn't feel like consulting G.B. about it. The cabin was sultry. Spread out on the lower bunk were half-a-dozen Dangerous Books – all volumes from Victor Gollancz's Left Book Club: *Barbarians at the Gate* by Leonard Woolf, *Home to India* by Ram Rau, *India Today* by R. Palme Dutt, *Soviet Communism: a New Civilisation* – two notorious volumes of whitewash by the Webbs.

'Well, what about it?'

'Would you mind, Robin, just taking these through the customs tomorrow in your luggage? They won't search yours, but they will mine.

Of course I did my bit for the Indian independence movement and there was no trouble. When we met again, forty years later in Delhi, Parvati was still a communist and an incorruptible MP for Keralla, one of the most successful left wing administrations in Asia. Still beautiful, her black, wiry hair was just beginning to turn grey.

Topees or Terais

My next vivid memory is of meeting Jock Harrison and Jimmy Waller at Rawalpindi. People who were in favour of Indian independence wore soft, floppy 'Terai' hats. Jock articulated the hat code after meeting a strange fellow on the Zemu Glacier, one Marco Pallis, who had shocked the British Resident by wearing the wrong headgear. Marco was ahead of his time in other matters too. Waller wore a cork topee and so did I because I hadn't learned the code yet. Waller was certainly not as blimpish as his letter or his hat might suggest. At one of his recent postings he had been in the habit of spending hours in the local prison visiting Jawaharlal Nehru, and had learnt a lot from him.

---

* In 1937, when Anthony Serrailier (later, ICS) and I made the first ascent of the Radcliffe Camera, we were in two minds about whether to hoist a Red Flag or a Union Jack. Patriotism prevailed and the Daily Mail decided that perhaps Oxford wasn't decadent after all. David Cox and Nulli Kretschmer replaced the flag with a white hankerchief ten days later, so saving the authorities a certain amount of trouble.

Then came the houseboat days in Srinagar and the gentle march over the Zoji La, skiing for two or three miles from the Zoji crest. Down into the arid gorges of Indus and Shyok. Marvellous, those granite cliffs and precarious paths linking the villages and the foaming apricot orchards. Jock claimed that he could spit a stone right over the Indus gorge.

Jimmy Roberts and his two Gurkhas made a rapid journey across the Deosai Plains to catch up the main Masherbrum party just above the Shyok junction. We had a feast that night – curried chicken, with green Chartreuse from Grenoble. Jimmy's energy, wit and sparkle were very good for us. With his family connections with Wilfrid Noyce and General Bruce and his early love of mountains, one felt that he was destined for a life in the great mountains and with mountain people. He and Jock were to become my incomparable friends and were to remain so for over half a century.

Reading Jimmy Waller's letter 60 years later, one can see behind the Boys Own Paper phrases a remarkable prescience. His ideas on equipment, clothes, tents, dehydration, acclimatisation, and on the timing of the reconnaissance, were all very sound. For a small expedition, his views on leadership were sensibly Shiptonian. The 'lesser breeds' attitude was characteristic of the time and place. But what about the secrecy? I think this was largely a reflection of Waller's feeling that he had got onto a good thing: so why tell everybody? Which is odd, if you consider that there were probably only two other expeditions active in the Karakoram that year.

Our equipment was, for 1938, both simple and up-to-date. And being pre-war, meant no vibrams, no nylon rope, and Shetland combinations rather than down clothing. Waller had two double-deck 'Reggie Cooke' cookers – snow melting in the top pan, and all inside an aluminium sleeve. High-altitude tents and wind-proofs were of a new, proofed cotton, tougher than the usual Grenfell cloth. Boots were mainly Lawrie's, nailed with his 'Everest' clinkers. Mine had an extra layer of asbestos in the sole – 'to reduce heat loss'! – though I suspect that it soaked up moisture and refroze just like the rest of the leather. Graham Brown had a special, hickory-shafted, folding axe that he had used on The Pear Buttress and the first vertical-partitioned sleeping bag I had seen. Underneath were Li-los which occasionally popped.

A 'recce' which became serious

The reconnaissance went very much according to plan. During the second week Jock and I found the route, up Scaly Alley, past the icefall and up to the Dome, which most subsequent parties have used. T.G.B. was beginning to feel the altitude and was getting tetchy. He started to advocate a rather unlikely route, up the steep southern ridge which bounds the main south-east face on its left. It would have been extremely long and hazardous. After several days of snow, Jock and I, who were the best acclimatised members of the party, managed to get a camp (7) – one tent – at about 24,000ft on the SW face. That face always seems to have been free from major avalanches. No big ice cliffs above; but even so we were very mindful of recent Nanga Parbat disasters. Neither the Walmsley-Whillans-Downes expedition of 1957, which very nearly reached the summit crest, nor the Americans, in their successful 1960 expedition, experienced more than minor snow slides on the face.

In one repect Jimmy Waller and all of us were seriously ill-informed. We still thought of the Karakoram weather as dominated by the monsoon. Only later did we understand that the Karakoram pattern is far more 'Alpine' and influenced by the tail-end of the westerly system. Had we realised this and had we been less apprehensive about avalanches, we might have just sat it out when things went wrong. Especially if we had known about snow holes *and* had had a shovel! When the snow avalanche buried Jock and me in that snug little tent at about 24,000ft, we burrowed out into a pre-dawn blizzard of driving snow. We retrieved our boots, one axe and some other gear and groped our way down into the storm.

'It can't take more than two hours,' we thought. Couldn't it? It was almost dark again before we found a comfortable crevasse and some shelter from the wind. By then our hands were going black and our toes were like ivory. By the morning it was sunny again and from the edge of our crevasse we could see Jimmy Waller waving an axe at Camp 6. At the next camp down we enjoyed a drink and G.B. was cross and said it would have been all right if we had taken his advice. His toes and Passang Phutar's were frostbitten too. But we all hobbled down to Hushe. From then on, Jock was carried and I sat on a horse for the long trek back to Srinagar. I remember sitting under a mulberry tree at the rest house in Khapalu reflecting about it all.

'Ah well, even if you can't do any more climbing, you'll be able to get a red MG and nip around North Wales.'

Jock Harrison was more seriously frostbitten than I was. He eventually lost almost half his feet, though his hands were tidier than mine. I was able to climb more than he was, mainly because my surgeon left a more generous flap over the foot amputations. Jock went to New Zealand after marrying a NZ nurse from his army hospital in London. He eventually became a founder and bursar of the first Outward Bound school in New Zealand. Had it not been for our disaster, he might well have become a great soldier-statesman, perhaps rivalling Wavell or Alexander. Both Waller and Roberts had distinguished and varied war service. The former retired, soon afterwards, to the Isle of Jersey. Somewhere there, I believe there is still an unedited version of the Masherbrum film he had made.

You don't really need many fingers for old-fashioned rock climbing. A month before the war started, John and Joy Hunt took me up my first rock climb, in Borrowdale. There was no MG. I was posted to the Sudan which I had been led to believe was flat. But it wasn't – there were good hills around the edges. My Sudanese pupils were a bit puzzled by my frostbite and found it easier to imagine an encounter with a crocodile.

News came of Jimmy Roberts' death after this article was in proof. I remember him, vividly, in Pokhara, thirty years after these events. Talk about expeditions, sweet and sour, about Tiger Tops, the future of trekking, his fancy pheasant farm; all to do with his ideas and hopes for his adopted clan of Sherpas. Four of them gave me a wonderful trip round the southern slopes and valleys of Annapurna. Much of the Sherpa's guts, integrity and fun was reflected in Jimmy's wrinkled glance; something too of the grace and greatness of the hills – Machapuchare rising sublimely above the mists to the north.

JOHN JACKSON

The Prophet of Mulbek Gompa

(*Plates 54 and 55*)

On a day late in October 1944, I was with a group of fighter pilots on the Ladakh side of the Zoji La. A cold and biting wind blew straight down the valley, rattling the wooden shutters of our caravanserai where a pine log fire warmed the main room. The wind whipped down the sooty chimney, frequently filling the dwelling with smoke, making eyes smart and shed salt tears. A good strong smell of frying eggs and soya links was mixed with that of wood smoke, damp clothes, steaming leather boots and body sweat. Outside the wind was increasing in its strength and ferocity, blowing great globs of snow almost horizontally to the east from whence appeared a line of pack mules and many men. With heads down against the cutting wind and cold of snow, they forced their way along the track to the rest house at Matayan. When the line of travellers arrived, I was delighted to recognise my friends Harry Tilly and Gordon Whittle who were returning with their party from a journey to the Wakka-Chu, and to the Buddhist gompa of Mulbek.

The gompa of Mulbek! Later, I came to know it well. The path to the gompa, which is steep and lined with prayer-flags, winds behind the back of the aiguille before leading to the door of the monastery. The gompa was built on a massive block of limestone laid down over 200 million years earlier when the subcontinent of India was close to Antarctica and slowly moving northwards in the Tethys sea. The 'red hat' lamas are members of a sect which practises a lamaism less strict than those who wear the yellow hat, for they still retain some of the customs of the earlier Bon religion of Tibet. Their long robes are the colour of old red wine, and on their feet they wear a special type of *cratpa* (felt boots) with turned-up toes and calf length uppers of brilliant crimson colour.

Neither of the lamas who received me when I first visited the monastery spoke Hindustani and no method of communication was possible, but their gestures were friendly, their faces all smiles and I followed them into the flat-roofed building. Light filtered into passages through narrow wood-framed slits and lit up rows of wooden prayer-wheels, wooden drums with a central spindle round which the drum can revolve. The hollow drum is filled with carefully folded papers on which have been printed many Buddhist prayers. A light touch of the finger causes these to revolve, and each turn of the wheel is the equivalent of saying many thousands of prayers.

Wheels vary greatly in size, type and colour and some which are little larger than a bobbin are held in the hand. This type have drums made of copper embossed with lively lotus patterns, figures of Buddha and the prayer *Om Mani Padme Hum*. As the band rotates clockwise the drum turns and a chain with a piece of lead attached swings outward, helping the rotation by centrigugal force. Larger wheels, some of them twenty feet high, are turned by water-power. Bright colours are popular, though sometimes in this and similar monasteries age and neglect have turned them to a dull brown. From Ladakh to Sola Khumbu and beyond they have the same in construction and meaning, and, like the torcho or the chorten, symbolise to the traveller the high mountain and plateau country of Central Asia.

The passageway led off into a room smelling strongly of rancid butter which was burning in small brass goblets – a tiny wick giving forth a small amount of light. Clothed Buddhas and idols were placed side by side in rows, one above the other. Cymbals, drums, flutes and huge ten-foot trumpets (Saung Daungs) littered the floor. Ceremonial masks covered the walls. It was a dusty room conveying an atmosphere of great age.

The drone of a voice attracted me to another small ill-lit alcove. Again butter lamps were burning, this time by a small table on which was propped a gompa book. A sharp-eyed, bald-headed monk sat cross-legged by the book, reading aloud at tremendous speed. His was a chanting voice that maintained one note, dropping only slightly at the end of a sentence or a page. Occasionally there was a bubbly, sucking noise; the monk swallowed, paused for a moment and then the rustle of paper indicated the turning of a page. Here time was of no importance.

After we had fed Harry and Gordon and provided them with steaming hot mugs of tea, Harry told us of their visit to the gompa and of their meeting with the Head Lama. Whilst in a trance he had told them that in the following year (1945) the war in the west would end, with the defeat of Germany. A less credible part of the prophecy was that the war in the east would also end in the same year and, most dramatically, with the use of a weapon that would be catastrophic in its power. It was a strange story and one not easy to believe. Even so, Tilly's description of Mulbek, of butter tea and gompa books, devil masks, incense shrines and images of Buddha, made me want to visit that distant place and meet the man of prophecy.

I did so on several occasions, but it was in August 1945, when I had returned to Kashmir again, that the improbable prophecy came true. I had been with Bill Starr on a mountain reconnaissance in the Matayan area of Ladakh. We had been attracted by a beautiful pyramidal-shaped peak at the head of the Matayan nullah. Something about its purity of line and the virgin innocence of its snows drew us like a magnet. We climbed it by the north ridge and, despite the lack of gripping technical problems, each foot of ascent set our spirits soaring. Strangely, that day we both felt an exceptionally strong sense of freedom and exhilaration; then finally at the summit a peace that all mountains of age, durability and isolation can give.

We found a cairn built by Gordon Whittle and Ralph Stokoe and realised that this was none other than 'Cumberland Peak' of which they had made the first ascent the year before. To the north we could see the Karakoram, the highest points disappearing into a cloud base at some 24,000ft, and were elated at making this second ascent – the first by the north ridge. Quietly we added stones to the cairn that linked us with our friends and reminded us of days shared with them on other mountains.

A few days later, on 19 August, we sat cooling our feet in the cold glacial waters of the Sind River below Gund. A pale-faced group of young men, air crews fresh out from Britain, walked towards us along the dusty track.

'Hi! What's the latest news of the war?', we asked, having been a week away in Ladakh.

'Don't you know?' they exclaimed, 'the war ended four days ago!'

'But that's impossible! How?'

'A bomb! Enormously powerful. Catastrophic! At one blast it destroys whole towns or cities. Two Japanese cities, Nagasaki and Hiroshima, have been totally demolished and the Japs ended the war before more bombs could be used. Yes – it's all over!'

It was a hot summer's day in the Sind valley with the sun blazing down from a clear azure sky, but I felt the hairs curl on the back of my neck. I remembered the evening in Matayan the previous year, and the recounting of the prophecy by the Head Lama of Mulbek, as told to Harry and Gordon. suddenly it was cold, as if a chill wind was blowing out from the barren lands to the east.

'Which was the day the war ended?' I asked.

'On the 15th of August,' was the answer – and I realised it was the day we had climbed Cumberland Peak and experienced such a great sense of freedom and peace.

I have told the story of the prophecy to many people and it has never failed to impress. Though inexplicable, it is true!

SIDNEY NOWILL

Adventures in Zanskar and Lahul

(*Plates 51–53*)

In mid-June 1983 the land route over the western Himalaya from Kashmir to Ladakh was still closed by snow. I had been trekking in Kashmir with my wife Hilary and we had wanted to move over to Ladakh to watch the Tibetan Buddhist rites and dances at the Hemis Monastery. But buses were not yet able to get through. We decided, therefore, to hire a horse and a ponyman from near Baaltal, and proceed on foot. At the Zoji La the local roads people were starting to cut through the drifts, and we found ourselves walking with 50ft walls on either side. Later, it became a matter of selecting the hardest snow for the horse to walk on.

After various vicissitudes, we reached the grim locality of Kargil at 2am, in utter darkness, after a 21-hour day. Three days later, feeling rather smug, we watched the Hemis Festival in the company of the other visitors who had flown in from Delhi. (The Zoji La was opened a fortnight later.)

After some travels in Ladakh, we returned by bus to Kargil via Lamayuru, and patiently made our presence felt there by letting it be known that we wanted a horse, to undertake a short expedition in northern Zanskar. On our outward journey, with the help of the Baaltal horse, we had made a dump in Kargil of a wooden packing case of stores bought in the bazaar in Srinagar, including the fuel and a cooker (plus the all-important 'pricker'). Patience was eventually rewarded after three days, when a young man approached us saying he knew of a ponyman with a horse in Pannikar (or Suru); he would effect the introduction – and it was only three hours by jeep from Kargil.

The prospect of penetrating the wild lands of northern Zanskar held great allure. We felt an agreeable tingle of excitement as the jeep bumped south on its way to Suru, and glaciated Himalayan peaks hove into view. After locating the horse and its owner, we undid the packing case and tipped the contents into two orange tarpaulin bags with eyelets and padlocks, previously made for the purpose in Istanbul. As the ponyman was not a linguist, means of communication were minimal; but I pointed up to a high ridge, saying 'Pukartse La', having resolved to enter Zanskar by the shorter (in miles) but more exacting, and higher route (also known as Parkatchik La).

We were not disappointed. After a tedious and seemingly never-ending ascent, which made me wonder what we were doing, a final crest became discernible. Then suddenly, bursting into view without warning, surged the 7000m peaks of Nun and Kun, across the intervening Suru Valley, rising 3000m higher than where we stood. It's one of the great views of the Himalaya – I had read about it, of course – but nothing prepares the traveller for the sudden revelation.

The descent to Parkatchik was steep, and the day was far spent. There was little visibility in the dim crepuscular light. We were not yet properly organised in a travel mode and had to spend the night on the sooty floor of a flea-ridden hovel. Domestic hens and cocks had settled down singly for the hours of darkness in small niches in the wall above our heads, emitting the odd unpredictable squawk. There was a whirlwind in the night, and a few flakes of snow.

Next day we were confronted by the passage of the Suru Gorges, made hazardous by the need to traverse slopes of hard snow which had completely buried what we believed must be the track to Rangdom, the Pensi La and Padum (jeepable only in midsummer). Twice we had to unload the horse and make a portage, returning to cut steps for the animal which the ponyman, walking backwards, encouraged and pulled forwards by the bridle, while I advanced uphill from behind, holding the horse's tail. Hilary watched this bizarre performance with horror. One slip could have precipitated our pack-horse into the roaring Suru, thundering along 200 feet below us, with waves five or six feet high. Luckily we had our ice-axes, but missed the reassurance of crampons.

The rest of the trip passed without incident. Every night we would put the tent up and marvel at the extraordinarily clean, moistureless atmosphere. There was no recession of planes to be discerned. Peaks that were 30 miles away stood out with the same intense sharpness and gradation of colour as landscape features only three miles distant. Towards sunset the fierce frost drove us into our tent early. We would retire to deal with the paraffin cooker, prick the cooker holes, and hope that it would work. The ponyman had warm equipment, but slept out, at or under whatever exiguous shelter could be found. Minimum night temperatures were typically between minus 10° and minus 12°C.

Studying the rudimentary map which was all we had to guide us, we had been intrigued to notice that there was a locality called Gulmatangze on the way east along the Suru Valley to our goal at Rangdom. Having expected to come upon three or four houses at least, we were surprised to find that the great metropolis of Gulmatangze had no houses or dwellings of any kind. It just consisted of a few large boulders and a wind-break, surrounded by Himalayan peaks, and inhabited by a single family and their animals.

We stopped and tarried with these hardy people, unable to communicate except by signs, but conscious of receiving from them an unmistakable flow of benevolence, friendship and welcome. They even offered us food, of which they had very little. We offered in return a little salt, which was happily accepted. It was difficult to leave Gulmatangze. We felt relaxed and exhilarated by these fellow human beings. They lived in unimaginable privation and poverty, yet seemingly in harmony with their surroundings and the universe – asking for nothing but the temporary gift of life, in the great wheel of Buddhist existence.

On the fourth day of our leisurely journey, with the glaciers and snow peaks of Nun and Kun behind us, we saw ahead the half-dozen houses of Juldo, their prayer flags fluttering in the late afternoon light. Suddenly we felt the pull of Zanskar. It had become real. The rest of the world had vanished. Here was a country of seven or eight thousand souls, half of them monks, living under conditions scarcely imaginable to the average Westerner. This remote land is one of the highest and coldest inhabited areas on earth. In endless solitude and silence, it lies sundered for two-thirds of the year from the rest of the planet. No crime of any sort had been recorded there. Imbued with the quietude, non-aggression and respect for all life implicit in ancient Buddhism, these people laboured for the few months in summer when nature was benign, to garner the crops that would sustain life during the rest of the year – an activity in which all who could participated, including the monks from the monasteries.

We erected our tent at a certain remove from the houses. After a discreet interval we received the welcoming visit of a couple of Juldo ladies wearing heavy clothing against the evening frost. The next day we walked over rough terrain to the Monastery of Rangdom, almost invisible under the huge scarps of a stratified mountain which towered above it. We spent some time with the Gelupta or yellow-cap monks who lived there. While making the passage of a wide area of shallow glacial rivers lying across our route, we came across the only folk who crossed our path during this 1983 journey into Zanskar. They were Elaine Brook and a Sherpa companion, carrying huge packs. Unlike the elderly Nowills, these people were real travellers, beholden to no one, unsupported and free. We saluted their endurance and physical strength with admiration.

Our whole 1983 expedition, from Kargil to Kargil, had cost us a total of £80, including numerous items donated to the ponyman upon our return to Parkatchik and the cost of the stores and fuel bought in Srinagar. It was the remotest travel we had ever accomplished, and left us determined to return to these haunting landscapes, but with bigger ambitions, for a more serious enterprise. As it happens, this was just about the time when trekking groups began to change the ethos of the Zanskaris under the assaults of Il Turismo over the Shingo La (from Himachal Pradesh). But you cannot change the world. Hilary and I remained under the spell of Zanskar, and resolved to come back.

Impediments began to emerge shortly afterwards, including cancer of the lip and the start of single vessel coronary heart disease. The two consultants threatened to forbid solar radiation, on the one hand, and conditions of anoxia (if upward movement was included), on the other. But the resulting delay was only temporary, as our wish to return to Zanskar had become a compulsion.

By 1985 I had decided that the following year would see us back in the western Himalaya for a much more ambitious programme. Invited to join us were Francis Meynell, an old friend living in Capetown, and Robert Jones, a highly experienced American alpinist, and my occasional companion of more than three decades of mountain endeavour. The suggested programme was a crossing of the icy desert lands of northern Lahul via the Baralacha La, starting from Darsha, to be followed by entry into Zanskar over the 5300m Phirtse La; from there we would seek to reach the uniquely impressive and semi-troglodytic monastery of Phuktal before moving back into southern Zanskar, with exit over the Shingo La.

There were two prior necessities: firstly, good research and preparation, and secondly (in my case), a long, thorough and slow training and acclimatisation programme. The former presented no problem for a hardened old expeditioner, and we soon agreed a 22/23-day chart of movements. As to the latter, one obviously had to grow the mandatory three-month beard to satisfy the dermatologist and spend six prior weeks of mountain activity to head off criticism from the other consultant.

After a few snowy weeks in the Aladag mountains of southern Turkey, I solicited the company of an admirable cicerone from Skye. Jean Thomas led me up classic trips like the Tour Ronde, carried through in the slowest of slow motion. This was no hardship for Jean, who was also a watercolour painter of some repute, and able to enjoy the mountain scene quietly. I had climbed the Peuterey Ridge of Mont Blanc 19 years previously, and now we looked at leisure towards this incomparable sweep of mountain form. But Jean had never actually seen the summit of Mont Blanc. So I said 'all right, I'll take you.'

For most readers of the AJ, the Goûter route must be regarded as a 'wearisome plod' ; but for the writer, on his final visit to the mountain, it had reverted to the status of dreamland. It would be unthinkable to participate in the morning rush. So Jean and I slipped out of the Goûter hut at exactly midnight. First party out, we stepped into a universe of upper glaciers picked out in the last rays of a setting moon, now retreating behind the ridges of the Bionnassay. The slopes ahead of us glinted sharply. Our crampons squeaked as the prongs bit into iron-hard snow.

In old age ambitions begin to fade. Finally they are muted. One becomes more receptive then – more open – to the immanence of the planetary firmament. At these great heights, the slow rhythms of a night march under the stars provided unalloyed pleasure.

It took us all of fourteen hours to climb to the summit of Mont Blanc and return to the Goûter. Could this be a record?

Some days later Hilary and I were on a flight to India and bound for Kashmir, where further activity followed in the shape of ten days of high-altitude trekking. If the writer had not reached his optimum of training and acclimatisation by then he obviously never would. So we moved over to Himachal Pradesh.

Francis, Bob, Hilary and I emerged from a 13½ hour journey from Manali to Darsha, over the Rothang Pass (it's only 140km, but we had a breakdown on the way), to erect tents in the dark on a stubbly field at Darsha. It was an inauspicious start, and precursor of more troubles to follow. But THE EXPEDITION HAD BEGUN!

We had agreed in advance for two riding horses, with riding saddles, to be provided. But the next morning, when we asked to see the riding saddles after the ponyman had made an appearance, the request was greeted with derision. There was only one riding horse, equipped with a wooden saddle reinforced with protuberant iron slats. Darsha has an unfortunate reputation, and our unco-operative ponymen confirmed it. One pack-horse was loaded to the exclusion of all else by their enormous and tattered communal tent. However, we packed up and set out for Patseo at 4300m – an easy stage of 15 kilometres.

The second day we moved on to Upper Zing Zing Bar, 300m higher, and put up our tents by the old Shiva temple, following the route of a military road, still under construction, to Leh. Sharp stones and rocks littered the site, so we had an uncomfortable night. The next morning, however, the brilliant mountain light and the peaks around us started to lift our spirits, which improved further when we saw that the last monsoon clouds were being left behind. Crossing the 5000m Baralacha La was part of our next stage. This pass is the gateway to the frozen wastes of northern Lahul, and it turned out to be the gentlest and easiest we had ever traversed. Only the prayer flags and the sheets of edelweiss, never before seen in such profusion, told us that we had reached the top. We were now above the summit of Mont Blanc.

After the Baralacha La we turned left and north, off the route of the military road, and finally north-west into vast landscapes tilting upwards, with small glaciers all around. The sky had turned to the darkest of deep blue. The air was implausibly clear. Again, no recession of planes. One morning we saw the moon rise with the same blaze of blue-diamond effulgence as a moon riding at the zenith. The humidity must have been virtually nil. It was hot at midday, in conditions of extreme solar radiation, but very cold at night. Of snow there was not a sign anywhere except on very high peaks. This could perhaps represent the highest snowline in the world at, say, 6000m, or slightly higher.

In the mornings the cook would get up early but the ponymen were slow to stir. They often didn't strike their tent until 10am. We sometimes left before them and struck out on our own, having agreed on a general direction to follow. When we departed together they would immediately roar off ahead of us in a cloud of dust. But they were co-operative when it came to rivers. At any serious river crossing they would wait to help us. Rivers are the only serious risk in this area. The only fatalities to travellers have occurred as a result of the hazard of drowning; or of being ground to pieces in glacial torrents.

One of our predecessors on the trek had told me that we should on no account spend just one night on the Lingti Ground. 'Spend two,' she had said. 'It's Paradise. So why not savour it?' Lingti was perhaps the highlight of our journey. We felt like Tennyson's Lotos Eaters, looking well on the beautiful world, surrounded by the wonder of the mountain scene and untroubled by doubt. The sky was blue and nearby diaphanous cloudlets looked like the backdrop of a stage. Several days of travel separated us from all other humans. It *was* paradise, and we did stay two nights.

The next day we started a difficult march to the locality of Khamerup. It was a hard stage, with complicated route-finding and numerous deep nullahs to cross and climb back out of. Despite resort to Diamox, I began to find the exertion troublesome and breathing difficult. When we finally arrived at Khamerup in the warm afternoon, this reputedly most dangerous of the rivers was thundering along and looked quite impassable. We didn't even attempt it, but put the tents up and awaited the morrow. By early morning and after a night of severe frost the flow of water from the glaciers had considerably diminished, and the water level had gone down two feet. For once the ponymen got up early. One of them made a trial crossing, mounted. I was next. Eventually everyone was over, plus all our food and equipment.

The landscape was now tilting inexorably upwards. We were being hemmed in. The next stage was the penultimate stage in northern Lahul. We were bound for our highest camp at Chumik Marpo – the summer site (I had read) of a group of yak breeders. But when we arrived at Chumik Marpo there was no trace or sign of their previous presence. These are lonely lands, and during the whole of our trek we had only met one shepherd and one itinerant Zanskari on a horse.

On the way up to Chumik Marpo one of the horses had fallen. It was carrying the fuel tank, and also the flour sack. But after checking the tank and detecting no damage, I had it re-loaded. Next morning we had a very unpleasant surprise. We were seated as usual on stones, waiting for our morning chapattis to appear. But when they did, the first mouthful revealed that disaster had struck. There had been an invisible pin hole in the tank and the constant jogging of the horse had allowed the fuel to seep away. The flour-sack was now useless, impregnated with paraffin. And we had no fuel left. Worse was to follow. A full-scale search revealed that some of our stores had been plundered by the ponymen. Other items had succumbed to the high noonday temperatures and become inedible. There were, however, biscuits left, and some tins of cheese.

Furthermore, Francis was feeling unwell and unable to move. Bob and Hilary, though, were in excellent form and represented a positive asset on our balance sheet. Bob's reaction was a tonic to morale. 'Let's leave Francis in camp for a quiet day. And the rest of us can nip up to the Phirtse La. Perhaps we'll glimpse K2! The La is only five or six hundred metres above us.' We took one horse, which I mounted for spells of 10-15 minutes, or until the iron crossbars became intolerable to bruised thighs. In a little over 2½ hours we were up at the La. Our two double-dial 7000m Thommen altimetres gave an adjusted height reading of 5300m +/– 50m. It's a 17,000ft pass, anyway.

Hilary and Bob went up a small peak east of the pass hoping to catch a glimpse of the great peaks of the Karakoram, but remote clouds obstructed their view. As we went down back to camp, I began to consider our options: we had little food and no fuel. The view from Phirtse La was impressive, but the way off the La and down into Zanskar lay over a tilted glacier that looked uninviting. I reckoned we needed seven to eight days more to complete the journey via Phuktal and back over the Shingo La. This looked problematical, to say the least, given the fuel and food situation.

We had been given the opportunity, thanks to Bob Jones, of getting a decent Satellite map from the Library of Congress; but I had decided to refuse it, as the risks from being caught with something like that in such an area were unacceptable. Our rather rudimentary 1:200,000 map indicated an escape route over a very high pass to the west. If surmounted, this could save several days of food and travel and land us in Zanskar at Kargiyah, only a couple of days from the Shingo La, on a route which commercial trekking parties were now using.

I decided it was that or nothing. The next day we struck camp at Chumik Marpo, beginning already to feel hungry; and attacked the climb to a rarely attained goal, the Surichun La. Francis and I took turns on the 'riding horse'. Slowly we gained ground, mounting to the highest rim of the upsweeping landscape. It took 6½ hours of strenuous activity before a panoply of peaks and glaciers started to meet our gaze. The horses were stopping to pant, with rasping breath, every minute or so; only a prodigious effort, with pounding hearts, landed us finally, in the late afternoon, on the actual pass of Surichun La, 5760m (18,900ft). On our left and lower down was a wall of ice about 250m high, which we skirted on the descent, to establish camp at 5210m on the Zanskar side. Otherwise we had walked on dry rocks or stones.

Next morning all the streams had frozen solid. It was our highest campsite ever. And we had no fuel. From there we went down on bad ground to a valley which led us in to Kargiyah in southern Zanskar. Our first glimpse of houses and chortens brought us an emotional feeling of reunion. And also a sense of deliverance.

I sent two ponymen to Purne to seek fuel and food. They returned twelve hours later with a little fuel, but no food. A day later we stopped for a midday rest, and exiguous snack, at the spring under the cliffs of the holy peak of Gumbaranjon. All around us were blue poppies. It was an Anniversary – and the day when this traveller was entering the second half of his seventh decade. We celebrated the occasion with one last tin of shrimps and a few biscuits.

Three days later we all made Darsha again, each losers of between 20 and 25lbs; but gainers of memories to bank for ever.

C A RUSSELL

One Hundred Years Ago

(with extracts from the *Alpine Journal*)

(*Plates 72–76*)

January, 1898, has been an extraordinary month in the High Alps. A succession of cloudless days following on one of the smallest falls of snow on record has made winter climbing much less laborious than it usually is. After an ascent of Piz Sella on Jan. 12, I went on the 19th to Boval, the little club hut by the Morteratsch Glacier. I was accompanied by a friend and two guides, and on the 20th, in summerlike weather, we made the ascent of Piz Palü, taking many photographs *en route*. The following day we went up another big mountain, Piz Zupo, 13,100 feet, and plied the camera again diligently on its head and sides. Though a cloudless day, there was a little wind, and on the top we felt somewhat chilly after an hour's stay. Indeed, my friend had to retire to bed with a slightly frost-bitten toe when we got home, and all our food and drinkables were frozen even by our return at 3.30 p.m. to the Morteratsch restaurant.

The favourable conditions experienced by Mrs Elizabeth Main[1] and P H Cooke during their climbs from the Boval hut with the guides Martin Schocher and Christian Schnitzler were enjoyed in many parts of the Alps during the opening weeks of 1898. On 28 January Frederick Gardiner and his wife Alice, accompanied by Ulrich, Rudolf, Hans and Peter Almer and a porter, reached the summit of the Wetterhorn after a night at the Gleckstein hut.

The weather throughout the expedition was superb. This is believed to be the second winter ascent of the Wetterhorn by a lady, the previous one having been made by Miss Brevoort[2] in 1874.

Another expedition of note, on 21 March, was the first ascent under winter conditions of Piz Morteratsch by E L Strutt and L C Rawlence with Schocher.

During the winter months the development of ski mountaineering was continued by small groups of enthusiasts at several of the principal resorts. On 5 January Wilhelm Paulcke and Robert Helbling attempted to climb the Dufourspitze, the highest peak of the Monte Rosa group, on ski, reaching a height of 4200m before Helbling became too ill to continue. Several weeks later, on 23 March, a ski ascent of the Dufourspitze – the first ski ascent of a 4000m peak – was completed by Oskar Schuster with Heinrich Moser.

The low temperatures and heavy snowfalls experienced in most Alpine regions during the spring and early summer were followed by a long spell of settled weather which continued throughout the mountaineering season.

> Not since 1881 has there been such a hot summer in the Alps as this one. The wonderful beauty of the weather during the last few weeks has made the climbing season quite a record one and seldom have the guides had more to do. There is a great deal of snow but it is in admirable condition. The Matterhorn is being ascended from the Swiss side by three or four parties daily and has also been traversed from the Italian side on at least three occasions.

One of the first parties to take advantage of the ideal conditions was that of Victor de Cessole who had commenced his exploration of the Maritime Alps. On 29 July de Cessole and Louis Maubert with Jean Plent and B Piacenza opened a fine route to the S, highest summit of the Punta dell' Argentera by way of the Promontoire Buttress and the W face. In the Graian Alps an outstanding route was followed on 13 August when J P Farrar with Daniel Maquignaz and Johann Köderbacher junior made the first complete traverse from the Gran Paradiso to Mont Herbetet.

In the Mont Blanc range on 17 August the Duke of the Abruzzi, the leader of the successful expedition to Mount St Elias (5489m) during the previous year, accompanied on this occasion by Giuseppe Petigax, Lorenzo Croux and Alphonse Simond made the first ascent of the Aiguille Sans Nom, on the ridge between the Aiguille du Dru and the Aiguille Verte. A few days later, on 22 August, the same party with Cesare and Felice Ollier in place of Simond made the first ascents of Punta Margherita[3] and Punta Elena[4] on the W ridge of the Grandes Jorasses after approaching the ridge from the south by way of the Rocher du Reposoir. Farrar and his party climbed Mont Blanc on 16 August after completing the second[5] traverse of the narrow ridge from the Aiguille de Bionnassay to the Dôme du Goûter and three days later reached the gendarme now known as Pointe Farrar[6] during an attempt to scale the Grands Montets ridge of the Aiguille Verte.

On 7 August on the Aiguille de Blaitière Sydney Spencer, with Christian Jossi senior and Hans Almer, took advantage of the favourable snow conditions above the Nantillons glacier to make the first ascent of the couloir which now bears his name. Later in the month, on 25 August, Adolfo Hess with Croux and Cesare Ollier completed the first ascent, by way of the SE ridge, of the Aiguille de la Brenva, one of the peaks associated in later years with the exploits of Gabriele Boccalatte and other famous climbers. Other new routes included the N ridge of the Tour Noir, climbed on 23 July by a party which included Théodore Aubert and the guide Maurice Crettez, and the NE ridge of Mont Maudit, ascended by

J S Masterman with Albert and Benedikt Supersaxo on 31 July during a traverse of Mont Blanc.

In the Arolla district on 18 August the unclimbed S summit of La Singla, the long rock ridge above the Otemma glacier, was reached by Ettore Canzio and Felice Mondini with Giacomo Noro as porter. A few days later, on 27 August, an expedition to the Petite Dent de Veisivi ended in tragedy when John Hopkinson, his son Jack and his daughters Alice and Lina fell to their deaths from a point high on the S face.

Further along the chain, on 12 July, Herbert Speyer accompanied by Ambros Supersaxo and Xavier Imseng and assisted by the favourable snow conditions was able to complete a new route to the summit of the Lagginhorn by way of the W face and the S ridge. On 2 September Hans Lorenz and Eduard Wagner made the first guideless ascent of the Schaligrat, the SW ridge of the Weisshorn. A week later, on 9 September, this formidable party completed another magnificent climb by making the first guideless ascent of the NW, Zmutt ridge of the Matterhorn. Another notable expedition was the first ascent, on 21 September, of the NNW, known as the N, ridge of the Weisshorn by Hans Biehly with Heinrich Burgener.

In the Bernese Oberland on 17 August C A Macdonald with Rudolf and Peter Almer made the first ascent of the NW ridge of the Klein Schreckhorn. On the southern side of the range a youthful visitor at the Belalp Hotel was Geoffrey Winthrop Young who on 3 September with Clemenz Ruppen reached the summit of the Gross Fusshorn by way of the unclimbed S ridge.

To the east in the Bernina Alps two notable expeditions were completed: the first ascent, on 22 July, of the NE face of Piz Scerscen by H C Foster with Martin Schocher and Ben Cadonan; and earlier in the season on 21 June the first traverse from the S, Italian side of the Porta da Roseg or Güssfeldtsattel, the high pass between Piz Scerscen and Piz Roseg, by Anton von Rydzewski with Christian Klucker and Mansueto Barbaria. The descent of the very steep ice wall on the N, Swiss side of the pass was one of Klucker's greatest achievements.

In the Dolomites J S Phillimore and the Rev A G S Raynor continued their exploration of the region and completed a number of new routes; on 17 August with Antonio Dimai, Michel Innerkofler and Zaccaria Pompanin they reached the summit of the Antelao after climbing the S face, an outstanding exploit for the period. Another fine achievement, on 21 July, was the first ascent of the W ridge of the Marmolada di Penia by Hans Seyffert and a friend, Dr Dittmann, with the guide Luigi Rizzi.

At the end of the season, on 24 September, a notable expedition was completed in the Dauphiné by Eugène Gravelotte accompanied by Maximin, Casimir and Devouassoud Gaspard and Joseph Turc. After ascending a new route up the N face of the Meije along the line of a couloir rising to the Brèche Zsigmondy – the Gravelotte couloir – the party climbed the Grand Pic before traversing the E, summit ridge to the Pic Central and descending to La Grave.

On 17 May the death occurred of the great guide Christian Almer senior, of Grindelwald. Later in the year Charles Pilkington, President of the Alpine Club, described Almer as

> ... that prince of guides, who for so many years led the fathers of the Alpine Club to victory, and never to disaster, and who, even in his old age, was able to guide their sons and show them how boldness could be allied with discretion, and that determination and experience were two of the greatest factors in mountaineering success ... .

On 20 August a famous mountain railway was officially opened to the public.

> It is a misfortune for that bold undertaking, the Gornergrat Railway, that a series of obstacles should have delayed the opening until almost the end of the Alpine Season. The whole of this truly marvellous line to the glacier-world has a length of little more than ten kilometres, or somewhat over six English miles.

Elsewhere in the Alps considerable progress was made in connection with other major engineering projects. The first section of the Jungfrau Railway, from Kleine Scheidegg to Eigergletscher Station, was inaugurated on 18 September and by the end of the summer work had commenced on the construction of the Simplon tunnel.

During the year many successful expeditions were completed in other mountain regions. In Norway W P Haskett Smith, Geoffrey Hastings and W C Slingsby visited the Lyngen Peninsula where on 15 July, accompanied by J Caspari, a schoolmaster, and E M Hogrenning as porter, they made the first ascent of Stortind[7] (1512m). Other unclimbed peaks ascended by the party, without Caspari, included Store Jaegervasstind (1540m) on 23 July and Store Lenangstind (1596m), the summit of which was reached at 11.45 pm on 25 July. Another visitor to the Lyngen district was Mrs Main who with Josef Imboden and his son Emil completed a number of climbs including, on 5 August, the second ascent of Stortind.

In the Caucasus the Hungarian explorer Maurice de Déchy made his sixth visit to the region, accompanied on this occasion by the botanist Professor Ladislaus Hollós and Dr Carl Papp as geologist and by the guide Unterberger from Kals.

> In the Western Caucasus the Karatchai district and the Klukhor group were visited. M. de Déchy, with the guide, ascended a peak, about 11,200ft., in the Chirukol Valley (a side valley of the Ullukam), mounting the Talichkang Glacier, and by a gap which affords a pass between the Chirukol Valley and the Nenskra Valley. ... The Klukhor group, entered by the Amanaus valley, proved to have only small

> glaciers and no great conspicuous peaks. Here the Tyrolese guide broke down from fatigue, and had to be sent back to his home from Batalpachinsk. In the Eastern Caucasus the glacier group of the Bogos was visited. Extensive botanical and geological collections were made, and M. de Déchy brought home a large collection of photographs of the high regions, which will complete those we already possess from the Central Caucasus.

In the Punjab Himalaya the Hon C G Bruce and another British officer, F G Lucas, took a party of Gurkhas over the Zoji La for training in mountain climbing and exploration. Starting on 20 July the party, accompanied by Bruce's wife who stayed with the main camp, spent several weeks in the Suru district of Ladakh and climbed a number of the neighbouring peaks. After Lucas had departed Bruce and his men carried out a reconnaissance of the Nun Kun group and reached or traversed several other summits, one team of Gurkhas traversing the S, highest Koh-i-nur peak (5136m).

Another party to visit the Suru district was that of Dr William Hunter Workman and his wife Fanny Bullock Workman who after cycling to Srinagar completed the first of their Himalayan journeys, reaching Leh on 27 June and continuing to the Karakoram Pass. In early October the Workmans, accompanied by a large party which included the guide Rudolf Taugwalder from Zermatt, set out from Darjeeling with the intention of following the Singalila ridge and crossing the Guicha La. This journey had to be abandoned in the face of numerous difficulties and the party returned to Darjeeling later in the month.

The principal undertaking of the year was Sir Martin Conway's expedition to the Andes and Tierra del Fuego. Accompanied by Antonio Maquignaz and Luigi Pellissier Conway arrived in La Paz at the end of August and decided to attempt the ascent of Illimani, the highest peak in the Cordillera Real. After reaching a high farmhouse where he was able 'to enlist the unwilling services of four or five Indians' Conway reconnoitred the mountain and on 5 September the party began to climb a steep gully leading towards the summit plateau. Addressing the Alpine Club in the following year Conway recalled that after arriving at the base of a wall of rock only two Indians, yielding to the temptation of large bribes, were willing to continue.

> The ascent of the wall was by no means easy. It was steep, and presented some points of real difficulty. At each of these difficulties, as they came, the Indians wished to turn back, and it was only by standing at the top and holding out small silver coins for them to climb for that I was able to tempt them forward. In this somewhat unusual fashion we slowly advanced until some two-thirds of the wall had been successfully climbed. Then there came a vertical gully filled with ice, in which steps had to be cut, and there the Indians absolutely

> declined to proceed; they threw down their burdens, turned tail, and descended.

Despite these difficulties Conway and the guides continued the ascent and early on 9 September reached the central summit.

> And now for the first time the final cone of Illimani came into view. This great mountain has a coronet of summits which surround a high plateau of snow, and differ from one another in altitude to a very slight extent. If we had not known by distant inspection which was the highest, we could not have discovered it from this point. As it was, there was no doubt; the peak lay right over against us, separated from us by an undulating snow-field toward which a gentle slope led down from our feet.

Later in the day after crossing the plateau the party completed the first ascent of the S, highest peak (6462m) of Illimani.

On 19 September Conway and his companions commenced the ascent of Ancohuma (6388m), the S, higher peak of the Sorata group[8] and five days later had reached a height of some 6000m before a deterioration in the weather forced them to abandon the climb. In the following month, on 10 October, the party had reached a point less than 100m below the summit when Conway, faced with a difficult crevasse and dangerous snow conditions, decided reluctantly to retreat.

Conway then travelled to Valparaiso where he made arrangements to attempt Aconcagua (6959m), the peak climbed during the previous year by the guide Mattias Zurbriggen and by Stuart Vines with Nicola Lanti as members of the expedition led by E A FitzGerald. Leaving Puente del Inca on 3 December with the guides, Anacleto Olavarria an expert muleteer, several porters and a number of mules Conway ascended the Horcones valley and established camps on the NW face. On 7 December after illness had forced Pellissier to return to a high camp at about 5640m Conway and Maquignaz reached the ridge between the N and S summits and continued over several undulations towards the N, higher summit before halting at 'the top of a peak near, and not many feet lower than, the highest peak.' Conway estimated this position to be 'within ten minutes of, and at the very outside 50ft. below, the highest point' but decided to descend because he was anxious to rejoin Pellissier as soon as possible and did not wish to be accused of jealousy if he continued to the actual summit reached by Zurbriggen, Vines and Lanti, being aware that they had 'made a record for altitude'.

Many years later Conway recalled[9] that there had been a further reason for his decision.

> I have often been asked why we did not stand on the highest point. The answer is simple. My old climbing companion, Edward FitzGerald,

> had in the previous year completed an elaborately-organised exploration of this district; his party, led by Zurbriggen, had made the first ascent of Aconcagua. They had spent several months in and about the Horcones valley and were popularly supposed to have been trying all the time to climb the peak, though as a matter of fact they did much else. FitzGerald's book[10] had not been published at the time of my ascent. I thought, and I believe correctly, that it would be harmful for the prestige of that book, just at the point of issue, if I were known to have accomplished in a week what was supposed to have taken FitzGerald's party several months.

Before leaving the region Conway visited Tierra del Fuego where on 31 December, with Maquignaz, he reached a height of some 1120m on Monte Sarmiento (2300m) before bad weather forced a retreat.

In the Canadian Rockies J N Collie, accompanied by H E M Stutfield and Hermann Woolley, spent six weeks exploring a large area to the north of the Canadian Pacific Railway. After cutting a new trail through difficult country they camped on the Athabasca Pass and on 18 August 'Stutfield shot three mountain sheep, saving the party from semi-starvation.' On the same day Collie and Woolley made the first ascent of Mount Athabasca (3491m), climbing the N ridge to the summit where they saw

> ... a vast ice-field probably never before seen by human eye, and surrounded by entirely unknown, unnamed, and unclimbed peaks.

The discovery of the Columbia Icefield is remembered as one of the great events in Canadian climbing history.

In Britain, with many strong parties in action, several notable new ascents were completed. In Wales the *Elliptical Route* on Lliwedd, climbed by J M Archer Thomson and Roderick Williams at Easter, was followed on 7 May by the first recorded ascent, as a rock climb,[11] of Twll Du or the Devil's Kitchen, the cleft in the central cliff of Clogwyn y Geifr above Llyn Idwal, by W R Reade and W P McCulloch. In the Lake District on 19 April O G Jones, leading G T Walker, forced a famous route – *Jones' Route Direct from Lord's Rake* – up the face of Scafell Pinnacle. In Glencoe the first ascent of the Church Door Buttress on Bidean nam Bian was completed, by way of the *Flake Route*, by Harold Raeburn, J H Bell, H C Boyd and R G Napier in July and on the Isle of Skye *Naismith's Route* on the Bhasteir Tooth was opened by W W Naismith and A M Mackay.

An important event was the publication of a revised edition of *A Guide to The Western Alps*, the classic work by John Ball, the first President of the Alpine Club. The new guide, edited by W A B Coolidge, was reviewed in the *Alpine Journal* where it was acknowledged to contain 'as much careful and well considered work as has, perhaps, ever been brought to bear on such a subject.' Other books published during the year included *The Annals of Mont Blanc* by C E Mathews and *With Ski & Sledge over Arctic Glaciers*, the account by Conway of his second expedition to Spitsbergen, undertaken in the previous summer.

In conclusion it is a pleasure to quote the following report published on 29 April and relating to a new climbing club formed during the year.

> Last night the inaugural dinner of 'The Climbers' Club' was held at the Café Monico, under the chairmanship of Mr. C E Mathews, the Birmingham Liberal Unionist leader, and an ex-president of the Alpine Club. The club already numbers 200 members, 80 of whom sat down at the first dinner. ... The inaugural of 'The Climbers' Club' was like a whiff of fresh mountain air in smoky London. The talk was all of gullies, and snow-slopes, and Cumberland fogs and 'P.Y.G.' and Sty-head pass, and the north fall of Lliwedd and such other things as delight the climber's soul. They were a very athletic, healthy-looking lot who surrounded the tables at the Monico last night.

REFERENCES

1 Better known as Mrs Aubrey Le Blond, the founder and first President of the Ladies' Alpine Club.
2 Miss M C Brevoort accompanied by her nephew W A B Coolidge, the guide Christian Almer senior, his son Ulrich and three porters had made the first winter ascent of the Wetterhorn on 15 January 1874.
3 Pointe Marguerite. Named by the Duke of the Abruzzi in honour of Queen Margherita of Italy.
4 Pointe Hélène. Named by the Duke after Hélène of Orléans, Duchess of Aosta, the wife of his eldest brother.
5 The first traverse had been completed by Miss Katharine Richardson with Emile Rey and Jean Baptiste Bich on 13 August 1888.
6 Named by Henri de Ségogne and party in 1925 after completing the first ascent of the Grands Montets ridge.
7 Stortind – Big Peak – is recorded for more than one height in the Lyngen district. The peak climbed by Slingsby's party was photographed by Hastings from Store Jaegervasstind. See *AJ19*, Plate facing 433, 1898-99.
8 The N peak is the famous Illampu (6362m).
9 Sir Martin Conway, *Mountain Memories*. London, Cassell and Company, Ltd, 1920.
10 E A FitzGerald, *The Highest Andes*. London, Methuen & Co, 1899.
11 Twll Du had been ascended under winter conditions by Archer Thomson and Harold Hughes in March 1895.

Area Notes 1997

EDITED BY JOSÉ LUIS BERMÚDEZ

Alps and Pyrenees	*Lindsay Griffin*
Russia and Central Asia	*Paul Knott*
Greenland	*Derek Fordham*
Scottish Winter	*Simon Richardson*
Middle East	*Tony Howard*
India	*Harish Kapadia*
Pakistan	*Lindsay Griffin & David Hamilton*
Nepal	*Bill O'Connor*
South America and Antarctica	*Chris Cheeseman*

LINDSAY GRIFFIN

Alps and Pyrenees 1996-1997

This report looks at selected activity, in terms of both exploration and technical performance, during the winter of 1996-97 and the following spring to autumn season. In preparing these notes Lindsay Griffin would like to acknowledge the assistance of Jérome Arpin, Valery Babanov, Gino Buscaini, Alain Delize, Stevie Haston, Robert Jasper, Andy Kirkpatrick, Igor Koller, Vlado Linek, Pat Littlejohn, François Marsigny, Neil McAdie, Martin Moran, Andy Parkin, Emanuele Pellizzari, Tony Penning, Michel Piola, Franci Savenc, Hilary Sharp, Pierre Tardivel, Paolo Vitali, Ed Watson and Matjez Wiegele. Technical grades are either French or UIAA unless otherwise stated.

New route descriptions or corrections and any information on Alpine Club members' activities will be most welcome and should either be sent to the Club or directly to: 2 Top Sling, Tregarth, Bangor, Gwynedd LL57 4RL. It is hoped that in the future all corrections and revised descriptions to routes that currently appear in Alpine Club guides will be published and acknowledged on the AC's web site (http: / / www.alpine-club.org.uk)

WINTER/SPRING 1996-1997

Pyrenees

Although seemingly little frequented by other than relatively local French and Spanish climbers, the high mountains of the Pyrenees have enormous potential for excellent winter routes. However, the ever-changing and unpredictable Mediterranean climate ensures that many of the best lines are often in condition for rather limited periods at a time.

Pic Blanc de Troumouse A new ice/mixed route was created on the 500m N Face of this 2957m peak above the Heas Valley at the beginning of March. *Bande de Sioux* was climbed by A Milhau and Jérome Thinières, and given an overall grade of TD+.

Peña Telera Two new, primarily rock routes were climbed on the main summit of this fine 2764m peak above Panticosa. *Senda de los Cuervos* (400m: 5+/6a but mainly 4/5) by Isidoro Sanches and Enrique Villasaur takes a rightward leaning crack line to the right of the classic *North Dièdre* (Abajo/Forn, 1970: ED1), finishing up the crest of the NW Ridge. *Directa a la Gran Diagonal* (350m: 5+) by Antonio Garno, Salvador Morales and Villasaur takes the obvious crack line below roofs to the right of Raquel (Fernandez and party, 1979: D+ in good névé) leading in to the 1971 winter classic *Gran Diagonal* (AD+).

Pico de Anayet Koldo Orbegozo and Iñaki Ruiz have climbed a new winter route on the E Face of this very famous 2559m summit to the N of the Peña Telera. *Atxarte Bizirik* (350m: D+/TD-: IV/4) links snow fields on the left side of the face, via icy ramps, narrow gullies and a crux water-ice pitch of 7m at 85°, before finishing up the top section of the N Face.

Pa de Sucre On the NE Face of this 2863m peak immediately N of the Aneto Massif, Joan Carlos Martin and Jordi Mena climbed a new route left of the NE Couloir. Named the *Salas/Montaner Couloir* and completed in December '96, the 300m route was mainly 50-65° with two hard sections, one of 80° and another of 5 and A1.

Tuc de Contesa Joan Jovier and Eduard Requeña climbed *Via del Dièdre* on the N Face of this 2786m peak situated above the Conangles Valley in the Besiberri Group. The overall grade was IV/5+ with two hard pitches to start (90° then 80°) but above, the climbing is escapable.

Posets Starting from the Viados Hut at 1740m, Eduard Abello and Joan Miguel Dalmau made the first ascent of the *Couloir Caribe* (350m: TD–), a mixed climb of 5 and 70° on the W Face of this major 3375m peak in the Central Pyrenees.

Pic du Midi d'Ossau Patrice Fauret, Philippe Martins and Christian Ravier climbed a hard new mixed/ice route, *Buffet Froid* (ED2: 700m: F5/5+ and 90°), on the N Face to the right of the two existing winter routes of *Ya du Grisou dans l'Tempo* (Berger/Thivel, 1993: TD+: 80°and 5+) and *Santa Coloma Couloir* (Thivel, solo, 1993: TD+/ED1: 75° and 5+). Remi Thivel took part in three important ascents on the S Face of the mountain during February. His opening gambit was the first winter solo ascent of the classic and somewhat exposed, vertical-to-overhanging S Pillar (de Bellefon/Despiau/Gremier/Ravier/ Ravier, 1956: 250m: TD+: 6b+, originally 5 and A2). On 8 February, with C Dupouy, he put up *Guignol's Band*, an ephemeral 700m ice runnel on the S Face at V/5– and on the following day the same pair put up a second line on the same part of the face, which they christened *Fortune Carrée* (also 700m and V/5–).

Gra del Fajol Petit On the NE Face of this 2563m top in the Cirque of the Ull de Ter (Far Eastern Pyrenees, south of the Canigou), Eduard Brocal and Marc Canela climbed a 155m (4-pitch) couloir which they named *Reservoir Dogs* (50-60° with a little mixed).

Pic Fachon The French climber, Daniel Lanne, climbed two new routes towards the end of January on this 2450m peak in the Balaitous Group. *Métamorphose* is a sustained 200m climb up a narrow ice runnel at TD+, while *Excelsa* takes the 200m chimney line to the left at ED1.

Los Picos de la Garganta On the 2559m **Pico Llana**, less than a kilometre W of the **Pico de Aspe** in the Western Pyrenees, Joserra Exkisable and Iñaki Ruiz made probably the first winter ascent of the original *Rabada/Navarro Route* up the N Chimney (300m: D+: 80° with rock to IV), a good example of an old rock route transformed into a very worthwhile winter excursion.

Ecrins Massif

Pic Sans Nom On the WNW Face Stéphane Benoist and Arnaud Guillaume put up a superb new rock route at the end of March. *Eloge de la Fuite* starts up the great NW Couloir, then immediately climbs the wall 50m left of the 1971 route in 14 pitches to the upper NW Ridge (6a and A2: two bivouacs on the wall).

Tête du Rouget On 8 March Jean Gleizes, Fabrice Gautier and Loic Barettaud made the first winter ascent of the *Le Trésor de Rackham de Rouget* (Cambon/Chapoutot, 1993: 470m: 15 pitches: ED1: 6c max), a fully bolted line up the great compact slabs in the centre of the S Face, left of the Girod Pillar. The rock was warm and snow-free but the approach and descent, in deep snow, interminable.

Mont Blanc Massif

Weather and conditions throughout most of the season were excellent, with the result that the Massif was often teaming with climbers, especially at the weekends. A good ice build-up on the N faces of the higher peaks had occurred during the autumn and a very heavy snowfall before Christmas, followed by a stable dry period, made access problems minimal. At lower altitudes, eg in the Aiguilles, conditions were somewhat thinner and the climbing much more taxing. Despite the wonderful weather and excellent conditions, surprisingly little innovatory climbing appears to have been achieved, alpinists seemingly content to repeat all the traditional hard classics, and the vast majority of these at the accessible venues.

Brouillard Arête Over 15-16 January, Patrick Berhault and Francis Bibollet made the second ascent of the E Goulotte of **Punta Baretti** (500m: TD) on the lower Brouillard Ridge. They claimed this as a new route, unaware at the time that it had first been climbed back in 1986 by the maestro Gian Carlo Grassi, with Sergio Rossi and Angelo Siri.

Mont Blanc du Tacul On the 9 March Robert Jasper and Daniela Klindt climbed *Vol de Nuit*, a hard new mixed route immediately right of the 1995 Gouault/Haston line *Scotch on the Rocks*. Branching out from below the first hard pitch of *Scotch*, the pair climbed 40m of Grade 8–, after which the difficulties were far less sustained (5 max). The pair returned on 2 April and this time made an on-sight ascent of *Scotch on the Rocks*. Jasper felt his own route to be the harder of the two and rated *Scotch* as IV/7M.

Grandes Jorasses *Michto* is a new route on the N Face of **Pointe Hélène** that follows a series of ephemeral goulottes between the two Polish Routes put up in 1970 and 1975. It was completed in just 14 hours on 3 March by the female

French guide Françoise Aubert and the well-known Jean-Christophe Lafaille. The hard climbing was characterised by thinly-iced runnels in compact rock, with protection sparse and difficult to arrange. A grade of VI/6 and A2/3 was awarded.

Aiguille du Plan In late March a new route on the N Face (exact line unknown) by K Bodin and S Montaz-Rosset was christened *Ou sont les Poulardes*?and given an Alpine ice grade of III/5+.

M Capucin du Requin On 25 January Laurent Fabre and Raphael Gaime climbed the couloir on the NE Face which starts right of **Pointe 2851m** and curves up behind the front face of the Capucin to a notch in its SE Ridge at *c*3000m. *Le Nez Rouge* was left equipped for a rappel descent and awarded a grade of III/5 and A1. The first three pitches gave 85-90° sections on particularly thin ice. Interestingly, most of this line, ascended as a summer route following the right branch of the couloir, was first climbed way back in the summer of 1914 by Ryan with Franz and Joseph Lochmatter during the second ascent of the Mayer-Dibona Ridge on the Requin.

Aiguille de Triolet Alpine Club members Steve Gould and David Rose completed three routes during the second week in March. Of note was their ascent of the N Face of the Triolet (700m: TD-), which has recently been undergoing a change in structure. The upper sérac barrier has all but disappeared to be replaced by a relatively safe set of rimaye walls. The pair also climbed the excellent NW Face of **Mont Dolent** (TD-), which gave 12 pitches to the summit ridge followed by a rappel descent from this point via well-equipped anchors. Their final route was the highly frequented *Lafaille Couloir* on **Mont Blanc du Tacul** (D+/TD– : rappel descent), normally the last of the popular routes on the E Face to vanish with the onset of spring weather.

The unfrequented S Face of the Triolet above the Triolet Glacier in Italy was the scene of a new 6-pitch mixed line, christened *Tibet Libre*, by Philippe Batoux and Patrick Gabarrou.

Les Droites The N Face was in perfect condition throughout the season and in March the *Ginat Couloir* finish to the *Classic Route* was getting more ascents than all other routes in the Argentière basin. At times there were up to six parties on the line the same day, reflecting the recent rise in climbing standards due to the increase in hard water-ice ascents throughout Europe. It was also rumoured that the 1994 Jasper/Roeper/Steinsburger offering *The Maria Callas Memorial Route* (1000m: ED3: 6a, A4 and Scottish 6) received a second ascent.

Tour des Droites On 18 April the well-known Spanish climber Joan Quintana put up a new line on the NW Flank. Climbing solo, Quintana branched out of the N Couloir of the Col de L'Aiguille Verte at a higher level than the 1994 Baudet/Cayrol/Ravenel route *Baptistoune* (TD/TD+), and climbed 4 steep mixed pitches more or less vertically below the summit of the Tour to join the 1994 route at the start of the last pitch. An ice/mixed grade of IV/4+ was quoted, together with additional rock difficulties of 5 and A1.

Aiguille Verte Chamonix guides Sylvain Frendo and Marc Ravanel climbed a new line on the NE Face Rock Triangle. The first two pitches (and crux) of the route were prepared on 17 January and the pair finished it off on 28 January, awarding an overall grade of ED1. However, it is difficult to see how their line can be entirely independent of the 1981 *Gabarrou/Vogler Route*.

Aiguille Sans Nom On 8-9 February Thierry Braguier (sadly killed while soloing on the Plan just one year later) and François Marsigny completed the long-awaited second ascent of the 1993 Backes/Twight route *There goes the Neighbourhood.* The French pair were able to confirm the grade (originally considered to be ED3/4) but in the excellent prevailing conditions were able to avoid the aid pitch (from which, according to Twight, a fall would be fatal) by a thin ice runnel which was not present at the time of the first ascent. A few days later Alexander Pautsch and Malte Roeper made a possible new start to the 1978 *Gabarrou/Silvy Directissima* (950m: ED2/3) on the same face. The two German climbers started to the right in a gully system between the two rock pillars. Although shattered and loose in summer, this gave fine mixed climbing at Scottish 4 and 5.

Petit Dru Dick Turnbull, with Frank Connell, added to his tally of winter ascents of the Six Great North Faces when he completed the classic *Allain/Leninger Route* (850m: TD). Conditions were quite lean and the climbing hard work though not technically difficult; mostly rock climbing in crampons with some aid (estimated winter grade: V/4+, F4 and A1). The pair took the normal descent to the Flammes de Pierre but suggest that a traverse of the Grand Dru is probably a safer option in winter.

Pointe du Génépi On 8 March, Lionel Chalon and Jacques Dreyer climbed a new 5-pitch route, *l'Echappé Belle*, on this small but popular rock tower just behind the Argentière Hut. The route more or less follows the crest of the ridge to the right of *Mort de Vive* and was sustained at F5c with two points of aid (6b all free).

Cumuls/Enchaînements There were a number of impressive linked ascents that took advantage of the fine weather and conditions during the winter. The most outstanding, indeed one of the finest and most demanding link-ups in the Massif to date, involved one of the great protagonists of the *enchaînement*, Patrick Berhault, and French ski champion Francis Bibollet. This pair began with an ascent of the 1977 *Brooks/Colton Route* on the West Summit of the **Droites** (ED2), then descended to the Leschaux Hut, where they slept just three hours before setting off for the 1976 *Colton/MacIntyre* (ED3) on the **Grandes Jorasses**. After a bivouac on the route, the summit was reached during late afternoon on the following day and the W Ridge of the Jorasses traversed through the dark to reach the Canzio Hut on the Col des Grandes Jorasses. A tiring day along the corniced Rochefort Arête led to the Torino Hut, where they spent a comfortable night before moving on to the Ghiglione Hut the next day. The following morning they set off for the *Cecchinel/Nominé* (1971: TD+/ED1) on the **Grand Pilier d'Angle** and, finding good conditions, steamed up the route, reaching the Eccles Huts that night (and a previous food dump left by Berhault). On the last day of their *cumul/enchaînement* they reached the summit of **Mont Blanc** via a fast ascent of the *Brouillard Hypercouloir* (Gabarrou/Steiner, 1982: ED2) which they fortunately found full of quality ice.

Jean-Marc Genevois and Patrick Pessi linked 4 faces above the Argentière Glacier in a marathon effort of 41 hours over 9-10 March. At 3am on the 9th the pair started up the N Face of the **Droites** (1050m: ED1), descended back to the Argentière Glacier, reportedly via the N Face of the Col de Courtes, dispatched the N Face of the **Triolet** (750m: TD–) in four hours, descended via the Col des Courtes, climbed the classic *Swiss Route* on **Les Courtes**, once again made the now all-too-familiar lengthy descent via the Col des Courtes and finally climbed the Couturier Couloir on the **Aiguille Verte** (900m: D).

Avalanches and Rockfalls Following the huge rock fall on the Brenva Face in 1996 a second and even more monstrous landslide occurred in the same region on 16 January. The fall originated from a section of the Brenva Spur and covered most of the upper Brenva Glacier, spilling debris down as low as 1500m. The blast flattened thousands of trees on the opposite side of the Val Veni and appears to have killed at least two skiers. Some days later, during the night of 24-25, the huge sérac to the right (E) of the Rocher Whymper on the SW Flank of the **Grandes Jorasses**, broke off and sent a gigantic avalanche (estimated at 15,000 cubic metres) down to the Val Ferret.

But the most notable cataclysm occurred in September when a huge rock fall occurred on the West Face of the **Dru**. The resulting impact was so great that it registered as far away as Sîon in the Rhone Valley, where it was recorded as between 2.0 and 2.5 on the Richter Scale. The top of the fall appears to have been in the region of the first big roof on the *Harlin/Robbins American Directissima* and it would seem that the lower section of this route, plus the lower sections of the neighbouring *French Directissima* below the *Red Shield,* the 1986 Camison/ Grenier route *Absolu,* the 1975 *Thomas Gross Route*, Catherine Destivelle's 1991 creation and possibly, but not certainly, the lower part of the *Bonatti Pillar* have all been destroyed. Two days later another smaller but significant fall occurred and the combined effect produced a huge rock scar that is now clearly visible from the valley. Certain geologists believe that all this recent activity is the result of a current 'tipping' of the entire range.

Gran Paradiso

Becco di Valsoera Nicknamed the Dru of the Gran Paradiso, the Becco has superb rock that has been compared in quality to that found on the walls of the Grand Capucin. On the 450m W Face, Manlio Motto and Rocco Sansano made the first winter ascent of the 1992 Remy bothers route *Agrippine* (380m: 15 pitches: 7b or 6b obl and A1). The pair climbed the route on 1st March after two previous attempts. A week later they were back in the company of Gianni Predan and on 8 March made the first winter ascent of Motto and Predan's own 1992 route *Nel Corso del Tempo* (350m to the top of the *Torre Staccata* (7a+: 6b+ obl). Both routes are rated ED2/3 but are well-bolted.

Becco della Tribolazione On the perfect rock of this dramatic collection of aiguilles, Motto was again responsible for making the first winter ascents of two of his own routes, both on the S Face. On 8 February he climbed *Pin Up* (Motto/Satore, 1996: 480m: 6a+, 5+ obl) with Sansano, and on 22 February with Giovanetto he climbed the 190m *Motto/Satore Route*, also put up in 1996, with maximum difficulties of 7a+ (6b+ obl).

Bregaglia

Pizzo Cengalo A remarkable linked ascent of two routes on the N Face took place in mid-March when Frank Jourdan first soloed the 1966 *Kasper Pillar* (1100m: ED1: VI and A1 with 70°: has been climbed all free in summer at VII) finishing up the *Classic North Face Route* (Borghese/Schnitzler/Schocher, 1897: TD–/TD: ice grade V/3) and then followed this with the technically harder and very rarely climbed *Renata Rossi Route* (Klinovsky/Silhan, 1989: 1200m: ED2/3: IV+ rock: VI/5 and 90° ice), which also joins the *Classic Route* after *c*600m.

Cima degli Alli On 9 February Dante Bazzana, Luca Biagini, Valentina Casellato, Luca Mesirca and Luca Passerini climbed a new route following the line of the obvious couloir on the NW Face of **Punta 2678m**, overlooking the upper Romilla Valley. The couloir was 400m (D) with snow/ice up to 75° and mixed terrain at IV+.

Precipizio degli Asteroidi On the huge S Face above the Mello Valley, Gabor Berecz and Thomas Tivadar spent six days during a period of fine weather at the end of February and the beginning of March creating a 9-pitch big-wall route which they christened *Kortykiraly.* This appears to be the third major aid route on this wall put up by Tivadar and was given an overall American rating of VI, 5.10a and A4. Bolts were apparently used quite sparingly and mostly at belays.

Ortler

Gran Zebrú This 3851m peak east of the Ortler gave up one of its secrets on 23 March when local activists Chiesa and Piccoli climbed a direct route up the S Face following a line of ephemeral ice runnels. *Ghost Zebru* was graded TD and had two crux sections; a 20m water-ice pitch at 90-95° and a section of rock at V and A1. On 5 August the *Voie Normale* was the scene of the year's worst Alpine accident when seven climbers fell to their deaths from an altitude of *c*3700m while descending from the summit.

Adamello

Punta della Val Rossa A little before the official winter season Fregoni, Inselvini and Piccoli climbed *L'Illuminata*, a new 750m, TD mixed line (IV/4+ and A1) on the SSE Face of this 2743m peak above the Val Miller on the western fringes of the range.

SUMMER

Ecrins Massif

More than usual snow cover during the summer allowed many parties to tackle some of the great high mountain classics. Two great classics appear to have been particularly popular, with an estimated 40 or so ascents of the 1956 *Couzy/ Desmaison Direct* on the NW Face of the **Olan** (1100m: ED2 but straightforward to the upper 500m diamond-shaped headwall: 5+/6a with a little A1 above or 6c all free) and more than 50 ascents of the *South Face Direct* on the **Meije** (Allain/Leininger, 1935: 800m: TD–/TD: 5+ maximum).

Pic Sans Nom The guru of Ecrins climbing, Jean-Michel Cambon, author of *Aurore Nucléaire* (ED1/2: 500m: 6b, 6a obl), the popular modern classic of the N Face and still considered to be the finest rock route above the Glacier Noir, put up another new route on the far left side of the face with Olivier Mansiot and Karine Maz. *Une Septentrion pour Rire* is 500m and TD (6a+: 5+ obl).

Ailefroide On the 3953m western and highest summit, Toni Clarasso, Cyrille Copier and Valérie Homage spent two days towards the end of May on a new line up the NW Face right of the 1957 *Coupé/Girod* but left of the *Czechoslovakian Route*. Natural protection was used throughout and the 1100m climb given an overall grade of ED1 (34 pitches sustained at 4–5+ with one of 6c and A2). Over two days in October, Pascal Dauger and Arnaud Guillaume climbed a new 1000m route up the steep pillar left of the 1975 *Voie des Dalles* on the NW Face of the Central Summit (3927m). *Le Pilier des Temps Maudits* is ED1 (6a+ and A1). Prior to this, Guillaume had soloed a new route up the very left side of the face to hit the Costa Rouge Arête some 300m below the summit at a prominent rock pinnacle called the **Tour du Géant (3618m)**. His 700m line merited an overall grade of TD– (5+).

On the N Face of the 3907m **Pointe Fourastier**, Grégoire Sauget made a partial first solo ascent in August of the *Pilier des Séracs* (Cambon/Francou, 1981: 5+ maximum) then descended from the base of the hanging glacier. He returned in early October to bag the first solo of the *Triangle Route* on the buttress to the left (Coqueugniot/Kelle/Mandin, 1966: D) but this time continued to the summit.

Tête de la Maye Cambon and Mansiot have squeezed yet another route on to these granite slabs above La Bérarde. *Du Cinq à Tire Larigo* should immediately become popular as it has an overall grade of D+ (5 max), making it very accessible to many visiting climbers.

Pointe des Cinéastes A new route of 250m was climbed at TD/TD+ by Codan, Elichabe and Vincent on the SW Flank of this easily accessible 3205m rock peak above the Glacier Blanc Hut.

Les Bans On the SE Face of this elegant mountain at the head of the Entraigues Valley, the experienced Ecrins pioneers Mr and Mrs Cambon, Pierre Chapoutot, Olivier Mansiot and Etienne Roi have put up *Ouvrez les Bans*, a fully-bolted 350m TD with considerable 'high mountain ambience', plus a long and difficult approach up the Glacier des Bans.

Grande Ruine In the spring, Chene and Dorner climbed a new 700m mixed route on the N Face which they christened *Mountain Wilderness* (TD– : 5: 50°). Their line lies a little to the right of the *Original 1938 Route* up the prominent rock pillar directly below the summit (Boniface/Colomb/Germain: 700m: D). The rock is (not surprisingly) rather poor and therefore needs to be well iced for the climb to be in condition.

Ski Descents

Pierre Tardivel, as ever, was active in this field, making the first ski descent (his 58th first descent overall) of the 700m N Couloir of the E Summit (3416m) of **Le Sirac**. Later in the year he climbed and skied, in a single day, both the elegant *Couloir Gravelotte* (D in ascent but 60° at the base) and the *Couloir des Corridors* (D: 50°) on the N Face of the **Meije**.

Vanoise/Tarentaise

Sélonge On this 250m-high, steep granite slab in the Chapieux Valley, on 2 June Jérome Arpin and Sylvain Empereur opened *Canyon ou Via Ferrata, mais ou sont passés les guides locaux d'antar?* (250m: TD; 6b obl). Only 6 bolts were placed (4 of these on belays) and the climb is considered poorly protected and very serious. Later, Empereur made the second solo ascent and fifth overall ascent of the very run out *Décapsulongle* (Cayrol/Erhrad/Guillemian, 1991: ED1/2: 7a, 6c obl) in 4 hours.

Barmes du Ché *L'Ivresse du Spit Honneur* is the name of the latest new route on the Barmes du Ché, a 250m limestone wall lower down the Chapieux Valley and about 6km from Bourg St Maurice. Put up in 17 hours during September and October by Arpin and Empereur, this superb ED1/2 route is situated right of Arpin's previous 1994 route *Pente et Fracas* (ED1: 6c+, 6b obl). It offers seven pitches with maximum difficulties of 6b obl and A2+. The second sustained aid section overhangs by some 15m.

Bazel Empereur made the first solo ascent in just 3½ hours during August of *13 en Colère* (10 pitches: now ED2: 7a+, 6b+ obl due to crucial holds breaking from the hard eighth pitch). The vast 350-400m high dolomitic wall of **Bazel** (3441m) lies above the Prarion Hut (Val d'Isère) and offers a number of classic routes from the 1970s such as the 400m high *Central Pillar* (Bozon/Dupont, 1970: TD: old V+).

Grand Bec de Pralognan On 13 April Jean Christophe Berrard and Lionel Ricard climbed a new *Directissima* up the N Face. The 650m mixed route was given an overall grade of D (technical ice grade of 4) and features 5 pitches of 75°.

Mont Pourri Empereur made the second solo ascent of the Direct Route *Sunset Boulevard* (350m: ED1: 6c, 6a obl) on the W Face of this 3782m summit. The line was first soloed, in winter, by Antoine Cayrol.

L'Epéna Three fine new routes were completed on the vast N Face of this multi-summited peak immediately N of **La Grande Casse**. The main mass of rock in the centre of the wall had remained unclimbed until the notable Ecrins activists Pierre Chapoutot and Olivier Mansiot, together with Mathier Lacolle and René Rol, created *In Bocca al Lupo* over two days in July and August. This is an 800m, TD (but a total of 26 pitches with almost 1000m of climbing), mostly at a steady 4 to 5c but with two pitches of 6a. There are very few possibilities for natural protection using nuts or Friends, so the route was equipped with around 80 bolts.

The face was visited again in September by the ubiquitous Patrick Gabarrou who, together with Laurent Bouvet, put up *A Toi l'Ami*, 16 long pitches with bold 6c obl climbing to the right of *In Bocca al Lupo*.

The third route in 1997 was actually the completion of a line called *Zélix* on the NW Face of the W Summit. Seven pitches of this route had been climbed and named in 1994, noted in a topo guide in 1996, but never completed until last August/September when another seven pitches were added by Deslandes, Mérel and Scanu. The completed TD+ line (6a obl) joins the 1966 *Swiss Route* on the NNW Pillar after 450m (14 pitches) and follows it for a last 100m of easier climbing to the top.

Other new routes were put up on the W Face of the **Roc de la Valette (2600m)** and on the impressive N Face of the **Grand Glière** to the west of the Epéna but unfortunately no details have been forthcoming.

Ski Descents

La Grande Casse Pierre Tardivel made the first ski descent of the rocky and complex 700m NW Face (sections of 55° and serious stonefall danger).

Mont Blanc Massif

The summer was notable for generally poor weather with much uncharacteristic snowfall. This in turn appears to have led to a great many accidents, some involving multiple tragedies. In early August four young Spanish climbers fell to their deaths from the region of the Chandelle on the Central Pillar of Frêney, while only a few days prior to this three Italians died after a 1000m fall from high on the Aiguille du Midi's Frendo Spur. In contrast, early to late autumn proved, once again, an excellent period to be tackling the big mixed routes and ephemeral ice runnels. Several fine ascents were achieved.

Conscrits Hut The new CAF hut, with bed space for 84 in a variety of accommodation from 18-bed dormitories to 4-bed rooms, opened in April. The hut is located at a slightly lower altitude than the previous building and is run from a huge bank of solar panels making it, theoretically, self-sufficient in energy. Reservations are essential: telephone 04 79 89 09 03.

Grand Capucin In recent years Michel Piola has taken it upon himself to re-equip several of his most popular routes in the Mont Blanc Massif. At all times he appears to have followed criteria that maintained the style of the first ascent and did not use drilled equipment when it was possible to employ natural removable alternatives such as nuts and Friends etc. Earlier this year Flaviano Bessone, a contributing editor to the Italian magazine *Alp*, proposed to help Piola with his project by donating the bolts and paying Piola for his time. The declared project for last summer was *Gulliver's Travels*, Piola's ground-breaking route on the Grand Capucin put up in 1982 with fellow Swiss Pierre Alain Steiner. *Alp* marketed this idea under the title *Monte Bianco 2000 Granito Securo* and gained the commercial backing of various climbing manufacturers. More routes were obviously in the pipeline.

The proposal brought immediate outrage from the French bastions of the GHM and FFME, not least because the Grand Cap lies in the French sector of the Massif and Italians were paying Swiss to meddle in their affairs. These two organisations also had highly laudable concerns about the further demise of adventure climbing in the region.

But despite all the protests Piola, with Bessone and the Italian guide Giovanni Bassanini, went ahead with the project on 5 September. The three replaced the existing 7 drilled anchors with 10mm or 12mm stainless steel bolts and removed two other bolts which they deemed too close to the existing route. *Gulliver's Travels* is now a much safer but less well-equipped route and climbers will still be unable to clip their first protection bolt until part-way up pitch five.

Prompted by near-accidents to descending parties due to stonefall in the couloir coming down from the Col des Aiguillettes, the same three also equipped a new rappel line straight down the wall taken by *Elixir*, *Flagrant Délire* and *Gulliver's Travels*. This gives a line of descent to the base of the Cap that should be totally free from objective danger.

The other notable event on the Grand Cap last summer concerned an almost completed project on the right side of the E Face by the former French World Cup Champion Arnaud Petit. Spreading his efforts over 5 days in August with the help of Pascal Baudin, Stéphanie Bodet and Jean-Paul Petit, Arnaud Petit climbed (and equipped) 12 pitches of his line from the ground up. The route climbs close to the ancient direct start to the Bonatti before breaking out right to cross *Directe des Capucins* and following a superb 30m dièdre capped by a roof. This last pitch was finally redpointed at 8a+. Above, the route continued directly up the walls right of *Directe des Capucins*, then up the final steep and seriously exposed pillar right of the Bonatti. This pillar involved another pitch of 8a but included a move of 7a (obl) which Petit climbed past before placing a protection bolt. The *Voie Petit* was climbed, according to the author, in the most adventurous style that he could manage, thereby leaving a route that would still be very difficult for future parties. Petit hopes to free the route in one continuous push this year, adding an independent last pitch. If this is achieved he may well set new standards in high-altitude, multi-pitch, Alpine rock climbing.

Mont Blanc du Tacul Excellent conditions in November prompted many parties to tackle the ice/mixed routes overlooking the Vallée Blanche and Stevie Haston's two mixed lines to the right of the Martinetti Pillar, *Pinocchio* and *Scotch on the Rocks*, received many ascents. *Pinocchio* was rated 6 and *Scotch* 7 or 7+.

Prior to this, AC member and Chamonix resident Andy Parkin, with Harry Taylor, put up *Nonestop* on 15 September in the centre of the E Face. The 800m line links rarely-formed, steep ice runnels immediately right of the *Boccalatte Pillar* (Central Spur) and was given a grade of IV/6 with rock to 5+ and A2. However, it is rumoured that this route had probably been climbed in the past by the talented Italian Ezio Marlier.

On 17 November, the same pair returned to climb the narrow couloir immediately left of the *Piliers du Sérac* and immediately right of Jasper's *Vol de Nuit*. *Slave to the Rhythm* (350m: IV/6+) features a hard 90° first pitch and finishes with a classic ice runnel left of the Damilano Pillar. It proved relatively popular in the following weeks.

Pointe de Lépiney In 1994 Philippe Batoux, Emmanuel Pélissier and Benoît Robert climbed and equipped 13 pitches up the right side of the E Face (right of the 1988 Anker/Piola Strappazzon route *Je t'ai conquis, je t'adore*) and despite not completing the route, gave it the name *Le Versant Du Soleil*. Last summer Batoux and Robert eventually returned to add two further pitches to the top of the face, one of which formed the crux (7b+ or 7a with one point of aid). The rest of the route is very sustained at 6b to 6c and features very thin slab climbing.

Aiguille de Blaitière On 3 August, Piola and Vincent Sprungli completed a 17-pitch route up the formidable E-facing pillar below a pointed pinnacle high on the long and crenellated SE Ridge. The pinnacle, for which the two Swiss propose the name *Point Gidéon*, was most likely a previously virgin summit and the route, *Oublié ta Vie*, offers plenty of sustained and exposed climbing with maximum difficulties of 6b+.

Pointes des Nantillons On the E Face of the First Point (2921m), Philippe Batoux and Benoît Robert discovered a superb route up the crest of the pillar left of the section known as Little Yosemite. Their 10-pitch route, christened *Le Nom de la Rose*, is very sustained at 6c with a crux pitch of 7a and comes highly recommended by the authors.

Aiguille de Roc On 22 August 1982 two young Swiss created one of the first rock climbs in the 'modern idiom' on the sunny granite of the **Envers des Aiguilles**. The 9-pitch route climbed directly up the beautiful slabby walls of the lower E Face of the Roc, then finished on a vast area of terraces some 300m above the glacier and far removed from any summit. Descent was effected by rappel, equipping the stances with bolt belays. At F4 to 5 with a one-move crux of 5+/6a, *Children of the Moon* became an instant classic and a route still synonymous with the new wave of exploration by Michel Piola on the compact slabs and walls of the Mont Blanc Massif.

On 5 August, with old friends Gérard Hopfgartner and Vincent Sprungli, Piola re-equipped the belay bolts and created two difficult variants plus a more direct finish to the terraces. Several days later he returned with Sprungli and added 9 more pitches above the terraces, involving largely naturally protected climbing, to give a superb 6a (one move of 6b), 18-pitch outing now called *Children of the Moon*; Integral.

Pointe Elisabeth On 23 August Lionel Chalou, Jacques Dreyer and Steve Meder squeezed another route onto the SE Face of this *c*2850m tower on the right side of the Trélaporte Glacier and named after Elisabeth Maertens or 'Babeth', the well-known guardian of the Envers Hut for more than 25 years. *Le Monde l'Envers* (or *Pas de Charlotte pour les Ouvreurs*), which starts more or less at the lowest point of the face close to the crest of the east pillar, gives 7 pitches at 5b to 6a+ with two points of aid, or 6b+ all free.

Aiguille de l'M Two teenage brothers (both sons of the French guide Dominique Potard) have claimed a new route to the left of the classic NNE Ridge. *Le Rapin du Toi* has a crux of 5+/6a but the upper section of the route, at least, has certainly been climbed before.

Mont Rouge de Peuterey Tony Penning and Andy Tierney climbed a short new route on the NE Face of the 2941m **Mont Rouge**, which lies in a tranquil corner of the Fauteuil des Allemands opposite the Noire Hut. Their climb takes a prominent corner to the right of the 1933 *Ottoz Route* and was climbed in 4 long pitches at British E3 5b, before continuing close to the crest of the N Ridge (easy at first then E2 5b on good granite) to finish on the top of the 'Second Tower'.

Grandes Jorasses Over the three days 26-28 September, Olivier Larios and François Marsigny made an ascent of the fabled *No Siesta* (VII– and A2: 90°), a line of thin narrow goulottes and difficult mixed climbing on the left flank of the Croz Spur, first put up on 21-23 July by Slovakian climbers Stanislav Glejdura and Jan Porvaznik. The route as a whole comprises 38 pitches, many giving hard mixed climbing and the last four to the summit ridge taking Marsigny a full 7 hours to lead. A second repeat took place from 31 October to 2 November by two young French alpinists, Stéphane Benoit and Yannick Graziani, who confirmed the level of commitment and technical difficulty.

Monts Rouges du Triolet The Second Point (3289m), or subsidiary top of the 3327m Central Summit of the Monts Rouges, has two long quasi-modern classics on its West Pillar: *Le Chamois Volants* (710m: 18 pitches: 5c max and obl) and *Kermasse Folk* (750m: 19 pitches: 5c max, 5a/b obl). On 30 July, Manlio Motto, Piola and Benoit Robert put up *Les 101 Dalmaziens*, a homogeneous climb at 6a/6a+ which is quite airy in parts and climbs the walls right of *Kermasse Folk*, finishing atop the Second Tower. On the lower slabs of the Point, reached in only 20 minutes from the hut, Motto, Piola and Robert added the strenuous *Le Secret de Ben* (3pitches: 6c) to the left of the 1996 Azzalea/Motto route *A Loba Loba* (6 pitches: 6b, 6a obl).

Paroi des Titans The latest 'fashion spot' is the huge 400m high walls that lie a few metres from the path leading up to the Triolet Hut and about 45 minutes walk from the valley. On 8 July Motto and Piola created the 12-pitch *Vénus ou bien Venise*, a totally equipped route with max difficulties of 6a+. Later in the season up to 30 climbers a day could be found at grips with this route over a fine weekend, elevating it to almost mega-classic status. On 11 September Motto made the first solo ascent in 5 hours. Over two days, 7 and 24 August, Motto, Piola and Robert climbed the 9-pitch *Titanic* to the right of *Vénus* and created a much more committing climb with maximum difficulties of 6c.

Flammes de Pierre On 28 October Andy Parkin made a solo ascent of a new ice/mixed line on the right side of the W Face of the Flammes de Pierre Ridge. Christened *PF*, this 500m line takes a rightward slanting gully at IV/5 with thin 80° ice.

Aiguille Sans Nom Over 17-18 September, while the neighbouring **Dru** was shedding a sizable portion of its W Face, the late Thierry Braguier and Russian climber Valery Babanov put up a new route on the N Face of the Aiguille Sans Nom, left of the classic *Gabarrou/Silvy Directissima. Russian Roulette* climbs 300m of complex mixed terrain between the *Boivin/Vallençant* and the *Gabarrou/Silvy*, all threatened by the great hanging sérac barrier, to reach the central snow slopes. Above, 4 hard new pitches on the mixed ground of the upper face led to a junction with the *Gabarrou/Silvy* above its difficulties. The 900m line was given an overall grade of ED3 with rock to F6b and A3, and an ice/mixed rating of V/6.

Aiguille du Moine François Pallandre, Richard Perez and various friends created a fine rock route on the NW Face of Point 3190m. Approached in 1¼ hours from the Charpoua Hut, the aesthetic 10-pitch line of *Sale Athée* follows a very steep series of cracks at 6a+ to 7a+ with a final and crux pitch of 7c.

Grand Darrey The steep pillars of compact granite situated on the massive S Face close to the A Neuve Hut are a very recent discovery and the first route here, *Illusions* (Chèvre/Pouget: 6b), was only climbed in 1996. Later that year Motto and Piola climbed *E la Nave Va* at a pleasant 5c to 6a (7 pitches). Piola returned in 1997 and with Robert added *L'Arête des Druids*, a very pleasant 8-pitch climb up the crest that leads to the summit of the Third Tower on the SE Ridge. The difficulties were quite reasonable (5b to 5c) and the authors strongly recommend continuing up the ridge to the summit of the Darrey. The same pair also added the steep *L'Homme est un Loup pour l'Homme* to the Second Tower. This gives 7 pitches with difficulties of 5c to 6a+.

Ski Descents

Emanuele Ballot and Pierre Tardivel have again been the two prominent performers in this field, with Ballot skiing part of the N Face of the **Grand Charmoz** (8 rappels made to link sections up to 60°), the Left Branch of the Y Couloir on the **Aiguille Verte** (55°) and the Lagarde Couloir on the **Droites** (starting 150m down from the top at the base of the rock barrier: 70m of 60°). Tardivel stole the show, however, by completing his 5-year dream of skiing all three faces of **Mont Dolent**. In July he made an audacious descent of the NW Face to the Argentière Glacier (three rappels in the 80° goulotte).

Gran Paradiso Massif

Gran Paradiso Highly criticised has been the retro-bolting and fixing of rope on the summit ridge of this 4061m peak, yet another example of a high mountain excursion brought down to its lowest level to appease those who feel the ascent should take place with minimum risk and self-reliance.

On the **Punta Marco**, a fine rock tower on the flanks of the mountain, Edoardo de Marchi and Maurizio Oviglia added the 11-pitch *Via Alison* (dedicated to Alison Hargreaves). The *c*330m route was climbed from the ground up over two days, equipped with 44 bolts (natural protection still essential) and has difficulties of 6c+ (6b obl). An easy ascent from the top leads to the summit of the Paradiso in one hour.

Becco di Valsoera In late summer Manlio Motto made the first solo ascent of *Sturm und Drang*, the hardest route on the 450m W Face at 7a and A3+ (7b+ with only two points of aid). A bivouac was necessary at half height.

Orco The Orco was also the scene of a small 'rassemblement' in August devoted to aid climbing and many short routes and several longer climbs from A1 to A3+ were put up over 5 days by a variety of performers including Christophe Moulin and Jean-Marc Troussier.

Valais

As usual, little has come to light concerning new activities in the Valais Alps, though heavy snow cover early in the season led to the ice/mixed routes being in superb condition providing they were climbed when well-frozen. In a single night on or about the 18-19 July André Georges, the well-known guide from the Arolla Valley, made a remarkable solo enchaînement of 5 N Faces: the 1100m N Face of **Mont Collon**; the 350m N Face of the **Petit Mont Collon**; the N Face of the **Pigne d'Arolla** (300m from the final rimaye); the 650m N Face of **Mont Blanc de Cheilon** and finally the 600m N Face of **La Ruinette** (a total guidebook ascent time alone of over 30 hours with difficulties up to TD). By the time you read this the Alpine Club will have published the first of two new volumes to the area: Valais Alps West.

Breithorn On 28 July Slovenians Tadej and Urban Golob plus Dusan Polenik climbed a new line on the NW Face of the Central Summit of the **Zermatt Breithorn**. The 700m *Nektar* was given an overall grade of ED2, a modern ice grade of V/6, and featured rock/mixed at IV+. However, the trio felt that their line would be very rarely found in condition.

Matterhorn One of the most significant and widely publicised (and criticised) events throughout the Alps in 1997 was the establishment of a new hut (the Lonza Bivouac Hut) below the Zmutt Ridge, immediately followed by the outrageous news that the Zermatt guides, in an act of blatant commercialism, were to equip part of this classic but serious route with fixed anchors. At the time of writing the job has started but not been completed and the outcry from many climbers and federations throughout the World, not least from the President of the UIAA, so far appears to have gone unheeded.

Bernese Oberland

Eiger The big news of late summer was the probable second ascent of the highly coveted *Ghilini/Piola Route* (1400m: ED3/4: 33 pitches to F7a and A4) by top Slovakian climbers Jaro Dutka and Martin Heuger. This 1983 creation climbs right of the Rotefluh above the tunnel entrance on the N Face, then directly up the pillar above. After seven days on the wall the Slovaks had reached the end of pitch 28 when they were hit by a bad storm. They sat it out and finally reached the West Flank on day 11. Dutka is no stranger to the Eiger having spent 13 days on the wall in the winter of '96 climbing 54 out of 62 pitches of the neighbouring and still unrepeated 1976 *Czechoslovakian Route* (VI and A4), before being forced down by constant spindrift avalanches.

Adamello

Val di Fumo Although little known outside the 'local' climbing community, the recently developed granite slabs close to the Refugio Val de Fumo give classic friction climbing on a par with the famous Val de Mello. A number of routes up to 12 pitches in length and VII– in standard have been created (and equipped).

Bregaglia/Masino

The well known local activist Gianluca Maspes, with the prolific new-router Manlio Motto and other partners, created around 15 first ascents on the southern side of the range, including lines on the famous Picco Luigi Amedeo, Punta Rascia and Pizzo di Zocca. Several of these are detailed in the following section.

Sasso Manduino On this remote and unfrequented peak at the western end of the range, Gualtiero Colzada and Mario Sertori climbed the 360m *Le Radici del Cielo* (VII+ obl) on the SE Face.

Monte Qualido On 2-3 May Gianluca Maspes made the first solo ascent of one of the most famous big-wall climbs in the region, *La Spada nella Roccia*. The 570m-high line on the E Face of Monte Qualido was put up in 1989 by Tarcisio and Ottavio Fazzini plus Norberto Riva in three days and given a grade of VIII (VIII– obl) and A4. The route is considered one of the most complex and difficult mixed free and aid climbs in the Central Alps and appears to have been repeated only once in its entirety. The route is characterised by a huge detached flake called La Foglia and on the first ascent the wide crack on the overhanging right side was aided on tied-off, custom-made piping 17-27 cm in length. In 1996 Ermanno Salvaterra is reported to have boldly free climbed all three pitches of the flake using layback techniques but did not complete the entire route.

Maspes also made a totally committing layback of the flake before continuing up poorly protected slabs (at one point making a pendulum off two skyhooks) to the top. A portaledge bivouac was made below the flake. In terms of difficulty and overall commitment this was widely considered to be one of the most significant solo ascents to have taken place in the Central Alps.

Later in the year Simone Pedeferri and Marco Vago climbed the entire route completely free and on-sight up to the top of La Foglia. The two pitches leading to the base of the flake, originally VII+ and A2, then A4, were reassessed at F7b and, somewhat surprisingly, F6b+. Above the flake, sections had to be worked owing to the less than perfect protection but the aid was eliminated at 7a/7a+ maximum.

The well-tested team of Sonja Brambati, Adriano Carnati and Paolo Vitali completed a new 19-pitch line christened *Mediterraneo* (6c+, 6b/c obl) up the steep and compact walls between the 1982 Boscacci/Masa/Merizzi route *Il Paradiso Può Attendere* (950m of climbing: VII and A3 or IX– all free as climbed in 1995 by Beranek, Koller and Machaj) and Brambati, Carnati and Vitali's own route *Melat* (700m: VII+ obl and A2) put up in 1993. Not long after, the talented local climber Simone Pedeferri managed to climb the route with only two points of aid at around 7c+.

Brambati, Carnati and Vitali also opened a new 4-pitch route immediately to the left which they named *Qualifalaise*. This 120m line starts with magnificent slab climbing at 6a to 6b+ before finishing up a thin crack at 7a+ (6b+ obl). There was also much praise for the repeat ascent of *Mellodramma* by Taglialegna and partner. This 18-pitch aid route (VII and A3) was climbed capsule style over seven days in two separate pushes.

Finally, Pedeferri free climbed the first half of the Fazzini route *Pejonasa Wall*, situated on the front face of the **Precipizio degli Asteroidi** (the SE-facing flank of the Qualido). The old A2 pitch around Il Naso was negotiated at 7b.

Pizzo Cengalo On the first tower of the S Ridge, normally avoided when climbing the classic *Vinci Route*, Maspes, Motto and Giovanni Ongaro put up the 230m *Don Carlos* on 27 September. The route has maximum technical difficulties of VII+ (VII obl).

The *Vinci Route* itself saw a number of ascents including one from Alpine Club members Neil McAdie and Andy Perkins, who felt the route to be slightly overgraded and completed the round trip from the start of the climb in four hours. They note that the new descent goes directly down the W Face from the last belay on the ridge and is very quick and easy with seven long rappels off double-bolt anchors.

Two new routes were put up on the left side of the E Face, the first by Marco Beltramini and Mario Sertori called *Il Volo del Picchio* (250m: VII/VII+) and the second just to the left by the same pair plus Gualtiero Colzada called *Le Fessure del Desiderio* (245m: VII+).

Punta Baroni Maspes and Ongaro created the bold *Mondi Sommersi* (400m: VII/VII+ obl) on the SE Face, a wall best known for its demanding 1969 offering *Sondrio City* (350m: VII/VII+ all free). No bolts were placed on the route.

Pizzo Torrone Occidentale (Punta 2987m) Using a backrope on four of the six pitches, Maspes made the first solo ascent of the 1993 Motto/Predan/Vogler route *Complicazioni Collaterali* (300m: VIII, VII+ obl) on the wall to the right of the Gugiatti (SW) Pillar.

Torrone Valley Two new routes have been created close to the recently revamped Manzi-Pirrotta Hut. Each has five pitches and involves largely crack climbing. One is attributed to Simone Pedeferri and partner while the other was put up by Paolo Cucchi and friends.

Meridiana del Torrone The Covelli brothers have added another hard aid climb to the vertical or overhanging 500m high E Face of the Meridiana. This is the very impressive golden granite wall on the left side of the entrance to the Torrone Valley which is home to the unrepeated 1988 route *Outlandos d'Amour* (Meloni/Tassoni/Villotta: VII and A2/3). Although no clear details are available, it seems likely the Covellis completed their original project, which proposed a line through the famous Meridiana Roof situated high on the face and projecting at least 30m.

Corni Bruciati On 10 October Maspes and Carlo Perlini investigated the NW Face of a point on the long rocky crest of the Bruciati dubbed the Torre Andrea and came back with the 200m line of *Innominata*. This route was climbed using only natural protection and had difficulties of VI+/VII–.

PAUL KNOTT

Russia and Central Asia 1997

Thanks are due to all those who have contributed information: in particular, Vladimir Birukov, Liana Darenskaya, Lindsay Griffin, Vladimir Komissarov, Vladimir Kopylov, Sergei Kurgin, Ivan Yarovoi. Information on many of these areas can be sporadic, so reports are always gratefully received. These should be sent via the Alpine Club.

The Pamir

Activity in this region was again somewhat inhibited by the unstable situation in Tadjikistan. Kidnapping of Western hostages has been reported, as well as various security incidents involving foreigners.

Despite these concerns a British/Russian team organised by Andrew Wielochowski (EWP) and Sergei Semiletkin again visited the Muzkol region. Their overland journey from Osh was uneventful apart from one routine border check. The range was approached from the W side giving access to a number of unclimbed peaks. Ascents began on 12 August with **Salters Peak (5660m)** at 2A. Three days later **Muzkolski (5895m)** was climbed by its NE Ridge at 3A. During the same period another group climbed **North Muzkol (6129m)** via SE slopes. On 19 August two climbers reached the summit of **Panorama (5929m)** from the W at 3A. The following day a different group summited on **Fay's Peak (6115m)** via the NW Ridge at an overall grade of 5A. An ascent was also made of **Odinakaya (5687m)**.

The Pamir Alai

The Laylak area has continued to attract the attention of climbers seeking high standard rock faces. In 1997 activity was concentrated in the Ak-Su valley, notably on the N Faces of Ak-Su (5217m) and neighbouring peaks.

A tentative, though probably incomplete, route status for the North Wall of Ak-Su is:

1 *Budianov* 5B (1983); E Ridge; VI, 5.9, A1; descent route.
2 *Korshunov* 5B (1985); VI, 5.9, A2; L buttress N Wall; 2+ ascents.
3 *Kavunenko* 6A (1984); L pillar N Wall; VI, 5.10, A2; 6+ ascents.
4 *Popov* 6B (1986); Centre N Wall; VI, 5.10, A3+; 2+ ascents.
5 *Shabalin* 6B (1994); through 'nose'; VI, 5.11, A3+; 2+ ascents.
6 *Ruchkin-Odintsov* 6B (1996) VI, 5.11, A3+; 1 ascent + variant.
7 *Chaplinski* 6B (1988); Centre N Wall; VI, 5.10, A3; 4+ ascents.
8 *Moschnikov* 6B (1984); Couloir N Wall; VI, 5.10, A3; 4+ ascents + 1997 variant.
9 *Kostenko* 6A (1988); variant of Moschnikov; VI, 5.10, A3; 2+ ascents.
10 *Troschinenko* 6A (1982); N Wall; VI, 5.10, A2; 10+ ascents.
11 *Klenov* 6B (1996); R part of N Wall; VI, 5.11, A3; 1+ ascents.
12 *Pershin* 6A (1988); R part of N Wall; VI, 5.10, A3; 1+ ascents + variant.
13 *Vedernikov* 6A (1986); R part of N Wall; VI, 5.10, A2; 3+ ascents.

14 *Vasiljev* 6A (1984); VI,5.10, A2; R pillar of N Wall; 2+ ascents.
15 '*1990 English route* on the dangerous ice R of Vasiljev pillar.'
16 *Klenov* 6B (1997); R of Ruchkin-Odintsov.
17 *Shabalin* (1997); mixed with A3-A4; R of Moschnikov.

In summer 1997 several teams climbed routes on this face as part of the Russian Mountaineering Championships. From 5-14 August a team from Ekaterinburg led by Alexander Klenov climbed a new variant in the centre of the N Face. The team was awarded first place in the Championships. The route, graded 6B, involved hard aid climbing in its middle section. A team from Perm led by A Shavriovich, climbing from 7-16 August, made the second ascent of the 1994 *Shabalin Route*. They were awarded second place in the Championships.

From 29 July to 5 August a more direct variant on the *Moschnikov Route* was climbed by Andrei Antonov, Ilias Tukhvatulin and Pavel Shabalin. The route sees no sun and so the rock was ice-covered for long sections. This ground was covered using the ice-fifi technique, the fifi being used in place both of sky hooks and of small knifeblades. The pick required sharpening and straightening on each pitch. Finally from 19 to 22 August a Krasnoyarsk team led by P Kuznetsov climbed the *Troschinenko Route* in only 39 hours on the move.

Teams were also active on the steep N Face of **Slesov Peak (4240m)**, also known as the **Russian Tower**. The *Morozov Route* was repeated by a team led by Sergei Pugachev, taking from 18-20 July. Most of the route was climbed free. A new variant on the *Semiletkin Route* was climbed from 22-27 July by Vladimir Lebedev, Andrey Pashkin and Sergei Semiletkin. In September British and American teams were active in the same area. To the R of the Russian Tower, as seen from base camp in the Ak-Su valley, is a previously unclimbed rock formation on which a new route was climbed by Dave Green and Paul Pritchard. The route took the W Face and, after a total of 6 days' effort, was wholly free climbed at a bold 5.12b with the use of only 8 hand-drilled bolts. The 1200m line was given the name *The Great Game*, and the rock feature **Wall of Dykes**. (*See article 'Ak-Su: The Wall of Dykes' by Paul Pritchard, pp109-116.*)

On the nearby **Central Pyramid (3850m)**, a new line was climbed by Americans Topher Donahue and Kennan Harvey taking black streaks on the R side of the W Face. The route, given the name *Black Magic*, had crux moves of 5.12a and was shortly afterwards repeated by Noel Craine and Johnny Dawes. Donahue and Harvey, together with Stephanie Davis and Patience Gribble, also climbed a free variant on the 1991 *Voie Française* at 5.12a. A significant variation in the middle section was christened the *Yellow Moon*. The same team also freed the 1988 *Russian Direct Route* on the face at 5.12b, taking approximately five days. On the opposite side of the valley Davis made a solo ascent of the 1993 French *North East Pillar* on **Pik 1000 Years of Russian Christianity**, confirming the grade at 5.9.

The Caucasus

After several years' absence climbers have returned to the Nakhar valley in the **Western Caucasus**. A team from Makhachkala led by Sergei Smotrov made the second ascent of the 1977 *Kovtun Route* on the NW Face of **Bolshoi Nakhar (3784m)**. The route, at 5B with over 650m of climbing, took from 26 to 30 July.

Routes on this face are awkward to access from the glacier and are susceptible to the unstable weather of this region.

The same group from Makhachkala also climbed an interesting area of rock walls on the W Face of **Kiukiurtliu (4639m)** in the Elbrus massif. From 5 to 9 August they made the fifth ascent of the 1981 *Lukashvili Route*, which takes the centre of the face at 6A with an average angle of 83°. The face reportedly also has a good quality unclimbed direct line, with an average angle around 90° and long overhanging sections. The area is approached via Karachaevo-Cherkessia rather than the more usual Baksan Valley. Further E in the range, a group from North Ossetia consisting of S Egorin, I Afanasiev and V Ivanov climbed the R part of the E Face of **Suganbashi** at 6A.

The Tien Shan

Access arrangements for the region are little changed for 1998, except for compulsory insurance for climbing and trekking in the Alptourzones. In addition a Kyrghyz Embassy has been established in London, enabling Kyrghyz visas to be obtained in Britain.

A noticeable trend in 1997 was the increase in activity of the Kyrghyz mountaineers. Ascents by local climbers have been reported in many of the ranges of the Tien Shan.

In the **Central Tien Shan** the 1997 summer season was unusually hot and dry. The characteristic afternoon snowfall during August was much less than usual, although reports differ. In total there were 260 visitors to the North and South Inylchek Glaciers. Of these 76 summited on **Khan Tengri (6995m)**, 48 of them from CIS countries, and 26 summited on **Pobeda (7439m)**. There were four fatalities – two Lithuanians on Pobeda, and a Russian and a Korean on Khan Tengri.

A team from Severodvinsk made the second ascent of the 1990 *Zhuravlev Route* on the NE Spur of Pobeda (7439m). This route, given 6A, lies to the L of the *Abalakov Route*. Snow conditions were such that progress was much easier at night. Sergei Penzov, M Ishutin and M Strelkov were on the move for 34 hours from 19 to 21 August, winning first place in the Russian high-altitude championships.

Also on **Pobeda** in August, a US team set out to make a ski descent of the *Abalakov Route*. Tyson Bradley and Dave Braun spent 9 days on the ridge, reaching 6700m and descending on free-heel gear. Julie Faure and Pete Keene abandoned the attempt at 5800m. Low on the route avalanches were the major hazard; 29 people were buried here in a 1950s disaster. The snow was extremely rotten and the team sank to their chests in many places. Above 6000m the snow was more supportive but the mixture of 3-foot *sastrugi* and scoured ice was challenging to ski. The summit had to be sacrificed owing to a clogged petrol stove.

On **Khan Tengri (6995m)**, a new route was climbed in late August by V Shamalo and D Kamarov. They took a couloir on the SW side of the mountain to search for the body of the fallen climber Yuri Krasnoukhov. They found the body and completed the route at 5B, the major difficulties being on the upper slabs. The body was later taken down by a rescue team, the first time for some years that financial circumstances have allowed such activity. The Khan Tengri race was held for the fourth time. Eight participated, the winner being Sergey Penzov with an out and back time of 12 hours 32 minutes from the South Inylchek base camp.

Also in the summer season, the first Kyrghyz ascent was made of **Peak Nansen (5697m)**, from the lower reaches of the S Inylchek Glacier. Climbers M Mikhailov, A Puchinin, A Manulik and V Akimov climbed via the NE Ridge at 5B.

In the upper reaches of the S Inylchek Glacier the first ascent was made of one of the last remaining unclimbed 6000m peaks in the area. **Peak Edelweiss (6000m)** was climbed by guides of the Tien Shan Mountaineering Camp led by Sergey Penzov.

In September several teams visited the much less well-known area the **Western Kokshaal-Too**. Climbing in this area has been inhibited by the proximity of the Chinese border, but access is now possible with the appropriate permit. An ISM group organised by Pat Littlejohn and Vladimir Kommisarov travelled by truck to the region of **Dankova (5982m)**. From the usual base camp for this area, a first ascent was made of nearby **Pik 4758m**, christened **Sababah**. **Pik Zenith (5180m)** was climbed by a new route, the E Ridge at AD+. The second ascent was made of **Pic de l'Entre Aide (5030m)**, also by a new route up the E Ridge at AD. Finally, a possible first ascent was made of a 4910m peak on the frontier which was named **Pik Serpentine**. Hard ice increased the difficulty of most of these routes.

The Western end of the same range, the region of **Kizil Asker (5842)**, was visited by the team of Christian Beckwith, Matthias Engelien, Brian Davison, Nick Green and Lindsay Griffin. After a fraught journey base camp was made in the Komarova Valley from which four first ascents were made. **Pic Lyev (4600m)** was climbed by its N Ridge. **Pic Jerry Garcia (5250m)** was climbed by two contrasting approaches to its N Ridge. **Pik 5225m** was climbed via a glacial bowl and granite headwall, and unofficially named 'Pic 37 Years of American Duct Tape'. Finally **The Unmarked Soldier (5400m)** was climbed by its N Face Couloir at Scottish III in deteriorating weather which thwarted further climbing.

Several of the above group also visited the more accessible, but still virtually deserted, **Ala-Archa** region just S of Bishkek. Beckwith and Engelien climbed the N Face of **Boks (4240m),** bare ice and stonefall greatly increasing the usual grade of 4A. The same team plus Garth Willis climbed an equally challenging couloir leading to **Teketor (4441m)**. Finally Beckwith and Griffin climbed the N Face of **Iziskatel (4570m)** via a 90° direct start.

Siberia and the Russian Far East

In the **Altai** in 1997 attention was focused on the Northern Chuiskiy range. In May local climber Valery Karpenko climbed **Maashey (4177m)** via the col between this peak and **Karagem (3972m)**, then traversed over peak Karagem to the Tamma Pass and hence to the Ak-Tru base camp. The col was reached from the north by a route sharing the same start as the Canny-Doyle route described opposite.

Later the Maashey valley was visited by the British/American team of Justin Canny, Mike Doyle, Bill Fischelis and Paul Knott. On 21 July two new routes were climbed on the N side of **Maashey**. Justin Canny and Mike Doyle climbed the NE Ridge, avoiding the lowest rocks via a snow ramp, while Bill Fischelis and Paul Knott climbed the N Ridge via a subsidiary summit *c*3750m. Unsettled weather and snow build-up precluded further routes of this standard but ascents were made of **Tamma (3700m)**, **Burevestnik (3800)**, **Ak-Tru (4044m)** and **Kurkurek (3989m)**. (*See MEF Report 97/39.*)

Local climbers Andrei Kolesnikov and Kostya Vinnikov, from Barnaul, made the first complete traverse of the peaks at the head of the Maashey Valley, from **Kurkurek (3982m)** to **Maashey**. The traverse took from 21 to 25 July and was carried out with a prior food dump near the Tamma Pass.

A team from Rubtsovsk was also active, making the third ascent of the 1967 *Budanov Route* on the NW Face of **Maashey**. Victor Sergeev, Evgeny Vinnikov and Andrei Drakin spent 31 July to 1 August on the mountain. The route has an average angle of 53° but is described as 'pouring with ice'.

In the **Katun Range** later in August a team proposed to make an 'extreme ski' descent of the N Face of **Bielukha East (4506m)**. The route was to have taken the so-called 'bottle', the couloir in the centre of the face between two icefalls. Maxim Ivanov, Igor Scherbakov and Dmitry Schitov ascended the classical route but called off the attempt to ski the N Face owing to avalanche danger.

In **Kamchatka** reports suggest that there has been little activity of note, due in part to the inability of local climbers to afford helicopter travel to remote areas.

An unusual trip took place in the N of Siberia, on the **Putorana Plateau** E of Norilsk. Sergey Kosin and Sergey Balaganski travelled 1000km by ski and 300km by raft. The raft was carried over the whole ski traverse, resulting in a combined sled and backpack weight of 75kg per person. From Norilsk the pair travelled via the Melkoye and Ayan Lakes to the village of Svetlogorsk on the Kureika River. The raft journey took them to the town of Igarka. The trip took 11 weeks from 16 April, during which time temperatures rose from the minimum of –35°C to above zero.

DEREK FORDHAM

Greenland 1997

The Inland Ice dominated much of the activity in Greenland during the year and in April claimed the lives of two members of a three-man Finnish expedition attempting to cross from the Ammassalik area to Sondre Stromfjord. The onset of a *piteraq* katabatic storm a few days after the expedition was flown onto the edge of the ice cap on 5 April prevented the team from erecting their tent and forced them to attempt to shelter under the collapsed flysheet. An emergency beacon was activated late on the day after the onset of the storm and a rescue helicopter arrived early the next day to find Tommi Heinonen (26) and Ari Mattila (27) dead. The survivor, Timo Polari (28), was the only one who, in the appalling conditions under the flysheet, had managed to put on some dry clothes.

There has been an increasing tendency in recent years for parties attempting the 'normal' ice cap crossing from Ammassalik to Sondre Stromfjord to choose to be helicoptered onto the ice, thus avoiding the difficulties of climbing up through the mountains. Some parties have even arranged to be helicoptered from the western margin of the ice, thus further side-stepping the real issues and challenge of crossing the Inland Ice. The experience of the Finns demonstrates that crossing the Inland Ice is still a serious undertaking and high on the Greenland ice cap little quarter can be expected.

The Danish Polar Centre gave permission for some 17 separate expeditions to cross the Inland Ice and among the more noteworthy was that of Swedes Claes-Goran Ersson and Erik Abrahamsson who flew to a glacier in the **Watkins Mountains** near **Gunnbjørnsfjeld (3710m)**, the highest peak in the Arctic. They started on 12 May with 120kg pulks and skied for 52 days to reach Thule Airbase in NW Greenland after a journey of 1653km, having used ski-sails for the last half of the traverse and travelled 140km on the their best day. Ronald Naar from Holland also took a three-man expedition to Gunnbjørnsfjeld in April, climbed the mountain and then skied 845km across the Inland Ice to Ilulissat on the west coast.

In June Frenchman Didier Drouet led a party from Ammassalik to Sondre Stromfjord. The five-person team included Valdemar Geisler, the first Greenlander to cross the Inland Ice. Drouet is now planning a solo south to north traverse of the Inland Ice.

An impressive west to east traverse was made by Christian Edelstam and Tomas Bergemalm from Sweden. They started from Sondre Stromfjord on 29 April with 125kg pulks and reached the Gunnbjornsfjeld area in 46 days after a 920km traverse in fine stable weather with only two days of high wind. As they skied to the glacier landing place where they were to meet their aircraft an extraordinary meeting took place. They came across a tent:

'Hello, there are two Swedes out here.'

The reply eventually came, 'Where are you from?'
'The west coast.'
'Aaah, from L.A.'
In the tent was an American expedition, led by Todd Burleson, which had been in the Gunnbjørnsfjeld area. Before being flown out by Twin Otter, Edelstam and Bergemalm made three attempts on Gunnbjørnsfjeld but on each occasion were driven back by bad weather.

The Norwegian South Pole veteran and Greenland tour operator Sjur Mordre was prevented by bad weather from flying in to Gunnbjørnsfjeld to make use of the large quantity of supplies he had left under a gigantic snow cairn in 1996. He did manage to organise a para-wing descent of the western edge of the Inland Ice from DYE 2, an abandoned early warning station on the ice cap, as well as a double dog-sledge crossing of the Inland Ice. Using dogs borrowed in East Greenland the expedition crossed to the western ice edge near Sondre Strom-fjord, paused to exchange members, and then returned to the east coast taking seven weeks for the round trip. Avoiding the bad weather which hampered Sjur Mordre, Edelstam and Bergemalm, Skip Horner from Montana managed to get up Gunnbjornsfjeld in early May with what he referred to as '... a senior citizen's expedition and probably the oldest party to summit'.

In the **Schweizerland** area of central East Greenland Paul Walker organised his usual collection of expeditions operating under the Tangent Expeditions banner. Problems with weather prevented some groups being flown to their intended destinations and three separate groups were flown to the Champs Elysées Glacier. After a heavy fall of snow good weather allowed a seven-man group under Nigel Edwards to make ten ascents, eight thought to be firsts. A team led by Paul Walker skied up the Champs Elysées Glacier and climbed eight new peaks, all in the region of 2400m, the most notable of which was **Tangent Peak (2420m)**. From the summits the group were able to look SE over the Pourquoi Pas Glacier to the area where the Karabiner Mountaineering Club Expedition had climbed in 1994 and beyond to the area first visited by University of London expeditions in 1968 and 1969 and more recently explored by the Oxford University expedition in 1996. A five-person all-women British expedition moved their base to the Kristians Glacier and made numerous ascents, notably the second ascent of **Point 2200m** above the Pourquoi Pas Glacier, first climbed by the KMC in 1994.

Tangent also provided the logistic support for a CAF expedition led by Bernard Gillet. The team were landed by helicopters on the Femstjernen glacier junction from where with some delays due to weather they climbed **Mont Forel (3360m)** by the SE ridge route before returning to the Femstjernen. Having chartered only one helicopter for the flight out, the expedition chose to abandon a large quantity of equipment on the glacier. Perhaps this wilful act of desecration, which was condemned by those in the area as forcefully as it will be by all who value unspoiled wilderness, is the inevitable result of access to such areas now being obtained so easily and with so little effort, as was the case with the CAF expedition.

Less controversial ascents of Mont Forel were made by three other expeditions; Jean Canceill led a five-strong French party on a 300km tour from the

Fenris Gletscher, north of Ammassalik, via the Jura Gletscher to the south side of Mont Forel which was climbed on 22 April by the SE ridge before the group skied out to the settlement of Kuummiut. A Norwegian group led by Eirik Tryti also started from the Fenris Gletscher and skied to the Mont Forel area where they made several first ascents in the Bredekuppel massif before, on 7 August, four members climbed Mont Forel by the NE face, using the route first attempted in 1984 by an Eagle Ski Club expedition, and linking with the standard SE ridge route. Later the same day one of the Norwegians, Jorn Hauge, made the first solo ascent of Forel, following his companions' route to the summit. The team then finished their successful expedition by climbing **Sydbjerg**, **Perfektnunatak** and a further outlying nunatak. The other ascent of Mont Forel was by a Swiss team led by Max Flick. They were helicoptered to the upper Paris Glacier on 9 July and made the ascent of the NE face two days later before commencing the long, but uneventful ski journey back to Tasilaq Fjord, hindered somewhat by bad visibility in the more southerly mountains.

In the south of Greenland two Scottish groups were active. At the end of July Pete Benson led the Scottish Torssuqatoq Spires Expedition to the area east of Nanortalik. A base camp was established at the head of Narssap Sarqua Fjord and from an ABC further inland a large number of first ascents of difficult rock routes were made in the very variable weather which is characteristic of this maritime area. A little to the north the Scottish South Greenland Expedition, composed of Douglas Campbell and Malcolm Thorburn, planned to make a south-north traverse over a section of the ice cap from Sermilik Fjord to Narssarssuaq during July and August but were prevented from so doing by pack ice in the southerly fjords. The pair rapidly revised their plans and made an arduous ascent onto the ice cap directly from Narssarssuaq and in generally good weather managed to reach a group of previously unvisited nunataks 30km in from the east coast. Here a number of first ascents of up to 2000m were made before returning to Narssarssuaq by the outward route.

Farther north on the East Greenland coast Arved Fuch's expedition boat *Dagmar Aasen* was frozen in to over-winter at Scoresbysund prior to attempting to 'follow the wake' of the German North Pole Expedition of 1868-70. That expedition had sought to break through the polar pack ice to find the 'open polar sea' so erroneously proposed by August Petermann the German geographer. One of the expedition's ships, the *Hansa*, was sunk and the crew, marooned on an ice floe, drifted for 200 days south along the East Greenland coast. So, one imagines 'the wake' will not be too closely followed!

SIMON RICHARDSON

Scotland 1996-97

It is a curious paradox, but the coldest and snowiest Scottish winters do not necessarily guarantee the best climbing. The 1996/97 Scottish winter may not have been a good season for classic ice routes, but from a mixed climber's perspective it was one of the best on record. Although a succession of storms and major thaws limited activity during the second half of the season, there were more high standard routes climbed than ever before. This was a direct result of the generally thin conditions, which focused the ever-growing band of Scottish winter activists away from traditional ice climbs onto more technical mixed and snowed-up rock routes.

A growing trend was the number of repeats of hard winter routes. Second ascents of the hardest Scottish winter climbs have been rare events in the past, but the newly completed series of SMC guidebooks and a more informative grading system have made the difficult routes more accessible. Unlike previous years which have been characterised by key activists seeking out new routes, many of the season's significant ascents were early repeats, aid eliminations and the straightening out of existing lines.

The definition of what constitutes a winter ascent was brought into question on several occasions. A major thaw in early January was followed by a long high pressure period which brought cold stable conditions to the hills. Under normal circumstances the settled weather would have been perfect for winter climbing, but with the crags stripped bare of snow it raised frustration levels. Undoubtedly, the North American 'dry tooling' approach influenced several climbers to venture onto 'snowed-up rock' climbs that were almost entirely bereft of snow or ice. In the main, the controversy was limited to those climbing existing routes, and, so far at least, those attempting first winter ascents of summer lines have restricted themselves to genuine winter conditions.

A selection of the season's important repeats and significant first ascents are described below. Full details can be found in the 1997 Scottish Mountaineering Club Journal.

Cairngorms

The Northern Corries of **Cairngorm** saw the first climbing of the winter, and by mid-November the easily accessible Coire an Lochain was in excellent mixed condition with the cliff well-hoared and the cracks free of ice. Robin McAllister and Stuart Mearns set the tone with the second ascent of the bold and technical *Prore* (VIII,8) which takes the rounded arête to the right of *Savage Slit*. The following weekend Al Powell and Pete Benson took advantage of the good conditions with the second ascent of *War and Peace* (VII,8), the steep wall on the right side of No.4 Buttress.

The most significant new route in the **Northern Corries** was *Migrant Direct* (VII,7) by Will Garrett and Ally Coull, which takes the prominent corner avoided by the original route. This stunning line had been investigated by several local climbers, and was a fine on sight performance for the young Edinburgh University pair. Later in the season, Brian Davison and Andy Nisbet solved two well-known problems by making the first free ascents of *Nocando Crack* (VII,8) and *Ventricle* (VII,9). Nisbet had made the futuristic first winter ascent of *Ventricle* (a steep summer HVS) with Colin MacLean way back in 1984, and since then a free ascent eliminating the two aid points had been a prime target.

The Loch Avon Basin saw one of the major events of the season, when visiting Slovenian Janez Jeglic and Andy Cave made the first free ascent of *Citadel* (VII,8). This long and sustained eight-pitch route on the **Shelter Stone** was first climbed by Murray Hamilton and Kenny Spence in February 1980, and has been referred to as the 'touchstone of Scottish mixed climbing'. Although the two crux pitches had been climbed free on separate occasions, and the route has achieved modern classic status with around a dozen ascents to date, no team had previously managed a completely free ascent. Also on the **Shelter Stone**, Davison and Nisbet made an important ascent of a long-standing problem with a complete winter ascent of *Consolation Groove* (VII,7). The original winter line climbed all bar 50m of *Raeburn's Buttress*. Davison and Nisbet climbed an independent winter route by following the turfy corner right of the original line and then trending left to below the smooth groove of the summer line.

Deep in the **Cairngorms**, the lonely **Beinn a'Bhuird** saw two major additions in December. First off the mark were Guy Robertson and Adrian Crofton who made two visits to Coire an Dubh Lochain before succeeding on *The Whip* (VII,7), the shallow groove system left of Bloodhound Buttress. In the more remote Garbh Choire, Chris Cartwright and Simon Richardson climbed *West Side Story* (VII,8), which takes the diagonal fault cutting across the W Face of Mitre Ridge. Late in the season, the ubiquitous Davison-Nisbet team had a productive day taking advantage of unusually good ice conditions on the N Wall of Squareface Buttress. They added four new ice routes including the prominent line of *Gold Coast Direct* (V, 5) up the L side of the wall.

In the **Southern Cairngorms**, big news on Creag an Dubh Loch was the third ascent of the very steep *Vertigo Wall* (VI,7) by Robin McAllister, Dave McGimpsey and Charlie French. The route was found in excellent condition just after New Year, and its reputation as one of the best mixed routes in Scotland was confirmed. Nearby, on **Lochnagar**, the Cartwright-Richardson team laid an old ghost to rest with the first ascent of *The Undertaker* (VII,7). This takes a rising traverse line on *The Stack*, to finish in a spectacular position up the undercut overhanging arête on the R edge of the buttress.

Northern Highlands

In Torridon, Andy Nisbet concluded an excellent run of early season routes with two very steep snowed-up rock climbs in Coire Mhic Fhearchair on **Beinn Eighe.** The summer HVS line of *Sting* (VII,7) on the Far East Wall was the first to fall. Nisbet had attempted the route several times over the past five winters and was finally successful with Martin Moran just after New Year.

The initial crux involved torquing up a thin crack with no footholds, and the second required blind hooking up a vertical wall well away from protection. Full of confidence, Nisbet then went on to make a winter ascent of *Samurai* (VII,7) with Jonathan Preston. By hooking chockstones up the overhanging wall above the Upper Girdle, it was possible to take a more direct line than the summer HVS. Narrow cracks and good incut holds make the quartzite cliffs of Coire Mhic Fhearchair ideally suited to this form of winter climbing which is best typified by the unrepeated 1993 Moran-Nisbet route *Blood Sweat and Frozen Tears* (VII,8) on the awesome West Central Wall.

Over the New Year period, Simon Richardson and Chris Cartwright climbed a winter route approximating to the summer line of *Enigma* on the front face of the forbidding Mainreachan Buttress on **Fuar Tholl**. Complex route finding meant the team were only successful on their second attempt, and due to the sustained nature of the climbing the route was thought to warrant VII,7. A couple of days earlier, Finlay Bennet and Jamie Fisher scooped the first winter ascent of *Bat's Gash* (V,6) on the remote N Face of **Beinn Lair**. This deep cleft to the left of Wisdom Buttress had been talked about by many teams over the years, but no-one was prepared to commit themselves to the six-hour approach. Further north on the lonely Cadha Dearg on **Seana Bhraigh**, Cartwright and Stuart Campbell made an important addition to the right of Geddes' Gully. *The Mercy Seat* (VII,6) starts left of Ruighe Ramp and takes a poorly protected line of weakness on the sensationally exposed NW prow of the crag.

Central Highlands

On **Aonach Mor**, Al Powell and Andy Benson scored a notable coup by climbing the overhanging groove system to the right of *Hurricane Arête*. *Alien Abduction* (VII,8) had hitherto been perhaps the finest unclimbed feature on the cliff. The second roof proved to be particularly blank and technical and demanded an axe rest and point of aid. Nearby on **Aonach Beag**, Powell and Benson added to their collection of difficult climbs on the Aonachs by making the second ascent of the steep and strenuous *Salmonella* (VII,8) on Raw Egg Buttress.

On Ben Nevis, Chris Cartwright and Simon Richardson found a serious ice climb on the previously unclimbed wall to the left of South Gully. *South Sea Bubble* (VII,7) finds its way through continuously overhanging terrain by linking two hanging ice smears with some bold mixed climbing to reach a free hanging icicle that leads through the final roof. The same team also made a good late season addition with an ascent of the striking fault cutting through the blank vertical wall to the right of Number Three Gully. *Darth Vader* (VII,8) had seen several previous attempts, and hints at the potential for difficult mixed climbing on a mountain which is best known for its ice climbs.

Southern Highlands

Arguably the most important ascent in the Southern Highlands was the second ascent of *The Screaming* (VIII,8) on **Beinn an Dothaidh** by Mark Garthwaite and Robin McAllister. This route had already seen off an earlier repeat attempt by a strong team in November, and McAllister provided some early excitement by taking a ground-sweeping fall on the first pitch when a block pulled.

Garthwaite demonstrated his well known strength and stamina by eliminating the axe rests on the crux pitch. This 20m continuously overhanging wall is climbed by thin torques and poor placements in well-spaced turf.

On the increasingly popular **Arrochar cliffs**, Dave McGimpsey and McAllister picked a major plum on **The Brack** when they climbed the steep crack system to the right of *Great Central Groove*. *Resolution* (VI,7) provided four very sustained pitches, with a steep crux groove near the top of the route. This route had been eyed up by several teams over recent years and is an important addition to the area. Further east, on the little known cliffs of **Meall nan Tarmachan** near Ben Lawers, Ken Crocket discovered six new grade III and IV routes in the company of Brian Dullea, Bob Richardson and Iain Smart. This area has seen one of the slowest developments of any Scottish winter cliff, since the first routes were recorded here by Raeburn way back in 1898. Clearly, there is still clearly plenty of scope for winter exploration in the Scottish mountains!

TONY HOWARD

Middle East 1997

Jordan

With the third edition of Tony Howard's *Treks and Climbs in Wadi Rum* now out, listing around 400 routes in the area, the pace of development has slowed. The main activists are still Albert Precht and Siggi Brochmeyer of Austria, who make an annual spring pilgrimage.

Spring 1997 got off to a poor start with cold *Hanseen* winds. This was followed by unusually high temperatures and it was not until late April that life settled down to normal. During this spell of peculiar weather Precht and Brochmeyer continued to add new routes on their favourite cliffs of **Vulcanics Tower** and **Makhman Canyon**. In the canyon they made two particularly hard routes, namely *Reise nach Kurdistan* (UIAA VII–) and *Geschenk Gottes* (UIAA VII+), to the top of **Jebel um Ishrin**. This latter route is 500m long, was climbed in 11 hours and was the scene of this team's first forced bivouac in Wadi Rum. The climbing is described as 'superb, with finger-tip dihedrals'.

Albert Precht also made a solo *enchaînement* up and down the 500m *Hiker's Road* (D+) on **Nassrani** followed by *Pillar of Wisdom* (TD–) on **Jebel Rum**, returning to camp down *Hammad's Route* (AD+).

Geoff Hornby and team added a few more big slab climbs and short test pieces out near **Burdah**, while we continued our exploration of the **Dead Sea Hills** for a forthcoming trekking guide. Interestingly, we were shown a newly discovered limestone cave in the far north, which looks as if it might be extensive. We hope to investigate next spring.

In the summer of 1997 three Bedouin from Rum (Sabbah Atieeq, Sabbah Eid and Atieeq Auda) visited the UK, sponsored by HM Queen Noor and the Tourism Ministry. They climbed in the Peak District, the Lakes and North Wales and attended courses at Plas-y-Brenin and Troll in rope techniques and mountain rescue to enable them to work more safely as guides.

Finally, big business has now discovered that there is money to be made in Rum and major investments and being made to develop the area for tourism with massive World Bank loans. We are trying to have as much input as possible into a scheme which, despite fine intentions, could marginalise the Bedouin community and the needs of climbers if commercial interests are allowed to dominate the project. If you have been to Rum and believe that the area should be protected as a National Park, with the local people playing a key role in its organisation and with the access needs of climbers protected, please send letters of support to : Tony Howard, c/o Troll, Spring Mill, Uppermill, Oldham OL3 6AA.

Libya

In spring 1997 Di Taylor and I were in Libya as guests of Wings Travel and Tours of Tripoli, checking out the potential for adventure tourism. Whilst we didn't find any obviously good climbing, there are some possibilities and also opportunities for short treks and caving. **Jebel Nafusa** south of Tripoli has a lot of known caves, some very extensive (over a kilometre) and others (sometimes man-made) have yet to be explored. Over 1000km east, between Benghazi and Tobruk, is the **Jebel Akhdar Massif**, the Green Mountains. Here too the rock is limestone and in places excellent but the crags we found were mostly small. Further east, just south of Tobruk, there is reputed to be a large limestone sea cliff which we didn't have time to visit.

There are, however, some impressive gorges with climbing opportunities, though the larger steeper cliffs looked yellow and rotten. Nevertheless these beautiful forested valleys have some nice walking and impressive cave entrances. The caves have provided human habitation since the time of early man and there are still some 'bandits' supposed to be living in them. Probably the best two gorges are Wadi Derna and Wadi Kouf. The latter is in the heart of the massif, close to the magnificent Greek and Roman cities of Cyrene and Apollonia which along with Sabratha and Leptis Magna near Tripoli are some of the best cities of their era outside Rome and Athens. These alone make Libya's coastal area well worth a visit.

Heading south, we crossed 100km of the amazing 200m high dunes of the Ramlat Dawada at the eastern end of the great Ubari Sand Sea *en route* to the **Akakus Towers** 1500km away in the far SW corner of Libya. The **Akakus** present an astonishing collection of weird sandstone towers and arches mostly 50-200m high. They rise from a vast desert of dunes and hamada covering an area of over 7000 square kilometres. Unfortunately, due to extremes of temperature, the rock is exfoliating badly and with virtually no rain the surface remains loose on both a small and a large scale. Climbers in desperate need of rock will find some single-pitch slabs and cracks to amuse themselves on, while some of the highest and largest towers way up on top of the plateau, with faces up to 300m, look more compact and solid – which is presumably how they have managed to stay up there. With no maps, however, getting to them looks very problematical.

The real attraction of the **Akakus** for its few visitors is an abundance of superlative rock art. The paintings and inscriptions of tribal life, elephants, giraffes, rhinos etc are amongst the best in Africa and date back 10,000 years. Photos we were shown of cliffs and cave drawings elsewhere in Libya revealed possibilities for short routes in **Haruj el Aswad** (Black Rocks), a basalt mass in central Libya, and also for longer mountain routes at **Jebel Arkno** and **Jebel Uweinat** in the far SE corner, on the Egyptian border. The same enthusiastic informant, a rock art specialist working with Wings, also told us that **Djebel Nuqay**, the northern arm of **Tibesti** which protrudes a long way into Libya, has potential for mountain routes.

Anyone wishing to visit any of these areas in this spectacular desert country should contact Isam Harus at Wings Travel and Tours, Tripoli (tel 00218 21 3331855; fax 3330881). They can arrange everything from visas and permits through to 4-wheel drives and guides.

HARISH KAPADIA

India 1997

The year 1997 was declared a year of celebration to commemorate the 50th Anniversary of Indian Independence. But unfortunately the weather was not in a celebratory mood and several expeditions had to face the wrath of the weather Gods. One expedition, specially organised for the occasion, was the traverse across the entire Himalayan range by a group of ladies.

A Walk Across The High Himalaya

A team of eight women traversed the entire Himalayan range from Arunachal Pradesh to the Eastern Karakoram. The team, led by Bachendri Pal, started from Bombila on 4 February 1997. They trekked through Bhutan, Sikkim, Nepal, Garhwal, Kinnaur, Spiti, Ladakh and the Karakoram.

Due to major differences which developed after four months on trek, the team split up at Dharchula, Kumaon. Three ladies left the main group and continued on a separate trek. They were Vineeta Muni, Sumita Roy and Malika Virdi. They were sponsored by the Himalayan Club. This group crossed 36 passes above 3000m, covering about 4500km on foot in 198 days (just over 6 months) of trekking. Their trek ended at the Karakoram Pass on 20 August 1997. They were accom-panied, in the final stages, by Jean Thomas. The other group ended their trek by reaching the Indira Col on the Siachen Glacier on 2 September 1997.

Garhwal

Satopanth (7075m) This was a super-fast climb by a very fit party of well-acclimatised instructors from the Nehru Institute of Mountaineering and led by their Principal, Col. Ajit Dutt. The expedition was organised as a refresher course for the instructors. Base camp (4680m) was established at Vasuki Tal on 7 July and advanced base camp (5200m) at Sundar Bamak the same day. Camp 1 (5920m) was set up on 8 July and Camp 2 (6400m) on the N Face five days later. Nine members reached the summit on 14 July following the traditional route on this 7000er. The round trip from ABC took only seven days.

Changabang N Face (6864m) A British team, led by Julie-Ann Clyma and Roger Payne, returned to this peak to complete the route left unfinished in 1996. The team consisted of several leading climbers from the UK and the US. After establishing base camp on 10 May, two separate routes were tried. Finally Brendan Murphy and Andy Cave reached the summit on 1 June – by a new route. Mick Fowler and Steve Sustad reached the summit ridge. As Brendan Murphy was setting up an abseil, an avalanche swept down, carrying Murphy away and narrowly missing others. His body was not found. (*See articles 'Changabang: A World Apart' by Andy Cave, pp3-11, and 'Mountain of Dreams, Mountain of Sorrows' by Julie-Ann Clyma, pp12-17.*)

Deoban (6855m) This peak is in the Kamet area. An Indian army team led by Maj. Anirudh Negi climbed it this year. Base camp was established on 1 September at Thada Udiar. Four camps were established on the mountain. On 19 September the summit was reached at 9.35am by Naik Subedar Dhanjeet Rai with LNK Topgey Bhutia and RFN Tenzing Sherpa. This difficult peak has not been climbed for a long time.

Changuch (6322m) This unclimbed peak near the Pindari Glacier was attempted by a British team consisting of Gary Murray, Brian James and Stephen Ferris. They attempted the peak from the glacier. Difficulties in crossing séracs and heavy snow on upper snowfields stopped them. (*See MEF Reports, ref. 97/26.*)

Bhagat Peak (5650m) and **The Garhwal Traverse** An Indian expedition from Bombay led by Harish Kapadia tried the ancient tracks in the Badrinath area of the Garhwal. They were the first to follow the routes pioneered by Shipton and Tilman in 1934.

In the first stage of the expedition the five-member team entered the Panpatia Valley and reached the icefall at its head. Their intention was to cross a high col to Madhyamaheshwar to prove an old legend. The icefall proved too difficult and long and the party gave up.

In the second stage Bhagirath Kharak Glacier was traversed and a high camp established on Deo Dekhni plateau. **Bhagat Peak** was climbed by Harish Kapadia and Nyima Sherpa on 19 June. Two other peaks were climbed the following day: **Deo Dekhni I (5400m)** and **Deo Dekhni II (5360m)**, both by Kaivan Mistry and Mingma.

Meanwhile Rajesh Gadgil and Monesh Devjani attempted to reach **Chaukhamba Col (6050m)** last crossed by C F Meade in 1912. They stopped at 4850m owing to wet snow conditions. The entire party then crossed two high passes (last crossed by Shipton and Tilman in 1936) **Shrak La (5700m)** and **Serga Col (5840m)**. Finally they returned via the Arwa valley to complete the exploration. (*See article 'In Famous Footsteps' by Harish Kapadia, pp53-58.*)

Draupadi Ka Danda (5716m) A 10-member Japanese team led by Kazuyoshi Kowdo climbed this small but important peak in the Bhilangna Valley. The summit was reached by the ENE Ridge. The leader and four other members reached the top on 3 August 1997.

Meru Central (6361m) A British team led by Owain Jones (with three members) made two attempts, twice reaching 6100m, on the E Face. Bad weather, crampon failure and high avalanche risk made them give up. Their route was the same as the Shark's Fin.

Thalay Sagar (6904 m) This peak, which sees many attempts and few successes, was climbed by an Australian team (Athol Whimp with three members), who reached the summit by the N Face on 19 September 1997. The summit was reached by Athol Whimp and Andrew Lindblade.

Several other popular peaks in the Garhwal were attempted, including **Shivling**, **Meru**, **Kamet**, **Kedarnath**, **Kedar Dome**, **Nanda Devi East** and others. Bad weather forced many teams to call off their attempts. On **Nandabhanar**, a peak near the Pindari Glacier, an Indian climber, K V Mohan, was killed when an avalanche hit the party.

Himachal Pradesh

Gya (6794 m) This unclimbed peak on the tri-junction of Spiti, Ladakh and Tibet has been an attraction to climbers for the past few years. This year no less than three expeditions attempted it from two directions. But the peak did not yield to any of them, though several other peaks near it were climbed.

Gya South-East (6680m) and others (from southern approach, Spiti). A three-member expedition from Bombay approached the unclimbed Gya from the Lingti valley in April-May 1997. Reaching base camp in near winter conditions they attempted the E Face of the SSW spur of Gya. They reached the SE Col. Finding the final ridge of Gya too difficult they turned SE to climb Gya SE. Dividing into different teams the other three peaks around the ridge were climbed. The last peak was near base camp. All the peaks climbed were first ascents and were given names by members of the expedition.

Gya North (6520 m) from the northern approach, Ladakh-Spiti. A young team from Delhi with three climbers wanted to climb Gya's NW Face in good style. After an attempt on the face Yousuf and Chaman followed the W Spur to establish three camps, the third one being almost on **Gyasumpa peak**, the point where the W Spur and N Ridge meet. From here, traversing the N Ridge with difficulties, these two reached the second high point on the ridge, at about 6520m, which they named Gya North. This was a first ascent of the peak.

Gyasumpa (6480m) from northern approach, Ladakh-Spiti. This was a large expedition consisting of climbers from seven countries from Asia and supported by many strong climbers from India. It was led by the experienced mountaineer Col H S Chauhan. They crossed Parang La and reached the base camp in the north. One member was evacuated owing to sickness. Their intention was to make the first ascent of **Gya (6794 m)**. Dividing in two large teams they climbed the W Spur and N Ridges. In all about 32 climbers reached the summit after fixing many metres of rope. Both the routes were of high technical calibre and required a good deal of care and effort. One party climbed to the W Spur from the N and the other party followed the N Ridge gained from S.

At first the expedition claimed the first ascent of Gya and all concerned were informed of this achievement. However upon scrutiny of their photographs, the leader declared that the team had climbed the much lower Gyasumpa (6480m). Literally meaning third peak of Gya, this peak was the one near which the Delhi group had established their Camp 3 a month before, climbing there easily from the S. The present expedition had turned in towards the peak one valley too soon and had mistaken Gyasumpa for Gya. (*See article 'In Pursuit of Gya' by Arun Samant, pp36-44.*)

Phawrarang (6349 m), Kinnaur. A Japanese team climbed this remote peak. The E Face to E Ridge route was climbed on 12 September by two members and on 13 September 1997 by a further two members. The team had excellent weather throughout.

Gepang Goh (6088 m), Lahul. This prominent peak can be observed from the popular Rohtang Pass. It is a group of several peaks and though of moderate height each of the peaks is difficult to climb. There are two known ascents in this group. The first was by General Charles Bruce (with the Swiss guide Heinrich Führer and 2 Gurkhas) in July 1912. 42 years later N Wollaston and R Platts are known to have climbed a peak here in 1954. The army team from Two JAK Rifles, Indian army, established a base camp near Khoksar on 6 July 1997. They approached the SE Face. A summit camp was established on 12 July. On 15 July a party left this camp at 5.15am reaching the peak at 12.45pm. Summiters were Gautam Thakur (instructor from Manali Mountaineering Institute), Rfn. Prem Chetri and Rfn. Dal Bahadur Gurung. The height of the peak, previously thought to be 5870 m, was revised by the present team as above.

Throne (5840m), S Parvati Valley, Kullu. Though small by Himalayan standards, this peak is a prominent feature in the S Parvati Valley. A Scottish expedition climbed it on 12 September 1997 by the NE Face and N Ridge. The summit was reached by Scott Muir (leader), D Proudfoot, G Lennox and K Kelly. The peak is situated near Pandu bridge, Manikaran.

Other peaks attempted or climbed in the area were **Chau Chau Kang Nilda** (Spiti), two unnamed 6000ers in the Baspa valley (Kinnaur), **Chandra Bhaga** and **Koa Rong**, both in Lahul.

Ladakh

Ladakh continues to be a popular destination. The high peaks of Nun and Kun were climbed and attempted by several teams. Kang Yissey was another popular destination.

But the real exploratory climbs were achieved in the Rupshu. The area has only been opened and known since 1995. I was a member of one of the early parties to climb in the area. We climbed **Lungser Kangri (6666m)** and **Chhamser Kangri (6622m)**. These were the highest peaks in Ladakh. But as they can be approached easily, they have been climbed at least three times each year since my first ascent. I do not know whether the mountain is blessing me or cursing me for opening up this onslaught! This year the remaining two major peaks in the area were climbed and one was attempted.

Kula (Chalung) (6546m) Rupshu, Ladakh. The peak is situated in Rupshu above Namshang La. It is known by both names. A Japanese team led by Tsuneo Suzuki (11 members) climbed it on 11, 13 and 15 July 1997 by the NW Ridge. This was the first ascent of the peak.

Pologongka (6632m), Rupshu, Ladakh. A British Expedition achieved some pioneering work in the area. It was led by M Ratty with T Willis, R Law, A Allcock. They climbed Pologongka, rising above the motorable pass of the same name, by the S Face (Ratty and Law with the Liaison Officer N Singh) on 20 August 1997. This was a first ascent. The expedition also attempted the S Face main buttress on **Chakura**, reaching 6000 m. This peak rises from the road near Chumathang. No wonder they gave the title 'Roadside Rupshu' to their article about this climb! (*See MEF Reports, ref. 97/34.*)

Sara Shua (6250m) Rupshu, Ladakh. The N Ridge was climbed by three members of an Italian expedition on 14 August, and repeated by three members on 17 August 1997. This is the peak on the western shores of Tso Moriri and was climbed by the Japanese in 1996 for the first time.

Lungser Kangri (6666m) and **Chhamser Kangri (6622m)**, Rupshu, Ladakh. This year it was a German team led by Dr Hans Dietrich Engel Hardt (three members) that took its turn on these peaks. Both the peaks were climbed.

1. Local 'club' climbers tackling a bolt-equipped cliff at Beauvoir near Poitiers. In Britain, such a cliff, similar to sections of Malham Right Wing, would probably be climbed using nuts. (*Ken Wilson*) (p175)

73. An early photograph of the Gornergrat Railway, with (*L to R*) Zinalrothorn, Schalihorn and Weisshorn. (*Brown Boveri*) (p238)

74. Mount Athabasca, with pack-train on the Saskatchewan glacier. (*J Monroe Thorington, 1923*) (p241)

Right
5. Koh-i-nur peaks from near Shisha Nag, E Liddar valley. (*The Hon C G Bruce, 1898*) (p239)

Below
6. F G Lucas (*L*) and the Hon C G Bruce with their climbing party of Gurkhas, 1898. (*The Hon Mrs C G Bruce*) (p239)

77. Ella Maillart, 1903–1997, at Chandolin in 1994, Dent Blanche behind. (*Janet Adam Smith*) (p337)

78. Walter Amstutz, 1902–1997. (p335)

. Yevgeniy Gippenreiter, 1927–1997. (p333)

Left
80. Jimmy Roberts on the Masherbrum Reconnaissance Expedition 1938. (*Robin Hodgkin*) (p222)

81. Jimmy Roberts, 1916–1997. (*John Cleare*) (p340)

Chhamser Kangri was climbed on 31 August from SW to NE by all members. Lungser Kangri was climbed from the SE by all members on 5 September 1997. Both these peaks are situated on the eastern shores of Tso Moriri Lake, Rupshu. We have not heard the last of them for sure.

Literature

Like every year many reprints of old classics were available. But of the original publications, *Exploring Kinnaur and Spiti* by Deepak Sanan and Dhanu Swadi fills a void of information about these areas. Sanan was a District Commissioner in both these areas and knows it first hand. The second edition of *Exploring the Hidden Himalaya* (Mehta and Kapadia) was issued as a paperback. It has an updated history of the range (to the end of 1997) and a set of new pictures.

Deaths

Though Lt. Col. J O M Roberts lived and died in Nepal he was an explorer well known in India. In fact he was the first visitor to Spiti and later to the Saser Kangri area. His climbs in the Dhaula Dhar were models of inspiration. Stationed in the Dalhousie Cantonment, he would turn mountaineer on Friday evenings, climb rocky peaks above Dharamsala and then report for the Monday morning parade. He was also a pioneer of what is now known as commercial trekking.

Two Himalayan scholars from Bengal also passed away. Uma Prasad Mukherjee (Hon. Member of the Himalaya Club) was a well known writer and inspired a generation of Himalayan lovers. S N Das was also a scholar of Bengali lores about the range.

Freedom Walk

As India celebrated its 50th year of Independence on 15 August 1997 we discovered that there were several extra holidays to celebrate the event. Many politicians were descending on Bombay, many events were planned and the celebrations would lead for certain to traffic jams and noise. So what could be a better way than to spend a week in the mountains? With friends I set off on a trek to the high Kush Kalyan plateau which contains several lakes. That prolific Himalayan writer Bill Aitken aptly called it 'the Lake District of the Garhwal'.

One evening we camped near a shepherd couple with their old father. I could not resist asking these nomads what they thought of Indian Independence today and that historic day exactly fifty years ago.

'I came to Kush Kalyan then,' the old man replied. 'We used to travel on foot from the plains, and even today we do the same. We have our flock with us.'

'What about the future?' I asked.

The young shepherd interjected, 'As long as I am alive I will be here and the yearly migration will continue in the same style.'

'But what is the effect of fifty years of Independence?' I persisted. 'What about freedom?'

He thought for a while and replied with a smile, as if it was a state of mind, 'We were always free.'

LINDSAY GRIFFIN & DAVID HAMILTON

Pakistan 1997

Thanks are due to Pakistan Ministry of Tourism, Xavier Eguskitza and Asem Mustafa Awan for their help in providing information.

1997 will be remembered as the year of the best weather conditions seen in the Karakoram for several decades. Low rainfall during the winter and spring meant that there were few problems with fresh snow at the start of the season. Long spells of settled conditions during June, July and August permitted a remarkably high number of climbing successes on both the high peaks and lower rock walls. Pakistan government figures show that 70% of this year's expeditions were successful compared with an average of 42% for the previous five years.

There were several notable climbing achievements recorded. A Korean party made the third ascent of **Gasherbrum IV** by a new route on the impressive West Face. A huge Japanese expedition split its resources between **Broad Peak**, **Gasherbrum I** and **Gasherbrum II** and successfully placed team members on each summit. The fine weather also suited those climbing big rock walls. A German team made the second ascent of **Latok II** by the unclimbed SW Face, while several groups succeeded on other hard technical rock routes. However the main news of the season was the increasing popularity of 'normal routes' on 8000m peaks and the relative decline of exploratory mountaineering on lesser-known objectives. In celebration of the nation's 50th anniversary the Pakistan authorities relaxed the normal restrictions on the number of permits issued for the 8000m peaks.

Ministry of Tourism statistics show that 57 expeditions from 16 countries received permission to climb peaks over 6000m. 23 of these expeditions came from Japan or Korea. A total of 40 expeditions concentrated on the five 8000m peaks, while the other 17 expeditions were spread over 11 different mountains. 29 expeditions succeeded in placing one or more members on the summit of an 8000m peak (73%), while 11 succeeding on a 6000m-8000m peak (65%). There were 9 fatalities among the 500 foreign climbers. Several Japanese groups included experienced Sherpas in their climbing teams. This is thought to be the first time since the 1930s that Nepalese mountaineers have visited the Pakistan Karakoram.

K2 (8611m) Despite record numbers of climbers on Pakistan's other 8000m peaks there were only two teams on K2. Seven Basque climbers led by José Ramón Aguirre attempted the 1994 route on the SSE Spur. They found this route to be more dangerous and avalanche threatened than previously reported and retreated from a high point of 7200m. Tanabe Osamu led a team of nine Japanese climbers and thirteen Nepalese Sherpas on a siege-style assault of the West Face. All climbers used oxygen above 7500m and over 3000m of rope was fixed. Three Japanese members reached the summit on 19 July, followed by four more Japanese and four Sherpas on 28 July. The exact line of their ascent is not known but it is thought to be a partial new route.

Broad Peak (8047m) Eight of the ten permits issued went to groups attempting the *Normal Route*. In addition two small teams tried the unclimbed SSE Ridge. Australian Andrew Lock, who had tried this route before in 1994 with a Swedish team, was joined this time by Rick Allen. Spanish brothers Alberto and Félix Iñurrategi had their eyes on the same line. Both pairs retreated from 7200m finding technical difficulties too great for an Alpine style ascent. Switching to the *Normal Route* the Spanish brothers made a very fast ascent of the Main Summit on 12 July, as did Andrew Lock on 7 August. Yoshio Matsunaga's Japanese group was first to establish itself on the *Normal Route* at the end of May. F Yokotagawa and Jeff Bubb (USA) were struck by an avalanche and killed, between C2 and C3, on 16 June. Six of the eight separate expeditions on the *Normal Route* were successful with approximately 25 climbers reaching either the Fore Summit or the Main Summit. (*See MEF Reports, ref. 97/38.*)

Gasherbrum I (8068m) Eight permits were issued for this peak which only a few years ago was the least popular of the Karakoram 8000m peaks. Permit sharing led to more than a dozen separate teams on the mountain all attempting to scale the *Japanese Couloir Route*. The large Japanese GUNMA group led by Nazuka Hideji did much of the early work preparing the route and fixing 600m of rope between C2 and C3. Seven members of this group reached the summit on 7 July followed two days later by 13 climbers from several other expeditions. It is thought that about 26 climbers in total reached the summit over a four-week period from early July to early August. Weather and snow conditions were close to ideal and with large numbers of climbers sharing the trail-breaking, the ascent was made less arduous than in previous years.

Gasherbrum II (8035m) More than 100 climbers assembled at base camp to attempt the *Normal Route* on G2. The Pakistan authorities had issued ten permits, but there were at least thirteen expeditions on the mountain. Some expeditions had secured permission for both G1 and G2 and a handful of climbers including Japanese, Koreans and Czechs summited on both peaks. Fred Barth's American team were the first to occupy base camp at the end of May and opened the route to C1 through the lower icefall. The large Japanese GUNMA group used their Sherpa staff to push the route out, fixing a large quantity of rope, breaking trail and establishing C2 and C3 before summiting on 8 July. Climbers from other expeditions were able to make use of the Japanese fixed ropes and a total of 30-35 people from a variety of countries are thought to have summited in the four weeks following the Japanese success. The only two unsuccessful teams on G2 both arrived at base camp during August and therefore missed the settled weather found in June and July.

Gasherbrum IV (7925m) The most remarkable ascent of the season was achieved by a Korean team led by Cho Sung-Dae who returned to complete the project that he started in 1995 : the *Central Spur* on the West Face. The 12-man team used a considerable amount of fixed rope, but most of the climbing above 6800m was done by four climbers, three of whom (Y Hak-Jae, B Jung-Ho, K Tong-Kwan) reached the summit on 18 July. This was only the third ever ascent of the mountain and the first time that the summit had been reached by a route on the W Face. The route has been graded at IV–/V+ on rock and mixed ground with ice sections of 70°-80° and is said to be threatened by considerable objective dangers. During their descent the Koreans discovered the body of Slavko Sveticic (Slovenia) who disappeared during a solo attempt on the face in 1995. Earlier in the season a strong four-man Basque team led by Miguel Rodriguez tried to make the second ascent of Gasherbrum IV's NW Ridge. They found the weather and snow conditions unfavourable and retreated from a high point of 7300m

Skilbrum (7360m) A large and well funded Japanese expedition containing many Himalayan veterans aimed to make the second ascent of this peak west of K2, first climbed by members of the Austrian Broad Peak expedition in 1956. Eight members of the 17-strong team reached the summit via the S Face on 17 August. Tragedy struck three days later when base camp in the Savoia Glacier was destroyed by a huge avalanche, killing expedition leader Hiroshima Mitsuo and five companions. Mitsuo was visiting Pakistan for the 56th time having made the second ascent of K2 with Ashraf Aman (Pakistan) in 1977. This freak accident accounted for 66% of the climbing fatalities recorded in 1997 which was in all other respects a very 'safe' year.

Masherbrum (7821m) on the southern watershed of the Baltoro was visited by a Spanish expedition led by Manuel Rodriguez. Bemused local staff report that the expedition members fell out with each other and abandoned their attempt without making any real impression on their intended SE Face route.

Three separate expeditions visited the **Trango Towers** in the lower Baltoro. On **Nameless Tower (6237m)** Walter Barker led a strong four-man group from the USA and Canada which succeeded in climbing a new line on the N Face. Their 900m 17-pitch route (VI, 5.10, A4, W13) *The Wall of Fiction* is reported to be right of the existing line of *Book of Shadows*. Seven Scandinavian climbers from Sweden and Norway led by Jan Stensten repeated the 1987 *Slovenian Route* on the S Face, with four of the party reaching the summit. On **Great Trango (6286m)** Lee Sang-Cho was the leader of a four-strong Korean group. Climbing from the Dunge Glacier they are thought to have succeeded in scaling a new route on the E Side of the peak.

Americans Mark Richey and John Bouchard were the latest climbers to attempt the compelling line of the N Ridge on **Latok I (7145m)**. Objective dangers caused by the warm weather forced them to give up after reaching a high point of 6000m. Perhaps the most outstanding achievement of the season was the first ascent of the SW Face of **Latok II (7108m)**, and second overall ascent of the peak. This was achieved in fine style by the talented four-man team of Thomas Huber, Alexander Huber, Toni Gutsch (all German) and Conrad Anker (USA). All four reached the summit on 19 July via a 1000m-long 'big-wall' route rising from the huge central couloir. Seven of the 25 pitches were given a grade of A3, and the whole route was graded at American VII. The Huber brothers had tried the peak previously in 1995. Two other members of the same expedition made the third overall ascent of the peak via another new route on the NW Ridge. Franz Fendt and Christian Schlesener graded their 1100m route VI+ and A3. Members of this expedition also climbed several smaller peaks surrounding the Uzun Brakk Glacier. Two pairs of climbers with previous experience of **Baintha Brakk (7285m)** returned to attempt to be the first to complete technical lines on the south side of this formidable mountain. Germans Jan Mersch and Jochen Hasse reached 6250m on the frequently tried S Pillar. The American pair Tom Nonis and Barry Rugo failed to get established on the SE Pillar owing to dangerous conditions low down on the approach to the route. It appears that the exceptionally warm and dry conditions that suited those on the big peaks and lower rock walls caused considerable risk of rockfall on more 'mixed' objectives.

Three expeditions visited the upper Chogolungma Glacier. The popular peak **Spantik (7027m)** received its annual visit from a French commercial group. Daniel Petraud led three clients to the top on 15 August and returned to make a fast solo ascent three days later. An Italian group on the same permit was unsuccessful, while a Basque group led by Pedro Vdaendo reached the summit.

Four Swiss climbers led by Dieter Fünfschilling attempted **Malubiting West (7453m)** the highest peak in the Malubiting group. Two members of the team reached the summit on 19 August after following the route of the first ascensionists (*1971 Austrian Route*) via the Polan La. This is thought to have been only the second ascent of this attractive peak. Three elderly Japanese climbers led by Narisue Yosuke attempted the unclimbed peak of **Phuparash 1 (6824m)** 12km west of Malubiting. Despite the use of high-altitude porters and fixed ropes they were reported to have been unsuccessful.

A large group of Iranian climbers scaled the attractive peak **Rakaposhi (7788m)** which dominates the Hunza Valley. The expedition was supported by the Mountaineering Federation of Iran and led by Ramin Baghini. Six climbers reached the summit by the long *SW Spur/Ridge Route* on 6 July. Two expeditions arrived at the base camp of **Diran (7257m)** in early August. A small Japanese team led by Hideki Nakayama was successful while a 12-member German commercial party led by Eckhard Radehose failed to climb the peak. It is thought that both groups were on the *Standard West Ridge Route*. On the other side of the Hunza Valley Yoshihumi Miyaji's six-member Japanese team was unsuccessful on **Hunza Peak (6230m)** immediately north of Bublimoting, first climbed by a British pair in 1991. For the first time in recent years no expeditions applied for permits to climb in the Pakistani part of the Hindu Kush.

Nanga Parbat (8125m) Fourteen permits were issued for Pakistan's most accessible 8000m peak. Ten of these groups concentrated on the *Kinshofer Route* on the Diamir Face while three teams chose less popular lines. Japanese climbers were unsuccessful on the *Schell Route*. The talented Czechs Leopold Sulovsky and Ludovit Zahoransky attempted an unclimbed line on the Rupal Flank without success. The hugely experienced pairing of Wojciech Kurtyka and Erhard Loretan made little progress on the unclimbed Mazeno Ridge owing to poor snow conditions. More than 30 climbers from eight separate expeditions reached the summit via the *Kinshofer Route*. A large joint Chinese/Pakistani expedition were first on the mountain and fixed ropes on the entire route to the top camp at 7400m. Eight climbers from this group summited on 15 June. Other teams made use of these ropes to summit during the weeks that followed. Catalan climber Joan Collet reached the summit with five others on

27 July but fell to his death during the descent three days later. The final permit of the year went to a Polish winter expedition led by Andrzej Zawada. They were reported to be still attempting the peak in late January 1998.

Several expeditions visited sub-6000m peaks throughout Pakistan's Northern Areas, attempting both steep rock walls and mixed mountaineering routes. The Pakistan Government does not collect statistics on these activities and it is therefore difficult to assemble comprehensive information.

All the British parties in the following survey were supported by the MEF and further details will be found in their reports on pages 298-300. A six-member British group climbed two separate routes on the unclimbed SE Face of **Beatrice (5800m)** above the Charakusa Glacier. The routes were about 200m apart on the face and both were 750m long. The Huxter/Pyke/Thomas line was possibly slightly harder than the Farquar/Meyers/Turner route, but both were 20 pitch climbs graded E3 6a A3+. (*See article 'Beatrice' by Louise Thomas, pp 117-125.*)

The well publicised ascent of **Shipton Spire (5852m)** in 1996 inspired two teams to visit the Upper Trango Glacier in 1997. The strong American pair Mark Synott and Jared Ogden claimed the second ascent of the spire via a new route christened *Ship of Fools.* This 27-pitch climb (VII, 5.11, A2, W16) was completed in 25 climbing days with the summit being reached on 6 August. Earlier in the season a Hungarian/German group (G Berecz, O Nadasdi, T Tivader) spent three weeks climbing on the slightly lower **East Tower**. They reported 21 pitches of excellent climbing (5.10, A4) but failed to reach the summit.

Two small British groups visited the Choktoi Glacier during the summer. Both parties narrowly failed to reach the summit of **Hanipispur South (6047m)** and found a variety of good climbing on rock and mixed objectives in the area.

Making his third visit to the Chogolungma area in as many years Dave Wilkinson's three-man British party made first ascents of three unnamed peaks above the Bolocho Glacier: **Bolocho V (5240m)** by the E Ridge, **Bolocho I (*c*6000m)** by the N Ridge and **Bolocho VI (*c*5200m)**.

Three groups attempted peaks in the infrequently visited Ghujerab range located between the Shimshal Valley and the Chinese frontier. A 7-member Pakistani civilian group aimed to climb **Koshik Peak (6100m)**, one of the many summits rising above the Khunjerab Pass. However the group seem to have been ill prepared for the endeavour and leader Muzaffar Faizi aborted the expedition in mid-August having only occupied base camp for one day.

A small British group hoped to climb **Zartgarbin (5850m)** above the Murkhun Valley but found the route impossible in the snow and weather conditions encountered in late August. A British women's expedition made two non-technical ascents of previously unclimbed peaks above the Shimshal Pass. **Rwadun Sar (5500m)** was climbed on 14 July by the NE Ridge, and **Zarsanic I (5900m)** on 17 July via the SW Ridge.

BILL O'CONNOR

Nepal 1997

I am grateful to Elizabeth Hawley for her help in compiling these notes.

Nepal had a relatively busy season although the post-monsoon period on the south side of Everest was slack, with only one, unsuccessful, expedition. The Tibetan side, on the other hand, was 'business as usual' with commercial expeditions continuing to dominate 8000m activity. There were quite a lot of groups visiting lower summits and some exploratory climbing, albeit very little. With 1998 designated Nepal Year by the government to encourage tourism, a list of new peaks have been made accessible and royalty-free. This is intended to encourage climbers to visit lesser-known areas and to relieve the pressure on the honey-pots of the Everest and Annapurna regions.

The sad news was the death of Lt Col J O M (Jimmy) Roberts who died at his home in Pokhara on 1 November. Jimmy had been intimately involved with mountaineering in Nepal since the country first opened its doors to Western climbers. Regarded as the father of organised trekking in the Himalaya, he was certainly responsible for getting the Nepalese authorities to designate 18 Trekking Peaks in 1975 and encouraged adventurous, low cost, Himalayan climbing. His knowledge, wit and encouragement will be missed by many of us. (*A full obituary and tributes appear on pages 340–344.*)

SPRING 1997

Ama Dablam (6828m) Only two groups attempted this most popular Khumbu peak in the spring. Both were on the SW Ridge. Neither were successful, each reaching a high point of 6100m.

Annapurna I (8091m) A South Korean team led by Kang Tae-Sun attempted the NE Buttress reaching a high point of 7250m. A Sherpa was killed in a fall.

Baruntse (7168m) An Austrian expedition led by Rudolph Mayr was unsuccessful on the SE Ridge. Although Western members did not go above base camp, two Sherpas reached a high point of 6400m on 2 May.

Cho Oyu (8201m) Undoubtedly the mountain for 'mail order mountaineers', at least 15 expeditions were active on this popular 8000er. The NW side is the route of choice, with 55 climbers reaching the summit between 27 April and 20 May. The only exception was an ascent of the N Ridge on 21 May by Georgi Kotov (Russia) and William Pierson (US).

Dhaulagiri 1 (8167m) A high level of activity concentrated on the NE Ridge with success achieved by expeditions from South Korea (27 April), Australia (25 May) and Japan (31 May). Spanish, Swiss and Venezuelan teams failed to climb the mountain, reaching high points of 7800m, 6900m and 7250m respectively.

Everest (8848m) Once again the 'mother of all mountains' was the scene of frenetic activity on both sides of the mountain. Most expeditions were cosmopolitan in make-up, reflecting their commercial nature. A total of 8 climbers/ Sherpas died on Everest but attracted little of the attention of the 1996 fatalities. Popular and well-known British climber Mal Duff died of illness at base camp while attempting the *South Col Route*.

On the *South Col/South East Ridge Route* 60 climbers reached the summit between 26 April and 27 May, with success for climbers from Indonesia, Russia, Nepal, UK, Iceland, Mexico, America, Canada, New Zealand, Finland, Australia, Malaysia and Latvia. A total of eleven expeditions attempted the route; nine were successful.

The *North Col/North Ridge Route* was equally busy with 16 expeditions. A total of 25 climbers from 6 expeditions reached the summit between 2 May and 29 May. There was success for Kazakh, Russian, Canadian, South Korean, Nepalese, French, Bulgarian, Slovenian, New Zealand and Tibetan nationals.

A variation ascent was made by a Russian team led by Kazbek Khamitsayev. Alexandre Zelinski and Sergei Sokolov climbed a rib on the N Face to reach the N Ridge which was followed to the summit on 24 May.

Gimmigela Chuli (Twins) (7350m) A British Services Expedition led by Pat Parsons made the first British ascent of this attractive peak on the N side of Kangchenjunga. They climbed a new route on the SW Ridge. The summit was reached on 10 May by Nigel Lane and Neil Peacock and on 12 May by Ted Atkins, Larry Foden, Rob Magowan and Tug Wilson. (*See article 'The Gimmigela Adventure' by Pat Parsons, pp126-132.*)

Kangchenjunga (8586m) Four expeditions attempted the N Face of the world's third highest mountain. A Slovak/Czech team lead by Jaryk Stejskal reached a high point of 8500m on 13 May. On 24 May Scott McKee (US) a member of Jonathan Pratt's Anglo/American expedition reached the summit. There were no other ascents.

Kanti Himal 2 minor unnamed peaks were climbed by a Japanese group led by Tamotsu Ohnishi during an exploratory trip to this attractive area N of Patrasi.

Lhotse (8501m) The W Face saw a lot of activity and success in the spring. A British/Finnish/Mexican group led by Andy Clarke had success when Alan Hinkes (UK) reached the summit on 23 May, along with Michael Jorgensen (Dan) and Christine Boskoff (US) who were part of a large multinational group active on the *South Col Route*. Between 24-26 May a total of ten Russian climbers reached the summit. Vladimir Bashkirov, the leader of this relatively large team, died of an undiagnosed cause.

Well-known Kazakh climber Anatoli Boukreev with Italian Simone Moro reached the top on 26 May. Sadly Boukreev, together with film-maker Dimitri Sobolev, was later killed by an avalanche low down on the S Face of Annapurna I. Simone Moro survived the accident.

A multinational team led by Agostino Da Polenza were also successful on the W Face when Abele Blanc (It), reached the summit on 27 May followed by Mario Panzeri (It), Salvatore Panzeri (It) and Jean Christophe Lafaille (Fr) on 28 May.

Makalu (8463m) A large Russian group led by Sergei Efimov climbed a new route on the W Face next to the W Pillar. Five climbers reached the summit on

21 May. Two climbers died. One was killed by rock fall. The other died of exhaustion and illness. Three other expeditions attempted the NW Ridge, but without success.

Nemjung (7140m) A combined American, Canadian and Australian team led by Charles Armatys attempted the SW Ridge without success. They reached a high point of 6100m

Numbur (7855m) The N Face was attempted by a Russian team led by Victor Koslov. They reached a high point of 7100m.

Pumori (7165m) Two expeditions attempted the SE Face/SW Ridge, but without success. A high point of 6700m was reached on 21 May.

Shanti Shikhar (Shartse II, Peak 38) (7591m) A Russian team led by Alexandre Iakovenko attempted the S Ridge at the start of Lhotse Shar's SE Ridge. Their attempt failed at 6400m on 27 April.

Tukuche (6920) Dutch climber Bart Voos made a solo ascent of the NW Ridge on 10 April. Two other expeditions attempted the SW and NW ridges in May but without success.

AUTUMN 1997

Ama Dablam (6828m) After a quiet spring it was business as usual on this popular peak with 12 expeditions swarming up the fixed ropes and jostling for tent space on limited ledges. One can imagine the scene as Russian, Georgian, Japanese, German, American, British, Polish, Portuguese, French, Swiss, Latvian, New Zealander, Australian, Hong Kong Chinese, Austrian and Nepalese climbers moved up and down the mountain. In all 76 ascents were made between 7 - 30 October. Only one expedition, an Austro/German team led by Peter Habeler, was unsuccessful, retreating from a high point of 6200m on 28 October.

Annapurna I (8091m) An Italian team led by Maco Bianchi reached a high point of 6100m on the N Face on 25 September.

Annapurna IV (7525m) An attempt on the NW Ridge by a Swiss/German expedition failed at 6400m on 20 October. A German group led by Manfred Salcher reached a high point of 6200m on 21 October.

Annapurna South (7219m) A Belgian expedition failed low down (4900m) on the E Ridge.

Baruntse (7168m) A German expedition led by Christoph Hoester climbed the SE Ridge. On 15 October Silke Bock, Jan Bracker and Falk Descher reached the summit. They were followed on 22 October by 14 members (including two Sherpas), of a French/ Italian expedition led by Denis Etienne and Marc Lubin who also reached the summit via the SE Ridge. The route was repeated later in the season by an Anglo/American team led by Roger Hassol. Hassol and Curtis Cote reached the summit on 5 November. Earlier in the season Dutch, Swiss and Italian teams failed on the mountain.

Cho Oyu (8201m) Once again the NW side of the mountain was very busy. 22 expeditions visited the mountain, all going for the same route. A high percentage of the teams were commercially organised and the success rate was high. A South Korean team led by Park Young-Seok was the first to summit on 19 September when five climbers reached the top. By the end of September 58 people from 22 countries had been successful.

Dhampus (6012m) A Japanese team led by Kazuhiko Tokutake turned their attention to this lesser peak (after failing on Tukuche). Five members and two Nepalese reached the summit on 15 October.

Dhaulagiri I (8167m) Three members of a Spanish expedition led by Jesus Martinez reached the summit on 24 September via the NE Ridge. Bulgarian Nikolai Petkov summited on 25 September, also via the NE Ridge, while French, German, Swiss, Austrian, Japanese, Russian and Ukrainian teams were unsuccessful.

Everest (8848m) Events this season were most unusual for this particular mountain. No one climbed it post-monsoon, but not for want of trying. Eleven expeditions, with only one on the Nepal side, attempted the mountain. Few went above 8000m. The well-known Swiss climber Jean Troillet reached 8700m on the North Ridge. Conditions were undoubtedly poor. A South Korean climber was killed on the North Col route.

Fang (Varaha Shikhar) (7647m) A South Korean expedition led by Yu Jae-Hyung were unsuccessful in their attempt on the E Face. One member was killed in a fall.

Ganesh II (7111m) A Japanese attempt on the NE side of this attractive mountain failed at 5200m on 6 October.

Gaurishankar (7134m) Yasushi Yamanoi led a Japanese attempt on the N Face without success. On 23 October they reached a high point of 6300m.

Jannu (7710m) Attempts were made on the N Face and SE Ridge in early October. Both failed at *c*6000m.

Lhotse (8501m) Two members of an Italian expedition, Sergio Martini and Fausto De Stefani claimed an ascent of the W Face on 15 October. On 18 October two South Korean climbers and Kaji Sherpa reached the top by the same route. They were followed on 21 October by Japanese climbers Kenichi Nagaoka and Shoji Sakamoto. A Spanish group failed in their attempt on the W Face.

Lobuche East (6119m) A strong trio led by Slovenian Tomaz Humar with compatriot Janez Jelic and Mexican Carlos Carsolio made a new route up the NE Face of this attractive 'trekking peak', reaching the summit on 1 October. The peak now has several high-standard routes and a relatively straightforward normal route up the SE flank.

Makalu (8463m) Three groups attempted the standard route on the NW side without success. A Swiss team led by Christophe Berclaz reached 8000m on 10 October.

Makalu II (Kangchungtse) (7678m) Sue Fear led an Australian group on a successful ascent via the S Ridge on 10 October. Sue Fear, Matthew Gregory, John Maraz and Nima Dorje Tamang reached the summit. A Czech/Slovakian group attempted the same route but without success. They reached 7300m.

Manaslu (8163m) It was an unusually busy post-monsoon on the NE Face of Manaslu. Eight expeditions including a total of 11 nationalities put 21 climbers on the summit between 19 September and 9 October.

Nuptse (7861m) Hans Kammerlander attempted the SW Ridge to the E peak, retreating from a high point of 6600m on 18 October. A Slovenian group led by Tomaz Humar turned their attention to the W Face of Nuptse, after warming up on Lobuche East and Pumori. Humar and Janez Jeglic climbed a new route to the NW Summit (7742m) on 31 October.

Pumori (7165m) Slovenian Tomaz Humar made an unsuccessful attempt on the S Pillar retreating from 6250m on 9 October. The same expedition led by Humar then turned its attention from the SE Face/Ridge to the E Ridge with success when five Slovenian members reached the summit on 15 October. There were five other expeditions attempting the same route all without success. Three Slovakian climbers died in a fall having reached 6800m.

Patha Hiunchuli (7246m) French and Canadian teams attempted routes on the S and NE sides of this peak without success. The French reached 6200m on the NE Face.

Raksha Urai (6593m) An Austrian group led by Guenther Mussnig attempted the NE Face of Peak III and the SE Face of Peak IV, both without success.

Tilicho (7134m) A Swiss group led by Hans Rauner failed in its attempt to climb the N Ridge.

Tukuche (6920) A Japanese attempt on the N Ridge failed at 6300m

CHRIS CHEESEMAN

South America and Antarctica 1997

Argentina

Appalling weather and heavy snowfall during the main climbing season put a miserable end to many climbers' aspirations in this area.

Atacama, notable for volcanoes, has received the attention of surveying teams attempting to map the area accurately and to clarify the heights of its peaks.

Some of the more notable climbs include a new route on the SE Face of **Cerro Pollone (2579m)** by Italians Luigi Crippa and Lorenzo Nadali. *Mastica e Sputa* takes an ice couloir alongside a rock pyramid giving 500m of climbing up to 90° at ED1. The second ascent was only a matter of weeks later by a French team. The NE ridge of **Piergiorgio** was climbed by another Italian team, this time Maurizio Giordani and Gian Maspes, after they returned to finish an attempt on the NW Face from the previous season. Finding their fixed ropes shredded, and less than enthusiastic to start again, they turned their attention to a 600m route from the col between **Piergiorgio** and **Cerro Pollone** and reached the allegedly unclimbable summit mushroom of **Piergiorgio** after 70° ice, 6a rock and a section of A2. They dubbed the route *Esperando la Cumbre*.

The twin-summited **Aguja Bifida (2394m)** saw two ascents of its W Face by another strong Italian team (Paolo Cavanetto, Roberto Giovannetto, Manilo Motto, Gianni Predan and Cesare Ravaschietto). The first of the routes, *Hielo y Fuego*, climbed over excellent rock in 16 pitches up to 6b and A3, overall grade ED2. The second route, *Su Patagonia*, was slightly shorter at 15 pitches but, again over superb rock, gave slightly harder climbing at 6b+ and A2.

Bolivia

Much climbing activity seems to centre around a relatively small number of mountains, particularly **Huayna Potosi (6088m)** (a good contender for the 'Most Climbed Hill in South America' award) and **Illimai (6439m)**. The continuing construction of new roads, often commercially promoted to serve mines, promises to open many more areas of this fine country to mountaineers. Aeroplane debris was reportedly found on Huayna Potosi only a stone's throw from, but invisible to, the Normal Route.

Attempts to provide high quality mapping for the Apolobamba area seem to have been thwarted for the present, but the relative inaccessibility of this area did not prove to be a problem for many foreign teams visiting the area, several of them British. A lavish expedition from the Army saw this team ascend **Chaupi Orco (6044m)** in the Cordillera Apolobamba by a variation of the SSE ridge (PD+).

In the same area, a team under the leadership of Pete Marshall climbed a number of peaks as first British ascents and new routes. New routes were climbed on the W Ridge of **Katantica Central (5610m)** (AD+) (new route and first British ascent), the NW Ridge of **Katantica Este (5592m)** (PD), the N Face of **Pt 5560m** (AD) (new route and first British ascent) and the SE Ridge of **Katantica Sur (5300m)** (PD) (new route and first British ascent). (*See MEF Report 97/2.*)

Acamani (5666m) saw a new route on its W Face at AD+ by Jason Currie and Mark Ryle, giving its first British ascent. The hazards of the mountain were apparently insignificant in comparison with the hazards of Bolivian bus drivers and muleteers during their approach to the mountain!

Chile

Permits are now required for any climb in the Torres del Paine National Park. At about $140 per climber (estimates vary considerably), they have not reached Himalayan proportions, but the tangled web of bureaucracy has not been scaled down accordingly. Money from this source does appear to be finding its way back into the park. A fire in the refuge hut at the Japanese camp destroyed the equipment of several expeditions but no climbers were injured. Rumours abound that the park authorities are considering removing all climbers' huts in the area owing to the alleged fire risk that they present to the forest.

Atrocious weather stopped many climbs on the big routes before they began. Of the routes which were completed, an American team (Bonetti and Schneider) took the second ascent of the 1992 route *Caveman* on **Cuerno Norte**, estimating the grade at an increased A3. A bold attempt at the W Face of the **Central Tower of Paine** got a team led by Noel Craine over the major difficulties (E3, E5, A2+) and to within what looked like 7 pitches of easy ground to the summit, but appalling weather destroyed their fixed ropes, preventing any summit bid. (*See article 'On the Central Tower of Paine', pp102-108.*)

There are tentative reports of two new ascents on the W Face of the **North Tower**, although further information is not forthcoming. This face offers steep granite climbing with numerous cracks offering good potential. The Americans Scott Lazar, Michael Pennings and Cameron Tague arrived in the area and beat the **North Tower** (*Ultima Esperanza*), **South Tower** (*Aste Route*) and **Central Tower** (*Via de las Mamas*) into complete submission in just a few days of climbing.

The Shield saw a number of good attempts at new routes on the impressive E Face, but attempts by Swiss and Italian teams were beaten back by the bad weather.

First ascents of **Immaculado**, **Mirador del Hielo**, **Punta Ilusion**, **Punta Aparicion** and **Cerro Cuatro Vientos** were achieved by members of the Arved Fuchs expedition, its main aim being to complete the South Patagonia Ice Cap. More climbing on this ice cap was undertaken by Guglielmetti, Howard, Osses and Buracchio, their efforts rewarded with the first ascent of an ice peak **Cerro Timonel (1330m)** located near the Fiordo de las Montanas.

Peru

The Cordillera Blanca area seems to be proving extremely popular, with reports of new routes abounding – too many to mention them all in this summary. Particularly noteworthy was the ascent of a new line on the W Face of

Yanapacha (5460m) on 80° rock up to V+, although this appears to be close to other existing routes on the face. A Slovenian party (Meglic and Soklic) reached the Normal Route on **Huandoy Norte** after ascending on the E Face, but failed to complete the climb. A PD+ route on the aesthetically pleasing **Piramide de Garcilaso (5885m)** has been climbed by Andy Clarke and Brett Wolf. Actually bivouacking on the summit, Slovenian climbers Markovic and Meglic climbed a 500m route on the N Face of **Nevado Chirup** giving *Eleven Joints* at an overall grade of ED3.

One of the hardest routes in this range appears to be the new route on the W Face of **Chacraraju Main (6001m)** by the Slovakians Debelak, Minar, Oblak and Tomaz giving 945m of climbing at an overall grade of ED4 with technical difficulties up to VII+ and A3 on superbly steep ground up to 95°.

The rarely visited peak of **Palcaraju (5900m)** gave Spanish climbers Pedro Gonzalez and José Polanco the opportunity to climb *Un Rayo de Sol* at ED1. They descended the SE Ridge without reaching the summit.

A British team consisting of Phil Best, Simon Cooke, James Hall, Gordon Midgley and Nick Wallis visiting the Cordillera Vilcanota climbed what may be the virgin summit of **Nevado Mullucocha (5400m)**, approaching via the N Ridge on 50-60° snow and ice, as well as climbing a new route on **Jatunriti (6106m)** via its fluted N Ridge. The previous British team to visit the area had their tents set alight by local bandits while they were sleeping inside.

Finally, Hywel and Ingram Lloyd, with five friends, climbed in the Cordillera Blanca, making their valley base the small town of Huaraz. Hywel writes that July (winter in Peru) is the best time to climb there, although it is usually thought of as the dry season. AC member Peter Mitchell, with Mike Spencer and local climber Emilio Henostroza, climbed **Huascaran Sur (6768m)**, the highest peak in Peru, while Hywel and Ingram, with Claudio Henostroza, climbed **Urus (5420m)** and **Ishinca (5530m)**. The whole party, which also included Jenny Spencer and AC members John and Sue Hare, climbed **Vicos (5325m)**. Other peaks climbed by members of the party included **Kuriikashajana (5510m)**, **Millisharaju (5500m)** and **Ishinca (5530m)**. The trip was rounded off with a visit to Cuzco and Machu Picchu. Hywel Lloyd commented, 'All in all, a pretty successful and enjoyable visit to a fascinating country with enthralling people.'

Antarctica

Reports of significant activity in the frozen wastes are very thin on the ground. The only expedition worth mentioning was led by Norwegian Ivar Erik Tollefsen, well known for his previous expeditions to this remote area. On this occasion Tollefsen led a team to Sor Rondane area in Queen Maud Land, previously unvisited by climbers – unsurprisingly since they lie a further 600km beyond the base camp of the 1994 expedition! Tollefsen, Caspersen, Aastorp and Staver spent 17 days climbing the stunning 830m high SE Face of **Rondespiret**. 20 sustained pitches of mixed climbing gave grades of VI+ and A3+.

Mount Everest Foundation Expedition Reports 1997

SUMMARISED BY BILL RUTHVEN

Each year the Mount Everest Foundation supports a number of expeditions undertaking exploration in one form or another amongst the high mountains of the world. As well as 'Approval' – which in itself sometimes has the effect of opening other purses – most expeditions which are not already well funded also receive a grant, typically ranging between £200 and £1500. Whilst this only represents a small proportion of the overall cost of an expedition, the moral support and the promise of a few hundred pounds during the preparatory stages of an expedition can sometimes make the difference between it going and not going.

All that the MEF asks in return is a comprehensive report. Once received, copies are lodged in the Alpine Club Library, the Royal Geographical Society and the British Mountaineering Council where they are available for consultation by future expeditioners. In addition, some reports – up to and including 1994 expeditions – have recently been given to the Alan Rouse Memorial Collection in Sheffield Central Library.

The following notes are based on reports that have been received during 1997, and are divided into geographical areas.

AMERICA – NORTH

97/17 Alaskan Walls 1997 Jerry Gore (with Silvo Karo from Slovenia). May-June 1997

After a week of high standard rock climbing in Yosemite, this pair flew into Ruth Gorge to find it unseasonably warm. As a result, attempts on the S Face of Mt Bradley, 2774m, and the S Face of Mt Dickie, 2909m, both failed due to rock and ice fall and the lack of safe lines. A five-day attempt on Mt Barrille, 2332m, involving climbing up to 'new wave A4' (one pitch took 13 hours to lead) ended at 3/4 height after Gore was struck by a rock and ice avalanche, with the rope being cut and Karo having a near-death experience.

97/22 British Thunder Mountain & Mount Hunter 1997 Paul Ramsden (with Jim Hall and Nick Lewis). May-June 1997

After five attempts on the Central Spur of Thunder Mountain (*c*3350m) this team switched its attention to the gully line on the left, which was climbed in a continuous 42-hour round trip. The route, which they called *Dream Sacrifice*, involved 1070m of climbing at Alpine grade E2, but predominantly on ice at Scottish V/VI. They also made the first ascent of Mount Providence, 3414m, by an 1100m Alpine D, Scottish III route on its S Face, but did not attempt Mount Hunter.

97/44 British Foraker Traverse 1997 Geoff Hornby (with Tom Nonis of USA). May 1997

Having planned to make the first traverse of Mts Crosson and Foraker from north to south, this team was disappointed on arrival in Alaska to find that two local climbers had just beaten them to it. Rather than repeat the route, they decided to fly to Ruth Gorge to look at a new route on Mt Bradley, 2774m. However, with bad weather forecast as they flew in, they changed plans yet again and repeated the Central Couloir on the N Face of Mt Barrille, 2332m, the next day. They were lucky, as from then on the weather became steadily worse, preventing any further mountaineering activity.

AMERICA – SOUTH

97/1 British Cerro Aguilera 1997 Julian Freeman-Attwood (with Frank MacDermot and Skip Novak). April-May 1997

On arrival in Chile, this team found that the first mate of the sailing vessel *Pelagic* had been injured and hence forced to return to the UK. Without him, Novak was not prepared to navigate the hazardous waters round Aguilera. They therefore turned their attention to Tierra del Fuego and, in particular, the unclimbed Mt Aosta, *c*1524m, but were refused permission to enter the fjords to the north. In the worst weather they had ever encountered in the area (and that's saying quite a lot!) they attempted a route on Mt Italia, *c*2134m, in the Darwin Ranges, but were beaten by deep soft snow and an underlying tangle of rotting tree-trunks and roots.

97/2 Walsall/Bolivia '97 Pete Marshall (with Yossi Brain, Eamonn Flood and Dean Wiggin). May-June 1997

In recent years the Cordillera Apolobamba in Northern Bolivia has not been very popular with British climbers. 1997 saw a change, and this was one of five MEF-supported expeditions that headed for the area. With the advantage of Brain's experience (he works as a Guide in the area), this team planned to climb new routes and make first British ascents in the Katantica group. Unfortunately, the leader was unable to climb owing to sickness, but the rest of the team repeated routes on Pt 5550 and Katantica Oeste, 5630m. They also made the first British ascents of Katantica Central, 5610m (by a new route on the W Ridge), Katantica Este, 5592m, Pt 5560m (AD, the N Face) and Katantica Sur, 5300m. Moving over to the Cordillera Real they found and buried the remains of a Spanish climber who had been missing for three years, but gave up plans to try a new route on Illimani, 6462m, owing to the onset of gale force winds.

97/6A Torres del Paine Noel Craine (with Roger 'Strappo' Hughes and Simon Nadin). January-March 1997

On arrival at the foot of the Central Tower of Paine, 2454m, this team discovered that their original objective of the S Ridge was already occupied by a strong Swiss party, so they turned their attention to a new big-wall route on the W Face. In a period of six weeks of some of the worst weather in living memory, they climbed pitches between E3 and E5, with artificial sections of A2+, to within six pitches of the summit, leaving fixed ropes and all their lead gear at this spot before descending. After about a week of waiting, the weather seemed to improve slightly, so they made their bid for the summit. However, they found that continual lashing by the wind had frayed the fixed ropes, making them unusable and their lead ropes inaccessible, so they had no option but to clear what they could and descend. (*See article 'On the Central Tower of Paine', pp 102-108.*)

97/8 UK Peru 1997 - Cordillera Central Paul Hudson (with Pamela Caswell, Ken Findlay, Stuart Gallagher, Peter Holden, Ken Mosley, Christopher Woodall and David Wynne-Jones). July-August 1997

The Cordillera Central is a little-visited area of Peru, 100km E of Lima, with a number of spiky peaks. This team found that there had been a considerable reduction in glaciation since the maps were drawn in 1969, with some 50% reduction in snow and ice cover. They succeeded in making first British ascents of three mountains: Quepala, 5422m, Padrecaca 5362m (by two routes) and also Nevado Ticilla, 5897m.

97/12 BMES Chile '97 Dr Alex Wright (with lots of victims: Maggie Beazley, Stephen Brearey, Ian Chesner, Timothy Clarke, Richard Clayton, Peter Forster, Daniel Hale, Peter Hillenbrand, Helen Hoar, Christopher Imray, Brian Johnson, Barry Lester, Andrew MacLennan, Ian MacLennan, John Milles, Damian Mole, Jon Morgan, John Simmons, Sarah Walsh - mainly doctors themselves). January 1997

Having developed new equipment for determining the status of cerebral oxygenation in a non-intrusive manner, doctors in the Birmingham Medical Research Expeditionary Society were keen to test it in the field. This was done by driving 20 volunteers (aged 24 to 59) rapidly from sea level (300km N of Santiago) to Pasa del Agua Negra at 4680m, intermediate measurements being taken at 2770m and 3650m. A clinical trial of medroxyprogesterone as a prophylactic for acute mountain sickness was also investigated, with no significant side effects being evident, although a full analysis of all the results will occupy the scientists for some time.

97/13 British Women's Patagonia Celia Bull (with Donna Raupp from USA and Geraldine Westrupp as climbers, Alison Thomas as support and Bill Hatcher as photographer). January-February 1997

Patagonia's reputation for having the worst weather in the world was confirmed by this team's experience. Of 28 days in the field, only one full and two half days were free from almost continuous rain or snow, with strong winds adding to the experience. As a result, their hopes of making the first all-female ascent of the 1963 Bonington/Whillans route on the Central Tower of Paine, 2454m, were well and truly dashed: in fact they did not even touch rock above Col Bich at 1850m. And then, as if the weather was not enough, the refugio at Base Camp burnt down, destroying much of their fuel, food and equipment. This expedition was the recipient of half the Alison Chadwick Memorial Grant for 1997.

97/20 British Cordillera Apolobamba 97 Bob Dawson (with Dick Gasson, Jan Lancaster and Mark Thompson). July-September 1997

This was another expedition hoping to make first ascents in this less popular area of the Andes, choosing to operate in the area between Paso Osipal and Sunchuli. They succeeded in climbing Cuchillo I (5650m), Yanarco (5600m) and Pts 5600m and 5550m.

97/29 Edinburgh University Mountaineering Club Apolobamba 1997 Jane McKay (with Tom Bridgeland, Sam Chinnery, Rob Goodier, Paul Schweizer and Heather Smith). July-August 1997

This group set out to explore the Sorel Oeste group, and climb as many new routes as possible. Experiencing good weather throughout, they succeeded in making new routes on the W Face of Sorel Este, 5471m, the NW Face of Katantica Oeste, 5630m, and the S Ridge of Sorel Oeste, 5641m. They also made the first traverse of the ridge from south of Palomani all the way north to just below Chaupi Orco, reaching a maximum height of 6400m on Illimani.

97/33 Manchester Apolobamba Andy MacNae (with Andy Dougherty). July-August 1997

In something of a roving expedition this pair visited three separate areas: Condirriri, Apolobamba and Illimani. Despite the worst weather in the area for many years, they achieved a probable seven first British ascents at grades up to TD.

97/48 Cordillera Apolobamba '97 Will Payne (with Andrew Macleod, Dafydd Morris, Hugh Morris, Gareth Roberts and Peter Ward). June-July 1997

After making first ascents of a number of peaks, this team decided to provide their own names to identify them: Devil's Elbow, 5350m; The Tower, 5100m; K4, 5500m; K5, 5250m; K8, 5350m and K9, 5100m. They also climbed the S Ridge/S Face of Cololo, 5916m. The routes varied from F to AD.

GREENLAND AND ARCTIC AREAS

97/15 Scottish South Greenland 1997 Malcolm Thorburn (with Douglas Campbell). July-August 1997

This two-man team planned to carry out a ski traverse across the ice cap from Sondre Sermilik Fjord to Narssarssuaq, making one-day first ascents of as many peaks as possible *en route*. However, bad pack-ice prevented them from accessing Nanortalik, so they used their intended descent route to gain the ice cap instead. This enabled them to cover a large area of unexplored territory and make several first ascents of peaks up to 2000m and AD–, although they also recorded failure on others due to approach difficulties.

97/28 1997 Scottish Torssuqatoq Spires Pete Benson (with Andy Benson, Kenton Cool and Al Powell). July-August 1997

The rock spires of Cape Farewell have become very popular with British climbers over recent years. After several flights and a boat trip from Nanortalik, this team set up Base Camp at the head of Narssap Sarqa Fjord. On the first night, their main tent was destroyed by a gale, so they moved into a dilapidated hut instead. Fortunately from then on the weather was generally very good and, as a a result, the team achieved an incredible eight free big-wall climbs of 400m to 800m on Agdlerussakasit, 1763m; Magic Arrow, 1200m; Maujit Qaqarssuasia (1560m); Navianorpoq, 1550m; and Tikaguta, 1350m – all up to ED2 and AD2.

HIMALAYA - INDIA

96/32A British Sikkim 1996 Doug Scott (with Phil Bartlett, Mark Bowen, Mike Clarke, Paul Crowther, Julian Freeman-Attwood, Lindsay Griffin and Skip Novak). September- November 1996

Until 1962, Sikkim was a popular haunt of British climbers, but then the 'Inner Line' was drawn, and everything changed. However, following a barrage of letters from Scott and various others, this expedition was allowed into the area with the hope of making the first ascents of Chombu, 6362m, and/or Gurudongmar West, 6630m. Unfortunately precipitation on most days with little consolidation made for a high avalanche risk, so they had to content themselves with a most useful reconnaisance of the two main peaks, plus the first ascent of Pt 5745m, which they named Chombu East. (*See article 'The British Sikkim Expedition 1996', pp45-52.*)

97/7 Chandra Bhaga Colin Knowles (with Ian Carey, Titch Kavanagh, Andy Phillips, Tracey Purchase,. Dave Reynolds, and Chris Smart, plus LO Gurpal Singh). August-September 1997

Most members of this 'Red Rope' expedition were making their first visit to the Greater Ranges, and selected the Lahul area of India as a suitable area to cut their teeth. The first ascent of CB11, 6044m, was their principal objective, and five members of the team achieved this by a couloir on the NW Face. Following the expedition, they renamed the mountain 'Independence Peak'.

97/14 Changabang North Wall 1997 Julie-Ann Clyma (with Andy Cave, Mick Fowler, Brendan Murphy, Roger Payne and Steve Sustad). May-June 1997

Some of this party had to abort on this mountain in 1996 owing to the sickness of one member. This year, Clyma and Payne spent 10 days on the face, reaching the Ice Tongue just above the second icefield. They sat out terrible storms before abseiling off without incident. Meanwhile, Cave and Murphy reached the summit on 1st June, having made the first ascent of the North Face. Following a day behind, Fowler and Sustad reached the summit ridge but Sustad slipped on 'balled up' crampons and the pair fell 200ft. Sustad sustained chest injuries and the four climbers teamed up to descend on the S side of the mountain. At around 6000m an avalanche tragically hit Murphy while he was setting up an abseil and he was swept down the face. It was not possible either to locate or recover his body. Our sympathy goes out to Brendan's family and friends. Julie-Ann Clyma, as an individual, was the recipient of half the

Alison Chadwick Memorial Grant for 1997. (*See articles 'Changabang: A World Apart', pp3-11, and 'Mountain of Dreams, Mountain of Sorrows', pp12-17.*)

97/26 Changuch 1997 Gary Murray (with Stephen Ferris and Brian James). September-October 1997

After spending a week in the Kumaon region moving camps up to *c*5400m to acclimatise, this team climbed to 5600m on Lamchir West, hoping to spot a possible route on the S Face of Changuch, 6322m. But then the weather broke and made further climbing impossible, so no attempt could be made on their main objective.

97/30 1997 British Bhagirathi III Steve Callen (with Dave Birkett, John Dunne and Jason Pickles). August-September 1997

Impossible Star on the W Face of Bhagirathi III, 6454m, currently has 7 aid pitches, but this team hoped to be able to eliminate them, and thus climb the route 'free'. However, to have any hope of achieving this, a long spell of good weather would be essential: unfortunately, although quite good when they arrived at BC, it rapidly deteriorated, covering the entire face in snow and ice for the duration of their stay.

97/34 Rupshu Mike Ratty (with Anne Allcock, Richard Law and Trevor Willis). July-August 1997

Although refused access to this area of Ladakh in previous years, persistence paid off, and this time a permit was forthcoming. They hoped to make first ascents of Chakura, 6529m, and/or Pologongka, 6632m, both 'roadside' mountains well away from the Tibetan border. Climbing at Alpine grade AD they reached 6000m on the former before snow conditions became too soft and tiring to progress further. They had more success on Pologongka, reaching the summit in ideal conditions at F on mixed rock and snow.

97/37 Scottish Himalayan 1997 Scott Muir (with Kevin Kelly, Gordon Lennox, Malcolm McIlrath, and David Proudfoot with Ajay Makin as LO). August-September 1997

From the summit of the Kullu Eiger in 1996 (*96/24*) this leader spotted The Throne, rising to 5840m above the Parbati Valley, and thus the present expedition was spawned. An attempt on the very steep and dangerous NE Face reached 5400m with climbing to ED, E1/2, Scottish III, A2 before the weather forced a retreat. The long N Ridge proved to be a more practical option, and was climbed direct to the top at Scottish II/III, with an enormous overhanging cornice guarding the summit.

HIMALAYA – NEPAL

97/9 British Services Gimmigela 1997 Pat Parsons (with Ted Atkins, Huan Davies, Bob Ewen, Larry Foden, Andy Gibson, Marty Hallett, Paul Hart, Bert Lane, Pea Peacock, Rob Magowan, Dave Sheridan, Callum Weeks and Tug Wilson). March-June 1997

When this expedition was first proposed, Gimmigela, 7350m, (*aka* 'The Twins') in the NE corner of Nepal had never been climbed. It was therefore a huge disappointment that it received two ascents by Japanese climbers whilst the present trip was being planned. Nevertheless they carried on, with the hope of making the first British ascent by the SW Ridge, which would be a new route. In this they were successful, with Lane and Peacock reaching the summit on 10 May followed two days later by Atkins, Foden, Magowan and Wilson. (*See article 'The Gimmigela Adventure', pp126-132.*)

97/51 Challenge 8000 1997 Alan Hinkes. March-August 1997
Having climbed eight of the world's 8000m peaks, Hinkes planned to finish off the other six in one continuous expedition. Extremely generous sponsorship from Berghaus enabled him to 'buy into' other teams' permits, and make occasional use of helicopters to transfer between base camps. After reaching the summit of Lhotse, 8511m on 23 May, he flew via Lukla to attempt Makalu, 8481m, but already the monsoon was moving in, with higher temperatures and rockfall making any attempt suicidal. Kangchenjunga, 8598m, was also out of the queston at this time, so he made a brief visit back home to 'recharge his batteries' (with beer and fish and chips). He then flew to Pakistan for an attempt on Nanga Parbat, 8125m, which had already received some ascents that season. A week after dumping some equipment near Camp I he discovered that it had been stolen, but then some flour on a chapati caused him to sneeze so violently that he seriously injured his back. He crawled down some 600m until a helicopter could fly him to Islamabad for treatment. The 1997 attempt was over, but he is determined to return in 1998. (*See article 'Challenge 8000: a Progress Report', pp83-88.*)

HIMALAYA – CHINA AND TIBET

97/4 British Nanchen Tangla John Town (with Huw Davies). July-August 1997
Always on the lookout for obscure peaks, this year Town selected Jomo Gankar (*aka* Qunghoganeze), 7048m, in central Tibet, some 100km NNW of Lhasa, and W of the road to Golmud. The lower one-third of the mountain turned out to be far more technical than had been anticipated, and they ran out of fixed rope at 5900m, necessitating a retreat whilst it was still possible. On the plus side, they were almost certainly the first foreigners to visit the N side of the mountain, as a result of which they observed many unclimbed 6000m peaks. No doubt they will return.

97/31 British Sepu Kangri 1997 Chris Bonington (with Charlie Clarke, Jim Curran, Jim Fotheringham, Jim Lowther, John Porter and Duncan Sperry). April-June 1997
During a reconnaissance trip in 1996 (*96/17*), Bonington and Clarke identified the NE Ridge of Seamo Uylmitok as probably the most feasible route to the summit of Sepu Kangri, 6950m, the highest unclimbed peak in the

Nyain-Qen-Tanghla Mountains of NE Tibet. This proved to be knife-edged and gendarmed, so they transferred to the NE Face instead. Having reached a height of 6050m, a possible site for Camp 3 and maybe three days to the summit, the weather broke and the entire face was covered with well over half a metre of snow: the expedition was over. Meanwhile, taking advantage of some of the expedition's wealth of modern technology, Clarke had telephoned a colleague at Bart's in London – just like that! – to ask for advice on the treatment of a desperately ill local woman. As a result of this long-distance consultation, she made a complete recovery. Clarke should be more than welcome to return with the team in 1998, when they hope to reach the summit of Sepu Kangri.

97/36 New Zealand Aghil 1997 John Nankervis (with John Cocks, Tom Davies, David Ellis, Kristen Foley, Dominic Hammond and John Wild). August-October 1997

The rarely visited Aghil Mountains lie between the Shaksgam and Zug Shaksgam rivers in Xinjiang Province. The peaks in the north proved to be very difficult to access owing to narrow gorges and very loose rock, so the team moved further up the Shaksgam to the Dong Skyang Glacier. From here, they were successful in climbing three mountains: making the second ascent of Pk 5959m and first ascents of Pk 6068m and Pk 6648m. Moving a little further up the glacier they then made the first ascent of an unnamed peak, *c*6340m, and took in an extraordinary vista from a 'humble mound' of 4798m, which they feel must have been visited before.

KARAKORAM – PAKISTAN

97/18 Joint North Wales Beatrice Mike 'Twid' Turner (with Grant Farquhar and Steve Mayers plus Louise Thomas with Glenda Huxter and Kath Pyke). August-September 1997

This was actually two separate expeditions – one all-male and one all-female – each attempting new big-wall routes on the SE Face of Beatrice, 5900m, above the Charakusa Glacier. Both teams were successful, the men climbing *The Excellent Adventure* (750m, ED+ A3+) and the girls climbing *Hateja* ('strong willed determined lady') (750m, ED+ A3+). The female team was the recipient of the Alison Hargreaves Grant. This originated as a posthumous 'Achievement Award' presented by Cosmopolitan/American Express: Alison's family most generously passed the money on to the MEF which decided to award it as a one-off grant to a deserving female climber or expedition in 1997. (*See article 'Beatrice', pp117-125.*)

97/23 British Choktoi Guy Willett (with Alex Franklin, Will Garrett, Rhona Hatchell and Colin Spark). June-August 1997

This expedition to the Choktoi Glacier had several aims, in some of which they were very successful. On Hanipispur South, 6047m, they failed to make the first ascent when forced back at *c*6000m, only two or three rope-lengths from the summit, owing to bad snow conditions (AD). They did achieve the first ascent of an independent peak, *c*5400m, (E of Latok IV) by its NW Ridge (also AD), and reached *c*5800m on the unclimbed Choktoi peak, 6166m, retreating at an impasse on the S Face after climbing at A2 and Scottish V/VI. On the 'Doug Scott Spur' of a 5000m+ sub-peak of Latok III (A1/2 and VS) they grossly underestimated the time it would take and aborted: on a different (higher) sub-spur, they were weathered off after some sustained climbing at E2.

97/25 Pinnacle Club 1997 Karakoram Annabelle Barker (with Pru Cartwright, Margaret Clennett, Sally Macintyre and Sue Williscroft). June-July 1997

When climbing nearby in 1986, the leader spotted an attractive unnamed peak near to Shuwert in Shimshal, and determined to return to locate and climb it. This expedition was the result. Unfortunately Williscroft had to return home early owing to a recurrent chest infection, but the rest of the team made the first ascent of Rwadun Sar, *c*5500m, via its badly corniced NE Ridge, and then of their basic target, Zarsanic I, 5900m, via its long but not unduly difficult SW Ridge.

97/27 British Bolocho 1997 Dave Wilkinson (with Andy Forsyth and Stewart Muir). July-August 1997

From the summit of Haramosh II in 1995, this leader saw a K2-like peak to the west, and set his heart on climbing it. An attempt in 1996 (*96/23*) from the Kero Lungma Glacier proved that the local map was unreliable, and that the mountain was actually located above the Bolocho Glacier. With the undoubted advantage of knowing where it was, he returned in 1997. The Glacier basin is surrounded by peaks which they gave the unimaginative but practical names (working from N to S) of Bolocho I to Bolocho VII: the target peak thus became Bolocho I. In the best weather Wilkinson had ever experienced in the Karakoram, the team acclimatised by climbing Bolocho V, *c*5240m, at Scottish III/IV, but Muir then rested a recurrent ankle injury whilst the others climbed Bolocho I, *c*6000m, by its N Ridge (D/TD & Scottish III/IV). As a bonus, all three plus the cook's assistant then climbed Bolocho VI, *c*5200m.

97/35 British Karakoram Colm Coffey (with Pete Cox, Stephen Gale, Craig Lyle and Chris Smith). August-September 1997

As the Markhum region of the Karakoram was closed until 1986, Zartgarbin, 5850m (*aka* Saue Gerdan), had only received one previous attempt, and that was by a team from a British school. Examination of photographs taken on that occasion led the present team to think that it would be possible to ascend a relatively straightforward snow couloir to gain the NE Ridge. However, a series of hot summers in the intervening years had made drastic changes to the terrain, and the anticipated snow turned out to be bare ice. Cox suffered a chest complaint, so he and his partner turned back leaving Coffey and Smith to continue to 5300m, where a shortage of ice screws forced them to abandon the attempt. As they arrived back at BC a storm broke, with some of the heaviest rain experienced in Pakistan for over 100 years.

97/38 Scottish-Australian Broad Peak 97 Rick Allen (with Andrew Lock of Australia). June-August 1997

Although thoroughly investigated by Kurtyka and Kukuczka in 1980, the S Ridge of Broad Peak, 8047m, still awaits its first ascent. This duo hoped to attempt it last year, but were refused a permit. Armed with one this year they reached 7200m before being forced to turn back because the climbing was too hard. At this stage, Allen had to return to the UK, but Lock stayed on, and later reached the summit solo by the original (W Face) route.

97/40 Sheffield Karakoram 1997 Mark Harris (with Richard Garnett, Dean Grindell and Oliver Howard). June-August 1997

This team visited the Choktoi Glacier with the intention of making first ascents of as many peaks as possible. They were successful in climbing a subsidiary summit, 5800m, of the Biacherai Towers by an easy couloir on the NW face, and the N Face/Arête of a rock buttress, 5400m, on Latok III with pitches up to E2, 5c. Hanipispur Spur provided good mixed climbing up to Scottish 3, whilst an attempt on Hanipispur S Summit (6047m) was aborted at 5900m, when two of the team were badly affected by the altitude.

CENTRAL ASIA AND THE FAR EAST

97/39 Northern Chuiskiy Paul Knott (with Michael Doyle from UK plus Justin Canny and Bill Fischelis from the USA). July-August 1997

The Maashey Valley is virtually unknown, and had never previously been visited by British or American climbers. Hence this enterprising team had no problems in finding something 'new' to climb. They started by putting up two new 23-hour epic routes on Maashey, at 4177m the highest peak in the Chuiskiy mass: N Ridge (up to VS) and NE Ridge, descent in each case being via the 'normal' W Ridge route (Russian 4A). Moving to the eastern end of the Maashey Wall, they then made first British/American ascents of Burevestnik, 3700m and Tamma, 3200m, and finally put up new routes on Ak-Tru, 4044m and Kurkurek, 3989m.

97/45 Anglo-American Kokshaal-Too Lindsay Griffin (with Brian Davison and Nick Green from UK, Christian Beckwith and Garth Willis from USA and Mattias Engelien from Germany). August-September 1997

The American/German portion of this team limbered up on ice/mixed routes of Scottish IV/V on peaks up to 4600m in the Ala Archa before heading for Kokshaal-Too, the most southern range of the Tien Shan, in Kyrghyzstan on its border with China. With 17 summits over 5000m and 60 between 4000m and 5000m, this is likely to become a popular area with Western climbers if the problems of access can be sorted out, but the present group faced virtually every setback known to mountaineering expeditions. Despite this, they did achieve their aim of making some first ascents: Pic Lyev, 4600m, Pic Jerry Garcia, 5250m, the Unmarked Soldier, 5400m and Pt 5225. Pitch difficulty was up to Scottish 5 mixed.

Book Reviews

COMPILED BY GEOFFREY TEMPLEMAN

The First Fifty Years of the British Mountaineering Council
A Political History
Edited by Geoff Milburn
with Derek Walker and Ken Wilson
BMC, pp xiv+320, £16.99

So the British Mountaineering Council, a little winded, on occasion bewildered, is still standing and looking pretty good as it enters the second half of its first century. That people celebrated the milestone at all is something to marvel at, given the tortuous and risky path the organisation has sometimes followed. And I can't avoid the conclusion that the biggest threats to its survival lurk just over the horizon, not defeated in the past. A collapse in funding, the threat of a competitor, the fragmentation of climbing into a range of different activities with little in common with each other, increasing pressures on the countryside, and so on; for a politicised voluntary body with a handful of professional staff, the future looks ominous.

But to begin at the beginning. In his introduction to this weighty volume, Geoff Milburn quotes G A Dummett on the BMC's prospects in 1946: 'It will succeed only in so far as it receives the full support of each and every mountaineer.' Under that criterion, the BMC failed years ago. One of the representative body's defining features is the underwhelming interest shown in it by the very people it champions. But then such pious expectations were unrealistic even then, writing from the ivory towers of Cambridge.

The reality is that the BMC has always been a committee designed by a committee of clubs, a kind of organisational camel, ponderous and of a ridiculous appearance – it can't possibly work! – but actually quite good at coping when things get hot since whoever has stamina in the desert survives. And the BMC has proved very good indeed at survival. In the late 1980s, when a slinky sport-climbing club dared to offer an attractive alternative to the matronly old BMC, the old battleaxe swatted the challenge aside without pausing for breath.

But what is it about the organisation that creates such ardent but almost constantly disgruntled support? 'Oh!' says the average climber. 'The BMC!' The eyes roll heavenward and there is a despairing shrug of the shoulders, as though he or she were commenting on some national joke, like the Millennium Dome or railway privatisation.

But quick as a flash they will come back: 'Although it does a lot of good work for access and conservation, doesn't it? And their insurance is very good, isn't it?' Well, sort of. The BMC has made serious mistakes over the years and adopted policies without sufficient debate, alienating one group in the interests of keeping or attracting another. It is poorly understood and undemocratic, is run by people with a strong sense of duty and is consequently unresponsive to the large majority of climbers who are not remotely as committed, making the BMC seem rather worthy and dull, at least formerly.

It wins and keeps the affection of so many climbers because of the huge voluntary contribution the organisation needs to survive. Even though the majority of climbers contribute at most a cheque and more probably nothing at all to its survival, the BMC is held in esteem because a fraction of climbers give up evenings and weekends to consider and develop ideas about every aspect of climbing. The fruits of their Sisyphean labours are minuted and accumulate, giving the BMC more impetus, making it appear like some unstoppable force. It is a rock for us to cling to or rail against, but at least it is there, like a favourite maiden aunt. (When crisis looms we can hide in her skirts and appeal for help. 'Do something!')

It has also meant, on the whole, that the BMC has escaped criticism in public, since nobody likes to be seen beating up old ladies. There have been bitter, even savage debates, particularly over training, but the level of scrutiny the representation of our sport is placed under barely exceeds vague indifference. Had the BMC been more open and those watching its activities a little more objective and enthusiastic then perhaps its current direction would be more focused. Instead it finds itself organising climbing competitions and events with the obvious consequence of attracting new participants while at the same time claiming to stick to a policy of doing the exact opposite. It concerns itself with defending adventure climbing while supporting those aspects of modern climbing which are most corrosive to – ghastly misnomer – 'traditional' climbing.

That is not to say that the BMC necessarily deserves duffing up. I am regularly astonished at how capable and thoughtful officers and volunteers are in the execution of their duties. It's simply that disapproval is heaped on anyone daring to criticise or question policies or actions. It's unpatriotic in some fundamental way to attack the BMC, as though we were perpetually at war and those opposed to the BMC's course were giving aid and comfort to the enemy. So it's unsurprising that a history of the BMC by the BMC should leave the interested reader feeling both impressed and irritated and the lay reader utterly confused. Unless you have a working knowledge of the role, function and history of the BMC and its politics, the book might as well be in Greek; it reads like a company history which lacks the saving grace of an Index.

Of immense benefit is the gathering together of experiences and lists, photographs and individuals, setting limits and giving a structure to what seems so limitless and confusing. The photographs particularly are a constant source of delight, comprehensive and representative, expertly captioned and a valuable source in themselves. There are enough wry observations and thoughtful analyses to breathe life into what might otherwise have been dessicated, not least Dave Gregory's contribution on writing guidebooks. Like I said, camels have their uses.

What this book is not, however, is a history of the BMC. As I understood it at school, history takes all the evidence it can muster and makes an objective assessment of what happened and why. This doesn't happen here. Nobody in this book doubts that the BMC should exist, for instance, or acknowledges that sometimes they were the ones wearing the black hats running the sherriff out of Dodge. It isn't comprehensive and it doesn't examine important issues that require it.

The prime illustration of this is the so-called 'Brazilgate' scandal involving the former General Secretary Dennis Gray. References to this incident are dropped into the text like small unexploded bombs for reviewers to trip over. The consequence is that a question mark, hopefully not permanent, is left over Gray's considerable contribution. The chronology at the back of the book refers to a 'bogus training scheme' in Brazil which prompted a clearly discomforting question from the Sports Council. Geoff Milburn makes a gnomic reference in his introduction. "Would, or should we publish the facts of 'Brazilgate'?" he asks. (Imagine if you knew nothing of the BMC's history and read this comment. What possible sense could be derived from it?)

In his chapter on the 1990s, Derek Walker elaborates slightly on this scandal but we are left with something which is more suggestion than explanation. I can understand the motives of the committee in their guarded references to this incident, but it should have been examined in full or not at all. The consequence of episodes like this in a 'political history' is a weakening of credibility.

So the book is a bit of a camel, just like the parent who spawned it. It's frustrating, entertaining, well-meaning and occasionally exclusive but, also like its parent, I am pleased that it is there. I am also pleased that the BMC is running climbing and not an exploitative growth-hungry organisation with half an eye on the International Olympic Committee. Whether the Alpine Club is still celebrating the British Mountaineering Council in another fifty years is less certain.

Ed Douglas

The Ordinary Route
Harold Drasdo
The Ernest Press, 1997, pp258, £12.50

One of the minor pleasures of reading this exceptional book is a persistent question: what is the craft skill which enables Drasdo to exert such a magic touch? The book isn't perfect. One or two chapters near the end could have been omitted without loss. And perhaps you need to have been in or at least, like me, near the golden age of British democratised climbing (1950-1960) to appreciate some of the goings on. But the book will endure; as good poetry does.

Drasdo's art partly shows in his non-self-centredness. He leaves you guessing about his own story, about the outcome of his wife's illness, about his jobs. But National Service isn't let off the hook: 'it made a man of me' and, one begins to see, a subversive too. The texture is always open and one's imagination is drawn in. The embroidery is thick at times. But that's the way with tradition. We could never have had tapestries without those stitching, gossiping, lore-enhancing ladies and their variant rememberings. The book is more of a shrub than a tree: no Deep Theme. The asides and branches are what make it: a chapter on hitch-hiking, the theology of falling (off), the Zen of sea and cliffs, the virtues of Catalan as a language for climbing guides, a lovely excursion into Ireland (he does let on, somewhere, that he knows a lot of Yeats by heart), an idyll in Yosemite and a brilliant paragraph which portrays Menlove Edwards finely. Many characters keep bobbing up but they are not name-dropped. You bump into them; the way you did.

It all starts with a bunch of teenage friends from Bradford making a group, making a club, an expedition to Helvellyn, to Langdale. Wall End Barn was their smoky shrine and Sid Cross one of their prophets. Then after a few years they have a reunion. Some of the lads are becoming rich; some aren't. Many of Drasdo's best yarns come from his unpicking and reworking the braid which started at Wall End Barn. He highlights three climbs which, for him, epitomise those golden Fifties when 'individuals and subcultures could remain untouched ... by the mass media'. The first is Deer Bield Crack which was part of 'our ambition to repeat all the great classics of the Lakes'.

> In ... 1951 I found myself spending a night in the Grasmere Youth Hostel with Pete Greenwood, ... an outstanding climber but his restless energy diverted him into very varied adventures. He ran into problems with policemen, licensees, hostel wardens, girls, other climbers. A Berserker spirit ruled his nature. In the barn one crowded night he insistently provoked a Bradford area gritstoner known as Pablo ... considerably bigger than the tormentor. From the dimly lit further end of the barn we heard a solid smack as he hit Pete, and then, an alarming crack as Pete's head struck the crudely cobbled floor.

And that was only the beginning of the story.

Deer Bield Crack eventually succumbed. To me it has a magic name. I had heard about it in the 1930s but never got there. So many names echo from it: A T Hargreaves, Graham Macphee, Dick Barry, John Jenkins. Drasdo suggests it has an 'anima' character. He is free with such interpretive offerings but I know what he means. His account of their snow-drifting ascent in stockinged feet is very much of the period and in tune with the crag's menacing, untameable beauty.

Drasdo's second strand of memory from that decade is the saga of his own attempts on, and first ascent of, North Crag Eliminate. (Here, as with several of his climbs, one yearns for a Heaton-Cooper style drawing to help one's inner vision.) It's a good, long-drawn account, ending with the following, so characteristic of the 1930-1960 age.

> I had no hammer but happened [!] to be carrying two or three pegs. Using a loose rock from the floor of the niche I tapped a peg awkwardly in. ... (one month later, on the entertaining second ascent, Joe Brown [pulled] the peg out by hand.) But it looked real and often that's all that's needed.

Reminiscent of Collie sixty years earlier in Moss Ghyll: ' ... the rock was smooth, so I took my axe and fashioned a step.'

We get further clues to Drasdo's world-view when, also in Langdale, he mourns the skills that went to the building of the Barn.

> The walls are neatly coursed, stream-dressed rubble, levelled on crude slate stringing. Any earth packing washed out centuries ago. The roof is slated in the diminishing courses characteristic of older Lakeland buildings ... [but] recently it's been meticulously restored. A melancholy shell. A spear of grief runs through me.

He is stricken by the hollow compromises of the heritage industry. The poet in him not only mourns the loss of friends and youthful optimism but also the dying of all those rural skills and focused lives which created their barn.

There is a touch both of the anarchy and the vitality of William Morris about Drasdo. Also of Wordsworth. It's a long time since I've read a mountain book which stirred me as this did: a far from ordinary route through the hills of memory.

Robin Hodgkin

Deep Play

Paul Pritchard

Bâton Wicks, 1997, pp192, £16.99

I don't suppose many Alpine Club members have been to Disneyland Paris, but amongst the many spectacular rides is one based on a flight simulator. The unfortunate 'passengers' are thrown into various galactic wars, plunged into bottomless chasms, crashed into alien spacecraft and generally shaken, vibrated and frightened out of their wits (well, I was anyway). All this happens while you are strapped into a seat that scarcely moves at all. If you haven't experienced this and don't want to go all the way to Paris to do so, then for £16.99 you can buy Paul Pritchard's first book *Deep Play* and enjoy/suffer a remarkably similar set of sensations, for this book is no smooth roller-coaster. It picks you up by the scruff of the neck and doesn't let you go again until the last page.

The book is actually a collection of articles, most of them originally published in the climbing magazines but modified and sometimes rewritten for this book. Unlike many such collections, these hang together well and become more than the sum of their parts. Pritchard's writing is direct, uncompromising, occasionally naïve; always honest, sometimes painfully so, and redolent with echoes of Menlove Edwards whom the author acknowledges (together with Joe Tasker) as a major influence. His account of a near-fatal accident on Gogarth in which he suffered serious injuries and nearly drowned has an intensity and ghastly surreal aura that rivals passages in Joe Simpson's *Touching the Void*.

Occasionally I was frustrated by the 'stream of consciousness' style and couldn't quite work out basic questions of who, what, when and where. I realised, too late, that at the end of the book there are explanatory notes to each chapter. I think it would have been worth the trouble to integrate this important information into the main text, but this is my only minor quibble.

The central theme of *Deep Play* is an intense questioning of the author's lifestyle, living at the absolute edge of extreme climbing. Suffering physical deprivation, abject poverty, and ever-changing relationships, good and bad, with his small band of fellow-travellers, Pritchard gives us a brilliant insight into the sometimes crazy world of the modern climber. Compelling essays on ascents that range from free climbing on Sron Ulladale, mind-blowing aid climbing on the Central Tower of Paine and on Asgard are contrasted with gritty descriptions of life in Llanberis and a childhood in Lancashire. Strangely, I was reminded of Hermann Buhl's classic *Nanga Parbat Pilgrimage*, though Pritchard's writing is still essentially in the tradition of 'British understatement'. Appalling difficulties are coolly described, but Pritchard's admissions of his own fears and self-doubt are recorded with a frankness that is almost shocking.

The book is a worthy winner of this year's Boardman Tasker Award, breaking with recent tradition by actually being a book about mountains and climbing. Pritchard emerges as a gifted writer who, we must hope, will produce more of the same. Whether he can only do it while he is performing at the highest standards is a question he will have to resolve one day, hopefully in the distant future.

This was a book that made me wish I was young again, but also quite relieved that I will never climb remotely near to Paul Pritchard's standards. Turning the last page I unclipped my imaginary seat belt, got up from my comfortable armchair and doddered off to solo a circuit of increasingly easy routes at Burbage North. My brain was still spinning with thoughts and memories of Trango, Patagonia and those far away places that still have the power to inspire and bewitch.

Jim Curran

Against the Wall
Simon Yates
Jonathan Cape, 1997, pp176, £14.99

In the autumn of 1991, Simon Yates, Sean Smith, Paul Pritchard and Noel Craine travelled down to Patagonia to attempt a new line on the Central Tower of Paine. This book is the story of the climb, but it is also a self-analysis of Simon Yates' climbing life over the last ten years.

The first ascent of *El Regalo de Mowana* on the 1200m East Face of the Central Tower of Paine was an outstanding achievement. The climb, made in fine style without bolts, received acclaim throughout the mountaineering world. It also marked the beginning of British involvement in the new league of alpine big wall routes which are at the cutting edge of today's technical mountaineering game. Recent British successes on Baffin, Greenland and Trango have all fed off the experience and confidence generated by the Paine route.

Simon tells the story well. The team soon found themselves on a steep learning curve as they taught themselves how to put up a new big wall route in an alpine environment. How the mountaineering experience of Yates and Smith was combined with the rock-climbing skills of Pritchard and Craine makes fascinating reading. Technical climbing can often appear tedious on the written page, but Simon has an easy style which captures the full atmosphere of being high on a big Patagonian wall. The reader is soon finding himself aiding on poor gear up icy cracks, jumaring up fixed lines, taking long leader falls and sitting out fierce storms. In the event, despite a long and determined struggle in which the whole team nearly made the summit, it was only Pritchard and Smith who had the time and mental resources to go back for a final try and eventual success.

The book is interspersed with Simon's climbing experiences over the last ten years. Flashbacks to Minus One Gully on the Ben, the Central Couloir on the Jorasses, all add to the depth of the book. Simon Yates did of course gain notoriety as 'the man who cut the rope' in Joe Simpson's *Touching the Void*. One cannot help thinking that one motive for writing the book was an opportunity to put his side of the story. It is no surprise, therefore, that the last flashback is to that awful snow slope on the Siula Grande. Here we find Yates sitting without anchors in a collapsing stance with Joe swinging on the rope 150 feet below. He is clear that ultimately he made the right mountaineering decision to cut the rope. After all, they did both survive.

It is this same mountaineering judgement which will not allow Yates to go back up the frayed fixed ropes on Paine for one last try. It is clearly a difficult personal decision, and the very act of making it allows Yates to reassess the direction of his life. I, for one, hope that this new direction does not lead to less climbing, for I look forward to the possibility of further writing from Simon, and reliving more of his full and varied adventures.

Simon Richardson

Into Thin Air
Jon Krakauer
Macmillan, 1997, £16.99

There are two images in Jon Krakauer's *Into Thin Air*, a compelling and hugely successful account of the deaths on Everest in the pre-monsoon season of 1996, that stuck in my mind as being superbly illustrative of everything that is currently wrong with climbing the highest mountain on Earth. The first centres on Yasuko Namba, a middle-aged Japanese businesswoman, who despite limited credentials as a mountaineer and a previously poor performance on the mountain, rallied on summit day to power her way up the final few hundred metres. She had, says Krakauer, 'the summit in her cross-hairs'. This idea of the mountain as quarry, with its echoes of tiger-shoots in the jungles of the Terai, seems apt. Self-glorification through a struggle with nature has long been an occupation of people with too much money and not enough respect.

The other image is of the team Krakauer joined as a reporter for the American magazine *Outside*. As Krakauer waits at the South Col, a place whose windswept misery clearly made an impact on his psyche, he reflects on the hollowness of his experience: 'In this godforsaken place, I felt disconnected from the climbers around me – emotionally, spiritually, physically – to a degree I hadn't experienced on any previous expedition. We were a team in name only, I'd sadly come to realise.'

The vacuum that lies at the heart of this book is a lack of emotional engagement. Krakauer quite likes most of the people he shares the mountain with, but they are acquaintances only, not friends. There is no shared dream or common purpose, in sharp contrast to expeditions of an earlier age like that which made the first ascent in 1953. When Yasuko Namba is found the morning after her ascent, exposed on the South Col with a three-inch carapace of ice over her face and close to death, the misery is compounded by a sense that she and the others who lived or died on the mountain did so in wretched solitude.

This impression has prompted a rash of negative publicity in the United States and Europe, the theme of which is the death of a noble ideal. The last time newspapers were interested in Everest, Ed Hillary and Tenzing Norgay were reaching the summit, the Americans Tom Hornbein and Willi Unsoeld were pioneering the West Ridge, Chris Bonington's team were plotting their way up the South-West Face. These were great endeavours and now, public opinion believes, we are left with cynicism and greed. The attitude is reinforced by the garbage and dead bodies apparently strewn on the mountain, a physical manifestation of the mountain's corruption. Among mountaineers, however, there has been some discomfort from the inquisitorial nature of Krakauer's account. While the general public – in the West at least – are used to enquiries and criticism if something goes wrong, we are usually reluctant to point a finger at individuals so accusingly. Krakauer has no such misgivings and is critical of the Seattle-based guide Scott Fischer and his Russian employee Anatoli Boukreev. In the latter case, Krakauer has no sympathy for the Russian's *laissez-faire* attitude, which he correctly identifies as being a cultural difference from the usual American abhorrence of fatalism.

Fischer's lead Sherpa, Lopsang Jangbu, is also criticised and the young tyro was forced to defend himself in the American press shortly before he too was killed on Everest in the autumn season of 1996. Krakauer's attitude to the Sherpas is strangely disengaged. He dutifully fills us in on the background of the more important ones, tells us about some of their quirky customs, but there is a powerful divide in the relationship between the climbers and their 'servants' who, in effect, climbed the mountain for them.

Jon Krakauer's additional title for his book is 'A personal account of the Everest disaster'. All the way through the book I couldn't help wondering which tragedy he meant. The multiple deaths of those terrible days and nights in May 1996, or something else? Certainly, there have been many other tragedies on Everest. Statistically, 1996 was a pretty safe year allowing for the numbers who were active on the mountain, a point Krakauer makes in his concluding remarks.

This particular tragedy got so much attention partly because of the final hours of Rob Hall, who said goodbye to his wife for the last time over his radio as he froze to death near the south summit, but also because some of the climbers involved were well-known Americans whose colleagues at base camp had lots of very sophisticated communications equipment with which to keep in touch with the world's media.

This instant access to the dramas enacted on Everest's slopes has been one of the most significant changes in recent years. Problems encountered by mountaineers are played in real time, not reported at a later date when the immediacy has gone. And physical access to the mountain has also speeded up. Helicopters fly to Shyangboche, cutting weeks off the approach endured by John Hunt and his team. The convenience of such rapid communications has cut the real story of Everest – the story, if you like, of Chomolungma – out of the agenda. The real story of Everest is not about the private aspirations of men and women who enjoy climbing, but the story of those who live and work in the Khumbu, who bring up their families and follow their *dharma* in the shadow of the mountain.

While the general public are riveted by what they perceive as a tragedy, the real story is more hopeful. Western environmentalists may warn that the Khumbu is being spoiled, but there is a convincing argument to be made that the management of the region is a success, albeit a qualified one. The numbers visiting may have increased exponentially in the last twenty years, but much of the region's allure has been effectively preserved.

Ultimately, Jon Krakauer's account is a catharsis of the guilt he felt following those harrowing hours. Guilt at survival, guilt over the death of the guide Andy Harris and his failure to notice the young New Zealander's distress, guilt at the pain he caused relatives of the dead in his uncompromising assessment. It is a horrifying story brilliantly told. But it is not the story of Everest, more a comment on the over-confidence of people who believe that wealth and position make the slightest difference when a storm settles on the roof of the world.

Ed Douglas

Dark Shadows Falling
Joe Simpson
Jonathan Cape, 1997, pp 207, £15.99

This is the second book which I have read by the same author. The first, unique in its category, described in compelling terms a personal experience almost beyond human belief, when survival was achieved by means of an indomitable will in the face of seemingly impossible odds. In some ways this latest book is a natural sequence to that experience. It is about Mount Everest, more specifically about the behaviour of people towards their fellow-creatures when faced with the extreme conditions which any ascent of Mount Everest must involve. There are two obvious reasons for the author's obsession with this theme. Firstly, only someone who has actually experienced the sensation of a resurrection to life from almost certain death could summon such emotional reactions towards the apparent disregard shown by climbers for those in distress high up on the mountain; secondly, because of the author's own lurking desire, not explicitly stated but implied on three separate occasions, to climb the mountain himself.

No press reporter could surpass the exposure which Simpson provides of the circumstances under which Everest is climbed today, with his blow-by-blow accounts of emergencies on the north and south sides of the mountain – many inevitable, a few avoidable – resulting in a growing series of deaths. Writing of this *genre* is all very well if the object is to stir the emotions, or to cater to a demand for mountain melodrama. But since the author must have had additional motives for writing this book, it seems a pity that he has made no attempt to probe into cause and effect, nor to examine the ethical and moral attitudes which led to the situations he describes. How many of the eleven persons stranded at night in a storm at 8000 metres were physically and mentally prepared for the situation in which they found themselves? For what reasons were they pushed to such an extremity – arrogance, ignorance, vanity, false expectations, value for money? The author does not delve deeply into these matters and some of his more cynical opinions seem to conflict with the emotional approach he adopts elsewhere in the book. Guiding on Mount Everest, for instance, is referred to as a 'lucrative flagship' for the guide; Everest is described as 'another holiday destination ... from which *everyone* (my italics) benefits'; and, 'it will always be a significant social asset' to ascend the mountain. Those are some of the ideas which the author propagates.

Simpson joins the current chorus of blame heaped upon the media for the depths to which some forms of climbing have sunk, forgetting that press reporting is fairly consistent in its style, being generally exaggerated and often inaccurate. But he appears to overlook or even tacitly to condone the behaviour of people who, by playing with their own lives, involve, with full knowledge, the lives of others. The attitude of the Japanese climber, whose remarks are quoted on page 48, is essentially defensible: 8500 metres on Everest, where each human being is himself precariously balanced on a knife-edge, is not the place to attempt to repair the follies of others. Those who do not treat a mountain with respect forfeit their right to be there. It is difficult not to label the behaviour of such people as reflecting the values of some sections of present-day society, and their actions have led to a growing series of events which has brought some areas of Himalayan activity into disrepute. One hopes devoutly that the minority which they represent will grow increasingly aware of the spreading distaste for their attitudes and actions.

Himalayan history is filled with accounts of valiant deeds performed under exceptional circumstances, when calculated risks taken by competent mountaineers have had an unfortunate outcome owing to unforeseeable events. The golden principle of mutual help has always been the guiding factor. But the alarming pace of change evident all around us today has resulted in an emphasis on individualism, which, in the Himalaya, has tended to mean 'every man for himself', and the adoption of a different set of ethical values. There are no miracles: there is no easy way, and there are always clear warning signals – individual capacity and skill, current form, weather signs, the time factor. The survivors are those who heed the signals; to ignore them is to accept the possibility of disaster, and worse, to assume selfishly that others ought to endanger their lives in a rescue attempt.

The book includes episodes from the author's expedition to Pumori in the autumn of 1996, recorded largely in the form of conversations between members of the party. Some of the moralising reveals ambivalent attitudes to perceptions which are condemned elsewhere. In his summing-up at the end, I cannot quite make out whether the author's specious argument, that if others behave badly why should not we do so, is seriously intended.

There are deeper issues involved. The attraction of the masses towards Everest and K2 could be curbed if the authorities in China, Nepal, and Pakistan were to adopt a different policy for issuance of permits. A moratorium for two or three years on expeditions to those two mountains might have the effect of calming the growing hysteria, and would provide an opportunity for cleaning-up operations. But we do not live in an ideal world, and the importance of foreign exchange earnings for all concerned will almost certainly dictate the policy of the authorities in the end.

There is no substitute for self-restraint on an individual level. If some of the follies and disasters graphically described in this book help to stir the majority sufficiently to make them raise their hand and say 'Enough', I think it will have served some purpose.

Trevor Braham

Spirits of Place
Jim Perrin
Gomer Press, 1997, pp250, £17.50

> There is a phrase in Welsh, *dyn ei filltir sgwar* ("a man of his own square mile") that in a sense defines D J Williams's literary project. It might sound simple, but the web of interdependence, knowledge, role and responsibility implicit in that phrase is intricate and profound. Its design is comprehensible, the individual's relationship to it defined. It's not some web site you can log in and out of at will. As a literary work *Hen Dy Ffarm* was the expression of a historical moment and a nation where scale was human and appropriate – where the *filltir sgwar* could both contain and satisfy aspiration. Perhaps the reason why I so passionately love this small country is that the diminishing echo of that moment remains. (p. 238)

This wish to close in and say not just well but exquisitely what can be said about a particular land – Wales – and its culture is increasingly Perrin's ambition. This collection of essays and radio talks, his third, includes fewer climbing pieces than previously, and its comments on modern climbing convey as much by omission as by invective. One of the most complex and civilised of men, certainly one of the most talented who currently makes a living from our sport, Perrin sees an increasing simplification and lack of sophistication in the game, and it dismays him. He is a traditionalist, for whom climbing is about adventure before it is about anything else, and for whom 'spontaneous adequacy, not planning and conquest, is [the] lynch-pin.' The reason is the same as it has always been: adventure opens our eyes and enables us to see. Perrin is above all a writer who wishes to see and to encourage others to do so, who views blindness as a spiritual failing.

If, as I think, mountaineering's full experience involves both ultimate blindness and the most penetrating awareness, and if the contemporary Everest circus (say) can be thought of as a good example of the former, then it is clear that Perrin's ambition is to stake out the opposite ground. He is one of two contemporary British mountain writers (the other is Joe Simpson) whose talent clearly deserves an audience beyond his own *milieu.* But his larger ambition, and it is not an absurd one, is to stand in the great tradition of radical British essayists whose concerns are much wider: environmental, social and ultimately political.

I do not know how successful this project will be. The work is in any event still ongoing. This latest contribution to it is organised into four sections: pieces written (or rewritten) for radio broadcast – these are all good, very fresh; portraits and obituaries; articles on climbing and the climbing scene culled almost entirely from his columns in *Climber* and *The Great Outdoors*; and 'sketches from a journey through Wales', which takes us on a long walking project southwards from Snowdonia, with wonderful portraits of people and places interwoven with a contemplative sadness at the creeping *embourgeoisement* of rural Wales.

I still think his climbing writing is the most consistently successful aspect of his output. He is one of very few writers who can bring alive the description of a rock climb – something which in most hands comes across as banal, tedious, blind; who can describe its aftermath with fresh phrases each time: 'chastened laughter from prisoners on parole who know they must go back, are unsure which is captivity, which is release'. It was Perrin's ability to write about climbing in this collection which led me to change my initial view that he lets in too much political comment. I still think some of this is too polarised – to see the Tories as *always* the bad guys, the socialists *always* as the keepers of decent values is too simple and it can be artistically unwise – party political comment can be too much of the moment, can jar with more timeless concerns. But one has to accept that without such comment not only would Jim not be Jim, but his work would be far less sharp, far less powerful. I was left at the end of the collection feeling that his artistic judgement, the main point at issue here, was right after all. Much of what he has to say cannot be satisfactorily divorced from contemporary political comment. One of the climbing pieces here, *Judas Climbers and the Trees*, which tackles the environmental stand-off at the site of the Newbury bypass and denigrates some climbers who earned considerable sums by offering their expertise to the authorities, drew criticism when it first appeared. Who was this man to pass judgement on others? Well, someone whose ethical analyses I would put some faith in.

Perrin is above all a writer – and a man – of passion, and must produce his best writing in that context. His descriptions of place, so much at the heart of the book, need to be approached differently from the run-of-the-mill essays which make up the bulk of the fare in outdoor magazines and journals. The value of these is generally to introduce a place or area, tell one how to get there, and send one off full of enthusiasm to experience it first hand. This is entirely good. But with work of Jim's quality and density, the situation is somewhat different. His essays are not always easy. There is too much in them, too much knowledge and literary allusion for that. They make me want to go there, but much more; they make me want to experience it, and *then* read what he has to say.

Jim is an interpreter of landscape; and true landscape art, whether in the medium of writing, pictures, or music, has value in itself. It not only feeds off the land it celebrates but interprets its hidden or subtle features and so returns something to it. Real art recognises that perception is not a passive activity, that the interpretation of the artist can alter the way we see and appreciate things. Art is then not mere self-expression – something which can slip so easily into self-indulgence – but something of immense social value. Whatever one's final judgement, I do think that Perrin is in the class of writers who should at least be discussed and criticised in that context.

It is a select and distinguished group in any age. It is one which Perrin is inclined to interpret as overwhelmingly Celtic. I feel a slight unease here. At the beginning of his marvellous portrait of Dervla Murphy he writes that the tale 'takes place in Ireland – a place to which I go frequently, especially since the alternative, going the other way, is to arrive in England and I'm not sure I'd like that.' This is certainly true to Jim's feelings. He is of 'the Celtic fringe', using the phrase geographically, not disparagingly, but it seems oversimplified for the subtlety of Jim's character. Is Celtic Culture truly the last repository of contemplative decency in modern Britain? Do we Anglo-Saxons really have nothing to offer? Quite possibly. But I would like to see the evidence. Jim is a great romantic, and like all romantics can overdo his enthusiasms, delineate too starkly his likes and dislikes.

For all his intelligence, it is the emotion behind his writing which is the key to its power. If the Murphy portrait is good, the one of Michael Foot, that 'close reasoner and ... loose dresser', is even better. Some of the other portraits, those where a close personal involvement is lacking, are not as good. I don't think Perrin is a particularly good obituarist, possibly because his natural style is cramped by the requirements of the genre – the need to record a life's events, to get the information down. And ironically, the sheer decency of the man doesn't always help. No one is seriously criticised in a Perrin obituary; everyone is too much an irreplaceable character. All this might be true, but it does not make for a powerful read.

Spirits of Place is as distinguished as one would expect. It is meticulously sub-edited, suitably designed, expensively produced, well illustrated by sharp and good black and white photographs, and published by Gomer Press of Llandysul, a quintessentially Welsh press in whose select literary list Perrin clearly takes pride. It is presumably not destined for best-seller status. It requires time and care. And this is as it must be. I think it was Blake who insisted that it was time above all that was needed for the spiritual life to flourish. Perrin has given the best part of his life so far to trying to see beyond the obvious in landscape and what we do there, and to express those moments when life does seem infinitely precious, whether in the company of people or the land. Absorbing what he has to say is bound to take time. You cannot 'skim' Perrin.

Phil Bartlett

The Death Zone
Matt Dickinson
Hutchinson, 1997, £16.99

'I'm not a climber,' the author said to me. 'I got to the top of Everest by a fluke, filming Al Hinkes's ascent.' I took him at his word and then I read his book. He had never been to the Alps, never climbed by the light of a head torch, never even been to the highest summits of the UK. But in a sense he had been training for Everest for all of his adult life – as a determined and resourceful survivor. At Durham University he joined the Exploration Society, got a first job as a trek leader in the Atlas Mountains and became an adventure film maker, joining teams who were proving 'that it's not all been done'. Most of these journeys demanded that Dickinson himself be part of the proof, with none of the 'fine wine at grand hotels and away in the Land Cruiser in the morning' that mars David Roberts' new collection of 'adventure' essays. For every project, Dickinson wanted both the toughest journey and the most challenging filming.

Thus he came to be filming the third Everest attempt by the 60-year-old thespian, Brian Blessed, whose money had been taken (again) by *Himalayan Kingdoms Expeditions*, with Al Hinkes along for support. Ascending from the north, Blessed was turned around just above the North Col and Al Hinkes became the focus of the film which was shown on Channel 4 on 26 August 1997. Dickinson became the 27th Briton to summit and the first to film on the summit and return.

So is the book of the film worth reading? I found it fascinating, a gripping read, honest, and revealing in more ways than it perhaps intended. Everest is presented in the book as an opportunity to sort himself out and make some decisions. All those requests for the wild caver or rafter or climber or surfer to 'do it one more time' for the camera were beginning to haunt him with their near misses. Then there is the matter of the ethics of filming Brian Blessed's third attempt. Dickinson raises the issue. He has recently admitted that he sought the advice of British guides on the chances of Blessed reaching the summit. He became a convinced fan of the Blessed project. When sensible decisions had to be taken above the North Col, Dickinson admits that he was an angry and naive contributor to that discussion, seeing his film project turned around by the voices of experience.

Should he film the body of an Indian climber over whom he has to step, knowing that, after the huge news interest in the disaster of a few days before, ITN would want his footage and that this was part of the reality? He was there to film anyway. 'I could not bring myself to film the dead man,' seems more an emotional than an ethical decision. Earlier he had admitted in the book that 'the truth was that the mountain had dehumanised me and hardened my emotional response.' This is grist to the mill of Joe Simpson's *Dark Shadows Falling*, the more so, I think, because Dickinson has not had the apprenticeship of loss as a part of the climbing community.

Dickinson manages to convey well the real climbing, emotional waves and final summit fever of his summit day. It is amazing what he carried to the top: two useless litres of frozen juice, a video camera, an SLR camera, his mum's Xmas pud and a throw-away fun camera with which he took summit stills. That he descended to the same unresolved personal problems with which he began is no surprise, but does raise the suspicion that lifestyle issues are in the book to help make a good story. This is certainly what he achieves, (unintentional) warts and all.

Terry Gifford

Chomolungma Sings the Blues. Travels round Everest
Ed Douglas
Constable, 1997, pp226, £18.95

Members of the Alpine Club will find this book worth reading for the first page alone. Our member Ed Douglas brings his writing skills to bear on the Club as it is today in a description to delight us all.

The book is an account of his travels over a three-year period to the base camps on the Rongbuk and the Khumbu glacier approaches to Mount Everest, supported by a travel fellowship from the Winston Churchill Memorial Trust. The author's concern that we might think that there is 'nothing more to be said about tired old Everest that had not been said a thousand times before' is allayed even before he leaves the Club Library. The ghosts of past Everesters begin to materialise as soon as you read the Acknowledgements and inevitably continue right through to the Epilogue. He does not even need to name Mick, Dougal and Nick for familiar faces to be evoked, but this is not a morbid account. It is a reflective piece by a journalist who reports and interprets for us what he sees and what he is told by all the people he meets, not only climbers and Sherpas but lawyers and bike boys in Kathmandu as well.

A difficulty that a journalist can get into by frank reporting of his sources is that his account may bring retribution onto any of them. Moreover, his partisan assessment of Chinese measures to suppress Tibetan nationalism might just delay the issue of a visa to visit Tibet in the future. But Ed Douglas may not wish to travel over that dismal crossing at Zhangmu and Nyalam ever again, an antipathy I recall feeling fervently after several experiences of the Friendship Highway ten years ago.

While giving his unequivocal support to the Free Tibet campaign, Douglas would have given us a more balanced account by reporting the Chinese point of view as well. Their publications used to be readily available in Tibet as well as in Beijing. When last I saw the ruins at Shegar it was in the company of military friends when we climbed to the top of the Dzong. If there ever was an airstrike on the fort by MIG bombers, as he reports, it was not apparent to us then. In spite of these minor carpings, anyone who has travelled in these parts recently will identify with the grim experience that Douglas describes and appreciate this account. Back in Kathmandu he is on safer ground, and is not prisoner to the schedule imposed on all organised parties in Tibet, with one of which he had been obliged to travel. In Kathmandu he had more time for research and he records a wealth of detail. He succeeds in his aim to do a comprehensible analysis of the success, or otherwise, of aid projects in Nepal. He discusses the dire environmental state of Kathmandu with its contaminated water, smog and traffic. His anecdotal approach is entertaining; his story of lingams belies his prudish response to temptations later to be put in his way in the Khumbu by his mischievous Sherpa guide. He is aware of the ironies of Kathmandu ('irony' is a word he uses a lot), such as Eco-tour advertisements glimpsed through exhaust haze across the street.

Trekking on to the Khumbu, I warmed to his opinions on the name Sagarmatha (Chomolungma is much preferred) and 'garbage hobbyists'. He applauds the sensible efforts of the Sagarmatha Pollution Control Committee, as well as those who offer a trash recovery bonus to encourage Sherpas to bring rubbish off the mountains when they are descending empty-handed after a carry. He hopes the focus of Western concern will now shift to the more important issues of poor sanitation and air pollution. There is a delightful exposition on potatoes which brought back fond memories of platefuls of hot buttered 'rigis' served at Base Camp. He parallels the development of lodges all along the trekking trails as far up as Gorak Shep with that of huts in the Alps a century earlier. (And is there not a parallel between what happened to the Matterhorn, such as a dancing bear on the summit, and TV broadcasts from the top of Everest?) He pays handsome tribute to Jimmy Roberts for introducing trekking to Nepal, which I am sure he would have appreciated if he had lived to see publication of this book.

Douglas makes several assessments of recent fatalities on Everest. His unflattering verdict on the first Sherpani's ascent will doubtless upset some in Kathmandu, but as a seasoned reporter he is no doubt prepared to take the rough with the smooth. He was himself at Base Camp in the Spring 1996 season and gives a first-hand description of some of the protagonists. Of the 33 climbers who went for the top, five were to die, including Rob Hall and Scott Fischer. (And Anatoli Boukreev who played a key role in the event has now gone too.) His climber's overview of the tragedy and its subsequent recriminations are well judged and make riveting reading. He weaves all this in with other triumphs and failures, yet he makes no bones about having no wish to try to climb Everest himself. He freely admits that, while he scorns those who are only interested in Everest for its fame, some of them are climbers he respects. He calls it the $64,000 question: why climb Everest at all?

This is a well-written book which will appeal to anyone with an interest in an up-to-date account of the Everest scene.

Henry Day

The Duke of the Abruzzi. An Explorer's Life
Mirella Tenderini & Michael Shandrick
The Mountaineers/Bâton Wicks, 1997, pp190, £17.99

The Duke of the Abruzzi was the grandson of King Vittorio Emanuele II of Italy. During vacations from training for the Italian navy, he explored the Gran Paradiso massif, a hunting area popular with the royal family. By 1890, aged 17, he had developed a passion for mountaineering, largely inspired by his aunt, Queen Margherita of Italy.

By the time he was 21 the Duke of the Abruzzi had completed, with guides from the Val d'Aosta, a number of fine Alpine climbs in the Mont Blanc range and the Monte Rosa group. Other notable climbs included his ascent of the Zmutt ridge of the Matterhorn with Mummery, Collie and the guide Josef Pollinger in 1894. Two years later, after completing one of his long voyages with the Italian navy and faced with an unexpected obstacle to his plans to lead an expedition to Nanga Parbat, the peak on which Mummery had lost his life in 1895, the Duke decided to attempt the ascent of Mount St Elias in Alaska.

So started his famous trio of mountaineering expeditions: the ascent of Mount St Elias in 1897, the exploration of the Ruwenzori mountains in 1906 when he climbed most of the major summits, and in 1909 the attempt on K2 by the ridge now named after him. These expeditions, which are described in this book, may be familiar to British climbers through the series of books by Filippo de Filippi, published by Constable at the time, with Vittorio Sella's magnificent photographs. Not so well known, perhaps, at least among mountaineers, was the Duke's Arctic expedition of 1899-1900, an attempt to reach the North Pole which achieved the 'farthest north' at that time.

The authors, however, relate more than just the adventurous side of the Duke's life, and describe his naval and (reluctant) political career. They also tell the story of his love for a young American heiress, which foundered, amidst much publicity, as a result of opposition from the Italian royal family. In the latter part of his life, the Duke established a communal farming village in Italian Somaliland and carried out further exploration into the interior. There he died in 1933, much loved by the local people.

The Duke of the Abruzzi is a name well known and revered among mountaineers everywhere but, until now, details of his life were almost unknown outside Italy. It is a pity, therefore, that this book, the result of a study of some excellent sources of reference, is marred by poor proof-reading, many careless errors and confusing contradictions which detract from the value of the historical content. For instance, the Duke did not learn during his voyage in the *Cristoforo Colombo* – which was his *first* voyage round the world (page 26) – that a fifth expedition had failed to climb Mount St Elias (page 27); the Duke did not plan to mount an expedition in 1896 and did not climb in the Alps in 1896 (page 28); the Duke was not Sella's monarch (page 104); in 1887 Francis Younghusband was not 'Sir' and was not a colonel (page 105); and Freshfield did not map and study the Kangchenjunga region in 1899-1902 but was there in 1899 only (pages 106-107).

The book, which includes a useful bibliography, contains a number of interesting photographs, many of which were taken by Sella, relating to an exciting and colourful life.

Geoffrey Templeman
C A Russell

The First Descent of the Matterhorn
A Bibliographical Guide to the 1865 Accident and Its Aftermath
Alan Lyall
Gomer Press, 1997, pp 674, £45

'The Matterhorn rises above Zermatt like ... ' How many magazine and newspaper articles include this sentence? Just fill in your own simile. I've proffered a few myself over the years, most slightly embarrassing to recall. But as readers this time are Alpine Club members I should not need to be topographically literal. You've seen it. So as a metaphor look at it as a giant Question Mark. Extend the great triangle above the east face, the classic view from Zermatt, and it is not difficult to visualise. Then you have a mountain that has spawned questions from the technical to the philosophical like no other.

One of the first of the 'Whys', of course, was *The Times* of 27 July 1865, just thirteen days after the first tragic ascent: 'Why is the best blood of England to waste itself in scaling inaccessible peaks ... ' etc. But no doubt Edward Whymper and the Taugwalders were turning over the questions and judicious answers even as they descended after the accident. Alan Lyall's compendious labour of love corrects past distortions of the Matterhorn saga and answers many questions. In the five months I have owned a copy it has proved of invaluable assistance in writing three Matterhorn-related articles. Yet it too cannot help but raise deeper questions as others are answered. And when it gets down to the conflicts of interest of the hotelier Joseph Clemenz who chaired the accident inquiry, and Arnold Lunn's virulent 'allergy' to Whymper, then we really are in *X Files* territory, or Peter Wright-style machinations, for an older generation. The mind swims and there is no distant shore of certainty.

Over the decades, the climbing fraternity has been split between those who say Whymper displayed callous indifference to the deaths of Hudson, Hadow, Douglas and Michel Croz, and those who believe he avoided casting blame to spare the feelings of the bereaved and the reputations of the Taugwalders. Thanks to Frank Smythe's confused interpretation of the Cowell memorandum, detractors Lunn and Carl Eggar were even able to suggest that Whymper accused the Taugwalders of plotting to murder him so that they could profit from the publicity of being the sole survivors.

Alan Lyall, after calling all the witnesses and commentators, basically confirms Whymper's own account in *Scrambles* and concludes that much of the criticism levelled at the AC's past vice-president (1872-74) was 'unjustified'. The 674-page guide draws together scores of contemporary documents, including letters to *The Times*, private correspondence and a first English translation of the Enquiry Report, and subjects their verities and inconsistencies to thorough analysis. Lyall is, after all, a lawyer. Is 'The First Descent of the Matterhorn' a lawyer's title, though? Lyall is fastidious about detail and, I know, scathing about newspaper distortions. Yet the title has the mocking flippancy of a *Guardian* headline. One senses a publisher's pressure for something snappy and that the sub-title 'A Bibliographical Guide to the 1865 Accident and Its Aftermath' might have been Lyall's first choice. It is more accurate, though too forbidding for what is, in fact, an absorbingly readable tome. The biographical sketches of 60 of the characters involved in the early years of the Matterhorn's notoriety are perhaps Lyall's greatest contribution to the endless debate. Of course nothing has changed about the immediate cause – the blundering Hadow slipped at the wrong moment and that was that. Lyall concludes that the inexperienced youth was in the party because neither Hudson, who invited him, nor Croz, their guide, believed there was any prospect of getting onto the trickier rock above the shoulder.

But it is the Taugwalders who dominate the saga. The biographical sketch of Old Peter Taugwalder alone runs to 16,000 words and does not leave a favourable impression – easily unnerved and prone to drink is being kind. The picture of his son, Young Peter, is blacker; the first to see the commercial gain from the disaster. Whymper may have wanted to spare the Taugwalders any blame for the accident but over the succeeding years plenty leaked out to besmirch their characters. Deservedly so? Lyall offers little mitigation. The disturbing side to this is how it chimes with our stereotypes. Here were a pair of Zermatt guides whose first concerns were next season's profit and the reaction of the rival guides' company in Chamonix, one of whom – Croz – had been killed. The Enquiry – the report of which Lyall had translated into English – amounted to little more than a cover-up. Clemenz, apparently, did not want further to provoke the Zermatt families who already distrusted him as an incomer. Even a Swiss newspaper protested at the secrecy over answers given to his enquiry. Yet the aura of secrecy continues. When recent enquiries were made about Old Peter's *Führerbuch*, which has never surfaced, the response was that even if it still existed 'nobody was going to see it'.

The stubborn, parochial defensiveness of the Zermatt guides has been in evidence most recently over their equipping of the Matterhorn's Zmutt ridge. Commerce is at the bottom of it again – the bolts and stanchions on the hitherto untamed route followed the gift of a hut from the Swiss chemical giant Lonza AG. When I telephoned to get the guides' side of the story, one of the first things their president told me was that he was a descendant of Old Peter Taugwalder. 'I know all about that,' he began. The tone was oddly challenging, since I hadn't asked about 1865. But thanks to Alan Lyall, I know all about it too. Do not be deterred by the price.

Stephen Goodwin

Alpi Retiche
Renato Armelloni
Alpi Pusteresi
Favio Cammelli with Werner Beikircher
Sardegna
Maurizio Oviglia
Club Alpino Italiano and Touring Club Italiano, 1997, approx. L65,000 each

In 1997 the CAI/TCI under the guidance of their General Editor Gino Buscaini (who is also an AC member) published three new guides. In common with their volume on the Bernina (reviewed in AJ102) each comes with a sturdy softback cover and beautiful colour pictures, photodiagrams and maps, enhancing the CAI's already established reputation for producing probably the best definitive guidebook to any alpine area under its remit.

The Retiche is a region of lower altitude peaks that many will have seen, yet never visited. It lies south of the Engadine between the popular honey-pots of the Bernina and Ortler Alps. AC members made first ascents of several of the main peaks during the mid-19th century but thereafter pioneering became the preserve of locally based mountaineers. Because of its generally arid nature during the summer months and mainly poor quality limestone, the Retiche is a collection of peaks that will appeal most to the adventurous mountaineer happy to reach altitudes of little more than 3000m by non-technical routes. Having said that, the highest summit, the 3439m Cima de Piazzi, has a fine little glaciated north face, while the 3233m Corno di Dosdé offers a 350m wall of solid gneiss with an eight-pitch ED2/3. Like the Albula to the north-west, the Retiche contains considerable areas of wild country that offer good walking/scrambling as well as extensive ski touring during the winter/spring. The new guide documents all this well and also includes a small section on valley cragging and icefall climbing.

The Pusteresi straddles the Austro-Italian border to the north-east of Brunico and south of the Zillertal. It is even less familiar to foreign climbers than the Retiche and, strangely, appears to have no equivalent name in German. The region has around 50 mountains rising above 3000m and the rock is generally gneiss, though certain peaks offer good quality granite. The best-known summit is the 3435m Callalto (Hochgall) in the Vedretta de Ries (Rieserferen Group) with its 350m Eisnase route (TD+/ED1) and on the snowless south side 800m pillars of solid, compact granite. The highest summit, the 3498m Pico de Tre Signori (Dreiherrenspitze) to the north, sports technically one of the hardest mixed routes in the Eastern

Alps. However, the majority of the climbs described in this guide are far more modest in standard and the many relatively short rock scrambles and snow routes will appeal to the alpinist operating at AD and below. The guide also features useful sections on the ski mountaineering potential and icefall climbing during the winter months.

Probably of most interest to British climbers will be the first comprehensive guide to the now internationally famous rock walls and crags on the island of Sardinia. It presents an interesting departure from traditional mountain venues for the CAI/TCI but not an illogical one. The interior of the island has walls of perfect 'Verdon' limestone up to a full 500m in height, the potential of which was first realised back in the early 1980s by luminaries such as Gogna and Manolo. Oviglia has spearheaded activity in the last decade, introducing ground-up, bolt-protected climbing on some of the bigger compact walls, while seemingly respecting traditional ethics on all the established lines. The majority of the routes described in his guide rely on natural protection and are graded under the UIAA system. Those that don't are generally distinguished by a French rating. In keeping with other CAI publications, this guide concentrates on climbs with an 'alpine' character. These can be as diverse as long multi-pitch offerings on dramatic limestone sea cliffs and short granite routes high in the mountains. Pure sport climbing is covered by topos in a small appendix and a somewhat more lengthy section deals with various excellent walking excursions throughout the interior, over terrain that can often feel quite wild and remote (the highest summit reaches 1823m and is often extensively snow covered in winter). The 100 or so excellent colour prints, photodiagrams, etc, really inspire and have effectively added yet another climbing venue to the list of those I simply have to visit.

Lindsay Griffin

Icefields
Thomas Wharton
Jonathan Cape, 1997, £9.99

It was reported locally at the time, but many UK alpinists may not have heard about the fall into a crevasse by Dr Edward Byrne on the Arcturus Glacier in the Canadian Rockies. He wedged upside down sixty feet from the surface, unconscious. In order to haul him out, his partners had to cut his rucksack away. As he recovered in Jasper, Byrne recalled seeing in the depths of the glacier ice a pale human figure with wings. He could never be certain about what exactly he saw, but this image haunted him for the rest of his life.

The time was actually 1898 and, in an era when retreating glaciers across the globe are giving up their secrets, this might have appeared to be a weirdly contemporary story. In fact it was the starting point of the first novel by the Canadian Thomas Wharton. This intriguing, understated, poetic novel won the Grand Prize at the 1995 Banff Mountain Book Festival and was shortlisted by the Boardman Tasker judges here.

So, back in England after the 1898 expedition, Byrne is restless and returns to Jasper, eventually building a hut on a nunatak in the Arcturus Glacier for his regular summer glaciological research. He appears to be calculating the moment when the section of ice into which he fell will peel off at the terminus. Meanwhile his relationships with a series of enigmatic women reveal as much about his psychological and emotional handicaps as they do about the history of tourist development in the Rockies. Sara is the daughter of an abandoned servant 'acquired' in India. Fraya is a lone woman explorer and climber. Elspeth keeps an extraordinary glasshouse linked to a hot spring and becomes the manager of the glacier visitor centre. What the tourists can see in later years is the grown fruit of Dr Byrne's rucksack.

The narrative picks up the stories of several characters in several short sections which can feel frustratingly fractured at first, but the book is worth hanging in with. It is as haunting and echoing as an ice cave that cannot give up all its secrets at once.

Terry Gifford

Storms of Silence
Joe Simpson
Jonathan Cape 1996, pp304, £17.99
Vintage 1997, ppvi+330, £7.99 (paperback, fewer photos)

It must be difficult for an author to follow a best-seller such as Joe Simpson's *Touching the Void*, and the successful *This Game of Ghosts*. The present book is a curious mixture of essay-like writing, rather over-long conversation pieces and wonderful passages describing parts of Nepal – so well written that they made me long to return there yet again.

Throughout the book, from the end of the first three chapters (about an expedition to the Langtang), there runs the thread of aggression and modern-day violence, comprising everything from a nasty brutish scene in a pub (really rather tedious) to Simpson's thoughts on Chinese atrocities in Tibet. He returns to Peru, for the most successful summer's climbing he ever had, and visits Yungay, the town buried in 1970 by a mud slide following an earthquake. This sets off a train of thought about Belsen, which he had visited as a schoolboy.

There is an odd chapter about training in various gymnasiums, and another on his fear of flying. It seems that he is an introverted character, who wants his readers to know what he is thinking and feeling most of the time. Is this a good thing? The book is very readable, simply because Simpson writes so well, but this reader was left with the thought that there is a lot of padding, and that it lacks cohesion.

Sally Westmacott

Traumberge Amerikas. Von Alaska bis Feuerland
Edkehard Radehose
Bergverlag Rother, 1996, pp 191, npq

The High Andes. A Guide for Climbers
John Biggar
Andes, 1996, pp 160, £16

The main contribution of these two books lies in their many pages of useful information regarding individual peaks of the New World, and the particular problems those peaks may pose to the expeditionary mountaineer. The scope of each book differs only slightly. The German work is more a collection of contributions by the author himself and by other climbers (including the very experienced Andeanist Herbert Ziehenhardt) on several peaks, ranging from Alaska to Patagonia (but not 'Feuerland'). The Scottish work is an Andean guidebook with basic information conveyed in a direct style. Statistics for both books are impressive. Radehose's guide surveys a total of 32 peaks, each one covered by a long description of climbing conditions to be found, illustrated with 133 top quality colour pictures and 30 colour maps. There is also an index. Alaska is represented by Mount McKinley and by four other peaks; the rest, all Andean, are mostly Peruvian ice peaks and Chilean desert volcanoes. Biggar's book deals purely with the Andes and it surveys 165 peaks in all, covered by means of a brief description of access and normal route, of other routes and of existing maps. It also offers 8 colour photos, 50 sketch maps, 72 line drawings (of normal routes), 8 short appendices and 2 indexes.

Both works seem to prefer the Peruvian Andes to the rest. Both were well prepared and designed to get a climber started on the road to the more representative peaks of the American continent. If any adverse remark is to be made it would be about the height of the peaks. The authors don't always use the most recent figures. Still, the amount of up-to-date information is remarkable and the Biggar book, in particular, promises to be of great practical value in the field.

Evelio Echevarría

Visions of Snowdonia. Landscape and Legend
Jim Perrin
BBC Books, 1997, pp 224, £18.99

Jim Perrin, our most eloquent mountain essayist and controversialist, describes the theme of this elegant book as a celebration of 'Snowdonia's richness, history, cultural texture and beauty'. Although a Mancunian born, Perrin's ancestral roots are Welsh and his lyrical writing echoes a genuine *hiraeth* for the land of his adoption. From Giraldus Cambrensis's 12th century tour of Wales through to Jan Morris, the best travel books about the Principality have been written by Anglo-Welsh or English writers. Although Perrin's vision is determinedly Welsh, his *Visions of Snowdonia*, illustrated with Ray Wood's hauntingly beautiful photographs, joins these ranks.

Perrin's journey through Cambria's northern hills and vales has the intensity of a pilgrimage. His *Landscape and Legend* draws comparison with Simon Schama's kaleidoscopic *Landscape and Memory* in examining the effect that mountains have had in shaping man's culture and imagination. But although Perrin paints an altogether more intimate picture on a smaller canvas, this is an ambitious book extending beyond landscape and legend to embrace history, literature and art (with a dash of socio-political polemic thrown in), and combining powerful descriptive passages (for example, his account of Castell y Bere on p.208) with an empathy for country and people:

> ... the broken walls of Castell y Bere trail haphazardly around the summit of this surprising rocky outcrop, where the ubiquitous spleenwort grows. A cool wind drifted from the mountain as I entered its green curtilage. Thyme was spreading and violets discreetly blooming. In months to come the delicate harebells would wave here. The place is still. Seven hundred springs have passed since the murderous commotions of war, since the siege and the fall, the blood and the cries at noon ...

But this poetic voyage through the Cymric heartland can never have been intended as a comprehensive artistic and literary compendium. Contemporary Welsh writers are freely quoted but the older poets less so and there are virtually no references to the many English writers and artists who, at least from Leland's 1536–9 *Itinerary in Wales* onwards, have recorded illuminating accounts of their travels through Snowdonia. Thus, although Wordsworth, the founding father of British romantic poets and himself a Snowdon ascensionist, is quoted, there is nothing of Southey, Shelley, Thomas Love Peacock, Tennyson (who wrote his Arthurian verse at Bala) or even Thomas Gray, whose poem *The Bard* inspired John Martin's dramatic depiction of Edward I's army marching through the Pass of Llanberis. This is the archetypal revolutionary picture with its wild-eyed, streaming-haired poet-seer perched barefoot on an overhanging crag clutching his harp and cursing the English invaders.

Painters of Snowdonia fare little better. Richard Wilson and John Dickson Innes get their due, but there is no reference to the romantic 19th century Welsh mountain paintings of Turner, Varley, Cox and Leman. Turner's magnificent *Dolbadarn Castle* (1800), the stronghold above Llyn Peris where the patriot hero Owen Glendower was imprisoned, was the culmination of his paintings of Wales.

Although Winthrop Young and Tilman get a mention, this is not intended as a mountaineering book. However, some reference to Lord Lyttleton's first sporting ascent of Snowdon in 1756 and the Reverend William Bingley's first British rock climb of Clogwyn du'r Arddu's Eastern Terrace in 1799 might have added historical perspective.

Snowdonia offers more than one nation's heritage, but it is probably appropriate that the theme and flavour of the book should primarily be local. The narrative is interleaved with cameos of contemporary local characters – artists, writers, National Park Wardens, RSPB officers, naturalists, farmers, mountain-bikers and clerics – whose lives have been shaped by their mountain environment. A spoonful of Perrin polemic enriches the stew and many of Jim's arrows – touristic and municipal philistinism; landscape desecration and degradation (notoriously, the Welsh Water Authority's destruction of Pont Scethin and the Forestry Commission's planting of 600,000 acres of coniferous forest: 'the biggest environmental catastrophe in Britain this century') and conservation issues generally strike home.

Wales is a land of legend which stretches back to the dawn of folk memory (its fairies and lake maidens supposedly reflect Bronze Age man's clash with the new Iron Age culture) through to Merlin, Arthur and a host of naturalistic superstitions about wells, caves, standing stones and circles, inundations, dragons and the like. The *Mabinogion* was a masterpiece of European medieval literature yet the portrayal of legend in the context of this journey through landscape was for me a less convincing aspect of this generally excellent book. Although legends, ancient and modern, are seamlessly interwoven into the narrative, their interposition sometimes arrests its flow. Many myths are so obscure that without detailed elucidation and explanation, their significance is lost. Two important source books might profitably have been added to the reading list: Carr & Lister's magisterial *The Mountains of Snowdonia* (Bodley Head,1925) and *Snowdon Biography* by Winthrop Young, Sutton and Noyce (Dent, 1957)

. However, these are minor quibbles. *Visions of Snowdonia*'s enchantment lies in the lyricism and conviction of Jim Perrin's writing and Ray Wood's evocative photographs. Both capture the essential spirit of *Eryri* ('the home of the eagles'), the Welsh name for these mountains which sadly, like the eagles, has been supplanted by the prosaic 'Snowdonia'.

J G R Harding

Hypoxia and the Brain
Proceedings of the 9th International Hypoxia Symposium, 1995
Editors: J R Sutton, C S Houston, G Coates
Queens City Printers Inc., Burlington, Vermont, USA, 1995, US$45.00

These Proceedings contain a wealth of information not only on the effects of oxygen lack on the brain but on many other subjects, notably the development of the foetus in utero and the effect of oxygen lack on vessels in the lung.

For mountaineers and others it has been known for over a century that the organ most sensitive to oxygen lack is the brain, and there are numerous accounts of hallucinations, personality changes, profound lack of judgement and speech disorders in the mountains. Exhaustion and cold also have mental effects. Those who advocate 'character building' in the mountains, an increasingly discredited concept, should be made aware of this.

These regular meetings held in North America at two-year intervals are mainly for medical scientists and enable those who work on the subject of oxygen lack, from whatever cause, to discuss advances and understand trends. These Proceedings should be studied by all concerned with the subject of oxygen transfer in human beings – a subject of critical importance to all mountaineers.

Michael Ward

High Altitude Medicine
Herb Multgren
Multgren Publications, Stanford, California, USA, 1997, US$45 (inc. p&p)

This is the latest in the now considerable number of major textbooks on high-altitude medicine. It is not comprehensive, since it omits any discussion of cold and cold injury. But it does embrace many other important topics that are either new or not normally covered, such as medico-legal aspects and a section on women at altitude. Mountaineering doctors will find a great deal of useful information in this book and being so reasonably priced it is excellent value for money.

Herb Multgren, who died just after the book was published, was a very highly respected Emeritus Professor of Medicine at Stanford University in California. He made major contributions to our understanding of high altitude pulmonary oedema, and climbed extensively in Europe, and in North and South America. He was an excellent teacher and companion. Both medical and mountaineering libraries should certainly have this book on their shelves, and many doctors who climb will wish to buy it.

Michael Ward

Guido Monzino
Rita Ajmone Cat
Alberti Libraio, 1997, pp216, npq

Our late member Guido Monzino was one of Italy's leading mountain and Arctic explorers, and this book describes all his major expeditions. From 1955 onwards Monzino organised expeditions every year, sometimes twice a year, to the Alps, Patagonia, the Sahara, Karakoram, Ruwenzori, Mount Kenya and Kilimanjaro, and many times to Greenland, culminating in his 1971 trip to the North Pole and in 1973 to Everest. Every expedition is briefly described, with a complete list of participants and many photographs.

There are photos, too, of the Villa Barbianello, Monzino's home on the shores of Lake Como. Anyone who has visited this glorious house and the museum Monzino established there will wonder how he could bear to leave it so often to go expeditioning around the world!

Annapurna Circuit. Himalayan Journey
Andrew Stevenson
Constable, 1997, pp224, £18.95

Andrew Stevenson's first book describes his two-month trek through Manang and Muktinath and over the Thorong La with a trip up to Annapurna base camp to finish. The Annapurna circuit has been described many times, but this book is rather different. For one thing, it is light on scenic descriptions, and for another there are no illustrations. Stevenson's interest is in the people who inhabit the area, and in his fellow back-packers, some of whom he joins up with on his travels. His book gives an in-depth picture of the lives of the hill people of Nepal, and also shows how standards of behaviour are deteriorating among some of the youth in Pokhara and Kathmandu. He is less than complimentary on the attitudes of many of his fellow travellers. Although the book is expensive for one with no photographs, it is worth acquiring a copy to read such a well-written travel book on the Annapurna region.

THE ALPINE CLUB LIBRARY ALSO RECEIVED THE FOLLOWING BOOKS DURING 1997:

Classic Rock. Great British Rock Climbs Compiled by Ken Wilson
Bâton Wicks, 1997, pp256, £19.99 Revised edition with added historical commentary, new colour plates and revised gradings.

Spy on the Roof of the World Sydney Wignall
Canongate, 1996, ppxviii+268, £16.99

Hamish's Mountain Walk & Climbing the Corbetts Hamish Brown
Bâton Wicks, 1997, pp704, £16.99

50 Best Scrambles in the Lake District Bill O'Connor
David & Charles, 1997, pp144, £9.99

On Foot in the Lake District. 1) Northern & Western Fells 2) Southern & Eastern Fells Terry Marsh. *David & Charles, 1997, pp128, £14.99 each*

Walking in Cornwall John Earle. *Cicerone Press, 1996, pp176, npq*

Cornish Rock. A Climbers' Guide to Penwith Rowland Edwards & Tim Dennell. *Cicerone Press, 1997, pp266, £18.99*

50 Classic Routes on Scottish Mountains Ralph Storer
David & Charles, 1997, pp112, £14.99

Britain's Highest Peaks. The Complete Illustrated Route Guide
Jeremy Ashcroft. *David & Charles, 1997, pp184, £12.99*

Winter Climbs in the Lake District Bob Bennett, Bill Birkett & Brian Davidson. *Cicerone Press, 3rd edition, 1997, pp192, £14.99*

East of Himalayas. Mountains and Valleys of Yunnan, Sichuan, SE Tibet and Myanmar Tamotsu Nakamura. *Yamakei, 1996, pp330* (in Japanese)

Descent into Chaos. The Doomed Expedition to Low's Gully
Richard Connaughton. *Brassey's, 1996, ppxiv+142, £14.95*

Kinabalu Escape. The Soldiers' Story Rick Mayfield with Bob Mann
Constable, 1997, pp282, £7.95

Stasera si mette al bello ed io partiro domattina per le montagne ... Lettere e scritti alpini di Costantino Perazzi (Novara 1832–Roma 1896)
Giuseppe & Paolo Sitzia. *C.A.I., 1996, pp238, npq*

Histoire Monumentale des Deux Savoies. La Memoire de la Montagne.
Gilbert Gardes *Horvath, 1996, pp392, FF195*

Les Alpinistes Victoriens Michel Tailland. *Presses Universitaires du Septentrion, 1996, 2 vols., pp1-425, 426-695, FF345*

Trekking en Bariloche. *Club Andino Bariloche, 1995, pp120*

Amor Por Carta. Recuerdos de un Andinista. *Club Andino Bariloche, 1995, pp82*

Annapurna. The First Conquest of an 8000-metre Peak Maurice Herzog.
Pimlico, 1997, ppxxii+246, £10.00

November Jon Barton, Paul Evans & Simon Norris.
Vertebrate Graphics, 1996, £4.95

Scrambles Amongst the Alps in the Years 1860–69 Edward Whymper
Dover Publications (New York), 1996, ppxviii+468, £13.95. A 'slightly reorganised' republication of the 5th edition.

Central Apennines of Italy. Walks, Scrambles & Climbs Stephen Fox
Cicerone Press, 1996, pp144, £8.99

Cape Rock Julian Fisher
Nomad Mountain Publications, 1996, ppiii+145

Mountain Memories. Wolverhampton Mountaineering Club 1951–1996
Hilary Clark, 1997, pp168, £6.50

Montana Magica. Veinticinco Anos de Expediciones Navarras Extraeuropeas Gregorio Ariz Txoria Errekan, 1996, *pp120, npq*

Heart of the Himalaya. Journeys in Deepest Nepal David Paterson
Peak Publishing, 1997, pp144, £14.95

Zen Explorations in Remotest New Guinea Neville Shulman
Summersdale, 1997, pp160, £12.99

A Climbing Guide to Crafnant Tony Shaw. *Mynydd C.C., 1997, pp94*
Escursioni in Val Divedro, Alpe Veglia, Devero Gianfranco Francese.
Pro Loco Val Divedro, 1996, pp258

Fotografia e Alpinismo. Storie parallele. La fotografia di montagna dai pionieri all'arrampicata sportiva Giuseppe Garimoldi
Priuli & Verlucca, Torino, 1995, pp312

Skye and the Hebrides. Rock and Ice Climbs. S.M.C., 1996, £19.95
Vol 1 The Isle of Skye John R MacKenzie & Noel Williams, *ppxvi+352*
Vol 2 The Outer Hebrides, Rum, Eigg, Mull & Iona Dave Cuthertson, Bob Duncan, Graham Little & Colin Moody, *ppxii+324*

Arran, Arrochar and the Southern Highlands. Rock and Ice Climbs
Graham Little, Tom Prentice & Ken Crocket. *S.M.C., 1997, ppxiv+386*

Mountain Moments. A Miscellany Celebrating 40 Years of the Army Mountaineering Association *Ed.* Lt Col A J Muston, *1997, pp80*

Walking in Italy's Gran Paradiso Gillian Price
Cicerone Press, 1997, pp192, £9.99

Primiero Nelle Immagini di Nanni Gadenz Sandro Gadenz, Marco Toffol & Luigi Zanetel. Introduction by Reinhold Messner
Casse Rurali, Primiero, 1996, pp165

Trekking in Bolivia. A Traveller's Guide Yossi Brain, Andrew North & Isobel Stoddart. *Cordée, 1997, pp224, £10.95*

Planning a Wilderness Trip in Canada and Alaska Keith Morton *Rocky Mountain Books/Cordée, 1997, pp384, £16.95*

Alpinismo e Cultura Giovanni Rossi. *Club Alpino Accademico Italiano, 1996, pp112*

Oz Rock. A Rock Climber's Guide to Australian Crags Alastair Lee *Cicerone Press, 1997, pp176, £10.99*

Vaud. Guide to Lac Léman–Lake Geneva, Jura and Alpine Regions Elisabeth Upton-Eickenberger. *U-Guides (Cordée), 1997, pp296, £12.95*

A series of 8 rock-climbing/bouldering guides (+2 supplements) to climbing areas in Poland. Malgorzata & Jan Kielkowscy, 1992–1997

Rescue. True Stories from Lake District Mountain Rescue John White. *Constable, 1997, pp214, £16.95*

The Munros in Winter. 277 Summits in 83 Days Martin Moran *David & Charles, 1997, pp240, £9.99*

Alps 4000. 75 Peaks in 52 Days Martin Moran. *David & Charles, 1997, pp240, £9.99*

L'Incanto del Giappone Fosco Maraini. *Museo Nazionale della Monagna 'Duca degli Abruzzi', Walter Weston, C.A.I., 1996, pp132*

Above the Horizon Rosemary Cohen *Allison & Busby, 1997, pp256, £7.99.* A mountaineering novel

K2. El Maximo Desafio (The Ultimate Challenge) Chile K2 1996 Expedition Rodrigo Jordan. *Rodrigo Jordan Fuchs, 1996, pp136, npq*

The Mountain Weeps Ian R Mitchell *Stobcross Press, 1997, pp128, £7.99* Short Stories

Tree of Crows Lewis Davies. *Parthian Books, 1996, pp102, £4.99* A mystery novel.

Trekking in Nepal. A Traveller's Guide Stephen Bezruchka. *Cordée, 1997, pp384, £12.95* 7th edition

In Memoriam

COMPILED BY GEOFFREY TEMPLEMAN

The Alpine Club Obituary 1997		Year of Election	
Yevgeniy B Gippenreiter		1984	(Hon 1984)
Walter Hermann Amstutz		1929	(Hon 1975)
Ella Maillart	LAC	1938	(Hon 1938)
Bernard Pierre		1949	(Hon 1981)
James Owen Merion Roberts		1937	
Lyman Spitzer		1984	
Hamish Gordon Nicol		1962	
Harry Leighton Stembridge		1955	
Malcolm R D Duff	ACG	1984	
Brendan Joseph Murphy		1986	
Malcolm Graham Rutherford		1972	
H C Sarin		1983	(Hon 1983)
George Tod		1955	
John Llywelyn Jones		1974	
Denis Percy Pierrepont Brimble		1944	
Ian H Ogilvie		1958	
Hilary St.Vincent Longley-Cook		1946	

Included this year are obituaries for Sybil Washington and Tom Peacocke, who died in 1995 and 1996 respectively.

The In Memoriam list for 1997 again includes many names well-known in the mountaineering world and, in particular, a high number of Honorary Members from abroad.

There are some members listed above for whom no obituaries have been received, and I would be pleased to include any of these in next year's *Alpine Journal.*

Geoffrey Templeman

Yevgeniy B Gippenreiter 1927-1997

British mountaineers who climbed in the Caucasus in 1958 and the Pamirs in 1962 remain grateful to Yevgeniy Gippenreiter for his role as an official in the Soviet Central Sports Council in helping to secure them permission from the authorities of the Bulganin-Khrushchev era. As a fluent English speaker, he was remarkably successful at dealing with Soviet bureaucracy and for maintaining cordial links with British mountaineers during the Cold War. He was elected an Honorary Member of the Alpine Club in 1984.

Gippenreiter accompanied Soviet sporting teams abroad in the 1950s as their interpreter, and in 1956 he visited the Alpine Club with Yevgeniy Beletski to give an account of Russian mountaineering. In 1957 the first chink in the climbing Iron Curtain appeared with the visit of Joyce Dunsheath to Elbrus, accompanied by Gippenreiter, while her husband, an atomic scientist, attended a Moscow conference. The following summer a British group, including John Hunt, George Band and Chris Brasher, was granted permission to climb in the spectacular Ushba and Bezingi regions of the Caucasus, continuing a tradition begun in 1868 by Freshfield, Moore and Tucker. Yevgeniy had been principally responsible for the trip, and by then had become a good friend to the British.

Gippenreiter started climbing in 1951, and went on to organise international mountaineering camps in the Soviet Union. He climbed Mount Communism and Peak Lenin and was made a Master of Sport. His later contributions were as a research worker, with a doctorate in biology, becoming a specialist in the fields of top performance sports, high altitude and space physiology. He was involved in the preparation and results of the Soviet Mount Everest Expedition in 1982 and was co-author of *Acute and Chronic Hypoxia* (1977) and *Physiology of Man at High Altitude* (1987). He was a vice-president of the International Society for Mountain Medicine and a member of the medical commission of the International Union of Alpine Associations.

A lean handsome figure with a Stalinesque moustache and an infectiously good-humoured gleam in his dark eyes, he was a great talker and an outspoken raconteur. Visiting England in 1993, he disclosed that his father had been a doctor at the court of Tsar Nicholas II and had been honoured for his services. This meant that, by the laws of succession, Yevgeniy himself qualified as a member of the reconstituted Russian Nobility Assembly, a connection he would scarcely have mentioned during the Communist era. He was delighted when his membership was confirmed, and overjoyed when he and his wife Lidia were presented to the Queen at the RGS in 1993.

On his last visit to England, in December 1996, he attended the Alpine Club's annual dinner. He is survived by his wife and two sons.

George Band

John Hunt writes:
I first met Yevgeniy ('Eugene' to most of his British friends) in 1954, when I was invited to give a lecture on the first ascent of Everest before an audience of sceptical Soviet mountaineers. Eugene, with his excellent command of English, contributed to their conversion and this led to the establishment of some lasting friendships. That historic encounter opened the door to further exchanges. Charles Evans visited Moscow in 1955 to lecture on his Kangchenjunga expedition; Yevgeniy Beletski came to Britain the following year to tell us about climbing in the Soviet Union. These overtures led to a series of expeditions in the USSR, and meets in Britain in which climbers of both countries took part.

It was a great moment for the Climbers' Club in 1957 when, following an initiative by John Neill, I received a telegram from Eugene inviting a group of British climbers to visit the Caucasus in the following year. The BMC followed up that event by inviting a Russian group to sample climbing in Britain. It was an offer which I had some difficulty in 'selling' to the (then) Minister of Sport in the Kremlin, who did not consider our cliffs and crags worthy of the attention of Soviet mountaineers! The crowning event during that period of developing co-operation occurred in 1962, when another British group, jointly sponsored by the Alpine Club and the Scottish Mountaineering Club, was invited to join a group of Russians to climb in the Western Pamirs. So much for the chronology of events during the Fifties and early Sixties, during which Eugene played a leading part in opening the doors of opportunity for British (and other) mountaineers from Western Europe to meet and climb in the Soviet Union and to entertain Soviet climbers in our country.

But my tribute to Eugene is anecdotal rather than historical. I recall sharing a tent with him and the renowned Georgian climber Josef Kachiani during an ascent of Pik Kavkaz in 1958 when we talked far into the night, munching dried fish from the Caspian Sea and other Russian delicacies emerging from Josef's enormous sack. In a very different setting, I escorted Eugene and Yevgeniy Beletski to Glasgow by the overnight sleeper train in 1960, to meet Scottish climbers. Our fare on that occasion was caviar, eaten with toothbrush handles, and vodka from tooth-mugs.

During their visit in 1960, I recall climbing Main Wall on Cyrn Las with Eugene, Anatoli Ovchhinikov and 'Misha' Khergiani, when 'Misha' surprised us by producing a large stone, which he had secreted in his pocket to facilitate the final crack. That episode was followed by a hair-raising canoe trip in Llyn Mymbyr when Eugene, true to his dare-devil character, persuaded me, against all the rules of the Plas y Brenin Centre, to borrow one of their fleet of canoes which we proceeded to board in our climbing clothes and mountain boots. Some way out from the shore, Eugene, a non-swimmer, succeeded in capsizing the craft, which led to a dramatic rescue operation by the Centre staff.

But the most enduring of all my memories of Eugene were of the expedition to the Pamirs in 1962. There was a moment of supreme joy, when Eugene and I embraced on reaching the summit of a virgin peak: Pik Sodruchestvo ('Concord'). By contrast, when Wilfrid Noyce and Robin Smith lost their lives tragically on Pik Garmo, the accident imposed a severe strain on the relations between the British group and some Soviet mountaineers who were at our base camp at that time. I will never forget the staunch support Eugene gave us during those painful days.

In the following years our friendship continued, albeit that the occasions to meet were less frequent, such as conferences of the UIAA in London and elsewhere and celebratory occasions in Zermatt and Chamonix. In 1993 Eugene came to London and visited North Wales during the events which marked the 40th anniversary of the first ascent of Everest. At the RGS he met the Queen and bemused her with an animated account of Russian achievements in the mountains. He was, in fact, an aristocrat at heart, for his father had served at the Court of Tsar Nicholas II. To his great joy, his title as a Russian Count was restored to him after the collapse of Communism, and the prefix 'von' was added to his name.

As a climber Eugene had a good record of achievements in his own country, which earned him the distinction of a Master of Sport. He was strong, bold and carefree to the point of rashness. I recall watching him with some apprehension when he insisted on taking the lead on the upper buttresses of Dykh-Tau in the Caucasus, choosing a most unpromising line with great vigour. That 'do-or-die' approach may have accounted for the accident he suffered on Cloggy in 1960.

In middle life Eugene studied mountain physiology, obtained a Doctorate and played an important role in preparing the Soviet team which climbed Everest by a new route on the South-West Face in 1982. All who knew this lovable person will remember him for his exuberance, his sense of fun and, above all, for the warmth of his friendship to the privileged few who knew him well.

Dr Walter Amstutz 1902 - 1997

Walter Amstutz, who died on 6 August 1997, was in many ways a unique person. He combined an active and resolute mind with physical skills and great personal charm, qualities which enabled him to achieve notable successes in the wide diversity of activities which filled his life. He was probably the last man alive who had participated in the first European downhill and slalom ski races ever organised. During the 1920s he became a leading Swiss skier, winning over 20 important competitions. He co-founded the Swiss Academic Ski Club in 1924, of which he was later elected Honorary Chairman, and he also inaugurated and edited their yearbook *Der Schneehase*. As a climber he was equally active; he began climbing at the age of 12 and, 70 years later, his tally of ascents, too numerous to detail here, was over 800 on mountains all over the world, including a number of first ascents. In 1924 he made the first ski descent of the Eiger, and the first ski traverse of the Jungfrau. His life encompassed almost a century in the development of mountaineering and skiing; and in 1990, at the age of 88, he qualified as a ski glider.

Walter Amstutz was born in 1902 in Brienzwiler, but moved a short time later to Mürren where his parents owned the Pension Alpina. He was sent to the village school where 28 pupils, crowded into one room, were instructed by a single teacher. At Lauterbrunnen, 950m below, he attended secondary school; since there was no cable-car then, and the cog railway did not operate in winter, he skied down about 9km to school, and climbed back to Mürren on skins in 1¾ hours. It was the Lunn Travel Agency, founded by Arnold Lunn's father, that popularised ski holidays in Mürren for the British, and someone once remarked that by 1924 'Mürren was practically a British Crown colony'. A close friendship grew between Walter Amstutz and Arnold Lunn who was older by 14 years. The development of slalom and downhill ski racing, pioneered by Arnold Lunn, in which Walter Amstutz began to excel, coincided with Walter's university studies. He undertook undergraduate and graduate courses in Bern, Zürich, Munich, and London in art, law, and geology, and obtained his doctorate in economics at the University of Bern.

In 1929 Walter Amstutz took up an appointment in St Moritz as Public Relations and Sports Director. It was there that he was largely responsible for turning downhill skiing into a popular sport. In 1930 he invented the Amstutz Spring which, attached to the rear of a boot, steadied and provided flexibility to the heel. He sold 10,000 of them. With the profits, he launched into a new entrepreneurial career from which he never looked back. Leaving St Moritz in 1939, his interest in graphic design led him to turn towards publishing. In 1938, with Walter Herdeg, formerly graphic artist for the Kurverein St Moritz, he co-founded an advertising agency in Zürich, which was later turned into a publishing company. During the 1940s, he and his partner started an international journal, *Graphis*, for applied arts; and in 1962 he produced *Who's Who in Graphic Art*, a 900-page reference book in three languages. After selling the firm to his partner, Walter Amstutz founded the small but elite publishing company De Clivo Press, which began to produce some very distinguished publications such as *Turner in Switzerland*, a volume dedicated to J M W Turner's Swiss and Alpine water-colours, and an English translation of Albrecht von Haller's epic poem *Die Alpen*. For an art-lover, volumes superbly produced to such rigid standards as these are a delight to handle. Walter Amstutz was a seeker after perfection. He used to say, 'Appreciating the value of the last few percentage points of perfection is something you are born with. My father was artistic and my grandfather was a renowned wood-carver.' Walter Amstutz's business interests led to various company directorships, amongst which was the chairmanship for over 40 years of Massey-Ferguson Switzerland.

In 1930 Walter Amstutz married the English novelist Eveline Palmer. Success in his business interests enabled him to establish two homes: a large one at Mannedorf by the lake of Zürich, which was filled with books, maps, and paintings, including a magnificent collection of Japanese prints. He had built, in 1935, a chalet for his mother in Mürren, which he enlarged later for himself and his family, covering its walls with Alpine paintings and prints. One of Walter Amstutz's mottos, carved on the exterior of the chalet, was 'Happiness shall always be found by those who dare and persevere. Wanderer, do not turn round, march on and have no fear.'

King Albert I of Belgium, a passionate alpinist, died in 1934 undertaking a solo rock-climb. Walter Amstutz had the privilege of skiing with him in 1929, and during four subsequent seasons he joined the King on his climbs in various parts of the Alps. Much impressed by the King's strength of character, and shocked by his premature death, Walter Amstutz decided to establish a memorial in his honour, adopting as its motto the King's own maxim, 'La Volonté, la Qualité maîtresse de L'Homme.' The King Albert I Memorial Foundation presents periodic awards for outstanding achievements in the general field of mountaineering.

Walter Amstutz was a member of the Founding Council of the Swiss Foundation for Alpine Research Zürich, which has sponsored expeditions to several of the world's ranges, also publishing annually between 1946-1969 *Berge Der Welt*, which appeared from 1953 in an English version as *The Mountain World*. Walter Amstutz contributed articles to the publication, as he did to *Der Schneehase*, to the *Alpine Journal* and other publications. He was as fluent in English as he was in German.

In 1975 Walter Amstutz was made an Honorary Member of the Alpine Club. He was also an Honorary Member of the Ski Club of Great Britain, and of the Groupe de Haute Montagne. In 1984, he had the rare distinction of receiving an Honorary OBE for 'important contributions to relations between Switzerland and Great Britain'

Walter Amstutz's wife died in 1993. He is survived by his daughter, Yvonne, her husband, three grandchildren, and two great-grandchildren.

Trevor Braham

Ella Maillart 1903-1997

Ella Maillart was invited to be an Honorary Member of the Ladies Alpine Club in 1938, on the strength of her travels among mountains – Caucasus, Tien Shan, Pamir, Karakoram. Born and brought up in Geneva, the Alps for her were more for skiing than climbing (she was a member of the Swiss skiing and sailing teams). From the time she left school, restless and dissatisfied, she made her own plans and paid her own way – mainly by journalism and the books which she found wearisome to write. In *Cruises and Caravans* (1943), one of a series aimed at the young, she gave her juniors advice based on her own experience: you must want to travel enough to give up everything to that end, but first – and this may be the hardest part – you have to discover that it's what you really want to do.

She herself had thrashed about for some years, trying her hand at acting, teaching, filming (with intervals of sailing small boats round the English coast and in the Mediterranean), before going to Moscow in 1930 where she studied film and rowed in the Alimentation Workers' eight. There she joined a party to cross the Caucasus, north to south, on foot. Her book on the trip, *Parmi la jeunesse russe*, helped to finance her next venture in 1932 to Kazakhstan and Kyrghystan. Without a proper visa she travelled across the Tien Shan mountains, on to Tashkent and Samarkand, Bokhara and Khiva, noting the effects of Soviet modernisation, herself at ease in a world where 'heat does not come in pipes, ice in boxes, sunshine in bulbs'. She wanted, as far as any passing stranger can, to enter into the lives of those she travelled among. She journeyed as they did – by crammed Turksib trains, lorries that kept breaking down, on the deck of an Oxus paddle-boat, on camel-back with a caravan across the desert of Kizil Kum, usually humping her own baggage. At Khiva she lodged with the Uzbek postmaster; in the desert by the frozen Aral Sea, she slept in Kazakh yurts.

From the last spur of the Tien Shan, at the frontier with China, she had looked longingly into forbidden Sinkiang and determined to travel there some day. Three years later her chance came when she was sent to Manchuria by *Le Petit Parisien* to report the Japanese occupation, and there met Peter Fleming, reporting for *The Times*. Somewhat reluctantly they agreed to join forces for an attempt to travel from Peking to Kashmir. This seven-month journey across the Taklamakan desert and Sinkiang, then closed to foreigners – memorably described in Fleming's *News from Tartary* (1936) and her *Forbidden Journey* (1937) – gave her an international reputation and made her much in demand as a lecturer.

A journey in 1939 through Persia and Afghanistan ended in India, where she spent the war years, mostly in a hut near Madras – a time when she embarked on a different kind of exploration. She talked to holy men, she learnt to meditate, and lost some of her restlessness (the book of tributes by her friends to mark her 80th birthday is titled *Voyage vers le Réel*). On her return to Switzerland she found the right haven for her new serenity in the high village of Chandolin, which looks up the Val d'Anniviers to the Dent Blanche. From there she set out on new ventures to Nepal, Tibet, the South Pacific, supporting herself and her own travels by conducting tours to India, China, Java, Korea, the Yemen, and by her books and lectures.

In 1978 Peter Lloyd, then President, asked me to have Kini – as all her friends called her – to stay for the Alpine Club Annual Dinner. This was the first of many visits, and led to a friendship that meant much to me. I was pleased to be able to introduce her to my neighbour Kate Grimond, Peter Fleming's daughter, who was keen to hear what Kini really thought of her father on their great journey. Had he irritated her? Kini pondered:

'Yes, when he borrowed my toothpaste, and squeezed the *middle* of the tube'.

In 1981 René Fedden and I were in Chandolin and saw much of her. One day at Achala, that chalet always so welcoming to Alpine friends, we all signed a postcard of greetings to another Honorary LAC (later AC) Member, Freya Stark: two great travellers who had early discovered what they wanted to do and, each in her own way, splendidly achieved it.

I last saw Kini in 1994, in Chandolin. We were waiting for the bus that would take me down to St Luc. I started to take her photograph: she, the expert photographer, ordered me to move: 'I must have the Dent Blanche behind me'. When the bus came she bade the driver take care of me and not rush the hairpin bends. Then she asked me to greet Kate Grimond – adding 'I think Peter and I managed very well – you see, we were both very intelligent people'.

Janet Adam Smith

Bernard Pierre 1920-1997

Bernard Pierre, who was elected to membership of the Alpine Club in 1949 on the recommendation of Geoffrey Winthrop Young and who became an Honorary Member in 1981, was a man of many parts. Decorated with the Croix de Guerre for his services in the Second World War, and made an Officer of La Légion d'Honneur and a Doctor at Law, he combined the professions of a banker and a stockbroker. He possessed an expert knowledge of the textile and oil industries and, in all those subjects, his writings were published.

His outstanding literary achievements were as a writer about his climbs and mountaineering expeditions: in the Saharan Hoggar mountains, the Ruwenzori massif, the Caucasus, the Elburz mountains of Iran, the Western Himalaya and the Andes. In the Western Alps he made numerous climbs of a high order of difficulty, his various companions being Lionel Terray, Louis Lachenal, Jean Franco and, most frequently, Gaston Rébuffat. Among some outstanding ascents were the North Ridge of the Aiguille des Deux Aigles and the North Face of the Aiguille Noire de Peuterey by the Voie Ratti.

Further afield, Bernard Pierre was a member of a French expedition which made the first ascent of Nun (7135m) in Kashmir. He led a Franco-Iranian expedition which made the first ascent of Demavand (5671m) by its East Arête. He was a member of the Franco-American expedition which first climbed Salkantay (6271m) in the Peruvian Andes. There are other first ascents to his credit in the Hoggar and Ruwenzori ranges.

Early in his climbing career, in 1947, he met John Barford and Michael Ward, who persuaded him to climb in North Wales. He was elected to membership of the Climbers' Club in 1949 and to honorary membership in 1996. He was a member of the Groupe de Haute Montagne.

In his later years Bernard took to travel writing in the *genre* of Jan Morris, placing on record, in very readable fashion, the stories of some of the great rivers: the Nile, the Mississippi, the Danube and the Ganges.

On a personal note, my climbs with Bernard, apart from a short season in the Dauphiné which included the South Face of the Aiguille Dibona by the Voie Boell with Pierre Allain, were of a less prestigious and more relaxed order. Between 1950 and 1952 he was a regular guest at our house in Fontaine-le-Port on the outskirts of Fontainebleau Forest. Almost every weekend, with other French climbing friends ('*bleausards*') we enjoyed ourselves on the strenuous bouldering climbs in the Forest. He endeared himself to my wife Joy and our French-speaking daughters. That close family relationship, which later embraced his talented and charming wife Roselyne, endured throughout the subsequent years. He was a man of deep affections and marvellous *joie de vivre*.

I shall always be grateful to Bernard for his brilliant translation of *The Ascent of Everest* for the publishers Amiot-Dumont.

John Hunt

Lt Col J O M Roberts, LVO, MBE, MC 1916-1997

Jimmy Roberts, the Himalayan mountaineer and explorer, who had made his home in Pokhara, Nepal, died there in November 1997, aged 81. He was one of the fast-dwindling band of pioneers who not only played a full part in the golden age of Himalayan mountaineering but also made it possible for countless others to experience the joys of trekking in that beautiful range.

Born and brought up in India, he joined the Indian Army in 1937 after education in England. His initiation to the hills was made in the Lake District, Norway and Austria, and he joined the 1st Gurkha Rifles, based at the Punjab hill station Dharamshala, because (in his own words) 'I wanted to climb in the Himalaya – not just one expedition, but a whole lifetime of mountaineering and exploration. It worked.' The Dhaula Dhar range, sweeping to 18,000ft directly above Dharamshala, provided a suitable launching pad. Every weekend or leave would be spent climbing or scrambling on the Mon, Two Gun Peak or the Indrahar Pass, or savouring with his retriever Rumple the solitude and grandeur of the mountains from the hut at Lakha. In 1938 he joined the expedition to Masherbrum (25,660ft) and experienced the dangers of high-altitude mountaineering for the first time. Seeing his companions losing fingers through frostbite strengthened his resolve to temper his own ambitions with necessary caution.

Next year came the war and an end to mountaineering until 1946. Among the first to volunteer for service with the newly-formed 153 Gurkha Parachute Battalion, he commanded the first operational drop into Burma, winning the Military Cross. Later he fought in the desperate hand-to-hand battle at Sangshak when the Japanese advance into India was halted. Roberts led a counter-attack, forcing the enemy off the perimeter. In their official account, the Japanese said they had been fought 'to a standstill'. Typically, he never mentioned these events, even to his friends.

After the war, long spells of leave were not difficult to get. Roberts made full use of such opportunities. In Kulu, he made the first ascent of White Sail Peak (21,148ft). According to Harish Kapadia, he was the first to enter the Spiti mountains, where he made the first ascent of Dharmsura. Kapadia also records him as being the first to explore Saser Kangri. In 1947 he led an expedition to that peak. Later that year he joined me for two memorable months climbing in the Alps. In glorious weather, we climbed ten major and many lesser peaks, several such as the Weisshorn, Dom-Täschhorn, Piz Palü, and the Matterhorn (via the Zmutt ridge) by traverse.

In 1952 Roberts was considered, among others, for leadership of the 1953 Everest expedition, though I doubt if he ever knew of this. Later, John Hunt asked him to bring up the vital oxygen cylinders, the transportation of which had been delayed. At Base Camp John Hunt invited him to join the expedition, but Roberts declined and instead went alone to explore the area to the east of Lukla, where he made the first ascent of Mera (21,247ft). The following year he achieved another first ascent, that of Hiunchuli (23,782ft) in West Nepal.

By then he was commanding the Western Gurkha Recruiting Depot at Lehra, from which, on a clear day, the spectacular peak of Machapuchare (22,950ft) could be seen. We were both drawn to it; our letters proposing an attempt crossed in the post. While I organised the expedition in the UK, Roberts made a reconnaissance, discovering the large unmapped area to the south of Annapurna, now known as the Annapurna Sanctuary and a popular trek objective. He also saw the lower part of what he hoped would be a feasible route up Machapuchare ('The Fish Tail').

Next year, under his leadership, the expedition forced a route from the north to the foot of the final great precipitous North Face. The lead climbers, Noyce and Cox, made a valiant attempt on the summit, retreating only 150ft below it when hard snow turned to blue ice, making step cutting too slow for the top to be reached before an approaching storm threatened to cut off their descent. Earlier, Roger Chorley had become paralysed with polio. Roberts organised his evacuation and accompanied the party carrying him to the hospital in Pokhara. Roberts returned, but by then had missed much of the climb. It was a typically unselfish gesture.

In 1960 Roberts led the successful British/Indian/Nepalese expedition to the last unclimbed 26,000ft peak, Annapurna II (26,041ft). This was the first of Chris Bonington's many Himalayan first ascents.

After three years (1958-61) as Military Attaché in Kathmandu, Roberts decided to settle in Nepal. He retired from the Army and set up the first trekking agency, Mountain Travel. He believed that the delights of trekking could be enjoyed by a wider public, not just by climbers. He was right.

Mountain Travel prospered and soon became a multi-million dollar business. This was not to Roberts' liking; he preferred dealing personally with individuals, discussing their needs and tailor-making their treks, advising on routes, choosing the sirdar, Sherpas and porters. So he sold the business, but retained a directorship. His initiative started an industry which has become a major source of income for Nepal. There are now no fewer than 350 trekking agencies in the country, but Mountain Travel (now, after a commercial merger with Tiger Tops, called Tiger Mountain) is the most experienced and prestigious.

In 1963 he joined the American Everest expedition as its logistics organiser, and helped that party to make the first traverse of the summit. Later, in 1971, Norman Dyhrenfurth asked Roberts to join his International Everest Expedition, this time as joint leader. The tensions which arose from the multinational composition of the party made for a far-from-happy expedition, and Roberts admitted that his 'childish' belief that all climbers were gentlemen was severely shaken.

Roberts retired from the Army in 1961, after a distinguished military career. He had won the Military Cross and was mentioned in dispatches in the campaign in Burma; he was made MBE for his part in the Emergency campaign in Malaya against the communist terrorists and again mentioned in dispatches. In 1961 he was made MVO (later converted to LVO) for helping to arrange the visit of HM The Queen to Nepal, and he received the Nepalese decoration Gorkha Dakshina Bahu for accompanying HM The King of Nepal on his state visit to Britain.

In retirement in Pokhara, Roberts built a house and started a pheasant farm, breeding rare species for their conservation. He spent his last years with the latest generation of his Rumples* among the people he loved, Gurkhas and Sherpas, in the land he loved, in full view of his much-loved Machapuchare, the Fish Tail. There he was visited by his many friends, from notables such as HRH The Prince of Wales, to the lowliest of Sherpas, all of whom held him in the highest esteem.

Shy, modest, but kindly, charming and courteous, he was at heart a loner and shunned publicity. He had great inner strength and was happy to live by his own judgements and values. Genial and generous, with a keen sense of humour, he held forthright opinions, had no time for humbug, and was not slow to say so. Latterly, he was afflicted by ill-health. After three hip operations, he needed regular painkillers which made it necessary to have blood transfusions, some 'on draught' direct from Sherpa donors. Typically, he made light of these burdens and never complained.

Jimmy Roberts had a profound influence on trekking and mountaineering in Nepal, where he was acknowledged to be the most experienced figure in that area of activity. He was also universally respected for the integrity of his character and achievements. A plane was chartered to bring his many friends from Kathmandu to his funeral in Pokhara. The King of Nepal sent a personal message of condolence. In accordance with his wishes,

* As one dog died, Jimmy's next dog was called by the same name. The latest has been taken in by Bobby, the Gurung boy who looked after Jimmy latterly.

Jimmy Roberts was cremated on the banks of the Seti River which flows from his beloved Machapuchare.

Charles Wylie

Robin Hodgkin writes:
In 1938 Jimmy Roberts and two Gurkhas made a rapid journey across the Deosai Plains to catch up the main Masherbrum party just above the Shyok junction. We had a feast that night – curried chicken, with green Chartreuse from Grenoble. Jimmy's energy, wit and sparkle were very good for us. Though he and I only occasionally met in later years, we remained close friends. With his family connections with General Bruce and Wilfrid Noyce and his early love of mountains, one felt that he was destined for a life in the great mountains and with mountain people.

I remember him, vividly, thirty years later in Pokhara. Talk about expeditions, sweet and sour, about Tiger Tops, the future of trekking, his fancy pheasant farm; all to do with his ideas and hopes for his adopted clan of Sherpas. Four of them gave me a wonderful trip round the southern slopes and valleys of Annapurna. Much of the Sherpa's guts, integrity and fun was reflected in Jimmy's wrinkled glance; something too of the grace and greatness of the hills – Machapuchare rising sublimely above the mists to the north.

John Cleare writes:
Jimmy Roberts was the unassuming genius of the Himalayan Golden Age and for nearly thirty years his name would be mentioned in awed tones by young mountaineers and trekkers in Nepal. It is said in Kathmandu that had he not actually made the first ascent of any particular peak, it was probably he who had first noticed it, first explored the route to it and made the first serious reconnaissance of its slopes. Though he found time for all who cared to consult him and obviously delighted in discussing their plans, he showed little patience for arrogance or those he sensed as glory-seekers. Low-key and comparatively unsung himself, he once complained that the very number of modern Himalayan expeditions and the accompanying publicity and ballyhoo had devalued mountaineering to the status of league football.

Jimmy was interested in everything appertaining to the mountains, from birds and flowers to people and photography, and proved delightful company on the march, taking great pains to explain everything that was new or strange to a young whipper-snapper on his first Himalayan expedition.

My first contact with Jimmy was in the late sixties when, with the Nepalese mountains closed for climbing, he had been invited to lead a future International Expedition to Dhaulagiri, in which I was involved. Thus I knew him on paper – I knew his terse yet humorous writing – before I eventually met him in person in 1971. By this time the expedition had changed its objective to Everest's then-virgin South-West Face. In due course it amalgamated with Norman Dyhrenfurth's American team with the same goal, and by the time it eventually took the field it had become the sort of enterprise about which Jimmy must have had considerable qualms. The 1971 International Expedition reached Base Camp with 24 members from 13 countries, led jointly by Dyhrenfurth and Jimmy Roberts and followed by huge media interest. It was hardly Jimmy's style.

Despite prolonged bad weather and rampant sickness, the lead climbers, Whillans and Haston, pushed to within 1500ft of the top but unfortunately several of the team proved to be incompatible prima donnas. For my own part, this had been my first taste of a big expedition and I returned home wiser but, like all of us, with incredible respect for Jimmy Roberts. He had been a pillar of calmness, common sense and dispassion when all that had once seemed a noble enterprise was collapsing around us. But it was the end of his active mountaineering for he was already in considerable pain from damaged hips and several times he returned to England for hip replacements.

Always he would share his encyclopaedic knowledge of Nepal. Aware that expensive permits and complex bureaucracy were inhibiting small, frugal, expeditions climbing in his own style, he would advise that a basic permit to *trek to a viewpoint* – rather than to *expedition to a mountain* – might with discretion cover a multitude of sins. 'I've pointed many small trekking parties – who I happen to know are competent climbers – at interesting unclimbed peaks,' he once told me 'and I just happen to know too that there've been ropes and crampons and ice-screws in their porters' baskets. And as long as the peaks aren't big or famous I've not asked embarrassing questions.' He added 'Never be surprised to find a cairn on a supposedly virgin summit.'

But that state of affairs could never last and eventually Jimmy persuaded the Tourist Ministry to release eighteen so-called Trekking Peaks up to 22,000ft in height which could be attempted with a minimum of formality, several of them officially unclimbed at the time and many of them still serious undertakings today. Needless to say it revolutionised the ethos of climbing in Nepal – and indeed in the other Himalayan countries.

Many climbers of my generation owe him much, not least our enjoyment of and our attitude towards Himalayan mountaineering. It was a very special experience to sit with Jimmy into the small hours, sipping a dram or two, talking of a subject dear to us both, until Machapuchare – his mountain – took shape in the approaching dawn. It was a great privilege to have known Jimmy Roberts.

Lyman Spitzer 1914 -1997

Lyman Spitzer, Jr. was born in Toledo, Ohio on June 26, 1914 and died in Princeton, NJ on March 31, 1997. He attended Yale University and earned a Doctorate from Princeton in 1938, spending a formative year at Cambridge along the way. During the Second World War he was the director of a sonar analysis group for the US Navy. In 1947 he returned to Princeton as Chairman of the Department of Astronomy and Director of the Observatory. During the 32 years he held these positions he built one of the world's leading programs in astrophysics. He received many academic honours, including the rare distinction of foreign membership in the Royal Society of London, the Gold Medal of the Royal Astronomical Society, the US National Medal of Science and the prestigious Crafoord Prize of the Swedish Academy of Sciences.

He pioneered the study of the dynamics of stellar systems and the structure of the gas between the stars. He was a leader in developing magnetic confinement for controlled thermonuclear fusion, and founded the Princeton Plasma Physics Laboratory. In 1946 he published a prescient paper on "Astronomical Advantages of an Extra-Terrestrial Observatory", which developed the concept of space-based telescopes, and for the next forty years carefully shepherded his brainchild to fruition. These efforts culminated with the launch of the Hubble Space Telescope in 1990 (an early version was known as the LST or Large Space Telescope, but many astronomers claimed the initials stood for Lyman Spitzer's Telescope). He continued to conduct research up to the day of his death.

Lyman began climbing on trips to Zermatt and the Tetons. Then around 1964 his climbing entered a more technical phase through association with colleagues on weekends in the Shawangunks, trips to the White Sands Missile Range in New Mexico and ice climbing in Huntington Ravine on Mt Washington, in New Hampshire.

In 1965 he participated in an Alpine Club of Canada expedition to Baffin Island. There he climbed Mt Asgard and made the first ascent of Mt Thor, which he did by the north ridge with Don Morton. Afterwards Lyman walked alone some 32 miles down the Weasel Valley and along the fiord to the town of Pangnirtung in order to return home ahead of the rest of the expedition. In 1967 he joined George Wallerstein and other astronomical colleagues in the Canadian Rocky Mountains east of Prince George, BC. There he made first ascents of Mt Walrus, Mt Petrie, and Mt Plaskett, the latter two named by the climbers after two prominent Canadian astronomers. Lyman returned to Canada in 1970 to climb Mt Waddington from the Tiedemann Glacier.

His climbing activity accelerated rapidly after his retirement in 1979. He travelled twice to the Dolomites, where he made guided ascents of the Sella Towers, Cima della Madonna, Rosetta Peak, Vajolet Towers, and many others. He also visited many climbing areas in the United States, including the Flat Irons, Eldorado Canyon, Lumpy Ridge and the Jackson-Johnson route on Hallet's Peak in Colorado, Seneca Rocks in West Virginia, the Needles in South Dakota, White Horse and Cathedral Ledges in New Hampshire, Devil's Tower in Wyoming, the Kor-Ingalls Route on Castleton Tower in Utah and Joshua Tree in California, as well as many routes in the Shawangunks. In 1976 the Princeton University authorities were unsettled to find him climbing Cleveland Tower, the high point of the campus. He spent hundreds of days climbing at the Shawangunks, where he led climbs up to 5.8 in difficulty. This activity contributed to the case for his election as a member of the Alpine Club at age 70 and he continued to climb until age 80.

He also climbed and hiked extensively with his wife Doreen (née Canaday), their four children, and their grandchildren; two of his grandchildren are enthusiastic climbers and to commemorate this influence his family wore climbing slings at his memorial service. Lyman had a very long reach – both physically and metaphorically – which he used to good advantage. He treated everyone the same, regardless of age, power, or title, with unfailing quiet courtesy, rigid integrity, ruthless intolerance of sloppy thinking, and a touch of humour and rebellion. His lucidity of scientific exposition and enthusiasm for mountaineering – as well as music, good food and many other activities – will be fondly remembered by all who knew him. Many of his friends and colleagues regard him as a role model for both their personal and professional life.

Scott Tremaine & Sverre Aarseth

Hamish Gordon Nicol 1929-1997

Hamish Nicol, outstanding alpinist of the immediate post-war generation, died on 17 May. He was above all an enthusiast, for mountains, for climbing – no weather was ever too foul; for his family; for his work – 'being a GP is the best job in the world'; for singing, with the local choral society; for fishing, writing, mountain biking in the Cotswolds, canoeing in Canada; and for his friends. His forthright and attractive personality, and his care for others, made him very many friends. Seven hundred people, climbers, patients, colleagues, friends and family, attended his funeral in Stratford upon Avon. For most, if not all of us, he is unforgettable.

He was born in Hong Kong, was sent to school in England but evacuated to Canada in 1940 with his mother, while his father returned to Hong Kong in time to be interned by the Japanese. Living in Edinburgh after the war, he attended Fettes (which he disliked) and at the age of 17 went to Edinburgh University to read English, French and Economics. It was here that he was first initiated into mountaineering, but his fascination with mountains and climbing had begun ten years earlier. It was no doubt prompted by the fact that his father was a keen hill walker. While still at Fettes, sent to a summer French course at Grenoble, Hamish had made a start; he climbed the Croix de Belledonne with an equally inexperienced friend. Afterwards, he recorded, 'the only thing I now wanted to be was a first-class mountaineer'.

National Service intervened in 1947 and gave him further opportunities for climbing; he was commissioned in the Royal Artillery. He went up to

Balliol in 1949, flirted briefly with Geology, and then switched to Medicine which was indeed his true *métier*. On arrival in Oxford, with an active Alpine season just past and much varied Scottish experience already behind him, he joined the OUMC and at once made his presence felt. The general standard at that time was not high, the occasional Severe being the limit of many members' ambition. Hamish, with Tom Bourdillon, aimed higher. Their 1950 Alpine season, during which they made first British ascents, guideless of course, of the West Face of the Purtscheller, the Roc-Grépon traverse and the North Face of the Petit Dru, was an inspiration to British alpinists, signalling their ability to tackle the fine rock routes put up by continental climbers between the wars.

At Easter 1951, attempting the unclimbed Zero Gully on Ben Nevis with the primitive equipment of those days, Hamish came off, the ice-piton belays failed, and he and Anthony Rawlinson fell some 600ft. Carried unconscious to Fort William, they were lucky to escape with their lives. Hamish suffered a fractured skull, with consequent deafness in one ear. His enthusiasm was undimmed and that summer, he did the Mer de Glace of the Grépon with John Sims, returning home frustrated at the lack of more challenging opportunities in a poor season. Next year in the Alps he had another mishap, when his companion tripped while they were moving together on an ice slope and pulled him down the Envers des Aiguilles glacier into a crevasse. Hamish was slightly concussed and broke his jaw badly. This was a disaster, as he himself related: 'A successful 1952 season would have strengthened my claims for a place on Everest in 1953. As it was, I could not possibly be considered, having suffered two falls in quick succession ... I was written off as dangerous, and given a place as a reserve.'

Instead of Everest there were several superb Alpine seasons. The list of major routes is impressive: in 1953, the Old Brenva in bad conditions with Mike Cunnington, the West Face of the Pointe Albert (the first ED climbed by a British rope in the Western Alps) with Alan Blackshaw, the South Face of the Aiguille Noire with Pat Vaughan, the NW Ridge of the Grands Charmoz, the South Ridge of the Pointe Gugliermina, the South Face of the Géant, and the Route Major, all with Ted Wrangham. In 1955 he was with Tom Bourdillon again. The weather was variable, but they climbed the North Ridge of the Peigne, the East Ridge of the Crocodile and the West Face of the Noire de Peuterey. It then rained for five days. Having practised the techniques of artificial climbing on an overhanging tree in Tom's Buckinghamshire garden, they were keen to exercise their skills on a suitably taxing climb so, when the rain stopped, they made for the East Face of the Grand Capucin. With deep snow on the ledges, such as they were, it took them a full two days. It was the fifth ascent, but no difficult climb of this type had been done before by British climbers. The West Face of the Petit Dru was also on their list, but icy conditions ruled it out.

The accident in 1956 to Tom Bourdillon and Dick Viney, another close friend, ended Hamish's great period in the Alps. A man of deep feeling, he was profoundly affected by this tragedy, which stayed with him for the rest of his life. Moreover, he was at this time desperate to establish himself in his profession, his student grants having run out, and for this reason had already declined John Hartog's invitation to join his Muztagh Tower party. He did not climb for four years and never returned to the ambitious routes that had previously been his passion.

In 1958 Hamish married Mary Walker, also a doctor. Two years later they went to live in Stratford, joining Dr Archibald McWhinney's practice in Rother Street where he became senior partner in 1982. He loved doctoring. Earlier, he had held appointments as obstetrician/gynaecologist and anaesthetist. While in general practice he took a course in hypnotism, to enable him to help patients with psychological problems. He was casualty officer at Stratford for many years. He extended his medical experience by an exchange for three months with a GP in Adelaide and by being medical officer, sometimes also leader, of several treks in Nepal.

Nicol family holidays were spent skiing, canoeing down French rivers or through the Canadian wilderness, but Hamish's love of the hills, and his restless spirit, would not let him give up climbing for good. He had a modest Alpine season in 1960, and in 1963 did the Firmin-Hicks route on Mount Kenya with Alan Wedgwood and Robert Chambers, going on to climb a new rock route on Point Peter and to ascend Kilimanjaro. Further Alpine seasons followed, but his most notable achievement was his membership of Alan Blackshaw's trans-Alpine ski traverse in 1972, the first by a British party, for which he acted as medical officer, of course skiing the whole way, in spite of being in his own view a mediocre skier. In the 1970s and later, winter ski mountaineering largely took over from the now crowded summer scene.

One of the achievements of which he was most proud was his work with the ambulance service in South Warwickshire. Hamish was of the opinion, not shared by more conservative members of the NHS, that ambulance crews, first on the scene of an accident, should be trained in advanced life-support skills. Against opposition, he devised and implemented a training programme, awarding green arm-bands to those who passed. This was in 1976, ten years before paramedics were generally recognised. His 'Green Bands' undoubtedly saved lives.

He was always very active in British hills, attending meets of the AC and the Climbers' Club and organising many of them. He was the first to leave the hut in the morning, rain or shine, enthusing one or two others to get a move on. Many of his closest friends were members of the Climbers' Club, of which he became President in 1972. His prime achievement as President was the admission of women to the club. The annual Scottish camping and climbing trip, mostly with CC friends, was a highlight of the last several years for those taking part, and it was Hamish who was the mainspring. He was a keen fisherman. Disclaiming any particular expertise (or any need for a fishing licence away from the road), he often supplied his companions with trout which, with suitable quantities of whisky, made for memorable evenings in camp.

Hamish was a great companion on the numerous treks in mountain country in which he took part. In 1965 he was a member of John Hunt's Duke of Edinburgh Award party which climbed in the Tatras. He was with the 'Everest Anniversary' treks of 1978 and 1993. Always quickly away after a halt (to the dismay of some of his companions), he was slowed in recent years by painful osteoarthritis of the hip, but pressed on nevertheless. Two years before the inevitable operation, he climbed Mount Tasman on his 59th birthday, with a guide. After the operation in 1990, he continued active climbing and trekking. No artificial hip has ever had such punishment; the Cradle Mountain–Lake St Clair walk in Tasmania; the Corsican GR20 in 1994 and Nepal again in the autumn; the Tour de Mont Blanc; *via ferrate* in the Dolomites, the Rolwaling in 1996; and of course the usual climbing, walking and mountain biking.

He fell while climbing an old favourite on the Cornish cliffs on Easter Day, and died after a determined fight for life for some weeks. His friends could hardly believe that Hamish had not succeeded in that struggle. We will miss him. He was unique. We will miss the 'dear boy' of his greeting, the stimulus of his company, his beaming face at a party, his strength and encouragement and joy on a climb. Our hearts go out to Mary and her family.

Michael Westmacott

John Hunt writes:

In making the difficult choice of my companions for the 1953 Everest Expedition, I was determined to include a few representatives of the up-and-coming generation of British climbers who, without Himalayan experience, were showing great promise in the Western Alps. Hamish Nicol was on my short-list. He and his companion Tom Bourdillon had earned the respect of leading European mountaineers in the early 1950s by their achievements in the massif of Mont Blanc. I first met them in 1950 at Chamonix, that Mecca of mountaineers, on their return from making the first British ascent of the North Face of the Petit Dru. I vividly recall the impact which that achievement made on the international climbing community.

The competition to join the attempt on Everest was fierce; I finally invited Hamish to be one of the reserves, who would fill unforeseen gaps in the team, and who would join us if, failing in our attempt during the spring of 1953, we decided to launch a second expedition after the monsoon. From that time onwards, Hamish became a member of the Everest 'family' which – alas diminishing – has met to climb and trek and socialise, with our families, ever since. During those reunions, whether in Snowdonia, the Alps, or the Himalaya, I came to appreciate the true qualities of this remarkable man.

There is nothing to compare with the test of facing dangers and difficulties at one end or other of a climbing rope, or of walking across an amphitheatre of high mountains, to appreciate the worth of one's companions. Whether it was during those anniversary meets in North Wales or the Himalaya; or joining Polish or Czech climbers in the High Tatras; or on some cliff or Alpine peak, Hamish always passed that test with flying colours. He possessed dynamic energy and enthusiasm, great physical strength and technical skill, which invigorated his companions. Above all, Hamish was a very human, caring person. I shall remember him, not only for the treks and climbs we shared together, but also for the time we spent in some camp site, where he and his wife Mary would work for hours coping with a surgery of local people, for whose ailments no other medical help was readily available.

I shall recall Hamish grieving when we buried his friend Tom Bourdillon at Visp in Switzerland, after the sad accident which befell Tom and Dick Viney in 1956. I join with all his other friends in grieving for Hamish now.

Thomas Arthur Hardy Peacocke 1907-1996

Tom Peacocke was a member of the Club for 63 years. He had been resident in a nursing home for some time and his death was not unexpected, but with him passed a singular character, a very experienced and devoted mountaineer, and a much loved and respected schoolmaster in the old style.

He was born in India, of a service family. There are photographs of him with his ayah, and already there was the piercing look of purpose and single-mindedness that stayed with him to the end of his life. He was educated at Wellington and University College Oxford, taking his degree in Chemistry, with the intention of teaching. Although subsequently a member of the OUMC and taking part in their meets, he did not go to the Alps until 1928, when he took up a post at a small British-run school at Chateau d'Oex. This gave him his jumping-off point for both climbing and skiing, and he never looked back. He was elected to the Club in 1932, with a long list of routes, mostly guideless, to his credit. His well-known book *Mountaineering*, in the Sportsman's Library series, published in 1941, makes clear the wealth of experience of Alpine and British climbing he had amassed in the previous decade.

During the war he was involved with ski-troop training, principally with the Lovat Scouts in the Cairngorms, then in the Rockies and finally in the Apennine hinterland near Rome. Here he had a narrow escape in a windslab avalanche which killed four men, and in which Tom went over a cliff and said he felt himself very close to death and 'outside his body'.

After the war, he engaged in his main spell of teaching and housemastering at St John's School, Leatherhead. According to a number of his pupils, he was a never-to-be-forgotten teacher of Chemistry (and, one suspects, a very good one). At this time, and later during his last few years teaching, at

Charterhouse, Tom was a regular visitor to South Audley Street. He served on the Committee, and was involved in the organisation of the Centenary celebrations. He continued to climb and ski in the Alps, and took regular parties of boys skiing and climbing, the latter usually in Wales. Richard Owen was invited by a mutual friend to join one of his parties at Helyg in 1960, and records this experience:

'Teatime at the end of our first day was enlivened by the arrival of an avalanche of telegrams for Tom. Some were on the old buff paper, some the new Greetings sort, so whatever it was, it didn't look like an unspeakable disaster. These were being delivered in relays by a breathless youth in a peaked cap on a red Post Office motorbike. Curiosity grew to fever pitch, but well-mannered as we were, nobody had the bottle to ask. So it was Tom who suddenly broke the silence by blurting out 'I suppose I'd better tell you the ghastly truth – I've got engaged to be married.' His exact words, I promise you. The thought lingered all week amongst us that here was one of the great exponents of bachelor schoolmastering who had succumbed graciously and unexpectedly at last, and who had timed the announcement to mischievous perfection.'

In his 60th year Tom had a good season in New Zealand during which he climbed Mt Cook. Later, one of his many contributions to the *Journal* records a circuit in 1977 of the mountains of Andorra, where he and his wife Constance had moved shortly after his retirement. In the last decade of his life, they moved back to this country and settled in South Devon.

Tom was in some ways the quintessential old-fashioned public school master. He had definite ideas as to what was right and what was not, and would express them directly, but with an old-fashioned courtesy. It was predictable that when the Honorary Secretary decided, in 1986, to edge into the modern age and discard the Esq from members' addresses, Tom would be the one to protest. But there was never a trace of stuffiness about him when it came to listening to new ideas, or encouraging younger climbers. He was an enthusiast for what they had done and planned to do. He was truly a gentleman.

Richard Owen & Michael Westmacott

Harry Leighton Stembridge 1902-1997

Harry Stembridge was one of those fortunate men who lived a very full and active life almost to the end. He died peacefully at his home in Crakehall, Bedale, on 12 February 1997 at the age of 94. He was a man of many interests and talents, including water-colour painting, poetry, climbing, skiing, mountaineering, potholing, bird watching, fishing, gardening, cricket, scouting, village life and the activities of his family and friends. But perhaps his outstanding quality was his ability to make friends easily and to encourage young people in whatever was their talent or interest.

Harry joined the family clothing manufacturing business in Leeds, founded by his father, and later became its Managing Director. His first wife died in 1952; they had one son David, who shared his father's interest in the outdoors. Harry married again in 1967; his second wife Betty had three children of her own. The two families soon blended into one very caring unit. Such was the character of the man.

Mountaineering was an abiding interest in Harry's life, which he exploited to the full. Living in Huby, within walking distance of Almscliff Crag, it was not surprising that he and his brother Frank climbed there regularly, particularly as there had been members of Yorkshire Ramblers' Club climbing there since before the turn of the century. In 1949 he published an illustrated guide, *Almscliff, a key to climbs*. Harry also potholed extensively, not only in his native Yorkshire, but also in Northern Ireland where he was involved in the discovery of several new and complex systems. He was also an experienced skier, and his visits to the Alps included ski touring in Austria. He climbed wherever there was rock, be it in England, Scotland or Wales. His ventures abroad included mountaineering in the Lofoten Islands, Pyrenees, Dolomites, Northern Greece and Corsica.

Harry joined the Alpine Club in 1955 after several seasons in the Alps with his brother Frank and other friends. Characteristically he made many friends in the Club and visited a variety of mountain areas with them. On his retirement, in 1960, he took on the role of Liaison Officer for the Duke of Edinburgh Award Scheme and then County Commissioner for Scouts in Central Yorkshire. He was also on the Board of the Outward Bound School in Eskdale.

In 1960 Harry skied the High Level Route from Saas Fee to Forclaz with his son David, Dick Cook, Eric Arnison, Tom Price and Joe Renwick. In 1963 he was in Peru with Alf Gregory, when he and Alf climbed three peaks over 18,000ft, one of which was a first ascent. Their highest summit was Nevada Pisco at about 19,000ft. Then came a visit to the Polish Tatras and a trek to Everest Base Camp with Bob Chadwick and Eric Shipton.

In 1933 he joined the Yorkshire Ramblers' Club, becoming the President from 1954 to 1956. He was elected an Honorary Member in 1977 by acclaim at the Annual General Meeting, an honour he richly deserved. He maintained a special interest in the YRC to the end of his life. I remember as a new member how welcome he made me feel, encouraging me in all aspects of my life.

At the YRC Annual Dinner in 1955, inspired by Charles Evans, the Chief Guest, the idea of a regional club mounting an expedition to the Himalaya was born. Harry provided the enthusiasm and was the driving force, along with Cliff Downham and Stanley Marsden. Eighteen months later the expedition set out for the Jugal Himal, the objective being the 23,255ft Lonpo Gang ('The Great White Peak').

Until a year before his death Harry kept a diary of day-to-day events, days spent roaming the countryside, climbing, recording the wild flowers or unusual birds seen in his lovely garden. During a visit weeks before his death he told me of the happy life he had had and how lucky he had been in it and in his family. He will be sadly missed by his wife Betty, children David, Patrick, Madeleine, Katherine and by his grandchildren. He will, I am sure, not be forgotten by his many friends in the climbing world, and in the village of Crakehall.

David Smith

Sybil Washington 1916-1995

Sybil was born into a family of military traditions. Her father, General Cameron, fought at Omdurman, commanded in India and had postings in Northern Ireland and Dover Castle. Sybil was educated at Bath and Edinburgh University. In 1942 she married Peter Washington, a farmer in Berkshire.

Early climbing was in the Dachstein. Later, as part of her degree course, she spent a year in Geneva. There she climbed on the Salève and had weekends in Chamonix. Returning to Edinburgh she discovered Scottish climbing. Holidays were snatched from farm and family and she climbed many classics in Scotland. There were also marathon drives to Wales and the Lakes.

The return to the Alps was in 1946. The weather was not kind but it was a happy visit. As her family became more independent, Alpine holidays became regular events and from 1961 she climbed in the Alps most years. Zermatt was a fine centre and so was Saas Fee. Other areas she visited were the Bernina, Bregaglia, Chamonix and the Dauphiné. The Dom was hard work in 1975 but the next year she found form in the Alpes Maritimes. She also made one visit to the Pyrenees.

Age began to bite but she still enjoyed walks in the Val Ferret, from Almagell and especially from La Grave and Ailefroide. Her last trip was in 1992. The weather was cold but the views of the Meije were wonderful as ever. Walking was helped by the use of two sticks, but the joy was still there.

A H Hendry

Malcolm R D Duff

Mal Duff was a great driver. In the mid-80s the track up to Ben Nevis was used for time trials. Keys had been obtained, not necessarily from the Forestry Commission who were regarded as an objective danger. The record from the dam at the top to the start of the tarmac was 14 minutes. I often put my helmet on before getting into Mal's car. The rush of adrenalin started early when you were climbing with Mal. The fun often carried on late into the night as he was never known to turn down the possibility of a party. He would have loved his funeral. Police sealed off his home village of Culross in Fife and the church was packed with his friends and family. Meanwhile, at the same time, in Everest Base Camp where Mal died peacefully of a heart attack on 23 April, a group of clients and fellow guides gathered to drink whisky and tell stories about their friend and sing increasingly incoherent renditions of 'Flower of Scotland'.

Mal hated being bored. Underneath the sleepy eyes was a hyperactive brain. An unimaginative guide can make his job tedious both for himself and his clients. If you were a client of Mal's you were likely to find yourself on new ground. He was one of the very best west coast Scottish winter climbers, excelling at all types of climbing. *Un Poco Loco*, with Andy Cave, climbs very steep ground near *Crypt Route* on Bidean Nam Bian in Glencoe, *Postman Pat* on Creag Meagaidh climbed with Andy Perkins involves super-steep icicle climbing. *Point Blank* and *Ring the Alarm* on Ben Nevis climb very thinly-iced slabs. All were well-known problems. Other, easier new routes, including several grade Vs, were climbed with clients. Some clients, such as Andy Cave, Tony Brindle and Sandy Allan, went on to become fine guides themselves.

For Mal, the Scottish winter would always be his first love. However, the Himalaya beckoned, where the resilience, strength and mountain sense gained in Scotland really served him well. Nepal, and especially the Khumbu, was his favourite area, although he did once go to Pakistan and make the second ascent of Mustagh Tower. His climbing CV was notably well-rounded in these days of 8000-metre tickers.

Amongst other achievements he reached the summits of Cho Oyu and Shisha Pangma with clients, climbed a technical new route Alpine style with Ian Tattersall on Mera, reached the summit of Pumori with his wife Liz and climbed a new route on Parchamo with Joe Simpson, after which they were both lucky to survive a 600ft fall.

He also had some excellent failures, the lot of anyone learning the Himalayan game. Attempts on Nuptse, first with Brian Sprunt, then with Sandy Allan, and on Lhotse Shar, again with Sandy Allan, were fine attempts by two men climbing Alpine style. So it was inevitable that he wouldn't try Everest the easy way. The first attempt after the deaths of Joe Tasker and Peter Boardman on the unclimbed North-East Ridge of Everest in 1985 reached 8200m and was regarded, by the fairly inexperienced team, as a relative success, as there had been no accidents and everyone came back friends. Mal went back, to try the Normal Route in the winter of 1993 with a group of regular and territorial army soldiers. The expedition reached the South Col but was literally blown off the mountain, a storm destroying every tent above Base Camp.

That trip led to Mal joining the Territorial SAS. He was over the maximum age for applying but got a special dispensation and had no problem passing selection. After all, he said, walking up hills with a big rucksack was what he did for a living. His chosen speciality was as a medic which involved periods of training at casualty departments of hospitals, work he found fascinating.

Some other things about Mal: he was a fiercely patriotic Scot; it was fun to innocently ask him where he had been born (Kenya). He did not have an ounce of malice in him. He was near the very top of his profession and had the respect of his few peers. He was best man at my wedding, putting in many painstaking hours of preparation to ensure everything went smoothly. He was a fine man and many people will miss him.

Jon Tinker

Brendan Joseph Murphy 1963-1997

Climbers often take on the characteristics of the mountains and cliffs that they love, or vice versa. Nick Dixon's routes are thin, John Dunne's are large in character and stature and Dawes's are quirky, bold and slightly insane. In mountaineering terms, the extraordinary climbs of Brendan Murphy rank alongside the achievements of the leading stars mentioned yet, like the mountains he climbed, they were relatively unknown to the wider population.

Brendan was a legend in his own lifetime amongst the tight-knit group of mountaineers operating away from the 8000m circus, at the very highest levels on steep technical terrain, applying the techniques of Scottish winter and Alpine face to the Himalaya.

Even amongst that small family, Brendan rarely talked of his own achievements. Much of the material for this obituary has come from its other members: Rob Durran (with whom Bren did the first Irish winter ascent of the North Face of the Eiger), Dave Wills (first complete winter ascent of *Divine Providence* and two attempts on the North Ridge of Latok I), Andy Cave (first ascent of the North Face of Changabang) and of course his long-standing partner Kate Phillips (with whom he made the first Irish ascent of Ama Dablam).

If he was reticent to talk about his own achievements or difficulties with his peers, amongst strangers he was modest almost to the point of secrecy. Some climbers met him last winter, reading a book in the café in Fort William. Asking him what he'd done elicited the response 'Oh, you know – had a good day.' Further questioning revealed that this 'good day' had involved driving solo from Cambridge overnight, dossing by the roadside, then soloing *Minus One* and *Astral Highway*. The following day he soloed *Galactic Hitch-hiker* and then drove back to Cambridge where he had a Ph.D in Computer Sciences and was working as a research scientist in high level networking systems.

His steady solid climbing style was ideally suited to the uncertain world of snow and ice climbing, yet he was no slouch as a rock climber either, having incredible strength and stamina 'for a mountaineer'. He was once established just below the crux of *Lord of the Flies* when a party arrived to do the Corner. They duly completed the route and abbed off two hours later, with Bren still hanging at the crux making absolutely sure the key sideways hex runner was placed to his satisfaction before committing himself (successfully, of course) to the crux in incredibly hot and greasy conditions.

This resistance to poor conditions was a legendary Murphy trait, though it more often applied to extremes of cold and wet than heat. He would simply appear to be unaffected by conditions where the rest of us would be seriously worried about long-term survival. During his first winter ascent of the Eiger, the weather conditions went completely pear-shaped on the third day. He and Rob Durran pressed on, with Brendan producing brews by holding the stove between his knees inside a bivvy bag. On Ama Dablam, it was his apparent lack of concern at the snowfall and poor visibility which gave Kate the confidence to push on to the summit. To this day, I cannot decide whether he felt the same discomfort, pain and fear as the rest of us in those marginal situations that mountaineering so often presents us with. I rather suspect that he did, but his equanimity, calm and positive approach enabled him to stay chilled out in situations that he liked to refer to as 'good sport' or 'character-building'.

Whether on the hill or off it, this strength of character made him a unique person to be with, as his semi-detached (from reality) attitude would result in all sorts of excitement. He was so often late in turning up from down south for rock-climbing weekends that the phrase 'The Late Brendan Murphy' still makes me laugh (when he arrived he would always have a daysack full of lager with him). He frequently ran out of petrol, the last time being on our way back from the Alps at Christmas, yet for Murphy this was just another opportunity to build our characters.

He was always losing things; his wallet and passport falling out of his rucksack strapped to the back of a motorbike on the way to catch a flight to Spain; his watch on the floor of a base camp shelter, every hour it would bleep, followed by a frantic couple of minutes searching in the darkness.

Kate tells a classic Murphy story where, after berating her for leaving her wallet in the Grindleford café, he then left his trousers in Outside, lost his car keys at Froggatt and then locked both his spare key and his pit in the car. Throughout all these minor epics, he remained totally unfazed, as if he knew that, whatever happened, it would all be okay.

This faith in a positive outcome to problems extended to his dealings with people, and earned him respect from a wider community than just the people with whom he climbed. In all the years that I climbed with Brendan, I never heard him utter a bad word about anyone, even Captain Camembert, the liaison officer from hell on our Gasherbrum IV trip in 1993. His rapport with the porters and other locals was obvious, evidence of a deep concern for their welfare. He provided many novice climbers at the Cambridge University MC with heaps of encouragement, enthusing them through his own positive approach. Good looking and charismatic, he attracted lots of attention from women, and people of all ages, genders and walks of life found him easy to talk to. Even London yuppies, focused on the complexities of financial dealings in the City, found him 'almost human – with very nice teeth'.

Bren's own finances were remarkably uncomplicated. His tastes were simple and unpretentious, his gear was always well-worn and he was happy to live on cheese toasties, coffee and wine. His money went on trips to go climbing, whether by motorbike to the Lakes, by car to Scotland, or by plane to the Himalaya.

It is those very special climbing days which will endure, above all the time we spent together on the North West Face of Cerro Kishtwar in autumn 1991. Lost rucksacks, an approach through Ladakh to avoid the unrest in Kashmir, an encounter with a psychotic American trekker in Zanskar, and 17 days of the most technical mixed climbing imaginable, in capsule style, made this the most enjoyable trip of my life. Throughout the entire expedition, even when we made the desperately difficult decision to turn back on day 15, just 150m from the summit, he retained that perfect blend of determination mixed with calm in the face of adversity.

I am convinced that he retained this inner peace and calm approach even as he was struck by the avalanche that carried him to his death. It is the one comfort that I can take from this appalling loss.

Like artists whose work only becomes valuable after their deaths, Bren's achievements were just starting to be recognised at the time that he left for his second attempt on the North Face of Changabang. Climbed in pure Alpine style, it epitomised his approach to mountaineering and the character traits demanded by such an outrageous route, climbed in weather conditions that could only be described as character-building. It will remain as a monument to one of the finest mountaineers of the last decade.

Andy Perkins

Malcolm Rutherford 1941-1997

Malcolm Rutherford distinguished himself on some long and demanding alpine climbs well before his election to the Alpine Club. But, with some exceptions, his companions had usually been service colleagues so, until his election to the Club committee, this kindly and very accomplished man was not widely known to members.

The son of a former Chief Constable, Malcolm began a life-long love affair with Scottish hills while still at Gordonstoun on a two-year naval scholarship. A school expedition to the Austrian Alps and several successive summers with the RNMC in the Valais and elsewhere were precursors to an outstanding season in 1962. With Nick Estcourt (they had all but started their climbing careers together) he went first to the Atlas and then to the Bernina and Bregaglia for a veritable feast of classic climbs. Moving next to Mont Blanc, and by now supremely fit, they climbed the south ridge of the Aiguille Noire de Peuterey, bivouacking on the summit, before tackling the Grandes Jorasses by the Arête des Hirondelles. 'Inclement weather' (sic) denied them this prize but not their next route, Mont Blanc by the Peuterey Ridge, made more memorable by a bivouac in a severe storm, a second night in the Vallot hut and descent via the Dôme du Goûter to Courmayeur. He was still barely 21. As often as not facilitated by service afloat, Malcolm lost no opportunity to widen his experience with visits to Greece, the Chilean Andes, Patagonia and Norway, soon adding skiing and ski mountaineering to his repertoire. Throughout, he was an enthusiastic member of the RNMC, serving as Honorary Secretary, Chairman and, for the last ten years of his naval career, President of what by then had become the Royal Navy & Royal Marines Mountaineering Club. Already a valued committee member of the Alpine Ski Club, he was elected to the committee of the Alpine Club in 1991, chairing the House Sub-Committee from 1992 to 1993 and bearing much of the considerable burden involved in the Club's move to new premises.

Malcolm Rutherford's naval career began conventionally enough at Dartmouth. 35 years later it culminated in his promotion to Vice-Admiral to take charge of the defence systems and equipment programme for all three services, as well as assuming the role of Chief Naval Engineer Officer. As a young lieutenant, his external London degree in electrical engineering had been augmented by a diploma in nuclear reactor engineering, a passport to ten absorbing years, afloat and ashore, in the submarine service. Always the opportunist, he also qualified as a naval diver and, somewhat out of context perhaps but very happily, completed the Italian interpreter's course, part of it in Florence where he met Fleur, his future wife.

Alongside his proven engineering skills lay a developing talent for people, which was to be recognised in subsequent appointments carrying increasingly senior rank. An exceptionally difficult tri-service task during the Gulf War led to his appointment as CBE, yet he and Fleur still found the energy and time to cycle the length of France. Two years previously he had competed in both the London and New York marathons. Uniquely for an engineer, Malcolm's next post was that of Naval Secretary with the rank of Rear Admiral and, two years later, it came as no surprise when he was promoted to Vice-Admiral. In all these jobs Malcolm's outgoing character and clear thinking endeared him to his colleagues, while his exceptional talent with people won the confidence of all three services. His naval climbing chums of all ranks had long held him in similar regard: 'inspirational', 'tremendously supportive', 'you always knew where you stood with him'. His close involvement with the higher management of the Joint Service Everest Expeditions of 1988 and 1992 was a natural consequence. In typical Rutherford style he trekked to the Everest area with Mike Kefford's 1992 party, accompanied by Fleur, and climbed Island Peak for good measure. 1996 brought success to the Services on Gasherbrum I under Malcolm's chairmanship. He, more than anyone, must have been thrilled by the success of the RN & RMMC on Gimmigela in 1997.

Some months after taking up his last appointment he and Fleur joined several of us on holiday in Corsica. But he was not well and a brain tumour was diagnosed soon after his return home. Astonishingly, a bare six weeks after major surgery, Malcolm was back at his desk showing the same determination and courage which were ever his hallmarks. The discomfort and anxiety of the ensuing treatments he bore with cheerful fortitude, continuing to appear regularly at Charlotte Road and at the RGS ... and taking up golf. He retired from the Navy in 1996 and joined GEC-Marconi briefly as director of its defence systems division.

His death, at 56, is a severe loss to the Club for, had he lived, Malcolm would surely have served it well. The loss to his adored family is incalculable. His many friends will remember him, strong, modest, humorous, invariably courteous, always considerate. There was no malice in him. He was, truly, a man for all seasons.

John Peacock
with thanks to Steve Jackson, RN&RMMC

Sir Charles Evans 1918-1995

Tony Trower adds a personal tribute to those in last year's volume:
I would like to make one small addition to the wonderful and justifiable tributes which have been paid to Charles Evans. I count myself among the most fortunate members of the Alpine Club that I climbed with him in the Alps in 1947 and 1949 and in Kulu in 1951 when we failed to get to the top of Deo Tibba. Because of his commitment to this little expedition, he felt unable to accept an invitation to participate in the Everest Reconnaissance – so typical of him.

I spent a delightful hour with him and Denise and Peter within the last three months of his life. It is a joy to my wife and me that the friendship endures into the next generation between Chuck and Caroline and my eldest son and his wife.

Alpine Club Notes

OFFICERS AND COMMITTEE FOR 1998

President	Sir Christian Bonington CBE
Vice Presidents	L N Griffin
	Dr M J Esten
Honorary Secretary	G D Hughes
Honorary Treasurer	A L Robinson
Honorary Librarian	D J Lovatt
Honorary Editor	Mrs J Merz
Committee Elective Members	D D Clark-Lowes
	Col M H Kefford
	W H O'Connor
	K Phillips
	W J Powell
	D W Walker
	J F C Fotheringham
	J M O'B Gore
	A Vila
Extra Committee Members	Ed Douglas
	M W Fletcher
	G C Holden

OFFICE BEARERS

Librarian Emeritus	R Lawford
Honorary Archivist	Miss L Gollancz
Honorary Keeper of the Club's Pictures	P Mallalieu
Honorary Keeper of the Club's Artefacts	R Lawford
Honorary Keeper of the Club's Monuments	D J Lovatt
Chairman of the Finance Committee	R F Morgan
Chairman of the Guidebooks Editorial & Production Board	L N Griffin
Chairman of the House Committee	M H Johnston
Chairman of the Library Council	G C Band
Chairman of the Membership Committee	M W Fletcher
Assistant Editors of the *Alpine Journal*	J L Bermúdez
	G W Templeman

Assistant Honorary Secretaries:

Annual Winter Dinner	M H Johnston

ALPINE CLIMBING GROUP

GENERAL, INFORMAL, AND CLIMBING MEETINGS 1997

14 January	General Meeting: Simon Clark, *Pumasillo*
21 January	Informal Meeting: Jerry Gore *Greenland*
11 February	General Meeting: Dave Wills, *Latok – No Success Like Failure*
18 February	Informal Meeting: Rupert Hoare, *More Alpine Classics*
25 February	Informal Meeting: Jim Perrin, *Don Whillans – So I 'it 'im*
11 March	General Meeting: Alan Hinkes, *Climbing the 8000ers*
18 March	Informal Meeting: Nick Clinch, *The Land of Up and Down*
22-23 March	ACG/AC Aviemore Winter Dinner and Meet
25 March	Informal Meeting: Ed Douglas, *The Hand of Fatima*
5-6 April	North Wales Regional Dinner, Lecture and Meet
15 April	General Meeting: Elaine Brook, *Nepal*
22 April	Informal Meeting: Derek Walker, *Don't leave it too late, matey!*
29 April	Informal Meeting: Sir John Johnson, *The Simien Mountains*
13 May	General Meeting: Lindsay Griffin, *Sikkim in 1996*
17-18 May	Derbyshire Meet and Informal Dinner: Roger Mear, *Antarctic since 1985*
20 May	Informal Meeting: Steve Jackson, *British Services Gasherbrum I Expedition*
21 May	Alpine Ski Club Lecture: Rachel Duncan, *Spitsbergen*
27 May	Informal Meeting: Ernst Sondheimer, *A Plant Addict in the Eastern Himalaya*
10 June	General Meeting: Roy Ruddle & Mike Pescod, *The Club's Caucasus Meet*
26 July-16 Aug	Alpine meet: Randa, Zermatt Valley (with ABMSAC & CC)

28 Aug-8 Sept	Cornwall Meet (jointly with CC)
9 September	General Meeting: Mick Fowler, *North Face of Changabang*
23 September	Informal Meeting: Larry Foden, *British Services Gimmigela Expedition*
27-28 Sept	Lakes Meet and out of London Dinner Lecture: Chris Bonington, *Sepu Kangri – Unknown Tibet*
8 October	Alpine Ski Club Lecture: Stephen Goodwin, *Remote Turkey*
14 October	General Meeting: Paul Pritchard, *reading from* 'Deep Play' *and talking about the Ak-Su region of Kyrghyzstan*
18 October	Ski Mountaineering Symposium (with ASC and ESC)
28 October	Informal Meeting: Alpine Meet evening
1 November	Annual Symposium and Meet at Plas y Brenin, *South America*
11 November	General Meeting: Peter Berg, *Scrambles Amongst the Alps*
25 November	Val d'Aosta Evening, *Skyrunning*
12 December	Annual General Meeting John Harding, *A Traveller's Miscellany*

The Annual London Dinner was held on 13 December at The Great Hall, St Bartholomew's Hospital. The principal guest was Paul Piana. The toast to the guests was proposed by Jerry Gore.

THE ALPINE CLUB LIBRARY 1997

There have been three Council meetings during the year. The computerisation of the catalogue system has continued thanks to the willingness of our librarian, Margaret Ecclestone, to work some 50 extra hours per month. The loading of the backlog, since the last published catalogue, was completed in October 1996 and since then she has been gradually transferring the information from the published catalogue; there are now some 10,000 items on computer. At this rate the whole project, including 500 bound volumes of tracts, will take three to four years. In March an application was made to the National Lottery Charities Board for a grant towards the project costs. Sadly, owing to the huge number of applications received, we were informed in October that, in common with four out of every five applicants, we had been unsuccessful. We therefore made a further application, in November, to the alternative Heritage Lottery Fund. To prevent the work being held up, and to cover further possible disappointment, we are in the process of seeking grants from other private sources. Meanwhile we are financing the project from our own resources.

Work continues on the Himalayan Index. It now includes also the Karakoram, Hindu Kush and China. At present the Index lists 2500 peaks, 5000 attempts or ascents, 4300 references and 30,000 climbers' names.

Eventually it is planned to include all peaks over 6000m in the countries of the former Soviet Union, thus completing the tally for Asia. Originally logged on SUPERFILE, which is now obsolete, the output is now available in Microsoft ACCESS form or in dBase3, which several overseas users find more helpful. Since start-up, over £15,000 has been invested in the Index and, in return for financial contributions, it is available to overseas alpine associations in the US, Switzerland, Spain and India.

In memory of our late member Frank Solari, who contributed so much to the Library, the Club and the British Mountaineering Council over the years, the Library Council agreed to assist in the underwriting of the 50-year history of the BMC which was duly published in April. Another important event in which our members participated was the summer exhibition 'Sublime Inspiration – the Art of Mountains from Turner to Hillary' at the Abbot Hall Gallery, Kendal. This was the finest assemblage of mountain paintings seen together in recent years and included a large number from the Club's collection, many of which had never been on public view before.

Two unusual gifts have been received: a Doctoral Thesis by Michel Tailland of Grenoble University, entitled 'Les Alpinistes Victoriens' covering in great detail the early history of the Club (*see opposite page*). The second was Edward Whymper's engraved alpenstock, kindly donated by the widow of the late Ralph Jones, which now joins Whymper's tent, lecture slides and ice-axe which are already among the Club's unique possessions (*further details on page 364*). In addition, we continue to be grateful for donations of books and journals, in particular those received this year from the late Professor R J Brockenhurst, Lady Greenacre, Mr C Fox and Lady Evans.

The Library's investment portfolio continues to be handled prudently by Flemings, providing for more than half our annual operating expenses. The abolition of ACT 25% credit for UK equities will progressively affect dividend income for charities. However, it is expected that dividend growth will outweigh any loss of income in the medium term. Renewal of members' expired covenants is more than ever appreciated to help fill the gap.

Ever mindful of possible disaster affecting the Club's valuable collection, a small working group has been set up to review and refine our Disaster Plan against fire or flood. We have joined an organisation 'Document S.O.S.' which provides technical services and a disaster control manual.

As always, the Council is greatly indebted to its core of volunteer workers. Rachel Rowe, the librarian at the Royal Geographical Society and the member of Council nominated by the RGS, resigned at the end of 1996. We were grateful for her constructive comments and that she will remain a useful point of contact. She is succeeded on the Council by Michael Westmacott.

George Band
Chairman of the Library Council

THE BOARDMAN TASKER MEMORIAL AWARD FOR MOUNTAIN LITERATURE

The 15th award ceremony was held at the Alpine Club on 17 October 1997. The judges were Peter Gillman (Chairman), Dawson Stelfox and John Porter. The winning book was *Deep Play* by Paul Pritchard (Bâton Wicks). Shortlisted were *Into Thin Air* by Jon Krakauer (Macmillan), *Spirits of Place* by Jim Perrin (Gomer Press), *Dark Shadows Falling* by Joe Simpson (Jonathan Cape), *Icefields* by Thomas Wharton (Jonathan Cape) and *Against the Wall* by Simon Yates (Jonathan Cape).

LES ALPINISTES VICTORIENS

The Club has been presented with a copy of a two-volume doctoral thesis entitled 'Les Alpinistes Victoriens' by Michel Tailland, published by the Université Versailles-Saint-Quentin-en-Yvelines, which members may wish to be aware of, since it covers the early history of the Club in some detail. Whilst being, naturally, in French, it is easily understandable by those with even a limited knowledge of that language and contains many quotations in English from classic British authors, as well as numerous tables and 'graphiques' of statistics, and a good bibliography.

The thesis, which runs to nearly 700 pages, is in five main parts:

1. The origins of alpinism, covering the early travellers and grand tours, up to the early 1850s.
2. Clubs and men. The formation of the Alpine Club is dealt with in considerable detail, together with the Journal, and gives brief details of all early members. The social and intellectual mix of these early climbers is also discussed, followed by the formation of other clubs both British and continental, and a chapter on female alpinists of the time.
3. 'Genèse d'une pratique sportive.' The genesis of the sport of mountaineering, with chapters on equipment.
4. 'Les Representations'. Chapters on the conditions that travellers and mountaineers could expect to find in the Alps, hotels, guides and comments on the local inhabitants.
5. The final section is entirely 'graphiques': 91 graphs and tables specifying: How many first ascents were made by British climbers? How many Alpine Club members went to university? How old were they when they joined the Club? Which public schools did they go to? – and so on.

EDWARD WHYMPER'S ALPENSTOCK

The Club is delighted to have received Edward Whymper's alpenstock, most generously donated by Susan Jones, the widow of the late Ralph Jones who died suddenly on 3 May 1997. Ralph was a member of the Climbers' Club and Rucksack Club and became a personal friend when we were both on the first post-war British party to climb in the Caucasus in 1958.

The alpenstock was purchased in the 1970s by Susan's father Tony Jones, a keen skier, from an antique dealer who had acquired it in a house clearance sale. Tony gave it to Ralph with the suggestion, prompted by the writer, that it might eventually be presented to the Alpine Club. This was duly arranged on 11 November 1997 at the appropriate occasion of Peter Berg's recreation of the lecture first given by Whymper in 1896 using his set of lantern slides, which have been in the Alpine Club archives since 1945.

There seems little doubt that the alpenstock was genuinely owned by Whymper. It is 170cm long overall, with a steel ferrule at the base, and is topped by a curved chamois horn (for use as a 'sky-hook'?) fixed firmly to the wooden staff by two copper splints held by brass rivets. A silver plaque near the top of the staff states: 'This staff was used by the English mountaineer Edward Whymper 1840-1911 *Per Callem Collem*'. On the side opposite the plaque is engraved the date 1863. Below this, engraved spirally around the staff in the fashion of those days, are thirty place names presumably visited by Whymper during his travels including Zermatt, Breuil, Cormayeur (*sic*), Chamonix, Montenvers, etc.

Looking through the engravings in Whymper's *Scrambles Amongst the Alps* there does not appear to be an illustration of this alpenstock although there are similar examples. The date on it – 1863 – is two years before his ascent of the Matterhorn and the disastrous descent on 14 July 1865. Up until about that time, the clients carried alpenstocks and only the guides, who were expected to do all the step-cutting, carried ice-axes (read, for example, A W Moore's account of crossing the ice-arête on the first ascent of the Old Brenva route on 15 July 1865). Later on, the more experienced climbers started to take their own ice-axes, especially, of course, for guideless climbs. On page 349 of *Scrambles* Whymper gives a detailed description of his ice-axe, which was modelled on that of Melchior Anderegg. Both this axe and Whymper's tent, together with the above-mentioned lantern slides, are owned by the Club, so perhaps his alpenstock has now reached its natural home among the Club's treasured possessions.

George Band

THE 1997 AC/ASC/ESC SKI MOUNTAINEERING SYMPOSIUM

The joint AC/ASC/ESC Ski Mountaineering Symposium, held at Charlotte Mason College, Ambleside, on 18 October 1997, was a sell-out even before being publicised in the AC's July Newsletter. The College's 150 'lecture ceiling' was comfortably exceeded and 105 participants enjoyed an excellent post-symposium dinner. Although the emphasis was practical rather than 'inspirational', our President, just flown in from Buenos Aires, set the tone with his last-minute opening introduction and, after a mandatory afternoon work-out on the crags, closed official proceedings with a sparkling post-prandial encomium.

The four-slot plenary morning session was prefaced by John Harding's presentation on **Ski Mountaineering in the Less Frequented Ranges** of Spain, Svalbard, Corsica, Greece and Turkey, which are all accessible to those with limited holidays and an exploratory bent. Bill O'Connor outlined a **Leadership Strategy** based on pre-trip planning and best tour practice, stressing the importance of information sources, preparation, practice and essential kit. Bill advocated mega-shovels as a partial antidote to some chilling avalanche statistics. Jim Kerr's **Survival, Rescue and Related Equipment** spoke about navigation, equipment and weight considerations, and the practical problems of avalanche evaluation and rescue. He also offered a wealth of tips on kit, survival and rescue. Blyth Wright, co-ordinator of the Scottish Avalanche Information Service, gave a polished professional account of **Avalanche Safety and Risk Assessment**, stressing the value of forecasting, preliminary and site-specific assessments; we learned, for instance, that Rutschblok tests are four times more effective than Shovel Shear tests and that 43% of Scottish avalanche victims are experienced or very experienced mountaineers. Dr Rodney Franklin's virtuoso prestissimo performance on **Mountain Medicine and First Aid** covered major and minor injuries, fractures and sprains, hypothermia, frostbite, HAPO & HACO causes and treatment, sun damage and medical kits. His invaluable five-page medical handout would, on its own, have been enough to make symposium attendance worthwhile.

As a kick-off to the afternoon's practical sessions, Rob Collister gave an inspirational and instructional slide presentation of his ski mountaineering expeditions to New Zealand, Nepal, Kullu, Kishtwar, as well as the Rockies, Coast and Hayes Ranges of North America.

Thereafter, participants were divided into groups for practical sessions, with Rob Collister and Jim Kerr demonstrating **Crevasse and Avalanche Rescue and Transceiver Techniques**, Blyth Wright illustrating the most recent technological advances in **Avalanche Assessment**, and Bill O'Connor holding audiences spellbound with his **Equipment Expositions and Updates**.

In this summary, it is not possible to do justice to the quality and content of the lecturers' various presentations and practical sessions. They all imparted a wealth of information within very limited time slots, often at breakneck speed but always with panache, finishing to the minute without recourse to the Chairman's second bell. Their contributions, if collected into a book, would make an invaluable ski mountaineering manual.

The three sponsoring clubs are indebted to the lecturers; to all those who assisted with printing, publicity and registration (particularly Ingram Lloyd); to Nigel Estlick for an inspiring ESC display stand; to the host college for providing a most congenial venue; and to Patrick Fagan, John Harding and Bill O'Connor for organising the Symposium. The 'Golden Rule' at Ambleside did a roaring trade and the three clubs shared a modest profit of £1,343.

Overall, this second Ski Mountaineering Symposium was a resounding success. One sample feedback suggestion – that a future symposium might cover a two-day weekend – may not be practicable, but future organisers might consider smaller numbers for longer practical workshop sessions, perhaps giving attendees some scope for choice.

ALPINE CLUB SYMPOSIUM 1997: MOUNTAINEERING IN SOUTH AMERICA

With ever increasing expense, restrictions and bureaucratic issues affecting expeditions to the Himalaya and Karakoram, the annual Alpine Club Symposium provided a timely reminder that a wealth of excellent mountaineering can be enjoyed elsewhere by parties of all abilities, without the huge administrative deterrents provided by the Himalayan kingdoms. South America was the subject, Plas y Brenin the venue and the Symposium took place on Saturday, 1st November.

The event was introduced by the President, Chris Bonington. It was then chaired for the rest of the day by Lindsay Griffin, who began proceedings with a whistle-stop journey down the length of the continent, giving an indication as to exactly what the audience had let themselves in for. The aim of the Symposium was to show the vast array of different climbing available, from the completely non-technical to the depressingly demanding, and in areas that ranged from internationally famous to almost unknown. The hope was to inspire, and to maintain the momentum speakers were limited to around 15 minutes a talk.

The top of the continent, Venezuela, was the subject for both George Band and Lindsay Griffin who took the audience through several climbs in the little-known but easily accessible Sierra Nevada de Mérida south of Lake Maracaibo. John Biggar spoke about the wild and beautiful volcanoes that characterise southern Bolivia and the Chilean Atacama Desert; while, moving further south, Skip Novak showed typical fierce conditions in the hostile environment of Tierra del Fuego. Slipping across to the east, Barbara James talked about life on the Falkland Islands and presented slides of rarely visited corners.

Big wall enthusiasts in the audience were well-catered for by Noel Craine and Paul Pritchard; the former showed a recent near miss on a new route on the Central Tower of Paine, while the latter demonstrated the variety of excellent but largely unknown (to British climbers at least) granite venues accessible from Rio de Janeiro. Noel's talk was previewed by vintage footage from the 1960s courtesy of Derek Walker. Derek added commentary to an informative 8mm film taken during a reconnaissance flight over the Torres del Paine.

George Band returned to the stage to talk about the first ascent of the spectacular yet little-known Huagaruncho in Peru's Central Cordillera, while south of Cuzco, the almost equally unfrequented Cordillera Vilcanota was the scene of a bandit attack, graphically described by Lindsay Griffin, and some interesting first ascents, plus rather strange medical research which was illustrated by Simon Cooke.

Bolivia was covered by two lecturers: Andy MacNae gave a lightning tour of the increasingly popular Cordillera Apolobamba while Lindsay Griffin gave a brief insight into the potential for exploratory climbing that still exists in the Cordillera Real.

The special guest for the day was the New England mountaineer Mark Richey. Mark, who arrived along with his delightful family and parents, is undoubtedly one of the world's most accomplished mountaineers, though best known for his exploits in Peru during the late 1970s and 1980s. Earlier in the day he gave a short talk on some of his guiding experiences in Ecuador, concentrating on the standard routes up the popular volcanoes but also showing slides of an unsuccessful attempt on the very active Sangay. As the final speaker of the day he was let loose for around 40 minutes to take the audience through an outstanding selection of climbs in the Cordillera Blanca and Huayhuash, climaxing with an awesome and nail-biting ascent (and descent) of his still unrepeated route on the East Face of Cayesh.

Refreshments during the day and a worthy Symposium dinner that evening were provided, once again, by catering manager Bryn Roberts and his staff. Many thanks are due to Plas y Brenin and individual staff involved in hosting the event, Sheila Harrison and club members who helped with the organisation, and naturally to all the speakers who generously gave up their time to make it such a memorable day. *

* *Thanks are due to Lindsay Griffin for organising this well-run and most enjoyable Symposium. Ed.*

THE 11TH INTERNATIONAL FESTIVAL OF MOUNTAINEERING LITERATURE

University College of Bretton Hall, Yorkshire, 22 November 1997

Harold Drasdo is one of this country's most serious and thoughtful climbing writers. With fifty years of climbing, exploring and writing behind him, it was fitting that he should open this 11th festival with its theme of 'Frontiers'. Reading from his extraordinary book *The Ordinary Route* (The Ernest Press) Drasdo described the delights and vicissitudes he had experienced as the writer of 'the slowest-selling guidebook in the Western World' (Lliwedd) and made us laugh and think by turns. What is written in guides, he told us, conditions our response to cliffs and climbs – and therefore to ourselves as climbers and writers. Drasdo's wit, his dry, self-deprecating humour and his seriousness of intent were warmly received by the capacity audience.

Rosemary Cohen then gave us a feisty reading from her first novel *Above the Horizon* (Allison & Busby) which pushes at boundaries of both gender and language. Seb Grieve – a climber who boldly goes where few have gone before – delivered a droll disquisition on the language games he plays to roll back the limits of the possible on dangerous first ascents.

Joe Simpson delivered a moving tribute to a recently-retired giant of the publishing world, Tony Colwell of Jonathan Cape. It was Colwell who, as his editor, helped Simpson make *Touching the Void* an international best-seller. Among his great successes were nine books shortlisted and three winners of the Boardman Tasker Award; he was a sad loss to climbing writers worldwide.

The first half of the afternoon was dominated by the Everest debate, and Ed Douglas's reading from his recent book *Chomolungma Sings the Blues* (Constable) set the tone for further exploration. Although Douglas disparaged his own efforts ('a superficially informed travel book') he held our attention by his evocative if ultimately bleak picture of a mountain region where only language and truth can cross dubious international frontiers.

Matt Dickinson then presented an illustrated lecture based on his film of the actor Brian Blessed making yet another attempt to climb Mount Everest. Dickinson talked about the ethical problems confronting him and Alan Hinkes, as other mountaineers lay dying in their tents and on the route. He stressed that, for him, this was a professional assignment. When Andy Cave joined Joe Simpson, Ed Douglas and Matt Dickinson to consider and debate their respective books – *Dark Shadows Falling* (Jonathan Cape), *Chomolungma Sings the Blues* (Constable) and *The Death Zone* (Hutchinson) – the temperature rose appreciably. The debate centred on the 'honeypot' of Everest and the spate of deaths following the disaster described in Jon Krakauer's *Into Thin Air* (Macmillan), which the panel was also considering. Certainly the hyperbole evident in some of these titles almost matched the scale of the fees paid to commercial companies who offer to 'guide' up Everest; and the foregrounding of death and human ignominy in their pages was reviled by some who questioned whether the myths matter more to us now than the mountain. Connected to summit sufferings by phone and satellite, are we not in danger of becoming voyeurs? It was Douglas who pointed out that Nepal had changed irrevocably under the pernicious influence of Western culture and, by extension, of mountaineering itself.

After such a journey into disturbing territory, the audience listened quietly to Peter Gillman's adjudication of the Boardman Tasker Award. He and Dawson Stelfox, with John Porter, had judged Paul Pritchard's *Deep Play* (Bâton Wicks) the 1997 winner because, amongst other things, it was at the frontier of the sport and the writing balanced its sense of achievement, being neither self-inflationary nor deprecating. Wider media interest had endorsed this popular and well-selling choice – though one or two in the audience marvelled that Drasdo's *The Ordinary Route* had not even made it to the short list.

Another of Dr Gifford's discoveries, Sid Marty, warmed us up with his unique brand of humour, song and lighthearted poetry. Then, as always, we forgathered in the Lawrence Batley Gallery for a viewing of mountain paintings. Andy Parkin, guide and extreme mountaineer, was exhibiting, and his bold and starkly dramatic scenes, drawn predominantly from the Alps and from a depth of self-knowledge, kept the audience looking long.

Finally, Jim Curran introduced the keynote speaker, Paul Piana. Curran claimed that he had been the first to spot Piana as a speaker: 'He jumped onto the stage and said "Live your life like a thrown knife". All very well, of course, but my life's been lived more like a thrown Yorkshire pudding!' After an introduction like that he could take us anywhere. But Paul, from Wyoming (where there are more unclimbed big walls than in the whole of Europe) startled us by recollecting that it was our own John Cleare's atmospheric photos for Tony Smythe's *Rock Climbers in Action in Snowdonia* (Secker & Warburg, 1966) that had first 'turned him on to climbing'. 'That Rusty Baillie on *Cenotaph Corner*,' he said, 'real neat.' Indeed, just like the small and well-honed Piana himself – and his climbing stories and slides of Wyoming Big Walls, way out on the edge of the known world. 'Come on over,' he called to us all, 'there's one unclimbed in my back garden; you can see it in your imagination.' And we could, too – just as Harold Drasdo told us we could: 'Climbing is, after all, substantially an activity of the imagination.'

Tim Noble

INTERNATIONAL CLIMBERS MEET

The first international climbers' meet to be hosted by the Nepalese Mountaineering Association (NMA) was held over 28-31 May 1997 to coincide with the anniversary of Everest's first ascent. It was attended by some 60 climbers representing 20 different nationalities and included many well-known Himalayan Mountaineers and commercial operators. It is the NMA that administers climbing on the 18 'trekking' peaks. All other peaks in Nepal on the permitted list are administered by the Government through the Ministry of Tourism. The aim of the meet was to provide an open forum for the discussion of the current state of Himalayan mountaineering and, if possible, to propose ways and means to improve and develop the situation for the benefit of all concerned. Although these discussions were widely based, there was understandably a certain bias towards the predicament in Nepal.

Naturally the topics discussed were fairly predictable and included (a) ways to encourage Himalayan mountaineering at national and international levels, (b) commercial expeditions to high mountains, (c) current mountaineering trends which lead to increased risk, (d) bureaucratic hurdles and (e) the present policies adopted by Himalayan countries and expedition personnel to protect the mountain environment and culture.

It was noted that relative interest in the high mountains amongst climbers had reached a plateau, and in a growing number of countries (eg Japan) was actually on the decline. Reasons for this were cited as the increasingly heavy bureaucracy and cost of mounting an expedition, especially the high costs for relatively low altitude peaks, and in the case of Nepal, few unexplored or unclimbed peaks open for climbing.

In many countries (including Britain) there has been a marked swing in the last few years away from the Himalaya and towards the challenging regions of South America, Alaska, etc, where access is so much easier and less stressful or costly.

It was agreed that commercial expeditions have a role to play in enabling 'tourists' to experience high mountain climbing albeit at a low technical level, and in the bringing of work and therefore money to the local communities of the mountain regions. However, there was real concern that the risks of high-altitude climbing, especially beyond the magic 8000m mark, were being played down. There was a general agreement that climbers operating over 8000m needed to be self-supporting. There was also a belief that some commercial operators were cutting their prices and increasing risks to clients without the clients' awareness.

It was noted that few trekkers or tourists die of AMS when they are alone. It was suggested that peer group pressure when on a trek, significant expedition or personnel sponsorship on an expedition, and in the case of Everest, very high personal costs for one chance at a crack at the world's highest summit, can often force people beyond their limits. The extensive use of fixed ropes on commercial expeditions has given the impression that the highest mountains can be climbed by people with little or no climbing experience. Although this has certainly been the case, it is also true that many have got into serious trouble. There was general agreement that unsuitable clients should be weeded out of the team before they precipitate a dangerous situation for other members.

When it came to the bureaucratic nightmares often experienced in Himalayan countries there was unanimous agreement that by far the most serious problem concerned Liaison Officers. It was believed that many of these problems could be solved either by having permanent LOs in particular areas who could deal with all the expeditions on site (eg Everest Base Camp) or by allowing a Sherpa/Sirdar to assume these duties (as is the case in China). There was some suggestion that a fund be started to finance the cleaning of Base Camp approaches by locally based people during the off-seasons. However, it was also felt that in Nepal a letter of credit for the Garbage Deposit was far more acceptable than a cash deposit, as the latter has proved difficult to recover at the end of the expedition.

At the end of the Meet nine recommendations were made and will go forward to the Nepalese Government for consideration:

1 Simplify the permit application procedures.
2 Reduce bureaucracy and costs of Nepalese mountaineering in order to encourage young mountaineers to go to the Himalaya.
3 Open more unclimbed peaks at a low cost.
4 Reconsider the whole issue of the need for liaison officers, replacing them by a central, locally-based service.
5 Investigate the feasibility and costs of constructing a permanent build ing at Everest Base Camp to house a central Liaison Officer service, communications and medical centre plus storage facilities. Consider the construction of similar buildings at other major base camp sites.
6 Set the fee for all peaks less that 6000m at zero (as in Pakistan) or at a very low level.
7 Replace the need for a cash Garbage Deposit with a Letter of Credit.
8 Abolish the need for recommendation letters from the National Federations and accept the recommendation of the expedition leader.
9 Start a fund to finance off-season cleaning of popular Base Camp approaches.

The Meet was felt to have been particularly fruitful and a similar one is to be organised for 1998. However, unless some of the recommendations are accepted by the Government and become reality by the time of this next event, it is unlikely that the 1998 Climbers' Meet will receive much, if any, support from visiting mountaineers.

Ian McNaught-Davis,
President, Union Internationale des Associations d'Alpinisme

RUBBISH ON EVEREST

A lot of publicity has focused recently on the environmental damage inflicted on 8000-metre peaks by those who venture on their slopes. Eloquent pleas have been made for the world's highest mountains to be treated with greater respect. Everest is, for obvious reasons, the mountain that non-climbers are interested in and there is no doubt that damage to the culture of mountaineering has been caused by the myth that its slopes are covered in litter.

I have now been on five expeditions to Everest, on three different routes and in all three climbing seasons – winter, spring and autumn. The three expeditions that I've led have placed 29 Westerners and Sherpas on the summit. By the early 1990s the mountain was becoming increasingly popular. We in the UK were lucky to have been associated with early exploration and success. For other countries a first national ascent became a matter of prestige, and massive resources were thrown at making a successful ascent. 'Expedition style' was, with a few honourable exceptions, almost defined by an Everest expedition. I saw this still happening in the spring of 1997 when Indonesian and Malaysian teams were under immense pressure from home to climb the mountain and money was of no object to get the 'result'.

Because most of these groups were 'one offs' perhaps not enough care was taken in clearing up after the expedition. The early 1990s saw several commercial expedition companies regularly operating on Everest. The South Col had become covered in expedition detritus, notably oxygen cylinders. In 1994 Scott Fischer and Brent Bishop started to offer a cash bonus for Sherpas to bring down cylinders. Nowadays most operators do the same. The current price is £10 a cylinder. A Sherpa will carry a load to the South Col and bring down up to six cylinders. This adds up to a very good day's wage in a country with a per capita annual income of less than $300.

The Nepalese and Chinese governments understandably view Everest as a resource. They have each in their way responded to concerns raised about rubbish on Everest. The Chinese have rubbish dumps at base camp which are cleared at regular intervals. Less successfully they have erected unspeakable toilets at base camp as well. The Nepalese have instituted rigorous rules. All oxygen cylinders have to be re-exported; batteries have to be exported even if they were bought in Kathmandu; tin cans have to be taken down to Kathmandu and even faecal waste at base camp has to be deposited in barrels and carried to a landfill site lower down the valley. Sherpa staff are getting more educated about rubbish. The best commercial operators have formed a trade association, International Guiding Operators 8000, and one of the Articles of Association places great emphasis on keeping the mountain environment clean.

There is certainly an ethical problem with corpses. Currently on the North Ridge one apparently has to walk past six bodies on the summit day. Many bodies are blown away in winter, covered with snow or are cut away. Some bodies remain frozen into the slopes and remain fixtures for many years. My view is that one should deal with this tragic problem on a case by case basis. If it does not put further lives at risk, then I believe that corpses should be placed in as private a position as possible. This could mean lowering them into a crevasse, cutting them away or burying them. If this is not possible then I strongly believe that photographs should not be published. Mountaineering is not war; the corpses are normally identifiable and one should think above all of the distress and offence given to the deceased's relatives.

Of course there will always be traces of man's passage on Everest, but these are surprisingly few considering the conditions of great stress under which people operate at these extreme altitudes. In many ways these have become a red herring, distracting attention from the very real problems of population growth, lack of education and mismanagement of resources from which a developing country like Nepal suffers.

John Tinker

IGO 8000

After the great Everest accident in 1996, Russell Brice, the well-respected New Zealander guide, brought together surviving operators in Kathmandu and suggested some kind of trade association for companies guiding the 8000m peaks. The disaster had proved graphically that no company can guarantee safety at nearly 9000m. However, there was a feeling that amongst the plethora of commercial and semi-commercial expeditions, some took their responsibilities more seriously than others. The better organised expeditions frequently found themselves helping other expeditions in trouble, which ruined things for their own clients because they ended up subsidising incompetent amateurs.

What is proposed is a new association – International Guiding Operators 8000. Initial members will include Himalayan Experience, Out There Trekking Expeditions, Himalayan Kingdoms and Guy Cotter's New Zealand-based Adventure Consultants. It is hoped that others will come on board, provided they agree to the terms of the association. Those terms are quite stringent. Members will have to have organised at least two 8000m expeditions in the past. They will have to abide by all local legal requirements. They will have to provide adequate medical and rescue facilities; proper sanitation arrangements; sufficient staff, whose names are published in promotional brochures, along with all the other details, so that prospective clients will know exactly what they are paying for.

For each person going to Everest or any other 8000m peak this is a new, fresh, personal adventure, and if anyone is going to be charged large amounts of money to facilitate that adventure, then it is right that they should have the benefit of an approved, accepted standard of professionalism. The top operators provide such a service, with fixed ropes on all awkward sections, Sherpas and other experienced staff organising camps, comprehensive medical facilities including Gamow bags, radio links between camps, and satellite communications to the outside world.

The UIAA Expeditions Commission, chaired by Joss Lynam, is thinking along the same lines. It is hoped that their Code of Practice will be equally stringent so that it can be adopted automatically by IGO 8000 members.

Stephen Venables

UIAA RECOMMENDED CODE OF PRACTICE FOR HIGH ALTITUDE GUIDED COMMERCIAL EXPEDITIONS

The following Code was approved by the General Assembly of the UIAA at its meeting at Kranjska Gora, Slovenia on 4 October 1997:

Definition This Code applies to commercial expeditions attempting 8000m peaks which offer to guide or accompany climbers above Base Camp.

It is not concerned with the many expeditions which employ trekking agencies to supply transport etc to Base Camp, and may also supply Base Camp services and high altitude porters.

Rationale A variety of organisations offer to take clients on 8000m peaks. They vary from those which provide a full service to the summit or nearly to the summit, to those where there is minimal support for clients above Base Camp. However, it is difficult for clients to deduce from brochures exactly what is offered in terms of guiding and support, and whether it corresponds to their needs. This Code supplies clients with pointers to assist them in making an informed choice.

High Altitude Warning Mountaineers climbing at very high altitude, especially above 8000m, are at the limit of their mental and physical powers and may not be capable of assisting others as has always been traditional in mountaineering. This fact is of particular importance to mountaineers of limited experience who rely on professional guides to bring them safely up and down 8000m peaks.

THE CODE

1 The leader or chief guide, and as many as possible of the other guides, should have experience at least to the altitude of the peak to be climbed.
[There is no qualification appropriate to high altitude guiding, so the term 'guide' does not imply that the person holds a professional qualification. Clients can only judge from the previous experience of the guides, who may be Westerners or Sherpas or other local mountaineers.]

2 The staff on the mountain must be adequate for the aims of the party and the services offered.

3 A doctor in the party is very desirable but at the very least advance arrangements must be made for medical help. Advance arrangements must also be made for evacuation assistance in case of emergency.

4 The minimum safety equipment available must be walkie-talkie radios, a satellite phone, medical oxygen, and recommended First Aid supplies.

5 Advertising must give a true picture of all the difficulties and dangers involved, and avoid promising the impossible. Biographical information about the team should be included.

6 Clients should not usually be accepted for 8000m peaks unless they have previous altitude experience to 6-7000m.

7 Information supplied in advance should include a clear statement of the guiding and support offered.

8 The expedition must take account of the *UIAA Environmental Objectives and Guidelines* and follow the *UIAA Expeditions Code of Ethics.*

Contributors

JOSÉ LUIS BERMÚDEZ is a lecturer in the Department of Philosophy, University of Stirling. He took up climbing too late and has been making up for lost time in the Alps, Caucasus and Himalaya. In July 1997 he climbed Gasherbrum I (Hidden Peak). Co-author (with Audrey Salkeld) of *On the Edge of Europe: Mountaineering in the Caucasus.*

ANDY CAVE lives beneath the gritstone edges of Derbyshire, and splits his time between guiding and researching folklore and dialect at Sheffield University.

CHRIS CHEESEMAN is currently trying to be a doctor. In the past he has managed to blackmail former employers into giving him time off to go to India, Nepal and South America to climb obscure peaks. He has plenty of exciting ideas for further expeditions, but no money.

JULIE-ANN CLYMA studied Physiology before moving to Britain from New Zealand in 1985. She has climbed extensively in the Alps of Europe and New Zealand, and has participated in 12 expeditions to Peru, Alaska, Pakistan, Nepal, Kazakhstan and India.

NOEL CRAINE lives in North Wales, attempting to work as a biologist with an interest in epidemiology in between trips and holidays. He enjoys a wide range of climbing types from big wall climbing to bouldering and has been privileged to climb with an interesting range of mountaineers. He has a particular enthusiasm for the sea cliffs around Britain.

JIM CURRAN, formerly a lecturer at the University of the West of England, is now a freelance writer and film-maker. He has taken part in many expeditions to the Himalaya and South America. Books include *K2, Triumph and Tragedy* and *Suspended Sentences*.

P M DAS is an officer of the Indian Police Service seconded to the Punjab cadre, decorated with the Police Medal for Gallantry and the Police Medal for Meritorious Services. His experience includes high treks and climbs in many parts of the Indian Himalaya and the Karakoram. He has served as Principal of the Mountaineering Institute at Gangtok, and while training for Everest 1996, climbed Mana, 7273m, by the difficult N route and three peaks over 6000m in Ladakh during the cold season.

DEREK FORDHAM When not dreaming of the Arctic, Derek practises as an architect and runs an Arctic photographic library. He is secretary of the Arctic Club and has led 21 expeditions to the Canadian Arctic, Greenland and Svalbard to ski, climb or share the life of the Inuit. In 1996 he led a successful expedition to Gunnbjørnsfjeld, the highest peak in the Arctic.

JULIAN FREEMAN-ATTWOOD is a forestry manager who lives on the Shropshire/Welsh border. He has climbed in the Himalaya, Africa, The Antarctic and Sub-Antarctic, specialising in unclimbed peaks in little-known areas. He is becoming increasingly interested in sailing/mountaineering trips, having once part-owned Tilman's Pilot Cutter *Baroque.*

ASHLEY GREENWOOD is a lawyer, formerly in the Colonial and Diplomatic legal services. He began climbing at school, has been President of CUMC and the ASC and has climbed extensively in every continent during 67 years.

LINDSAY GRIFFIN is a magazine editor/journalist living in North Wales who, despite dwindling ability, still pursues all aspects of climbing with undiminished enthusiasm. Exploratory visits to the Greater Ranges are his main love, and a return to Bolivia in 1996 marked his first visit to the South American mainland for a decade. Now convinced that this length of absence was inexcusable, he is making every endeavour to return before 2006.

DAVID HAMILTON earns a precarious living organising trekking, mountaineering and ski touring expeditions to the world's great mountain ranges. He has spent the last eleven summers in northern Pakistan leading more than 30 groups on a variety of unpredictable projects in the Karakoram and Hindu Kush ranges. Other mountain adventures, in Africa, South America, Russia and the Alps, ensure that David is seldom to be found at home.

J G R HARDING, a retired City solicitor, formerly served in HM Colonial Service, South Arabia. He has climbed and skied extensively in Europe, Asia, Africa and Australia. He was President of both the Alpine and Eagle Ski Clubs, a Vice-President of the Alpine Club and Hon Legal Adviser to the MEF for 15 years.

ALAN HINKES aims to become the first Briton to climb the fourteen eight-thousanders. This is his 'Challenge 8000'. By November 1997 he had climbed nine eight-thousanders, leaving five to be climbed before he achieves his goal. He is a British Mountain Guide (UIAGM) and writes a monthly column in *Trail* magazine, 'Hinkes on Hills'. He has a 14-year-old daughter, Fiona.

ROBIN HODGKIN spent 15 years teaching in the Sudan's education service. In the 1960s he was headmaster of Abbotsholme School in Derbyshire and in the 1970s was a lecturer at the Department of Educational Studies, Oxford University. He is married with nine grandchildren. A recent book, on what education really is, was *Playing and Exploring* (Methuen 1985).

TONY HOWARD, a founding partner of Troll Safety Equipment, led the first ascent of Norway's Troll Wall in 1965 and wrote the Romsdal guide. His expeditions include Arctic Norway, Canada, South Georgia and Greenland. He has climbed extensively across North Africa and the Middle East from Morocco to Iran. He 'discovered' and wrote the guide to Wadi Rum. Recently he rediscovered Egypt's forgotten Red Sea Mountains.

JOHN JACKSON has climbed and explored in the Alps, Greenland, Africa and the Andes. His experience in the Himalaya dates from 1944 and includes first ascents in Kashmir, Ladakh, Garhwal, Sikkim and Nepal. A reserve member of the 1953 Everest expedition, he was also a member of the British team which made the first ascent of Kangchenjunga in 1955.

HARISH KAPADIA has climbed in the Himalaya since 1960, with ascents up to 6800m. He is Hon Editor of both the *Himalayan Journal* and the *HC Newsletter*. In 1993 he was awarded the IMF's Gold Medal and in 1996 was made an Honorary Member of the Alpine Club. He has written several books including *High Himalaya Unknown Valleys, Spiti: Adventures in the Trans-Himalaya* and, with Soli Mehta, *Exploring the Hidden Himalaya*..

PAUL KNOTT works on the Faculty at Al Akhawayn University, situated in Morocco, where he enjoys the undeveloped climbing scene. He delights in visiting obscure mountain ranges and has climbed in most regions of Russia and Central Asia. After two visits he also retains a fascination for the deep snow and storms of the St Elias range in the Yukon.

JIM LOWTHER's first expedition was to Greenland in 1982. Since then he has re-visited the country a further 8 times making numerous first ascents (about 40 in total) and doing some long ski and sledge trips including a traverse of the ice cap in 1987. He sailed there with Bonington and Knox-Johnston in 1991 to climb in the Lemon Mountains and has since accompanied Chris to Kinnaur (India), Lemon Mountains (again) and Tibet (Sepu Kangri).

PAUL MOORES is a full-time mountaineer with a UIAGM Carnet. He owns a climbing shop and guiding business in Scotland and is a member of the Glencoe Mountain Rescue Team. He also works as a technical consultant to film companies, TV, and industry. He has climbed extensively in the Himalaya, Andes, Alaska, Africa and Patagonia, always returning to climb hard new routes in Scotland and the Alps.

SIDNEY NOWILL OBE, born in Istanbul, has climbed and trekked in Turkey very extensively over several decades, as well as in the Alps and Dolomites. He has been active also in Ecuador, Iran, Patagonia, the Western Himalaya and Nepal. His publications number 14, of which 10 relate to Turkey. For the last 27 years he has enjoyed a rather tenuous connection with Shell.

BILL O'CONNOR is a UIAGM mountain and ski guide who spends much of his time climbing and guiding abroad, with more than 30 summer Alpine seasons and 23 Himalayan expeditions in the bag. A one-time guidebook editor for the AC, he is the author of several books including a soon-to-be-published volume on the Lake District where he lives.

PAT PARSONS joined the Royal Marines in 1974. After completing the Mountain Leader Course he commanded the Mountain and Arctic Warfare Cadre from 1988 to 1991. He has climbed extensively in the Alps and the Himalaya, including Phabrang and Manaslu North, and the 1988 British Services Everest Expedition. He has also climbed Kilimanjaro, Mt Kenya and Mt McKinley.

JONATHAN PRATT worked for several years as a mining engineer in the USA. Since 1986 he has climbed in N and S America, New Zealand and Africa and has taken part in many Himalayan expeditions. He has climbed Everest and Lhotse and has made first British ascents of Hidden Peak (Gasherbrum I) and Makalu. In 1993 he made the first complete British ascent (including safe return) of K2.

PAUL PRITCHARD has done many new routes on Gogarth, in the mountains and on slate. He has climbed on big walls in the Alps, Patagonia, Brazil, North America, the Himalaya and on Baffin Island. In 1997, with Dave Green, he climbed an all free 1200m route on an unclimbed peak in the Ak-Su Valley, Kyrghyzstan. *The Great Game* was graded 5.12b. In the same year his book *Deep Play* won the Boardman Tasker Memorial Award for Mountain Literature.

KEV REYNOLDS has climbed in the Alps, Atlas, Caucasus, Turkey and extensively in the Pyrenees, and now makes an annual pilgrimage on trek in the Himalaya. A former Youth Hostel Warden, he is a freelance writer and lecturer.

SIMON RICHARDSON is a petroleum engineer based in Aberdeen. Experience gained climbing in the Alps, Andes, Himalaya and Alaska is put to good use most winter weekends whilst exploring and climbing in the Scottish Highlands.

C A RUSSELL, who formerly worked with a City bank, devotes much of his time to mountaineering and related activities. He has climbed in many regions of the Alps, in the Pyrenees, East Africa, North America and the Himalaya.

BILL RUTHVEN has been Hon Secretary of the Mount Everest Foundation since 1985. When not suffering the inconvenience of trying to earn a living as an aeronautical engineer, he used to be a keen mountaineer, traveller and photographer. Having worn out his back carrying heavy rucksacks up hills for 50 years, he is now confined to a wheelchair, so is wearing his fingers out writing about them instead.

ARUN SAMANT is a consulting structural engineer living in Bombay. He is a Committee Member of the Himalayan Club and has made 13 first ascents including White Peak (6102m) in Garhwal, Sondhi (6480m) in Eastern Karakoram and Num Themga (6024m) in Spiti. He has contributed many climbing and technical articles to magazines and Himalayan Journals.

DOUG SCOTT CBE is a leading high-altitude and big-wall climber, who has pioneered new routes on many of the world's most difficult mountains. Through his Specialist Trekking Co-operative, he helps the Sherpas and Tamangs he has used on previous expeditions in Nepal to improve their conditions of labour. AC Vice-President 1992-93. BMC Vice-President from 1994.

JOE SIMPSON (ACG) has climbed extensively in the Alps, Andes and the Greater Ranges, making first ascents as well as guiding groups on treks and climbs. In 1989 his bestseller *Touching the Void* won the Boardman Tasker Award and the NCR Award for Non-Fiction. His other books, *The Water People*, *This Game of Ghosts*, *Storms of Silence* and *Dark Shadows Falling* are all currently in print published by Jonathan Cape (hardback) and Vintage (paperback).

ERNST SONDHEIMER, retired academic and Editor of the *Alpine Journal* from 1987 to 1991, climbed the Inaccessible Pinnacle as his first Munro in 1946 and has since then enjoyed roaming the hills of the world, with emphasis on Scotland and the Swiss Alps. In his Third Age he has trekked in Bhutan and Tibet and has taken to cultivating alpine plants in his garden.

WALDEMAR SOROKA has been climbing since 1980, first in the Tatras and then on Mount Kenya and in the Alps, the Himalaya and the Karakoram. He has taken part in seven expeditions, including Broad Peak in 1990 and again in 1995. In 1996 he led the successful expedition to Annapurna North-West Ridge. He lives in Gdansk and is a director of a poligraphic firm there.

GEOFFREY TEMPLEMAN, a retired chartered surveyor, has greatly enjoyed being an Assistant Editor of the *AJ* for the past 26 years. A love of mountain literature is coupled with excursions into the hills, which are becoming less and less energetic.

LOUISE THOMAS is a UIAGM Mountain Guide working at Plas y Brenin. Six years ago, with Mike Turner, she climbed her first big wall – the unclimbed SW Face of Cuernos Norte, Paine. Since then she has climbed new routes and big walls in Greenland, Patagonia, North America, Europe and Africa, as well as Pakistan where, in 1997 with an all-women's team, she climbed a hard 750m new route on the rock peak Beatrice above the Characusa Valley

VADIM VASILJEV was born in Leningrad in 1961 and has been climbing and skiing for over 20 years. After graduating from the Leningrad Electrical Engineering Institute in 1984, he spent six further years at the Institute researching acousto-optics. He then became involved in the adventure travel business and in outdoor equipment trading and now works for W L Gore & Associates, GmbH, as a consultant.

MICHAEL WARD CBE was a member and Medical Officer of the 1951 and 1953 Everest Expeditions. He is a consultant surgeon (retired) who has combined exploration in Nepal, Bhutan, Kunlun and Tibet with high altitude research. Honorary Member of the Alpine Club 1992.

KEN WILSON is a publisher of mountaineering books. Sometime architectural photographer and founding editor of the magazine *Mountain*, his compilations include *Hard Rock*, *Classic Rock* and *The Games Climbers Play*. He also adapted the (Dumler/Burkhart) latest edition of Blödig's *Vier Tausender die Alpen* for publication in Britain and America (also France and Poland) as *The High Mountains of the Alps*. He has climbed regularly (though modestly) since 1958 and maintains a keen interest in mountaineering politics and ethics.

Index

1998 Vol 103

NOTES FOR CONTRIBUTORS

The *Alpine Journal* records all aspects of mountains and mountaineering, including expeditions, adventure, art, literature, geography, history, geology, medicine, ethics and the mountain environment.

Articles Contributions in English are invited. They should be sent to the Hon Editor, **Ed Douglas, 93c Junction Road, London, N19 5QX** (*e-mail* ed_douglas@compuserve.com) or to the Production Editor, **Johanna Merz, 14 Whitefield Close, Putney, London SW15 3SS.** Articles should be in the form of typed copy or on disk with accompanying hard copy. Their length should not exceed 3000 words without prior approval of the Editor **and may be edited or shortened at his discretion.** Authors are asked to keep a copy. It is regretted that the *Alpine Journal* is unable to offer a fee for articles published, but authors receive a complimentary copy of the issue of the *Alpine Journal* in which their article appears.

Articles and book reviews should not have been published in substantially the same form by any other publication.

Maps These should be well researched, accurate, and finished ready for printing. They should show the most important place-names mentioned in the text. It is the authors' responsibility to get their maps redrawn if necessary. This can be arranged through the Production Editor if required.

Photographs Only top quality photographs will be accepted. Prints (any size) should be black and white, with glossy finish if possible. They should be numbered (in pencil) on the back and accompanied by captions on a separate sheet (see below). Colour transparencies, in 35mm format or larger, should be originals (**not copies**).

Captions These should be listed **on a separate sheet** and should give title, author and approximate date when the photograph was taken.

Copyright It is the author's responsibility to obtain copyright clearance for both text and photographs, to pay any fees involved and to ensure that acknowledgements are in the form required by the copyright owner.

Summaries A brief summary should be included with all 'expedition' articles.

Biographies Authors are asked to provide a short biography, in not more than 60 words, listing the most noteworthy items in their climbing career and anything else they wish to mention.

Deadline: **copy and photographs should reach the Editor by 1 January of the year of publication**.